Case Studies in Finance Managing for Corporate Value Creation

FOURTH EDITION

Robert F. Bruner

Boston   Burr Ridge, IL   Dubuque, IA   Madison, WI   New York
San Francisco   St. Louis   Bangkok   Bogotá   Caracas   Kuala Lumpur
Lisbon   London   Madrid   Mexico City   Milan   Montreal   New Delhi
Santiago   Seoul   Singapore   Sydney   Taipei   Toronto

McGraw-Hill Higher Education

A Division of The *McGraw-Hill* Companies

CASE STUDIES IN FINANCE: MANAGING FOR CORPORATE VALUE CREATION
Published by McGraw-Hill/Irwin, a business unit of The McGraw-Hill Companies, Inc., 1221 Avenue of the Americas, New York, NY, 10020. Copyright © 2003, 1999, 1994, 1990 by The McGraw-Hill Companies, Inc. All rights reserved. No part of this publication may be reproduced or distributed in any form or by any means, or stored in a database or retrieval system, without written consent of The McGraw-Hill Companies, Inc., including, but not limited to, in any network or other electronic storage or transmission, or broadcast for distance learning.

Some ancillaries, including electronic and print components, may not be available to customers outside the United States.

This book is printed on acid-free paper.

domestic   2 3 4 5 6 7 8 9 0 DOC/DOC 0 9 8 7 6 5 4 3 2
international   1 2 3 4 5 6 7 8 9 0 DOC/DOC 0 9 8 7 6 5 4 3 2

ISBN 0-07-233862-8

Publisher: *Steve Patterson*
Sponsoring editor: *Michele Janicek*
Editorial coordinator: *Barbara Hari*
Executive marketing manager: *Rhonda Seelinger*
Producer, media technology: *Melissa Kansa*
Project manager: *Destiny Rynne*
Production supervisor: *Rose Hepburn*
Director of design BR: *Keith J. McPherson*
Supplement producer: *Joyce J. Chappetto*
Cover designer: *Maureen McCutcheon*
Cover illustrator: *©Richard Tuschman Images*
Typeface: *10/12 Times Roman*
Compositor: *Carlisle Communications, Ltd.*
Printer: *R. R. Donnelley*

Library of Congress Cataloging-in-Publication Data
Bruner, Robert F., 1949–
    Case studies in finance: managing for corporate value creation / Robert F. Bruner. — 4th ed.
      p. cm. — (The McGraw-Hill/Irwin series in finance, insurance, and real estate)
    Includes bibliographical references and index.
    ISBN 0-07-233862-8 (alk. paper)— ISBN 0-07-119927-6 (international ed.: alk. paper)
    1. Corporations—Finance—Case studies. 2. International business
enterprises—Finance—Case studies. 3. Decision-making—Case studies. 4. Women
executives. I. Title. II. Series
    HG4015.5.B78 2003
658.15—dc21   2002025549

INTERNATIONAL EDITION ISBN 0-07-119927-6
Copyright © 2003. Exclusive rights by The McGraw-Hill Companies, Inc. for manufacture and export. This book cannot be re-exported from the country to which it is sold by McGraw-Hill. The International Edition is not available in North America.

www.mhhe.com

The McGraw-Hill/Irwin Series in Finance, Insurance and Real Estate

CONSULTING EDITOR
Stephen A. Ross
Franco Modigliani Professor of Finance and Economics *Sloan School of Management*
Massachusetts Institute of Technology

FINANCIAL MANAGEMENT

Benninga and Sarig
Corporate Finance: A Valuation Approach

Block and Hirt
Foundations of Financial Management
Tenth Edition

Brealey and Myers
Principles of Corporate Finance
Seventh Edition

Brealey, Myers and Marcus
Fundamentals of Corporate Finance
Third Edition

Brooks
FinGame Online 3.0

Bruner
Case Studies in Finance: Managing for Corporate Value Creation
Fourth Edition

Chew
The New Corporate Finance: Where Theory Meets Practice
Third Edition

DeMello
Cases in Finance

Grinblatt and Titman
Financial Markets and Corporate Strategy
Second Edition

Helfert
Techniques of Financial Analysis: A Guide to Value Creation
Eleventh Edition

Higgins
Analysis for Financial Management
Seventh Edition

Kester, Fruhan, Piper and Ruback
Case Problems in Finance
Eleventh Edition

Nunnally and Plath
Cases in Finance
Second Edition

Ross, Westerfield and Jaffe
Corporate Finance
Sixth Edition

Ross, Westerfield and Jordan
Essentials of Corporate Finance
Third Edition

Ross, Westerfield and Jordan
Fundamentals of Corporate Finance
Sixth Edition

Smith
The Modern Theory of Corporate Finance
Second Edition

White
Financial Analysis with an Electronic Calculator
Fourth Edition

INVESTMENTS

Bodie, Kane and Marcus
Essentials of Investments
Fourth Edition

Bodie, Kane and Marcus
Investments
Fifth Edition

Cohen, Zinbarg and Zeikel
Investment Analysis and Portfolio Management
Fifth Edition

Corrado and Jordan
Fundamentals of Investments: Valuation and Management
Second Edition

Farrell
Portfolio Management: Theory and Applications
Second Edition

Hirt and Block
Fundamentals of Investment Management
Seventh Edition

FINANCIAL INSTITUTIONS AND MARKETS

Cornett and Saunders
Fundamentals of Financial Institutions Management

Rose
Commercial Bank Management
Sixth Edition

Rose
Money and Capital Markets: Financial Institutions and Instruments in a Global Marketplace
Eighth Edition

Santomero and Babbel
Financial Markets, Instruments, and Institutions
Second Edition

Saunders and Cornett
Financial Institutions Management: A Risk Management Approach
Fourth Edition

Saunders and Cornett
Financial Markets and Institutions: A Modern Perspective

INTERNATIONAL FINANCE

Beim and Calomiris
Emerging Financial Markets

Eun and Resnick
International Financial Management
Second Edition

Levich
International Financial Markets: Prices and Policies
Second Edition

REAL ESTATE

Brueggeman and Fisher
Real Estate Finance and Investments
Eleventh Edition

Corgel, Ling and Smith
Real Estate Perspectives: An Introduction to Real Estate
Fourth Edition

FINANCIAL PLANNING AND INSURANCE

Allen, Melone, Rosenbloom and Mahoney
Pension Planning: Pension, Profit-Sharing, and Other Deferred Compensation Plans
Ninth Edition

Crawford
Life and Health Insurance Law
Eighth Edition (LOMA)

Harrington and Niehaus
Risk Management and Insurance

Hirsch
Casualty Claim Practice
Sixth Edition

Kapoor, Dlabay and Hughes
Personal Finance
Sixth Edition

Skipper
International Risk and Insurance: An Environmental-Managerial Approach

Williams, Smith and Young
Risk Management and Insurance
Eighth Edition

In dedication to my wife,

Bobbie

and it's you or whatever a moon has always meant
and whatever a sun will always sing is you.

from *i carry your heart with me (i carry it in*
e. e. cummings

ABOUT THE AUTHOR

Robert F. Bruner is Distinguished Professor of Business Administration and Executive Director of the Batten Institute at the Darden Graduate School of Business Administration, University of Virginia. His work has been published in journals such as *Financial Management, Journal of Accounting and Economics, Journal of Applied Corporate Finance, Journal of Financial Economics, Journal of Financial and Quantitative Analysis,* and *Journal of Money, Credit, and Banking.* His research has concentrated on corporate finance, particularly mergers, restructurings, and corporate financing policies. He is the coauthor of *Finance Interactive,* multimedia tutorial software in finance, and of *The Portable MBA.* He has received numerous awards for teaching and casewriting in the United States and Europe. Industrial corporations, financial institutions, and government agencies have retained him for counsel and training. He has served the Darden School, professional groups, and community organizations in various positions of leadership.

CONTENTS

P A R T   3   ESTIMATING THE COST OF CAPITAL

P A R T   4   CAPITAL BUDGETING AND RESOURCE ALLOCATION

P A R T   5   MANAGEMENT OF THE FIRM'S EQUITY: DIVIDENDS, REPURCHASES, INITIAL OFFERINGS

P A R T   6   MANAGEMENT OF THE CORPORATE CAPITAL STRUCTURE

FOREWORD

With pleasure I introduce the reader to Bob Bruner's *Case Studies in Finance*. I have known Bob's work for over a decade. On two occasions he has won INSEAD's award for "Outstanding Teacher in the Elective Courses." His case studies have won numerous recognitions, including "European Case of the Year" from the European Case Clearinghouse. A number of the cases in this volume were conceived, researched, or tested on one of Bob's visits to INSEAD. He exemplifies the practice-oriented scholar who has a vision of finance in a global arena. He travels widely, listens wherever he goes, and translates his learnings into material that is accessible both to the serious practitioner and novice in finance.

This book and its three previous editions have helped shape the case literature in finance. Organizations and markets have changed dramatically over the past two decades. Students and instructors have needed materials that focused on current concepts, current institutions, and current best practices, while retaining enduring insights that remain at the core of professional mastery. Bob Bruner has responded to this need with cases that:

- **Link managerial decisions to capital markets and the expectations of investors.** In these cases, the valuation task links managers and markets. The cases require the student to study the needs of investors through the lens of financial markets.
- **Survey issues of contemporary interest to practitioners and scholars.** These issues include agency problems, option valuation, real options, financial innovations, investing in emerging markets, and contests for corporate control.
- **Apply rigorous analytic techniques to the resolution of classic problems.** Many of these applications reinforce lessons covered in standard texts. Others help the student define best practice where the texts may disagree. In all instances, the student is called to offer analysis, rather than opinion.

This collection of cases will help students, scholars, and practitioners sharpen their decision-making ability. And it will advance further the case literature in finance.

Gabriel Hawawini, Dean, and
Henry Grunfeld Chaired Professor of Investment Banking
INSEAD
Fontainebleau, France, and Singapore

PREFACE

The inexplicable is all around us. So is the incomprehensible. So is the unintelligible. Interviewing Babe Ruth[1] in 1928, I put it to him "People come and ask what's your system for hitting home runs—that so?" "Yes," said the Babe, "and all I can tell 'em is I pick a good one and sock it. I get back to the dugout and they ask me what it was I hit and I tell 'em I don't know except it looked good."

Carl Sandburg[2]

Managers are not confronted with problems that are independent of each other, but with dynamic situations that consist of complex systems of changing problems that interact with each other. I call such situations messes. . . . Managers do not solve problems: they manage messes.

Russell Ackoff[3]

ORIENTATION OF THE BOOK

Practitioners tell us that much in finance is inexplicable, incomprehensible, and unintelligible. Like Babe Ruth, their explanations for their actions often amount to "I pick a good one and sock it." Fortunately for a rising generation of practitioners, tools and concepts of modern finance provide a language and approach for excellent performance. The aim of this book is to illustrate and exercise the application of these tools and concepts in a messy world.

Focus on Value: The subtitle of this fourth edition remains *Managing for Corporate Value Creation*. Economics teaches us that value creation should be an enduring focus of concern because value is the foundation of survival and prosperity of the enterprise. The focus on value also helps managers understand the impact of the firm on the world around it. These cases harness and exercise this economic view of the firm. It is the special province of finance to highlight value as a legitimate concern for managers. The cases in this book exercise valuation analysis over a wide range of assets, debt, equities, and options, and a wide range of perspectives, such as investor, creditor, and manager.

Linkage to Capital Markets: An important premise of these cases is that managers should take cues from the capital markets. The cases in this volume help the student learn to look at the capital markets in four ways. First, they illustrate important players in the

---

[1]George Herman "Babe" Ruth (1895–1948) was one of the most famous players in the history of American baseball, leading the league in home runs for 10 straight seasons, setting a record of 60 home runs in one season, and hitting 714 home runs in his career. Ruth was also known as the "Sultan of the Swat."

[2]Carl Sandburg, "Notes for Preface," in *Harvest Poems* (New York: Harcourt Brace Jovanovich, 1960), p. 11.

[3]Russell Ackoff, "The Future of Operational Research Is Past," *Journal of Operational Research Society* 30, 1 (1979): 93–104.

capital markets (such as the cases on Warren Buffett, Jeanne Mockard, and the Fidelity Magellan Fund). Second, they exercise the students' abilities to interpret capital market conditions. Third, they explore the design of financial securities, and rationalize the use of exotic securities in support of corporate policy. Finally, they help students understand the implications of transparency of the firm to investors, and the impact of news about the firm in an efficient market.

Respect for the Administrative Point of View: The real world is messy. Information is incomplete, arrives late, or is reported with error. The motivations of counterparties are ambiguous. Resources often fall short. These cases illustrate the immense practicality of finance theory in sorting out the issues facing managers, assessing alternatives, and illuminating the effects of any particular choice. A number of the cases in this book present practical ethical dilemmas or moral hazards facing managers. Most of the cases (and teaching plans in the associated instructor's manual) call for *action plans* rather than mere analyses or descriptions of a problem.

Contemporaneity: All cases in this book are set in 1995 or after. Fully 61 percent of these cases are new, or significantly updated. The mix of cases reflects the global business environment: 41 percent of the cases in this book are set outside the United States, or have strong cross-border elements. Finally the blend of cases continues to reflect the growing role of women in managerial ranks: 44 percent of the cases present women as key protagonists and decision makers. Generally, these cases reflect the increasingly diverse world of business participants.

PLAN OF THE BOOK

The cases may be taught in many different combinations. The sequence indicated in the Contents corresponds to course designs used at Darden. Each cluster of cases in the Contents suggests a concept module, with a particular orientation.

1. **Setting Some Themes.** These cases introduce basic concepts of value creation, assessment of performance against a capital market benchmark, and capital market efficiency that reappear throughout a case course. The numerical analysis required of the student is relatively light. The synthesis of case facts into an important framework or perspective is the main challenge. The case "Warren E. Buffett, 1995" sets the nearly universal theme of this volume: the need to think like an investor. The cases about Federal Express and UPS and Coca-Cola versus Pepsico (in the third section) use "economic profit" (or EVA®) to explore the origins of value creation and destruction, and its competitive implications for the future.

2. **Financial Analysis and Forecasting.** In this section, students are introduced to the crucial skills of financial-statement analysis, break-even analysis, ratio analysis, and financial statement forecasting. One case ("The Body Shop, 2001") takes the student step by step through the preparation of forecasts, both by hand and with the aid of a computer-spreadsheet program. Other cases address issues in the analysis of working-capital management, and credit analysis.

3. **Estimating the Cost of Capital.** This module begins with a discussion of "best practices" among leading firms. The cases exercise skills in estimating the cost of capital for firms and their business segments. The cases aim to exercise and solidify students' mastery of the capital asset pricing model, the dividend-growth model, and the weighted average cost of capital formula. The new case, "Nike, Inc." presents an introductory exercise in the estimation of weighted average cost of capital. "Teletech Corporation, 1996," explores the implications of mean-variance analysis to business segments within a firm, and gives a useful foundation for discussing value additivity.

4. **Capital Budgeting and Resource Allocation.** The focus of these cases is the evaluation of investment opportunities and entire capital budgets. The analytical challenges range from simple time-value-of-money problems to setting the entire capital budget for a resource-constrained firm. Key issues in this module include the estimation of free cash flows, the comparison of various investment criteria (NPV, IRR, payback, and equivalent annuities), the treatment of issues in mutually exclusive investments, and capital budgeting under rationing. The new case, "Genzyme/Geltex Joint Venture Investment," explores the economics of staged investing versus investing in a lump sum.

5. **Management of Shareholders' Equity.** This module seeks to develop practical principles about dividend policy and share issues by drawing on concepts about dividend irrelevance, signaling, investor clienteles, bonding, and agency costs. "Eastboro Machine Tools" explores decisions about dividends and share repurchase through the lenses of a range of theoretical concepts, including signaling, clientele effects, and residual policies. The new case, "eBay Inc.," considers numerous issues in initial public offerings, including underpricing, choice of comparables, and underwriter risk.

6. **Management of the Corporate Capital Structure.** The problem of setting capital structure targets is introduced in this module. Prominent issues are the use and creation of debt tax shields, the role of industry economics and technology, the influence of corporate competitive strategy, the trade-offs between debt policy, dividend policy, and investment goals, and the avoidance of costs of distress. "Polaroid Corporation, 1996" addresses the classic trade-off between optimizing the capital structure optimality and providing financial flexibility. "MCI Communications Corp." assesses the value of debt tax shields. The new case, "Threshold Sports LLC," considers the trade-offs between debt and equity financing for the rapidly growing firm.

7. **Analysis of Financing Tactics: Leases, Options, and Foreign Currency.** While the preceding module is concerned with setting debt targets, this module addresses a range of tactics a firm might use to pursue those targets, hedge risk, and exploit market opportunities. Included are domestic and international debt offerings, swaps of various types, recapitalizations, warrants, and convertibles. With these cases, students will exercise techniques in securities valuation, including the use of option-pricing theory. This module includes three new cases. "Amtrak: Acela Financing" gives an exercise in the analysis of lease financing proposals. "Corning Inc." presents an introduction to the valuation of convertible bonds. And the case "Enron's Weather Derivatives" gives the opportunity to evaluate an innovation in security design.

8. **Valuing the Enterprise: Acquisitions and Buyouts.** This module exercises students' skills in valuing the firm. The focus includes valuation using DCF and multiples, techniques of valuing highly leveraged firms, reallocation of value in financial distress, and

distribution of joint value in merger negotiation. This module features seven new cases, including two merger negotiation exercises, and a technical note on hostile takeovers. "Yeats Valves and Controls Inc." is an introductory-level company valuation case that can be paired with "TSE International Corporation" (found in the instructor's manual) to create a negotiation exercise. "Chrysler Corporation" is an advanced problem in valuation and transaction design that may be paired with "Daimler-Benz" in the instructor's manual to create a negotiation exercise. "Palamon Capital Partners" is a new case dealing with cross-border private equity investing. "General Mills' Acquisition of Pillsbury" considers the use of contingent value rights in M&A transactions. "Printicomm's Proposed Acquisition of Digitech" explores the use and valuation of earnout proposals. "Structuring Repsol's Acquisition of YPF" considers the interplay of price, form of payment, and financing in the design of M&A transactions. And "The Hilton–ITT Wars" explores the dynamics of hostile takeovers, and the difficult decisions managers must make. The cases in this module are excellent vehicles for end-of-course classes, student term papers, and/or presentations by teams of students.

This edition offers a number of cases that give insights about investing or financing decisions in emerging markets. These include "Paginas Amarelas," "Deutsche Brauerei," "Kota Fibres," "Rosario Acero," "Star River Electronics," and "Structuring Repsol's Acquisition of YPF."

SUMMARY OF CHANGES TO THE FOURTH EDITION

The fourth edition represents a substantial change from the third edition.

This edition offers 25 new and significantly updated cases, or 61 percent of the total number. All of the cases are set in 1995 or after. Time marches on. In the interest of presenting a fresh and contemporary collection, older cases have been updated and/or replaced with new case situations. Several of the most favorite "classic" cases from the first three editions are available online from McGraw-Hill/Irwin; instructors who adopt this edition may copy them for classroom use. All cases and teaching notes have been edited to sharpen the opportunities for student analysis.

The book continues with a strong international aspect (17 of the cases, 41 percent, are set outside the United States or feature significant cross-border issues). Also, the collection continues to feature women decision makers and protagonists prominently (18, or 44 percent, of the cases.)

SUPPLEMENTS

The case studies in this volume are supported by various resources that help make student engagement a success:

- Spreadsheet files support student and instructor preparation of the cases. They are located on the book's website at www.mhhe.com/bruner4e.

- A guide to the novice on case preparation, "Note to the Student: How to Study and Discuss Cases" follows this Preface.
- Six cases in the instructor's resource manual provide counterparty roles for two negotiation exercises, or present detailed discussions of case outcomes (i.e., the "B" case to cases appearing in this volume). These supplemental cases can significantly extend student learning and expand the opportunities for classroom discussion.
- An instructor's resource manual of about 1,000 pages contains teaching notes for each case. Each teaching note includes suggested assignment questions, a hypothetical teaching plan, and a prototypical finished case analysis.
- Web site addresses in many of the teaching notes. These provide a convenient avenue for updates on the performance of undisguised companies appearing in the book.
- Notes in the instructor's manual on how to design a case method course, on using computers with cases, and on preparing to teach a case.
- A companion book by Robert Bruner titled "Socrates' Muse: Reflections on Effective Discussion Leadership," is available to instructors who adopt the book for classroom use.
- Several "classic" cases and their associated teaching notes were among the most popular and durable cases in the first three editions of *Case Studies in Finance*. Instructors adopting this volume for classroom use may request permission to reproduce them for their courses.

ACKNOWLEDGMENTS

This book would not be possible without the contributions of many other people. Colleagues at Darden who have taught, coauthored, contributed to, or commented on these cases are Yiorgos Allayannis, Sam Bodily, Karl-Adam Bonnier, Susan Chaplinsky, John Colley, Bob Conroy, Ken Eades, Mark Eaker, Bob Fair, Jim Freeland, Sherwood Frey, Bob Harris, Mark Haskins, Charles Meiburg, Jud Reis, Michael Schill, William Sihler and Robert Spekman. I am grateful for their collegiality and for the support of the Darden School Foundation, the Batten Institute, the Citicorp Global Scholars Program, and INSEAD for my casewriting efforts.

Lee Remmers of INSEAD contributed the case, "Merton Electronics," which I am delighted to present in this collection.

Colleagues at other schools provided worthy insights and encouragement toward the development of the four editions of *Case Studies in Finance*. I am grateful to the following persons (listed with the schools with which they were associated at the time of my correspondence or work with them):

Michael Adler, Columbia
Raj Aggarwal, John Carroll
Turki Alshimmiri, Kuwait Univ.
Ed Altman, NYU
James Ang, Florida State
Paul Asquith, M.I.T.

Geert Bekaert, Stanford
Michael Berry, James Madison
Randy Billingsley, VPI&SU
Gary Blemaster, Georgetown
Rick Boebel, Univ. Otago, New Zealand
Oyvind Bohren, BI, Norway

John Boquist, Indiana
Michael Brennan, UCLA
Duke Bristow, UCLA
Ed Burmeister, Duke
Kirt Butler, Michigan State
Don Chance, VPI&SU
Andrew Chen, Southern Methodist
Barbara J. Childs, Univ. of Texas at
    Austin
C. Roland Christensen, Harvard
Thomas E. Copeland, McKinsey
Jean Dermine, INSEAD
Michael Dooley, UVA Law
Barry Doyle, University of San Francisco
Bernard Dumas, INSEAD
Peter Eisemann, Georgia State
Javier Estrada, IESE
Ben Esty, Harvard
Thomas H. Eyssell, Missouri
Pablo Fernandez, IESE
Kenneth Ferris, Thunderbird
John Finnerty, Fordham
Joseph Finnerty, Illinois
Steve Foerster, Western Ontario
Günther Franke, Konstanz
Bill Fulmer, George Mason
Louis Gagnon, Queens
Dan Galai, Jerusalem
Jim Gentry, Illinois
Stuart Gilson, Harvard
Robert Glauber, Harvard
Mustafa Gultekin, North Carolina
Benton Gup, Alabama
Jim Haltiner, William & Mary
Rob Hansen, VPI&SU
Philippe Haspeslagh, INSEAD
Pekka Hietala, INSEAD
Rocky Higgins, Washington
Pierre Hillion, INSEAD
Laurie Simon Hodrick, Columbia
John Hund, Texas
Daniel Indro, Kent State
Thomas Jackson, UVA Law
Pradeep Jalan, Regina
Michael Jensen, Harvard

Sreeni Kamma, Indiana
Steven Kaplan, Chicago
Andrew Karolyi, Western Ontario
James Kehr, Miami Univ. (Ohio)
Kathryn Kelm, Emporia State
Carl Kester, Harvard
Herwig Langohr, INSEAD
Dan Laughhunn, Duke
Ken Lehn, Pittsburgh
Saul Levmore, UVA Law
Wilbur Lewellen, Purdue
Scott Linn, Oklahoma
Dennis Logue, Dartmouth
Paul Mahoney, UVA Law
Paul Malatesta, Washington
Wesley Marple, Northeastern
Felicia Marston, UVA (McIntire)
John Martin, Texas
Ronald Masulis, Vanderbilt
John McConnell, Purdue
Catherine McDonough, Babson
Richard McEnally, North Carolina
Wayne Mikkelson, Oregon
Michael Moffett, Thunderbird
Nancy Mohan, Dayton
Ed Moses, Rollins
Charles Moyer, Wake Forest
David W. Mullins, Jr., Harvard
James T. Murphy, Tulane
Chris Muscarella, Penn State
Robert Nachtmann, Pittsburgh
Tom C. Nelson, University of Colorado
Ben Nunnally, UNC-Charlotte
Robert Parrino, Texas (Austin)
Luis Pereiro, Universidad Torcuato di
    Tella
Pamela Peterson, Florida State
Larry Pettit, Virginia (McIntire)
Gordon Philips, Maryland
Tom Piper, Harvard
John Pringle, North Carolina
Ahmad Rahnema, IESE
Al Rappaport, Northwestern
Allen Rappaport, Northern Iowa
Raghu Rau, Purdue

David Ravenscraft, North Carolina
Henry B. Reiling, Harvard
Lee Remmers, INSEAD
Jay Ritter, Michigan
Richard Ruback, Harvard
Art Selander, Southern Methodist
Israel Shaked, Boston
Dennis Sheehan, Penn State
J.B. Silvers, Case Western
Betty Simkins, Oklahoma State
Luke Sparvero, Texas
Richard Stapleton, Lancaster
Laura Starks, Texas
Jerry Stevens, Richmond
John Strong, William & Mary
Marti Subrahmanyam, NYU
Anant Sundaram, Thunderbird
Rick Swasey, Northeastern
Bob Taggart, Boston College
Udin Tanuddin, Univ. Surabaya, Indonesia
Anjan Thakor, Indiana
Thomas Thibodeau, Southern Methodist

Clifford Thies, Shenandoah Univ.
James G. Tompkins, Kenesaw State
Walter Torous, UCLA
Max Torres, IESE
Nick Travlos, Boston College
Lenos Trigeorgis, Cyprus
George Tsetsekos, Drexel
Peter Tufano, Harvard
James Van Horne, Stanford
Nick Varaiya, San Diego State
Theo Vermaelen, INSEAD
Michael Vetsuypens, Southern Methodist
Claude Viallet, INSEAD
Ingo Walter, NYU
J.F. Weston, UCLA
Peter Williamson, Dartmouth
Brent Wilson, Brigham Young
Kent Womack, Dartmouth
Karen Wruck, Ohio State
Fred Yeager, St. Louis
Betty Yobaccio, Framingham State
Marc Zenner, North Carolina

I am also grateful to the following practitioners (listed here with affiliated companies at the time of my work with them):

Norm Bartczak, Center for Financial Strategy
Bo Brookby, First Wachovia
W.L. Lyons Brown, Brown-Forman
Bliss Williams Browne, First Chicago
George Bruns, BankBoston
Ian Buckley, Henderson Investors
Ned Case, General Motors
Daniel Cohrs, Marriott
David Crosby, Johnson & Johnson
Jinx Dennett, BankBoston
Barbara Dering, Bank of New York
Ty Eggemeyer, McKinsey
Geoffrey Elliott, Morgan Stanley
Christine Eosco, BankBoston
Catherine Friedman, Morgan Stanley
Charles Griffith, AlliedSignal
Ian Harvey, BankBoston
David Herter, Fleet Boston

Christopher Howe, Kleinwort Benson
Paul Hunn, Manufacturers Hanover
Kristen Huntley, Morgan Stanley
James Gelly, General Motors
Ed Giera, General Motors
Denis Hamboyan, Bank Boston
Betsy Hatfield, Bank Boston
Thomas Jasper, Salomon Brothers
Andrew Kalotay, Salomon Brothers
Mary Lou Kelley, McKinsey
Francesco Kestenholz, UBS
Eric Linnes, Kleinwort Benson
Peter Lynch, Fidelity Investments
Mary McDaniel, SNL Securities
Jean McTighe, BankBoston
Frank McTigue, McTigue Associates
Michael Melloy, Planet
David Meyer, J.P. Morgan
Jeanne Mockard, Putnam Investments

Pascal Montiero de Barros, Planet
Lin Morison, BankBoston
John Muleta, PSINet
Dennis Neumann, Bank of New York
John Newcomb, BankBoston
Ralph Norwood, Polaroid
Marni Gislason Obernauer, J.P. Morgan
Michael Pearson, McKinsey
Nancy Preis, Kleinwort Benson
Joe Prendergast, First Wachovia
Luis Quartin-Bastos, Planet
Jack Rader, FMA
Christopher Reilly, S.G. Warburg
Gerry Rooney, NationsBank
Emilio Rottoli, Glaxo
Craig Ruff, AIMR
Barry Sabloff, First Chicago
Linda Scheuplein, J.P. Morgan
Keith Shaughnessy, Bank Boston
Jack Sheehan, Johnstown

Katrina Sherrerd, AIMR
John Smetanka, Security Pacific
John Smith, General Motors
Raj Srinath, AMTRAK
Rick Spangler, First Wachovia
Kirsten Spector, BankBoston
Martin Steinmeyer, MediMedia
Stephanie Summers, Lehman Brothers
Sven-Ivan Sundqvist, Dagens Nyheter
Peter Thorpe, Citicorp
Katherine Updike, Excelsior
Tom Verdoorn, Land O'Lakes
Blaine Walgren, California State University,
   Fullerton
David Wake Walker, Kleinwort Benson
Frank Ward, Corp. Performance Systems
Ulrich Wiechmann, UWINC
Scott Williams, McKinsey
Harry You, Salomon Brothers

Research assistants working under my direction have helped gather data and prepare drafts. My principal assistant for this fourth edition was Jessica Chan. She distinguished her contribution through solid mastery of finance, tenacious attention to detail, lucid drafting, a gifted focus on learning rather than teaching, and joyful passion for ideas. Research assistants who contributed to various cases in this and previous editions include Darren Berry, Anne Campbell, David Eichler, Dennis Hall, Jerry Halpin, Peter Hennessy, Casey Opitz, Katarina Paddack, Chad Rynbrandt, Michael Schill, John Sherwood, Jane Sommers-Kelly, Thien Pham, Carla Stiassni, Sanjay Vakharia, Larry Weatherford, and Steve Wilus. I have supervised numerous others in the development of individual cases—those worthy contributors are recognized in the first footnote of each case.

A busy professor soon learns the wisdom in the adage "Many hands make work light." I am very grateful to the staff of the Darden School for its support in this project. Excellent editorial assistance at Darden was provided by Stephen Smith (the unflappable lead editor for this edition). Betty Sprouse and Ginny Fisher gave stalwart secretarial support. Donald Aielli, Sherry Alston, and Michael Hamm helped with archiving and administering the case collection. Outstanding library research support was given by Karen Marsh and Frank Wilmot. The patience, care, and dedication of these people are richly appreciated.

At McGraw-Hill/Irwin, Michele Janicek served as Sponsoring Editor, and Barbara Hari served as Development Editor and Editorial Coordinator on this edition. Destiny Rynne was Project Manager on this edition. Mike Junior, Vice President, recruited me into this project years ago; the legacy of our early vision-setting continues in this edition.

Of all the contributors, my wife, Barbara McTigue Bruner, and two sons, Jonathan and Alexander, have endured great sacrifices to see this book appear. As Milton said, "They also serve who only stand and wait." Development of this fourth edition would not have been possible without their fond patience.

All these acknowledgments notwithstanding, responsibility for these materials is mine. I welcome suggestions for their enhancement. Please let me know of your experience with these cases, either through McGraw-Hill/Irwin, or at the coordinates given below.

Robert F. Bruner
Distinguished Professor of
Business Administration and
Executive Director of the Batten Institute

> Darden Graduate School of Business
> University of Virginia
> Post Office Box 6550
> Charlottesville, Virginia 22906
> Email: brunerr@virginia.edu[*]
> Web site: http://faculty.darden.edu/brunerb/

Individual copies of all the Darden cases in this and previous editions may be obtained promptly from McGraw-Hill/Irwin's *Primis Online* (www.mhhe.com/primis/) or from Darden Educational Materials Services (telephone: 434-982-2192; email: dardencases@virginia.edu). Proceeds from these case sales support casewriting efforts. Please respect the copyrights on these materials.

---

[*] Students should know that I am unable to offer *any* comments that would assist their preparation of these cases without the prior express request of their instructors with agreement by me.

NOTE TO THE STUDENT: HOW TO STUDY AND DISCUSS CASES

Get a good idea and stay with it. Dog it and work at it until it's done, and done right.

—Walt Disney

You enroll in a "case method" course, pick up the book of case studies or the stack of loose-leaf cases, and get ready for the first class meeting. If this is your first experience with case discussions, the odds are that you are clueless and a little anxious about how to prepare for this course. That's fairly normal but something you should try to break through quickly in order to gain the maximum from your studies. Quick breakthroughs come from a combination of good attitude, good "infrastructure," and good execution—this note offers some tips.

GOOD ATTITUDE

Students learn best that which they teach themselves. Passive and mindless learning is ephemeral. Active, mindful, learning simply sticks. The case method makes learning sticky by placing you in situations that require invention of tools and concepts *in your own terms.* The most successful case students share a set of characteristics that drive self-teaching:

1. **Personal initiative, self-reliance.** Case studies rarely suggest how to proceed. Professors are more like guides on a long hike: they can't carry you, but they can show you the way. You must arrive at the destination under your own power. You must figure out the case on your own. To teach yourself means that you must sort ideas out in ways that make sense to you, personally. To teach yourself is to give yourself two gifts: the idea you are trying to learn, and greater self-confidence in your own ability to master the world.

2. **Curiosity, a zest for exploration as an end in itself.** Richard P. Feynman, who won the Nobel Prize in Physics in 1965, was once asked whether his key discovery was worth it. He replied, "[The Nobel Prize is] a pain in the. . . . I don't like honors. . . . The prize is the pleasure of finding the thing out, the kick in the discovery, the observation that other people use it [my work]—those are the real things; the honors are unreal to me."[1]

---

[1]Richard P. Feynman, *The Pleasure of Finding Things Out* (Cambridge, Mass.: Perseus Publishing, 1999), 12.

3. **A willingness to take risks.** Risk-taking is at the heart of all learning. Usually one learns more from failures than successes. The banker Walter Wriston once said, "Good judgment comes from experience. Experience comes from bad judgment."

4. **Patience and persistence.** Case studies are messy, a realistic reflection of the fact that managers don't manage problems, they manage messes. Initially, reaching a solution will seem to be the major challenge. But once you reach *a* solution, you may discover other possible solutions, and face the choice among the best alternatives.

5. **An orientation to community and discussion.** Much of the power of the case method derives from a willingness to *talk* with others about your ideas and/or your points of confusion. This is one of the paradoxes of the case method: you must teach yourself, but not in a vacuum. The poet T. S. Eliot said, "There is no life not lived in community." Talking seems like such an inefficient method of sorting through the case, but if exploration is an end in itself, then talking is the only way. Furthermore, talking is an excellent means of testing your own mastery of ideas, of rooting out points of confusion, and, generally, of preparing yourself for professional life.

6. **Trust in the process.** The learnings from a case-method course are impressive. They arrive cumulatively over time. In many cases, the learnings continue well after the course has finished. Occasionally, these learnings hit you with the force of a tsunami. But generally, the learnings creep in quietly, but powerfully, like the tide. After the case course, you will look back and see that your thinking, mastery, and appreciation have changed dramatically. The key point is that you should not measure the success of your progress on the basis of any single case discussion. Trust that, in the cumulative work over many cases, you will gain the mastery you seek.

GOOD INFRASTRUCTURE

"Infrastructure" consists of all the resources that the case student can call upon. Some of this is simply given to you by the professor: case studies, assignment questions, supporting references to textbooks or articles, and computer data or models. But you can go much farther to help yourself. Consider these steps:

1. **Find a quiet place to study. Spend at least 90 minutes there for each case study.** Each case has subtleties to it, which you will miss unless you can concentrate. After two or three visits, your quiet place will take on the attributes of a habit: you will slip into a working attitude more easily. Be sure to spend enough time in the quiet place to give yourself a chance to really engage the case.

2. **Get a business dictionary.** If you are new to business and finance, some of the terms will seem foreign; if English is not your first language, *many* of the terms will seem foreign if not bizarre. Get into the habit of looking up terms that you don't know. The benefit of this becomes cumulative.

3. **Skim a business newspaper each day; read a business magazine; follow the markets.** Reading a newspaper or magazine helps build a *context* for the case study you are trying to solve at the moment, and helps you make connections between the case study and current events. The terminology of business and finance that you see in the publica-

tions helps reinforce your use of the dictionary, and hastens your mastery of terms you will see in the cases. Your learning by reading business periodicals is cumulative. Some students choose to follow a good business news web site on the Internet. These have the virtue of being inexpensive and efficient, but they tend to screen too much. Having the printed publication in your hands, and leafing through it, helps the process of *discovery,* which is the whole point of the exercise.

4. **Learn the basics of spreadsheet modeling on a computer.** Many case studies now have supporting data available for analysis in spreadsheet files, such as Microsoft Excel. Analyzing the data on a computer rather than by hand both speeds up your work and extends your reach.

5. **Form a study group.** The ideas in many cases are deep; the analysis can get complex. *You will learn more and perform better in class participation by discussing the cases together in a learning team.* Your team should devote an average of an hour to each case. High-performance teams show a number of common attributes:
   a. Members commit to the success of the team.
   b. The team plans ahead, leaving time for contingencies.
   c. The team meets regularly.
   d. Team members show up for meetings and are *prepared* to contribute.
   e. There may or may not be a formal leader, but assignments are clear. Team members meet their assigned obligations.

6. **Get to know your professor.** In the case method, students inevitably learn more from one another than from the instructor. But the teacher is part of the learning infrastructure, too: a resource to be used wisely. Never troll for answers in advance of a case discussion. Do your homework; use classmates and learning teams to clear up most questions so that you can focus on the meatiest issues with the teacher. Be very organized and focused about what you would like to discuss. Remember that teachers like to learn, too: if you reveal a new insight about a case or bring a clipping about a related issue in current events, the professor and student both gain from their time together. Ultimately, the best payoff to the professor is the "aha" in the student's eyes when he or she masters an idea.

GOOD EXECUTION

Good attitude and infrastructure must be employed properly—one needs good execution. The extent to which a student learns depends on how the case study is approached. What can one do to gain the maximum from the study of these cases?

   1. Reading the case. The very first time you read any case, look for the forest, not the trees. This requires that your first reading be quick. Do not begin taking notes on the first round; instead, read the case like a magazine article. The first few paragraphs of a well-constructed case usually say something about the problem—read those carefully. Then quickly read the rest of the case, seeking mainly a sense of the scope of the problems and what information the case contains to help resolve them. Leaf through the exhibits, looking for what information they hold rather than for any analytical insights. At the conclusion of the first pass, read any supporting articles or notes that your instructor may have recommended.

2. Getting into the case situation. Develop your "awareness." With the broader perspective in mind, the second and more detailed reading will be more productive. The reason is that, as you now encounter details, your mind will be able to organize them in some useful fashion rather than inventorying them randomly. Making links among case details is necessary for solving the case. At this point, you can take the notes that will set up your analysis.

The most successful students project themselves into the position of the decision maker because this perspective helps them link case details as well as develop a stand on the case problem. Assignment questions may help you do this; but it is a good idea to get into the habit of doing it yourself. Here are the kinds of questions you might try to answer in preparing every case:

- Who are the protagonists in the case? Who must take action on the problem? What do they have at stake? What pressures are they under?
- In what business is the company? What is the nature of its product? What is the nature of demand for that product? What is the firm's distinctive competence? With whom does it compete?[2] What is the structure of the industry? Is the firm comparatively strong or weak? In what ways?
- What are the goals of the firm? What is the firm's strategy in pursuit of these goals? (The goals and strategy might be explicitly stated, or they may be implicit in the way the firm does business.) What are the firm's apparent functional policies in marketing (e.g., push-versus-pull strategy), production (e.g., labor relations, use of new technology, distributed production vs. centralized), and finance (e.g., the use of debt financing, payment of dividends)? Financial and business strategies can be inferred from analysis of financial ratios and a sources-and-uses-of-funds statement.
- How well has the firm performed in pursuit of its goals? (The answer to this question calls for simple analysis using financial ratios, such as the DuPont system, compound growth rates, and measures of value creation.)

The larger point of this phase of your case preparation is to broaden your awareness of issues. Perhaps the most successful investor in history, Warren Buffett, said, "Any player unaware of the fool in the market probably *is* the fool in the market." Awareness is an important attribute of successful managers.

3. Defining the problem. A common trap for many executives is to assume that the issue at hand is the real problem most worthy of their time rather than a symptom of some larger problem that *really* deserves their time. For instance, a lender is often asked to advance funds to help tide a firm over a cash shortfall. Careful study may reveal that the key problem is not a cash shortfall but rather product obsolescence, unexpected competition, or careless

---

[2]Think broadly about competitors. Mark Twain wrote, in *A Connecticut Yankee in King Arthur's Court,* "The best swordsman in the world doesn't need to fear the second best swordsman in the world; no, the person for him to be afraid of is some ignorant antagonist who has never had a sword in his hand before; he doesn't do the thing he ought to do, and so the expert isn't prepared for him; he does the thing he ought not to do; and it often catches the expert out and ends him on the spot."

cost management. Even in cases where the decision is fairly narrowly defined (such as in a capital expenditure choice), the "problem" generally turns out to be the believability of certain key assumptions. Students who are new to the case method tend to focus narrowly in defining problems and often overlook the influence that the larger setting has on the problem. In doing this, the student develops narrow specialist habits, never achieving the general-manager perspective. It is useful and important for you to define the problem yourself, and in the process, validate the problem as suggested by the protagonist in the case.

4. Analysis: run the numbers and go to the heart of the matter. Virtually all finance cases require numerical analysis. This is good because figure-work lends rigor and structure to your thinking. But some cases, reflecting reality, invite you to explore blind alleys. If you are new to finance, even these explorations will help you learn.[3] The best case students develop an instinct for where to devote their analysis. Economy of effort is desirable. If you have invested wisely in problem definition, economical analysis tends to follow. For instance, a student might assume that a particular case is meant to exercise financial forecasting skills and will spend two or more hours preparing a detailed forecast, instead of preparing a simpler forecast in one hour and conducting a sensitivity analysis based on key assumptions in the next hour. An executive rarely thinks of a situation as having to do with a forecasting method or discounting or any other technique, but rather thinks of it as a problem of judgment, deciding on which people or concepts or environmental conditions to bet. The best case analyses get down to the *key bets* on which the executive is wagering the prosperity of the firm and his or her career. Get to the business issues quickly, and avoid lengthy churning through relatively unimportant calculations.

5. Prepare to participate: take a stand. To develop analytical insights without making recommendations is useless to executives, and drains the case-study experience of some of its learning power. A stand means having a point of view about the problem, a recommendation, and an analysis to back up both of them. The lessons most worth learning all come from taking a stand. From that truth flows the educative force of the case method. In the typical case, the student is projected into the position of an executive who must do something in response to a problem. It is this choice of what to do that constitutes the executive's "stand." Over the course of a career, an executive who takes stands gains wisdom. If the stand provides an effective resolution of the problem, so much the better for all concerned. If it does not, however, the wise executive analyzes the reasons for the failure and may learn even more than from a success. As Theodore Roosevelt wrote:

> The credit belongs to the man[4] who is actually in the arena—whose face is marred by dust and sweat and blood . . . who knows the great enthusiasms, the great devotions—and spends himself in a worthy cause—who, at best, if he wins, knows the thrills of high achievement—and if he fails, at least fails while daring greatly so that his place shall never be with those cold and timid souls who know neither victory nor defeat.

6. In class: participate actively in support of your conclusions, but be open to new insights. Of course, one can have a stand without the world being any wiser. To take a stand

---

[3]Case analysis is often iterative: an understanding of the big issues invites an analysis of details—then the details may restructure the big issues and invite the analysis of other details. In some cases, getting to the "heart of the matter" will mean just such iteration.

[4]Today, a statement such as this would surely recognize women as well.

in case discussions means to participate actively in the discussion and to advocate your stand until new facts or analyses emerge to warrant a change.[5] Learning by the case method is not a spectator sport. A classic error many students make is to bring into the case-method classroom the habits of the lecture hall (i.e., passively absorbing what other people say). These habits fail miserably in the case-method classroom because they only guarantee that one absorbs the truths and fallacies uttered by others. The purpose of case study is to develop and exercise *one's own* skills and judgment. This takes practice and participation, just as in a sport. Here are two good general suggestions: (1) defer significant note-taking until after class and (2) strive to contribute to every case discussion.

7. Immediately after class; jot down notes, corrections, and questions. Don't over-invest in taking notes during class—that just cannibalizes "airtime" in which you could be learning through discussing the case. But immediately after class, collect your learnings and questions in notes that will capture your thinking. Of course, ask a fellow student or your teacher questions that will help clarify issues that still puzzle you.

8. Once a week, flip through notes. Make a list of your questions, and pursue answers. Take an hour each weekend to review your notes from class discussions during the past week. This will help build your grasp of the flow of the course. Studying a subject by the case method is like building a large picture with small mosaic tiles. It helps to step back to see the big picture. But the main objective should be to make an inventory of anything you are unclear about: terms, concepts, and calculations. Work your way through this inventory with classmates, learning teams, and, ultimately, the instructor. This kind of review and follow-up builds your self-confidence and prepares you to participate more effectively in future case discussions.

CONCLUSION: FOCUS ON PROCESS, AND RESULTS WILL FOLLOW

View the case-method experience as a series of opportunities to test your mastery of techniques and your business judgment. If you seek a list of axioms to be etched in stone, you are bound to disappoint yourself. As in real life, there are virtually no "right" answers to these cases in the sense that a scientific or engineering problem has an exact solution. Jeff Milman has said, "The answers worth getting are never found in the back of the book." What matters is that you obtain a way of thinking about business situations that you can carry from one job (or career) to the next. In the case method, it is largely true that *how you learn is what you learn.*[6]

---

[5]There is a difference between taking a stand and pigheadedness. Nothing is served by clinging to your stand to the bitter end in the face of better analysis or common sense. Good managers recognize new facts and arguments as they come to light, and adapt.

[6]In describing the work of case teachers, John H. McArthur has said, "How we teach is what we teach."

PART 1

Setting Some Themes

Warren E. Buffett, 1995

On August 25, 1995, Warren Buffett, the CEO of Berkshire Hathaway, announced that his firm would acquire the 49.6 percent of GEICO Corporation that it did not already own. The $2.3 billion deal would give GEICO shareholders $70.00 per share, up from the $55.75 per share market price before the announcement. Observers were astonished at the 26 percent premium that Berkshire Hathaway would pay, particularly since Buffett proposed to change nothing about GEICO, and there were no apparent synergies in the combination of the two firms. At the announcement, Berkshire Hathaway's shares closed up 2.4 percent for the day, for a gain in market value of $718 million.[1] That day, the S&P 500 Index closed up 0.5 percent.

The acquisition of GEICO renewed public interest in its architect, Warren Buffett. In many ways, he was an anomaly. One of the richest individuals in the world (with an estimated net worth of about $7 billion), he was also respected and even beloved. Though he had accumulated perhaps the best investment record in history (a compound annual increase in wealth of 28 percent from 1965 to 1994)[2] Berkshire Hathaway paid him only $100,000 per year to serve as its CEO. Buffett and other insiders controlled 47.9 percent of the company, yet he ran the company in the interests of all shareholders. He was the subject of numerous laudatory articles and three biographies,[3] yet he remained an intensely

---

[1] The change in Berkshire Hathaway's share price at the date of the announcement was $609.60. The company had outstanding 1,177,750 shares.

[2] Buffett's initial cost per share in Berkshire Hathaway in 1965 was about $17.578. On August 25, 1995, the price per share closed at $25,400.

[3] Robert G. Hagstrom, Jr., *The Warren Buffett Way,* (New York: John Wiley & Sons, 1994); Andrew Kilpatrick, *Of Permanent Value: The Story of Warren Buffett* (Birmingham, Ala.: AKPE, 1994); Roger Lowenstein, *Buffett: The Making of an American Capitalist* (New York: Random House, 1995).

private individual. Though acclaimed by many as an intellectual genius, he shunned the company of intellectuals and preferred to affect the manner of a down-home Nebraskan (he lived in Omaha), and a tough-minded investor. In contrast to other investment "stars," Buffett acknowledged his investment failures quickly and publicly. Though he held an MBA from Columbia University and credited his mentor, Professor Benjamin Graham, with developing the philosophy of value-based investing that guided Buffett to his success, he chided business schools for the irrelevance of their theories of finance and investing.

Numerous writers sought to distill the essence of Buffett's success. What were the key principles that guided Buffett? Could these be applied broadly in the late 1990s and into the 21st century, or were they unique to Buffett and his time? From an understanding of these principles, analysts hoped to illuminate Berkshire Hathaway's acquisition of GEICO. Under what assumptions would this acquisition make sense? What were Buffett's probable motives in the acquisition? Would the acquisition of GEICO prove to be a success? How would it compare to the firm's other recent investments in Salomon Brothers, USAir, and Champion International?

BERKSHIRE HATHAWAY, INC.

The company was incorporated in 1889 as Berkshire Cotton Manufacturing, and eventually grew to become one of New England's biggest textile producers, accounting for 25 percent of the country's cotton textile production. In 1955, Berkshire merged with Hathaway Manufacturing and began a secular decline due to inflation, technological change, and intensifying competition from foreign competitors. In 1965, Buffett and some partners acquired

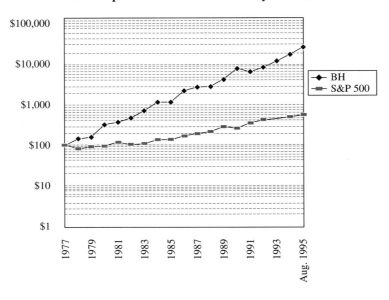

Share price of Berkshire Hathaway vs. S&P 500 Index

control of Berkshire Hathaway, believing that the decline could be reversed. Over the next 20 years, it became apparent that large capital investments would be required to remain competitive and that even then the financial returns would be mediocre. In 1985, Berkshire Hathaway exited the textile business. Fortunately, the textile group generated enough cash in the initial years to permit the firm to purchase two insurance companies headquartered in Omaha: National Indemnity Company and National Fire & Marine Insurance Company. Acquisitions of other businesses followed in the 1970s and 1980s.

The investment performance of a share in Berkshire Hathaway had astonished most observers. In 1977, the firm's year-end closing share price was $89.00. On August 25, 1995, the firm's closing share price was $25,400.00. In comparison, the annual average total return on all large stocks from 1977 to the end of 1994 was 14.3 percent.[4] Over the same period, the Standard & Poor's 500 Index grew from 107 to 560. Some observers called for Buffett to split the firm's share price, to make it more accessible to the individual investor. He steadfastly refused.

In 1994, Berkshire Hathaway described itself as "a holding company owning subsidiaries engaged in a number of diverse business activities."[5] **Exhibit 1** gives a summary of revenues, operating profits, capital expenditures, depreciation, and assets for the various segments. By 1994, Berkshire's portfolio of businesses included:

- *Insurance Group.* The largest component of Berkshire's portfolio focused on property and casualty insurance, on both a direct and reinsurance basis. The investment portfolios of the Insurance Group included meaningful equity interests in ten other publicly traded companies. The equity interests are summarized in **Exhibit 2,** along with Berkshire's share of undistributed operating earnings in these companies. Because the earnings in some of these companies could not be consolidated with Berkshire's under GAAP rules, Buffett published Berkshire's "look-through" earnings[6]—as shown in **Exhibit 2,** the share of undistributed earnings of major investees accounted for 40–50 percent of Berkshire's total "look-through" earnings. **Exhibit 3** summarizes investments in convertible preferred stocks[7] that Berkshire Hathaway had made in recent years, serving as a "white squire" to major corporations—each of these firms had been the target of actual or rumored takeover attempts.
- *Buffalo News.* A daily and Sunday newspaper in upstate New York.
- *Fechheimer.* A manufacturer and distributor of uniforms.
- *Kirby.* A manufacturer and marketer of home cleaning systems and accessories.
- *Nebraska Furniture.* A retailer of home furnishings.
- *See's Candies.* A manufacturer and distributor of boxed chocolates and other confectionery products.
- *Childcraft and World Book.* A publisher and distributor of encyclopedias and related educational and instructional material.

---

[4]*Stocks, Bonds, Bills, and Inflation* (Chicago: Ibbotson Associates, 1994), 10.

[5]Berkshire Hathaway, Inc., 1994 Annual Report, 6.

[6]"Look-through" earnings were calculated as the sum of Berkshire's operating earnings reported in its income statement, plus the retained operating earnings of major investees not reflected in Berkshire's profits, less tax on what would be paid by Berkshire if these earnings had been distributed to Berkshire. (The presentation used a 14 percent tax rate, the rate Berkshire paid on dividends it received.)

[7]Convertible preferred stock was preferred stock that carried the right to be exchanged by the investor for common stock. The exchange, or "conversion," right was like a call option on the common stock of the issuer. The terms of the convertible preferred stated the price at which common shares could be acquired in exchange for the principal value of the convertible preferred stock.

- *Campbell Hausfeld.* A manufacturer and distributor of air compressors, air tools, and painting systems.
- *H.H. Brown Shoe Company; Lowell Shoe, Inc.; and Dexter Shoe Company.* A manufacturer, importer, and distributor of footwear.

In addition to these businesses, Berkshire owned an assortment of smaller businesses[8] generating about $400 million in revenues.

BERKSHIRE HATHAWAY'S ACQUISITION POLICY

The GEICO announcement renewed general interest in Buffett's approach to acquisitions. **Exhibit 4** gives the formal statement of acquisition criteria contained in Berkshire Hathaway's 1994 Annual Report. In general, the policy expressed a tightly disciplined strategy that refused to reward others for actions that Berkshire Hathaway might just as easily take on its own. Therefore, analysts scrutinized the criteria to assess where they might offer winning ideas to Buffett.

One prominent example to which Buffett referred was Berkshire Hathaway's investment in Scott & Fetzer in 1986. The managers of Scott & Fetzer had attempted a leveraged buyout of the company in the face of a rumored hostile takeover attempt. When the Labor Department objected to the company's use of an employee stock ownership plan to assist in the financing, the deal fell apart. Soon the company attracted unsolicited proposals to purchase the company, including one from Ivan F. Boesky, the arbitrageur. Buffett offered to buy the company for $315 million (which compared to its book value of $172.6 million). Following the acquisition, Scott & Fetzer paid Berkshire Hathaway dividends of $125 million, even though it earned only $40.3 million that year. In addition, Scott & Fetzer was conservatively financed, going from modest debt at the acquisition to virtually no debt by 1994. **Exhibit 5** gives the earnings and dividends for Scott & Fetzer from 1986 to 1994. Buffett noted that in terms of return on book value of equity, Scott & Fetzer would have easily beaten the Fortune 500 firms.[9] The annual average total return on large company stocks from 1986 to 1994 was 12.6 percent.[10]

BUFFETT'S INVESTMENT PHILOSOPHY

Warren Buffett was first exposed to formal training in investing at Columbia University, where he studied under Professor Benjamin Graham. The coauthor of a classic text, *Security Analysis,* Graham developed a method of identifying undervalued stocks (i.e., stocks

---

[8]These included companies in conduit fittings, marketing motivational services, retailing fine jewelry, air compressors, sun and shade control products, appliance controls, zinc die-cast fittings, automotive compounds, pressure and flow measurement devices, fractional horsepower motors, boat winches, cutlery, truck bodies, furnace burners, compressed gas fittings, and molded plastic components.

[9]This exempts from the comparison firms emerging from bankruptcy in recent years. Buffett's observation was made in Berkshire Hathaway's 1994 Annual Report.

[10]*Stocks, Bonds, Bills, and Inflation.*

whose price was less than "intrinsic value"). This became the cornerstone of the modern approach of "value investing." Graham's approach was to focus on the value of assets such as cash, net working capital and physical assets. Eventually, Buffett modified that approach to focus also on valuable franchises that were not recognized by the market.

Over the years, Buffett had expounded his philosophy of investing in his CEO's letter to shareholders in Berkshire Hathaway's annual report. By 1995, these lengthy letters had accumulated a broad following because of their wisdom and their humorous, self-deprecating tone. The letters emphasized the following elements:

1. *Economic reality, not accounting reality.* Financial statements prepared by accountants conformed to rules that might not adequately represent the *economic* reality of a business. Buffett wrote:

   > Because of the limitations of conventional accounting, consolidated reported earnings may reveal relatively little about our true economic performance. Charlie and I, both as owners and managers, virtually ignore such consolidated numbers. . . . Accounting consequences do not influence our operating or capital-allocation process.[11]

   Accounting reality was conservative, backward-looking, and governed by generally accepted accounting principles (GAAP). Investment decisions, on the other hand, should be based on the economic reality of a business. In economic reality, intangible assets such as patents, trademarks, special managerial know-how, and reputation might be very valuable, yet under GAAP, they would be carried at little or no value. GAAP measured results in terms of net profit; in economic reality, the results of a business were its *flows of cash.*

   A key feature of Buffett's approach defined economic reality at the level of the business itself, not the market, the economy, or the security—he was a *fundamental analyst* of a business. His analysis sought to judge the simplicity of the business, the consistency of its operating history, the attractiveness of its long-term prospects, the quality of management, and the firm's capacity to create value.

2. *The cost of the lost opportunity.* Buffett compared an investment opportunity against the next best alternative, the so-called "lost opportunity." In his business decisions, he demonstrated a tendency to frame his choices as "either/or" decisions rather than "yes/no" decisions. Thus, an important standard of comparison in testing the attractiveness of an acquisition was the potential rate of return from investing in common stocks of other companies. Buffett held that there was no fundamental difference between buying a business outright and buying a few shares of that business in the equity market. Thus, for him, the comparison of an investment against other returns available in the market was an important benchmark of performance.

3. *Value creation: time is money.* Buffett assessed intrinsic value as the present value of future expected performance.

   > [All other methods fall short in determining whether] an investor is indeed buying something for what it is worth and is therefore truly operating on the principle of obtaining value for his investments. . . . Irrespective of whether a business grows or doesn't, displays volatility or smoothness

---

[11]Berkshire Hathaway, Inc., 1994 Annual Report, 2.

in earnings, or carries a high price or low in relation to its current earnings and book value, the investment shown by the discounted-flows-of-cash calculation to be the cheapest is the one that the investor should purchase.[12]

Enlarging on his discussion of "intrinsic value," Buffett used an educational example:

> We define intrinsic value as the discounted value of the cash that can be taken out of a business during its remaining life. Anyone calculating intrinsic value necessarily comes up with a highly subjective figure that will change both as estimates of future cash flows are revised and as interest rates move. Despite its fuzziness, however, intrinsic value is all-important and is the only logical way to evaluate the relative attractiveness of investments and businesses.
>
> To see how historical input (book value) and future output (intrinsic value) can diverge, let us look at another form of investment, a college education. Think of the education's cost as its "book value." If it is to be accurate, the cost should include the earnings that were forgone by the student because he chose college rather than a job. For this exercise, we will ignore the important noneconomic benefits of an education and focus strictly on its economic value. First, we must estimate the earnings that the graduate will receive over his lifetime and subtract from that figure an estimate of what he would have earned had he lacked his education. That gives us an excess earnings figure, which must then be discounted, at an appropriate interest rate, back to graduation day. The dollar result equals the intrinsic economic value of the education. Some graduates will find that the book value of their education exceeds its intrinsic value, which means that whoever paid for the education didn't get his money's worth. In other cases, the intrinsic value of an education will far exceed its book value, a result that proves capital was wisely deployed. In all cases, what is clear is that book value is meaningless as an indicator of intrinsic value.[13]

To illustrate the mechanics of this example, consider the hypothetical case presented in **Exhibit 6.** Suppose an individual has the opportunity to invest $50 million in a business—this is its "cost" or "book value." This business will throw off cash at the rate of 20 percent of its investment base each year. Suppose that instead of receiving any dividends, the owner decides to reinvest all cash flow back into the business—at this rate, the "book value" of the business will grow at 20 percent per year. Suppose that the investor plans to sell the business for its "book value" at the end of the fifth year. Does this investment create value for the individual? One determines this by discounting the future cash flows to the present at a cost of equity of 15 percent—suppose that this is the investor's opportunity cost, the required return that could have been earned elsewhere at comparable risk. Dividing the present value of future cash flows (i.e., Buffett's "intrinsic value") by the cost of the investment (i.e., Buffett's "book value") indicates that every dollar invested buys securities worth $1.23. Value is created.

Consider an opposing case, summarized in **Exhibit 7.** The example is similar in all respects except for one key difference: the annual return on the investment is 10 percent. The result is that every dollar invested buys securities worth $0.80. Value is destroyed.

Comparing the two cases in **Exhibits 6** and **7,** the difference in value creation and destruction is driven entirely by the relationship between the expected returns and the discount rate: in the first case, the spread is positive; in the second case, it is negative.

---

[12]Berkshire Hathaway, Inc., 1992 Annual Report, 14.
[13]Berkshire Hathaway, Inc., 1994 Annual Report, 7.

Only in the instance where expected returns equal the discount rate will "book value" equal intrinsic value. In short, book value or the investment outlay may not reflect economic reality: one needs to focus on the prospective rates of return, and how they compare to the required rate of return.

4. *Measure performance by gain in intrinsic value, not accounting profit.* Buffett wrote:

> Our long-term economic goal . . . is to maximize the average annual rate of gain in intrinsic business value on a per-share basis. We do not measure the economic significance or performance of Berkshire by its size; we measure by per-share progress.[14]

The gain in intrinsic value could be modeled as the value added by a business above and beyond a charge for the use of capital in that business. The gain in intrinsic value was analogous to "economic profit" and "market value added," measures used by analysts in leading corporations to assess financial performance. Those measures focus on the ability to earn returns in excess of the cost of capital.

5. *Risk and discount rates.* Conventional academic and practitioner thinking held that the more risk one took, the more one should get paid. Thus, discount rates used in determining intrinsic values should be determined by the risk of the cash flows being valued. The conventional model for estimating discount rates was the Capital Asset Pricing Model (CAPM), which added a risk premium to the long-term risk-free rate of return (such as the U.S. Treasury bond yield).

Buffett departed from conventional thinking by using the rate of return on the long-term (e.g., 30-year) U.S. Treasury bond to discount cash flows.[15] Defending this practice, Buffett argued that he avoided risk, and therefore should use a "risk-free" discount rate. His firm used almost no debt financing. He focused on companies with predictable and stable earnings. He or his vice chairman, Charlie Munger, sat on the boards of directors where they obtained a candid, inside view of the company and could intervene in decisions of management if necessary. Buffett wrote:

> I put a heavy weight on certainty. If you do that, the whole idea of a risk factor doesn't make sense to me. Risk comes from not knowing what you're doing.[16]
>
> We define risk, using dictionary terms, as "the possibility of loss or injury." Academics, however, like to define "risk" differently, averring that it is the relative volatility of a stock or a portfolio of stocks—that is, the volatility as compared to that of a large universe of stocks. Employing databases and statistical skills, these academics compute with precision the "beta" of a stock—its relative volatility in the past—and then build arcane investment and capital allocation theories around this calculation. In their hunger for a single statistic to measure risk, however, they forget a fundamental principle: it is better to be approximately right than precisely wrong.[17]

6. *Diversification.* Buffett disagreed with conventional wisdom that investors should hold a broad portfolio of stocks in order to shed company-specific risk. In his view, investors

---

[14]Ibid., 2.

[15]The yield on the 30-year U.S. Treasury bond on August 25, 1995, was 6.86 percent. The beta of Berkshire Hathaway was 0.95.

[16]Quoted in Jim Rasmussen, "Buffett Talks Strategy with Students," *Omaha World-Herald,* January 2, 1994, p. 26.

[17]Berkshire Hathaway, Inc., 1993 Annual Report, and republished in Andrew Kilpatrick, *Of Permanent Value: The Story of Warren Buffett* (Birmingham, Ala.: AKPE, 1994), 574.

typically purchased far too many stocks rather than waiting for the one exceptional company. Buffett said,

> Figure businesses out that you understand, and concentrate. Diversification is protection against ignorance, but if you don't feel ignorant, the need for it goes down drastically.[18]

7. *Investing behavior should be driven by information, analysis, and self-discipline, not by emotion or "hunch."* Buffett repeatedly emphasized "awareness" and information as the foundation for investing. He said, "Anyone not aware of the fool in the market probably is the fool in the market."[19] Buffett was fond of repeating a parable told him by Benjamin Graham:

> There was a small private business and one of the owners was a man named Market. Every day Mr. Market had a new opinion of what the business was worth, and at that price stood ready to buy your interest or sell you his. As excitable as he was opinionated, Mr. Market presented a constant distraction to his fellow owners. "What does he know?" they would wonder, as he bid them an extraordinarily high price or a depressingly low one. Actually, the gentleman knew little or nothing. You may be happy to sell out to him when he quotes you a ridiculously high price, and equally happy to buy from him when his price is low. But the rest of the time you will be wiser to form your own ideas of the value of your holdings, based on full reports from the company about its operation and financial position.[20]

Buffett used this allegory to illustrate the irrationality of stock prices as compared to true intrinsic value. Graham believed that an investor's worst enemy was not the stock market, but oneself. Superior training could not compensate for the absence of the requisite temperament for investing. Over the long term, stock prices should have a strong relationship with the economic progress of the business. But daily market quotations were heavily influenced by momentary greed or fear, and were an unreliable measure of intrinsic value. Buffett said,

> As far as I am concerned, the stock market doesn't exist. It is there only as a reference to see if anybody is offering to do anything foolish. When we invest in stocks, we invest in businesses. You simply have to behave according to what is rational rather than according to what is fashionable.[21]

Accordingly, Buffett did not try to "time the market" (i.e., trade stocks based on expectations of changes in the market cycle)—his was a strategy of patient, long-term investing. As if in contrast to "Mr. Market," Buffett expressed more contrarian goals: "We simply attempt to be fearful when others are greedy and to be greedy only when others are fearful."[22] Buffett also said, "Lethargy bordering on sloth remains the cornerstone of our investment style,"[23] and "The market, like the Lord, helps those who help themselves. But unlike the Lord, the market does not forgive those who know not what they do."[24]

---

[18]Quoted in *Forbes* (October 19, 1993), and republished in Andrew Kilpatrick, *Of Permanent Value,* 574.

[19]Quoted in Michael Lewis, *Liar's Poker* (New York: Norton, 1989), 35.

[20]Originally published in Berkshire Hathaway, Inc., 1987 Annual Report, 1987. This quotation was paraphrased from James Grant, *Minding Mr. Market* (New York: Times Books, 1993), xxi.

[21]Peter Lynch, *One Up on Wall Street* (New York: Penguin Books, 1990), 78.

[22]Berkshire Hathaway, Inc., 1986 Annual Report, 16.

[23]Berkshire Hathaway, Inc., 1990 Annual Report, 15.

[24]Berkshire Hathaway, Inc., *Letters to Shareholders, 1977–1983,* 53.

Buffett scorned the academic theory of capital market efficiency. The Efficient Markets Hypothesis (EMH) held that publicly known information was rapidly impounded into share prices, and that as a result, stock prices were "fair" in reflecting what was known about a company. Under EMH, there were no bargains to be had and trying to outperform the market would be futile. "It has been helpful to me to have tens of thousands turned out of business schools taught that it didn't do any good to think," Buffett said.[25]

> I think it's fascinating how the ruling orthodoxy can cause a lot of people to think the earth is flat. Investing in a market where people believe in efficiency is like playing bridge with someone who's been told it doesn't do any good to look at the cards.[26]

8. *Alignment of agents and owners.* Explaining his significant ownership interest in Berkshire Hathaway, Buffett said, "I am a better businessman because I am an investor. And I am a better investor because I am a businessman."[27]

As if to illustrate this sentiment, he said,

> A managerial "wish list" will not be filled at shareholder expense. We will not diversify by purchasing entire businesses at control prices that ignore long-term economic consequences to our shareholders. We will only do with your money what we would do with our own, weighing fully the values you can obtain by diversifying your own portfolios through direct purchases in the stock market.[28]

For four of Berkshire's six directors, over 50 percent of their family net worth was represented by shares in Berkshire Hathaway. The senior managers of Berkshire Hathaway subsidiaries held shares in the company, or were compensated under incentive plans that imitated the potential returns from an equity interest in their business unit, or both.

GEICO CORPORATION

Berkshire Hathaway began purchasing shares in GEICO in 1976, and by 1980 had accumulated a 33 percent interest (34.25 million shares) for $45.7 million. During the period 1976–1980, GEICO's share price had been hammered by double-digit inflation, higher accident rates, and high damage awards that raised the costs of its business more rapidly than premiums could be increased. By August 1995, that stake had grown to 50.4 percent of the firm's shares (because GEICO had repurchased some of its own shares while Berkshire had maintained its holdings) and the original stake of $45.7 million had grown in value to $1.9 billion.[29] Also, GEICO had paid an increasing dividend each year (see **Exhibit 8**). From 1976 to 1994, the average annual total return on large company stocks was 13.5 percent.[30]

---

[25]Quoted in Andrew Kilpatrick, *Of Permanent Value,* 353.
[26]Quoted in L. J. Davis, "Buffett Takes Stock," *New York Times,* April 1, 1990, 16.
[27]Quoted in *Forbes,* (October 19, 1993), and republished in Andrew Kilpatrick, *Of Permanent Value,* 574.
[28]"Owner-Related Business Principles" in Berkshire Hathaway's 1994 Annual Report, 3.
[29]This assumes the pre-announcement GEICO share price of $55.75.
[30]*Stocks, Bonds, Bills, and Inflation,* 10.

In explaining the decision to acquire the rest of the shares in GEICO, Buffett noted:

- The firm was the seventh-largest auto insurer in the United States, underwriting policies for 3.7 million cars.
- The firm's senior managers were "extraordinary" and had an investment style similar to Buffett's. These managers would add depth to Berkshire Hathaway's senior management bench and provide continuity in case anything happened to Buffett (age 65) or Munger (age 72).
- The firm was the lowest-cost insurance provider in the industry.

Some analysts sought to test the suitability of Buffett's $70-per-share offer for GEICO using the discounted-cash-flow approach. On July 7, 1995, *Value Line Investment Survey* published a forecast of GEICO's dividends[31] and future stock price within a range of possible outcomes.

***Value Line* Forecast Information**

	Low End of Range	High End of Range
Forecasted Dividends		
1996	$1.16	$1.16
1997	$1.25	$1.34
1998	$1.34	$1.55
1999	$1.44	$1.79
2000	$1.55	$2.07
Forecasted Stock Price in 2000	$90.00	$125.00

Value Line also presented evidence consistent with a cost of equity for GEICO of 11 percent.[32] GEICO had outstanding 67,889,574 shares as of April 30, 1995. Analysts noted that the timing of Berkshire Hathaway's bid followed closely Walt Disney Company's bid to buy Capital Cities/ABC for $19 billion.

CONCLUSION

Conventional thinking held that it would be difficult for Warren Buffett to maintain his record of 28 percent annual growth in shareholder wealth. Buffett acknowledged that "a fat wallet is the enemy of superior investment results."[33] He stated that it was the firm's goal to meet a 15 percent annual growth rate in intrinsic value. Would the GEICO acquisition serve the long-term goals of Berkshire Hathaway? Was the bid price appropriate? What might account for the share price increase for Berkshire Hathaway at the announcement?

---

[31]GEICO paid dividends quarterly, though *Value Line* presented only an annual forecast. Annual figures are given here for simplicity.

[32]Analysts used the Capital Asset Pricing Model to estimate GEICO's cost of equity. *Value Line* estimated GEICO's beta at 0.75. (In comparison, Berkshire Hathaway's beta was 0.95.) The equity market risk premium was about 5.5 percent. And the risk-free rate estimated by the yield on the 30-year U.S. Treasury bond was 6.86 percent.

[33]Quoted in Garth Alexander, "Buffett Spends $2bn on Return to His Roots," *Times* (London), August 17, 1995.

EXHIBIT 1
Business Segment Information, Berkshire Hathaway, Inc. (dollars in millions)

Segment	Revenues		Pretax Opng. Profit[2]		Capital Expenditures		Depreciation		Identifiable Assets	
	1994	1993	1994	1993	1994	1993	1994	1993	1994	1993
Insurance	$1,437	$1,591	$639	$961	$0.9	$1.2	$0.9	$0.8	$18,494	$16,127
Candy	216	201	47	40	4.1	4.3	4.1	4.1	69	70
Encyclopedias	191	199	24	19	0.1	0.7	1.4	1.5	76	75
Home-cleaning systems	207	193	44	41	1.0	1.5	4.2	5.3	42	49
Home furnishings	245	209	17	21	22.6	5.3	6.2	2.7	128	101
Newspaper	151	145	54	50	5.2	3.6	2.2	1.9	48	45
Shoes	609	370	76	40	17.9	4.4	10.2	5.2	673	642
Uniforms	151	122	14	13	4.6	1.0	2.5	1.8	95	88
Other	639	568	(192)[1]	60	10.7	13.0	18.0	17.3	1,712	2,324
Total	$3,847	$3,599	$722	$1,246	$67.1	$35.0	$49.6	$40.5	$21,338	$19,520

[1]Includes pretax charge of $269, representing an other-than-temporary decline in value of investment in USAir Group, Inc., preferred stock.
[2]Before interest expense.
N.B. Columns may not sum to the total because of rounding.

Source: Berkshire Hathaway, Inc., 1994 Annual Report.

EXHIBIT 2
Major Investees of Berkshire Hathaway, and "Look-Through Earnings"
(dollars in millions)

Berkshire's Major Investees	Berkshire's Approximate Ownership at Year-end		Berkshires Share of Undistributed Operating Earnings (in millions)	
	1994	1993	1994	1993
American Express Co.	5.5%	2.4%	$ 25	$ 16
Capital Cities/ABC	13.0	13.0	85	83
Coca-Cola	7.8	7.2	116	94
Federal Home Loan Mtge.	6.3	6.8	47	41
Gannett	4.9	—	4	—
GEICO	50.2	48.4	63	76
Gillette	10.8	10.9	51	44
PNC Bank	8.3	—	10	—
Washington Post	15.2	14.8	18	15
Wells Fargo	13.3%	12.2%	$73	$ 53
Berkshire's share of undistributed earnings			$ 492	$422
Hypothetical tax on these earnings			(68)	(59)
Reported operating earnings of Berkshire			606	478
Total "Look-through" earnings of Berkshire			$1,030	$841

Source: Berkshire Hathaway, Inc., 1994 Annual Report, 13.

EXHIBIT 3
Berkshire's Investments in Private Purchases of Convertible Preferred Stocks

	Dividend Yield on Par Value	Year of Purchase	Cost ($mm)	Market Value ($mm at December 1995)
Champion International Corp.[1]	9.25%	1989	$300	$ 388
First Empire State Corp.[2]	9.00	1991	40	110
The Gillette Company[3]	8.75	1989	600	2,502
Salomon, Inc.[4]	9.00	1987	700	728
USAir Group, Inc.[5]	9.25	1989	358	215

[1]The Champion International issue could be converted into common shares at $38.00 per share. At August 25, 1995, Champion International's common share price was $57.50. By December 31, 1995, Champion's share price had fallen to $42.75.
[2]The First Empire issue could be converted into common shares at a conversion price of $78.91 per share. First Empire has the right to redeem the issue beginning in 1996. At August 25, 1995, First Empire's common share price was $184.50.
[3]The Gillette issue could be converted into common stock at $25.00 per share, and carried a mandatory redemption by Gillette after 10 years. In February 1991, following the highly successful introduction of the Sensor razor, Gillette announced that it would redeem the issue at $31.75, which effectively forced Berkshire to convert its holding into common stock. Berkshire converted, and received 12 million common shares, or 11 percent o
f Gillette's total shares outstanding. At August 25, 1995, Gillette's share price was $43.00.
[4]The Salomon issue could be converted into common stock at $38.00 per share. If Berkshire did not convert the preferred stock, Salomon would redeem it over five years, beginning October 1995. At August 25, 1995, Salomon's common share price was $37.125.
[5]The USAir issue could be converted into common shares at $60 per share. If Berkshire did not convert the series into common stock, USAir would have to redeem the preferred in 10 years. At August 25, 1995, the USAir common share price was $8.50.

Source: Berkshire Hathaway, Inc., 1995 Annual Report, 16.

EXHIBIT 4
Berkshire Hathaway Acquisition Criteria

We are eager to hear about businesses that meet all of the following criteria:

1. Large purchases (at least $10 million of after-tax earnings).
2. Demonstrated consistent earning power (future projections are of no interest to us, nor are "turnaround" situations).
3. Businesses earning good returns on equity while employing little or no debt.
4. Management in place (we can't supply it).
5. Simple businesses (if there's lots of technology, we won't understand it).
6. An offering price (we don't want to waste our time or that of the seller by talking, even preliminarily, about a transaction when the price is unknown).

The larger the company, the greater will be our interest: we would like to make an acquisition in the $2–3 billion range.

We will not engage in unfriendly takeovers. We can promise complete confidentiality and a very fast answer—customarily within five minutes—as to whether we're interested. We prefer to buy for cash, but will consider issuing stock when we receive as much in intrinsic business value as we give.

Our favorite form of purchase is one fitting the pattern through which we acquired Nebraska Furniture Mart, Fechheimer's, Borsheim's, and Central States Indemnity. In cases like these, the company's owner-managers wish to generate significant amounts of cash, sometimes for themselves, but often for their families or inactive shareholders. At the same time, these managers wish to remain significant owners who continue to run their companies just as they have in the past. We think we offer a particularly good fit for owners with such objectives and we invite potential sellers to check us out by contacting people with whom we have done business in the past.

Charlie and I frequently get approached about acquisitions that don't come close to meeting our tests: We've found that if you advertise an interest in buying collies, a lot of people will call hoping to sell you their cocker spaniels. A line from a country song expresses our feeling about new ventures, turnarounds, or auction-like sales: "When the phone don't ring, you'll know it's me."

Besides being interested in the purchase of businesses as described above, we are also interested in the negotiated purchase of large, but not controlling, blocks of stock comparable to those we hold in Capital Cities, Salomon, Gillette, USAir, and Champion. *We are not interested, however, in receiving suggestions about purchases we might make in the general stock market.*

Source: Berkshire Hathaway, Inc., 1994 Annual Report, 21.

EXHIBIT 5
Scott & Fetzer, Book Value of Equity, Earnings,
and Dividends, 1986–1994

	Beginning Book Value	Earnings	Dividends	Ending Book Value
1986	$172.6	$40.3	$125.0	$87.9
1987	87.9	48.6	41.0	95.5
1988	95.5	58.0	35.0	118.5
1989	118.5	58.5	71.5	105.5
1990	105.5	61.3	33.5	133.3
1991	133.3	61.4	74.0	120.7
1992	120.7	70.5	80.0	111.2
1993	111.2	77.5	98.0	90.7
1994	90.7	79.3	76.0	94.0

Source: Berkshire Hathaway, Inc., 1994 Annual Report, 7.

EXHIBIT 6
Hypothetical Example of Value Creation

Assume:
- 5-year investment horizon, when you liquidate at "book" or accumulated investment value
- initial investment is $50 million
- no dividends are paid, all cash flows are reinvested
- ROE = 20%
- Cost of equity = 15%

Year	0	1	2	3	4	5
Investment or **Book** Equity **Value**	50	60	72	86	104	124

Market Value (or "Intrinsic Value") = PV @ 15% of 124 = $61.65
Market/Book   = $61.65/50.00 = 1.23
Value created: $1.00 invested becomes $1.23 in market value.

Source: Casewriter analysis.

EXHIBIT 7
Hypothetical Example of Value Destruction

Assume:
- 5-year investment horizon, when you liquidate at "book" or accumulated investment value
- initial investment is $50 million
- no dividends are paid, all cash flows are reinvested
- ROE = 10%
- Cost of equity = 15%

Year	0	1	2	3	4	5
Investment or **Book** Equity **Value**	50	55	60	67	73	81

Market Value (or "Intrinsic Value") = PV @ 15% of $81 = $40.30
Market/Book   = $40.30/50.00 = 0.80
Value destroyed: $1.00 invested becomes $0.80 in market value.

Source: Casewriter analysis.

EXHIBIT 8
GEICO Dividend Payment History

Year	GEICO Dividend per Share	Total Dividends to Berkshire Hathaway
1976	$0.00	$ 0.00
1977	0.01	0.34
1978	0.04	1.37
1979	0.07	2.40
1980	0.09	3.08
1981	0.10	3.43
1982	0.11	3.77
1983	0.14	4.80
1984	0.18	6.17
1985	0.20	6.85
1986	0.22	7.54
1987	0.27	9.25
1988	0.33	11.30
1989	0.36	12.33
1990	0.40	13.70
1991	0.46	15.76
1992	0.60	20.55
1993	0.68	23.29
1994	1.00	34.25

Note: Total dividends to Berkshire were estimated by multiplying the per-share dividend times 34.25 million shares, Berkshire's holdings in GEICO. This presentation assumes that all of Berkshire's shares in GEICO were acquired in 1976.
Source of annual dividends per share: *Value Line Investment Survey.*

The Fidelity Magellan Fund, 1995

1988: The only thing that sets him apart is this: for ten years now, he has been the best mutual fund manager alive. . . . "Around Fidelity," says one former marketing aide, "Peter Lynch is God."[1]

1991: Morris Smith does things his way at Fidelity Magellan—but he gets the same old stellar results.[2]

1993: If young Jeff Vinik keeps up his torrid performance as manager of Fidelity's Magellan Fund, his shareholders might soon forget there ever was a Peter Lynch. . . . Vinik is now the hero.[3]

In the autumn of 1995, investors in the Magellan Fund of Fidelity Management & Research Company (FMR) could look back on a remarkable record of performance: an average annual total return of 22.7 percent per year over the previous 15 years, which surpassed the

---

[1]Joseph Nocera, "The Ga-Ga Years," *Esquire* (February 1988): 87.
[2]Geoffrey Smith, "Peter Lynch? Who's Peter Lynch?" *Business Week* (May 20, 1991): 118.
[3]"Who Needs Peter Lynch? Upstart Magellan Manager Scores Big" *Barron's* (June 21, 1993): 36.

return on the Standard & Poor's 500 Index (S&P 500) by 7.77 percent per year. In addition, the fund beat the broad market average for the previous 10, 5, and 3 years—results that Fidelity advertised in soliciting new investors to the fund. These results stood in stark contrast to the historical performance of equally ambitious and talented managers of other mutual funds. Furthermore, the results contrasted with conventional theories suggesting that in markets characterized by high competition, easy entry, and informational efficiency, it would be extremely difficult to "beat the market" on a sustained basis. Observers wondered what might explain Magellan's performance.

Of special note was that the fund had delivered superior performance despite turnover in its management. The fund's long-standing and highly successful manager, Peter Lynch, retired in 1990 at the age of 46. His replacement was Morris Smith, who retired in 1992 at the age of 34. *His* replacement was the present manager, Jeffrey Vinik, now 36. The financial press noted that all three managers "beat the market" during their tenure.

The Magellan Fund was the largest equity mutual fund in the world, with nearly $51 billion in net assets in late 1995. FMR, the parent of Fidelity Investments, which provided management and advisory services to the fund's shareholders, was a privately held company, managing 223 funds. Fidelity's revenue in 1992 was $1.84 billion; net income was $94 million.[4] Fidelity's assets under management in 1995 were nearly $390 billion. Wide acknowledgment placed Fidelity among the most innovative—and aggressive—mutual fund advisers in the industry.

THE U.S. EQUITY MARKET

Institutional investors, or "money managers," who managed pension funds and mutual funds on behalf of individual investors dominated the market for common stocks in the United States in the mid-1990s. While statistics still revealed that households, life insurance companies, personal trusts (i.e., those managed by bank trust departments), and nonprofit institutions held the majority of shares of common stock, the percentage had been declining over the previous 30 years. Indeed, at the end of 1994, equity mutual funds owned only 13 percent of the almost $6 trillion of market value of American common stock—private pension funds owned slightly more than 13 percent.

But the aggregate figures somewhat masked the explosive growth of mutual funds from 1979 to 1995. Over this period, assets of all mutual funds grew from $95 billion to $2.6 trillion. Moreover, the percent of individual investors who owned mutual fund shares rose from 15.8 percent to about 33 percent between 1981 and 1995.

More importantly, the sheer dominance of money managers appeared not in assets held but in their trading muscle—their ability to move huge sums of money into and out of stocks on short notice. Accordingly, money managers were the principal price setters (or "lead steers") in the stock market. Approximately 90 percent of all trades on the New York Stock Exchange (NYSE) involved institutional investors. The rising dominance of institutional in-

---

[4]Alyssa A. Lappen, "Fidelity Grapples with Gigantism," *Institutional Investor* (September 1995): 90.

vestors resulted in the growth of trading volume, average trade size, and especially in block trading (i.e., individual trades of more than 10,000 shares) which was virtually nonexistent 30 years ago but by 1986 accounted for about half of the trading volume.

MUTUAL FUND INDUSTRY

Mutual funds served several economic functions for investors. First, they afforded the individual investor the opportunity to diversify his or her portfolio efficiently (i.e., own many different stocks) without having to invest the sizable amount of capital usually necessary to achieve efficiency. Efficiency was also reflected in the ability of mutual funds to exploit scale economies in trading and transactions costs, economies unavailable to the typical individual investor. Second, in theory, mutual funds provided the individual investor the professional expertise necessary to earn abnormal returns through successful securities analysis.

A third view was that the mutual fund industry provided "an insulating layer between the individual investor and the painful vicissitudes of the marketplace":

> This service, after all, allows individuals to go about their daily lives without spending too much time on the aggravating subject of what to buy and sell and when, and it spares them the even greater aggravation of kicking themselves for making the wrong decision. . . . Thus, the money management industry is really selling "more peace of mind" and "less worry," though it rarely bothers to say so.[5]

In the 10 years from 1985 to 1995, the number of mutual funds grew from 1,528 to 6,683.[6] This total included many different kinds of funds, each pursuing a specific investment focus and categorized into several acknowledged segments of the industry: aggressive growth (i.e., capital appreciation-oriented), equity-income, growth, growth and income, international, option, specialty, small company, balanced, and a variety of bond or fixed-income funds.[7] Funds whose principal focus of investing was common stocks comprised the largest sector of the industry.

To some extent, the growth in number and types of mutual funds reflected the increased liquidity in the market and the demand by investors for equity. But more importantly, it reflected the effort by mutual fund organizations to segment the market, (i.e., to identify the specialized and changing needs of investors, and to create products to meet those needs). One important result was a broader customer base for the mutual fund industry as well as deeper penetration of the total market for financial services.

Another important result of this development was that it added a degree of complexity to the marketplace that altered the investment behavior of some equity investors. In particular, this tended to encourage fund switching, especially from one type of fund to another within a

---

[5]Contrarious, "Good News and Bad News," *Personal Investing* (August 26, 1987): 128.

[6]"The Seismic Shift in American Finance," *Economist* (October 21, 1995): 75; Morningstar Mutual Funds, September 29, 1995.

[7]Aggressive growth funds seek to maximize capital gains. Current income is of little concern. Growth funds invest in more well-known companies with steadier track records. Growth and income funds invest in companies with longer track records that are expected to increase in value and provide a steady income stream. International funds invest in foreign companies. Option funds seek to maximize current returns by investing in dividend-paying stocks on which call options are traded. Balanced funds attempt to conserve principal while earning both current income and capital gains.

family of funds. This reflected the greater range of mutual funds from which to choose, the increased volatility in the market, and the increased trend toward timing-oriented investment strategies. In short, as the mutual fund industry grew, mutual fund money became "hotter" (i.e., it tended to turn over faster).

The performance of a mutual fund could be evaluated in terms of its total returns to investors as calculated by:

$$\text{Annual total return} = \frac{\text{Change in net asset value} + \text{Dividends} + \text{Capital gain distributions}}{\text{Net asset value (at the beginning of the year)}}$$

Net asset value (NAV) was computed as total assets, less liabilities, and divided by the number of mutual fund shares outstanding. Computing the annual total return in this manner took into account annual management fees, and did not take into account front-end or back-end "loads."

Mutual fund advisers received compensation under various schemes that featured variations on two components:

Initial payments: Nearly three-quarters of all mutual funds were sold under some kind of commission, sales fee, or "load." The load could be as large as 8.5 percent of the investor's principal. Back-end loads (i.e., redemption fees) were also possible.

Annual fees: Annual management fees ranged from under 0.5 to over 2 percent of fund assets. Some funds also charged a separate fee for marketing and promotion expenses, which could run up to 2 percent of assets.

The net effect of these payments on shareholder returns could be dramatic.[8] Another drag on returns to shareholders was the tendency of funds to keep 10 percent of assets in cash—5 percent to meet redemptions, and 5 percent to meet unexpected bargains. In comparison, Magellan carried only 1.4 percent in cash before the stock market crash in October 1987, ultimately forcing Peter Lynch to dump $1 billion worth of shares in the market in order to meet unexpectedly high redemptions.[9]

PERFORMANCE OF THE MUTUAL FUND INDUSTRY

Exhibit 1 reveals that the average return on 1,841 domestic equity funds over the 1-, 5-, and 10-year periods was below that of the Wilshire 5000 Index of common stocks, and barely exceeded the S&P 500 over the three- and five-year range. Indices such as the Wilshire, S&P 500, Dow Jones, and Value Line, each were measures of the investment performance

---

[8]For instance, suppose that you invested $10,000 in a fund that would appreciate at 10 percent annually, and that you sold out after three years. Also, suppose that the advisory firm charged annual fees of 2 percent and a redemption fee of 4 percent. The fees would cut pretax profit by 35 percent—from $3,310 to $2,162.

[9]One observer of the industry, economist Henry Kaufman, warned that a sudden economywide shock from interest rates or commodities prices could spook investors into panic-style redemptions from mutual funds, who themselves would liquidate investments and send securities prices into a tailspin. Unlike the banking industry, which enjoys the liquidity afforded by the Federal Reserve System to respond to the effects of panic by depositors, the mutual fund industry enjoys no such government-backed reserve.

of hypothetical portfolios of stock.[10] In each of the recent years, only about one-quarter of all equity mutual funds provided returns (before fees and expenses) greater than the S&P 500. The performance of pension funds was similar.

The two most frequently used measures of performance were (1) the percentage annual growth rate of net asset value assuming reinvestment (i.e., total return on investment), and (2) the absolute dollar value today of an investment made at some time in the past. These measures were then compared to the performance of a benchmark portfolio such as the Wilshire 5000 or the S&P 500. However, academicians criticized these approaches because of their failure to adjust for the riskiness of the mutual fund. Over long periods, as **Exhibit 2** shows, different types of securities yielded different levels of total return. But **Exhibit 3** shows that each of these different types of securities was associated with different degrees of risk (measured as the standard deviation of returns). The relationship between risk and return was reliable on average and over time. For instance, it should be expected that a conservatively managed mutual fund would yield a lower return—precisely because it took fewer risks.

After adjusting for the riskiness of the fund, academic studies reported that mutual funds were able to perform up to the market on a gross returns basis; however, when expenses were factored in, they underperformed the market. For instance, Michael Jensen, in a paper published in 1968, reported that gross risk-adjusted returns were −0.4 percent and that net risk-adjusted returns (i.e., net of expenses) were −1.1 percent. In 1977, Main updated the study and found that for a sample of 70 mutual funds, net risk-adjusted returns were essentially zero. Some analysts attributed this general result to the average 1.3 percent expense ratio of mutual funds and their desire to hold cash.[11]

Most mutual fund managers relied on some variation of two classic schools of securities analysis:

> *Technical analysis:* This involved the identification of profitable investment opportunities based on trends in stock prices, volume, market sentiment, Fibonacci numbers, etc.[12]
> *Fundamental analysis:* This approach relied on insights afforded by an analysis of the economic fundamentals of a company and its industry: demand and supply, costs, growth prospects, etc.

While variations on these approaches often produced supernormal returns in certain years, there was no guarantee that they would produce such returns consistently over time.

---

[10]The Dow Jones indices of industrial companies. transportation companies, and utilities reflected the stocks of a small number (e.g., 30) of large "blue-chip" companies, all traded on the New York Stock Exchange. The S&P 500 was an index of shares of the 500 largest companies, traded on both the New York and American Stock Exchanges. The Value Line Index reflected 1,400 different companies. The Wilshire was the broadest index, and covered 5,000 companies—virtually the entire universe of regularly traded shares. As the index sample became larger, it reflected a greater weighting of smaller, high-growth companies.

[11]Jeffrey M. Laderman, "The Best Mutual Funds," *Business Week* (February 22, 1988): 64.

[12]The sequence, named for Leonard Fibonacci (1175–1240) consisted of the numbers 1, 1, 2, 3, 5, 8, 13 and so on. Each number after the first two equals the sum of the two numbers before it. No academic research associates this sequence with a consistent ability to earn supernormal returns from investing in the market.

Burton Malkiel, an academic researcher, concluded that a passive buy-and-hold strategy (of a large diversified portfolio) would do as well for the investor as the average mutual fund:

> Even a dart-throwing chimpanzee can select a portfolio that performs as well as one carefully selected by the experts. This, in essence, is the practical application of the theory of efficient markets. . . . The theory holds that the market appears to adjust so quickly to information about individual stocks and the economy as a whole, that no technique of selecting a portfolio—neither technical nor fundamental analysis—can consistently outperform a strategy of simply buying and holding a diversified group of securities such as those that make up the popular market averages. . . . [O]ne has to be impressed with the substantial volume of evidence suggesting that stock prices display a remarkable degree of efficiency. . . . If some degree of mispricing exists, it does not persist for long. "True value will always out" in the stock market.[13]

Many academicians accepted this view. They argued that the stock market followed a "random walk," where the price movements of tomorrow were essentially uncorrelated with the price movement of today. In essence, this denied the possibility that there could be momentum in the movement of common stock prices. According to this view, technical analysis was the modern-day equivalent of alchemy. Fundamental analysis, too, had its academic detractors. They argued that capital markets were informationally efficient and that the insights available to any one fundamental analyst were bound to be impounded quickly into share prices.

By implication, these academic theories were highly critical of the services provided by active mutual fund managers. Paul Samuelson, the Nobel Prize-winning economist, said:

> [E]xisting stock prices already have discounted in them an allowance for their future prospects. Hence . . . one stock [is] about as good or bad a buy as another. To [the] passive investor, chance alone would be as good a method of selection as anything else.[14]

Various popular tests of this thinking seemed to support it. For instance, *Forbes* magazine chose 28 stocks by throwing darts in June 1967 and invested $1,000 in each. By 1984, the $28,000 investment was worth $131,697.61 for a 9.5 percent compound rate of return. This beat the broad market averages and almost all mutual funds. *Forbes* concluded, "It would seem that a combination of luck and sloth beats brains."[15]

Yet, the nagging problem remained that there were still *some* superstar money managers—like Peter Lynch, Morris Smith, and Jeffrey Vinik—who, over long periods of time, greatly outperformed the market. In reply, Professor Burton Malkiel suggested that beating the market was much like participating in a coin-tossing contest where those who consistently flip heads are the winners.[16] At the first flip, half of the contestants are eliminated. At the second flip, half of the surviving contestants are eliminated. And so on until on the seventh flip only eight contestants remain. To the naive observer the ability to flip heads consistently looks like extraordinary skill. By analogy, Professor Malkiel suggested that the success of a few superstar portfolio managers could be explained as luck.

---

[13]Burton G. Malkiel, *A Random Walk Down Wall Street* (New York: Norton, 1990), 186, 211.

[14]Paul Samuelson, quoted in Malkiel, *A Random Walk Down Wall Street,* 182.

[15]*Forbes* (summer 1984), cited in Malkiel, *A Random Walk Down Wall Street,* 164.

[16]Malkiel, *A Random Walk Down Wall Street,* 175–76.

As might be expected, the community of money managers received the academic theories with great hostility. And even in the ranks of academicians, dissension appeared in the form of the "investment behaviorists" who suggested that greed, fear, and panic are much more significant factors in the setting of stock prices than the mainstream theory admits. For instance, the stock market crash of October 1987 seemed to many to be totally inconsistent with the view of markets as fundamentally rational and efficient. Professor Lawrence Summers of Harvard argued that the crash was a "clear gap with the theory. If anyone did seriously believe that price movements are determined by changes in information about economic fundamentals, they've got to be disabused of that notion by [the] 500-point drop."[17] Professor Robert Shiller of Yale said, "The efficient market hypothesis is the most remarkable error in the history of economic theory. This is just another nail in its coffin."[18]

Academic research exposed other inconsistencies with the efficient markets hypothesis. These included apparently predictable stock price patterns indicating reliably abnormally positive returns in early January of each year (the "January effect"), and a "blue Monday" effect where average stock returns are negative from the close of trading on Friday to the close of trading on Monday. Other evidence suggested that stocks with low P/E multiples tended to outperform those with high P/E multiples. Finally, some evidence emerged for positive serial correlation (i.e., "momentum") in stock returns from week to week or month to month. These results were inconsistent with a random walk of prices and returns. Yet, despite the existence of these anomalies, the efficient markets hypothesis remained the dominant paradigm in the academic community.

FIDELITY MAGELLAN FUND

Exhibit 4 presents a summary of the Magellan Fund as it stood in mid-1995 and of its performance over the previous 15 years. Morningstar Mutual Funds, a well-known statistical service reporting on mutual fund performance, gave Magellan a five-star rating, its highest for investment performance. **Exhibit 5** gives a comparison of Magellan's return versus other "growth-stock oriented" mutual funds. The long-term performance results suggested that Magellan tended to outperform the market in bull[19] markets and underperform the market in bear markets. This was attributed to the fund managers' conscious strategy of staying fully invested at all times rather than attempting to time the extent of market investments.

The other striking fact about Magellan's recent financial results was its sheer rate of growth. As early as 1988, one journalist wrote that:

> Because of its enormous size, Magellan can no longer beat the market the way it once could. Lynch himself advises people looking for big gains to try another fund. But they won't.[20]

---

[17]B. Donnelly, "Efficient-Market Theorists Are Puzzled by Recent Gyrations in Stock Market," *The Wall Street Journal,* October 23, 1987, 7.

[18]Ibid.

[19]A "bull market" was a period of time in which stock prices were generally rising. A "bear market" was a period of time in which stock prices were generally declining.

[20]Nocera, "The Ga-Ga Years," 88.

Yet, despite its size, the fund continued to outperform the broad market averages. In 1995, however, one pension fund consultant said,

> The fewer stocks in a portfolio, the more stock selection drives performance. The more names, the more performance is driven by [industry] sectors. And funds [like Magellan] that were built as stock selection vehicles become far less so as time goes on. Magellan in the early 1980s had eye-popping numbers that just cannot be repeated, even with big sector bets.[21]

One popular explanation for the fund's performance was the unusual skill of its managers. Peter Lynch was an adherent of the fundamental analysis approach to investing. In his book on equity investing, he wrote:

> It seemed to me that most of what I learned at Wharton, which was supposed to help you succeed in the investment business, could only help you fail. . . . Quantitative analysis taught me that the things I saw happening at Fidelity couldn't really be happening. I also found it difficult to integrate the efficient market hypothesis . . . with the random walk hypothesis. . . . Already I'd seen enough odd fluctuations to doubt the rational part, and the success of the great Fidelity fund managers was hardly unpredictable. It also was obvious that Wharton professors who believed in quantum analysis and random walk weren't doing nearly as well as my new colleagues at Fidelity, so between theory and practice, I cast my lot with the practitioners.[22]

The following are Lynch's "favorable attributes" of stocks to invest in:

1. It sounds dull—or even better, ridiculous.
2. It does something dull.
3. It does something disagreeable.
4. It's a spin-off.
5. The institutions don't own it, and the analysts don't follow it.
6. The rumors about it: it's involved with toxic waste and/or the Mafia.
7. There's something depressing about it.
8. It's a no-growth industry.
9. It's got a niche.
10. People have to keep buying it.
11. It's a user of technology.
12. The insiders are buyers.
13. The company is buying back shares.[23]

In summary, Peter Lynch said, "I continue to think like an amateur as frequently as possible." After accumulating an impressive performance record, Peter Lynch retired on May 31, 1990, at the age of 46. He confessed to being burned out by 80-hour weeks that left him without enough time for his wife and three daughters, and noted that his father had died of cancer at the age of 46.

Morris Smith assumed the helm of the Magellan Fund just months before the market slump beginning in late 1990. At the time, Magellan's assets were $13 billion. He had been hired by Fidelity in 1982, and rose to manage its OTC Portfolio Fund, which posted an out-

---

[21]Lappen, "Fidelity Grapples with Gigantism," 83.
[22]Peter Lynch, *One Up on Wall Street* (New York: Simon & Schuster, 1989): 34.
[23]Ibid., 122–36.

standing performance record during his tenure. In contrasting his investing strategy with Peter Lynch's, Smith said,

> I've never been married to one strategy, and I always try to interpret the market as it is. Peter and I are both bottom-up types of investors . . . visiting companies, a lot of hands-on research. . . . [I]t's difficult for me to analyze what the differences are.[24]

Still, investors were skeptical that Peter Lynch's performance would be maintained: "The probabilities aren't in favor of anyone doing as well as Peter Lynch," wrote Charlie Hooper, editor of *Mutual Fund Strategist.*[25] Indeed, the *Boston Globe* instituted a "Morris Watch" column in its Sunday business section, tracking Magellan's performance each week, looking for the stumble that would differentiate him from Peter Lynch.

The stumble never occurred. Smith configured Magellan's investments conservatively, and successfully rode out the market decline of 1990–91. Indeed, in 1991 he beat the S&P 500 by 10.5 percent. Then in April 1992, Smith stunned the investment community with the announcement that he would retire from the fund. The 34-year-old manager, an Orthodox Jew, planned to move to Israel to spend more time with his wife and children and study the Talmud. He claimed not to have had the time to read a book for leisure since 1982.

Smith's successor, Jeffrey Vinik, joined Fidelity in 1987, having graduated from Duke University and Harvard Business School. Within two years, he became an assistant to Peter Lynch, and then won appointments to be the manager of increasingly prominent Fidelity funds, including Contrafund, and Growth & Income Fund. When Vinik, age 32, assumed responsibility for the Magellan Fund, its assets had risen to $22 billion. One observer said, "If you're running a $22 billion fund, you're basically buying the market,"[26] implying that investors would be better off allocating their wealth to an index fund that closely mirrored the performance of the S&P 500, and doing so with lower costs. In reply, Vinik said flatly, "My goal is to beat the S&P."[27] He had allocated the fund's assets to nearly 500 issues of common stock, but had concentrated almost half of the fund in the technology sector. One observer called Vinik a "manic" trader, pointing to the very high turnover rates of previous portfolios he had managed—for the year to August 1995 the turnover rate for the fund was 120 percent, indicating that Vinik had executed nearly $60 billion of trades so far that year. Notwithstanding the complexity of his portfolio and his high trading volume, Vinik said that he would continue leaving the office at 5:30 P.M., limiting workweeks to 60–65 hours: "My family was the first thing I thought about when I was approached about the job. I feel like I can handle it—stress is part of the job."[28] Vinik was reported to own at least 30,000 shares in FMR, worth about $100 apiece, and to earn more than $1 million per year.[29]

In part, Magellan's remarkable growth in assets was due to its superior investment performance—supported by a deep talent pool of portfolio managers and a research staff

---

[24]Sharon Harvey, "Mr. Smith Goes to Magellan," *Institutional Investor* (March 1991): 131–32.

[25]John Waggoner, "Magellan's New Star," *USA Today,* April 5, 1991, 1B.

[26]Quotation of Sheldon Jacobs, editor of *No-Load Fund Investor,* in Thomas Watterson, "Jeffrey Vinik's Nest Egg," *Boston Globe,* January 17, 1993.

[27]Ibid.

[28]Geoffrey Smith, "Morris, We Hardly Knew Ye," *Business Week,* (May 11, 1992): 40.

[29]Lappen, "Fidelity Grapples with Gigantism," 86.

over 100 strong. Internal research was supplemented with research purchased from numerous external analysts. But industry observers also credited the growth, in part, to aggressive marketing by FMR, the parent company. Roger Servison, an FMR executive said, "We want to own [the financial consumer's] brain. We want them to think of us as their primary financial provider."[30] FMR's chief executive officer, Ned Johnson, said,

> Oh, [growth] isn't an end. It's every day—the challenge of running and improving the businesses, being rewarded, and also providing something of value to others. It's like collecting or like playing a professional sport. It's a desire to win, yes, but it's also the desire to produce something that has value to many people.[31]

Nevertheless, other observers saw FMR as a company driven toward aggressive growth, with a highly competitive internal culture, that might lead to the firm's ultimate downfall. One journalist wrote:

> As the assets of the chief Fidelity funds swell . . . their portfolio managers may well feel compelled, in the ultracompetitive Fidelity climate, to take added risks to sustain their impressive, growth-fund-style returns. "The more money you manage and the more fields you are in," notes the marketing head of a major competitor, "the greater the chances that you will be on the playground when a big mortar hits."[32]

CONCLUSION

Judged from almost any perspective, the performance of the Magellan Fund was remarkable. Its long-run, market-beating performance defied conventional academic theories. And its ability to achieve this performance in the face of the fund's staggering size challenged most pragmatists who believed that the fund would eventually become a clone of the broad market.

Investors, academicians, and market observers wondered about the sources of Magellan's superior performance, and about its sustainability into the future. As of mid-1995, was it rational for the equity investor to buy shares in Magellan?

---

[30]Ibid., 78.
[31]Ibid., 80.
[32]Ibid., 82.

EXHIBIT 1
Morningstar Comparison of Performance of Mutual Fund Categories and Broad Market Indexes

Benchmark Performance

No. of Funds	Objective	TR% YTD 09-08-95	Total Return% through 08-31-95				Annualized			Annual Returns							
			1Mo	3Mo	6Mo	1Yr	3Yr	5Yr	10Yr	1987	1988	1989	1990	1991	1992	1993	1994
1841	**Domestic Stock**	**27.14**	**0.97**	**10.14**	**18.43**	**20.45**	**14.77**	**15.53**	**13.25**	**1.20**	**15.78**	**25.25**	**-5.74**	**37.02**	**9.32**	**12.86**	**-1.54**
93	Aggressive Growth	33.77	1.24	16.11	23.96	26.86	19.45	18.79	14.36	-2.97	15.42	27.17	-8.29	53.59	8.49	19.49	-3.56
132	Equity-Income	20.38	0.99	4.60	12.65	13.91	11.18	12.99	11.53	-2.23	16.05	21.35	-5.78	26.70	9.19	13.20	-1.73
811	Growth	27.85	0.81	10.35	18.93	20.31	14.47	15.37	13.59	2.82	14.82	27.55	-4.52	37.36	8.30	11.61	-1.86
460	Growth and Income	24.03	0.61	6.21	15.40	16.98	12.50	13.58	12.49	2.22	15.11	23.66	-4.55	28.84	8.25	10.99	-1.15
345	Small Company	30.35	1.74	15.47	22.06	25.98	19.30	19.38	13.98	-2.32	19.91	22.81	-10.1	49.21	14.09	16.94	-0.69
656	**International Stock**	**6.85**	**-1.64**	**3.74**	**11.79**	**-2.22**	**12.29**	**7.99**	**14.06**	**11.23**	**15.76**	**23.22**	**-11.5**	**14.94**	**-3.53**	**38.98**	**-2.99**
54	Diversified Emerging Market	-0.01	-2.05	1.71	12.03	-15.71	13.73	11.00	11.21	0.23	10.50	28.11	-9.74	18.10	0.26	72.16	-9.60
41	Europe Stock	15.18	-2.88	3.32	12.39	8.39	10.55	4.99	12.52	15.95	7.00	25.69	-5.37	7.28	-7.93	26.45	2.55
310	Foreign Stock	4.81	-1.58	3.63	11.33	-3.89	11.67	7.62	14.82	8.25	16.97	21.92	-11.6	12.57	-4.43	37.94	-2.20
89	Pacific Stock	0.93	-2.00	1.13	8.11	-8.99	13.89	6.07	15.50	32.42	22.66	27.70	-19.8	13.68	-3.98	57.82	-8.17
162	World Stock	14.12	-1.10	6.18	14.43	5.15	13.04	10.39	12.77	5.68	13.64	22.54	-9.81	21.93	-0.38	31.61	-2.27
284	**Specialty Stock**	**20.35**	**1.25**	**7.69**	**16.76**	**14.78**	**14.99**	**13.18**	**11.93**	**7.55**	**6.87**	**27.38**	**-9.38**	**24.78**	**5.24**	**30.65**	**-4.13**
15	Communication	23.52	1.81	12.80	20.46	16.83	22.22	21.40	16.39	6.59	21.89	45.01	-13.1	29.61	16.16	32.11	-1.98
16	Financial	31.71	4.18	11.43	20.70	17.72	21.36	26.21	13.14	-11.4	19.03	24.84	-15.7	58.98	35.08	16.75	-2.78
18	Health	27.46	2.07	13.04	17.34	24.99	13.02	16.78	17.71	0.27	11.61	38.50	14.99	63.76	-4.69	3.76	4.26
38	Natural Resources	16.20	0.23	3.29	14.58	7.14	10.31	6.61	8.46	9.33	9.80	29.41	-8.60	6.26	2.89	21.86	-2.64
42	Precious Metals	7.93	1.15	5.53	18.37	-1.69	14.15	3.48	5.95	36.79	-17.7	25.65	-23.8	-3.89	-15.2	84.97	-11.7
32	Real Estate	7.80	0.96	5.53	9.77	5.03	10.79	10.92	—	-7.68	15.60	10.57	-16.6	33.11	12.74	22.63	-4.34
27	Technology	52.83	1.43	24.09	41.13	58.36	33.23	26.61	15.71	2.92	2.36	22.20	-2.57	47.46	12.57	20.91	15.23
80	Utilities	14.94	1.18	2.92	9.33	10.34	7.29	11.41	9.92	-7.00	11.61	26.95	-0.45	20.81	9.31	14.39	-8.87
16	Unaligned	26.06	0.13	9.50	17.70	15.62	15.97	16.32	15.37	-4.99	24.24	23.63	-9.19	33.54	10.60	21.48	-5.84
498	**Hybrid**	**17.95**	**0.71**	**4.74**	**12.15**	**13.19**	**9.88**	**11.78**	**11.19**	**3.50**	**11.12**	**17.85**	**-0.14**	**23.58**	**7.36**	**12.46**	**-2.74**
166	Asset Allocation	18.40	0.66	4.74	12.16	14.49	10.35	11.95	9.93	2.44	9.73	15.97	1.19	21.96	8.14	11.98	-1.76
278	Balanced	18.86	0.88	5.03	12.44	13.92	9.91	12.25	11.70	1.70	12.61	19.12	-0.43	26.22	7.41	11.17	-2.42
54	Multiasset Global	12.28	0.05	3.19	10.64	6.75	8.69	9.52	10.11	15.14	7.28	17.32	-2.06	16.60	5.16	20.36	-4.56
381	**Specialty Bond**	**12.09**	**-0.10**	**1.81**	**9.23**	**10.00**	**8.00**	**11.94**	**9.80**	**3.02**	**11.39**	**4.26**	**-2.67**	**28.19**	**11.38**	**17.00**	**-4.94**
42	Convertible Bond	17.31	0.76	6.58	13.14	11.56	11.78	13.65	10.90	-3.96	11.92	14.47	-6.04	28.55	13.81	15.50	-4.58
131	Corp Bond–High Yield	12.20	0.16	2.26	8.07	10.46	9.44	13.56	9.70	2.02	12.82	-0.48	-9.96	36.58	17.39	18.84	-3.71
58	Multisector Bond	11.76	0.35	1.67	8.38	9.80	6.74	10.58	9.81	1.40	13.05	6.88	1.40	24.39	8.31	14.65	-5.03
150	World Bond	10.69	-0.75	0.15	9.47	9.26	5.10	7.72	8.79	15.97	5.12	6.16	13.46	13.22	2.60	16.38	-6.21
642	**Corporate Bond**	**10.27**	**0.99**	**1.50**	**6.64**	**8.87**	**5.48**	**8.55**	**9.14**	**2.14**	**8.02**	**10.98**	**7.09**	**14.84**	**6.19**	**9.26**	**-3.00**
390	Corp Bond–General	11.30	1.10	1.55	7.26	9.69	6.21	9.27	9.45	2.20	8.66	10.82	6.27	16.39	7.39	10.30	-3.50
211	Corp Bond–High Quality	9.54	0.94	1.43	6.02	8.64	5.56	8.20	8.73	2.41	7.14	11.65	7.63	14.25	6.35	8.33	-2.05
211	Corp Bond–High Quality	9.54	0.94	1.43	6.02	8.64	5.56	8.20	8.73	2.41	7.14	11.65	7.63	14.25	6.35	8.33	-2.05
41	Short-Term World Income	4.57	0.26	1.43	4.06	2.78	1.45	3.74	—	-9.26	10.15	-14.3	13.43	7.99	-0.73	6.33	-2.93
646	**Government Bond**	**9.78**	**0.96**	**1.25**	**5.94**	**8.17**	**4.68**	**8.13**	**8.72**	**1.46**	**7.37**	**12.59**	**8.34**	**14.30**	**6.02**	**7.68**	**-3.50**
67	Govt Bond–Adj-Rate Mortgage	3.25	0.46	0.33	2.44	1.12	1.47	5.90	—	-1.24	5.91	12.33	8.27	10.53	4.68	3.90	-2.77
378	Govt Bond–General	10.14	1.01	1.31	6.11	8.62	4.90	7.89	8.12	1.50	6.64	11.93	8.38	14.01	6.05	8.00	-3.58
134	Govt Bond–Mortgage	10.92	0.96	1.52	6.36	9.42	4.98	8.06	8.38	2.16	7.68	12.92	9.39	14.64	6.43	7.10	-3.40
67	Govt Bond–Treasury	11.77	1.14	1.36	7.41	10.59	6.33	9.50	11.86	-0.03	9.86	14.44	6.50	15.41	6.20	10.86	-4.11
1735	**Municipal Bond**	**10.89**	**1.04**	**0.73**	**4.56**	**7.08**	**6.05**	**7.99**	**8.29**	**-1.00**	**10.85**	**9.44**	**6.11**	**11.44**	**8.63**	**11.84**	**-5.88**
164	Muni Bond–California	11.47	1.08	0.37	4.46	6.89	5.98	7.98	8.18	-2.41	10.95	9.68	6.58	11.01	8.42	12.12	-6.77
502	Muni Bond–National	10.33	0.99	0.93	4.61	7.06	5.95	7.90	8.38	-0.18	10.38	9.28	6.12	11.35	8.42	11.25	-5.07
126	Muni Bond–New York	10.99	1.09	0.65	4.68	6.73	5.94	8.19	8.18	-1.76	10.64	9.32	5.21	12.93	9.42	12.27	-6.56
943	Muni Bond–Single State	11.07	1.05	0.70	4.53	7.18	6.16	8.04	8.17	-1.38	11.43	9.56	6.20	11.28	8.65	12.10	-6.09
6683	**Total Fund Average**	**15.77**	**0.66**	**4.39**	**10.76**	**11.17**	**9.76**	**11.33**	**11.34**	**1.95**	**12.07**	**17.28**	**-0.42**	**23.11**	**7.37**	**14.69**	**-3.51**
	S&P 500 Index	**26.87**	**0.25**	**5.97**	**16.79**	**21.42**	**13.83**	**15.10**	**15.19**	**5.26**	**16.61**	**31.68**	**-3.12**	**30.48**	**7.62**	**10.06**	**1.32**
	Lehman Bros Aggregate	**—**	**1.21**	**1.72**	**7.79**	**11.30**	**6.75**	**9.61**	**9.95**	**2.76**	**7.89**	**14.53**	**8.96**	**16.01**	**7.40**	**9.75**	**-2.92**
	U.S. 90-Day Treasury Bill	**—**	**0.44**	**1.34**	**2.75**	**5.47**	**4.02**	**4.45**	**5.63**	**5.83**	**6.67**	**8.11**	**7.51**	**5.41**	**3.46**	**3.02**	**4.27**

Index Performance

Index	Total Return% through 08-31-95				Annualized			Index	Total Return% through 08-31-95				Annualized		
	1Mo	3Mo	6Mo	1Yr	3Yr	5Yr	10Yr		1Mo	3Mo	6Mo	1Yr	3Yr	5Yr	10Yr
Domestic Stock								**Government and Corporate**							
Wilshire 5000	0.98	8.49	17.98	21.95	14.80	15.93	14.53	Lehman Bros Corp	1.61	2.07	9.58	13.48	7.96	10.79	10.71
Wilshire 4500	2.33	13.57	20.15	22.42	16.93	17.73	13.14	Lehman Bros Govt	1.17	1.57	7.72	10.90	6.74	9.56	9.62
Russell 2000	2.07	13.55	20.09	20.79	19.23	19.00	11.86	Lehman Bros ARM	0.61	1.39	4.62	8.22			
S&P MidCap 400	1.85	11.52	18.51	20.48	16.18	19.66	16.47	Lehman Bros Mortgage	1.04	1.79	6.99	10.94	6.14	9.07	10.11
International Stock								**Municipal Bond**							
MSCI EAFE	-3.81	0.38	9.33	0.49	12.17	7.01	15.34	Lehman Bros Muni	1.27	1.34	5.91	8.34	6.78	8.64	9.42
MSCI World	-2.25	2.56	12.13	8.24	12.51	9.65	14.06	Lehman Bros CA Muni	1.26	0.86	5.57	8.42	—	—	—
MSCI Europe	-3.87	2.10	12.51	10.65	12.19	9.15	16.00	Lehman Bros NY Muni	1.40	1.34	6.10	7.74	—	—	—
MSCI Pacific	-3.77	-1.20	6.47	-7.57	12.25	5.15	14.81	**Specialty Bond**							
MSCI Latin America	0.90	5.13	17.76	-27.13	10.62	25.73	—	First Boston High Yield	0.28	2.51	8.95	13.21	10.74	15.51	—
MSCI Emerging Markets	-3.42	-2.50	3.71	-18.27	15.58	13.70	—	Salomon Bros World Govt	-5.72	-4.75	8.27	16.67	9.64	13.41	14.84

Morningstar Mutual Funds

EXHIBIT 2
Long-Term Cumulative Returns on Major Asset Categories

Wealth Indices of   Year-End 1925 = $1.00
Investments in the
U.S. Capital Markets

From 1925 to 1994

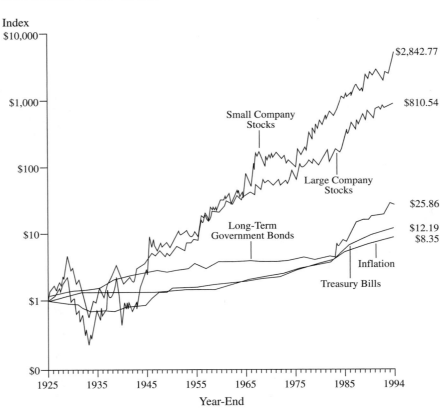

Source: Ibbotson Associates.

EXHIBIT 3
Mean Returns and Standard Deviation of Returns by Major Asset Categories

Basic Series:
Summary Statistics of
Annual Total Returns

From 1926 to 1994

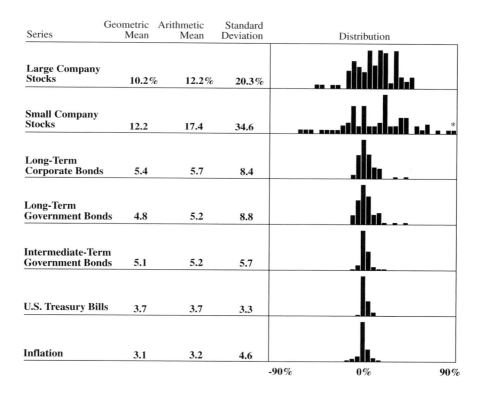

Series	Geometric Mean	Arithmetic Mean	Standard Deviation	Distribution
Large Company Stocks	10.2%	12.2%	20.3%	
Small Company Stocks	12.2	17.4	34.6	
Long-Term Corporate Bonds	5.4	5.7	8.4	
Long-Term Government Bonds	4.8	5.2	8.8	
Intermediate-Term Government Bonds	5.1	5.2	5.7	
U.S. Treasury Bills	3.7	3.7	3.3	
Inflation	3.1	3.2	4.6	

-90%   0%   90%

*The 1933 Small Company Stock Total Return was 142.9 percent.

Source: Ibbotson Associates.

EXHIBIT 4
Morningstar Report on Fidelity Magellan Fund

Fidelity Magellan

	Ticker	Load	NAV	Yield	SEC Yield	Assets	Objective
	FMAGX	3.00%	$90.69	0.4%	---	$51613.0 mil	Growth

Fidelity Magellan Fund seeks capital appreciation. The fund invests primarily in common stocks and convertible securities, with up to 20% of assets invested in debt securities of all types and qualities. It features domestic corporations operating primarily in the United States, domestic corporations that have significant activities and interests outside the U.S., and foreign companies. No limitations are placed on total foreign investment, but no more than 40% of assets will be invested in companies operating exclusively in one foreign country.

The fund closed to new investment in 1965 and reopened in 1981.

Portfolio Manager(s)

Jeffrey N. Vinik, CFA. Since 7-92. BS'81 Duke U.; MBA'85 Harvard. Vinik is a portfolio manager with Fidelity Investments. He joined the company in 1986 as an analyst covering the energy and computer-services industries. Previously, he was an equity block trader with First Boston. He began his investment career in 1981 as a securities analyst with Value Line.

Performance 08-31-95

	1st Qtr	2nd Qtr	3rd Qtr	4th Qtr	Total
1991	20.23	-0.14	9.06	7.70	41.03
1992	-0.70	0.65	1.73	5.25	7.02
1993	8.62	6.42	8.21	-0.34	24.66
1994	-1.59	-4.49	5.43	-0.90	-1.81
1995	8.44	15.77	---	---	---

Trailing	Total Return %	+/- S&P 500	+/- Wil 5000	% Rank All	% Rank Obj	Growth of $10,000
3 Mo	16.88	10.91	8.39	5	10	11,688
6 Mo	30.44	13.65	12.46	2	5	13,044
1 Yr	31.61	10.19	9.66	4	7	13,161
3 Yr Avg	21.12	7.29	6.32	5	10	17,768
5 Yr Avg	20.91	5.81	4.98	6	9	25,840
10 Yr Avg	19.12	3.93	4.58	3	3	57,505
15 Yr Avg	22.70	7.77	8.33	1	1	215,182

Most Similar Funds in MMF

Fidelity Contrafund	Strong Fit
Fidelity Stock Selector	Strong Fit
Putnam Vista A	Fair Fit

Tax Analysis

	Tax-Adj Return %	% Pretax Return
3 Yr Avg	18.46	87.4
5 Yr Avg	18.04	86.3
10 Yr Avg	16.15	84.5
Potential Capital Gain Exposure		32% of assets

Analysis by Patricia Brady 09-29-95

Despite its critics' forecasts, Fidelity Magellan Fund is still every inch the iconoclast.

When Peter Lynch–the standard by which all future Magellan managers will be measured–stepped down, it was to a chorus of negative prophesies. The media suggested that if Magellan grew any larger it couldn't help but become an S&P 500 surrogate, especially in the hands of someone other than Lynch.

In current manager Jeff Vinik's hands, the fund is now more than three times as large as it was then, but it has become even more an individual. When Lynch left, the fund had a 96% correlation with the S&P 500, compared with a current 65%. Vinik has also decreased the number of stocks in the portfolio to fewer than 500, down from 1,200 under Lynch. Also, although Lynch was known for taking bold positions, his sector choices–especially near the end of his tenure–resembled the S&P 500. Vinik, on the other hand, is now making huge bets in some sectors; he is also avoiding

many stocks in the S&P, including energy and nondurables, because he dislikes their long-term prospects.

It's unlikely that Vinik will radically change the fund's weightings any time in the near future. That's partly pragmatic: A $51 billion fund can hardly follow each market gyration. Also, Vinik invests for the long term; for example, he explains the fund's huge technology weighting by saying that he pays little attention to the current overall valuation of the sector, and focuses only on its strong long-term prospects.

Vinik's faith in technology has worked wonders for existing shareholders: The fund has enjoyed an excellent run under his guidance, including a spectacular 1995. Prospective investors, however, might do well to consider technology's recent run and current valuations. While the fund should continue to be a long-term star, it would be painful to buy just before a short-term drop.

Address	82 Devonshire Street
	Boston, MA 02109
Telephone	800-544-8888
Advisor	Fidelity Management & Research
Subadvisor	FMR (U.K.)/FMR (Far East)
Distributor	Fidelity Distributors
States Available	All
Report Grade	A+
Income Distrib	Semiannually

Historical Profile

Return	High	
Risk	Average	
Rating	★★★★	
	Highest	

95%	92%	90%	97%	81%	84%	93%	98%

	1984	1985	1986	1987	1988	1989	1990	1991	1992	1993	1994	08-95	History
	33.69	45.21	48.69	40.10	48.32	59.85	53.93	68.61	63.01	70.85	66.80	90.69	NAV
	2.03	43.11	23.74	1.00	22.77	34.58	-4.51	41.03	7.02	24.66	-1.81	36.36	Total Return %
	-4.24	11.37	5.07	-4.26	6.16	2.90	-1.39	10.54	-0.60	14.60	-3.13	11.88	+/- S&P 500
	-1.02	10.55	7.65	-1.36	4.82	5.41	1.67	6.82	-1.96	13.38	-1.74	11.03	+/- Wilshire 5000
	1.18	1.94	0.90	1.65	2.27	2.22	1.51	2.18	2.00	1.12	0.19	0.59	Income Return %
	0.85	41.17	22.85	-0.65	20.50	32.36	-6.02	38.85	5.01	23.54	-2.00	35.76	Capital Return %
	61	4	11	51	9	7	70	13	58	11	33	2	Total Rtn %Rank All
	29	2	7	63	13	20	52	32	57	6	52	5	Total Rtn %Rank Obj
	0.37	0.65	0.46	0.72	0.90	1.24	0.83	1.30	1.25	0.75	0.13	0.33	Income $
	3.69	1.78	6.84	9.02	0.00	3.82	2.42	5.43	8.82	6.50	2.64	0.00	Capital Gains $
	1.04	1.12	1.08	1.08	1.14	1.08	1.03	1.06	1.05	1.00	0.99	0.96	Expense Ratio %
	1.47	2.79	1.95	1.18	1.33	2.13	2.54	2.47	1.57	2.11	1.07	0.39	Income Ratio %
	85	126	96	96	101	87	82	135	172	155	132	120	Turnover Rate %
	1954.4	4136.0	7405.5	7800.1	8971.1	12699.6	12325.7	19257.1	22268.9	31705.1	36441.5	51613.0	Net Assets ($mil)

Risk Analysis

Time Period	Load-Adj Return %	Risk %Rank[1] All	Risk %Rank[1] Obj	Mstar Score Return	Morningstar Risk-Adj Rating
1 Yr	27.66				
3 Yr	19.90	72	40	1.70 0.78	★★★★
5 Yr	20.17	72	35	1.78 0.80	★★★★★
10 Yr	18.75	68	37	2.16 0.90	★★★★★
Average Historical Rating (117 months)				5.0 ★s	

[1] 1=low, 100=high

Other Measures

		Standard Index S&P 500	Best Fit Index SPMid400
Standard Deviation	10.79		
Mean	19.89	Alpha	5.6	4.8
Sharpe Ratio	1.48	Beta	1.11	0.97
		R-Squared	65	73

Portfolio Analysis 03-31-95

Total Stocks: 466
Total Fixed-Income: 43

Share Chg (09-94) 000	Amount 000		Value $000	% Net Assets
2067	11158	IBM	913586	2.30
-141	16110	Motorola	880009	2.21
14709	18312	General Motors	810298	2.04
9709	25007	Oracle Systems	781478	1.96
820	8783	Intel	745423	1.87
3098	13697	Columbia/HCA Healthcare	588950	1.48
883	6570	FNMA	534609	1.34
1232	6673	CSX	525483	1.32
503	4214	Hewlett-Packard	507308	1.27
-88	6564	Micron Technology	498887	1.25
	3155	Nokia Pfd	460244	1.16
3	12810	Lowe's	441948	1.11
-19	4974	Texas Instruments	440199	1.11
2024	7317	Computer Associates Intl	434459	1.09
607	7660	Caterpillar	426104	1.07
1132	7729	Applied Materials	426067	1.07
9297	12053	Compaq Computer	415835	1.04
5390	7383	Conrail	414343	1.04
205	9395	Merrill Lynch	400475	1.01
9327	10027	Digital Equipment	379773	0.95
835	10464	Silicon Graphics	371479	0.93
-67	9653	General Instrument	335449	0.84
233	5682	Advanced Micro Devices	324573	0.82
510	5665	3Com	320764	0.81
914	5993	LSI Logic	314654	0.79

Investment Style

Style Value Blend Growth		Stock Portfolio Avg	Rel S&P 500	Rel Objective
Price/Earnings Ratio		21.3	1.13	0.98
Price/Book Ratio		4.2	1.04	0.99
5 Yr Earnings Gr %		19.6	1.82	1.14
Return on Assets %		10.2	1.25	1.09
Debt % Total Cap		23.9	0.86	0.92
Med Mkt Cap ($mil)		4094	0.26	0.62

Special Securities % of assets

● Private/Illiquid Securities	Trace
○ Structured Notes	0
● Emerging-Markets Secs	Trace
○ Options/Futures/Warrants	Yes

Composition % of assets 07-31-95

Cash	1.9
Stocks	97.7
Bonds	0.4
Other	0.0

Index Allocation % of stocks

S&P 500	56.1
S&P Mid	17.0
US Sm Cap	22.1
Foreign	6.3

Sector Weightings

	% of Stocks	Rel S&P
Utilities	0.1	0.01
Energy	1.1	0.12
Financials	11.5	0.98
Industrial Cyclicals	17.4	1.01
Consumer Durables	7.3	1.56
Consumer Staples	0.1	0.01
Services	13.2	1.64
Retail	3.7	0.71
Health	3.0	0.31
Technology	42.7	3.70

Investment Style History

Equity
Average Stock %

Growth of $10,000

- Investment Value ($000) of Fund
- Investment Value ($000) S&P 500

▼ Manager Change
~ Partial Manager Change
► Mgr Unknown After
◄ Mgr Unknown Before

Performance Quartile (Within Objective)

Minimum Purchase	$2500	Add: $250	IRA: $500
Min Auto Inv Plan	$2500	Systematic Inv: $100	
Date of Inception	05-02-63		

Expenses & Fees

Sales Fees	3.00%L		
Management Fee	0.30%+0.52% max/0.27% min(G)+/-0.2%P		
Actual Fees	Mgt: 0.75%	Dist: ---	
Expense Projections	3Yr: $60	5Yr: $81	10Yr: $144
Annual Brokerage Cost	0.26%		

MORNINGSTAR Mutual Funds   215

EXHIBIT 5

Performance Comparison of Fidelity Magellan Fund versus Other Growth Funds

Fund Size (total assets in millions on Sept. 30, 1995)	Number of Funds in Category	Total Assets (in millions on Sept. 30, 1995)	Total Reinvested Performance (percentage increase in initial investment value from inception to Sept. 30, 1995)			
			10 Years	5 Years	1 Year	Year to Date
$250–$500	51	$ 18,697	306%	129%	26.8%	28.0%
$500–$750	17	10,742	318.7	144.1	27.3	28.6
$750–$1,000	19	16,517	328.6	155.9	29.1	30.6
$1,000–$2,000	36	48,519	321.9	145.5	26.9	28.7
$2,000+	23[1]	134,793	290.3	124.6	25.9	27.8
Fidelity Magellan Fund	**1**	**46,653[2]**	**514.5**	**181.0**	**37.6**	**38.9**

[1]The category of funds larger than $2 billion includes the results of Fidelity Magellan Fund in its performance statistics.
[2]This is the reported balance in May 1995. As noted in the case, the assets under management in the fall of 1995 were closer to $51 billion.

Source: Lipper Analytical Services, Inc., Lipper Mutual Fund Performance Analysis, September 1995.

Jeanne Mockard at Putnam Investments

On May 29, 1996, Jeanne Mockard considered three pairwise choices among possible investments for the two preferred stock mutual funds she managed for Putnam Investments. Institutional salespersons at other firms called her daily with offers to sell her preferred stocks. From various calls that day, she had culled six potential investments—but she limited her action to buying only three of these, to concentrate her buying power and to avoid unnecessary redundancy. The reality was that these investment opportunities might remain open only for a few hours. Other investors were almost certainly considering these opportunities. Competing with other institutional investors, she sought to improve the return on her fund within strict investment guidelines set by Putnam. Current capital market conditions were buoyant (see **Exhibit 1**). The yield curve[1] was moderately sloped, but had risen since the beginning of 1996, reflecting analysts' expectations of inflation as the U.S. economy completed its fifth year of expansion. And there were rumors of a change in the tax code that would affect the tax advantages enjoyed by corporate investors in preferred stocks. Mockard needed to decide quickly what action to take on these six investment opportunities.

---

[1]A yield curve was simply a graph of the market yields on U.S. Treasury securities by maturity. An example is given in Exhibit 1. A steeply rising curve would indicate that yields on debt instruments would vary significantly with maturity. A relatively flat yield curve would indicate that yields were relatively insensitive to maturity. The slope and height of the curve change with variations in market conditions.

PUTNAM INVESTMENTS

Mockard worked for a large, well-known investment management company located in Boston, Massachusetts. Owned by Marsh & McLennan, Putnam offered a family of 41 mutual funds available for investment by the general public. Putnam also managed funds for specific clients in the United States and globally, such as pension trusts, 401(k) plans, and charitable institutions that were not open to the public. Putnam's public funds were grouped into four investment categories and had assets of $147 billion.

1. *Growth funds* included 14 funds focusing on investing in fast-growing companies and sought to maximize the value of investment over time. These funds were segmented by region (e.g., United States, Asia, Europe), industry (e.g., health, natural resources), and size of company (e.g., small emerging companies, large established growth companies).
2. *Growth and income funds* as the name suggests, balanced their emphasis on growth and income investing. These included eight funds with specialties ranging from a balanced blend of stocks and bonds, or on a particular industry (e.g., utilities), and to a focus on particular securities (e.g., convertible securities).
3. *Tax-free funds* included seven funds aimed at investing in bonds and money-market instruments issued by states and municipalities in the United States. Income from these was exempt from federal income tax in the United States, and from certain state and local taxes.
4. *Income funds* sought to offer a regular stream of income through investing in bonds and dividend-paying stocks. These included 12 funds emphasizing current income (rather than growth) and varying among U.S. government debt securities, corporate debt, and corporate preferred stocks.

The two funds that Jeanne Mockard managed were classified as income funds.

Putnam was known in the financial community for its highly disciplined approach to investing. In recent years, the public had learned that prominent managers at other fund companies were pursuing investment strategies that deviated sharply from their advertised fund objectives. For example, one equity growth fund manager had deployed a significant portion of the fund's assets into U.S. government securities in the expectation of sharp interest rate changes. In another instance, equity funds had invested in interest-rate swaps and options. In a third case, a conservative equity fund was revealed to hold 10 percent of its assets in Mexican bonds. Fund investors were outraged, because these mutual funds had advertised that they would invest in growth stocks. Putnam funds were not involved in these unhappy incidents. Indeed, the company prided itself on the clarity of investment focus achieved at each fund, largely through careful delineation of excluded types of investments, and of investment concentration limits. The Putnam approach required managers who were disciplined "team players," not the solo "superstar" managers who had been lionized by the press in recent years.

Some money-management companies aimed to offer the highest returns in any investment category. Skeptics believed that this goal motivated fund managers to take unusual risks, since returns were largely determined by risks. Putnam, however, aimed more conservatively to rank in the top half of an investment category *consistently over time*.

PUTNAM PREFERRED-INCOME FUND AND PUTNAM DIVIDEND-INCOME FUND

The two funds that Mockard managed focused on investing in corporate preferred stocks. The Putnam Preferred-Income Fund was an open-ended fund with assets of about $121 million.[2] The Putnam Dividend-Income Fund was a closed-ended fund with assets of about $115 million.[3] Each fund held 70 to 90 separate issues of securities. The investment strategy for one of these funds was described as follows:

> The fund seeks to achieve its objective by investing at least 80 percent of its total assets (taken at current value) in investment-grade adjustable-rate preferred stock[4] and . . . common or preferred stocks, which pay dividends that are generally higher than the average dividend paid by the stocks included in the Standard & Poor's 500 Composite Stock Price Index. Under normal market conditions, the fund will invest at least 65 percent of its total assets in preferred stock. The fund may also invest up to 20 percent of its total assets in government and investment-grade corporate debt securities and high-quality, short-term money market instruments.[5]

The 65 percent limit was an absolute minimum; 80 percent was the target minimum. Mockard could not invest in securities rated less than Baa or BBB at the time of investment, nor could her funds hold more than 5 percent of their assets in any one issuer.

The Putnam Dividend-Income Fund currently held a three-star rating from Morningstar Mutual Funds, indicating average return and risk within its fund category. **Exhibit 2** presents the Morningstar report on Putnam Dividend-Income Fund at mid-1996. (The Putnam Preferred-Income Fund was not covered by Morningstar.)

PREFERRED STOCK

Preferred stock differed from common stock in having preference over the common in dividend payments and in distribution of assets in the event of liquidation of the firm. Because preferred stock was viewed legally as *equity,* it held no special right to draw the firm into bankruptcy proceedings. Preferred dividends were typically *cumulative,* meaning that if a preferred dividend payment were missed, the obligation to pay that dividend would remain, and would take precedence before any common dividends could be paid. Preferred stockholders usually had rights to elect some directors to the firm's board in the event that preferred dividends were not paid. Otherwise, preferred stockholders had no voting privileges.

---

[2]An open-ended fund had a variable number of shares outstanding, depending on the inflows into the fund by investors. Transactions in fund shares were between investors and the fund. The assets under management could vary due to changes in market value of fund assets and variations in the number of shares outstanding.

[3]A closed-ended fund had a fixed number of shares outstanding. Transactions in fund shares were between investors. The assets under management were relatively fixed as a result (i.e., except for changes in market values of fund assets).

[4]The dividend rates on adjustable-rate preferred stocks were adjusted every 90 days to reflect any changes in benchmark interest rates, such as the yields on U.S. Treasury securities.

[5]Putnam Preferred Income Fund Prospectus, April 1, 1996, 8.

Preferred shares typically carried a stated liquidation value, such as $25 per share. The dividend on the preferred stock could either be expressed in dollar terms per share, or as a "coupon rate" or "dividend yield of stated value" equaling the dollar dividend divided by the liquidation value. Because the market values of preferred stock typically fluctuated, preferred stock returns could also be quoted as "strip yields."[6]

A paradox was that preferred-stock dividend yields were often at or below yields on bonds of similar risk—even though preferreds were subordinate to bonds. If market returns were determined by risk, preferred yields should be higher. This paradox might be explained by an unusual tax feature of preferred stocks. Dividends from preferred stocks were subject to a "dividends received deduction" (DRD) of 70 percent when the owner of the shares was another corporation. This meant that 70 cents of every dollar of preferred dividends received by corporations would not be taxed. To compare the yields on preferred stock with other securities, it would be necessary to "gross up" the preferred stock yield to a pretax equivalent.[7] Thus, a preferred stock bearing a dividend yield of 7 percent would have a pretax equivalent yield to a corporate investor of 9.6 percent (where the corporate investor had a marginal tax rate of 35 percent). If the DRD were reduced to 50 percent, the pretax equivalent yield in this example would fall to 8.9 percent; if DRD were reduced to 20 percent, the pretax equivalent yield would fall to 7.8 percent. In comparison, **Exhibit 1** gives pretax yields on corporate bonds.

The comparison of standard preferred stocks to bonds was not completely inappropriate: both were regarded as fixed-income securities, and investors in either participated in the growth in value of the enterprise. The value of preferred stocks was sensitive to changes in interest rates. Finally, like debt, preferred stocks often could be redeemed (or "called") before maturity at the option of the issuer. But preferred stock usually ranked behind debt in priority in liquidation of the firm. Furthermore, the dividends paid on preferred stock were not deductible from income for purposes of computing corporate tax—unlike interest payments, which were deductible.

Given the similarities of preferred stock to debt, and yet the disadvantages of preferred compared to debt, many observers wondered what might motivate corporations to issue preferred stock. The range of answers suggested that preferred stock resolved difficult trade-offs in *managing the corporate capital structure.* For instance, preferred stock looked like equity to creditors (and therefore was thought to expand the borrowing base of the firm), but looked like a liability to common stockholders (and therefore increased the financial leverage of the firm). This hybrid-like nature of preferred stock was of special interest to firms facing a nontrivial risk of bankruptcy: accumulated unpaid dividends were not debts of a corporation and thus could not trigger bankruptcy proceedings. Preferred stock was equity, and yet it did not carry votes, it did not dilute the voting control of common stockholders. Finally, in regulated industries (such as electric power generation) it might be

---

[6]Strip yield was calculated as the dollar dividend/(current price − accumulated dividends).

[7]The estimate of a pretax equivalent yield of preferred stock assumes that in an efficient market securities of equivalent risk will offer the same return after taxes. Thus, the dividend yield of preferred stock (PDY) should have the following relationship to the pretax yields (YTM) of other securities that are not subject to the DRD:

$$(\%DRD \times PDY) + [(1 - \%DRD) \times (1 - t) \times PDY] = YTM \times (1 - t)$$

possible to pass the tax disadvantage of preferred dividends on to customers—electric utilities were large issuers of preferred stock.

In the spring of 1996, rumors circulated that the Clinton administration was considering reducing the dividends received deduction from 70 percent to 50 percent. This would
have the effect of somewhat lowering the attractiveness of preferred stock as an investment
medium for corporations.

Adjustable-Rate Preferred Stock

A special variety of preferred stock featured a coupon rate that would reset every 90 days
to float at a target level above some benchmark rate such as the market yield on U.S. Treasury securities. Adjustable-rate preferred stock (or "ARPS") was attractive to corporate
treasurers looking for an investment in which to place a firm's excess cash balance for a period of time. Because the yield varied, the market value of the investment would remain relatively fixed,[8] ensuring that the treasurer would not have to explain extraordinary gains or
losses in securities to his or her board of directors. In addition, the yields on ARPS offered
a premium return compared to yields on U.S. Treasury instruments or other short-term
money market instruments. For a corporate investor, this yield would be augmented by the
70 percent dividends received deduction.

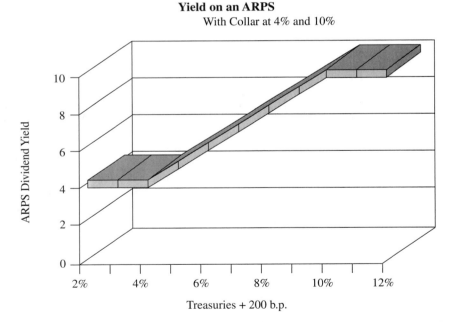

Yield on an ARPS
With Collar at 4% and 10%

Typically, the dividend yield on ARPS would be allowed to vary within a set range,
between a minimum and maximum. The upper and lower bounds formed a "collar." The

---

[8]The exception to this rule was when the market yields varied above the collar maximum or below the minimum.

figure above gives a graph of the possible yields offered an investor by a collar set at 4.0 and 10.0 percent. Suppose that within the collar, yields would be set to equal the yield on a specific U.S. Treasury security plus 200 basis points. The floor would protect the investor against an unusually low yield; the ceiling would protect the issuer against an unusually high yield. The width of the collar was a matter of choice to the issuer at the time the ARPS was originally issued. In general, a wider collar meant that the investor bore more uncertainty about the return to be received at the next reset date; a narrower collar meant less uncertainty.

JEANNE MOCKARD

Mockard joined Putnam Investments in 1990 upon completion of her MBA degree. Initially, she worked as a securities analyst. She assumed responsibility for the two funds in 1993. In May 1996, she held the title of senior vice president. Mockard described her work this way:

> I compete for securities, for good investments. There are only a couple of other funds with a specific focus on preferred stock like mine. However there are a large number of mutual funds with at least a little appetite for preferred stocks. In addition, I compete with large corporations like IBM and Disney who invest their excess cash directly into preferred stocks.
>
> On the other side, I compete for investors to buy shares in my funds. A few of the investors are private individuals, but most are corporations. The smaller firms that invest in the funds consider me their cash management/investment office. We offer them a chance to diversify their risk and gain ready access to market dealers who bring me their investment ideas.
>
> The size of my fund is a competitive advantage in this market. To make money here, you have to be a big player. People come to me when they want to do a deal. I network a lot, so that preferred stock traders call me; and so that I know whom to call. The market in preferred stocks is different from common equities where you have up-to-the-minute electronic information. Information about preferreds is exchanged more by word-of-mouth. Information is simply less available. Also, the market in preferreds is not as liquid as the market for common—I simply can't buy every issue that's out there. When an opportunity to invest does come along, I have to think carefully and strategically, since the opportunity may not reappear for a while.
>
> Though my focus is preferred stocks, I have to have an opinion on where interest rates are headed. Preferreds are income securities, and thus affected by changes in the interest rate environment. You need a real appreciation of the yield curve. Adjustable-rate preferreds trade off of the short end of the curve, because they are reset every 90 days against the short-term Treasury rate. Perpetual preferreds trade more in relation to the long end of the yield curve.
>
> I'm like a brand manager: I have a clear idea of my customer and the market segment I'm trying to serve. I can't be all things to all people. My goal is to invest mainly in perpetual preferred stocks, balanced with some adjustable-rate preferreds and sinking fund preferreds[9] to dampen the swings in value as interest rates move. I have to practice a strategy of "disciplined opportunism." I want to serve the investor and the mission of the fund. I also want to beat the

---

[9]Sinking fund preferreds are preferred stocks that have a scheduled amortization or repayment over time, similar to long-term debt. The preferred issue "sinks" as it is repaid.

Merrill Lynch preferred stock index—the benchmark for "the market" in the preferred stock arena; I aim to wind up in the top half of the league tables in my segment.

I spend 50 percent of my time traveling. I talk to companies to assess investment risk, and to anticipate the private actions of corporate executives beforehand. I go to conferences to get a sense of industry trends. The content of this work always surprises me. I love what I do. You have to be interested in everything. No two days are alike. It's not an orderly job. Market developments constantly require you to decide how to manage your time best.

PUTNAM'S ECONOMIC AND MARKET OUTLOOK

Dr. Robert Goodman, managing director and senior economic advisor at Putnam, described the company's outlook on the economy in the following way in his summer 1996 *Commentary:*

As we enter the second half of 1996, confusion and uncertainty about economic prospects abound. The confusion has manifested itself in a rise in long-term government bond yields to more than 7 percent and an equity market that has been stuck in a broad trading range for most of the year. While traders in both bonds and stocks are at risk in such environment, history suggests that investors with long-term horizons can take advantage of these circumstances.

Chief among the uncertainties currently facing investors is the prospect of increased inflation as we go forward. Anxiety about accelerating inflation stems from a rise in commodity prices, such as the recent spurt in gasoline prices, and the possibility of wage increases if economic growth should reaccelerate. In my view, both of these concerns have been exaggerated in the media and on Wall Street.

Since 1979, the bond market, battered by brutal experience, has imposed a very real and severe constraint on the ability of the Fed to pursue an inflationary monetary policy. The bond market vigilantes, as these defenders of price stability have been called, have been responsible for the downtrend in interest rates and inflation that took place throughout the 1980s and continues today. Should the Fed embark upon a policy deemed to be inflationary by bond market participants, bonds would be sold in anticipation of that inflation and long-term interest rates would rise.

. . . What we are likely to experience going forward are shifts in relative prices among commodities, reflecting supply and demand conditions in the marketplace. But these price changes should not be translated into a generalized inflation spiral.

Nevertheless, until investors accept this analysis, the bond market will be buffeted by fears of renewed inflationary pressure. It is quite possible, therefore, that for a time interest rates may rise to levels exceeding long-term equilibrium. In my opinion, long-term bond yields above 7 percent are not sustainable and, when they are available, represent good value relative to the average rate of inflation we are likely to experience over the longer run.

THE SIX INVESTMENT OPPORTUNITIES

Exhibit 3 presents data summarizing the three pairwise choices that Mockard needed to decide on soon. The exhibit gives information that she used to make buy-or-sell decisions quickly. This information included the credit ratings of the issues determined by Moody's and S&P (**Exhibit 4** gives the rating definitions of these categories). The "Ex date" was the next date in 1996 after which purchase of the security would not entitle the investor to the next quarterly dividend. The strip yield was calculated simply as the annual dividend of the security divided by the current price less accrued dividends. The "spread vs. 30 year" was the difference between the strip yield and the yield on the 30-year U.S. Treasury bond. YTC stands for yield to call, the preferred's internal rate of return yield calculated as if the issuer were to redeem the issue at the earliest possible date, indicated by "call date." These data were drawn by Mockard's assistant from a Bloomberg terminal.

- **Decision A:** An institutional salesperson at R. W. Baird had called to say that two preferred issues from Georgia Power had come on the market. These issues were perpetual preferreds and were similar in many respects. The Series Q carried a coupon of $1.9875 per share, while the Series R carried a coupon of $1.9375 per share.
- **Decision B:** An institutional salesperson at Salomon Brothers called to offer perpetual preferred issues on two different companies: Travelers Insurance and Merrill Lynch. The Travelers issue carried a coupon rate of 9.25 percent, whereas the Merrill Lynch issue carried a coupon rate of 9.00 percent.
- **Decision C:** An institutional salesperson at Lehman Brothers offered Mockard two different issues of adjustable-rate preferreds. One, issued by Texas Utilities, held a current coupon rate of 6.5 percent, and a collar that would permit coupon rates between 6.5 and 13 percent. The other issue, from Puget Sound, offered a current coupon of 6.31 percent and a collar that would permit coupon rates to vary between 4 and 10 percent.

Mockard needed to decide quickly between the alternatives within each pair of opportunities. As she turned to the data, she reflected on the possible impact of changes in the environment. Interest rates had been rising all spring; how would Putnam's interest-rate outlook affect the three decisions? Also, the Clinton administration might lower the DRD. How, if at all, should this possible change influence her thinking?

EXHIBIT 1
Capital Market Conditions
(May 29, 1996)

U.S. Treasury Obligations	Yield
90-day bills	5.18%
1-year notes	5.74
2-year notes	6.24
5-year notes	6.63
10-year bonds	6.85
30-year bonds	6.92

Long-Term Corporate Debt Obligations

AAA	7.63%
AA	7.73
A	7.99
BBB	8.26
BB+	8.60
BB/BB−	10.34
B	10.38

Other Instruments

Prime rate loans	8.25%
Discount rate	5.00
Certificates of deposit (90-day)	5.36
Commercial paper (6 months)	5.42

U.S. Treasury Yield Curve

Sources: Bloomberg Business News; Standard & Poor's *Current Statistics.*

EXHIBIT 2
Morningstar Report

Putnam Dividend Income

	Ticker	NAV	Mkt Price	Yield	Prem/Disc	Closed–End Mstar Category
	PDI	$10.77	$10.00	7.4%	-7.1%	Long–Term Bond

Prospectus Objective: Income

Putnam Dividend Income Fund seeks high current income eligible for the 70% dividends-received deduction consistent with preservation of capital.

The fund normally invests at least 65% of assets in dividend-paying stocks and investment-grade preferreds. It usually invests no more than 25% of assets in the utilities industry.

The fund redeemed all of its outstanding auction-rate preferred shares, in three stages, in 1993 and 1994, and releveraged with a private issue of auction-rate preferreds in March 1996.

Historical Profile

Return Average
Risk Average
Rating ★★★
Neutral

Premium/Discount %

—	—	—	7.8	3.8	-0.4	6.4	-2.4	-9.8	-10.8	-11.7	Average
—	—	—	10.3	10.0	6.9	10.6	10.9	-5.7	-8.4	-6.9	Highest
—	—	—	6.6	-5.9	-4.2	-2.5	-11.4	-15.7	-14.8	-16.9	Lowest

Month-End

Average Historical -3.0%

—	—	—	11.49	9.83	11.35	11.53	11.99	9.93	10.78	10.77	NAV
—	—	—	1.83*	-3.44	29.23	12.24	18.28	-7.65	17.31	6.67	NAV Total Return %
—	—	—	—	-12.40	13.23	4.84	8.53	-4.73	-1.16	3.84	+/- LB Aggregate
—	—	—	—	-9.86	9.70	3.71	2.11	-0.56	-12.62	7.36	+/- LB LT Govt/Corp
—	—	—	3.03*	10.86	13.51	10.61	10.59	7.53	8.73	6.76	Income Return %
—	—	—	-1.20*	-14.30	15.72	1.59	7.87	-15.05	8.56	-0.09	Capital Return %
—	—	—	—	85	26	18	1	66	95	23	Total Rtn % Rank Cat
—	—	—	1.01*	-14.78	31.59	24.45	-1.35	-9.48	17.45	13.89	Market Total Rtn %
—	—	—	0.35	1.22	1.17	1.16	1.13	0.81	0.73	0.62	Income $
—	—	—	0.00	0.02	0.02	0.00	0.38	0.26	0.00	0.00	Capital Gains $
—	—	—	—	—	2.02	1.64	1.70	1.42	1.07	1.23	Expense Ratio %
—	—	—	—	—	11.67	11.14	9.65	8.06	7.39	6.88	Income Ratio %
—	—	—	—	—	198	160	166	74	27	35	Turnover Ratio %
—	—	—	—	103.1	120.8	124.0	129.7	107.4	116.6	113.5	Net Assets $mil
—	—	—	—	74.0	74.0	74.0	74.0	0.0	0.0	60.3	Leverage Amount ($mil)

Avg Daily Volume	Shares Outstanding	Exchange
23,727 shares	10,821,255	NYSE

Portfolio Manager(s)

Jeanne L. Mockard, CFA. Since 3-93. BS'85 Tufts U.; MBA'90 Darden Graduate Business School. Mockard rejoined Putnam as an equity analyst in 1990 and has been a fund manager since 1993. She previously worked at Putnam as a client liaison from 1987 to 1988.

NAV Performance %

	1st Qtr	2nd Qtr	3rd Qtr	4th Qtr	Total
1994	-4.06	-1.84	0.55	-2.48	-7.65
1995	5.84	4.70	4.02	1.77	17.31
1996	0.11	1.52	1.57	—	—

Income Paid Monthly

1994	0.23	0.20	0.20	0.20	0.81
1995	0.19	0.18	0.18	0.18	0.73
1996	0.18	0.18	0.20	—	—

Trailing

	NAV Total Return %	+/- LB Agg	+/- LB LTGvt/Corp	%Rank All	%Rank Cat	Mkt Total Return %
3 Mo	5.24	1.42	-0.34	29	57	8.92
6 Mo	7.59	2.30	0.20	24	42	15.65
1 Yr	7.70	1.86	3.31	53	47	10.87
3 Yr Avg	4.86	-0.78	-0.68	69	85	4.49
5 Yr Avg	10.34	2.65	0.43	36	25	8.90
Incept Avg	9.87*	—	—	—	—	7.62*

Tax Analysis

	Tax Efficiency %	Rel Cat
3 Yr	17.0	0.44
5 Yr	57.8	0.98
10 Yr	—	—
Potential Capital Gain Exposure	% Net Assets	Rel Cat

Analysis by S. Olivia Barbee 11-22-96

On the whole, Putnam Dividend Income Fund's caution has served it well.

PDI doesn't do anything fancy. Manager Jeanne Mockard invests exclusively in bonds that qualify for the 70% dividends-received corporate deduction, emphasizing higher-quality issuers. She chooses from perpetual, adjustable-rate, and sinking-fund preferreds, but rarely makes rapid shifts; under her tenure, the fund's turnover has been moderate.

More important, Mockard has displayed a defensive bias. In 1994, all fixed-income funds struggled, but PDI could have lost its shirt because its electric-utilities stake (25% of assets) was walloped by deregulation fears, and the fund's leverage increased its exposure. PDI's losses were minimized, though, because Mockard gradually eliminated the fund's leverage in 1994 and moved into interest-rate-resistant adjustable-rate and sinking-fund preferreds.

Thus, the fund was able to finish 1994 with a non-catastrophic 7.7% loss. Despite releveraging early this year, PDI has also held its own in 1996's uncertain market, thanks again to its more-defensive holdings.

Of course, the fund's approach can work against it in rallies. Mockard kept the fund unleveraged throughout 1995's bull market because she didn't believe spreads were wide enough to justify releveraging. This may have been true, but PDI's lack of leverage held it back relative to its peers. The fund's excellent returns from 1991 through 1993 might indicate that it can be a bull-market vehicle. In 1991 and 1992, however, PDI held roughly a third of its portfolio in common stocks; recently, the fund's stock position has hovered around 10% or less.

This fund might not make the best total-return play, then. Still, its moderate risk scores and tax-advantaged income make it a solid choice for institutional investors.

Risk Analysis

Time Period	Risk %Rank[1] All	Risk %Rank[1] Cat	Morningstar[2] Return	Morningstar[2] Risk	Morningstar Risk-Adj Rating
3 Yr	33	38	0.01	0.81	★★
5 Yr	38	37	1.04	0.88	★★★
10 Yr	—	—	—	—	
Average Historical Rating (3 months)				3.0★s	

[1]1=low, 100=high [2]1.00 = Taxable Avg [3]1.00 = 90-day T-bill Rtn

Other Measures

Standard Deviation	5.40	Alpha	-0.7
Mean	4.88	Beta	0.95
Sharpe Ratio	0.01	R-Squared	69

Portfolio Analysis 06-30-96

Amount $000	Total Stocks: 102 Total Fixed-Income: 0	Maturity	Value $000	%Total Invest
190,537	McDermott Pfd $2.60		5,645	3.17
50,000	Duke Power Pfd $7		5,000	2.80
194,000	HF Ahmanson Pfd $2.10		4,996	2.80
190,000	Provident Pfd $2.025		4,845	2.72
217,000	New York Electric & Gas ARP		4,638	2.60
50,000	Chase Manhattan ARP		4,500	2.52
200,000	Georgia Power ARP		4,350	2.44
40,000	Baltimore Gas/Elec Pfd $6.99		3,950	2.22
175,000	Puget Sound Power & Lt ARP		3,938	2.21
40,000	Texas Utilities Electric A ARP		3,700	2.08
140,000	Detroit Edison Pfd $1.938		3,518	1.97
120,000	Boise Cascade Pfd $2.35		3,090	1.73
115,000	AON Pfd $2.00		2,961	1.66
116,000	PSI Energy Pfd $7.44		2,958	1.66
108,000	Travelers Group Pfd $2.313		2,795	1.57
111,000	LASMO Pfd $2.50		2,775	1.56
109,270	Lehman Brothers Cv Pfd $1.955		2,622	1.47
93,822	General Motors Pfd $2.275		2,568	1.44
30,000	BankAmerica ARP		2,528	1.42
29,800	Citicorp 2 ARP		2,514	1.41

Current Investment Style

Duration: Short Int Long
Quality: High Med Low

Not Available

Interest-Rate Stance

	Fund	Rel Cat
Average Effective Duration (years)	—	—
Average Effective Maturity (years)	8.1	0.6
Average Weighted Coupon (%)	—	—
Average Weighted Price (% of par)	—	—

Quality

Avg Credit Quality A
*Common stocks make up less than 25%

Credit Analysis % of bonds 09-30-96

US Govt	0
AAA/Aaa	62
AA/Aa	0
A/A	0
BBB/Baa	0
BB/Ba	4
B/B	27
Below B	2
NR/NA	4

Coupon Range

	% of Bonds	Rel Cat
0%	—	—
0% to 7%	—	—
7% to 8.5%	—	—
8.5% to 10%	—	—
More than 10%	—	—
1.00=Objective Average		

Composition % of assets 09-30-96

Cash	3.1	Bonds	0.0
Stocks	4.2	Other	92.7

Leverage Factor: 1.53

Address	One Post Office Square Boston, MA 02109	Reinvestment Plan: Yes Direct Purchase Plan: No
Advisor	Putnam Investment Management	Telephone: 617-292-1000 / 800-634-1587
Subadvisor	N/A	Fiscal Year End: June
Administrator	N/A	*Date of Inception: 09-28-89
Management Fee	0.75%	Report Grade: B
		Income Distrib: Paid Monthly

 **Mutual Funds**

41

EXHIBIT 3
Summary of Investment Opportunities

Decision	Broker	Security	Number of Shares	Moody's Rating	S&P Rating	Ex Date	Asking Price	Strip Yield %	Spread vs. 30 Year (b.p.)	YTC	YTC Spread (b.p.)[4]	Call Date	Call Price	30-Year Bond Yield
A	Baird	Georgia Power Series Q $1.9875 coupon	13,500	A2	A	6/13	$25.60	7.88%	+96	6.68	+117	6/2/97	$25.00	6.92
	Baird	Georgia Power Series R $1.9375 coupon	11,300	A2	A	6/13	$25.55	7.69	+77	6.73	+117	7/2/97	$25.00	6.92
B	Salomon	Travelers Series d, 9.25% coupon	212,500	A1	A	5/29	$25.80	8.96	+204	5.49	−14	7/1/97	$25.00	6.92
	Salomon	Merrill Lynch Series A 9.0% coupon	189,870	A1	A−	6/13	$28.875	7.92	+100	6.84	+26	12/30/04	$25.00	6.92
C	Lehman	Texas Util. Series A, ARPS, collar: 6.5–13% current coupon = 6.5%	50,000	Baa3	BBB	7/10	$92.18	7.12	+20[1]	—	—	—	—	6.92
	Lehman	Puget Sound Series B, ARPS, collar: 4–10%, current coupon = 6.31%	200,000	Baa1[2]	BBB+	7/18	$22.50	6.41	−51[3]	—	—	—	—	6.92

[1]The Texas Utilities ARPS yield was 103 percent of the 30-year Treasury bond yield (7.12/6.92).

[2]Puget Sound was listed for a possible downgrade by Moody's.

[3]The Puget Sound ARPS yield was 93 percent of the 30-year Treasury bond yield (6.41/6.92).

[4]Versus contemporaneous treasuries.

EXHIBIT 4
Standard & Poor's Risk Rating Definitions

AAA	Preferred stock rated AAA has the highest rating assigned by S&P. Capacity to pay dividends and meet redemption requirements is extremely strong.
AA	Preferred stock rated AA has a very strong capacity to pay dividends and meet redemption requirements and differs from the higher rated issues only in small degree.
A	Preferred stock rated A has a strong capacity to pay dividends and meet redemption requirements, although it is somewhat more susceptible to the adverse effects of changes in circumstances and economic conditions than preferred stock in higher rated categories.
BBB	Preferred stock rated BBB is regarded as having an adequate capacity to pay dividends and meet redemption requirements. Whereas it normally exhibits adequate protection parameters, adverse economic conditions or changing circumstances are more likely to weaken the capacity to pay dividends and meet redemption requirements for preferred stock in this category than in higher rated categories.
BB, B, CCC, CC, C	Preferred stock rated BBB, B, CCC, CC, and C is regarded, on balance, as predominantly speculative with respect to capacity to pay dividends and redemption requirements in accordance with the terms of the obligation. BB indicates the lowest degree of speculation and C the highest degree of speculation. While such preferred stock will likely have some quality and protective characteristics, these are outweighed by large uncertainties or major risk exposure to adverse conditions.

Source: Paraphrased from Standard & Poor's *Bond Guide.*

Ben & Jerry's Homemade, Inc.

Jerry:	*What's interesting about me and my role in the company is, I'm just this guy on the street. A person who's fairly conventional, mainstream, accepting of life as it is.*
Ben:	*Salt of the earth. A man of the people.*
Jerry:	*But then I've got this friend, Ben, who challenges everything. It's against his nature to do anything the same way anyone's ever done it before. To which my response is always, "I don't think that'll work."*
Ben:	*To which my response is always, "How do we know till we try?"*
Jerry:	*So I get to go through this leading-edge, risk-taking experience with Ben— even though I'm really just like everyone else.*
Ben:	*The perfect duo. Ice cream and chunks. Business and social change. Ben and Jerry.*

—Ben & Jerry's Double Dip

As Henry Morgan's plane passed over the snow-covered hills of Vermont's dairy land, through his mind passed the events of the last few months. It was late January 2000. Morgan, the retired dean of Boston University's business school, knew well the trip to Burlington. As a member of the board of directors of Ben & Jerry's Homemade over the past

This case was prepared by Professor Michael J. Schill with research assistance from Daniel Burke, Vern Hines, Sangyeon Hwang, Wonsang Kim, Vincente Ladinez, and Tyrone Taylor. It was written as a basis for class discussion rather than to illustrate effective or ineffective handling of an administrative situation. Copyright © 2001 by the University of Virginia Darden School Foundation, Charlottesville, VA. All rights reserved. *To order copies, send an e-mail to dardencases@virginia.edu. No part of this publication may be reproduced, stored in a retrieval system, used in a spreadsheet, or transmitted in any form or by any means—electronic, mechanical, photocopying, recording, or otherwise—without the permission of the Darden School Foundation.*

13 years, he had seen the company grow both in financial and social stature. The company was now not only an industry leader in the super-premium ice cream market but also commanded an important leadership position in social causes from the dairy farms of Vermont to the rainforests of South America.

Increased competitive pressure and Ben & Jerry's declining financial performance had triggered a number of takeover offers for the resolutely independent-minded company. Today's board meeting had been convened to consider the pending offers. Morgan expected a lively debate. Cofounders Ben Cohen and Jerry Greenfield knew the company's social orientation required corporate independence. In stark contrast, chief executive Perry Odak felt that shareholders would be best served by selling out to the highest bidder.

BEN & JERRY'S HOMEMADE

Ben & Jerry's Homemade, a leading distributor of super-premium ice creams, frozen yogurts, and sorbets, was founded in 1978 in an old gas station in Burlington, Vermont. Cohen and Greenfield recounted their company's beginnings:

> One day in 1977 we [Cohen and Greenfield] found ourselves sitting on the front steps of Jerry's parents' house in Merrick, Long Island, talking about what kind of business to go into. Since eating was our greatest passion, it seemed logical to start with a restaurant. . . . We wanted to pick a product that was becoming popular in big cities and move it to a rural college town, because we wanted to live in that kind of environment. We wanted to have a lot of interaction with our customers and enjoy ourselves. And, of course, we wanted a product that we liked to eat. . . . We found an ad for a $5 ice-cream-making correspondence course offered through Penn State. Due to our extreme poverty, we decided to split one course between us, sent in our five bucks, read the material they sent back, and passed the open-book tests with flying colors. That settled it. We were going into the ice cream business.
>
> Once we'd decided on an ice cream parlor, the next step was to decide where to put it. We knew college students eat a lot of ice cream; we knew they eat more of it in warm weather. Determined to make an informed decision (but lacking in technological and financial resources), we developed our own low-budget "manual cross-correlation analysis." Ben sat at the kitchen table, leafing through a U.S. almanac to research towns that had the highest average temperatures. Jerry sat on the floor; reading a guide to American colleges, searching for rural towns that had the most college kids. Then we merged our lists. When we investigated the towns that came up, we discovered that apparently someone had already done this work ahead of us. All the warm towns that had a decent number of college kids already had homemade ice-cream parlors. So we threw out the temperature criterion and ended up in Burlington, Vermont. Burlington had a young population, a significant college population, and virtually no competition. Later we realized the reason there was no competition: it's so cold in Burlington for so much of the year, and the summer season is so short, it was obvious (to everyone except us) that there was no way an ice cream parlor could succeed there. Or so it seemed.[1]

By January 2000, Cohen and Greenfield's ice cream operation in Burlington, Ben & Jerry's Homemade, had become a major premium ice cream producer with over 170 stores

---

[1]Ben Cohen and Jerry Greenfield, *Ben & Jerry's Double Dip* (New York: Simon & Schuster, 1997), 15–17.

(scoop shops) across the United States and overseas, and had developed an important presence on supermarket shelves. Annual sales had grown to $237 million, and the company's equity was valued at $160 million (see **Exhibits 1** and **2**). The company was known for such zany ice cream flavors as Chubby Hubby, Chunky Monkey, and Bovinity Divinity. **Exhibit 3** provides a selected list of flavors from a scoop-shop menu.

BEN & JERRY'S SOCIAL CONSCIOUSNESS

Ben & Jerry's was also known for its emphasis on socially progressive causes and community commitment. Although unique during its early years, Ben & Jerry's community orientation was no longer that uncommon. Companies such as Patagonia (clothing), Odwalla (juice), The Body Shop (body-care products), and Tom's of Maine (personal-care products) shared similar visions of what they termed "caring capitalism."

Ben & Jerry's social objective permeated every aspect of the business. One dimension was its tradition of generous donations of corporate resources. Since 1985, Ben & Jerry's donated 7.5 percent of its pretax earnings to various social foundations and community-action groups. The company supported causes such as Greenpeace and the Vietnam Veterans of America Foundation by signing petitions and recruiting volunteers from its staff and the public. The company expressed customer appreciation with an annual free cone day at all of its scoop shops. During the event, customers were welcome to enjoy free cones all day.

Although the level of community giving was truly exceptional, what really made Ben & Jerry's unique was its commitment to social objectives in its marketing, operations, and finance policies. Cohen and Greenfield emphasized that their approach was fundamentally different from the self-promotion-based motivation of social causes supported by most corporations.

> At its best, cause-related marketing is helpful in that it uses marketing dollars to help fund social programs and raise awareness of social ills. At its worst, it's "greenwashing"—using philanthropy to convince customers the company is aligned with good causes, so the company will be seen as good, too, whether it is or not. . . . They understand that if they dress themselves in that clothing, slap that image on, that's going to move product. But instead of just slapping the image on, wouldn't it be better if the company actually did care about its consumers and the community?[2]

An example of Ben & Jerry's social-values-led marketing included its development of an ice cream flavor to provide demand for harvestable tropical-rainforest products. The product's sidebar described the motivation:

> This flavor combines our super creamy vanilla ice cream with chunks of Rainforest Crunch, a cashew & Brazil nut buttercrunch made for us by our friends at Community Products in Montpelier, Vermont. The cashews & Brazil nuts in this ice cream are harvested in a sustainable way

---

[2]Ibid., 33.

from tropical rainforests and represent an economically viable long-term alternative to cutting these trees down. Enjoy! Ben & Jerry

Financing decisions were also subject to community focus. In May of 1984, Ben & Jerry's initiated its first public equity financing. Rather than pursue a broad traditional public offering, the company issued 75,000 shares at $10.50 a share exclusively to Vermont residents. By restricting the offering to Vermonters, Cohen hoped to provide that those who first supported the company be able to profit from its success. To provide greater liquidity and capital, a traditional broad offering was later placed and the shares were then listed and traded on Nasdaq. Despite Ben & Jerry's becoming a public company, Cohen and Greenfield did not always follow traditional investor-relations practices. "Chico" Lager, the general manager at the time, recalled the following Ben Cohen interview transcript he received before publication in the *Wall Street Transcript:*

TWST:	Do you believe you can attain a 15 percent increase in earnings each year over the next five years?
Cohen:	I got no idea.
TWST:	Umm-hmm. What do you believe your capital spending will be each year over the next five years?
Cohen:	I don't have any ideas as to that either.
TWST:	I see. How do you react to the way the stock market has been treating you in general and vis-à-vis other companies in your line?
Cohen:	I think the stock market goes up and down, unrelated to how a company is doing. I never expected it to be otherwise. I anticipate that it will continue to go up and down, based solely on rumor and whatever sort of manipulation those people who like to manipulate the market can accomplish.
TWST:	What do you have for hobbies?
Cohen:	Hobbies. Let me think. Eating mostly. Ping-Pong.
TWST:	Huh?
Cohen:	Ping-Pong.[3]

Solutions to corporate operating decisions were also dictated by Ben & Jerry's interest in community welfare. The disposal of factory wastewater provided an example.

In 1985, when we moved into our new plant in Waterbury, we were limited in the amount of wastewater that we could discharge into the municipal treatment plant. As sales and production skyrocketed, so did our liquid waste, most of which was milky water. [We] made a deal with Earl, a local pig farmer, to feed our milky water to his pigs. (They loved every flavor except Mint with Oreo Cookies. Cherry Garcia was their favorite.) Earl's pigs alone couldn't handle our volume, so eventually we loaned Earl $10,000 to buy two hundred piglets. As far as we could tell, this was a win-win solution to a tricky environmental problem. The pigs were happy. Earl was happy. We were happy. The community was happy.[4]

---

[3]Fred "Chico" Lager, *Ben & Jerry's: The Inside Scoop* (New York: Crown Publishers, 1994), 124–25.
[4]*Ben & Jerry's Double Dip,* 154.

Ben & Jerry's social orientation was balanced with product and economic objectives. Its mission statement included all three dimensions, and stressed seeking new and creative ways of fulfilling each without compromising the others:

Product. To make, distribute, and sell the finest quality all natural ice cream and related products in a wide variety of innovative flavors made from Vermont dairy products.

Economic. To operate the Company on a sound financial basis of profitable growth, increasing value for our shareholders, and creating career opportunities and financial rewards for our employees.

Social. To operate the Company in a way that actively recognizes the central role that business plays in the structure of society by initiating innovative ways to improve the quality of life of a broad community—local, national, and international.

Management discovered early on that the company's three objectives were not always in harmony. Cohen and Greenfield told of an early example:

One day we were talking [about our inability to make a profit] to Ben's dad, who was an accountant. He said, "Since you're gonna make such a high-quality product . . . why don't you raise your prices?" At the time, we were charging fifty-two cents a cone. Coming out of the sixties, our reason for going into business was that ours was going to be "ice cream for the people." It was going to be great quality products for everybody—not some elitist treat. . . . Eventually we said, "Either we're going to raise our prices or we're going to go out of business. And then where will the people's ice cream be? They'll have to get their ice cream from somebody else." So we raised the prices. And we stayed in business.[5]

At other times, management chose to sacrifice short-term profits for social gains. Greenfield tells of one incident with a supplier:

Ben went to a Social Ventures Network meeting and met Bernie Glassman, a Jewish-Buddhist-former-nuclear-physicist-monk. Bernie had a bakery called Greyston in inner-city Yonkers, New York. It was owned by a nonprofit religious institution; its purpose was to train and employ economically disenfranchised people [and] to fund low-income housing and other community-service activities. Ben said, "We're looking for someone who can bake these thin, chewy, fudgy brownies. If you could do that, we could give you some business, and you could make us the brownies we need, and that would be great for both of us." . . . The first order we gave Greyston was for a couple of tons. For us, that was a small order. For Greyston, it was a huge order. It caused their system to break down. The brownies were coming off the line so fast that they ended up getting packed hot. Then they needed to be frozen. Pretty soon, the bakery freezer was filled up with these steaming fifty-pound boxes of hot brownies. The freezer couldn't stay very cold, so it took days to freeze the brownies. By the time they were frozen, [they] had turned into fifty-pound blocks of brownie. And that's what Greyston shipped to us. So we called up Bernie and we said, "Those two tons you shipped us were all stuck together. We're shipping them back." Bernie said, "I can't afford that. I need the money to meet my payroll tomorrow. Can't you unstick them?" And we said, "Bernie, this really gums up the works over here." We kept going back and forth with Greyston, trying to get the brownies right. Eventually we created a new flavor, Chocolate Fudge Brownie, so we could use the brownie blocks.[6]

---

[5]Ibid., 21–22.
[6]Ibid., 60–62.

ASSET CONTROL

The pursuit of a non-profit-oriented policy required stringent restrictions on corporate control. For Ben & Jerry's, asset control was limited through elements of the company's corporate charter, differential stock-voting rights, and a supportive Vermont legislature.

Corporate Charter Restrictions

At the 1997 annual meeting, Ben & Jerry's shareholders approved amendments to the charter that gave the board greater power to perpetuate the mission of the firm. The amendments created a staggered board of directors, whereby the board was divided into three classes, with one class of directors being elected each year for a three-year term. A director could only be removed with the approval of a two-thirds vote of all shareholders. Also, any vacancy resulting from the removal of a director could be filled by two-thirds of the directors then in office. Finally, the stockholders increased the number of votes required to alter, amend, repeal, or adopt any provision inconsistent with these amendments to at least two-thirds of shareholders. See **Exhibit 4** for a summary of the current board composition.

Differential Voting Rights

Ben & Jerry's had three equity classes: class A common, class B common, and class A preferred. The holders of class A common were entitled to one vote for each share held. The holders of class B common, reserved primarily for insiders, were entitled to 10 votes for each share held. Class B common was not transferable but could be converted into class A common stock on a share-for-share basis and was transferable thereafter. The company's principals—Ben Cohen, Jerry Greenfield, and Jeffrey Furman—held effectively 47 percent of the aggregate voting power, with only 17 percent of the aggregate common equity outstanding. Non-board members, however, still maintained 51 percent of the voting power (see **Exhibit 5**). The class A preferred stock was held exclusively by the Ben & Jerry's Foundation, a community-action group. The class A preferred gave the foundation a special voting right to act with respect to certain business combinations and authority to limit the voting rights of common stockholders in certain transactions such as mergers and tender offers, even if the common stockholders favored such transactions.

Vermont Legislation

In April 1998, the Vermont Legislature amended a provision of the Vermont Business Corporation Act, which gave the directors of a Vermont corporation the authority to consider the interests of the corporation's employees, suppliers, creditors, and customers when determining whether an acquisition offer or other matter was in the best interests of the corporation. The board could also consider the economy of the state in which the corporation was located and whether the best interests of the company could be served by the continued independence of the corporation.

These and other defense mechanisms strengthened Ben & Jerry's ability to remain an independent, Vermont-based company and to focus on carrying out the threefold corporate mission, which management believed was in the best interests of the company, its stockholders, employees, suppliers, customers, and the Vermont community at large.

THE OFFERS

Morgan reviewed the offers on the table. Discussion with potential merger partners had been ongoing since the previous summer. In August 1999, Pillsbury (maker of the premium ice cream Häagen-Dazs) and Nestlé (maker of Nestlé-brand frozen treats and 22 percent owner of Dreyer's Grand) announced the formation of an ice cream joint venture. Ben & Jerry's had previously contracted with both Pillsbury and Dreyer's to distribute Ben & Jerry's products. Thus, with the merger, Pillsbury-Nestlé would become the largest distributor of Ben & Jerry's product. Concernt that the Pillsbury-Nestlé distribution channel was no longer advantageous motivated the Ben & Jerry's board to authorize Odak to pursue joint-venture and merger discussion with Unilever and Dreyer's. By December, the joint-venture arrangements had broken down, but the discussions had resulted in takeover offers for Ben & Jerry's of between $33 and $35 per share from Unilever and $31 from Dreyer's. Just yesterday Unilever had raised its offer to $36 and two private investment houses, Meadowbrook Lane Capital and Chartwell Investments, had made two seperate additional offers. The offer prices represented a substantial premium over the pre-offer announcement share price of $21.[7] See **Exhibit 6** for a comparison of investor-value measures for Ben & Jerry's and selected competitors.

Dreyer's Grand Ice Cream

Dreyer's Grand Ice Cream sold premium ice cream and other frozen desserts under the Dreyer's and Edy's brands and some non-branded labels. The Dreyer's and Edy's lines were distributed through a direct-store-delivery system. Total sales were over $1 billion, and company stock traded at a total capitalization of $450 million. Dreyer's was also involved in community-service activities. In 1987, the company established the Dreyer's Foundation to provide more focused community support, particularly for youth and K–12 public education.

Unilever

Unilever manufactured branded consumer goods, including foods, detergents, and other home and personal-care products. The company's ice cream division included the Good

---

[7]Recent food-company acquisitions included Kraft's $270-million acquisition of Balance Bar and Kellogg's $308-million acquisition of Worthington Foods. Balance Bar and Worthington—both health-food companies—sold at takeover premia of 76 percent and 88 percent, respectively. The mean acquisition premium offered by successful bidders in a large sample of U.S. multiple-bid contests was found to be 70 percent. See S. Betton and B. E. Eckbo, "Toeholds, Bid Jumps, and Expected Payoffs in Takeovers," *Review of Financial Studies* 13, no. 4 (winter 2000): 841–82.

Humor, Breyers, Klondike, Dickie Dee, and Popsicle brands, and was the largest producer of ice cream in the world. Good Humor–Breyers was headquartered in Green Bay, Wisconsin, with plants and regional sales offices located throughout the United States. Unilever had a total market capitalization of $18 billion.

Meadowbrook Lane Capital

Meadowbrook Lane Capital was a private investment fund that portrayed itself as socially responsible. The firm was located in Northampton, Massachusetts. The Meadowbrook portfolio included holdings in Hain Foods, a producer of specialty health-oriented food products. Meadowbrook proposed acquiring a majority ownership interest through a tender offer to Ben & Jerry's shareholders.

Chartwell Investments

Chartwell Investments was a New York City private-equity firm that invested in growth financings and management buyouts of middle-market companies. Chartwell proposed investing $30–$50 million in Ben & Jerry's in exchange for a convertible preferred-equity position that would allow provided that Chartwell to obtain majority representation on the board of directors.

Morgan summarized the outstanding offer details as follows:

Bidder	Offering Price	Main Proposal
Dreyer's Grand	$31 (stock)	• Maintain B&J management team
		• Operate B&J as a quasi-autonomous business unit
		• Encourage some social endeavors
Unilever	$36 (cash)	• Maintain select members of B&J management team
		• Integrate B&J into Unilever frozen desserts division
		• Restr3ict social commitments and interests
Meadowbrook Lane	$32 (cash)	• Install new management team
		• Allow B&J to operate as an independent company controlled under the Meadowbrook umbrella
		• Maintain select social projects and interests
Chartwell	Minority interest	• Install new management team
		• Allow B&J to continue as an independent company

CONCLUSION

Morgan doubted that the social mission of the company would survive a takeover by a large traditional company. Despite his concern for Ben & Jerry's social interests, Morgan recognized that, as a member of the board, he had been elected to represent the interests of shareholders. Financial reporter Richard McCaffrey expressed the opinion of many shareholders:

Let's jump right into the fire and suggest, depending upon the would-be acquiring company's track record at creating value, that it makes sense for the company [Ben & Jerry's] to sell. Why? At $21 a share, Ben & Jerry's stock has puttered around the same level, more or less, for years despite regular sales and earnings increases. For a company with a great brand name, about a 45 percent share of the super-premium ice cream market, successful new-product roll-outs, and decent traction in its international expansion efforts, the returns should be better. Some of the reasons for underperformance, such as the high price of cream and milk, aren't factors the company can control. That's life in the ice cream business. But Ben & Jerry's average return on shareholders's equity, a measure of how well it's employing shareholders' money, stood at 7 percent last year, up from 5 percent in 1997. That's lousy by any measure, though it's improved this year and now stands at about 9 percent. This isn't helped by the company's charitable donations, of course, but if you're an investor in Ben & Jerry's you knew this going in—it's an iron clad part of corporate culture, and has served the company well. Still, Ben & Jerry's has to find ways to create value.[8]

The plane banked over icy Lake Champlain and was beginning its descent into Burlington as Morgan collected his thoughts for what would undoubtedly be an emotional and spirited afternoon meeting.

---

[8]Richard McCaffrey, "In the Hunt for Ben & Jerry's," *Fool.com* (December 2, 1999).

EXHIBIT 1
Ben & Jerry's Homemade Financial Statements and Financial Ratios

		1999	1998	1997	1996	1995	1994
1	Net sales	$237.0	$209.2	$174.2	$167.2	$155.3	$148.8
2	Cost of sales	145.3	136.2	114.3	115.2	109.1	109.8
3	Gross profit	91.7	73.0	59.9	51.9	46.2	39.0
4	Selling, general & administrative expenses	78.6	63.9	53.5	45.5	36.4	36.3
5	Earning before interest and taxes	13.1	9.1	6.4	6.4	9.8	2.8
6	Net income	12.0	6.2	3.9	3.9	5.9	(1.9)
8	Working capital	$ 42.8	$ 48.4	$ 51.4	$ 50.1	$ 51.0	$ 37.5
9	Total assets	150.6	149.5	146.5	136.7	131.1	120.3
10	Long-term debt and obligations	16.7	20.5	25.7	31.1	32.0	32.4
11	Stockholders' equity	89.4	90.9	86.9	82.7	78.5	72.5
	Per share figures—						
	Sales	$31.34					
	Earnings	1.59					
	Book equity	$11.82					
	Gross margin (3/1)	38.7%	34.9%	34.4%	31.0%	29.7%	26.2%
	Operating margin (5/1)	5.5%	4.3%	3.7%	3.8%	6.3%	1.9%
	Net income margin (6/1)	5.1%	3.0%	2.2%	2.3%	3.8%	−1.3%
	Asset turnover (1/9)	1.6	1.4	1.2	1.2	1.2	1.2
	Working capital turnover (1/8)	5.5	4.3	3.4	3.3	3.0	4.0
	ROA (5*(1−40%)/9)	5.8%	3.7%	2.6%	2.8%	4.5%	1.4%
	ROE (6/11)	13.4%	6.8%	4.5%	4.7%	7.5%	−2.6%

Source: SEC filings.

EXHIBIT 2
Ben & Jerry's Homemade Stock-Price Performance

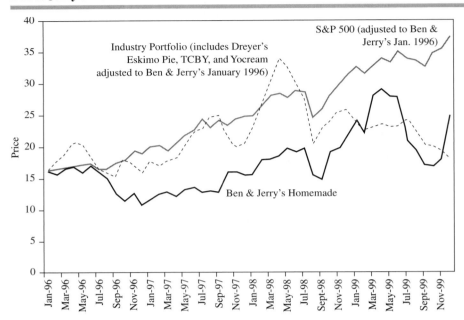

EXHIBIT 3
Ben & Jerry's Selected List of Flavors (January 2000)

Bovinity Divinity	Milk-chocolate ice cream and white-chocolate cows swirled with white-chocolate ice cream and dark fudge cows
Cherry Garcia	Cherry ice cream with cherries and fudge flakes
Chocolate Chip Cookie Dough	Vanilla ice cream with gobs of chocolate-chip cookie dough
Chocolate Fudge Brownie	Chocolate ice cream with fudgy brownies
Chubby Hubby	Chocolate-covered peanut-butter-filled pretzels in vanilla-malt ice cream with fudge and peanut-butter swirls
Chunky Monkey	Banana ice cream with walnuts and chocolate chunks
Coconut Almond Fudge Chip	Coconut ice cream with almonds and fudge chips
Coffee, Coffee, BuzzBuzzBuzz!	Coffee ice cream with espresso-fudge chunks
Deep Dark Chocolate	Very chocolaty ice cream
New York Super Fudge Chunk	Chocolate ice cream with white- and dark-chocolate chunks, pecans, walnuts, and chocolate-covered almonds
Peanut Butter Cup	Peanut-butter ice cream with peanut-butter cups
Phish Food	Milk-chocolate ice cream with marshmallow nougat, caramel swirls, and fudge fish
Pistachio Pistachio	Pistachio ice cream with pistachios
S'mores	Chocolate low-fat ice cream with marshmallow swirls and graham-cracker wedges
Southern Pecan Pie	Brown-sugar ice cream with roasted pecans, chunks of pecan-pie pieces, and a pecan-caramel swirl

EXHIBIT 4
Composition of Board of Directors

Name	Age	Office*	Year Elected
Jerry Greenfield	48	Chairperson, Director	1990
Ben Cohen	48	Vice Chairperson, Director	1977
Perry Odak	54	Chief Executive Officer, President, and Director	1997
Pierre Ferrari	49	Director, Self-Employed Consultant	1997
Jeffrey Furman	56	Director, Self-Employed Consultant	1982
Jennifer Henderson	46	Director, President of leadership-consulting firm Strategic Interventions	1996
Frederick A. Miller	53	Director, President of management-consulting firm Kaleel Jamison Consulting Group	1992
Henry Morgan	74	Director, Dean Emeritus of Boston University School of Management	1987
Bruce Bowman	47	Senior Director of Operations	1995
Charles Green	45	Senior Director of Sales and Distribution	1996
Michael Sands	35	Chief Marketing Officer	1999
Frances Rathke	39	Chief Financial Officer and Secretary	1990

*Occupations of directors who were neither employed at Ben & Jerry's nor The Ben & Jerry's Foundation, Inc., as of March 25, 1999, are as follows:

Ben Cohen: Co-founder of Ben & Jerry's, and served as a director at Blue Fish Clothing, Community Products, Inc., Social Venture Network, and Greenpeace International.

Pierre Ferrari: President of Lang International, a marketing-consulting firm.

Jeffrey Furman: Self-employed consultant.

Jennifer Henderson: Director of Training at the Center for Community Change, and President of Strategic Interventions, a leadership- and management-consulting firm.

Frederick A. Miller: President of Kaleel Jamison Consulting Group, a strategic-culture-change and management-consulting firm.

Henry Morgan: Retired Dean Emeritus of Boston University School of Management. Also served as a director at Cambridge Bancorporation, Southern Development Bancorporation, and Cleveland Development Bancorporation.

Source: SEC filings.

EXHIBIT 5
Beneficial-Ownership Structure of Ben & Jerry's Homemade

	Class A Common Stock		Class B Common Stock		Preferred Stock	
	Number of Shares	% Outstanding Shares	Number of Shares	% Outstanding Shares	Number of Shares	% Outstanding Shares
Ben Cohen	413,173	6.7%	488,486	61.5%	—	—
Jerry Greenfield	130,000	2.1%	90,000	11.3%	—	—
Jeffrey Furman	17,000	*	30,300	3.8%	—	—
Perry Odak	368,521	6.0%	—	—	—	—
Pierre Ferrari	8,121	*	—	—	—	—
Jennifer Henderson	1,138	*	—	—	—	—
Frederick A. Miller	4,345	*	—	—	—	—
Henry Morgan	5,845	*	—	—	—	—
Bruce Bowman	46,064	*	—	—	—	—
Charles Green	17,809	*	—	—	—	—
Frances Rathke	51,459	*	—	—	—	—
Crédit Suisse Asset Management	860,500	14.1%	—	—	—	—
Dimensional Fund Advisors	359,000	5.9%	—	—	—	—
All officers and directors (as a group of 15 persons)	1,115,554	18.2%	608,786	76.6%	—	—
The Ben & Jerry's Foundation, Inc.	—	—	—	—	900	100.0%
Total shares outstanding	6,121,493		794,539		900	

*Less than 1%.

Source: SEC filings.

EXHIBIT 6
Investor-Value Measures—Ben & Jerry's and Industry Comparables

	Price/Earnings	Price/Book
Dreyer's Grand	47.2	7.8
Eskimo Pie	30.7	1.1
TCBY Enterprises	12.5	1.2
Yocream International	9.4	1.8
Ben & Jerry's	13.2	1.7

Source: Casewriter analysis.

The Battle for Value: Federal Express Corporation vs. United Parcel Service of America, Inc. (Abridged)

We will produce outstanding financial returns by providing totally reliable, competitively superior global air-ground transportation of high priority goods and documents that require rapid, time-certain delivery.
—Federal Express Mission Statement

[We will] maintain a financially strong, manager-owned company earning a reasonable profit, providing long-term competitive returns to our shareowners.
—United Parcel Service Mission Statement

Federal Express is a leader of the pack in developing information systems aimed at keeping its customers informed and serving them better.
—Tom Peters, Liberation Management

This is probably one of the three or four defining moments for this company.
—John Alden, UPS Senior Vice President, referring to a major reengineering effort announced May 23, 1995[1]

Clearly, the competencies that are most valuable are those that represent a gateway to a wide variety of potential product markets. To take a financial analogy, investing in core competencies is like investing in options. A core competence leader possesses an option on participation in the range of end-product markets that rely on that core

---

[1]Robert Frank, "Efficient UPS Tries to Increase Efficiency," *The Wall Street Journal,* May 24, 1995, B1.

competence. . . . A core competence is a bundle of skills and technologies that enables a company to provide a particular benefit to customers. . . . At Federal Express the benefit is on-time delivery, and the core competence, at a very high level is logistics management.

—Gary Hamel and C. K. Pralahad, Competing for the Future

Then one day the company looked out upon its business and saw that times had changed. The practices had become "inoperative" because the strategies had become outdated. The strategies had become outdated because smaller upstart rivals and old foes had become more competitive. Profits declined. So UPS examined what its customers wanted, sought ideas from its employees, swallowed hard, and decided it had better start doing business differently—or there might not be any more business to do. So it did. Now UPS is living happily ever after once again. For now.[2]

On July 10, 1995, J.C. Penney announced the award to United Parcel Service (UPS) of a $1 billion, five-year contract for delivery services. This was the largest distribution contract ever awarded and represented a dramatic concentration of Penney's business with one carrier. "They're stealing business from each other. The question is, who can do it at the lowest cost?"[3] said one analyst. A J.C. Penney spokesperson confirmed that the additional UPS business was coming at the expense of other carriers—Penney's previously standing agreement with UPS had entailed shipments worth $160 million over three years. At the announcement, the stock price of Federal Express Corporation (FedEx) fell 2.33 percent; FedEx's total market value of equity declined $85 million.

The contract announcement surprised many observers. Federal Express had virtually invented customer logistical management, was widely perceived as innovative, entrepreneurial, and an operational leader. Business pundits applauded the company for its outstanding operational practices. In 1990, FedEx received the crowning acknowledgment of excellence by winning the coveted Malcolm Baldrige Award for quality. As Chairman Fred Smith explained: "Quality was really part of the culture from the outset. I think it came from the fundamental recognition that in providing time-definite transportation, quality was really all that we were selling."[4] So good was FedEx at this that they were generally credited with redefining the product.

UPS had also garnered awards and recognitions. But historically it had the reputation as big, bureaucratic, and an industry follower. However, UPS was shedding this image as it became an innovator and an increasingly tenacious adversary. UPS's transition had involved some rude awakenings, however, about the customer expectations that had changed. The announcement by J.C. Penney seemed to suggest that UPS was successfully making the transition into the new world of air-express package delivery.

The competition between FedEx and UPS for dominance of the $19 billion air-express delivery market foreshadowed an unusually challenging future:[5]

---

[2]Charles R. Day, "Shape Up and Ship Out," *Industry Week,* February 6, 1995.

[3]"UPS Gets $1 billion, 5-Year Contract from J.C. Penney," *Bloomberg Business News,* July 11, 1995.

[4]Peter Bradly, "Making Quality Fly; Federal Express's Quality Control," *Purchasing* (January 17, 1991).

[5]Virtually all of Federal Express's business activities were in the air-express segment of the package-delivery industry. But United Parcel had roughly 27 percent of its revenues derived from air express.

- Intensifying efforts at product innovation, customer focus, quality management, and reengineering.
- High and rising investment in the business. According to Fred Smith, the CEO of FedEx: "Anyone who's unwilling to spend on quality is really mapping a blueprint for liquidation."[6] For the future, analysts forecasted large investment outlays as each firm attempted to gain the upper hand through efficient, modern technology and infrastructure.
- Shifting market shares. FedEx's dominance of the overnight express package market was high; growth in that segment was slowing as the market matured. The new intensive battleground was in the market for two- and three-day delivery.

Against the backdrop of the J.C. Penney announcement, industry observers wondered how this titanic struggle would resolve itself, particularly for investors in those two firms. Was the performance of the firms in recent years an indication of the future?

FEDERAL EXPRESS CORPORATION

At the end of 1994, FedEx had nearly $6 billion in assets and net income of $204 million, on revenues of about $8.5 billion. FedEx had survived the lean years of 1991–93, and by 1994, the firm's financial ratios indicated an improvement (see **Exhibit 1**).

FedEx first took form as Fred Smith's term paper in a Yale economics course. Smith's strategy dictated that FedEx would actually acquire the planes for transport, whereas all other competitors used the cargo space on commercial airlines. In addition to using his own planes, Smith's key innovation was to apply a hub-and-spoke distribution pattern, which permitted cheaper and faster service to more locations than his competitors. Smith invested his $4 million inheritance, and raised $91 million in venture capital to launch the firm—this was the largest venture capital start-up in memory. In the early years FedEx experienced losses, and Smith would have been ousted from his chairmanship were it not for improved results and the support of his president. By 1976, FedEx finally saw a modest profit though, of $3.6 million on an average daily volume of 19,000 packages. Through the rest of the 1970s, FedEx continued to grow by expanding services, acquiring more trucks and aircraft, and raising capital. The formula was successful; in 1981, FedEx generated more revenue than any other U.S. air-delivery company.

By 1981, competition in the industry had started to rise. Emery Air Freight began to imitate FedEx's hub system and to acquire airplanes. UPS began to move into the overnight air market. The United States Postal Service (USPS) positioned its overnight letter at half the price of FedEx's, but quality problems and FedEx's now immortal "absolutely-positively-overnight" ad campaign quelled any potential threat from that quarter. In 1983, FedEx had reached $1 billion in revenues and seemed poised to own the market.

In 1990, FedEx received the prestigious Malcolm Baldrige National Quality Award from U.S. President George Bush. FedEx was the first service firm to win the award. FedEx had won 194 other awards for operational excellence since 1973. Part of this success could be attributed to deregulation and to operational strategy, but credit could also

---

[6]"Federal Express" Darden School Case. (UVA-OM-0721).

be given to FedEx's philosophy of "People-Service-Profit," which reflected an emphasis on customer focus, total quality management, and employee participation. In explaining its philosophy, the company's 1994 Annual Report stated: "We believe that by working as a team, we can produce exemplary service for our customers, which in turn will provide outstanding long-term financial returns for our stockholders." Extensive attitude surveying, a promote-from-within policy, an effective grievance procedure that sometimes resulted in a chat with Fred Smith himself, and a high emphasis on personal responsibility and initiative not only earned FedEx the reputation as a great place to work, but also helped to keep the firm largely union-free.

FedEx's entire history was set against a background of fundamental changes in the business environment. The first was deregulation in transportation. For instance, government deregulation of the airline industry in 1978 permitted larger planes to replace smaller planes, reducing the number of trips between cities—this permitted FedEx to purchase several Boeing 727s, which helped reduce its unit costs. Deregulation of the trucking industry in 1994 permitted FedEx to establish an integrated regional trucking system that would lower its unit costs further on short-haul trips, and to compete more effectively with UPS. And trade deregulation in the Asia-Pacific region permitted FedEx to establish a new base of operations there. The second major change was induced by inflation and rising global competitiveness—these forces compelled manufacturers to manage their inventories closely and to emulate "just-in-time" supply programs of the Japanese. This created a demand for rapid and carefully monitored movement of components. The third major force was technological innovation, which afforded advances in customer ordering, package tracking, and process monitoring.

UNITED PARCEL SERVICE, INC.

Founded in 1907, manager-owned UPS was the largest transportation company in America. Consolidated parcel delivery, both on-ground and through the air, was the primary business of the company. Service was offered to and from every address in the United States and Western Europe, and many addresses in other countries—it was the only express delivery company to service all areas of the United States (except northern Alaska). The company delivered between 10 and 20 million packages a day, 20 times the amount delivered by the United States Post Office. This translated into an estimated 80–90 percent market share of the entire domestic small package delivery market. UPS employed 303,000 people, owned 221 aircraft and 135,000 ground vehicles. UPS stock was owned by UPS managers, or their families, by former employees, or by charitable foundations owned by UPS. The company acted as the market-maker in its own shares, buying or selling shares at a "fair market value"[7] determined by the board of directors each quarter.

---

[7]In setting its share price, the board considered a variety of factors including past and current earnings, earnings estimates, the ratio of UPS common stock to debt of UPS, the business and outlook of UPS, and the general economic climate. The opinions of outside advisers were sometimes considered. The stock price had never decreased in value. The employee stock purchases were often financed with stock hypothecation loans from commercial banks. As the shares provided collateral for these loans, the assessment by the outside lenders provided some external validation for the share price.

The key to UPS's success was efficiency. According to *Business Week* reporter Todd Vogel, "Every route is timed down to the traffic light. Each vehicle was engineered to exacting specifications. And the drivers, all 62,000 of them, endure a daily routing calibrated down to the minute."[8] But this demand for machinelike precision met with resistance by UPS's unionized labor force. Of those demands, UPS driver Mark Dray said:

> drivers are expected to keep precise schedules (hours broken down into hundredths) that do not allow for variables such as weather, traffic conditions, and package volume. If they're behind, they're reprimanded, and if they're ahead of schedule, their routes are lengthened. Drivers make 100 to 120 deliveries a day[9]

In its quest for efficiency, UPS experienced several strikes resulting from changes in labor practices and driver requirements.

More aggressive and more vocal than ever before, the new UPS of 1995 was the product of extensive reengineering efforts and a revitalized business focus. UPS was girding itself for battle. UPS, although much larger than FedEx, had not chosen to compete directly in the overnight delivery market until 1982. According to observers, such a late entry typified the slow, plodding nature of the heavily unionized UPS.

In 1994, *Fortune* magazine ranked UPS as the tenth most-admired company in the United States—the magazine had ranked UPS as the most-admired transportation company for each of the preceding 10 years. The survey particularly cited UPS for its successful record as a long-term investment, and for its innovations in package-tracking capabilities with cellular technology.[10] Traditionally, the company had been the industry's low-cost provider. In recent years, the company had been investing heavily in information technology, aircraft, and facilities to support service innovations, maintain quality, and reduce costs.

At year-end 1994, UPS reported assets, revenues, and profits of $11.1 billion, $19.6 billion, and $943 million, respectively (see **Exhibit 2** for various financial ratios about the firm). The company's financial conservatism was reflected in its AAA bond rating.

COMPETITION IN THE EXPRESS DELIVERY MARKET, 1982–1995

Exhibit 3 gives a detailed summary of the major events marking the competitive rivalry between FedEx and UPS. Significant dimensions of this rivalry included increased customer focus, price competition, and business process reengineering with an emphasis on quality of service (see **Exhibit 4**). However, three dimensions of competition drew particular attention.

- *Globalization.* In 1984, FedEx entered the international delivery market with its first acquisition, Gelco Express, which delivered to 84 countries—this was followed quickly

---

[8]Todd Vogel and Chuck Hawkins, "Can UPS Deliver the Goods in a New World?" *Business Week* (June 4, 1990).

[9]Jill Hodges, "Driving Negotiations; Teamsters Survey Says UPS Drivers among Nation's Most Stressed Workers," *Star Tribune* (June 9, 1993).

[10]In 1994, UPS introduced electronic clipboards that communicated with cellular technology to a communications center in New Jersey. From there, delivery information could be forwarded to customers. As more manufacturers used express delivery companies to move inventory on a just-in-time basis, package-tracking capabilities became important.

with acquisitions in Britain, the Netherlands, and United Arab Emirates. In 1985, it established an airport hub in Brussels, aiming to build an intra-Europe delivery system, much as it had built in Memphis in the United States. In 1989, FedEx bought Tiger International for $883 million—the acquisition proved to be one of FedEx's costliest investments, augmenting the company's debt by 250 percent to $2.1 billion. FedEx bought Tiger only three weeks after learning it was for sale, claiming that it hurried the transaction to prevent UPS's purchase. UPS insisted that it had contemplated, but rejected, the purchase after deciding that it would not be profitable. An international delivery service, Tiger represented FedEx's hope to acquire an immediate (and profitable) presence in Europe—FedEx wanted Tiger's existing delivery routes and landing privileges for access to Europe, East Asia, and South America. The acquisition had given FedEx a 7 percent international market share. However, Tiger's fleet consumed enormous sums for extensive modifications to meet FAA standards and by 1991, international losses at FedEx amounted to $194 million. Then in 1992, with European demand remaining only a tiny fraction of the U.S. overnight demand, FedEx relinquished its hub in Europe by selling the Brussels operation to DHL. Analysts estimated that FedEx had lost $1 billion in Europe since its entry there. FedEx would continue to deliver to Europe, but rely on local partners. In total, between 1982 and 1994, FedEx had invested about $2.5 billion in its overseas operations.

- UPS did not break into the European market in earnest until 1988, with the acquisition of 10 European courier services. To enhance its international delivery systems, UPS created a system that coded and tracked packages, and automatically billed customers for customs duties and taxes. Throughout the 1988–1992 period, UPS seemed to announce the acquisition of local and regional distributors as rapidly as FedEx. Also, UPS expanded to Asia, using its own planes and canceling a contract previously held with Tiger International. Unfortunately, the company had not earned a profit on its international services; Kent Nelson speculated that UPS would not turn its first international profit until 1998, but said,

  > We could have had great difficulties sustaining the losses we had in international operations if we were a public company. It would have taken a lot of dancing and a lot of explaining, and somebody could have replaced me and dramatically cut our losses overnight by bailing out. If I were going after short-term profits, I might have chosen another course. But international is going to be one of our winners.[11]

- UPS hoped that its international service would account for one-third of total revenue by the year 2000. Donald Layden, UPS's international operations manager, commented "The overall strategy is for us to be the leading provider of package distribution services worldwide."[12] In May 1995, UPS announced that it would spend more than $1 billion to expand its European operations during the next five years. UPS noted that its first-quarter pretax international losses narrowed to $47 million from $77 million a year earlier.

Exhibit 5 presents segment data decomposing revenues, operating profit, and assets for both firms by domestic and foreign orientation. However, analysts noted that allocations

---

[11]"The Wizard Is Oz," *Chief Executive* (March 1994): 42.
[12]"UPS Optimistic about Shipping Its Strategy Worldwide," *Los Angeles Times,* July 4, 1992, D2.

between these segments were often a matter of judgment—for instance, how was a sorting facility to be allocated if it served both domestic and foreign routes?

- *Information technology.* Every package handled by FedEx was logged by a central computer system, COSMOS (Customer, Operations, Service, Master On-line System). This global computer network transmitted data from package movements, customer pick-ups, invoices, and deliveries to a central database at the Memphis headquarters. At every transition in the delivery cycle, the bar-coded data on each package was scanned and processed, allowing package movements to be tracked precisely. In 1992, COSMOS performed 250,000 of these transactions—each day. In 1993, FedEx introduced Powership 3, a desktop shipping system given to customers who shipped three or more packages a day. This system stored frequently used addresses, printed labels, requested a courier without a telephone, traced packages, and was connected directly to FedEx. Also in 1993, FedEx announced the introduction of three other technology systems aimed at more efficient handling or better control.

UPS had much catching up to do, according to Francis Erbrick, vice president of Information Systems: "If you went into our information services facility in 1985, you went into 1975 in terms of technology."[13] To catch up, UPS invested in an $80 million central data facility in New Jersey to link all of UPS's computers worldwide. From there, investment in information technology grew exponentially—by 1992, the cumulative total investment was $1.4 billion. "Nineteen ninety-two was the first year we spent more on computers than on vehicles," said UPS CEO Kent Nelson. "Initially that scared me, but information is just as important as packages." UPS planned on spending an additional $3.2 billion on information technology by 1996, including a worldwide computer network known as PRISM to handle customer requests, billing, and package tracing internationally. Later UPS introduced the Delivery Information Acquisition Device (DIAD), which scanned package bar codes and recorded customer signatures. These handheld units were carried by the drivers and once back in the truck, would connect with the central computer system by a Motorola cellular modem. Other technological improvements at UPS included the creation of optical character recognition equipment that could translate address labels or other documents to be saved directly on the computer without hand typing.

- *Service expansion and new service introduction.* FedEx launched Zapmail in 1984 at a cost of $100 million. Designed to capture the growing fax market before the machines were priced low enough to be universal, technical problems and the meteoric plunge in facsimile machine prices caused the service to fail and then close just two years later. The cumulative write-off on Zapmail was about $400 million.[14] FedEx responded to UPS's price competition by guaranteeing delivery by 10:30 A.M. instead of noon, as it had previously. The new competition from UPS spurred FedEx to further expand its geographic service to 95 percent of the United States from 74 percent. Throughout the 1980s, FedEx, armed with volume discounts and superb quality, went after big clients that had previously used UPS without thought. At the same time, FedEx continued to find new markets

---

[13]Resa W. King, "UPS Gets a Big Package—of Computers," *Business Week* (July 25, 1988).
[14]When FedEx announced the establishment of Zapmail in 1984, its stock price fell nearly $10.00 from the mid-$40s to the mid-$30s. Later, when Zapmail was terminated, FedEx's stock price rose $8.00 per share.

such as contract warehousing services for mission-critical inventory that could be delivered anywhere at a moment's notice.

This competition forced UPS to revise its strategy. The company began to copy FedEx's customer interfaces, such as installing 11,500 drop-off boxes to compete with FedEx's 12,000 boxes, 165 drive-through stations, and 371 express-delivery stores. Further, UPS began to pick up packages on the same day that the order was received, a service that FedEx had always offered—wherever and whenever a customer called. As UPS tried to enter FedEx's business, so too did FedEx enter UPS's. In 1990 FedEx entered UPS's core business: the two-day ground-delivery market. At the same time, UPS began to offer modest discounts to volume shippers. In 1993, UPS added a new and cheaper three-day delivery service to undercut FedEx's more expensive two-day service. Up until the summer of 1995, the race seemed to be one of how quickly each competitor could transform itself into the other. UPS had begun Saturday pickups and deliveries to match FedEx. FedEx bought $200 million in ground vehicles to match UPS. In January 1995, UPS bought SonicAir, a *same-day* delivery company, for $60 million.

The largest recent innovations entailed offering integrated logistics services to large corporate clients. These services were aimed at providing total inventory control, and included purchase orders, receipt of goods, order entry and warehousing, inventory accounting, shipping, and accounts receivable. For instance, the London design company, Laura Ashley, retained FedEx to store, track, and ship products quickly to individual stores worldwide. Similarly, Dell Computer retained UPS to manage its total inbound and outbound shipping.

One measurable impact of this competition between FedEx and UPS, investment spending, is given in **Exhibit 6**. Through 1989, net cash used for investment rose at an annualized rate of 27 percent at Federal Express and 17 percent at UPS. By 1994, UPS had outspent FedEx by a factor of nearly two to one. After the U.S. Congress deregulated intrastate trucking in October 1994, FedEx announced that it would augment its ground service with the purchase of 4,000 new trucks and an investment of $200 million in ground vehicles. Greg Smith, an analyst with the research consulting firm Colography Group, commented, "The more you can do with trucks, the more FedEx will buy and the more they'll become like UPS."[15]

Fred Smith, CEO of FedEx, argued that his company had compelled UPS to deliver packages faster. "UPS has had to adapt to all the innovations we have offered," he said. "The middle ground (two- and three-day delivery) is the battleground. In the next century, people will find it absurd not to move things by express. How many people go by bus today?"[16]

SHARES OF MARKET

Reflecting this competitive turbulence, the market shares of FedEx and UPS had changed over the preceding seven years, as illustrated in Table 1.

---

[15]Quoted in Joan Feldman, "The Price of Success; FedEx Is Solidly No. 1 in Express Shipping and Is Relying on Technology to Stay There Despite the Pressures of Rising Costs," *Air Transport World* (September 1994): 46.
[16]Richard Weintraub, "Delivering a Revolution: The Fierce Rivalry between FedEx and UPS Remakes Global Commerce," *Washington Post,* August 28, 1994.

TABLE 1
Express Delivery Market Shares

	1987	1991				1994		
	Air Overnight Package and Letter	Air Overnight Letter	Air Overnight Package	Air Deferred Packages and Letters	Air Overnight Letter	Air Overnight Package	Air Deferred Packages and Letters*
Federal Express	52.80%	56.80%	28.40%	35.10%	58.30%	29.40%	36.60%
Airborne	6.60	15.90	18.70	10.00	15.10	19.80	19.40
UPS	13.20	10.20	35.40	63.20	12.70	41.50	42.60
U.S. Postal Service	8.00	13.00	4.90	—	9.60	3.40	—
DHL	2.50	NA	8.50	—	2.90	2.70	—
Others	16.90	4.10	4.10	1.70	1.40	3.20	1.40
Total	100.00%	100.00%	100.00%	100.00%	100.00%	100.00%	100.00%

*1994 market share for deferred packages and letters reflects the research of the Colography Group, which indicated that some delivery services sold by UPS as "air delivery" actually traveled by truck and rail. In 1994 (but not 1991) that volume has been removed. This adjustment should be taken into consideration when comparing UPS's market share in the "Deferred Packages and Letters" category.

Source: Greg Smith of the Colography Group and *Business Week,* March 30, 1987.

PERFORMANCE ASSESSMENT

Virtually all interested observers—customers, suppliers, investors, and employees—watched the competitive struggle of these two firms for hints about the next steps in the drama. The conventional wisdom was that if a firm were operationally excellent, strong financial performance would follow. Indeed, FedEx had set a goal of "producing outstanding financial returns," while UPS targeted "competitive returns to shareholders." Had the two firms achieved their goals? Moreover, did the trends in financial performance suggest whether strong performance could be achieved in the future? In pursuit of these questions, the exhibits afford several possible avenues of analysis.

- *E.P.S., market values and returns.* **Exhibit 7** presents the share prices, E.P.S., and price-earnings ratios for the two firms. Also included is the annual total return from holding each share (percent gain in share price, plus dividend yield). Some analysts questioned the appropriateness of using UPS's "fair market value" share price because it was set by the board of directors rather than in an open market.
- *Ratio analysis.* Exhibits 1 and 2 present a variety of analytical ratios computed from the financial statements of each firm.
- *Economic profit analysis.* Also known as "Economic Value Added" (EVA) computed the value created or destroyed each year by deducting a charge for capital from the firm's net operating profit after taxes (NOPAT).

$$\text{EVA} = \text{Operating Profits} - \text{Capital Charge}$$

$$= \text{NOPAT} - (\text{K} \times \text{Capital})$$

The capital charge was determined by multiplying the weighted average cost of capital, K, times the capital employed in the business or operation.

- *Estimating capital.* Included in capital are near-capital items that represent economic value employed on behalf of the firm such as the present value of operating leases, amortized goodwill, and losses. The rationale for including losses and write-offs in continuing capital is that such losses represent unproductive assets, or failed investment. Were they excluded from the capital equation, the sum would only count successful efforts, and not accurately reflect the performance of the firm.
- *Estimating NOPAT.* Net operating profit after taxes (NOPAT) is calculated with a similar regard for losses and write-offs. Here the aim is to arrive at the actual cash generated by the concern. To do so, the estimates add increases in deferred taxes back into income because it is not a cash expense, and calculate the interest expense of the leased operating assets as if they were leased capital assets.
- *Estimating cost of capital.* The capital charge applied against NOPAT should be based on a blend of the costs of all the types of capital the firm employs, or the weighted average cost of capital. The cost of debt (used for both debt and leases) is the annual rate consistent with each firm's bond rating (BBB for FedEx, and AAA for UPS). The cost of equity may be estimated in a variety of ways—in the analysis here, the capital asset pricing model was employed.[17] FedEx's beta and cost of equity are used in estimating FedEx's cost of capital. Since UPS's beta was unobservable, the analysis that follows uses the average beta each year of FedEx, Roadway Package Services, and Airborne Express, UPS's publicly held peer firms.
- *Estimating EVA and MVA.* In **Exhibits 8 and 9** the stock of capital and the flow of NOPAT are used to calculate the actual return and, with the introduction of the WACC, the EVA. These exhibits present the EVA calculated each year, and cumulatively through time. The panel at the bottom of each exhibit estimates the market value created or destroyed (or "Market Value Added," [MVA]) over the observation period. MVA is calculated as the difference between the current market value of the company and its investment base. The market value created could be compared with cumulative economic value added. In theory, the following relationships would hold:

$$\text{MVA} = \text{Present value of all future EVA}$$

$$\text{MVA} = \text{Market value of debt and equity minus capital}$$

Thus,

$$\text{Market Value} = \text{Capital plus present value of all future EVA}$$

In other words, maximizing the present value of EVA amounted to maximizing the market value of the firm.

---

[17]The capital asset pricing model describes the cost of equity as the sum of the risk-free rate of return and a risk premium. The risk premium is the average risk premium for a large portfolio of stocks times the risk factor (or "beta") for the company. A beta equal to 1.0 suggests that the company is just as risky as the market portfolio; less than 1.0 suggests lower risk; greater than 1.0 implies greater risk. In July 1995, FedEx's beta was 1.13.

OUTLOOK FOR FEDERAL EXPRESS IN MID-1995

About 75 percent of FedEx's common shares were held by institutional investors, who, it could be assumed, were instrumental in setting the prices for the company's shares.[18] Typically, these investors absorbed the thinking of the several securities analysts and analytical services that followed Federal Express in 1995. The following excerpts indicate the outlook held by these analysts:

Analyst	Comments
Donaldson, Lufkin & Jenrette Securities P. R. Schlesinger May 26, 1995	As noted, the recent weakness in FDX stock appears, to us, more an indication of general concerns about the health of the economy and the implications for the air express market, and relatedly, renewed worries that Federal might not be able to reverse its domestic earnings declines by boosting prices. The added recent concern about its being vulnerable to US-Japan trade tensions might have added one too many worries for some holders. The stock has . . . underperformed the market. We continue our market performance rating on the stock.
Value Line M. M. Royce, June 23, 1995	The domestic operations have been suffering margin erosion. Federal is working to trim costs and get rid of less profitable business, and we expect fiscal 1996 will bring some relief. . . . Meanwhile, the international segment is running strong. Brisk traffic continues to lift revenues and margins, and the air courier is now tapping into the huge market in Asia to keep the momentum going. . . . This neutrally ranked stock is interesting for its 3- to 5-year appreciation potential, based on the increasing globalization of Federal's network. Indeed, foreign operations should provide the lion's share of profits by early next century.
Alex. Brown & Sons H. P. Boyle, Jr. March 14, 1995	The domestic business was a disappointment. Although volume growth remained robust (up 20.1%), cost per domestic package fell only 2.6% versus a revenue per package yield decline of 5.9%. Thus, the domestic operating margin was squeezed to 4.2% from last year's 6.7% level. The business mix shift toward lower-yielding deferred delivery products requires a more rapid reduction in the cost base than the company was able to achieve during the quarter. . . . we are raising our estimates for the remainder of the fiscal year and beyond. The international performance was spectacular, and we expect it to continue to offset the deterioration in domestic operating income. Given the outlook, we continue to rate the common shares "buy."

Federal Express paid no common stock dividend, which meant that returns to investors would derive entirely from capital gains.

CONCLUSION

Observers of the air-express package delivery industry pondered the recent performance of the two leading firms and their prospects. What had been the impact of the intense competition between the two firms? Which firm was doing better? The announcement about the J.C. Penney contract might contain clues about the prospects for competition in the future.

---

[18]Officers, directors, and employees of FedEx owned 10 percent of the shares. The remainder, about 15 percent, were owned by individual investors not affiliated with the company.

EXHIBIT 1
Analytical Financial Ratios, Federal Express Corporation

	1985	1986	1987	1988	1989	1990	1991	1992	1993	1994	
Activity Analysis											
Average days outstanding	47.43	47.83	44.92	43.43	46.41	47.73	47.28	45.79	44.08	43.23	365/receivables turnover
Working capital turnover	22.59	17.89	34.34	125.84	149.90	162.81	(233.91)	(47.22)	(82.89)	78.62	Sales/average net working capital
Fixed assets turnover	1.64	1.78	1.86	1.90	1.82	2.00	2.14	2.15	2.27	2.45	Sales/average net fixed assets
Total asset turnover	1.18	1.23	1.33	1.41	1.24	1.28	1.36	1.36	1.39	1.44	Sales/average total assets
Liquidity Analysis											
Current ratio	1.34	1.42	1.01	1.10	1.01	1.06	0.90	0.87	0.99	1.15	Current assets/current liabilities
Cash ratio	0.04	0.43	0.04	0.10	0.14	0.08	0.08	0.06	0.11	0.26	(Cash + Mkt securities)/current liabilities
Cash from operations ratio			0.92	1.08	1.17	0.47	0.63	0.37	0.52	0.53	Cash from operations/current liabilities
Defensive interval			1.11	1.51	3.28	1.96	2.38	3.20	2.54	3.18	(Cash + AR + Cash Taxes)/(Rents + Gross CAPEX)
Long-term Debt and Solvency Analysis											
Debt equity ratio	0.75	0.51	0.69	0.63	1.43	1.30	1.09	1.14	1.13	0.85	Total debt/total equity
Times interest earned	5.58	8.87	7.81	5.65	3.68	2.06	1.39	0.14	2.34	3.73	EBIT/interest expense
Fixed charge coverage ratio	4.78	3.71	1.73	1.55	1.47	0.46	(0.36)	(0.93)	0.27	0.49	Earnings before fixed charges and taxes/fixed charges
Capital expenditure ratio			0.60	0.93	0.55	0.87	1.02	1.04	0.91	1.95	Cash from operations/CAPEX
Cash from operations-debt ratio			0.53	0.65	0.31	0.24	0.43	0.29	0.39	0.47	Cash from operations/total debt
Profitability Analysis											
Margin before interest and tax	12.83%	13.37%	11.48%	9.77%	8.21%	5.52%	3.28%	0.30%	4.83%	6.26%	EBIT/Sales
Net profit margin	3.77	5.12	(2.06)	4.83	3.57	1.65	0.08	(1.51)	0.69	2.41	Net income/sales
Return on assets	5.98	6.74	(1.27)	7.29	5.73	4.08	2.04	(0.08)	2.40	4.17	(Net income + after-tax interest costs)/ average total assets
Return on total equity	9.90	13.82	(6.04)	15.58	13.07	7.37	0.36	(7.01)	3.31	11.37	Net income/average total equity
Financial leverage effect	29.42	38.32	(17.98)	49.47	43.48	29.89	2.34	(495.42)	14.28	38.51	Net income/operating income

	84–85	85–86	86–87	87–88	88–89	89–90	90–91	91–92	92–93	93–94	Compound Annual Growth Rate	
Growth												
Sales	41.19%	27.65%	23.51%	22.17%	33.07%	35.77%	9.60%	(1.80)%	3.42%	8.60%	17.31%	(85–94)
Total adjusted capital	20.98%	38.80	13.69	19.47	62.66	8.47	1.71	2.15	7.57	8.46	18.11	(84–94)
Book assets		15.29	19.95	19.90	53.76	3.92	1.62	(5.87)	1.90	(0.78)	11.98	(84–94)
Net income before unusual (gain) loss		38.87	N.M.F.	N.M.F.	(11.33)	(30.45)	(94.91)	N.M.F.	N.M.F.	86.11	4.40	(85–94)
Adjusted NOPAT		14.94	4.37	5.21	22.28	16.10	(36.43)	(8.76)	21.42	35.74	11.61	(85–94)
Net income		73.30	N.M.F.	N.M.F.	(1.69)	(37.27)	(94.91)	N.M.F.	N.M.F.	279.40	11.61	(85–94)
Operating income		33.02	6.02	4.03	11.85	(8.74)	(34.91)	(90.89)	154.24	40.69	8.31	(85–94)

Source: Federal Express annual report.

EXHIBIT 2
Financial Ratios, United Parcel Service

	1985	1986	1987	1988	1989	1990	1991	1992	1993	1994	Formula
Activity Analysis											
Average days outstanding	16.31	14.80	10.63	9.40	16.42	21.23	22.23	23.13	23.11	25.66	365/receivables turnover
Working capital turnover	175.90	382.90	77.65	(109.36)	(112.44)	101.75	124.67	140.99	543.54	313.87	Sales/average net working capital
Fixed asset turnover	3.28	3.26	2.84	2.53	2.42	2.44	2.54	2.64	2.71	2.69	Sales/average net fixed assets
Total asset turnover	1.83	1.70	1.59	1.52	1.51	1.54	1.60	1.68	1.78	1.71	Sales/average total assets
Liquidity Analysis											
Current ratio	1.01	1.03	1.16	0.78	1.11	1.04	1.08	1.03	1.00	1.04	Current assets/current liabilities
Cash ratio	0.31	0.30	0.40	0.22	0.26	0.08	0.14	0.06	0.12	0.09	(Cash + Mkt. securities)/current liabilities
Cash from operations ratio		1.00	1.12	1.36	0.60	0.60	0.85	0.69	0.83	0.68	Cash from operations/current liabilities
Defensive interval		1.40	0.81	0.62	1.31	1.13	1.58	1.71	1.83	1.50	(Cash + AR + Cash Taxes)/(Rents + Gross CAPEX)
Long-term Debt and Solvency Analysis											
Debt equity ratio	0.07	0.05	0.10	0.04	0.24	0.24	0.21	0.23	0.22	0.24	Total debt/total equity
Times interest earned	288.82	134.44	259.96	197.54	81.93	14.61	24.61	30.48	42.87	53.27	EBIT/interest expense
Fixed charge coverage ratio	10.38	22.66	13.57	16.76	(0.04)	(7.49)	2.18	3.23	14.90	13.16	Earnings before fixed charges and taxes/fixed charges
Capital expenditure ratio		1.62	1.14	1.34	0.98	0.94	1.53	1.56	1.60	0.96	Cash from operations/CAPEX
Cash from operations to debt ratio		10.38	4.80	13.54	1.33	1.28	1.92	1.68	2.06	1.43	Cash from operations/total debt
Profitability Analysis											
Margin before interest and tax	10.66%	13.44%	10.03%	9.75%	9.83%	7.73%	8.33%	7.74%	8.20%	7.95%	EBIT/sales
Net profit margin	6.97	7.76	8.10	6.88	5.61	4.39	4.66	3.12	4.55	4.82	Net income/sales
Return on assets	16.13	19.83	19.10	16.17	12.43	9.06	9.91	6.77	10.24	11.03	(Net income + after-tax interest cost)/average total assets
Return on total equity	25.99	29.76	28.53	24.44	20.49	16.59	18.72	13.59	21.13	21.96	Net income/average total equity
Financial leverage effect	65.40	57.75	80.78	70.56	57.06	56.72	55.96	40.40	55.54	60.63	Net income/operating income

Growth	84-85	85-86	86-87	87-88	88-89	89-90	90-91	91-92	92-93	93-94	Compound Annual Growth Rate
Sales	12.50%	12.14%	12.33%	13.94%	12.02%	10.10%	10.39%	9.98%	7.65%	10.08%	11.10% (84–94)
Total adjusted capital	27.58	21.19	23.19	5.02	33.74	5.71	8.55	6.69	3.62	13.90	14.48 (84–94)
Book assets	39.12	18.22	37.60	21.52	13.30	5.03	7.51	3.92	6.15	14.84	16.12 (84–94)
Net income before unusual (gain) loss	19.12	17.85	(6.61)	21.45	(8.61)	(13.94)	17.33	9.27	5.82	16.51	7.07 (84–94)
Adjusted NOPAT	–	1.93	(3.33)	10.94	0.89	(9.41)	(2.16)	12.26	3.03	9.89	2.44 (85–94)
Net income	–	40.39	17.22	(3.24)	(8.61)	(13.94)	17.33	(26.28)	56.86	16.51	7.88 (85–94)
Operating income	–	58.98	(16.20)	10.77	13.02	(13.42)	18.92	2.12	14.08	6.74	8.01 (85–94)

Source: United Parcel Services annual report.

EXHIBIT 3
Timeline of Competitive Developments

FedEx		UPS
Offers 10:30 A.M. delivery	**1982**	Enters Overnight Package Delivery
Increases service area 74% to 94% Later cutoff times Introduces technology to link services	**1983**	
Acquires GELCO: access to 83 countries	**1984**	
Sets up Brussels hub	**1985**	Begins making significant IT investment
Warehouse for IBM, National Semi-conductor, Laura Ashley	**1987**	TV advertising; lower rates
	1988	Offers automated customs service
Announces standard overnight service Announces reduced corporate rate Buys Tiger International International acquisitions	**1989**	Offers same-day pickup Invests $80 million in computer and telecommunications center International acquisitions
	1990	Offers delivery by 10:30 A.M.
	1991	Raises rates—32% for commercial, 16% for residential Launches DIAD system
Exits from Europe Offers 2-day delivery	**1992**	Offers Saturday delivery
Introduces PowerShip software Introduces business logistics services Allies with IBM, Kinko's, Claris, Radio Shack, Sam's, Connect Soft	**1993**	Offers HAZMAT shipping Offers logistics service Offers prepaid letter Offers Saturday pickup Offers 3-day service New ad campaign
Persuades UPS catalog customers to defect from UPS Buys 4,000 trucks Offers service through Internet	**1994**	DIAD fully functional Raises rates 3.9% Offers heavy package delivery Offers early A.M. service Offers service on Internet
	1995	Acquires SonicAir Offers same-day delivery Exclusive contract with J.C. Penney, $1 billion over five years

EXHIBIT 4
Pricing and Delivery of Comparable Packages
Comparative Pricing of Major Overnight Carriers: 1993, 1995
(two-pound package, Baltimore to Los Angeles)

Company	Same-Day	Next AM		Two-Day	
	1995	1993	1995	1993	1995
Federal Express					
Price	$159.00	$24.25	$24.25	$14.00	$14.00
Commitment		10:30 A.M.	10:30 A.M.	4:30 P.M.	4:30 P.M.
Airborne					
Price	$155.00	N/A	$25.00	$9.00	$9.00
Commitment			12:00 noon	3:00 P.M.	3:00 P.M.
United Parcel Service					
Price	$159.00	$18.50	$16.75	$10.50	$5.25
Commitment		10:30 A.M.	10:30 A.M.	4:00 P.M.	4:00 P.M.
U.S. Postal Service					
Price	N/A	$13.95	$15.00	N/A	N/A
Commitment		3:00 P.M.	3:00 P.M.		
DHL					
Price	$159.00	$24.25	$24.25	N/A	N/A
Commitment		12:00 noon	12:00 noon		
Price Premium of FedEx over UPS		**31.08%**	**44.78%**	**33.33%**	**93.10%**

Source: Alex Brown & Sons, Inc., 1993; telephone survey, 1995.

EXHIBIT 5
Segment Information
(in thousands of dollars)

	1986	1987	1988	1989	1990	1991	1992	1993	1994
United Parcel Service									
Domestic:									
Revenue						$13,694,728	$14,721,686	$15,822,558	$17,297,843
Income before income taxes						1,470,645	1,545,484	1,698,299	1,902,140
Identifiable assets						7,982,237	7,873,398	8,359,395	9,886,634
Foreign:									
Revenue						1,325,102	1,796,935	1,959,795	2,277,847
Loss before income taxes						(253,580)	(276,189)	(266,602)	(326,764)
Identifiable assets						876,174	1,164,419	1,214,436	1,295,770
Consolidated:									
Revenue						15,019,830	16,518,621	17,782,353	19,575,690
Income before income taxes						1,217,065	1,269,295	1,431,697	1,575,376
Identifiable assets						8,858,561	9,037,817	9,573,831	11,182,404
Federal Express									
Domestic:									
Revenues	$2,456,832	$2,924,742	$3,459,427	$4,144,827	4,784,887	5,057,831	5,194,684	5,667,964	6,199,940
Operating income (loss)	358,267	393,876	409,977	467,143	608,069	671,186	635,872	559,140	559,629
Identifiable assets				3,007,348	3,798,364	4,032,361	3,941,022	4,432,578	4,883,644
Foreign:									
Revenues	116,397	253,566	423,390	1,022,140	2,230,182	2,630,465	2,355,376	2,140,179	2,279,516
Operating income (loss)	$ (14,246)	$ (29,144)	$ (30,525)	(42,708)	(194,490)	(391,393)	(612,905)	(181,967)	(28,997)
Identified assets				$2,286,074	$1,876,709	$ 1,640,100	$ 1,522,164	$ 1,360,486	$ 1,108,854
Consolidated:									
Revenues	2,573,229	3,178,308	3,882,817	5,166,967	7,015,069	7,688,296	7,550,060	7,808,043	8,479,456
Operating income (loss)	$ 344,021	$ 364,743	$ 379,452	424,435	413,579	279,793	22,967	377,173	530,632
Identifiable assets				$5,293,422	$5,675,073	$ 5,672,461	$ 5,463,186	$ 5,793,064	$ 5,992,498

Source: United Parcel Service reports to shareholders and Federal Express annual reports, SEC, 10-K reports.

EXHIBIT 6
Comparative Capital Investment Information

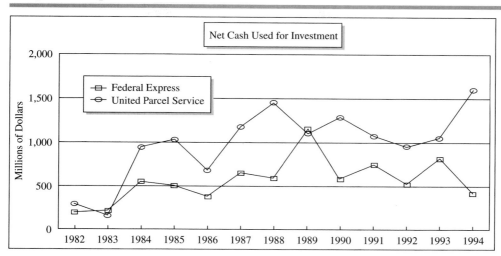

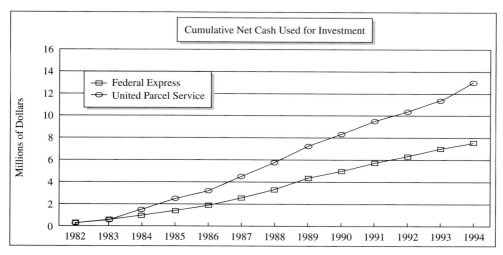

Source: Casewriter analysis of annual reports.

EXHIBIT 7
Equity Returns and Prices

	1981	1982	1983	1984	1985	1986	1987	1988	1989	1990	1991	1992	1993	1994	1995, Q2
Federal Express															
Stock Price, December 31	31.25	$37.13	$23.13	$34.50	$60.63	$63.13	$39.88	$50.63	$45.75	$33.88	$38.75	$54.50	$70.88	$60.25	$60.75
EPS	1.85	$2.03	$2.52	$1.61	$2.64	$2.65	$(1.26)	$3.56	$3.53	$2.18	$0.11	$(2.11)	$0.98	$3.65	$5.27
P/E multiple	16.89	18.29	9.18	21.43	22.96	23.86	n.m.f	14.20	12.96	15.56	350.51	n.m.f	72.00	16.51	11.53
Total capital appreciation return		18.80%	(37.71)%	49.19%	75.72%	4.12%	(36.83)%	26.96%	(9.63)%	(25.96)%	14.39%	40.65%	30.05%	(14.99)%	0.83%
Cumulative compound annual return		18.80%	(26.00)%	10.40%	94.00%	102.00%	27.60%	62.00%	46.40%	8.40%	24.00%	74.40%	126.80%	92.80%	94.40%
United Parcel Service															
Fair market value, December 31	$1.69	$2.31	$4.13	$6.25	$8.25	$10.25	$12.00	$13.38	$14.50	$15.25	$16.00	$18.50	$20.75	$23.50	$24.50
EPS	0.49	$0.49	$0.73	$0.71	$0.84	$0.99	$1.16	$1.12	$1.07	$0.95	$1.14	$0.87	$1.40	$1.63	—
Implied P/E multiple	3.48	4.70	5.69	8.87	9.82	10.34	10.33	11.90	13.54	15.98	14.08	21.33	14.86	14.45	—
Dividends per share	0.10	$0.16	$0.35	$0.34	$0.38	$0.39	$0.41	$0.43	$0.46	$0.47	$0.47	$0.49	$0.49	$0.54	—
Capital appreciation return		37.04%	78.38%	51.52%	32.00%	24.24%	17.07%	11.46%	8.41%	5.17%	4.92%	15.63%	12.16%	13.25%	4.26%
Income return		24.63%	22.52%	13.59%	11.59%	10.71%	10.44%	8.86%	7.68%	6.41%	7.27%	5.03%	7.11%	7.35%	—
Total annual return		61.66%	100.90%	65.11%	43.59%	34.96%	27.52%	20.32%	16.10%	11.59%	12.19%	20.65%	19.28%	20.60%	4.26%
Cumulative compound annual return		61.66%	224.78%	436.24%	669.96%	939.11%	1225.03%	1494.24%	1750.84%	1965.29%	2217.10%	2695.67%	3234.54%	3921.60%	4092.73%
Standard & Poor 500 Index Return, with Reinvestment															
Annual	(4.91)%	21.41%	22.51%	6.27%	32.16%	18.47%	5.23%	16.81%	31.49%	(3.17)%	30.55%	7.67%	9.99%	1.31%	20.22%
Cumulative		21.41%	48.74%	58.07%	108.90%	147.48%	160.43%	204.20%	300.00%	287.32%	405.64%	444.43%	498.81%	506.63%	629.28%
Cumulative Compound Annual Returns, Net of the Standard & Poor 500															
Federal Express		(2.61)%	(74.74)%	(47.67)%	(14.90)%	(45.48)%	(132.83)%	(142.20)%	(253.60)%	(278.92)%	(381.64)%	(370.03)%	(372.01)%	(413.83)%	(534.88)%
United Parcel Service		40.25%	176.04%	378.17%	561.06%	791.63%	1064.60%	1290.04%	1450.84%	1677.97%	1811.46%	2251.25%	2735.73%	3414.96%	3463.45%

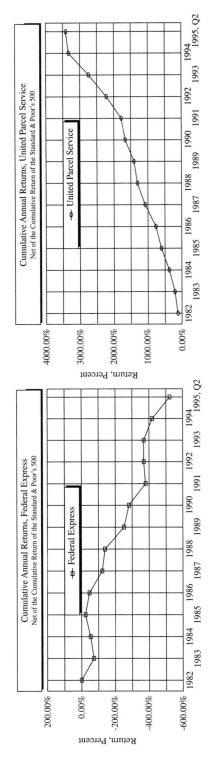

Cumulative Annual Returns, United Parcel Service
Net of the Cumulative Return of the Standard & Poor's 500

— United Parcel Service

Cumulative Annual Returns, Federal Express
Net of the Cumulative Return of the Standard & Poor's 500

— Federal Express

EXHIBIT 8
EVA Estimation, FedEx

	1985	1986	1987	1988	1989	1990	1991	1992	1993	1994
NOPAT	$ 235,029	$ 270,140	$ 281,950	$ 296,642	$ 362,744	$ 421,152	$ 267,728	$ 244,280	$ 296,612	$ 402,621
Beginning capital	$1,403,280	$1,981,285	$2,551,826	$2,901,126	$3,465,870	$5,637,746	$6,115,501	$6,220,035	$6,353,969	$ 6,834,676
RATE OF RETURN	16.75%	13.63%	11.05%	10.23%	10.47%	7.47%	4.38%	3.93%	4.67%	5.89%
WACC										
Long-Term Debt	$ 607,508	$ 561,716	$ 744,914	$ 838,730	$2,138,940	$2,148,142	$1,826,781	$1,797,844	$1,882,279	$ 1,632,202
PV Noncapitalized operating leases	$ 111,384	$ 291,264	$ 510,900	$ 488,929	$ 604,217	$ 996,153	$1,214,342	$1,246,275	$1,334,481	$ 1,567,249
PV of capital leases	$ 295,075	$ 299,228	$ 321,310	$ 319,165	$ 512,079	$ 467,755	$ 239,254	$ 225,800	$ 221,740	$ 199,004
Total	$1,013,967	$1,152,208	$1,577,124	$1,646,824	$3,255,236	$3,612,050	$3,280,377	$3,269,919	$3,438,500	$ 3,398,455
Average shares outstanding	46,970	49,840	51,905	52,670	52,272	53,161	53,350	53,961	54,719	56,012
Share price	$ 58.00	$ 66.00	$ 44.00	$ 49.00	$ 45.00	$ 34.00	$ 33.00	$ 55.00	$ 70.00	$ 57.00
Market value of equity	$2,724,260	$3,289,440	$2,283,820	$2,580,830	$2,352,240	$1,807,474	$1,760,550	$2,967,855	$3,830,330	$ 3,192,684
Tax rate	46.00%	46.00%	34.00%	34.00%	34.00%	34.00%	34.00%	34.00%	35.00%	35.00%
Long-term USG bonds	10.74%	8.14%	8.76%	9.11%	8.62%	8.81%	8.24%	7.61%	6.46%	7.43%
Yield of senior BBB-rated debt	12.19%	10.37%	10.55%	10.75%	10.35%	10.86%	10.12%	9.18%	8.55%	8.91%
Beta	1.35	1.30	1.15	1.10	1.10	1.05	1.05	1.15	1.20	1.25
Cost of equity	18.03%	15.16%	14.97%	15.05%	14.56%	14.48%	13.91%	13.82%	12.94%	14.18%
Cost of capital	**14.93%**	**12.68%**	**11.70%**	**11.95%**	**10.07%**	**9.61%**	**9.20%**	**9.75%**	**9.45%**	**9.86%**
EVA										
NOPAT/beginning capital	16.75%	13.63%	11.05%	10.23%	10.47%	7.47%	4.38%	3.93%	4.67%	5.89%
WACC	14.93%	12.68%	11.70%	11.95%	10.07%	9.61%	9.20%	9.75%	9.45%	9.86%
Spread	1.82%	0.95%	−0.65%	−1.73%	0.39%	−2.14%	−4.83%	−5.82%	−4.78%	−3.96%
× Beginning capital	$1,403,280	$1,981,285	$2,551,826	$2,901,126	$3,465,870	$5,637,746	$6,115,501	$6,220,035	$6,353,969	$ 6,834,676
Annual economic value added	**$ 25,583**	**$ 18,914**	**($16,596)**	**($50,079)**	**$13,620**	**($120,431)**	**($295,178)**	**($362,265)**	**($303,694)**	**($270,959)**
Cumulative Annual EVA	**$ 25,583**	**$ 44,497**	**$ 27,901**	**($22,178)**	**($8,557)**	**($128,988)**	**($424,166)**	**($786,431)**	**($1,090,125)**	**($1,361,084)**

FEDEX: MEASURES OF VALUE CREATION (billions)

	1985	1994	Change
CUMULATIVE EVA	0.026	(1.361)	(1.387)
Analysis of Market Value Added			
Book Value of Equity	0.815	1.925	1.109
Interest-Bearing Debt and Equivalents	1.014	3.398	2.384
CAPITAL (Book Value)	1.829	5.323	3.494
Market Value of Equity	2.724	3.193	0.468
Interest-Bearing Debt and Equivalents	1.014	3.398	2.384
CAPITAL (Market Value)	3.738	6.591	2.853
MARKET VALUE ADDED	**1.909**	**1.268**	**(0.641)**

Source: Casewriter analysis of annual reports.

EXHIBIT 9
Economic Profit Estimation, UPS

	1985	1986	1987	1988	1989	1990	1991	1992	1993	1994
NOPAT	$ 831,562	$ 847,624	$ 819,396	$ 909,046	$ 917,178	$ 830,912	$ 812,968	$ 912,629	$ 940,269	$ 1,033,291
Beginning Capital	$2,333,765	$2,977,489	$3,608,550	$4,445,420	$4,668,509	$6,243,546	$6,599,950	$7,164,016	$7,642,932	$7,919,479
RATE OF RETURN	35.63%	28.47%	22.71%	20.45%	19.65%	13.31%	12.32%	12.74%	12.30%	13.05%
WACC										
Long-term debt	$ 150,950	$ 113,882	$ 293,825	$ 140,009	$ 848,036	$ 854,687	$830,634	$862,378	$852,266	$ 1,127,405
PV Noncapitalized operating leases	—	—	—	—	—	$ 334,593	$451,534	$562,073	$621,874	$635,233
PV of capital leases	385,935	341,656	344,608	345,383	345,265	342,122	333,074	320,616	289,838	233,639
Total	$5,574,908	$ 455,538	$ 638,433	$ 485,392	$1,193,301	$1,531,402	$1,615,242	$1,745,067	$ 1,763,978	$1,996,277
Average shares outstanding	675,746	675,000	675,000	675,000	647,481	625,481	616,000	595,000	580,000	580,000
Share price	$8.25	$10.25	$12.00	$13.38	$14.50	$15.25	$16.00	$18.50	$20.75	$23.50
Market value of equity	$5,574,908	$6,918,750	$8,100,000	$9,028,125	$9,388,477	$9,538,588	$9,856,000	$11,007,500	$12,035,000	$13,630,000
Tax rate	46.00%	46.00%	34.00%	34.00%	34.00%	34.00%	34.00%	34.00%	35.00%	35.00%
U.S. Treasury bond yields (30-yr.)	10.74%	8.14%	8.76%	9.11%	8.62%	8.81%	8.24%	7.61%	6.46%	7.43%
Cost of debt (AAA-rated)	10.93%	9.02%	9.32%	9.55%	9.16%	9.34%	8.69%	8.27%	7.16%	7.80%
Beta	1.10	1.01	0.97	0.97	0.96	1.02	1.02	0.94	1.07	1.05
Cost of equity	16.66%	13.59%	14.00%	14.34%	13.82%	14.34%	13.75%	12.68%	12.21%	13.11%
Cost of capital	**15.72%**	**13.05%**	**13.42%**	**13.93%**	**12.94%**	**13.20%**	**12.62%**	**11.69%**	**11.25%**	**12.08%**
EVA										
NOPAT/beginning capital	35.63%	28.47%	22.71%	20.45%	19.65%	13.31%	12.32%	12.74%	12.30%	13.05%
WACC	15.72%	13.05%	13.42%	13.93%	12.94%	13.20%	12.62%	11.69%	11.25%	12.08%
Spread	19.92%	15.41%	9.28%	6.52%	6.70%	0.10%	−0.30%	1.05%	1.06%	0.97%
×Beginning capital	$2,333,765	$2,977,489	$3,608,550	$4,445,420	$4,668,509	$6,243,546	$6,599,950	$ 7,164,016	$ 7,642,932	$ 7,919,479
Annual economic value added	464,804	458,971	334,978	289,955	313,001	6,469	(19,902)	75,258	80,720	76,463
Cumulative Annual EVA	**464,804**	**923,775**	**1,258,753**	**1,548,708**	**1,861,710**	**1,868,179**	**1,848,277**	**1,923,534**	**2,004,255**	**2,080,718**

UPS: MEASURES OF VALUE CREATION (billions)

	1985	1994	Change
CUMULATIVE EVA	0.465	2.081	1.616
Analysis of Market Value Added			
Book Value of Equity	2.026	4.647	2.621
Interest-Bearing Debt and Equivalents	0.537	1.996	1.459
CAPITAL (Book Value)	2.563	6.644	4.080
Market Value of Equity	5.575	13.630	8.055
Interest-Bearing Debt and Equivalents	0.537	1.996	1.459
CAPITAL (Market Value)	6.112	15.626	9.514
MARKET VALUE ADDED	**3.548**	**8.983**	**5.434**

Source: Casewriter analysis of annual reports.

PART 2

Financial Analysis and Forecasting

The Financial Detective, 1996

Financial characteristics of companies vary for many reasons. The two most prominent drivers are industry economics and firm strategy.

Each industry has a financial norm around which companies within the industry tend to operate. An airline, for example, would naturally be expected to have a high proportion of fixed assets (airplanes), while a consulting firm would not. A steel manufacturer would be expected to have a lower gross margin than a pharmaceutical manufacturer, because commodity products like steel are subject to strong price competition, while highly differentiated products like patented drugs enjoy much more pricing freedom. Because of unique economic features of each industry, average financial statements will vary from one industry to the next.

Similarly, companies within industries have different financial characteristics, in part, because of varied strategies. Executives choose strategies that will position their company favorably in the competitive jockeying within an industry. Strategies typically entail making important choices in how a product is made (e.g., capital intensive versus labor intensive), how it is marketed (e.g., direct sales versus use of distributors), and how the company is financed (e.g., the use of debt or equity). Strategies among companies in the same industry can differ dramatically. Different strategies can produce arresting differences in financial results for firms in the same industry.

The following paragraphs describe two participants in a number of different industries. Their strategies and market niches provide clues to the financial condition and performance one would expect of them. The companies' common-sized financial statements and operating data as of early 1996 have been presented in a standardized format in **Exhibit 1**. It is up to you to

This case was prepared by Mark S. Bonney under the direction of Professor Robert F. Bruner. It was written as a basis for class discussion rather than to illustrate effective or ineffective handling of an administrative situation. Copyright © 1996 by the University of Virginia Darden School Foundation, Charlottesville, VA. All rights reserved. *To order copies, send an e-mail to* dardencases@virginia.edu. *No part of this publication may be reproduced, stored in a retrieval system, used in a spreadsheet, or transmitted in any form or by any means—electronic, mechanical, photocopying, recording, or otherwise—without the permission of the Darden School Foundation. Rev. 11/01. Version 2.0.*

match the financial data with the company descriptions. Also, try to explain the differences in financial results *across* industries.

HEALTH PRODUCTS

Companies A and B manufacture and market health care products. One firm develops, manufactures, and distributes ethical drugs (pharmaceuticals) to doctors and hospitals through a direct sales force. This firm holds a substantial number of patents on original research. In addition, it owns shares in joint ventures and small biotech firms as part of a strategy of tapping new research breakthroughs.

The other firm manufactures and nationally mass markets a broad line of over-the-counter remedies (i.e., nonprescription drugs), name-brand toiletries, and consumer baby-care products. Its products are sold to retailers and distributors from where they are sold directly to consumers. Brand development and management are a major element of this firm's mass-market-oriented strategy.

HOUSEHOLD APPLIANCES

The two home-appliance manufacturers are companies C and D. One focuses on manufacturing and marketing high-quality washers, dryers, dishwashers, and refrigerators under its own brand name. The strategy of this first company is to be the quality leader in the industry, and to charge commensurate prices.

The other company attempts to segment the market for the same products by selling under its own and three private-label brand names. In particular, this second firm is a captive supplier of private-label appliances on a large multiyear contract with one of the leading retailers in the United States.

COMPUTERS

Companies E and F sell computers and related equipment. One company is a mail-order seller of personal computers primarily to the consumer market. This firm is located in modest facilities in a rural region, and it outsources important elements of its manufacturing. The key strategy of this firm is to keep costs low, charge lower prices, and achieve higher unit sales volumes.

The other company sells its computers through dealers and a sales force. Many of this company's sales are to the business market. This firm has a leading brand name. More of this firm's manufacturing is internal (i.e., rather than outsourced). The key strategy of this firm is to be the quality and service leader in the industry, and to offer a broad product line in its segment.

RETAILING

Companies G and H are two retailers with different marketing emphases. One company is a large, national chain of department stores. This company sells, largely on credit, everything from automotive equipment and services to clothing and household items. Its properties are primarily leased.

The other firm is a rapidly growing chain of consumer home-improvement stores offering a large selection of home-improvement items at low prices. The firm has been called a "category killer" by virtue of its strategy to underprice the competition, advertise heavily, and enjoy large market share and unit-sales volumes. This firm's stores are in a "warehouse" format and are all leased.

HOTELS

Companies I and J are both operators of large hotel/motel chains. One of these two companies owns one of the largest food-service contractors in the country. This firm finances its hotels via off-balance-sheet limited partnerships. The company has significant assets in the form of food-service and hotel-management contracts. The key strategy of this firm is to manage, not own, its hotels.

The other firm operates a worldwide chain of high-quality hotels and motels in addition to a smaller line of casinos. The key strategy of this firm is to concentrate on the lodging and entertainment businesses, and to own its properties.

NEWSPAPERS

Companies K and L own newspapers. One has a large flagship newspaper that is sold around the country and around the world. Because the company is centered largely around one product, it has strong central controls. Competition for subscribers and advertising revenues in this firm's chosen segment is fierce.

The other firm owns a number of newspapers in relatively smaller communities throughout the Midwest. Some analysts view this firm as holding a portfolio of small local monopolies in newspaper publishing. This company has a significant amount of goodwill on its balance sheet stemming from acquisitions. Key to this firm's operating success is a strategy of decentralized decision making and administration.

BEER

Of the beer companies, M and N, one is a national brewer of mass-market consumer beers under a variety of brand names. This company also owns several theme parks.

The other company is one of a group of "microbrewers" with smaller production volume and higher prices. This company outsources much of its brewing activity and has recently completed a successful initial public offering (IPO) of its stock.

STEEL

Companies O and P manufacture and sell steel. One of the steel companies is a "mini mill." This company serves a specific segment of the steel market that is not as vulnerable to foreign competition. Being smaller, the firm can fill smaller production orders profitably. Not being as unionized as the rest of the industry, the firm enjoys lower labor costs. The key strategic emphases of this firm are low costs, low prices, and nimble service.

The other company is a large integrated steel producer able to provide a full range of products. While it has higher costs (mainly in labor), it aims to offset this with long production runs in the fulfillment of large contracts.

EXHIBIT 1
Common-Sized Financial Data and Ratios
(NMF = not meaningful)

	Health Products		Appliances		Computers		Retail		Hotels		Newspapers		Beer		Steel	
	A	B	C	D	E	F	G	H	I	J	K	L	M	N	O	P
ASSETS																
Cash and equivalents	7.6	7.5	6.7	1.9	9.5	15.1	1.8	1.4	13.3	5.5	1.9	2.7	0.9	47.7	7.5	8.8
Receivables	16.3	10.6	19.6	27.1	40.2	36.1	60.7	4.4	7.0	18.0	10.2	8.2	5.1	21.0	13.7	12.3
Inventories	12.7	5.8	12.5	13.2	27.6	20.0	12.2	29.7	0.4	4.5	3.3	1.3	5.5	12.1	13.0	13.4
Other current assets	7.8	4.8	4.0	3.2	6.2	5.9	5.1	0.8	2.7	6.3	3.3	1.5	2.7	4.3	1.3	1.7
Total current assets	44.4	28.7	42.8	45.4	83.5	77.1	79.8	36.3	23.4	34.3	18.7	13.7	14.2	85.1	35.5	36.2
Net fixed assets	29.1	29.4	33.0	22.8	14.2	15.1	15.3	60.7	55.4	20.7	19.3	37.8	63.9	8.0	45.0	63.8
Other assets	26.5	41.9	24.2	31.8	2.3	7.8	4.9	3.0	21.2	45.0	62.0	48.5	21.9	6.9	19.5	0.0
Total assets	100.0	100.0	100.0	100.0	100.0	100.0	100.0	100.0	100.0	100.0	100.0	100.0	100.0	100.0	100.0	100.0
LIABILITIES & EQUITY																
Accounts payable	9.0	7.1	6.7	12.5	17.7	20.9	18.5	11.2	10.0	20.0	4.3	4.6	6.4	11.2	8.8	9.3
Other ST liabilities	15.6	27.4	10.5	36.6	16.6	25.8	25.6	8.0	7.5	18.0	16.5	10.7	5.3	14.9	9.3	10.1
Total current liabilities	24.6	34.5	17.2	49.1	34.3	46.7	44.1	19.2	17.5	38.0	20.8	15.3	11.7	26.1	18.1	19.4
Long-term debt	11.8	18.0	25.3	12.6	3.8	1.0	30.3	9.8	34.9	20.1	13.5	18.9	30.9	2.4	22.1	4.7
Other liabilities	13.0	9.8	27.5	11.9	2.9	2.9	8.5	2.1	6.6	15.7	10.2	18.0	15.5	0.0	37.8	6.1
Total liabilities	49.4	62.3	70.0	73.6	41.0	50.6	82.9	31.1	59.0	73.8	44.5	52.2	58.1	28.5	78.0	30.2
Equity	50.6	37.7	30.0	26.4	59.0	49.4	17.1	68.9	41.0	26.2	55.5	47.8	41.9	71.5	22.0	69.8
Total liabilities & equity	100.0	100.0	100.0	100.0	100.0	100.0	100.0	100.0	100.0	100.0	100.0	100.0	100.0	100.0	100.0	100.0
Sales	100.0	100.0	100.0	100.0	100.0	100.0	100.0	100.0	100.0	100.0	100.0	100.0	100.0	100.0	100.0	100.0
Cost of Goods Sold (CGS)	33.1	27.9	74.0	75.6	77.0	83.3	65.5	72.3	44.4	21.9	40.3	54.1	65.7	48.8	87.5	83.8
Gross profit	66.9	72.1	26.0	24.4	23.0	16.7	34.5	27.7	55.6	80.1	59.7	45.9	34.3	51.2	12.5	16.2
Selling, general & admin (SG&A)	48.3	42.8	16.5	19.6	14.3	10.0	25.7	19.8	44.1	72.6	35.9	36.4	17.0	45.0	5.6	3.8
Loss/(Gain)	0.2	(1.0)	5.8	(0.7)	0.6	(0.4)	(0.1)	0.2	(15.1)	0.3	0.0	(2.0)	1.0	(0.8)	0.4	(0.3)
EBIT	18.4	30.3	3.7	5.5	8.1	7.1	8.9	7.7	26.6	5.2	23.8	11.5	16.3	7.0	6.5	12.7
Interest expense	0.8	4.2	1.7	1.7	0.0	0.0	3.9	0.0	7.5	0.6	2.7	2.0	2.2	0.2	1.5	0.3
Pretax income	17.6	26.1	2.0	3.8	8.1	7.1	5.0	7.7	19.1	4.6	21.1	9.5	14.1	6.8	5.0	12.4
Income taxes	4.9	6.8	2.5	1.2	2.7	2.4	2.0	3.0	7.0	1.8	8.0	3.9	5.5	(1.5)	1.9	4.5
Income before minority & extraordinary	12.7	19.3	(0.5)	2.6	5.4	4.7	3.0	4.7	12.1	2.8	13.1	5.6	8.6	8.3	3.1	7.9
Minority interests & extraordinary items	0.0	(14.6)	0.2	0.1	0.0	0.0	(2.2)	0.0	0.3	0.0	0.0	0.0	2.4	0.0	0.0	0.0
Net income/(loss)	12.7	33.9	(0.7)	2.5	5.4	4.7	5.2	4.7	11.8	2.8	13.1	5.6	6.2	8.3	3.1	7.9
MARKET DATA																
Beta	1.10	1.10	1.25	1.55	1.46	1.55	1.32	1.40	1.20	1.30	0.80	1.00	1.00	NMF	1.15	1.20
P/E ratio	23.0	24.5	13.7	19.0	17.2	11.2	15.5	32.3	25.8	24.9	19.1	21.2	19.4	56.0	9.2	18.2
Market/Book	6.1	5.7	3.4	2.1	2.9	3.3	3.8	4.7	2.4	1.8	3.4	1.8	3.8	6.8	1.6	3.6
Dividend payout ratio	34.4%	32.6%	NMF	48.0%	0.0%	0.0%	26.4%	12.3%	33.5%	14.1%	34.7%	39.9%	66.8%	0.0%	6.5%	9.0%
LIQUIDITY																
Current ratio	1.8	0.8	2.5	0.9	2.4	1.7	1.8	1.9	1.3	0.9	0.9	0.9	1.2	3.3	2.0	1.9
Quick ratio	0.3	0.2	0.4	0.0	1.5	0.3	0.0	0.1	0.8	0.1	0.1	0.2	0.1	1.8	0.4	0.5
ASSET MANAGEMENT																
Inventory turnover	2.8	2.1	6.9	6.8	2.7	17.7	5.7	5.7	48.0	51.2	27.6	35.6	12.2	8.7	9.4	10.6
Receivables turnover	6.9	4.4	6.2	4.2	5.4	11.2	1.8	51.8	7.1	13.0	8.4	9.2	18.1	11.6	9.6	12.8
(Net) Fixed asset turnover	3.7	1.6	4.2	5.2	14.4	28.3	7.5	3.9	0.9	11.0	4.6	2.0	1.6	31.2	3.0	2.5
DEBT MANAGEMENT																
Debt to assets	13.6%	31.2%	25.4%	38.2%	3.8%	2.2%	51.7%	9.8%	42.0%	20.1%	22.1%	19.0%	30.9%	2.5%	25.0%	4.7%
(LT) debt to equity	23.3%	47.7%	84.2%	52.4%	6.5%	2.0%	247.4%	14.4%	85.3%	76.5%	24.3%	39.6%	73.8%	3.4%	100.6%	7.7%
Times interest earned	24.2	7.2	2.2	3.2	NMF	NMF	2.3	289.2	3.6	8.8	9.0	5.7	7.5	42.5	4.3	47.6
DuPONT ANALYSIS																
Profit margin (1)	12.7%	19.3%	-0.5%	2.6%	5.4%	4.7%	3.0%	4.7%	12.1%	2.8%	13.4%	5.6%	8.6%	8.3%	3.1%	7.9%
Asset turnover (2)	112.4	46.8	131.3	115.5	211.0	388.1	99.2	235.6	48.9	248.1	84.1	74.0	97.8	279.0	128.4	161.1
Return on assets (1) × (2)	14.3%	9.0%	-0.7%	3.0%	11.4%	18.2%	3.0%	11.1%	5.9%	6.9%	11.3%	4.1%	8.4%	23.2%	4.0%	12.7%

The Body Shop International PLC 2001: An Introduction to Financial Modeling

Finance bored the pants off me; I fell asleep more times than not.[1]

—Anita Roddick, founder,
The Body Shop International

Roddick, as self-righteous as she is ambitious, professes to be unconcerned [with financial results]. . . . "Our business is about two things: social change and action, and skin care," she snaps. "Social change and action come first. You money-conscious people . . . just don't understand." Well, maybe we don't but we sure know this: Roddick is one hell of a promoter. . . . She and her husband, Gordon, own shares worth not far from $300 million. Now that's social action.[2]

One of our greatest frustrations at The Body Shop is that we're still judged by the media and the City by our profits, by the amount of product we sell, whereas we want, and have always wanted, to be judged by our actions in the larger world, by the positive difference we make.[3]

— Anita Roddick

---

[1] Anita Roddick, *Body and Soul* (London: Ebury Press, 1991), 105.
[2] Jean Sherman Chatzky, "Changing the World," *Forbes* (March 2, 1992): 87.
[3] Anita Roddick, *Business as Unusual* (London: Thorsons, 2000): 56.

This case was written by Susan Shank and John Vaccaro under the direction of Professors Robert Bruner and Robert Conroy as a basis for class discussion rather than to illustrate effective or ineffective handling of an administrative situation. The financial support of the Batten Institute for case development is gratefully acknowledged. *Copyright © 2001 by the University of Virginia Darden School Foundation, Charlottesville, VA. All rights reserved. To order copies, send an e-mail to* dardencases@virginia.edu. *No part of this publication may be reproduced, stored in a retrieval system, used in a spreadsheet, or transmitted in any form or by any means—electronic, mechanical, photocopying, recording, or otherwise—without the permission of the Darden School Foundation. Version 1.2.*

In the late 1990s, The Body Shop International PLC, previously one of the fastest growing manufacturer-retailers in the world, ran aground. Annual revenue growth of 20 percent in the early-to-mid-1990s had, by the late 1990s, slowed to around 8 percent. New retailers of naturally based skin- and hair-care products entered the market, bringing in intense competition for The Body Shop. Amid the competition, The Body Shop failed to maintain its brand image, becoming something of a mass-market line as it expanded into "almost every mall in America, as well as virtually every corner on Britain's shopping streets."[4]

Anita Roddick, founder of The Body Shop, stepped down as CEO in 1998[5] after numerous unsuccessful attempts to reinvent the company. Patrick Gournay, an executive from the French food giant Danone SA, came on board as CEO. However, problems persisted despite the management change. In fiscal-year 2001, revenue grew 13 percent, but pretax profit declined 21 percent. Gournay said of the results, "This is below our expectations and we are disappointed with the outcome."[6]

Nonetheless, Gournay was confident that a newly implemented strategy would produce improved results. The strategy consisted of three principal objectives: "To enhance The Body Shop brand through a focused product strategy and increased investment in stores; to achieve operational efficiencies in our supply chain by reducing product and inventory costs; and to reinforce our stakeholder culture."[7]

Suppose that Anita Roddick, the founder and cochair of the board of directors, and Patrick Gournay, CEO, came to you in the spring of 2001 for assistance in near-term and long-range planning for The Body Shop. As a foundation for this work, you will need to estimate The Body Shop's future earnings and financial needs. The challenge of this advisory work should not be underestimated: Anita Roddick is a strong-willed decision maker with little taste for finance and financial jargon. Your projections must not only be technically correct, but they must also yield practical insights and be straightforward. What you have to say and how you say it are equally important.

If you do not feel comfortable using **Exhibit 8** to prepare the next three years of financial statements and demonstrate The Body Shop's debt financing needs, you might be better served to scan the next few sections on basic financial modeling and concentrate on the last section of the case ("Ms. Roddick and Mr. Gournay Want to Know. . ."). From experience, however, a vast number of students have found the following exercises to be invaluable in their early understanding of financial modeling.

AN OVERVIEW OF FINANCIAL FORECASTING

In seeking to respond to Roddick and Gournay's request, you can draw on at least two classical forecasting methods and a variety of hybrids that use some of each method. The two methods are:

---

[4]Sarah Ellisan, "Body Shop Seeks a Makeover—U.K. Cosmetics Retailer Confirms Sale Talks with Mexico's Grupo Omnilife—A Long and Difficult Fall from Grace," *The Wall Street Journal Europe,* June 8, 2001.

[5]Anita Roddick remained on the company's board of directors and, together with her husband, Gordon Roddick, served as cochair.

[6]CEO report (The Body Shop International PLC preliminary results for the 53 weeks to March 3, 2001).

[7]Ibid.

T-account forecasting: This method starts with a base year of financial statements (e.g., last year). Entries through double-entry bookkeeping determine how each account will change and what the resulting new balances will be. While exactly true to the mechanics of how funds flow through the firm, this method is cumbersome and may require a degree of forecast information about transactions unavailable to many analysts outside (and even inside) a firm.

Percent-of-sales forecasting: This method starts with a forecast of sales and then estimates other financial statement accounts based on some presumed relationship between sales and that account. While simple to execute, this technique is easily misused. For instance, some naive analysts may assume that operational capacity can increase in fractional amounts with increases in sales—but can an airline company really buy only half a jumbo jet? Operational capacity usually increases in "lumps" rather than by smooth amounts. The lesson here is that when you use this technique, you should scrutinize the percent-of-sales relationships for their reasonableness.

The most widely used approach is a hybrid of these two. For instance, T-accounts are used to estimate shareholders' equity and fixed assets. Percent-of-sales is used to estimate income statements, current assets, and current liabilities, because these latter items may credibly vary with sales. Other items will vary as a percentage of accounts other than sales: tax expense will usually be a percentage of pretax income, dividends will vary with after-tax income, and depreciation will usually vary with gross fixed assets.

A FORECAST WITH PENCIL AND PAPER

As an introduction to financial modeling, we will walk through the construction of a forecasted income statement and balance sheet, first with pencil and paper (just visualizing the steps may suffice), and later with a spreadsheet. In either case, you are preparing a pro forma (or projected) income statement and balance sheet for The Body Shop for 2002 (income statement for the entire year; balance sheet for year-end). All values should be in pounds sterling. Use the following assumptions as a guide:

Sales:	£422,733,000 (a 13 percent increase over 2001)
Cost of goods sold:	38 percent of sales
Operating expenses:	50 percent of sales
Interest expense:	6 percent of debt (about the current interest rate)
Profit before tax:	Sales − COGS − Operating expenses − interest
Tax:	30 percent of profit before tax (the going corporate tax rate in Britain)
Dividends:	£10.9 million (same as previous three years)
Earnings retained:	Profit after tax − dividends
Current assets:	32 percent of sales
Fixed assets:	£110,600,000
Total assets:	Current assets + fixed assets
Current liabilities:	28 percent of sales
Debt:	Total assets − current liabilities − shareholders' equity
Common equity:	£121,600,000 plus retentions to earnings

Income statement: Begin with sales, and use it to estimate COGS and operating expenses. For the time being, leave interest expense at zero since we do not yet know the amount of debt. Estimate profit before tax, tax expense, profit after tax, dividends, and earnings retained.

Balance sheet: Estimate current assets (32 percent of sales) and add that to £110,600,000 to get an estimate for total assets. Next, estimate current liabilities (28 percent of sales) and common equity. Debt becomes the "plug" figure that makes the two sides of the balance sheet balance. This amount is your estimate of the external financing The Body Shop will need by year-end 2002. Estimate the plug by subtracting the amounts for current liabilities and common equity from total assets.

Iterate: Initially, you entered an interest expense of zero on the income statement. But this cannot be correct if debt is outstanding (or if excess cash is invested in interest-earning instruments). This is a classic problem in finance arising from the dependence of the income statement and balance sheet on each other: interest expense is necessary to estimate retained earnings, which is necessary to estimate debt; let's call this the problem of "circularity." The way to deal with this problem is to insert your best estimate of interest expense in the income statement (using 6 percent times debt), then re-estimate the plug figure, then re-estimate interest expense, and so on. By iterating through the two statements five or six times, you will come to estimates of interest expense and debt that do not change very much further. Stop iterating when changes get to be small.

A FORECAST WITH A SPREADSHEET MODEL

Fortunately, the tedium of iterating can be eliminated with the aid of a computer and spreadsheet software such as Excel. The specific commands reviewed here relate to Excel 2000. (These commands will appear in table form within the text.) The adaptation to other spreadsheet programs should be straightforward.

Now, try the same forecast for The Body Shop using a computer spreadsheet.

Setup. Start with a clean spreadsheet. Set the recalculation mode to MANUAL so that the model will iterate only when you press CALC (F9). Also, set the number of iterations to 1 so that you will be able to see Excel re-estimate the plug figure and interest expense. You can set the number of iterations higher (Excel's default is 100), but Excel will converge on a solution after five or six iterations, so a setting of 1 is best to see the iterations in action. The commands here are:

> Choose the **Tools** menu and then the **Options** menu item. Then choose the **Calculations** tab, select the button next to **Manual,** and enter 1 in **Maximum Iterations.** Be sure the box next to **Iterations** is checked.

Saving. As you develop your model, be sure to save it every five minutes or so just for insurance.

Format. Use the format in **Exhibit 1** as a guide to plan your worksheet. To facilitate sensitivity analysis, it is generally best to place the "Input Data" at the top of the worksheet.

Next, develop the income statement just as you did by pencil and paper. Use **Exhibit 2** as a guide. Be sure to tie the cells to the proper percentage rate in the Input Data section. The first time through, enter 0 for interest. (This is very important for the iteration to work properly.) We will return to it later.

Now do the balance sheet. Again, be sure to tie the balance sheet together by formulas.

With the basic format laid out, go back and enter the formula to calculate interest as "interest rate times debt." Press the F9 key and you should see the worksheet change. You should be able to press the F9 key several more times until the numbers stop changing, which means the model has converged to a solution. You should have interest as exactly 6 percent of long-term liabilities and a balance sheet that balances.

Once you have seen how this works, you may want to have the model converge without having to press CALC several times. In order to do this, you must set the number of iterations you wish the spreadsheet to perform. Set the number of iterations back to 100, Excel's default, and allow the computer to recalculate automatically.

Choose the **Tools** menu, and then the **Options** menu item. Then choose the **Calculations** tab, click on **Automatic,** and enter 100 in **Maximum Iterations.** Be sure the box next to **Iterations** is checked.

Note: Changing your iterations setting, combined with the circularity of the debt plug and interest expense (and later we'll add the circularity of data tables), can lead to some confusing situations. It's easy to forget where you have your iterations set (and that more data tables lead to more circularity). When comparing your work to someone else's, be sure that both of you have the same iterations setting and have hit F9 the same number of times (and that you have either no data tables or the same data tables).

Your worksheet should now look like **Exhibit 3**.

PROJECTING FARTHER

So far, you have managed to project The Body Shop's financial statements through 2002. Now extend your projection to 2003 and 2004. A simple way to do this is to copy your model for the two additional years. Before copying formulas from column B to columns C and D, make sure that any references to your Input Data (cells B3 through B12) are absolute references as opposed to relative references. (An absolute reference means that when you copy cells B16 through B35 to other parts of your spreadsheet, the cells are still linked back to the originals, for example, B5. Otherwise, the program assumes that the cells should be linked to new cells, for example, C5. To make a reference absolute, put in dollar signs— B3, instead of B3.) Now you should be ready to copy:

Select the range of your data by highlighting it in the worksheet. Choose the **Edit** menu and then the **Copy** menu item. Highlight the cells where you want the copy to go. Choose the **Edit** menu and then the **Paste** menu item.

Note that you will have to change the equity formula for 2003 and 2004. For 2003, make the formula equal to 2002's equity plus 2003's additions to retained earnings. Also, you should make sales grow by compounding. To do this, multiply 2002's sales times 2003's expected sales growth rate (say, 13 percent). As you enter these changes, you should see the effect ripple through your model.

WHEN DEBT IS NEGATIVE

Now modify the model to deal with the situation where the plug for debt is negative—this can happen routinely for firms with seasonal or cyclical sales patterns. Negative debt can be interpreted as excess cash. But this is an odd way to show cash; a nonfinancial manager (like Anita Roddick) might not appreciate this type of presentation. The solution is to add a line for "Excess Cash" on the assets side of the balance sheet and then set up three new lines below the last entry in the balance sheet:

Name	Formula
Trial assets	Current assets + Fixed assets
Trial liabilities and equity	Current liabilities + Equity
Plug	Trial assets − Trial liabilities

Now enter the formula for "Excess Cash":

$$= IF(PLUG < 0, -PLUG, 0)$$

Instead of the word "PLUG," you should use the cell address for the actual plug number. The formula for DEBT is:

$$= IF(PLUG > 0, +PLUG, 0)$$

See **Exhibit 4** for an example of how your spreadsheet should look. To see how these modifications really work, change your COGS/SALES assumption to 0.45 and press F9.

With excess cash, you should generate interest income instead of interest expense. To have your model treat interest as income rather than expense in the event of an excess cash balance, modify your interest expense formula as follows:

$$= +(B6*B34) - (B6*B28)$$

An example of finished results appears in **Exhibit 5**.

EXPLORE SENSITIVITIES

After your model replicates the exhibit, you are ready to conduct a sensitivity analysis on the pro forma years by seeing how variations in the forecast assumptions will affect the financing requirements. A financial analyst might want to try the following variations (or more than one in combination):

- Suppose sales in 2002 will be £500 million.
- Suppose COGS runs at 45 percent of sales.
- Suppose dividends are increased to 60 percent of net income.
- Suppose that The Body Shop must double its manufacturing capacity by adding a new £100 million facility in 2002.
- Assume inventories run higher than expected (model this by increasing current assets to 40 percent of sales).
- Assume that accounts-receivable collections improve so that current assets run at 28 percent of sales.
- Assume that operating expenses increase faster than sales.

What happens to the plug value (i.e., debt) under these different circumstances? In general, which assumptions in the Input Data section of your spreadsheet seem to have the biggest effect on future borrowing needs?

The "Data Table" is an invaluable tool for conducting a sensitivity analysis. It automatically calculates debt (or whatever else you want to focus on) as it varies across different values for a particular assumption, for instance, growth rates. In Excel, you can create a data table in a two-step process illustrated in the following examples. Suppose that you want to estimate The Body Shop's debt required and excess cash generated at COGS/SALES ratios of .35, .38, .40, .42, .44, .45, and .48.

1. **Set up the table.**   Move to a clean part of the spreadsheet and type the COGS/SALES ratios (.35, .38, .40, .42, .44, .45, and .48) in a column. At the top of the next column (one row above your first COGS/SALES ratio), enter the location of the value to be estimated, in this case, debt, or =B34. In the next column, type the cell location for excess cash, =B28. Your data table should be formatted as in **Exhibit 6**.
2. **Enter the data table commands.**

> Highlight the cells that contain your COGS/SALES ratios and your cell references to Debt and Excess Cash. (The cells to the right of your COGS/SALES ratios and below your cell references to Debt and Excess Cash are the cells to be filled in and should also be highlighted.)
>
> Choose the **Data** menu and then the **Table** menu item.
>
> In the **Column Input Cell** box, enter the cell where your COGS/SALES assumption is (B4).
>
> The computer will fill in the table.

The additional circularity brought about by data tables can lead to some confusing results. To avoid this, be sure at this point to set the number of iterations to *at least* 10. The result should look like **Exhibit 7**.

The data table in **Exhibit 7** reveals that, at COGS/SALES ratios of 45 percent, the firm will need to borrow. This should trigger questions in your mind about what might cause that to happen, such as a price war or a surge in materials costs. Your spreadsheet format can tell you about more sophisticated data-table formats. No financial analyst can afford to ignore this valuable tool. Armed with this tool, it's easy to go back and try the variations in other input assumptions listed above.

Note: Remember that data tables add more calculations that need to be iterated in your worksheet. When comparing your work to that of a fellow student, be sure your iterations are set the same and you have roughly the same data tables in your files.

MS. RODDICK AND MR. GOURNAY WANT TO KNOW. . .

Now that you have completed a simplified forecast, prepare a forecast based on the full range of accounts as actually reported by The Body Shop in 2001. **Exhibit 8** presents the results for the past three years. Please forecast all of the accounts individually for the next three years: you will see many familiar accounts, as well as some unusual accounts like minority interests. For most accounts, you should extrapolate by using the same percentage of sales borne out by the preceding years' experience. You might use an average of the three historical years. You might want to use just the most recent year, or if you notice a significant upward or downward trend in an account, you might want to try growing or shrinking the percentage in the future years. Use your judgment. Whatever assumptions you decide on, you should again isolate them at the top of your worksheet. This way you can easily change an assumption and have it flow through your worksheet. And this is very important for calculating sensitivities later, as you want to be able to point to one cell as the Column Input Cell in a data table.

Please make "overdrafts" the plug figure, and base interest expense (at 6 percent) on the overdrafts, current portion of long-term debt, and long-term liabilities. (If you skipped to this section without doing the exercise above, you may differ from your fellow students in your treatment of the case where debt is negative.)

Make your own assumptions regarding sales growth. Make other assumptions as needed. Prepare to report to Roddick and Gournay your answers to the following questions:

- How did you derive your forecast? Why did you choose the "base-case" assumptions that you did?
- Based on your pro forma projections, how much additional financing will The Body Shop need during this period?
- What are the three or four most important assumptions ("key drivers") in this forecast? What is the effect on financing need of varying each of these assumptions up or down from the base case? Intuitively, why are these assumptions so important?
- Why are your findings relevant to general managers like Roddick and Gournay? What are the implications of these findings for them? What action should they take based on your analysis?

In discussing your analysis with Roddick and Gournay, do not permit yourself to get mired in forecast technicalities or financial jargon. Focus your comments on your results; state them as simply and intuitively as you can. Do not be satisfied with simply presenting results. Link your findings to recommendations: key factors to manage, opportunities to enhance results, issues warranting careful analysis. Remember that Roddick plainly admits she finds finance boring; whenever possible, try to express your analysis in terms that she finds interesting: people, customers, quality natural products, and the health and dynamism of her business. Good luck!

EXHIBIT 1
Format for Developing a Spreadsheet Model

	A	B
1	Input Data	
2		
3	SALES	422,733
4	COGS/SALES	0.38
5	OPERATING EXPENSES/SALES	0.50
6	INTEREST RATE	0.06
7	TAX RATE	0.30
8	DIVIDENDS	10,900
9	CURR. ASSETS/SALES	0.32
10	CURR. LIABS./SALES	0.28
11	FIXED ASSETS	110,600
12	STARTING EQUITY	121,600
13		
14	INCOME STATEMENT	2002
15		
16	SALES	
17	COGS	
18	OPERATING EXPENSES	
19	INTEREST EXPENSE (INCOME)	
20	PROFIT BEFORE TAX	
21	TAX	
22	PROFIT AFTER TAX	
23	DIVIDENDS	
24	EARNINGS RETAINED	
25		
26	BALANCE SHEET	2002
27		
28	CURRENT ASSETS	
29	FIXED ASSETS	
30	TOTAL ASSETS	
31		
32	CURRENT LIABILITIES	
33	DEBT	
34	EQUITY	
35	TOTAL LIAB. & NET WORTH	

EXHIBIT 2
Spreadsheet Formulas to Forecast 2002 Financials

	A	B
1	**Input Data**	
2		
3	SALES	422,733
4	COGS/SALES	0.38
5	OPERATING EXPENSES/SALES	0.50
6	INTEREST RATE	0.06
7	TAX RATE	0.30
8	DIVIDENDS	10,900
9	CURR. ASSETS/SALES	0.32
10	CURR. LIABS./SALES	0.28
11	FIXED ASSETS	110,600
12	STARTING EQUITY	121,600
13		
14	INCOME STATEMENT	2002
15		
16	SALES	+B3
17	COGS	+B4*B16
18	OPERATING EXPENSES	+B5*B16
19	INTEREST EXPENSE (INCOME)	+B6*B33
20	PROFIT BEFORE TAX	+B16-B17-B18-B19
21	TAX	+B7*B20
22	PROFIT AFTER TAX	+B20-B21
23	DIVIDENDS	+B8
24	EARNINGS RETAINED	+B22-B23
25		
26	BALANCE SHEET	2002
27		
28	CURRENT ASSETS	+B9*B16
29	FIXED ASSETS	+B11
30	TOTAL ASSETS	+B28+B29
31		
32	CURRENT LIABILITIES	+B10*B16
33	DEBT	+B30-B32-B34
34	EQUITY	+B12+B24
35	TOTAL LIAB. & NET WORTH	+B32+B33+B34

EXHIBIT 3
Basic Forecasting Results for 2002

	A	B
1	Input Data	
2		
3	SALES	422,733
4	COGS/SALES	0.38
5	OPERATING EXPENSES/SALES	0.50
6	INTEREST RATE	0.06
7	TAX RATE	0.30
8	DIVIDENDS	10,900
9	CURR. ASSETS/SALES	0.32
10	CURR. LIABS./SALES	0.28
11	FIXED ASSETS	110,600
12	STARTING EQUITY	121,600
13		
14	INCOME STATEMENT	2002
15		
16	SALES	422,733
17	COGS	160,639
18	OPERATING EXPENSES	211,367
19	INTEREST EXPENSE (INCOME)	(1,171)
20	PROFIT BEFORE TAX	51,899
21	TAX	15,570
22	PROFIT AFTER TAX	36,329
23	DIVIDENDS	10,900
24	EARNINGS RETAINED	25,429
25		
26	BALANCE SHEET	2002
27		
28	CURRENT ASSETS	135,275
29	FIXED ASSETS	110,600
30	TOTAL ASSETS	245,875
31		
32	CURRENT LIABILITIES	118,365
33	DEBT	(19,520)
34	EQUITY	147,029
35	TOTAL LIAB. & NET WORTH	245,875

EXHIBIT 4
Adjusting to Reflect Excess Cash

	A	B
1	**Input Data**	
2		
3	SALES	422,733
4	COGS/SALES	0.38
5	OPERATING EXPENSES/SALES	0.50
6	INTEREST RATE	0.06
7	TAX RATE	0.30
8	DIVIDENDS	10,900
9	CURR. ASSETS/SALES	0.32
10	CURR. LIABS./SALES	0.28
11	FIXED ASSETS	110,600
12	STARTING EQUITY	121,600
13		
14	**INCOME STATEMENT**	**2002**
15		
16	SALES	422,733
17	COGS	160,639
18	OPERATING EXPENSES	211,367
19	INTEREST EXPENSE (INCOME)	+(B6*B34)-(B6*B28)
20	PROFIT BEFORE TAX	40,706
21	TAX	14,247
22	PROFIT AFTER TAX	26,459
23	DIVIDENDS	10,900
24	EARNINGS RETAINED	15,559
25		
26	**BALANCE SHEET**	**2002**
27		
28	EXCESS CASH	=IF(B40<0,-B40,0)
29	CURRENT ASSETS	135,275
30	FIXED ASSETS	110,600
31	TOTAL ASSETS	+B29+B30+B28
32		
33	CURRENT LIABILITIES	118,365
34	DEBT	=IF(B40>0,+B40,0)
35	EQUITY	137,159
36	TOTAL LIAB. & NET WORTH	+B33+B34+B35
37		
38	TRIAL ASSETS	+B29+B30
39	TRIAL LIABILITIES AND EQUITY	+B33+B35
40	PLUG: DEBT (EXCESS CASH)	+B38-B39

EXHIBIT 5
Finished Results for 2002, Reflecting Excess Cash

	A	B
1	**Input Data**	
2		
3	SALES	422,733
4	COGS/SALES	0.38
5	OPERATING EXPENSES/SALES	0.50
6	INTEREST RATE	0.06
7	TAX RATE	0.30
8	DIVIDENDS	10,900
9	CURR. ASSETS/SALES	0.32
10	CURR. LIABS./SALES	0.28
11	FIXED ASSETS	110,600
12	STARTING EQUITY	121,600
13		
14	**INCOME STATEMENT**	**2002**
15		
16	SALES	422,733
17	COGS	160,639
18	OPERATING EXPENSES	211,367
19	INTEREST EXPENSE (INCOME)	(1,171)
20	PROFIT BEFORE TAX	51,899
21	TAX	15,570
22	PROFIT AFTER TAX	36,329
23	DIVIDENDS	10,900
24	EARNINGS RETAINED	25,429
25		
26	**BALANCE SHEET**	**2002**
27		
28	EXCESS CASH	19,520
29	CURRENT ASSETS	135,275
30	FIXED ASSETS	110,600
31	TOTAL ASSETS	265,395
32		
33	CURRENT LIABILITIES	118,365
34	DEBT	0
35	EQUITY	147,029
36	TOTAL LIAB. & NET WORTH	265,395
37		
38	TRIAL ASSETS	246,875
39	TRIAL LIABILITIES AND EQUITY	265,395
40	PLUG: DEBT (EXCESS CASH)	(19,520)

EXHIBIT 6
Setup for a Forecast with Data Table

	A	B	C	D	E	F
1	**Input Data**					
2						
3	SALES	422,733				
4	COGS/SALES	0.38				
5	OPERATING EXPENSES/SALES	0.50		**Sensitivity Analysis**		
6	INTEREST RATE	0.06		Of Debt and Excess Cash		
7	TAX RATE	0.30		To COGS/SALES Ratio		
8	DIVIDENDS	10,900				
9	CURR. ASSETS/SALES	0.32		COGS/SALES	DEBT	Ex. CASH
10	CURR. LIABS./SALES	0.28			=B34	=B28
11	FIXED ASSETS	110,600		0.35		
12	STARTING EQUITY	121,600		0.38		
13				0.40		
14	**INCOME STATEMENT**	**2002**		0.42		
15				0.44		
16	SALES	422,733		0.45		
17	COGS	160,639		0.48		
18	OPERATING EXPENSES	211,367				
19	INTEREST EXPENSE (INCOME)	(1,171)				
20	PROFIT BEFORE TAX	51,899				
21	TAX	15,570				
22	PROFIT AFTER TAX	36,329				
23	DIVIDENDS	10,900				
24	EARNINGS RETAINED	25,429				
25						
26	**BALANCE SHEET**	**2002**				
27						
28	EXCESS CASH	19,520				
29	CURRENT ASSETS	135,275				
30	FIXED ASSETS	110,600				
31	TOTAL ASSETS	265,395				
32						
33	CURRENT LIABILITIES	118,365				
34	DEBT	-				
35	EQUITY	147,029				
36	TOTAL LIAB. & NET WORTH	265,395				
37						
38	TRIAL ASSETS	246,875				
39	TRIAL LIABILITIES AND EQUITY	265,395				
40	PLUG: DEBT (EXCESS CASH)	(19,520)				

EXHIBIT 7
Finished Forecast with Data Table

	A	B	C	D	E	F
1	**Input Data**					
2						
3	SALES	422,733				
4	COGS/SALES	0.38				
5	OPERATING EXPENSES/SALES	0.50		**Sensitivity Analysis**		
6	INTEREST RATE	0.06		Debt and Excess Cash		
7	TAX RATE	0.30		By COGS/SALES		
8	DIVIDENDS	10,900.00				
9	CURR. ASSETS/SALES	0.32		COGS/SALES	DEBT	Ex. CASH
10	CURR. LIABS./SALES	0.28			+B34	+B28
11	FIXED ASSETS	110,600		0.35	0	28,787
12	STARTING EQUITY	121,600		0.38	0	19,520
13				0.40	0	13,342
14	**INCOME STATEMENT**	**2002**		0.42	0	7,165
15				0.44	0	987
16	SALES	422,733		0.45	2,102	0
17	COGS	160,639		0.48	11,369	0
18	OPERATING EXPENSES	211,367				
19	INTEREST EXPENSE (INCOME)	(1,171)				
20	PROFIT BEFORE TAX	51,899				
21	TAX	15,570				
22	PROFIT AFTER TAX	36,329				
23	DIVIDENDS	10,900				
24	EARNINGS RETAINED	25,429				
25						
26	**BALANCE SHEET**	**2002**				
27						
28	EXCESS CASH	19,520				
29	CURRENT ASSETS	135,275				
30	FIXED ASSETS	110,600				
31	TOTAL ASSETS	265,395				
32						
33	CURRENT LIABILITIES	118,365				
34	DEBT	0				
35	EQUITY	147,029				
36	TOTAL LIAB. & NET WORTH	265,395				
37						
38	TRIAL ASSETS	245,875				
39	TRIAL LIABILITIES AND EQUITY	265,395				
40	PLUG: DEBT (EXCESS CASH)	(19,520)				

EXHIBIT 8
Historical Financial Statements (£ in millions)

	1999 (£)	1999 (% sales)	2000 (£)	2000 (% sales)	2001 (£)	2001 (% sales)
			Fiscal Year Ended February 28			
Income Statement						
Turnover	303.7	100.0	330.1	100.0	374.1	100.0
Cost of sales	127.7	42.0	130.9	39.7	149.0	39.8
Gross profit	176.0	58.0	199.2	60.3	225.1	60.2
Operating expenses						
− excluding exceptional costs	151.4	49.9	166.2	50.3	195.7	52.3
− exceptional costs[*]	4.5	1.5	0.0	0.0	11.2	3.0
Restructuring costs[†]	16.6	5.5	2.7	0.8	1.0	0.3
Net interest expense	0.1	0.0	1.5	0.5	4.4	1.2
Profit before tax	3.4	1.1	28.8	8.7	12.8	3.4
Tax expense	8.0	2.6	10.4	3.2	3.5	0.9
Profit/ (loss) after tax	(4.6)	−1.5	18.4	5.6	9.3	2.5
Ordinary dividends	10.9	3.6	10.9	3.3	10.9	2.9
Profit/ (loss) retained	(15.5)	−5.1	7.5	2.3	(1.6)	−0.4
			Fiscal Year Ended February 28			
Balance Sheet						
Assets						
Cash	34.0	11.2	19.2	5.8	13.7	3.7
Accounts receivable	27.8	9.2	30.3	9.2	30.3	8.1
Inventories	38.6	12.7	44.7	13.5	51.3	13.7
Other current assets	12.5	4.1	15.6	4.7	17.5	4.7
Net fixed assets	87.8	28.9	104.7	31.7	110.6	29.6
Other assets[‡]	0.0	0.0	6.0	1.8	6.7	1.8
Total assets	200.7	66.1	220.5	66.8	230.1	61.5
Liabilities and equity						
Accounts payable	13.0	4.3	20.5	6.2	10.7	2.9
Taxes payable	11.3	3.7	11.7	3.5	7.1	1.9
Accruals	10.8	3.6	15.6	4.7	11.5	3.1
Overdrafts	0.0	0.0	0.3	0.1	0.7	0.2
Other current liabilities	21.6	7.1	13.3	4.0	16.9	4.5
Long-term liabilities	28.0	9.2	36.7	11.1	61.2	16.4
Other liabilities[§]	1.7	0.6	1.0	0.3	0.4	0.1
Shareholders' equity	114.3	37.6	121.4	36.8	121.6	32.5
Total liabs. and equity	200.7	66.1	220.5	66.8	230.1	61.5

[*] Exceptional costs in 2001 included redundancy costs (4.6 million), costs of supply chain development (2.4 million) and impairment of fixed assets and goodwill (4.2 million). The exceptional costs of 4.5 million in 1999 were associated with closing unprofitable shops and an impairment review of the remaining shops in the U.S.
[†] Restructuring costs in 2001 and 2000 relate to the sale of manufacturing plants in Littlehampton, England, and to associated reorganization costs. Restructuring costs in 1999 arose from the realignment of the management structure of the business in the U.S. and the UK.
[‡] Other assets in 2001 and 2000 represented receivables relating to the sale of the company's Littlehampton manufacturing plant.
[§] Other liabilities included mostly deferred taxes.

Padgett Paper Products Company

Negotiations with Padgett Paper Products Company had been going on for almost a year. Francis Libris hoped the time had come when they could be pushed to a mutually satisfactory conclusion. If not, Padgett might seek another bank as its source of funds. Alternatively, Mr. Libris would be subject to criticism by his superiors for failing to deliver on his commitment to manage and structure the relationship properly. Libris was vice president of the Caslon Trust Company of Richmond, Virginia, one of Virginia's largest banks. He was responsible for the Broad Street Commercial Lending Center of the bank, to which Padgett's account was assigned because its small executive offices were on an upper floor of the same building in which the center was located. It was a significant account for the center and an important one to its profitability.

Padgett had borrowed small amounts off and on from Caslon since it had first established an account with the bank in 1947. Even the acquisition of several small companies (for less than $1 million each) in the 1980s did not require high levels of debt. The acquisition of a long-coveted competitor at an attractive price on short notice in early 1996 brought Padgett suddenly to the bank, asking for an additional $3.6 million loan. Combined with the $3.6 million already outstanding at that time, Caslon's total exposure could rise to $7.2 million, well in excess of the $5 million advised credit line that had been approved for the company. The request was granted nevertheless, under an internal guidance line of $8 million, and the rate was continued at prime. Mr. Libris had been working since then to structure the arrangements on a more orderly basis than 90-day notes with no protective covenants.

This case was prepared by Paul H. Hunn, Visiting Lecturer, whose cooperation is acknowledged with appreciation. It was written as a basis for class discussion rather than to illustrate effective or ineffective handling of an administrative situation. Copyright © 1996 by the University of Virginia Darden School Foundation, Charlottesville, VA. All rights reserved. *To order copies, send an e-mail to* dardencases@virginia.edu. *No part of this publication may be reproduced, stored in a retrieval system, used in a spreadsheet, or transmitted in any form or by any means—electronic, mechanical, photocopying, recording, or otherwise—without the permission of the Darden School Foundation. Rev. 9/99. Version 1.5.*

It was now January 1997. Libris hoped to have the new terms worked out so they could be reflected on the financial statements for the 1997 fiscal year that would end April 30. There was a chance that a negotiation completed before the auditors finished their field-work, roughly two months after the April ending of Padgett's fiscal year, could be incorporated in the auditor's report. Libris preferred, however, to have the agreement signed before the end of the fiscal year to avoid this complication.

Libris wondered whether he should take a fresh look at the situation. He had originally tried to persuade Padgett's management to finance part of the company's requirements in the form of long-term debt from a life insurance company. When the financial vice president declined the private-placement proposal, Libris decided to see how the loan could be repaid to the bank within the period initially suggested by his superiors. As time had gone on, he began to think that these constraints might not be appropriate to the situation and that a more creative solution might prove acceptable both to departmental senior management and to Padgett's management. Because Libris knew he would have to get the approval of his superiors before he undertook a different initiative with Padgett's management, time was getting exceedingly short. He had to develop both the implications of the original decision and of any alternatives that appeared more attractive.

PADGETT PAPER PRODUCTS COMPANY

Padgett Paper Products Company, a closely held but publicly traded (over-the-counter) company, manufactured a variety of stationery products including notebooks, loose-leaf binders, forms, and filler paper for students and record-keeping purposes. The company was over 100 years old. Its ownership remained primarily with the descendants of the founders, now a large and widely spread group. Few family members were active in the company's management, and the major connection with most of the owners came in the form of the quarterly dividend check. A few members of the family depended on the dividends for most of their income. Most of the shareholders considered Padgett just another investment and an illiquid one at that because the market for the company's stock was extremely thin. A significant payout was considered important by management.

Management, which was primarily professional, appeared competent, responsible, and reasonably effective. Its expertise was largely in operations, which were carried on at several plants in the Midsouth, and in marketing, which was controlled out of the executive office in Richmond. Management was not financially oriented, Libris had observed.

Padgett's customers were some 5,000 wholesalers and retailers in the United States and Canada. No single customer or small group of customers accounted for a substantial share of Padgett's sales. Terms were 2/10 net 30, but few customers took the discount. Many stretched payment for an additional 30 days. The business had a slight seasonal peak in the late summer when big back-to-school sales took place. Because the company tried to maintain level production to reduce unit cost in the highly competitive market, a seasonal variation of about $2 million occurred in its borrowing pattern. The peak occurred in the summer.

A consolidation had been taking place in the business since the late 1970s, initially caused by the high inflation rate of the period that made it difficult for small firms to finance their

current assets. Financial difficulties and inventory problems resulting from the subsequent recession in the early 1980s further reduced the level of the competition. Changes in the tax rules
periodically provided new impetus for the smaller companies to sell. The sharp drop in the stock
market in October 1987 had frightened some owners into selling out. Most recently, a sudden
increase in paper prices, which had risen over 50 percent from mid-1994 and exceeded the previous high prices of 1988–89, had again created financial strains for firms such as Tri-State
Tablet. These pressures had become great enough, and the price-earnings multiples attractive
enough because of the booming equity market, that many of the remaining owners (including
Tri-State's) put their firms on the market. Tri-State had not been able to pass all the price increases through to its customers because of strong competition from large, integrated paper companies. In Padgett's case, a drop in its tax rate helped compensate for smaller margins.

Over the years, many of Padgett's competitors had been acquired by national corporations with strong marketing skills and good financial resources. The response of Padgett's
management had been to acquire smaller companies that fit into its product or marketing
needs. The acquisition of its competitor, Tri-State Tablet Company, in April 1996 was the
culmination of these efforts.

Padgett's financial statements for fiscal year 1996 had been given an unqualified opinion
by the national CPA firm that audited them. Straight-line depreciation was used for reporting
purposes with accelerated depreciation used for taxes. Inventory had been valued on a lower of
cost (FIFO) or market basis despite the potential cash savings from the favorable tax effect of
a change to LIFO. Padgett's management had always concluded that it was not worth the complexity to change inventory accounting methods. Financial statements for the 1993–96 fiscal
years are presented in **Exhibits 1 and 2**. **Exhibit 3** is a standard computerized spread used by
Caslon's credit department to organize a company's financial statements for analysis.

PADGETT'S RELATIONSHIP WITH CASLON TRUST

Caslon Trust had historically been Padgett's only lending bank and was its only lending bank
in early 1997. Among other benefits of this relationship, Padgett used Caslon Trust as the depository for its substantial Virginia and federal tax payments. So far during the 1997 fiscal
year, Padgett's average collected balance with Caslon had been $524,000. Affiliated compa-
nies and subsidiaries had balances that had averaged $231,000. The loan balances outstand-
ing had ranged from $3.3 to $7.2 million, with an average of $5.05 million. The loan had last
been cleaned up for an extended period from March 31, 1993, to January 8, 1994.

Padgett maintained a small deposit relationship with the Phoenix Bank, a major North
Carolina bank that had long been soliciting a more important role in the company's financial
arrangements. In addition, several local banks were used to service the various plant locations.

The speed with which the Tri-State Tablet acquisition had been made had not allowed
for careful planning of the financial arrangements. Libris's group management had been reluctant to double the loan to Padgett without a carefully structured financial program as well
as appropriate protective covenants. With Libris's assurance that these questions could be
quickly resolved, the group's senior vice president had authorized the loan and established
a new temporary credit limit of $8 million. It had been expected, however, that the loan
would be formally structured long before January 1997, which was a source of embarrass-

ment to Libris. He knew he also would be embarrassed and his profit plan damaged if he should lose the account to Phoenix.

Once the dust created by the acquisition had settled down, Libris met with John Ruhl, Padgett's financial vice president, to discuss the company's plans. Based on these conversations, Libris and Caslon's credit department prepared a preliminary financial forecast for Padgett's 1997–2000 fiscal years. Summary figures from this forecast are presented in **Exhibit 4.**

Libris was distressed to note that, even under what he thought were assumptions that minimized the need for funds, Padgett would still have $4.4 million in short-term debt on the books at the end of the fiscal year 2000. Assuming the company could generate about $1 million in "undedicated" cash each subsequent year, a total of eight years would be required to retire the debt. This was considerably longer than the typical bank five-year term loan that a company of Padgett's size might expect. Caslon was willing to stretch to six years for important relationships, but a seven-year term loan would be considered a bit long for a company such as Padgett, which did not enjoy the financial flexibility afforded firms having easy entry to the public capital markets.

Libris decided that a need of this duration appropriately called for insurance company financing. After he had met with officers of several companies, he wrote Mr. Ruhl to propose a 12- to 15-year loan and to quote terms an insurance company might offer. (Libris's letter is reproduced as **Exhibit 5.**) He also pointed out that Caslon might be able to structure an arrangement that would allow the bank to take the seasonal needs while the insurance company would take the long-term core requirements of $5 million.

Ruhl's response was emphatically negative. While he appreciated the information, he reported that management believed the current long-term fixed rates were too high. Although it was tempting to take advantage of the fact that long-term corporate rates had not yet returned to their early-1995 peak, his board was somewhat pessimistic about the future of the economy. "Politicians like low rates before elections," he said, "but they pay the piper afterwards. I think they're pumping up the economy now. We'll probably have high rates soon after the election, and then we'll have a recession. Maybe that will be the time to lock in really low rates." He admitted, however, that a repeat of the interest-rate runup of the 1970s would again have a serious effect on Padgett.

Furthermore, Padgett's management did not like the idea of an elaborate set of covenants. Ruhl said that he particularly disliked the type of covenant that could throw the company in default without management's explicit action. "Violation of a debt-capital ratio, for instance," explained Ruhl, "could occur as the result of an adverse year rather than anything we do. I don't mind agreeing not to borrow or pay dividends if certain conditions would result, but I just don't see agreeing to a lot of things that are out of my control. I can't see getting tied up in all these technicalities." Ruhl indicated that he did not see anything wrong with the present, friendly, informal loan. "After all," he said, "if you don't like what we're doing—anything at all—you can call your entire loan at the end of any 90-day period. Isn't this better protection for you than fancy agreements?"

In the months that followed this disappointing outcome, Libris met frequently with Ruhl to get a thorough understanding of the business. He planned to prepare a forecast of future needs that would accurately reflect Padgett management's thinking and his own insights into the company. By late in 1996, preliminary estimates for the 1997 fiscal year were becoming available so Libris could incorporate them into his forecasts. The forecasts, which were prepared showing the effects of 5 percent, 10 percent, and 15 percent growth in sales over the 1998–2000 fiscal years, are included as **Exhibit 6**.

Ruhl thought that this effort was most helpful, although he noted that two last-minute changes should be incorporated in the planning. First, he had finally persuaded Padgett's directors that a shift to LIFO-inventory valuation would save more cash than the cost of implementing the system. LIFO would be adopted for the 1997 fiscal year, which would result in a tax benefit of $500,000. Second, management had decided to dispose of a redundant warehouse that had been part of the Tri-State acquisition. Management expected to receive $700,000 from the cash sale and tax refunds on the book loss.

ALTERNATIVES

Libris still thought that splitting the loan—maybe with the bank's own real estate department—had promise. For instance, Padgett owned outright a large, general-purpose warehouse. Its appraisal value of $3 million was more than the amount at which it was carried on the books. Although Libris was not an experienced real-estate lending officer, he believed the property would be attractive collateral for a mortgage loan. Another alternative might be to wait until the loan had been partly retired and then invite another bank to share the remainder for the duration of the repayment. Part of the loan could be rotated between banks to allow each a clean-up period of several months. Finally, he had discovered that Padgett's small Canadian operation was self-contained with a negligible amount of intercompany transfers and charges. With net current assets of $1.8 to $2.0 million to offer as collateral and no direct debt, the Canadian subsidiary could probably raise $1.0 million from Canadian banks. The Canadian banks would require "charge," a form of security agreement, against all current assets of the subsidiary.

Although U.S. banking law and practice were not identical with Canadian and British practice with respect to "floating liens," asset-based finance might offer useful alternatives. It would be expensive to take effective security against Padgett's receivables because the company had so many customers and the average account was small. A factoring arrangement might be suitable, in which Padgett could sell its accounts on a nonrecourse basis to a commercial finance company. Caslon Bank itself did not operate a factoring function, however. It would be necessary to find one that had experience in the paper-distribution business or else the costs of the factoring, which were usually about 2 percent of accounts purchased, would be too high. On the other hand, if Padgett factored its accounts, it could eliminate its credit department and would have no bad debts.

Caslon could always grant credit against the security of the accounts receivable even though the bank would not monitor the accounts as closely as a factor would. The loan would be limited to a percentage of receivables to provide some protection against losses. A security interest in the inventory also could be required, although the granting of this security could upset some major paper companies that were Padgett's sources of supply.

MONEY MARKET CONSIDERATIONS AND PRICING ASPECTS

Funds were readily available in the financial markets in January 1997. Although the prime rate had risen rapidly during 1994, rates had then declined modestly during 1995 and 1996 to 8 1/4 percent. The prime's low in recent years had been 6 percent from mid-1992 to early 1994. Thirty-day commercial paper was currently yielding 5.38 percent. The Treasury yield curve was relatively flat: 90-day bills yielded 5.04 percent; one-year notes, 5.6 percent; five-year notes, 6.10; 10-year bonds, 6.59 percent; and 30-year bonds, 6.73 percent. During the recent election campaign, however, there had been much debate about whether the economy was growing too slowly or too rapidly. Rates had therefore been very volatile. Whenever the market began to suspect that the Federal Reserve would raise rates to curb inflation, rates spiked up.

The interest-rate volatility was an issue that Libris would have to address in preparing a proposal for Ruhl. Should the loan (or loans) be priced at a fixed rate or at a floating rate? Fixed-rate loans were generally offered at a premium of 2 1/2 to 1 percent above the floating rate.

In adjusting the prime rate to the conditions of the borrower, Caslon bank officers often used what they termed a "risk-premium" system. This approach added or subtracted 25 basis points (1/4 percent) to the price for such factors as the size of the company's sales (add points for small size and lack of access to public markets), purpose, term, escalating versus level payments, debt profile, liquidity posture, and (subtract points for) relationship benefits (for example, balances, tax payments, and corporate trust). Of course, the final rate had to be checked against the market, which in Padgett's case was highly competitive as the result of Phoenix's interest.

Because of the complications that had already been experienced and that were likely to arise while completing the negotiations, Libris knew that he had no more time to collect information. He had to work quickly toward a satisfactory resolution of the loan structure with Padgett's management.

EXHIBIT 1
Income Statements for the Fiscal Years Ended April 30, 1993–1996 (thousands of dollars except per-share figures)

	1993	1994	1995	1996
Net sales	$26,331	$27,219	$36,897	$41,308
Cost of goods sold	15,728	16,077	21,937	24,555
Depreciation and amortization	*	510	667	739
	$10,603	$10,632	$14,293	$16,014
General and admin. expense	5,814	5,087	7,139	7,821
Selling expense	—	1,878	2,603	3,147
Operating expenses	$ 5,814	$ 6,965	$ 9,742	$10,968
Operating profit	$ 4,789	$ 3,667	$ 4,551	$ 5,046
Interest expense	—	32	220	379
Other expenses (income)	83	(42)	(39)	(71)
Profit before taxes	$ 4,706	$ 3,677	$ 4,370	$ 4,738
Income taxes	2,702	1,893	2,216	2,132
Profit after taxes	$ 2,004	$ 1,784	$ 2,154	$ 2,606
Number of shares (000)	1,000	1,115	1,116	1,118
Earnings per share	$ 2.00	$ 1.60	$ 1.93	$ 2.33
Dividends per share	1.00	1.00	1.00	1.00

*Included in cost of goods sold in 1993.
— Included in general and administrative expenses in 1993.

EXHIBIT 2
Balance Sheets as of April 30, 1993–96 (thousands of dollars)

	1993	1994	1995	1996
Assets				
Current assets				
Cash and securities	$ 1,691	$ 266	$ 658	$ 834
Accounts receivable	4,734	5,542	6,350	7,754
Inventory	7,276	7,743	10,959	14,360
Prepayments and other	233	194	153	563
Total current assets	$13,934	$13,745	$18,120	$23,511
Property, plant, equip.	—	8,718	11,265	12,468
Less: Accumulated depn.	—	3,384	4,912	5,209
Net prop., plant, equip.	$ 4,797	$ 5,334	$ 6,353	$ 7,259
Other assets	59	257	386	224
Total assets	$18,790	$19,336	$24,859	$30,994
Liabilities and Owners' Equity				
Current liabilities				
Short-term notes	$ —	$ —	$ 3,118	$ 7,221
Accounts payable	1,127	1,619	2,158	1,958
Accruals	395	397	703	1,014
Other current liabilities	271	251	418	824
Current portion, long-term debt	615	117	51	52
Total current liabilities	$ 2,408	$ 2,384	$ 6,448	$11,069
Long-term debt	338	221	507	455
Deferred taxes	538	568	714	756
Other liabilities	136	126	116	151
Total liabilities	$ 3,420	$ 3,299	$ 7,785	$12,431
Owners' equity				
Common stock	5,587	5,587	5,587	5,587
Retained earnings	9,783	10,450	11,487	12,976
Total owners' equity	$15,370	$16,037	$17,074	$18,563
Total liabilities and net worth	$18,790	$19,336	$24,859	$30,994

EXHIBIT 3

Cash Flow and Ratio Analysis, for the Fiscal Years Ended April 30, 1993–96 (figures in thousands of dollars)

	1993	1994	1995	1996
Sources				
Profit after taxes plus depn. and amort.*		$ 2,294	$ 2,821	$ 3,345
Deferred taxes		30	146	42
New long-term debt		—	337	—
New short-term debt		—	3,118	4,103
Accounts payable		492	539	(200)
Accruals		2	306	311
Other current liabilities		(20)	167	406
Other liabilities		(10)	(10)	35
Total sources		$ 2,788	$ 7,424	$ 8,042
Uses				
Dividends paid in cash		$ 1,117	$ 1,117	$ 1,117
Capital expenditure		979	1,575	1,530
Repayment of long-term debt		615	117	51
Accounts receivable		808	808	1,404
Inventory		467	3,216	3,401
Prepayments and other current assets		(39)	(41)	410
Other assets		198	129	(162)
Intangibles*		68	111	115
Total uses		$ 4,213	$ 7,032	$ 7,866
Change in cash and securities		$ (1,425)	$ 392	$ 176
Working capital	$11,526	$11,361	$11,672	$12,442

	1993	1994	1995	1996
Profitability				
Sales growth	n.a.	3.4%	35.6%	12.0%
Gross profit margin	40.3%	39.1	38.7	38.8
Operating expenses/sales	22.1	25.6	26.4	26.5
Pre-tax margin	17.9	13.5	11.8	11.5
After-tax margin	7.6	6.6	5.8	6.3
Return on aver. owners' equity	n.a.	11.4	13.0	14.6
Return on total assets	10.7	9.2	8.7	8.4
EBIT/total assets	25.0	19.2	18.5	16.5
Dividend payout	50.2	62.6	51.9	42.9
Turnover on Sales				
Receivables	5.6×	4.9×	5.8×	5.3×
Inventory	3.6	3.5	3.4	2.9
Accounts payable	23.4	16.8	17.1	21.1
Working capital	2.3	2.4	3.2	3.3
Fixed asset	5.5	5.1	5.8	5.7
Net worth	1.7	1.7	2.2	2.2
Leverage				
Total debt/owners' equity	22.3%	20.6%	45.6%	67.0%
Long-term debt/owners' equity	2.2	1.4	2.9	2.4
Interest coverage	n.a.	115.9×	20.9×	13.5×
Liquidity				
Quick ratio	2.7×	2.4×	1.1×	.8×
Current ratio	5.8	5.8	2.8	2.1

*Intangibles amortized as purchased.

EXHIBIT 4

Summary Figures from Preliminary Projection of Financial Position for the Fiscal Years Ending April 30, 1997–2000 (millions of dollars)

	1997	1998	1999	2000
Sources of Funds				
Net sales	$55.2	$60.7	$66.8	$73.5
Profit after taxes	3.3	3.6	4.2	4.8
Noncash charges	.9	.9	1.0	1.1
Cash generated from operations	$ 4.2	$ 4.5	$ 5.2	$ 5.9
Disposition of assets	.2	—	—	—
Total sources	$ 4.4	$ 4.5	$ 5.2	$ 5.9
Uses of Funds				
Dividends	$ 1.1	$ 1.1	$ 1.1	$ 1.1
Increase in working capital*	2.4	2.4	3.1	3.6
Capital expenditures	1.0	1.0	1.0	1.0
	$ 4.5	$ 4.5	$ 5.2	$ 5.7
Effect on Short-Term Debt				
*Including retirement of short-term debt	.7	.2	.8	1.1
Leaving a balance in short-term debt of	$ 6.5	$ 6.3	$ 5.5	$ 4.4

Assumptions:
1. 10% sales growth
2. 6 to 6 1/2% after-tax margin
3. Accounts receivable turnover 5.7 (17.5% of sales)
4. Inventory turnover 3.6 (27.8% of sales)
5. Accounts payable turnover 21.3 (4.7% of sales)

Totals may not add because of rounding.

EXHIBIT 5
Francis Libris's Letter Outlining Proposed Term-Loan Arrangement

Caslon Trust Company
Broad Street Commercial Lending Center
1111 Broad Street
Richmond, Virginia

Francis X. Libris
Vice President and Manager

May 15, 1996

Mr. John Ruhl
Vice President–Finance
Padgett Paper Products Company
Richmond, Virginia

Dear John:

Thank you for the opportunity last week to review the financial plans you have for Padgett. This letter sets forth our thoughts relating to the need for properly incorporating your bank loan into these plans.

Currently, Padgett has $6,853,000 outstanding in short-term 90-day notes, and we understand that an additional $1.0 to $1.5 million is likely to be borrowed to support new receivables of your new acquisition. This is in contrast with the circumstance of May 1994 when we financed your previous acquisition, and our loan outstanding increased from $500,000 to $1,850,000. At that time, an anticipated restructuring of the loan was postponed until a clearer definition of longer term corporate cash need could be ascertained.

In late 1995, we expressed an interest in discussing with you a restructuring of the loan then outstanding so that legitimately long-term funds could be sourced on a proper long-term basis. Our subsequent conversations and cash flow study were complicated by the anticipated major acquisition and its impact.

Enclosed is a copy of our most recent Padgett forecast, the results of which we have jointly reviewed. On balance, our feeling is that the forecast may tend to understate the cash requirement in that it assumes moderate sales growth, the upholding of traditional margins, and tight control over capital expenditures and dividends. The forecast does seem to indicate a long-term need of at least $5 million, which cannot be properly funded through the bank on anything resembling a full-payout term-loan basis.

Given what appears to be the clear nature of the need, it seems appropriate that financing discussions with an insurance company be initiated. This suggestion is rooted in our firm feeling that it is strategically unwise from the standpoint of the company, as well as that of the bank, to fulfill substantial long-term financial need through the continued use of 90-day notes.

On a confidential basis and without revealing your name, we have talked with three insurance companies within the last week. Discussions included the following generalized parameters for life insurance company lending:

amount:	no problem
term:	12–15 years
rate:	fixed, 9 1/2% minimum
payback:	level payments desired but flexibility offered, e.g., three years of grace
prepayment:	all want protection designed to discourage it; however, there are provisions for pre-payment without penalty if they were to turn you down for a requested increase in amount and you were able to obtain a commitment from another source
availability of money:	good

Caslon would continue to provide for Padgett's seasonal working-capital financing on a floating-prime-rate basis. Our pricing, based on the structure of the long-term debt outlined, would probably be prime plus 1/2 percent.

We all recognize the fact that interest rates have started to rise again. Our Economics Department does not feel that long-term interest rates will see reduced levels in the foreseeable future. Financing demands on the capital markets are expected to continue strong, inflation psychology seems to be rising, the deficits are not yet under control, and any advantage to be gained in avoiding the long-term market is, at best, marginal. It might, in fact, be dangerous.

For any needs consistent with prudent bank lending, Caslon Trust stands ready to finance your business. Our desire to assist in every way we can is complete and sincere.

Sincerely,

Frank

Francis X. Libris
Vice President

EXHIBIT 6

Projected Financial Statements for the Fiscal Years Ending April 30, 1998–2000 Assuming 5, 10, and 15 Percent Sales Growth

(dollars in millions except per-share figures)

	1996 Actual	1997 Est.	5% Growth 1998	1999	2000	10% Growth 1998	1999	2000	15% Growth 1998	1999	2000
A. Income Statements											
Sales, net	$41.32	$57.80	$60.69	$63.72	$66.91	$63.58	$69.94	$76.93	$66.47	$76.44	$87.91
Cost of sales	24.56	36.08	37.27	38.86	40.81	39.05	42.65	46.93	40.82	46.61	53.61
Depn. & amort.	0.74	0.94	0.91	1.00	1.10	0.91	1.00	1.10	0.91	1.00	1.10
General & admin.	7.82	10.23	10.75	11.29	11.87	11.27	12.42	13.69	11.81	13.64	15.72
Selling expense	3.15	4.61	4.84	5.09	5.35	5.08	5.60	6.15	5.30	6.11	7.03
Operating profit	$ 5.05	$ 5.94	$ 6.92	$ 7.48	$ 7.78	$ 7.27	$ 8.27	$ 9.06	$ 7.63	$ 9.08	$10.45
Interest expenses*	0.38	0.95	0.80	0.72	0.61	0.89	0.84	0.77	.97	1.01	1.05
Other exp. (income)	(.07)	(.71)	0.07	0.07	0.07	0.07	0.07	0.07	0.07	0.07	0.07
Pre-tax earnings	$ 4.74	$ 5.70	$ 6.05	$ 6.69	$ 7.10	$ 6.31	$ 7.36	$ 8.22	$ 6.59	$ 8.00	$ 9.33
After-tax earnings	2.61	3.42	3.63	4.01	4.26	3.79	4.42	4.93	3.95	4.80	5.60
Earnings per share on 1,118,000 shares	$ 2.33	$ 3.06	$ 3.25	$ 3.59	$ 3.81	$ 3.39	$ 3.95	$ 4.41	$3.54	$ 4.29	$ 5.01
Dividends per share	1.00	1.03	1.08	1.19	1.27	1.13	1.31	1.47	1.18	1.43	1.66

*Includes interest calculated on the cash deficit at 8 1/2%.

Note: Figures may not add because of rounding.

EXHIBIT 6 (continued)

B. Balance Sheets

	1996 Actual	1997 Est.	5% Growth			10% Growth			15% Growth		
			1998	1999	2000	1998	1999	2000	1998	1999	2000
Assets											
Cash (minimum)	$ .83	$ 1.17	$ 1.23	$ 1.29	$ 1.36	$ 1.29	$ 1.42	$ 1.56	$ 1.35	$ 1.55	$ 1.78
Excess cash	—	—	.01	.73	1.24	—	—	—	—	—	—
Acc. receivable	7.75	10.12	10.62	11.15	11.71	11.13	12.24	13.46	11.63	13.38	15.38
Inventory	14.36	16.18	16.99	17.84	18.74	17.80	19.58	21.54	18.61	21.40	24.61
Prepayments, etc.	.56	.23	.24	.26	.27	.26	.28	.31	.27	.31	.36
Total current assets	$23.51	$27.71	$29.10	$31.27	$33.32	$30.48	$33.52	$36.87	$31.86	$36.64	$42.14
Plant & equip.	12.47	13.27	14.27	15.27	16.27	14.27	15.27	16.27	14.27	15.27	16.27
Less: accum. depn.	5.21	6.04	6.95	7.95	9.05	6.95	7.95	9.05	6.95	7.95	9.05
Net plant & equip.	$ 7.26	$ 7.23	$ 7.32	$ 7.32	$ 7.22	$ 7.32	$ 7.32	$ 7.22	$ 7.32	$ 7.32	$ 7.22
Other	.22	.11	.11	.11	.11	.11	.11	.11	.11	.11	.11
Total assets	$30.99	$35.05	$36.54	$38.71	$40.65	$37.91	$40.95	$44.20	$39.29	$44.07	$49.47
Liabilities and Owners' Equity											
Short-term notes	$ 7.22	$ 7.45	$ 6.29	$ 5.50	$ 4.35	$ 6.29	$ 5.50	$ 4.35	$ 6.29	$ 5.50	$ 4.35
Acc. payable	1.96	2.72	2.85	3.00	3.14	2.99	3.29	3.62	3.12	3.59	4.13
Accruals	1.01	1.44	1.52	1.59	1.67	1.59	1.75	1.92	1.66	1.91	2.20
Other	.82	1.15	1.21	1.33	1.40	1.27	1.39	1.53	1.33	1.61	1.85
Current portion, LTD	.05	.05	.05	.05	.05	.05	.05	.05	.05	.05	.05
Total current liabs.	$11.06	$12.82	$11.93	$11.48	$10.61	$12.19	$11.98	$11.47	$12.45	$12.66	$12.58
Long-term debt	.46	.40	.35	.30	.25	.35	.30	.25	.35	.30	.25
Deferred taxes	.76	.80	.80	.80	.80	.80	.80	.80	.80	.80	.80
Other	.15	.20	.20	.20	.20	.20	.20	.20	.20	.20	.20
Cash deficit*	n	n	n	n	n	1.02	1.37	1.89	2.02	3.44	5.23
Total liabilities	$12.43	$14.22	$13.28	$12.78	$11.86	$14.56	$14.65	$14.61	$15.82	$17.40	$19.06
Common stock	5.59	5.59	5.59	5.59	5.59	5.59	5.59	5.59	5.59	5.59	5.59
Retained earnings	12.98	15.24	17.67	20.34	23.18	17.76	20.71	24.00	17.88	21.09	24.82
Total owners' equity	$18.56	$20.83	$23.25	$25.93	$28.77	$23.35	$26.30	$29.59	$23.47	$26.68	$30.41
Total liabilities & owners' equity	$30.99	$35.05	$36.53	$38.71	$40.63	$37.91	$40.95	$44.20	$39.29	$44.07	$49.47

*Includes interest calculated on the cash deficit at 8 1/2%.

EXHIBIT 6 (*continued*)

C. Cash Flow

	1997 Est.	5% Growth			10% Growth			15% Growth		
		1998	1999	2000	1998	1999	2000	1998	1999	2000
Sources										
After-tax earnings	$3.42	$3.63	$4.01	$4.26	$3.79	$4.42	$4.93	$3.95	$4.80	$5.59
Noncash charges	.94	.91	1.00	1.10	.91	1.00	1.10	.91	1.00	1.10
Funds from operations	$4.36	$4.54	$5.01	$5.36	$4.70	$5.42	$6.03	$4.86	$5.80	$6.69
Deferred taxes	.04	—	—	—	—	—	—	—	—	—
Accounts payable	.76	.14	.14	.14	.27	.30	.33	.41	.47	.54
Accruals	.43	.07	.07	.08	.14	.16	.17	.22	.25	.29
Other and miscellaneous current liabilities	.33	.06	.12	.07	.12	.12	.14	.17	.27	.24
Other liabilities	.05	—	—	—	—	—	—	—	—	—
Other assets	.11	—	—	—	—	—	—	—	—	—
Total sources	$6.08	$4.81	$5.34	$5.65	$5.22	$6.00	$6.67	$5.66	$6.79	$7.76
Uses										
Dividends	$1.16	$1.21	$1.34	$1.42	$1.26	$1.47	$1.64	$1.31	$1.59	$1.86
Capital expenditures	.80	1.00	1.00	1.00	1.00	1.00	1.00	1.00	1.00	1.00
Short-term debt	(.23)	1.16	.79	1.15	1.16	.79	1.15	1.16	.79	1.15
Long-term debt	.05	.05	.05	.05	.05	.05	.05	.05	.05	.05
Minimum cash	.34	.06	.06	.06	.12	.13	.14	.18	.20	.23
Accounts receivable	2.36	.50	.53	.56	1.01	1.11	1.22	1.52	1.74	2.01
Inventory	1.82	.81	.85	.89	1.62	1.78	1.96	2.43	2.79	3.21
Prepay & def. charge	(.33)	.01	.01	.01	.02	.02	.03	.04	.04	.05
Intangibles	.11	—	—	—	—	—	—	—	—	—
Total uses	$6.08	$4.80	$4.63	$5.14	$6.24	$6.35	$7.19	$7.69	$8.20	$9.56
Net cash flow	—	.02	.71	.51	(1.01)	(.35)	(.52)	(2.03)	(1.41)	(1.80)
Cumulative	—	.02	.73	1.24	(1.01)	(1.36)	(1.88)	(2.02)	(3.43)	(5.23)

EXHIBIT 6 (concluded)

	1996 Actual	1997 Est.	5% Growth			10% Growth			15% Growth		
			1998	1999	2000	1998	1999	2000	1998	1999	2000
D. Analytical Ratios											
Profitability											
Sales growth	12.0%	39.9%	5.0%	5.0%	5.0%	10.0%	10.0%	10.0%	15.0%	15.0%	15.0%
E.P.S. growth	20.7	31.4	6.2	10.3	6.3	10.8	16.5	11.2	15.5	21.4	16.5
Gross profit margin	38.8	35.9	38.6	39.0	39.0	38.6	39.0	39.0	38.6	39.0	39.0
Operating exp./sales	26.5	25.7	25.7	25.7	25.7	25.7	25.8	25.8	25.7	25.8	25.9
Pretax margin	11.5	10.3	10.0	10.5	10.6	9.9	10.5	10.7	9.9	10.5	10.6
After-tax margin	6.3	5.9	6.0	6.3	6.4	6.0	6.3	6.4	5.9	6.3	6.4
Return on average owners' equity	14.6	17.4	16.5	16.3	15.6	17.1	17.8	17.6	17.9	19.1	19.6
Return on total assets	8.4	9.8	9.9	10.4	10.5	10.0	10.8	11.2	10.1	10.9	11.3
EBIT/total assets	16.5	19.0	18.7	19.1	19.0	19.0	20.1	20.4	19.4	20.7	21.2
Dividend payout	42.9	33.8	33.3	33.3	33.3	33.3	33.3	33.3	33.2	33.2	33.2
Turnover											
Receivables	5.3×	5.7×	5.7×	5.7×	5.7×	5.7×	5.7×	5.7×	5.7×	5.7×	5.7×
Inventory	2.9	3.6	3.6	3.6	3.6	3.6	3.6	3.6	3.6	3.6	3.6
Accounts payable	21.1	21.3	21.3	21.3	21.3	21.3	21.3	21.3	21.3	21.3	21.3
Working capital	3.3	3.6	3.5	3.2	2.9	3.5	3.3	3.0	3.4	3.2	3.0
Fixed asset	5.7	8.0	8.3	8.7	9.3	8.7	9.6	10.6	9.1	10.4	12.2
Net worth	2.2	2.8	2.6	2.4	2.3	2.7	2.6	2.6	2.8	2.9	2.9
Leverage											
Total debt/owners' equity	67.0%	68.3%	57.1%	49.3%	41.3%	62.3%	55.7%	49.3%	67.4%	65.2%	62.7%
Long-term debt/owners' equity	2.4	1.9	1.5	1.1	0.9	1.5	1.1	0.8	1.5	1.1	0.8
Interest coverage	13.5	7.0	8.7	10.3	12.6	8.0	9.6	11.1	7.5	8.3	8.9
Liquidity											
Quick ratio	.8×	1.0×	1.0×	1.1×	1.3×	1.0×	1.1×	1.3×	1.1×	1.2×	1.4×
Current ratio	2.1	2.2	2.4	2.7	3.1	2.5	2.8	3.2	2.6	2.9	3.3
Working capital	$12.44	$14.89	$19.40	$29.98	$29.55	$18.29	$21.46	$25.23	$19.40	$23.98	$29.55

Kota Fibres, Ltd.

Mrs. Pundir, the managing director and principal owner of Kota Fibres, Ltd., discovered the problem when she arrived at the parking lot of the company's plant one morning in early January 2001. Trucks filled with rolls of fiber yarns were being unloaded, but they had been loaded just the night before and had been ready to depart that morning. The fiber was intended for customers who had been badgering Mrs. Pundir to fill their orders in a timely fashion. The government tax inspector, who was stationed at the company's warehouse, would not clear the trucks for departure because the excise tax had not been paid. The tax inspector required a cash payment, but in seeking to draw funds for the excise tax that morning, Mr. Mehta, the bookkeeper, discovered that the company had overdrawn its bank account again—the third time in as many weeks. The truck drivers were independent contractors who refused to wait while the company and government settled their accounts. They cursed loudly as they unloaded the trucks.

Now this shipment would not leave for at least another two days, and angry customers would no doubt require an explanation. Moreover, before granting a loan with which to pay the excise tax, the branch manager of the All-India Bank & Trust Company had requested a meeting with Mrs. Pundir for the next day to discuss Kota's financial condition and plans for restoring the firm's liquidity.

Mrs. Pundir told Mr. Mehta, "This cash problem is most vexing. I don't understand it. We're a very profitable enterprise, yet we seem to have to depend increasingly on the bank. Why do we need more loans just as our heavy selling season begins? We can't repeat this blunder."

This case was written by Thien T. Pham under the direction of Professor Robert F. Bruner as a basis for class discussion rather than to illustrate effective or ineffective handling of an administrative situation. The financial support of the Batten Institute is gratefully acknowledged. Copyright © 2001 by the University of Virginia Darden School Foundation, Charlottesville, VA. All rights reserved. *To order copies, send an e-mail to* dardencases@virginia.edu. *No part of this publication may be reproduced, stored in a retrieval system, used in a spreadsheet, or transmitted in any form or by any means—electronic, mechanical, photocopying, recording, or otherwise—without the permission of the Darden School Foundation. Version 1.1.*

COMPANY BACKGROUND

Kota Fibres, Ltd., was founded in 1962 to produce nylon fiber at its only plant in Kota, India, about 100 kilometers south of New Delhi. By using new technology and domestic raw materials, the firm had developed a steady franchise among dozens of small local textile weavers. It supplied synthetic fiber yarns used in weaving colorful cloths for making saris, the traditional women's dress of India. On average, each sari required eight yards of cloth. An Indian woman typically would buy three saris a year. With India's female population at around 500 million, the demand for saris would account for more than 12 billion yards of fabric. This demand was currently being supplied entirely from domestic textile mills that, in turn, filled their yarn requirements from suppliers such as Kota Fibres.

SYNTHETIC-TEXTILE MARKET

The demand for synthetic textiles was characterized by stable year-to-year growth and predictable seasonal fluctuations. Unit demand increased with both population and national income. In addition, India's population celebrated hundreds of festivals each year, in deference to a host of deities, at which saris were traditionally worn. The most important festival, the Diwali celebration in mid-autumn, caused a seasonal peak in the demand for new saris, which in turn caused a seasonal peak in demand for nylon textiles in late summer and early fall. Thus, the seasonal demand for nylon yarn would peak in midsummer. Unit growth in the industry was expected to be 15 percent per year.

Consumers purchased saris and textiles from cloth merchants located in villages around the country. A cloth merchant was an important local figure usually well known to area residents; the merchant generally granted credit to support consumer purchases. Merchants maintained relatively low levels of inventory and built stocks of goods only shortly in advance of and during the peak selling season.

Competition among suppliers (the many small textile-weaving mills) to these merchants was keen and was affected by price, service, and credit that the mills could grant to the merchants. The mills essentially produced to order, building their inventories of woven cloth shortly in advance of the peak selling season and keeping only maintenance stocks at other times of the year.

The yarn manufacturers competed for the business of the mills through responsive service and credit. The suppliers to the yarn manufacturers provided little or no trade credit. Being near the origin of the textile chain in India, the yarn manufacturers essentially banked the downstream activities of the industry.

PRODUCTION AND DISTRIBUTION SYSTEM

Thin profit margins had prompted Mrs. Pundir to adopt policies against overproduction and overstocking, which would require Kota to carry inventories through the slack selling season.

She had adopted a plan of seasonal production, which meant that the yarn plant would operate at peak capacity for two months of the year and at modest levels the rest of the year. This policy imposed an annual ritual of hirings and layoffs.

To help ensure prompt service, Kota Fibres maintained two distribution warehouses, but getting the finished yarn quickly from the factory in Kota to the customers was a challenge. The roads were narrow and mostly in poor repair. A truck could take 10 to 15 days to negotiate the trip between Calcutta and Kota, a distance of about 1,100 km. Except when they passed through cities, highways had only one lane. When two cars or trucks met, they had to slow down and squeeze past each other or else stop and wait for the traffic to pass. Journeys were slow and dangerous, and accidents frequent.

COMPANY PERFORMANCE

Kota Fibres had been consistently profitable. Moreover, sales had grown at an annual rate of 18 percent in 2000. Gross sales were projected to reach 90.9 million rupees (Rs) in the fiscal year ended December 31, 2001 (see **Exhibit 1**).[1] Net profits reached Rs2.6 million in 2000. **Exhibits 2** and **3** present recent financial statements for the firm.

REASSESSMENT

After the episode in the parking lot, Mrs. Pundir and her bookkeeper went to her office to analyze the situation. She pushed aside the several items on her desk to which she had intended to devote the morning—a letter from a field sales manager requesting permission to grant favorable credit terms to a new customer (see **Exhibit 4**), a note from the transportation manager regarding a possible change in the inventory policy (**Exhibit 5**), a proposal from the purchasing agent regarding the delivery lead times of certain supplies (**Exhibit 6**), and a proposal from the operations manager for a scheme of level annual production (**Exhibit 7**).

To prepare a forecast on a business-as-usual basis, Mrs. Pundir and Mr. Mehta agreed on various parameters. Cost of goods sold would run at 73.7 percent of gross sales—a figure that was up from recent years because of increasing price competition. Operating expenses would be about 6 percent of sales—also up from recent years to include the addition of a quality-control department, two new sales agents, and three young nephews in whom she hoped to build an allegiance to the Pundir family business. The company's income tax rate was 30 percent and, although accrued monthly, was actually paid quarterly in March, June, September, and December. The excise tax (at 15 percent of sales) was different from the income tax and was collected at the factory gate as trucks left to make deliveries to customers and the regional warehouses. Mrs. Pundir proposed to pay dividends of Rs500,000 per quarter to the 11 members of her extended family who held the entire equity

---

[1] At the time, the rupee was pegged to the U.S. dollar at the rate of 46.5 rupees per dollar.

of the firm. For years Kota had paid high dividends. The Pundir family believed that excess funds left in the firm were at greater risk than if the funds were returned to shareholders.

Mr. Mehta observed that sales collections in any given month had been running steadily at the rate of 40 percent of the last month's sales plus 60 percent of the sales from the month before last. The value of raw materials purchased in any month represented on average 55 percent of the value of sales expected to be made two months later. Wages and other expenses in a given month were equivalent to about 34 percent of purchases in the previous month. As a matter of policy, Mrs. Pundir wanted to see a cash balance of no less than Rs750,000.

Kota Fibres had a line of credit from All-India Bank & Trust Company, where it also maintained its cash balances. All-India's short-term interest rate was currently 14.5 percent, but Mr. Mehta was worried that inflation and interest rates might rise in the coming year. The seasonal line of credit had to be cleaned up for at least 30 days each year. The usual cleanup month had been October,[2] but Kota Fibres had failed to make a full repayment at that time. Only after strong assurances by Mrs. Pundir that she would clean up the loan in November or December had the bank lending officer reluctantly agreed to waive the cleanup requirement in October. Unfortunately, Kota Fibres' credit needs did not abate as rapidly as expected in November and December, and although his protests increased each month, the lending officer agreed to meet Kota's cash requirements with loans. Now he was refusing to extend any more seasonal credit until Mrs. Pundir presented a reasonable financial plan for the company that demonstrated its ability to clean up the loan by the end of 2001.

FINANCIAL FORECAST

Mr. Mehta hurriedly developed a monthly forecast of financial statements using the current operating assumptions (see **Exhibit 8**). As an alternative way of looking at the forecasted funds flows, Mr. Mehta also prepared a forecast of cash receipts and disbursements (**Exhibit 9**). The monthly T-accounts underlying the forecasts are given in **Exhibit 10,** and a summary of the forecast assumptions is in **Exhibit 11**.

Mr. Mehta handed over the forecast to Mrs. Pundir with a graph showing projected sales and month-end debt outstanding **(Exhibit 12)**. After studying the forecasts for a few moments, Mrs. Pundir expostulated,

> This is worse than I expected. The numbers show that we can't repay All-India's loan by the end of December. The loan officer will not accept this forecast as a basis for more credit. We need a new plan, and fast. We need those loans in order to scale up for the most important part of our business season. Let's go over these assumptions in detail and look for any opportunities to improve our debt position.

Then, casting her gaze toward the stack of memos she had pushed aside earlier, she muttered, "Perhaps some of these proposals will help."

---

[2]The selection of October as the loan-cleanup month was imposed by the bank on the grounds of tradition. Seasonal loans of any type made by the bank were to be cleaned up in October. Mrs. Pundir had seen no reason previously to challenge the bank's tradition.

EXHIBIT 1
Summary of Monthly Sales, Actual for 2000
and Forecast for 2001 (in rupees)

	2000 (Historical)	2001 (Forecast)
January	2,012,400	2,616,120
February	2,314,260	2,892,825
March	3,421,080	4,447,404
April	7,043,400	8,804,250
May	12,074,400	13,885,560
June	15,294,240	17,588,376
July	14,187,420	16,315,533
August	7,144,020	8,572,824
September	4,024,800	5,031,000
October	3,421,080	4,447,404
November	2,716,740	3,531,762
December	2,213,640	2,767,050
Year	**75,867,480**	**90,900,108**

EXHIBIT 2
Historical and Forecast Annual Income Statements (in rupees)

	1999 (Actual)	2000 (Actual)	2001 (Forecast)
Gross sales	64,487,358	75,867,480	90,900,108
Excise tax	9,673,104	11,380,122	13,635,016
Net sales	**54,814,254**	**64,487,358**	**77,265,092**
Cost of goods	44,496,277	53,865,911	66,993,380
Gross profits	**10,317,978**	**10,621,447**	**10,271,712**
Operating expenses	3,497,305	4,828,721	5,454,006
Depreciation	769,103	908,608	1,073,731
Interest expense	910,048	1,240,066	1,835,620
Profit before tax	**5,141,521**	**3,644,052**	**1,908,355**
Income tax	1,542,456	1,093,216	572,506
Net profit	**3,599,065**	**2,550,837**	**1,335,848**

EXHIBIT 3
Historical and Forecast Balance Sheets (in rupees)

	2000 (Actual)	2001 (Forecast)
Cash	762,323	750,000
Accounts receivable	2,672,729	3,715,152
Inventories	1,249,185	2,225,373
Total current assets	**4,684,237**	**6,690,525**
Gross PP&E	10,095,646	11,495,646
Accumulated depreciation	1,484,278	2,558,009
Net PP&E	8,611,368	8,937,637
Total assets	**13,295,604**	**15,628,161**
Accounts payable	759,535	1,157,298
Notes to bank (deposits at bank)	684,102	3,463,701
Accrued taxes	0	(180,654)
Total current liabilities	**1,443,637**	**4,440,345**
Owners' equity	11,851,967	11,187,816
Total liabilities and equity	**13,295,604**	**15,628,161**

EXHIBIT 4
Memo from Field Sales Manager

To: Mrs. G. Pundir
From: Mr. A. Bajpai

January 7, 2001

As you know, Pondicherry Textiles is considering us to be their prime yarn supplier for this year. Purchases would be in the neighborhood of Rs6,000,000 and are not reflected in our current sales forecast. Pondicherry would be one of our largest accounts. They have accepted our terms on price, but have asked for credit terms of 80 days, net. Unless we extend our credit terms, Pondicherry will not do business with us. We can expect that Pondicherry will purchase our yarn across the year in about the same pattern as our other customers.

If you approve this exception to our standard terms (45 days), the Pondicherry district sales office immediately will meet its quarterly sales quota. Please indicate your approval below.

Approved:

_____

EXHIBIT 5
Memo from Transportation Manager

To: Mrs. G. Pundir
From: Mr. R. Sikh

January 2, 2001

I have been tracking our supply shipments in the last six months as you asked me to. The new road between Kota and New Delhi has improved reliability of the shipments significantly. Our supplier's new manufacturing equipment is now running consistently, and they have been meeting their shipment dates consistently. As a result, I would propose that we reduce our raw-material-inventory requirement from 60 days to 30 days. This would reduce the amount of inventory we are carrying by one month, and should free up a lot of space in the warehouse. I am not sure if this will affect any other department since we will be buying the same amount of material, but it would make inventory tracking a lot easier for me. Please let me know so we can implement this in January.

EXHIBIT 6
Memo from Purchasing Agent

To: Mrs. G. Pundir
From: Mr. R. Mohan

January 5, 2001

Hibachi Chemicals of Yokohama has approached us with a proposal to supply us polyester pellets on a "just-in-time" basis from their plant in Majala (20 km away). These pellets account for 35 percent of our raw-material purchases. I am looking into the feasibility of this scheme—in particular, whether Hibachi can actually perform on this basis—and will report back in two weeks. If the proposal is feasible, it would reduce our inventory of pellets from 60 days outstanding to only 2 or 3 days.

EXHIBIT 7
Memo from Operations Manager

To: Mrs. G. Pundir
From: Mr. L. Gupta

January 7, 2001

You asked me to estimate the production efficiencies arising from a scheme of level annual production. In essence, there are significant advantages to be gained:

- Gross profit margin would rise by 2 or 3 percent, reflecting labor savings and production efficiencies gained from a stable work force and the absence of certain seasonal training and setup costs.
- Seasonal hirings and layoffs would no longer be necessary, permitting us to cultivate a stronger work force and, perhaps, suppressing labor unrest. You will recall that the unions have indicated that reducing seasonal layoffs will be one of their major negotiating objectives this year.
- Level production entails lower manufacturing risk. With the load spread throughout the year, we suffer less from equipment breakdowns and can match the routine maintenance better with the demand on the plant and equipment.

EXHIBIT 8
Monthly Forecast of Income Statements and Balance Sheets for 2001 (in rupees)

	January	February	March	April	May	June	July	August	September	October	November	December
Gross sales	2,616,120	2,892,825	4,447,404	8,804,250	13,885,560	17,588,376	16,315,533	8,572,824	5,031,000	4,447,404	3,531,762	2,767,050
Excise taxes	392,418	433,924	667,111	1,320,638	2,082,834	2,638,256	2,447,330	1,285,924	754,650	667,111	529,764	415,058
Net sales	2,223,702	2,458,901	3,780,293	7,483,613	11,802,726	14,950,120	13,868,203	7,286,900	4,276,350	3,780,293	3,001,998	2,351,993
Cost of goods sold	1,928,080	2,132,012	3,277,737	6,488,732	10,233,658	12,962,633	12,024,548	6,318,171	3,707,847	3,277,737	2,602,909	2,039,316
Gross profit	295,622	326,889	502,557	994,880	1,569,068	1,987,486	1,843,655	968,729	568,503	502,557	399,089	312,677
Operating expenses	454,501	454,501	454,501	454,501	454,501	454,501	454,501	454,501	454,501	454,501	454,501	454,501
Depreciation	84,130	84,130	87,047	87,047	87,047	89,964	89,964	89,964	92,880	92,880	92,880	95,797
Interest expense (income) (1)	11,058	24,825	70,867	158,210	268,352	362,187	363,212	259,568	145,898	80,686	50,025	40,731
Profit before taxes	(254,068)	(236,566)	(109,858)	295,123	759,168	1,080,835	935,979	164,697	(124,776)	(125,510)	(198,317)	(278,352)
Income Taxes	(76,220)	(70,970)	(32,957)	88,537	227,751	324,251	280,794	49,409	(37,433)	(37,653)	(59,495)	(83,506)
Net profit	(177,847)	(165,596)	(76,900)	206,586	531,418	756,585	655,185	115,288	(87,343)	(87,857)	(138,822)	(194,847)
Assets												
Cash (2)	750,000	750,000	750,000	750,000	750,000	750,000	750,000	750,000	750,000	750,000	750,000	750,000
Accounts receivable (3)	2,773,349	3,291,542	5,012,144	10,301,737	17,997,155	24,748,757	25,697,603	17,191,189	9,003,739	6,295,049	5,029,249	3,715,152
Inventories (4)	2,308,135	5,850,125	11,855,841	17,637,315	19,666,227	14,469,652	6,815,272	3,883,970	2,950,257	1,854,837	1,639,892	2,225,373
Total current assets	5,831,484	9,891,667	17,617,985	28,689,052	38,413,382	39,968,409	33,262,875	21,825,159	12,703,996	8,899,886	7,419,142	6,690,525
Net prop. plant & equip. (5)	8,527,237	8,443,107	8,706,060	8,619,013	8,531,966	8,792,002	8,702,038	8,612,075	8,869,194	8,776,314	8,683,434	8,937,637
Total assets	14,358,721	18,334,774	26,324,045	37,308,065	46,945,348	48,760,411	41,964,914	30,437,233	21,573,190	17,676,200	16,102,575	15,628,161
Liabilities and Owners' Equity												
Accounts payable (6)	1,614,553	4,010,818	6,805,539	8,842,088	8,142,024	3,883,534	1,935,531	1,614,553	1,110,950	690,358	1,039,007	1,157,298
Note payable—bank (7)	1,146,268	2,962,622	8,767,030	17,419,379	26,997,556	32,950,665	27,167,192	15,795,793	8,352,899	5,002,010	3,278,054	3,463,701
Accrued taxes (8)	(76,220)	(147,190)	(180,148)	(91,611)	136,140	0	280,794	330,203	0	(37,653)	(97,148)	(180,654)
Total current liabilities	2,684,601	6,826,250	15,392,421	26,169,856	35,275,720	36,834,199	29,383,517	17,740,548	9,463,849	5,654,715	4,219,913	4,440,345
Shareholders' equity (9)	11,674,120	11,508,524	10,931,623	11,138,209	11,669,627	11,926,212	12,581,397	12,696,685	12,109,341	12,021,484	11,882,662	11,187,816
Total liabilities & equity	14,358,721	18,334,774	26,324,045	37,308,065	46,945,348	48,760,411	41,964,914	30,437,233	21,573,190	17,676,200	16,102,575	15,628,161

(1) Interest expense = Notes Payable * 14.5%/12 months.
(2) See Exhibit 9.
(3) See panel 1, Exhibit 10.
(4) See panel 2, Exhibit 10.
(5) See panel 6, Exhibit 10.
(6) See panel 3, Exhibit 10.
(7) Plug figure.
(8) See panel 5, Exhibit 10.
(9) See panel 4, Exhibit 10.

123

EXHIBIT 9
Schedule of Cash Receipts and Disbursements for 2001 (in rupees)

	January	February	March	April	May	June	July	August	September	October	November	December
Assume:												
Sales	2,616,120	2,892,825	4,447,404	8,804,250	13,885,560	17,588,376	16,315,533	8,572,824	5,031,000	4,447,404	3,531,762	2,767,050
Purchases (1)	2,446,072	4,842,338	7,637,058	9,673,607	8,973,543	4,715,053	2,767,050	2,446,072	1,942,469	1,521,878	1,870,526	1,988,817
Debt outstanding	1,146,268	2,962,622	8,767,030	17,419,379	26,997,556	32,950,665	27,167,192	15,795,793	8,352,899	5,002,010	3,278,054	3,463,701
Receipts:												
Accts rcvble collected	2,515,500	2,374,632	2,726,802	3,514,657	6,190,142	10,836,774	15,366,686	17,079,239	13,218,449	7,156,094	4,797,562	4,081,147
New borrowings (repayments)	462,166	1,816,354	5,804,408	8,652,349	9,578,178	5,953,108	(5,783,473)	(11,371,400)	(7,442,894)	(3,350,889)	(1,723,956)	185,647
Disburs.:												
Accounts paid (2)	1,591,054	2,446,072	4,842,338	7,637,058	9,673,607	8,973,543	4,715,053	2,767,050	2,446,072	1,942,469	1,521,878	1,870,526
Capital expenditures	0	0	350,000	0	0	350,000	0	0	350,000	0	0	350,000
Interest payments	11,058	24,825	70,867	158,210	268,352	362,187	363,212	259,568	145,898	80,686	50,025	40,731
Excise tax paid	392,418	433,924	667,111	1,320,638	2,082,834	2,638,256	2,447,330	1,285,924	754,650	667,111	529,764	415,058
Operating expenses	454,501	454,501	454,501	454,501	454,501	454,501	454,501	454,501	454,501	454,501	454,501	454,501
Accrued income tax paid	0	0	0	0	0	460,390	0	0	292,770	0	0	0
Wages	540,958	831,665	1,646,395	2,596,600	3,289,026	3,051,005	1,603,118	940,797	831,665	660,439	517,438	635,979
Dividends	0	0	500,000	0	0	500,000	0	500,000	500,000	0	0	500,000
Subtotal: Disbursements	2,989,989	4,190,986	8,531,210	12,167,005	15,768,320	16,789,882	9,583,214	5,707,839	5,775,555	3,805,206	3,073,606	4,266,794
Receipts – Disbursements	(12,323)	0	0	0	0	0	0	0	0	0	0	0
BOP cash balance	762,323	750,000	750,000	750,000	750,000	750,000	750,000	750,000	750,000	750,000	750,000	750,000
EOP cash balance	750,000	750,000	750,000	750,000	750,000	750,000	750,000	750,000	750,000	750,000	750,000	750,000

(1) Equal to 55 percent of sales in period (T+2).
(2) Equal to purchases in period (T−1).

EXHIBIT 10
Forecast T-Accounts Supporting Financial Statements (in rupees)

	January	February	March	April	May	June	July	August	September	October	November	December
1. Schedule of Accounts Receivable												
Beginning of period	2,672,729	2,773,349	3,291,542	5,012,144	10,301,737	17,997,155	24,748,757	25,697,603	17,191,189	9,003,739	6,295,049	5,029,249
Plus sales	2,616,120	2,892,825	4,447,404	8,804,250	13,885,560	17,588,376	16,315,533	8,572,824	5,031,000	4,447,404	3,531,762	2,767,050
Less collections, last month (1)	885,456	1,046,448	1,157,130	1,778,962	3,521,700	5,554,224	7,035,350	6,526,213	3,429,130	2,012,400	1,778,962	1,412,705
Less collections, month before last (2)	1,630,044	1,328,184	1,569,672	1,735,695	2,668,442	5,282,550	8,331,336	10,553,026	9,789,320	5,143,694	3,018,600	2,668,442
End of period	2,773,349	3,291,542	5,012,144	10,301,737	17,997,155	24,748,757	25,697,603	17,191,189	9,003,739	6,295,049	5,029,249	3,715,152
(1) 40% of sales in period (T−1).												
(2) 60% of sales in period (T−2).												
2. Schedule of Inventories												
Beginning of period	1,249,185	2,308,135	5,850,125	11,855,841	17,637,315	19,666,227	14,469,652	6,815,272	3,883,970	2,950,257	1,854,837	1,639,892
Plus purchases (1)	2,446,072	4,842,338	7,637,058	9,673,607	8,973,543	4,715,053	2,767,050	2,446,072	1,942,469	1,521,878	1,870,526	1,988,817
Plus labor	540,958	831,665	1,646,395	2,596,600	3,289,026	3,051,005	1,603,118	940,797	831,665	660,439	517,438	635,979
Less shipments (COGS)	1,928,080	2,132,012	3,277,737	6,488,732	10,233,658	12,962,633	12,024,548	6,318,171	3,707,847	3,277,737	2,602,909	2,039,316
End of period	2,308,135	5,850,125	11,855,841	17,637,315	19,666,227	14,469,652	6,815,272	3,883,970	2,950,257	1,854,837	1,639,892	2,225,373
(1) Equal to 55 percent of sales in period (T+2).												
3. Schedule of Accounts Payable												
Beginning of period	759,535	1,614,553	4,010,818	6,805,539	8,842,088	8,142,024	3,883,534	1,935,531	1,614,553	1,110,950	690,358	1,039,007
+ Purchases (1)	2,446,072	4,842,338	7,637,058	9,673,607	8,973,543	4,715,053	2,767,050	2,446,072	1,942,469	1,521,878	1,870,526	1,988,817
− Payments (2)	1,591,054	2,446,072	4,842,338	7,637,058	9,673,607	8,973,543	4,715,053	2,767,050	2,446,072	1,942,469	1,521,878	1,870,526
End of period	1,614,553	4,010,818	6,805,539	8,842,088	8,142,024	3,883,534	1,935,531	1,614,553	1,110,950	690,358	1,039,007	1,157,298
(1) Equal to 55 percent of sales in period (T+2).												
(2) Equal to purchases in period (T−1).												

(continued)

EXHIBIT 10 (*continued*)

Forecast T-Accounts Supporting Financial Statements (in rupees)

	January	February	March	April	May	June	July	August	September	October	November	December
4. Schedule of Shareholder's Equity												
Beginning of period	11,851,967	11,674,120	11,508,524	10,931,623	11,138,209	11,669,627	11,926,212	12,581,397	12,696,685	12,109,341	12,021,484	11,882,662
Plus net profit	(177,847)	(165,596)	(76,900)	206,586	531,418	756,585	655,185	115,288	(87,343)	(87,857)	(138,822)	(194,847)
Less dividends	0	0	500,000	0	0	500,000	0	0	500,000	0	0	500,000
End of period	11,674,120	11,508,524	10,931,623	11,138,209	11,669,627	11,926,212	12,581,397	12,696,685	12,109,341	12,021,484	11,882,662	11,187,816
5. Schedule of Accrued Taxes												
Beginning of period	0	(76,220)	(147,190)	(180,148)	(91,611)	136,140	0	280,794	330,203	0	(37,653)	(97,148)
Plus monthly tax expense (@ 30%)	(76,220)	(70,970)	(32,957)	88.537	227,751	324,251	280,794	49,409	(37,433)	(37,653)	(59,495)	(83,506)
Less quarterly tax payments	0	0	0	0	0	460,390	0	0	292,770	0	0	0
End of period	(76,220)	(147,190)	(180,148)	(91,611)	136,140	0	280,794	330,203	0	(37,653)	(97,148)	(180,654)
6. Schedule of Property, Plant and Equipment												
Beginning gross PP&E	10,095,646	10,095,646	10,095,646	10,445,646	10,445,646	10,445,646	10,795,646	10,795,646	10,795,646	11,145,646	11,145,646	11,145,646
Plus capital expenditures	0	0	350,000	0	0	350,000	0	0	350,000	0	0	350,000
Ending gross PP&E	10,095,646	10,095,646	10,445,646	10,445,646	10,445,646	10,795,646	10,795,646	10,795,646	11,145,646	11,145,646	11,145,646	11,495,646
Monthly depreciation expense	84,130	84,130	87,047	87,047	87,047	89,964	89,964	89,964	92,880	92,880	92,880	95,797
Less cumulative depr'n.	1,568,408	1,652,539	1,739,586	1,826,633	1,913,680	2,003,643	2,093,607	2,183,571	2,276,451	2,369,332	2,462,212	2,558,009
Ending net PP&E	8,527,237	8,443,107	8,706,060	8,619,013	8,531,966	8,792,002	8,702,038	8,612,075	8,869,194	8,776,314	8,683,434	8,937,637

EXHIBIT 11
Forecast Assumptions

Ratio of:	
Income tax/profit before tax	30%
Excise tax/Sales	15%
This month collections of last month's sales	40%
This month collections of month-before-last sales	60%
Purchases/Sales two months later	55%
Wages/Purchases	34%
Annual operating expenses/Annual sales	6.00%
Capital Expenditures (every third month)	350,000
Interest rate on borrowings (and deposits)	14.5%
Minimum cash balance	750,000
Depreciation/Gross PP&E (per year)	10%
(per month)	0.83%
Dividends paid (every third month)	500,000

EXHIBIT 12
Trend of Certain Financial Accounts by Month (in millions of rupees)

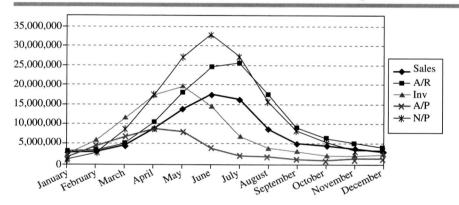

Deutsche Brauerei

In early January 2001, Greta Schweitzer arrived at Deutsche Brauerei[1] to participate in her first meeting of the board of directors. She had recently joined the board at the behest of her uncle, the managing director of the company. Lukas Schweitzer had told her that the board could use her financial expertise in addressing some questions that would come up in the near future, but he would not be specific as to the nature of those questions. The company was owned entirely by 16 uncles, aunts, and cousins in the Schweitzer family. Greta had received an MBA degree from a well-known business school and had worked for the past six years as a commercial-loan officer for a leading bank in Frankfurt, Germany. With the permission of the bank, she agreed to join the Deutsche Brauerei board.

The agenda for the January meeting of the directors consisted of three items of business: (1) approval of the 2001 financial budget, (2) declaration of the quarterly dividend, and (3) adoption of a compensation scheme for Oleg Pinchuk, the company's sales-and-marketing manager. Because she knew little about the company, Greta decided to visit it for a day before the first board meeting.

THE COMPANY

Deutsche Brauerei produced two varieties of beer, dark and light, for which it had won quality awards consistently over the years. Its sales and profits in 2000 were €92.1 million and

---

[1] In English, "Deutsche Brauerei" (DOI-cha BROI-reye) means "German brewery."

€2.9 million, respectively.[2] (See **Exhibit 1** for historical and projected financial statements.) Founded in 1737, the Deutsche Brauerei had been in the Schweitzer family for 12 generations. An etching of Gustav Schweitzer, the founder, graced the label of each bottle of beer.

The company was located in a village just outside Munich, Germany. Its modern equipment was capable of producing 1.2 million hectoliters of beer a year. In 2000, the company sold 1.173 million hectoliters. This equipment was acquired in 1994, following a fire that destroyed the old equipment.

Because of its efficiency improvements and slightly larger size, the new equipment increased the potential output of the brewery. This additional capacity remained unused, however, until late 1998. In that year, Deutsche Brauerei expanded into Ukraine. Following the dissolution of the USSR, Lukas Schweitzer had envisioned a significant new market for high-quality beer in eastern Europe, particularly in the former Soviet states, and resolved to penetrate that market. Ukraine was particularly attractive given its relatively larger population of 52 million and its strategic location within central and eastern Europe.

In 1995 and 1996, the Ukrainian government embarked on a wave of privatizations and market reforms. The Ukrainian government's posture convinced the Schweitzer family that it was a propitious time to enter the Ukrainian market. After analyzing various entry options, the Schweitzers decided to enter Ukraine through a network of independent distributors. Launched in 1998, Deutsche's beer was an overnight success. Accordingly, Lukas Schweitzer hired Oleg Pinchuk away from a major Ukrainian beer producer to market Deutsche's beer even more aggressively.

The beer won popularity for its full-bodied, malty taste. A factor extrinsic to the product—the fragmented nature of the Ukrainian beer industry—also provided easy entry opportunities for Deutsche Brauerei.

When the Russian debt crisis hit in 1998, the Ukrainian hryvna depreciated by around 50 percent against the deutsche mark within three months (see **Exhibit 2**). The depreciation of the hryvna resulted in lower revenue, profit, and asset values when translated into deutsche marks (Germany's currency in 1998). Because of the popularity of Deutsche's beer, however, the increase in Deutsche Brauerei's volume sales more than offset the negative currency effects.[3] By early 2001, Ukrainian consumers accounted for 28 percent of Deutsche's sales. Further, Ukraine had accounted for most of the unit growth in Deutsche's sales over the past three years.

In Germany, Deutsche Brauerei served its markets through a network of independent distributors. These distributors purchased Deutsche's beer, stored it temporarily in their own refrigerated warehouses, and ultimately sold it to *their* customers at the retail end of the distribution chain (e.g., stores, restaurants, and hotels). Oleg Pinchuk had adopted a different distribution strategy with regard to Ukraine.

LUNCH WITH UNCLE LUKAS

After driving down from Frankfurt, Greta's visit began with a luncheon meeting with Lukas Schweitzer. Now 57, Lukas had worked at the brewery for his entire career. His experience

---

[2]In January 2001, the euro could be exchanged for about US$0.94.

[3]For 2001 and 2002, the hryvna was not expected to depreciate materially against the euro. As Exhibit 2 shows, the hryvna had held steady since the Russian default. In January 2001, UAH1 was equivalent to €0.20.

had been largely on the production side of the brewery, where he had risen to the position of brewmaster before assuming general management of the company upon the retirement of his father. He said,

> Over the long history of this company, the Schweitzers have had to be brewers, not marketers or finance people. As long as we made an excellent product, we always sold our output at the price we asked. Then, in the 1990s, I realized that we needed more than just production know-how. The collapse of the Berlin Wall, and then the dissolution of the Soviet Union, convinced me that tremendous opportunities existed in eastern Europe. I hired Oleg Pinchuk to lead this initiative.
>
> I'm quite pleased with what Oleg has been able to accomplish. He has organized five distributorships, taken us from 0 to 211 customer accounts, and set up warehousing arrangements—in 30 months, and on a small budget! He really produces results. I am afraid I will have to pay him a lot more money next year, if I am to keep him. As it is, I paid him €81,440 in 2000, consisting of a base salary of €40,000 and an incentive payment of €41,440, which is calculated as 0.5 percent of the annual sales increase in Ukraine. As you know from my letter to the board of directors, I am proposing increases in both his base salary (to €48,500) and incentive payment (to 0.6 percent of the annual sales increase).
>
> Oleg was very helpful in pulling together the financial plan for 2001 [see Exhibit 1]. It shows handsomely rising sales and profits! Also, he prepared various analytical presentations, including a sources-and-uses-of-funds statement **[Exhibit 3]** and a detailed ratio analysis **[Exhibit 4]**. One very helpful analysis was the break-even chart[4] Oleg prepared **[Exhibit 5]**. It shows that, as we increase our volume above the break-even volume, our profits rise disproportionately faster.
>
> If we keep on this growth course, we'll exhaust our existing unused productive capacity by late 2001. The budget for 2001 calls for investment of €7 million in new plant and equipment. For 2002, Oleg has proposed that we invest €6.8 million in a state-of-the-art warehouse and distribution center in Ukraine. He argues that we won't be able to sustain our growth in Ukraine without these major investments. I haven't even begun thinking about how we will finance all this growth. In recent years, we have depended more on short-term bank loans than we used to. I don't know whether we should continue to rely on them to the extent we have. Right now, we can borrow from our long-standing Hausbank at a 6.5 percent rate of interest.[5] Our banker asked me to meet with him next week to discuss our expansion plans; I'm guessing that he can't wait to get more of our business!
>
> With the improved profits, I am proposing an increase in dividends for this quarter to a total of €698,000, one-fourth of the dividends projected to be paid in 2001. This should keep the Schweitzer family happy. As you know, half of our family stockholders are retirees and rely on the dividend to help make ends meet. We have traditionally aimed for a 75 percent dividend payout from earnings each year, to serve our older relatives.

Lukas Schweitzer had been quite talkative during the meal, allowing Greta little opportunity to ask questions or offer her own opinions. She was disquieted by some of the

---

[4]This chart shows the relationship between revenues, costs, and volume of output. For instance, revenues are calculated as the volume of hectoliters of beer sold times the unit price of €78.5 per hectoliter. Fixed costs (€24.6 million) remain constant as unit output varies, and are the sum of administration and selling expense plus depreciation. Variable costs are the sum of production costs, excise duties, and allowance for doubtful accounts, or €52.3 per hectoliter. At any given level of output, total costs are the sum of variable and fixed costs. Profits or losses are illustrated as the difference between the revenue and total-cost lines, but note carefully that "profit" here is implicitly defined as earnings before interest and taxes (EBIT). This analysis identifies the break-even volume, where revenues just equal total costs. Deutsche Brauerei's break-even volume was 938,799 hectoliters.

[5]In January 2001, the yield on short-term euro government debt was 4.58 percent.

statements she heard, however, and resolved to study the historical and forecast financials in detail. Then, quite abruptly, Uncle Lukas announced that lunch was done and he would take her to meet Oleg Pinchuk.

MEETING WITH OLEG PINCHUK

After the introductory pleasantries, Greta asked Oleg to describe his marketing strategy and achievements in Ukraine. He said,

> Our beer almost sells itself; discount pricing and heavy advertising are unwarranted. The challenge is getting people to try it and getting it into a distribution pipeline, so that when the consumer wants to buy more, he or she can do so. But in 1998, the beer-distribution pipeline in Ukraine was nonexistent. I had to go there and set up distributorships from nothing; there were willing entrepreneurs, but they had no capital. I provided the best financing I knew how, in the form of trade-credit concessions. First, I extended credit to distributors in Ukraine who could not bear the terms we customarily gave our distributors in western Germany. I relaxed the terms to these new distributors from 2 percent 10, net 40, to 2 percent 10, net 80.[6] Even on these terms, our distributors are asking for more time to pay; I plan to relax the payment deadline to 90 days. I am confident that we will collect on all of these receivables; my forecast assumes that bad debts as a percentage of accounts receivable will amount to only 2 percent.
>
> These distributors are real entrepreneurs. They started with nothing but their brains. They have great ambitions and learn quickly. Some of them have gotten past due on their payments to us, but I suspect that they will catch up in due course. Virtually all the retailers and restaurateurs we supply are expanding and enhancing their shops, buying modern equipment, and restocking their own inventories—all without the support of big banks like yours in Frankfurt! Most of these retailers can't get bank credit; their "bootstrap" financing is ingenious and admirable. A little delay in payment is understandable. Where we see great opportunity in these distributors, the banks see no collateral, low profits, negative cash flow, and high risk. I know these distributors better than the banks know them. I think we'll make a profit on our investment there. My analysis [see **Exhibit 6**] suggests that we are earning a very high return on our investment in receivables in Ukraine. We borrow at 6.5 percent from our bank in the West, and use those funds to finance receivables in Ukraine that give us a return of about 130 percent!
>
> I should add that the other parts of my marketing strategy involve field warehousing, to permit rapid response to market demand, and quite a lot of missionary activity, to see that our beer receives the proper placement in stores and restaurants. My policy on field inventories has been to support the fragile distributor network by carrying a substantial part of the inventory on behalf of the distributor. This resulted in a sizable increase in inventory for the company in 1999 and 2000.
>
> These new marketing policies have paid off handsomely in terms of our unit growth in the new federal states. Sales in Ukraine grew 47 percent in 2000—a rate of increase that I aim to sustain for the foreseeable future. Without my changes in credit and inventory policy, we would have realized only a small fraction of our current level of sales there. In 2001, I hope to establish five more distributors and place our beer in 100 more stores and restaurants.

---

[6]"2 percent 10, net 40" means that Deutsche's customer can take a 2 percent discount if payment is made within 10 days of invoice and that, otherwise, the full payment is due within 40 days.

Greta inquired about the signs of global economic recession. Oleg seemed relatively unconcerned. He said, "I don't think Ukraine will be affected. Last year the economy grew 7 percent, and this year it is predicted to grow 10 percent. I expect unit sales in Ukraine to rise significantly in 2001." At the close of their meeting, Greta asked for information on Deutsche's credit customers. Oleg supplied several files from which she extracted the summary information in **Exhibit 7.**

CONCLUSION

After a lengthy dinner that evening, at which she met the other directors, Greta returned to the information she had gathered that day. She would need to form an opinion on the three matters coming before the board the next day (the financial plan, the dividend declaration, and the compensation plan for Oleg). She also wanted to study the company's reliance on debt financing. The other directors would be interested to know why, if the company was operating so profitably above its break-even volume, it needed to borrow so aggressively. Greta also wondered about the wisdom of Deutsche's aggressive penetration of Ukraine: did rapid sales growth necessarily pay off in terms of more profits or dividends? All this would take more study. She yawned and then poured herself a cup of coffee before returning to scrutinize the numbers.

EXHIBIT 1

Historical and Projected Income Statements and Balance Sheets (fiscal year ended December 31; all figures in € thousands)

	1997 (Actual)	1998 (Actual)	1999 (Actual)	2000 (Actual)	2001 (Proj'd)	2002 (Proj'd)
Income Statements						
1 Sales: Germany	62,032	62,653	64,219	66,216	68,203	70,249
2 Sales: Ukraine	—	4,262	17,559	25,847	37,479	48,722
3 Net sales	62,032	66,915	81,779	92,064	105,682	118,971
Operating expenses:						
4 Production costs and expenses	32,258	35,366	44,271	49,827	61,393	71,609
5 Admin. and selling expenses	12,481	13,014	16,274	18,505	18,500	18,500
6 Depreciation	3,609	4,314	5,844	6,068	6,766	7,448
7 Excise duties	9,143	9,108	10,486	11,557	11,625	13,087
8 Total operating expenses	(57,491)	(61,802)	(76,874)	(85,957)	(98,284)	(110,644)
9 Operating profit	4,541	5,113	4,904	6,106	7,398	8,327
10 Allowance for doubtful accounts	(5)	(7)	(38)	(24)	(201)	(60)
11 Interest expense	(1,185)	(1,064)	(1,046)	(1,304)	(1,468)	(1,634)
12 Earnings before taxes	3,351	4,042	3,821	4,779	5,729	6,633
13 Income taxes	(1,132)	(1,396)	(1,510)	(1,864)	(2,005)	(2,322)
14 Net earnings	2,219	2,646	2,311	2,915	3,724	4,311
15 Dividends to all common shares	1,669	1,988	1,734	2,186	2,793	3,234
16 Retentions of earnings	550	658	577	729	931	1,078
Balance Sheets						
Assets						
1 Cash	5,366	8,183	9,813	11,048	12,682	14,277
2 Accounts receivable						
Germany	6,933	7,142	7,222	7,517	7,661	7,891
Ukraine	—	424	4,090	6,168	9,241	12,014
Allowance for doubtful accounts	(69)	(76)	(113)	(137)	(338)	(398)
3 Inventories	6,133	6,401	7,817	12,889	14,795	16,656
4 Total current assets	18,363	22,075	28,829	37,485	44,042	50,439
5 Investments & other assets	3,102	3,189	3,416	3,520	3,500	3,500
6 Gross property plant & equipt.	58,435	58,435	60,682	60,682	67,663	74,485
7 Accumulated depreciation	(23,404)	(27,719)	(33,562)	(39,631)	(46,397)	(53,845)
8 Net property plant & equipt.	35,031	30,716	27,120	21,052	21,266	20,639
9 Total assets	56,496	55,981	59,365	62,057	68,808	74,579
Liabilities and Stockholders' Equity						
10 Bank borrowings (short term)	2,987	10,236	12,004	13,089	17,862	21,372
11 Accounts payable	3,578	3,755	4,103	4,792	5,284	5,949
12 Other current liabilities	7,397	7,361	8,996	10,127	11,625	13,087
13 Total current liabilities	13,962	21,352	25,103	28,009	34,771	40,407
14 Long-term debt: Bank borrowings	16,107	7,544	6,601	5,658	4,715	3,772
15 Shareholders' equity	26,427	27,085	27,661	28,390	29,321	30,399
16 Total liabs. & stockholders' equity	56,496	55,981	59,365	62,057	68,808	74,579

Source: Casewriter analysis.

Note: Deutsche Brauerei purchased pension annuities for its employees from an outside insurance company. Thus, pension liabilities were not carried on the firm's balance sheet.

EXHIBIT 2
Historical Exchange Rates: Ukrainian Hryvna to Deutsche Mark/Euro

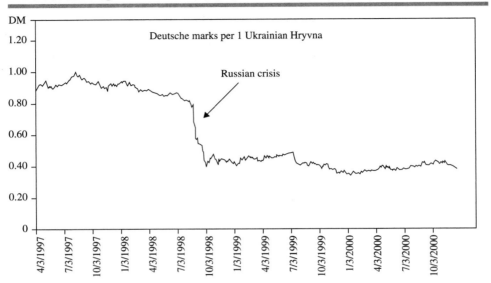

Source: http://www.oanda.com/convert/fxhistory.

EXHIBIT 3

Sources-and-Uses-of-Funds Statements (fiscal year ending December 31; all figures in € thousands)

	1998 (Actual)	1999 (Actual)	2000 (Actual)	2001 (Proj'd)	2002 (Proj'd)
Sources of Funds					
1 Net income	2,646	2,311	2,915	3,724	4,311
2 Increases in allowance for doubtful accts.	7	38	24	201	60
3 Depreciation	4,314	5,844	6,068	6,766	7,448
4 Increases in short-term debt	7,249	1,768	1,085	4,773	3,510
5 Increases in accounts payable	177	348	690	492	664
6 Increases in other current liabilities	(36)	1,635	1,131	1,498	1,462
7 **Total Sources of Cash**	**14,357**	**11,943**	**11,913**	**17,454**	**17,456**
Uses of Funds					
8 Dividend payments	1,988	1,734	2,186	2,793	3,234
9 Increases in cash balance	2,817	1,630	1,234	1,634	1,595
10 Increases in accts. receivable (Germany)	209	79	296	144	230
11 Increases in accts. receivable (Ukraine)	424	3,665	2,078	3,074	2,772
12 Increases in inventories	267	1,417	5,072	1,906	1,861
13 Increases in other assets	87	227	104	(20)	0
14 Reductions in long-term debt	8,563	943	943	943	943
15 Capital expenditures	0	2,247	0	6,980	6,822
16 **Total Uses of Cash**	**14,357**	**11,943**	**11,913**	**17,454**	**17,456**

Source: Casewriter analysis.

EXHIBIT 4
Ratio Analyses of Historical and Projected Financial Statements (fiscal year ended December 31)

	1997 (Actual)	1998 (Actual)	1999 (Actual)	2000 (Actual)	2001 (Proj'd)	2002 (Proj'd)
Profitability						
1 Operating profit margin (%)	7.3%	7.6%	6.0%	6.6%	7.0%	7.0%
2 Average tax rate (%)	33.8%	34.5%	39.5%	39.0%	35.0%	35.0%
3 Return on sales (%)	3.6%	4.0%	2.8%	3.2%	3.5%	3.6%
4 Return on equity (%)	8.4%	9.8%	8.4%	10.3%	12.7%	14.2%
5 Return on net assets (%)	6.5%	7.4%	6.9%	8.4%	9.3%	9.7%
6 Return on assets (%)	3.9%	4.7%	3.9%	4.7%	5.4%	5.8%
Leverage						
7 Debt/Equity ratio (%)	72.3%	65.6%	67.3%	66.0%	77.0%	82.7%
8 Debt/Total capital (%)	41.9%	39.6%	40.2%	39.8%	43.5%	45.3%
9 EBIT/Interest (×)	3.8	4.8	4.7	4.7	5.0	5.1
Asset Utilization						
10 Sales/Assets	1.10	1.20	1.38	1.48	1.54	1.60
11 Sales growth rate (%)	4.0%	7.9%	22.2%	12.6%	14.8%	12.6%
12 Assets growth rate (%)	6.0%	−0.9%	6.0%	4.5%	10.9%	8.4%
13 Receivables growth rate (%)	4.0%	9.1%	49.5%	21.0%	23.5%	17.8%
14 Receivables growth rate: Germany	4.0%	3.0%	1.1%	4.1%	1.9%	3.0%
15 Receivables growth rate: Ukraine	0.0%	NMF	863.5%	50.8%	49.8%	30.0%
16 Days in receivables	40.8	41.3	50.5	54.3	58.4	61.1
17 Days in receivables: Germany	40.8	41.6	41.0	41.4	41.0	41.0
18 Days in receivables: Ukraine	NMF	36.3	85.0	87.1	90.0	90.0
19 Payables to sales	5.8%	5.6%	5.0%	5.2%	5.0%	5.0%
20 Inventories to sales	9.9%	9.6%	9.6%	14.0%	14.0%	14.0%
Liquidity						
21 Current ratio	1.32	1.03	1.15	1.34	1.27	1.25
22 Quick ratio	0.88	0.73	0.84	0.88	0.84	0.84

Notes: These financial ratios show the performance of the firm in four important areas:

Profitability is measured both in terms of *profit or expense margins* (lines 1–3) and as *investment returns* (lines 4–6). Investors will focus on the latter measures of profitability.

Leverage ratios measure the use of short-term and long-term debt financing by the firm. In general, higher usage of debt increases the risk of the firm. Higher ratios of debt to equity and to capital (lines 7 and 8) suggest higher financial risk. The ratio of EBIT to interest expense measures the ability of the firm to "cover" its interest payments; lower levels of this ratio suggest higher risk (line 9).

Asset-utilization ratios measure the efficiency of asset use. For instance, the sales-to-assets ratio (line 10) shows how many € of sales are generated per € of assets; a higher figure suggests more efficiency, and a lower figure suggests less efficiency. Over the long term, differences in the growth rates of sales (line 11) and assets (line 12) can lead to production problems of over- or undercapacity. Days in receivables (lines 16–18) shows how many days it takes to collect the average credit sale; the longer it takes, the greater the investment in receivables.

Liquidity ratios measure the resources available to meet short-term financial commitments. The current ratio (line 21) is the ratio of all current assets to all current liabilities. The quick ratio (line 22) is the ratio of only cash and receivables (i.e., those assets that can be liquidated quickly) to all current liabilities.

EXHIBIT 5
Break-Even Chart for Deutsche Brauerei

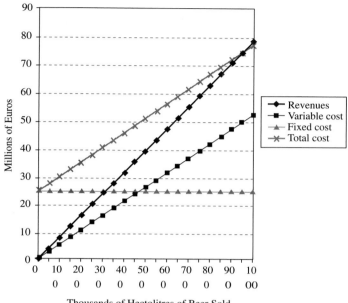

Thousands of Hectolitres of Beer Sold

Source: Casewriter analysis.

EXHIBIT 6
Oleg Pinchuk's Analysis of the Return on Investment from Investment in Accounts Receivable in Ukraine

To: Lukas Schweitzer
From: Oleg Pinchuk

The following table illustrates the high profitability we have achieved on our investment in receivables in Ukraine. We can look forward to a return of about 120–130 percent on our receivables from the East.
The return on investment is calculated as follows:

$$\text{Return on Investment} = \frac{\text{Marginal After-Tax Profit Contribution}}{\text{Required Marginal Investment}}$$

The numerator is simply the profits we earn on new sales each year in Ukraine. It excludes the fixed costs because we assume these costs have been covered: we want to focus only on the *marginal* events. Also, it assumes that, without the extension of credit, no sales growth would occur in Ukraine. The denominator is Deutsche's investment in the receivables. This is *not* the face amount of the receivables; it is only the cash outlay for the product underlying the receivable. Accordingly, for 2001, the calculation is:

$$\text{Investment in Accounts Receivable (AR)} = (\text{Variable Costs} \div \text{Sales}) \times \text{Change in AR}$$
$$= (\text{€}52.31 \div \text{€}78.49) \times \text{€}3{,}073{,}536 = \text{€}2{,}048{,}512$$

Assumptions

Revenue per HL (€)	78.49
Variable Costs per HL (€)	52.31
Contribution Percentage	33%
Tax Rate	35%

	1997 (Actual)	1998 (Actual)	1999 (Actual)	2000 (Actual)	2001 (Proj'd)	2002 (Proj'd)
Sales in Ukraine (€, thousands)	—	4,262	17,559	25,847	37,479	48,722
Change in sales (€, thousands)	—	4,262	13,297	8,288	11,631	11,244
Variable costs on the marginal sales	—	(2,841)	(8,863)	(5,524)	(7,752)	(7,494)
Contribution on the marginal sales	—	1,421	4,435	2,764	3,879	3,750
Taxes on the marginal contribution	—	(497)	(1,552)	(967)	(1,358)	(1,312)
Marginal After-tax Profits (€ thousands)	—	924	2,883	1,797	2,521	2,437
Variable Costs/Sales	—	67%	67%	67%	67%	67%
Change in accounts receivable, Ukraine (€ thousands)	—	424	3,665	2,078	3,074	2,772
Investment in Accts. Receivable (€ thousands)	—	283	2,443	1,385	2,049	1,848
Return on Marginal Investment in Receivables	0%	327%	118%	130%	123%	132%

EXHIBIT 7
Selected Information on Deutsche's Distributors in Ukraine

Deutsche Distributors by City:	Kharkiv	Dnipropetrovsk	Odessa	Donetsk	Kiev	Composite Ratios, German Beer-Distribution Industry
Income Data						
Net sales, 2000	€2,530,935	€2,024,748	€2,812,150	€843,645	€3,475,255	NA
Operating profit/sales	1.8%	2.2%	3.0%	1.1%	3.5%	3.7%
Pretax profit/sales	1.7	1.9	2.3	0.7	3.1	3.5
Assets (as % of total)						
Trade receivables	12.9%	13.5%	16.5%	19.5%	13.0%	12.0%
Inventory	15.1	19.0	30.0	25.0	22.0	31.0
Fixed assets	33.1	29.1	25.0	21.0	28.0	24.0
Total	100.0	100.0	100.0	100.0	100.0	100.0
Liabilities and Equity (as % of Total)						
ST bank borrowings	0.1%	2.1%	1.5%	2.5%	4.0%	15.0%
Trade payables	29.2	32.2	28.7	37.5	19.0	16.3
Total curr. liabs.	35.0	41.0	33.2	43.2	27.0	39.4
LT debt	2.5	0.0	3.0	0.0	5.0	16.0
Net worth	32.5	59.0	63.8	56.2	68.0	44.6
Total	100.0	100.0	100.0	100.0	100.0	100.0
Ratios						
Current ratio	1.1	1.2	1.1	0.9	1.6	1.4
Days' sales outstanding	27.7	25.9	27.4	39.5	19.8	19.4
Sales/assets	2.0	1.9	2.2	1.8	2.4	2.3
Pretax profit/assets	2.9%	3.6%	5.1%	1.3%	7.4%	8.0%
Debt/equity	8.0%	3.6%	7.1%	4.4%	13.2%	69.5%

Source: Casewriter analysis.

ServerVault: "Reliable, Secure, and Wicked Fast"

In early July 2000, Patrick Sweeney and Jim Zinn, respectively the president/CEO and CFO of ServerVault, prepared for a series of meetings with private investors and venture capital firms from which they hoped to raise the capital to grow their firm. ServerVault had been founded eight months before and had demonstrated the efficacy of its business model. Now Sweeney and Zinn sought to implement an ambitious plan of expansion. They knew that prospective investors would want an estimate of the firm's rate of cash consumption, known as the "burn rate." Therefore, they sought to have a forecast of the firm's Statement of Cash Flows (SOCF) prepared on a monthly basis for the next two and one-half years that would reflect their plan of expansion. From this they hoped to identify the timing and amount of funds to be sought in the firm's capital-raising program.

HOSTING-INDUSTRY OVERVIEW

Companies in the hosting industry offered businesses and individuals the infrastructure to operate Internet-based applications, ranging from simple Web sites to sites featuring complex commercial transactions. Web sites were streamed into the Internet from powerful desk-top-size computers, called "servers." Hosting companies offered physical space for these servers and supporting services. Web-hosting customers, like customers of other outsourcing services, used the service to avoid the attention and expense of maintaining hard-

This case was prepared by J. Chadwick Rynbrandt and Professor Robert F. Bruner from field research. Some financial data have been disguised; some other information has been simplified to clarify the issues. The case is intended to serve as the basis for classroom discussion rather than to illustrate effective or ineffective managerial action. Copyright © 2000 by the University of Virginia Darden School Foundation, Charlottesville, VA. All rights reserved. *To order copies, send an e-mail to* dardencases@virginia.edu. *No part of this publication may be reproduced, stored in a retrieval system, used in a spreadsheet, or transmitted in any form or by any means—electronic, mechanical, photocopying, recording, or otherwise—without the permission of the Darden School Foundation. Rev. 11/01. Version 1.5.*

ware or providing personnel to make Internet applications work. Hosting offered investors an "infrastructure play" in the Internet world. They offered an analogy to describe the role of hosting: "We are the arms merchant to the Internet. We don't care who's fighting, just as long as they continue to fight." Because infrastructure players supplied the capacity to compete on the fast-growing Internet and generated cash flows from their inception, the capital market rewarded these firms with high valuation multiples. According to one analyst, Web-hosting companies faced a bright future as "they ride two transforming tailwinds . . . growth of the Internet and the trend toward business outsourcing."[1]

The industry featured three hosting business models: shared, co-location, and managed. **Exhibit 1** summarizes the characteristics of each. At the most basic level, all types of hosting offered the minimum "power, pipes, and paint." That is, they rented space in a building with constantly available power and Internet connections. From there, the three business models varied:

- **Shared** hosting put multiple customers on one server, sharing memory, processing power, and server space. Customers who had simple Internet needs usually preferred this option where they shared a host-owned server with other customers. Leading shared hosting providers (with 1999 revenues in millions of dollars) were: PSINet ($555), Verio ($258), and Concentric ($147).[2]
- **Co-location** customers rented building space instead of hard drive space. Hosts in this segment targeted customers who owned and managed their own servers, but lacked highly powered and cooled space and reliable connection to the Internet. In some instances, co-location providers offered additional services such as data backup. Leading co-location hosting providers (with 1999 revenues in millions of dollars) were: BBN/GTE Internetworking ($1,036), Exodus Communications ($242), Qwest ($143), and Global Center ($79).
- **Managed** hosting introduced more value-added services to the hosting customer, mainly managing the equipment and applications of the customer. Companies who had a significant Internet presence or high volume e-commerce would be more likely to choose this complete outsourcing solution. Leading managed hosting providers (with 1999 revenues in millions of dollars) were: Digex ($59.8), IBM ($47), and Data Return ($7.1). ServerVault most likely would be classified in this segment, though Patrick Sweeney argued that ServerVault offered a much higher level of service than other firms in this group.

Hosting companies could differentiate themselves beyond type of service. Other important elements of hosting service were the level of physical and electronic security and the stability of power and Internet connections. Hosts offering the highest service provided completely reliable access to the server ("one hundred percent availability")—anything that might compromise access to the server, such as a damaged machine or a lost Internet connection would be mitigated through redundancy of capacity and system security.

Exhibit 2 shows the rapid growth expected in each of the three segments. By 2004, total revenues in the industry would approach $13 billion. The "managed" segment of service

---

[1]Jim Linnehan, Kevin Monroe, John Sharko, Peter DeCaprio, and Kent Siefers, "Hosting the New Economy: A White Paper on the Hosting Service Industry," Thomas Weisel Partners, March 29, 2000.

[2]Classification of firms into the three categories and their revenues are drawn from Linnehan et al., ibid.

was expected to account for the majority of growth. The "shared" and "co-location" segments, in contrast, would not see much growth and would likely turn into commodity markets. Pricing pressure would be strong, and, therefore, a hosting company that wanted to compete in that segment would need to find a differentiable service that made its customers less price sensitive. An alternative strategy was to acquire the services necessary to make it a player in the "managed" segment—recent announcements[3] of acquisition talks had generated a flurry of speculation about the industry.

SERVERVAULT'S BUSINESS

ServerVault was founded in early 1999, when Patrick Sweeney, a second-generation IT professional and a high-tech director at the real estate firm Trammell Crow, convinced Jim Zinn, former CFO of Capital One, to support his attempt to carve out a niche in the hosting industry. Zinn joined first as an investor and then as CFO of the start-up.

With ServerVault, Sweeney and Zinn created a company that served a segment of hosting customers who were Internet-reliant and security-savvy. ServerVault wanted customers whose Internet applications were so important that security and reliability drove the selection of a hosting provider. They were also targeting customers who wanted the end-to-end solution that "managed" hosting provided. At the core, ServerVault's promise was to provide "managed" hosting services that, according to the firm's motto, were "reliable, secure, and wicked fast."

ServerVault differentiated itself most clearly in the "secure" part of its promise. The firm offered seven layers of security protection **(Exhibit 3).** The result was a level of protection that met U.S. Department of Defense security standards. For example, the physical layer (i.e., the facility) included a vaultlike structure within an already-secure building. The vault, also known as the data center, contained row after row of server racks, each holding up to 25 machines. The vault was specially manufactured to be able to withstand the most destructive forces of nature. Reaching the vault required passing through a "man-trap" where visitors were screened for proper authorization to enter the facility. Once at the vault, only those ServerVault employees who had total security clearances could proceed inside; for security reasons, customers were required to take a virtual tour.

ServerVault's promises of reliability and speed were met by redundant bandwidth and power supply. Each facility had four to five providers of Internet access. Should access to one of them become unavailable, traffic was instantly rerouted to another available bandwidth. Similarly, each facility had multiple electricity generators that were able to provide ample electricity should a power outage occur.

ServerVault derived revenue from three sources: one-time setup fees for new servers, monthly hosting fees, and fees for additional value-added services. Each facility was designed to generate four or five times more revenue per square foot than those of competitors.

---

[3]Exodus Communications had announced preliminary talks to acquire Global Crossing Ltd.'s Global-Center Inc. unit for about $6.5 billion in stock. Nippon Telegraph & Telephone Corp. agreed to acquire Verio, Inc., and World-Com Corp. acquired Digex's parent, Intermedia Communications, Inc., for $3 billion in stock plus $3 billion in assumed debt.

The cash costs for the business occurred mainly upfront. Building each facility required a significant investment. The variable cost of adding servers and maintaining them was comparatively small. Thus, when a ServerVault facility reached maximum capacity, it produced a significant and reliable stream of cash that amply covered the total costs. The challenge for Sweeney and Zinn was to fill each facility as quickly as possible, because, once a facility had been built, the majority of expenses had been incurred. Every additional server hosted in a facility contributed a large profit over its variable costs. Patrick Sweeney mused that the hosting facilities were similar in their economics to a newly completed hotel waiting for guests.

PLANS FOR GROWTH

As Sweeney and Zinn looked forward, they faced a major decision regarding the pace of expansion. Their first small-scale facility in the Washington, D.C., area was complete and was starting to fill up. Given the "land rush" that was taking place in the hosting market, Sweeney and Zinn felt pressure to gain a first-mover advantage by building additional facilities as quickly as possible. They planned to build a second, full-sized facility in Dulles, Virginia, in September 2000. After that, they planned to establish a European presence in Dublin, Ireland, by opening a facility in January 2001. Other high-potential areas for future facilities included Silicon Valley, Boston, Austin (Texas), and Asia.

ServerVault faced two major constraints on its expansion. First, growth required employees. Each facility required 20 to 30 full-time employees, and ServerVault wanted to "hire only the best." But, as the best could be very hard to find, the job market affected the rate at which the firm could expand. In addition, ServerVault's corporate staff was still growing and refining their skills to optimally support the facilities.

The second constraint, cash, was even more pressing in the minds of Sweeney and Zinn. **Exhibit 4** shows the Statement of Cash Flows for the first six months of 2000 for ServerVault. After raising enough money in 1999 to start the first facility and build the corporate staff, ServerVault faced a cash crunch in May 2000. Accordingly, Sweeney and Zinn obtained a $2 million bridge loan from an Irish venture capitalist.[4] The $2 million would support operations for a few months, but in order to build any more facilities, a major capital infusion was needed. In the next few days, Sweeney and Zinn would need to decide how much capital they needed and when they needed it, given their growth plans.

FINANCIAL FORECAST

Answering those important questions required a monthly forecast of ServerVault's cash flows for the next three years. Sweeney and Zinn discussed several assumptions that would be needed to build the forecast:

---

[4]The bridge loan would convert into equity at the next issuance of equity. Because the Irish investor had invested its capital months before new equity would be issued, the Irish loan would convert to shares at a discounted price per share. So, for example, if new equity were issued in September 2000 at $10 per share, the Irish investor would be allowed to convert its $2-million loan to equity at a price of $8 per share.

- *Capital expenditures.* Each new facility would cost $5–$6 million and could hold approximately 5,000 servers, depending on size. Assuming that ServerVault could raise as much capital as it needed, Zinn estimated that it could add one more facility (Dulles) by the end of 2000, followed by one each quarter beginning in January 2001. Sweeney believed that the corporate staff could not support faster expansion. An alternative assumption for the forecast was for ServerVault to build a new facility only as it reached capacity in existing facilities.
- *Server costs.* Because ServerVault planned to own the servers in its facilities, it would need to purchase them as customer demand ramped up. ServerVault wanted to offer its customers a choice of server manufacturers. Zinn estimated that, on average, new servers (including the necessary software) would cost $3,000 each, representing an average mix of different configurations.
- *Server revenue.* Zinn compiled a forecast for growth in the number of servers hosted. He assumed a growth rate that started at 50 percent and gradually decreased to 10 percent by the end of the three-year period. His estimates are contained in **Exhibit 5.** For planning purposes, Zinn also estimated that the one-time setup fees for new servers would be $500 each (net of sales-force commissions).[5] Monthly recurring hosting fees were conservatively estimated to be $750 per server.
- *Services revenue.* Additional value-added services were offered on a server-by-server basis. Zinn believed that ServerVault would initially start at $50 of service revenue per server per month.
- *Operating expenses.* Each facility required people and bandwidth to run. Zinn and ServerVault's manager of Human Resources estimated that each facility would require 20 to 30 people at an average cost of $7,000 per month per person, including benefits. ServerVault's redundant bandwidth design would translate into monthly expenses of $25,000 per month for each facility. Two other operating expenses were relevant to the forecast—marketing and administrative. ServerVault's growth plans would require aggressive marketing in the form of advertising and discounts. Zinn believed that marketing expenses would be run at $100,000 per month for the rest of 2000, $150,000 per month during 2001, and $200,000 per month for 2002. As for administrative expenses, Zinn estimated that $50,000 per month would cover the corporate staff, utilities, and other miscellaneous items.

FINANCING NEEDS

Given their experience over the past months, Sweeney and Zinn knew that they would need funding soon. Friends, family, and "angel" investors[6] had provided the funds to get the business off the ground. Then, in May, the $2 million bridge loan came at a pivotal time, when

---

[5] The setup fee for new servers was actually projected to grow each year.

[6] Start-up companies typically went through different rounds of financing as they grew. In many cases, an entrepreneur's friends, family, or individual "angel" investors provided seed capital at the very beginning. Once those sources of funds ran dry, start-ups would then seek a significant investment from a venture-capital or private-equity fund to launch the high-growth phase of the business.

their cash balance had declined to about $100,000. They expected that a similar "crunch point" would arise in the future.

Accordingly, Sweeney and Zinn turned their eyes toward the two meetings that awaited them. Both were with venture capitalists who were interested in taking an equity stake in ServerVault in exchange for a cash investment. The amount to be raised would depend on capital-market conditions and the appetite of investors. One might hypothesize an issue of equity capital in July 2000 that would raise as little as $5 million or as much as $15 million. This reflected recent conditions in the market for "new economy" sector equities and for venture capital: between March and June 2000, the Nasdaq index had plummeted 40 percent, reflecting investor disillusionment with prospects in that sector. One journalist wrote:

> America's Internet companies continue to burn prodigious amounts of cash, raising the prospect that dozens more will disappear from the landscape over the next 12 months. But the deteriorating cash position of the Internet universe as a whole masks the fact that an important change is taking place: The players are rapidly becoming separated into winners and losers.[7]

Against this backdrop, Sweeney and Zinn knew that, among other topics, the investors would cover three questions. First, how long could ServerVault go on without any additional cash? Second, how much cash should they aim to raise in the next round of financing to keep the company going for 12 months beyond that point? Third, when would Server-Vault become a net producer of cash rather than a net user?

Patrick Sweeney observed as he reviewed the existing and potential competition in the managed segment of the hosting industry, "One big problem is that people are promising what they can't deliver. We *can* deliver what we promise. But the general gap between talk and delivery means we have to sell harder to our investors and customers." Nevertheless, he was confident that the market would recognize and reward ServerVault's value proposition.

Now was the time to seize this opportunity through a program of rapid expansion of the number of facilities. Investors would want to know: How much cash should the firm seek to raise? When? What would be ServerVault's burn rate and the key drivers of that rate?

---

[7]Jack Willoughby, "Smoldering: 'Net Companies, Still Burning Cash, Try to Conserve Tinder," *Barron's,* October 2, 2000, 38.

EXHIBIT 1
Comparison of Different Types of Hosting

	Shared	Co-location	Managed
Who is responsible for "power, pipes, and paint"?	Host	Host	Host
Who manages the equipment?	Host	Customer	Host
Is the server shared among customers or dedicated to one?	Shared	Dedicated	Dedicated
Are value-added services offered?	Rarely	Occasionally	Always
Who are the typical customers?	Small businesses and individuals that want a Web page	Businesses that own and manage their own servers	Businesses that want a complete, outsourced solution
What is the primary benefit?	Hard drive space on an Internet server	Building space for servers, with power, cooling, and connectivity	Security, application maintenance, and outsourced technical staff

EXHIBIT 2
Projected Size of Web-Hosting Segments

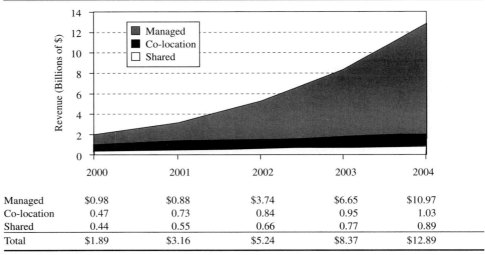

	2000	2001	2002	2003	2004
Managed	$0.98	$0.88	$3.74	$6.65	$10.97
Co-location	0.47	0.73	0.84	0.95	1.03
Shared	0.44	0.55	0.66	0.77	0.89
Total	$1.89	$3.16	$5.24	$8.37	$12.89

Source: Forrester Research, Inc.

EXHIBIT 3
Seven Layers of Security at ServerVault

Application

To support familiar Internet applications like HTTP, FTP, Telnet, and Mail, ServerVault provides robust messaging, security, and directory services, including redundant ACE servers for one-time password authentication and SSL certificate distribution for secure VPN-based systems management. Extensive use of parallel and load balancing systems ensures that your content is available.

Presentation

To provide data translation and reformatting between different applications, ServerVault has adopted the industry's best network management and monitoring solutions. The information from all of these systems flows through a single fault-tolerant real-time management application, and converts these network statistics into a real-time heads-up picture of current performance and emerging security threats.

Session

Providing logical connections between machines, the session layer supports information delivery for all Internet applications. This layer protects against DoS attacks, logs all session-level activity for trend analysis and demand planning, and flags any traffic sequences containing attack profiles or signatures.

Physical

ServerVault's connections to the outside world follow multiple physical paths and do not share dependencies on any external equipment. This makes it impossible for a single incident outside of our facilities to disrupt service. The data center itself is shielded and armored, and provides total protection from fire, shock, gases, moisture, and all electromagnetic wave energy from the outside world. Access to the facility is limited to ServerVault employees, and armed guards make sure it stays that way.

Transport

To ensure reliable communications from client and server, ServerVault's multi-layer network switches understand traffic classification at this layer in order to make sure time-sensitive or priority traffic is given preferred treatment.

Network

ServerVault's multiprovider attachments and private-peering provide fully fault-tolerant high-speed WAN connections that do not depend on any single carrier. In addition, multiple hosts can be viewed as one from the outside world, balancing the load for high-demand web sites, and providing another level of backup if any of the servers should fail.

Data Link

ServerVault's core network is fully fault-tolerant along all of its link-paths using technologies such as gigabit-channel Ethernet and multi-homing techniques. So, if a port or piece of equipment should fail, your service stays up. Guaranteed.

Source: Company brochure.

EXHIBIT 4
Statement of Cash Flows (direct method)

	Jan-00	Feb-00	Mar-00	Apr-00	May-00	Jun-00
Cash Flows from Operating Activities						
Operating revenues						
Setup	1,000	2,500	3,000	5,000	6,000	7,500
Hosting	2,420	6,440	10,480	18,540	26,200	35,480
Services	445	350	600	1,150	1,900	2,325
Total sources	3,865	9,290	14,080	24,690	34,100	45,305
Operating Expenses						
Bandwidth	(3,790)	(3,790)	(6,115)	(5,591)	(5,591)	(11,678)
Marketing	(3,500)	(22,250)	(51,750)	(57,250)	(51,750)	(79,800)
Salaries	(28,250)	(45,100)	(54,570)	(56,600)	(61,520)	(62,200)
G&A (including corp.)	(9,584)	(15,484)	(16,884)	(22,530)	(30,160)	(39,910)
Total uses	(45,124)	(86,624)	(129,319)	(141,971)	(149,021)	(193,588)
Net cash produced (used) by operating activities	(41,259)	(77,334)	(115,239)	(117,281)	(114,921)	(148,283)
Cash Flows from Investing Activities:						
Capital expenditures						
Computer hardware	(9,800)	(14,265)	(17,770)	(31,220)	(36,150)	(44,890)
Facilities	(10,180)	(81,100)	(29,540)	(27,590)	—	—
Net cash produced (used) by investing activities	(19,980)	(95,365)	(47,310)	(58,810)	(36,150)	(44,890)
Cash Flows from Financing Activities:						
External funding	47,500	50,000	10,000		2,000,000	
Net cash produced (used) by financing activities	47,500	50,000	10,000	—	2,000,000	—
NET MONTHLY CASH INFLOW (OUTFLOW)	(13,739)	(122,699)	(152,549)	(176,091)	1,848,929	(193,173)
CASH POSITION						
Beginning balance	575,000	561,261	438,562	286,013	109,922	1,958,851
Ending cash balance	561,261	438,562	286,013	109,922	1,958,851	1,765,678

EXHIBIT 5
Three-Year Forecast of Server Growth

	Jan-00	Feb-00	Mar-00	Apr-00	May-00	Jun-00	Jul-00	Aug-00	Sep-00	Oct-00	Nov-00	Dec-00
New facilities	0	0	0	0	0	0	0	0	1	0	0	0
Total facilities	1	1	1	1	1	1	1	1	2	2	2	2
New servers	3	5	6	10	12	15	25	35	65	90	115	135
Total servers	3	8	14	24	36	51	76	111	176	266	381	516

	Jan-01	Feb-01	Mar-01	Apr-01	May-01	Jun-01	Jul-01	Aug-01	Sep-01	Oct-01	Nov-01	Dec-01
New facilities	1	0	0	1	0	0	1	0	0	1	0	0
Total facilities	3	3	3	4	4	4	5	5	5	6	6	6
New servers	206	221	236	271	291	311	351	376	401	447	477	502
Total servers	722	943	1179	1450	1741	2053	2404	2780	3182	3628	4105	4607

	Jan-02	Feb-02	Mar-02	Apr-02	May-02	Jun-02	Jul-02	Aug-02	Sep-02	Oct-02	Nov-02	Dec-02
New facilities	1	0	0	1	0	0	1	0	0	1	0	0
Total facilities	7	7	7	8	8	8	9	9	9	10	10	10
New servers	547	547	582	647	692	737	807	862	917	997	1062	1132
Total servers	5153	5700	6282	6929	7621	8358	9165	10027	10945	11942	13004	14137

Source: Casewriter and company analysis.

PART 3

Estimating the Cost of Capital

"Best Practices" in Estimating the Cost of Capital: Survey and Synthesis

In recent decades, theoretical breakthroughs in such areas as portfolio diversification, market efficiency, and asset pricing have converged into compelling recommendations about the cost of capital to a corporation. By the early 1990s, a consensus had emerged prompting such descriptions as "traditional . . . textbook . . . appropriate," "theoretically correct" and "a useful rule of thumb and a good vehicle."[1] Beneath this general agreement about cost of capital theory lies considerable ambiguity and confusion over how the theory can best be applied. The issues at stake are sufficiently important that differing choices on a few key elements can lead to wide disparities in estimated capital cost. The cost of capital is central to modern finance touching on investment and divestment decisions, measures of economic profit, performance appraisal and incentive systems. Each year in the United States, corporations undertake more than $500 billion in capital spending. Since a difference of a few percent in capital costs can mean a swing in billions of expenditures, how firms estimate the cost is no trivial matter.

The purpose of this paper is to present evidence on how some of the most financially sophisticated companies and financial advisers estimate capital costs. This evidence is valuable in several respects. First, it identifies the most important ambiguities in the application of cost-of-capital theory, setting the stage for productive debate and research on their resolution. Second, it helps interested companies benchmark their cost-of-capital estimation

---

[1]The three sets of quotes come, in order, from Ehrhardt (1994), Chapter 1; Copeland et al. (1990), p. 190; and Brealey and Myers (1993), p. 197.

This chapter was written by Robert F. Bruner, Kenneth M. Eades, Robert S. Harris, and Robert C. Higgins. Bruner, Eades, and Harris are professors at the Darden School, University of Virginia. Higgins is a professor at the University of Washington. The authors thank Todd Brotherson for excellent research assistance, and gratefully acknowledge the financial support of Coopers & Lybrand and the University of Virginia Darden School Foundation. The research would not have been possible without the cooperation of the 37 companies surveyed. These contributions notwithstanding, any errors remain the authors'. This chapter appeared in *Journal of Financial Practice and Education* (Spring 1998), and appears here with the permission of the Financial Management Association International, University of South Florida, College of Business Administration, Tampa, FL 33620-5500 (telephone: 813-974-2084).

practices against best-practice peers. Third, the evidence sheds light on the accuracy with which capital costs can be reasonably estimated, enabling executives to use the estimates more wisely in their decision making. Fourth, it enables teachers to answer the inevitable question, "How do companies really estimate their cost of capital?"

The paper is part of a lengthy tradition of surveys of industry practice. Among the more relevant predecessors, Gitman and Forrester (1977) explored "the level of sophistication in capital budgeting techniques" among 103 large, rapidly growing businesses, finding that the internal rate of return and the payback period were in common use. Although the authors inquired about the level of the firm's discount rate, they did not ask how the rate was determined. Gitman and Mercurio (1982) surveyed 177 Fortune 1000 firms about "current practice in cost of capital measurement and utilization," concluding that "the respondents' actions do not reflect the application of current financial theory." Moore and Reichert (1983) surveyed 298 Fortune 500 firms on the use of a broad array of financial techniques, concluding among other things, that 86 percent of firms surveyed use time-adjusted capital budgeting techniques. Bierman (1993) surveyed 74 Fortune 100 companies reporting that all use some form of discounting in their capital budgeting and 93 percent use a weighted-average cost of capital. In a broad-ranging survey of 84 Fortune 500 large firms and Forbes 200 best small companies, Trahan and Gitman (1995) report that 30 percent of respondents use the capital asset pricing model.

This paper differs from its predecessors in several important respects. Existing published evidence is based on written, closed-end surveys sent to a large sample of firms, often covering a wide array of topics and commonly using multiple-choice or fill-in-the-blank questions. Such an approach often yields response rates as low as 20 percent and provides no opportunity to explore subtleties of the topic. Instead, we report the result of a telephone survey of a carefully chosen group of leading corporations and financial advisers. Another important difference is that the intent of existing papers is most often to learn how well accepted modern financial techniques are among practitioners, while we are interested in those areas of cost-of-capital estimation where finance theory is silent or ambiguous and practitioners are left to their own devices.

The following section gives a brief overview of the weighted-average cost of capital. The research approach and sample selection are discussed in Section II. Section III reports the general survey results. Key points of disparity are reviewed in Section IV. Section V discusses further survey results on risk adjustment to a baseline cost of capital, and Section VI offers conclusions and implications for the financial practitioner.

I. THE WEIGHTED-AVERAGE COST OF CAPITAL

A key insight from finance theory is that any use of capital imposes an opportunity cost on investors; namely, funds are diverted from earning a return on the next best equal-risk investment. Since investors have access to a host of financial market opportunities, corporate uses of capital must be benchmarked against these capital market alternatives. The cost of capital provides this benchmark. Unless a firm can earn in excess of its cost of capital, it will not create economic profit or value for investors.

A standard means of expressing a company's cost of capital is the weighted average of the cost of individual sources of capital employed. In symbols, a company's weighted-average cost of capital (or WACC) is

$$\text{WACC} = \left(W_{\text{debt}}(1 - t)K_{\text{debt}}\right) + \left(W_{\text{preferred}}K_{\text{preferred}}\right) + \left(W_{\text{equity}}K_{\text{equity}}\right) \qquad (1)$$

where:

K = Component cost of capital

W = Weight of each component as percent of total capital

t = Marginal corporate tax rate

For simplicity, this formula includes only three sources of capital; it can be easily expanded to include other sources as well.

Finance theory offers several important observations when estimating a company's WACC. First, the capital costs appearing in the equation should be current costs reflecting current financial market conditions, not historical, sunk costs. In essence, the costs should equal the investors' anticipated internal rate of return on future cash flows associated with each form of capital. Second, the weights appearing in the equation should be market weights, not historical weights based on often arbitrary, out-of-date book values. Third, the cost of debt should be after corporate tax, reflecting the benefits of the tax deductibility of interest.

Despite the guidance provided by finance theory, use of the weighted-average expression to estimate a company's cost of capital still confronts the practitioner with a number of difficult choices.[2] As our survey results demonstrate, the most nettlesome component of WACC estimation is the cost of equity capital; for unlike readily available yields in bond markets, no observable counterpart exists for equities. This forces practitioners to rely on more abstract and indirect methods to estimate the cost of equity capital.

II. SAMPLE SELECTION

This paper describes the results of a telephone survey of leading practitioners. Believing that the complexity of the subject does not lend itself to a written questionnaire, we wanted to solicit an explanation of each firm's approach told in the practitioner's own words. Though our interviews were guided by a series of questions, these were sufficiently open-ended to reveal many subtle differences in practice.

Since our focus is on the gaps between theory and application rather than on average or typical practice, we aimed to sample practitioners who were leaders in the field. We began by searching for a sample of corporations (rather than investors or financial advisers) in the belief that they had ample motivation to compute WACC carefully and

---

[2]Even at the theoretical level, Dixit and Pindyck (1994) point out that the use of standard net present value (NPV) decision rules (with, for instance, WACC as a discount rate) does not capture the option value of being able to delay an irreversible investment expenditure. As a result, a firm may find it better to delay an investment even if the current NPV is positive. Our survey does not explore the ways firms deal with this issue; rather we focus on measuring capital costs.

to resolve many of the estimation issues themselves. Several publications offer lists of firms that are well regarded in finance;[3] of these, we chose a research report, *Creating World-Class Financial Management: Strategies of 50 Leading Companies* (1992), which identified firms,

> selected by their peers as being among those with the best financial management. Firms were chosen for excellence in strategic financial risk management, tax and accounting, performance evaluation and other areas of financial management. . . . The companies included were those that were mentioned the greatest number of times by their peers.[4]

From the 50 companies identified in this report, we eliminated 18 headquartered outside North America.[5] Of those remaining, five declined to be interviewed, leaving a sample of 27 firms. The companies included in the sample are given in **Exhibit 1.** We approached the most senior financial officer first with a letter explaining our research, and then with a telephone call. Our request was to interview the individual in charge of estimating the firm's WACC. We promised our interviewees that, in preparing a report on our findings, we would not identify the practices of any particular company by name—we have respected this promise in the presentation that follows.

In the interest of assessing the practices of the broader community of finance practitioners, we surveyed two other samples:

- *Financial advisers.* Using a "league table" of merger and acquisition advisers presented in *Institutional Investor* issues of April 1995, 1994, and 1993, we drew a sample of 10 of the most active[6] advisers. We applied approximately[7] the same set of questions to representatives of these firms' merger and acquisition departments. We wondered whether the financial advisers' interest in promoting deals might lead them to lower WACC estimates than those estimated by operating companies. This proved not to be the case. If anything, the estimating techniques most often used by financial advisers yield higher, not lower, capital cost estimates.
- *Textbooks and trade books.* From a leading textbook publisher we obtained a list of the graduate-level textbooks in corporate finance having the greatest unit sales in 1994. From

---

[3]For instance, *Institutional Investor* and *Euromoney* publish lists of firms with the best CFOs, or with special competencies in certain areas. We elected not to use these lists because special competencies might not indicate a generally excellent finance department, nor might a stellar CFO.

[4]*Creating World-Class Financial Management: Strategies of 50 Leading Companies,* Research Report No. 1-110, Business International Corporation, New York, 1992 (238 pages), pages vii–viii. This survey was based upon a written questionnaire sent to CEOs, CFOs, controllers, and treasurers, followed up by a telephone survey.

[5]Our reasons for excluding these firms were the increased difficulty of obtaining interviews, and possible difficulties in obtaining capital market information (such as betas and equity market premiums) that might preclude using American practices. The enlargement of this survey to firms from other countries is a subject worthy of future study.

[6]*Activity* in this case was defined as four-year aggregate deal volume in mergers and acquisitions. The sample was drawn from the top 12 advisers, using their *average* deal volume over the 1993–95 period. Of these 12 firms, 2 chose not to participate in the survey.

[7]Specific questions differ, reflecting that financial advisers infrequently deal with capital budgeting matters and that corporate financial officers infrequently value companies.

these, we selected the top four. In addition, we drew on three trade books that discuss the estimation of WACC in detail.

Names of advisers and books included in these two samples are shown in Exhibit 1.

III. SURVEY FINDINGS

The detailed survey results appear in **Exhibit 2.** The estimation approaches are broadly similar across the three samples in several dimensions:

- Discounted cash flow (DCF) is the dominant investment-evaluation technique.
- WACC is the dominant discount rate used in DCF analyses.
- Weights are based on *market,* not book, value mixes of debt and equity.[8]
- The after-tax cost of debt is predominantly based on *marginal* pretax costs, and *marginal* or *statutory* tax rates.
- The capital asset pricing model (CAPM) is the dominant model for estimating the cost of equity. Some firms mentioned other multifactor asset pricing models (e.g., arbitrage pricing theory), but these were in the small minority. No firms cited specific modifications of the CAPM to adjust for any empirical shortcomings of the model in explaining past returns.[9]

These practices differ sharply from those reported in earlier surveys.[10] First, the best-practice firms show much more alignment on most elements of practice. Second, they base their practice on financial economic models rather than on rules of thumb or arbitrary decision rules.

On the other hand, disagreements exist within and among groups on how to apply the CAPM to estimate cost of equity. The CAPM states that the required return (K) on any asset can be expressed as

$$K = R_f + \beta(R_m - R_f) \tag{2}$$

where:

R_f = Interest rate available on a risk-free bond
R_m = Return required to attract investors to hold the broad market portfolio of risky assets
β = the relative risk of the particular asset

---

[8]The choice between target and actual proportions is not a simple one. Because debt and equity costs clearly depend on the proportions of each employed, it might appear that the actual proportions must be used. However, if the firm's target weights are publicly known and if investors expect the firm soon to move to these weights, then observed costs of debt and equity may anticipate the target capital structure.

[9]For instance, even research supporting the CAPM has found that empirical data are better explained by an intercept higher than a risk-free rate and a price of beta risk less than the market risk premium. Ibbotson (1994) offers such a modified CAPM, in addition to the standard CAPM and other models, in its cost of capital service. Jagannathan and McGrattan (1995) provide a useful review of empirical evidence on the CAPM.

[10]Gitman and Forrester (1977), and Gitman and Mercurio (1982).

According to CAPM, then, the cost of equity, K_{equity}, for a company depends on three components: returns on risk-free bonds (R_f); the stock's equity beta, which measures risk of the company's stock relative to other risky assets ($\beta = 1.0$ is average risk); and the market risk premium ($R_m - R_f$) necessary to entice investors to hold risky assets generally versus risk-free bonds. In theory, each of these components must be a forward-looking estimate. Our survey results show substantial disagreements on all three components.

Comments on Risk-Free Rates

Some of our best-practice companies noted that their choice of a bond market proxy for a risk-free rate depended specifically on how they were proposing to spend funds. We asked, "What do you use for a risk-free rate?" and heard the following:

- "Ten-year Treasury bond or other duration Treasury bond if needed to better match project horizon."
- "We use a three- to five-year Treasury note yield, which is the typical length of our company's investment. We match our average investment horizon with maturity of debt."

The Risk-Free Rate of Return

As originally derived, the CAPM is a single-period model, so the question of which interest rate best represents the risk-free rate never arises. But in a many-period world typically characterized by upward-sloping yield curves, the practitioner must choose. Our results show the choice is typically between the 90-day T-bill yield and a long-term Treasury bond yield. (Because the yield curve is ordinarily relatively flat beyond 10 years, the choice of which particular long-term yield to use is not a critical one.)[11] The difference between realized returns on the 90-day T-bill and the 10-year T-bond has averaged 150 basis points over the long run; so choice of a risk-free rate can have a material effect on the cost of equity and WACC.[12]

The 90-day T-bill yields are more consistent with the CAPM as originally derived and reflect truly risk-free returns in the sense that T-bill investors avoid material loss in value from interest rate movements. However, long-term bond yields more closely reflect the

---

[11]In early January 1996, the differences between yields on the 10- and 30-year T-bonds was about 35 basis points. Some aficionados will argue that there *is* a difference between the 10- and 30-year yields. Ordinarily the yield curve declines just slightly as it reaches the 30-year maturity—this has been explained to us as the result of life insurance companies and other long-term buy-and-hold investors who are said to purchase the long bond in significant volume. It is said that these investors command a lower liquidity premium than the broader market, thus driving down yields. If this is true, then the yields at this point of the curve may be due not to some ordinary process of rational expectations, but rather to an anomalous supply–demand imbalance, which would render these yields less trustworthy. The counterargument is that life insurance companies could be presumed to be rational investors too. As buy-and-hold investors, they will surely suffer the consequences of any irrationality and therefore have good motive to invest for yields "at the market."

[12]This was estimated as the difference in arithmetic mean returns on long-term government bonds and U.S. Treasury bills over the years 1926 to 1994, given in Ibbotson Associates (1995).

default-free holding period returns available on long-lived investments and thus more closely mirror the types of investments made by companies.

Our survey results reveal a strong preference on the part of practitioners for long-term bond yields. Of both corporations and financial advisers, 70 percent use Treasury-bond yield maturities of 10 years or greater. None of the financial advisers and only 4 percent of the corporations used the Treasury-bill yield. Many corporations said they matched the term of the risk-free rate to the tenor of the investment. In contrast, 43 percent of the books advocated the T-bill yield, while only 29 percent used long-term Treasury yields.

Beta Estimates

Finance theory calls for a forward-looking beta, one reflecting investors' uncertainty about the future cash flows to equity. Because forward-looking betas are unobservable, practitioners are forced to rely on proxies of various kinds. Most often this involves using beta estimates derived from historical data and published by such sources as Bloomberg, Value Line, and Standard & Poor's.

The usual methodology is to estimate beta as the slope coefficient of the market model of returns:

$$R_{it} = \alpha_i + \beta_i(R_{mt}) \tag{3}$$

where:

R_{it} = Return on stock i in time period (e.g., day, week, month) t
R_{mt} = Return on the market portfolio in period t
α_i = Regression constant for stock i
β_i = Beta for stock i

In addition to relying on historical data, use of this equation to estimate beta requires a number of practical compromises, each of which can materially affect the results. For instance, increasing the number of time periods used in the estimation may improve the statistical reliability of the estimate, but risks the inclusion of stale, irrelevant information. Similarly, shortening the observation period from monthly to weekly, or even daily, increases the size of the sample but may yield observations that are not normally distributed and may introduce unwanted random noise. A third compromise involves choice of the market index. Theory dictates that R_m is the return on the market portfolio, an unobservable portfolio consisting of *all* risky assets, including human capital and other nontraded assets, in proportion to their importance in world wealth. Beta providers use a variety of stock market indices as proxies for the market portfolio on the argument that stock markets trade claims on a sufficiently wide array of assets to be adequate surrogates for the unobservable market portfolio.

The following table shows the compromises underlying the beta estimates of three prominent providers and their combined effect on the beta estimates of our sample companies. Note, for example, that the mean beta of our sample companies according to Bloomberg is 1.03, while the same number according to Value Line is 1.24. **Exhibit 3** provides a complete list of sample betas by publisher.

Compromises Underlying Beta Estimates and Their Effect on Estimated Betas of Sample Companies

	Bloomberg*	Value Line	Standard & Poor's
Number of observations	102	260	60
Time interval	Weekly over 2 years	Weekly over 5 years	Monthly over 5 years
Market index proxy	S&P 500	NYSE composite	S&P 500
Sample mean beta	1.03	1.24	1.18
Sample median beta	1.00	1.20	1.21

*With the Bloomberg service it is possible to estimate a beta over many differing time periods, market indices, and smoothed or unadjusted. The figures presented here represent the base-line or default-estimation approach used if one does not specify other approaches.

Over half of the corporations in our sample (item 10, Exhibit 2) rely on published sources for their beta estimates, although 30 percent calculate their own. Among financial advisers, 40 percent rely on published sources, 20 percent calculate their own, and another 40 percent use what might be called "fundamental" beta estimates. These are estimates which use multifactor statistical models drawing on fundamental indices of firm and industry risk to estimate company betas. The best-known provider of fundamental beta estimates is the consulting firm BARRA.

Within these broad categories, the following comments indicate that a number of survey participants use more pragmatic approaches, which combine published beta estimates or adjust published estimates in various heuristic ways.

We asked our sample companies, "What do you use as your volatility or beta factor?" A sampling of responses shows that the choice is not always a simple one:

- "[We use] adjusted betas reported by Bloomberg. At times, our stock has been extremely volatile. If at a particular time the factor is considered unreasonably high, we are apt to use a lower (more consistent) one."
- "We begin with the observed 60-month covariance between our stock and the market. We also consider Value Line, BARRA, S&P betas for comparison and may adjust the observed beta to match assessment of future risk."
- "We average Merrill Lynch and Value Line figures and use Bloomberg as a check."
- "We do not use betas estimated on our stock directly. Our company beta is built up as a weighted average of our business segment betas—the segment betas are estimated using pure-play firm betas of comparable companies."

Equity Market Risk Premium

This topic prompted the greatest variety of responses among survey participants. Finance theory says the equity market risk premium should equal the excess return expected by investors on the market portfolio relative to riskless assets. How one measures expected future returns on the market portfolio and on riskless assets are problems left to practitioners.

Because expected future returns are unobservable, all survey respondents extrapolated historical returns into the future on the presumption that past experience heavily conditions future expectations. Where respondents chiefly differed was in their use of *arithmetic* versus *geometric* average historical equity returns and in their choice of realized returns on T-bills versus T-bonds to proxy for the return on riskless assets.

The arithmetic mean return is the simple average of past returns. Assuming the distribution of returns is stable over time and that periodic returns are independent of one another, the arithmetic return is the best estimator of expected return.[13] The geometric mean return is the internal rate of return between a single outlay and one or more future receipts. It measures the compound rate of return investors earned over past periods. It accurately portrays historical investment experience. Unless returns are the same each time period, the geometric average will always be less than the arithmetic average and the gap widens as returns become more volatile.[14]

Based on Ibbotson Associates' (1995) data from 1926 to 1995, the matrix below illustrates the possible range of equity market risk premiums depending on use of the geometric as opposed to the arithmetic mean equity return and on use of realized returns on T-bills as opposed to T-bonds.[15] Even wider variations in market risk premiums can arise when one changes the historical period for averaging. Extending U.S. stock experience back to 1802, Siegel (1992) shows that historical market premiums have changed over time and were typically lower in the pre-1926 period. Carleton and Lakonishok (1985) illustrate considerable variation in historical premiums using different time periods and methods of calculation even with data since 1926.

The Equity Market Risk Premium ($R_m - R_f$)

	T-Bill Returns	T-Bond Returns
Arithmetic mean return	8.5%	7.0%
Geometric mean return	6.5%	5.4%

Of the texts and trade books in our survey, 71 percent support use of the arithmetic mean return over T-bills as the best surrogate for the equity market risk premium. For long-term projects, Ehrhardt advocates forecasting the T-bill rate and using a different cost of equity for each future time period. Kaplan and Ruback (1995) studied the equity risk premium implied by the valuations in highly leveraged transactions and estimated a mean pre-

---

[13]Several studies have documented significant negative autocorrelation in returns—this violates one of the essential tenets of the arithmetic calculation, since if returns are not serially independent, the simple arithmetic mean of a distribution will not be its expected value. The autocorrelation findings are reported by Fama and French (1986), Lo and MacKinlay (1988), and Poterba and Summers (1988).

[14]For large samples of returns the geometric average can be approximated as the arithmetic average minus one-half the variance of realized returns. Ignoring sample size adjustments, the variance of returns in the current example is .09 yielding an estimate of $.10 - 1/2(.09) = .055 = 5.5\%$ versus the actual 5.8% figure. Kritzman (1994) provides an interesting comparison of the two types of averages.

[15]These figures are drawn from Table 2–1, Ibbotson (1995), where the R_m was drawn from the "Large Company Stocks" series, and R_f drawn from the "Long-Term Government Bonds" and "U.S. Treasury Bills" series.

mium of 7.97 percent, which is most consistent with the arithmetic mean and T-bills. A minority view is that of Copeland, Koller, and Murrin (1990, pp. 193–94) writing on behalf of the Corporate Financial Practice at McKinsey & Company: "We believe that the geometric average represents a better estimate of investors' expected returns over long periods of time." Ehrhardt (1994) recommends use of the geometric mean return if one believes stockholders are "buy-and-hold" investors.

Half of the financial advisers queried use a premium consistent with the arithmetic mean and T-bill returns, and many specifically mentioned use of the arithmetic mean. Corporate respondents, on the other hand, evidenced more diversity of opinion and tend to favor a lower market premium: 37 percent use a premium of 5 to 6 percent, and another 11 percent use an even lower figure.

Comments Regarding Market Risk Premium

"What do you use as your market risk premium?" A sampling of responses from our best-practice companies shows the choice can be a complicated one.

- "Our 400-basis-point market premium is based on the historical relationship of returns on an actualized basis and/or investment bankers' estimated cost of equity based on analysts' earnings projections."
- "We use an Ibbotson arithmetic average starting in 1960. We have talked to investment banks and consulting firms with advice from 3 to 7 percent."
- "A 60-year average of about 5.7 percent. This number has been used for a long time in the company and is currently the subject of some debate and is under review. We may consider using a time horizon of less than 60 years to estimate this premium."
- "We are currently using 6 percent. In 1993 we polled various investment banks and academic studies on the issue as to the appropriate rate and got anywhere between 2 and 8 percent, but most were between 6 and 7.4 percent."

Comments from financial advisers also were revealing. While some simply responded that they use a published historical average, others presented a more complex picture.

- "We employ a self-estimated 5 percent (arithmetic average). A variety of techniques are used in estimation. We look at Ibbotson data and focus on more recent periods, around 30 years (but it is not a straight 30-year average). We use smoothing techniques, Monte Carlo simulation, and a dividend discount model on the S&P 400 to estimate what the premium should be, given our risk-free rate of return."
- "We use a 7.4 percent arithmetic mean, after Ibbotson, Sinquefeld. We used to use the geometric mean following the then scholarly advice, but we changed to the arithmetic mean when we found later that our competitors were using the arithmetic mean and scholars' views were shifting."

Comments in our interviews (see box above) suggest the diversity among survey participants. While most of our 27 sample companies appear to use a 60-plus-year historical period to estimate returns, one cited a window of less than 10 years, two cited windows of about 10 years, one began averaging with 1960 and another with 1952 data.

This variety of practice should not come as a surprise, since theory calls for a forward-looking risk premium, one that reflects current market sentiment and may change with market conditions. What is clear is that there is substantial variation as practitioners try to operationalize the theoretical call for a market risk premium. A glaring result is that few respondents specifically cited use of any forward-looking method to supplement or replace reading the tea leaves of past returns.[16]

IV. THE IMPACT OF VARIOUS ASSUMPTIONS FOR USING CAPM

To illustrate the effect of these various practices, we estimated the hypothetical cost of equity and WACC for Black & Decker, which we identified as having a wide range in estimated betas, and for McDonald's, which has a relatively narrow range. Our estimates are "hypothetical" in that we do not adopt any information supplied to us by the companies but rather apply a range of approaches based on publicly available information as of late 1995. **Exhibit 4** gives Black & Decker's estimated costs of equity and WACCs under various combinations of risk-free rate, beta, and market risk premiums. Three clusters of practice are illustrated, each in turn using three betas as provided by S&P, Value Line, and Bloomberg (unadjusted). The first approach, as suggested by some texts, marries a short-term risk-free rate (90-day T-bill yield) with Ibbotson's arithmetic mean (using T-bills) risk premium. The second, adopted by a number of financial advisers, uses a long-term risk-free rate (30-year T-bond yield) and a risk premium of 7.2 percent (the modal premium mentioned by financial advisers). The third approach also uses a long-term risk-free rate but adopts the modal premium mentioned by corporate respondents of 5.5 percent. We repeated these general procedures for McDonald's.

The resulting ranges of estimated WACCs for the two firms are as follows:

	Maximum WACC	Minimum WACC	Difference in Basis Points
Black & Decker	12.80%	8.50%	430
McDonald's	11.60%	9.30%	230

The range from minimum to maximum is large for both firms, and the economic impact is potentially stunning. To illustrate this, the present value of a level perpetual annual stream of $10 million would range between $78 million and $118 million for Black & Decker, and between $86 million and $108 million for McDonald's.

Given the positive but relatively flat slope of the yield curve in late 1995, most of the variation in our illustration is explained by beta and the equity market premium assumption. Variations can be even more dramatic, especially when the yield curve is inverted.

---

[16]Only two respondents (one advisor and one company) specifically cited forward-looking estimates, although others cited use of data from outside sources (e.g., a company using an estimate from an investment bank) where we cannot identify whether forward-looking estimates were used. Some studies using financial analyst forecasts in dividend growth models suggest market risk premiums average in the 6 to 6.5 percent range and change over time with higher premiums when interest rates decline. See for instance, Harris and Marston (1992). Ibbotson (1994) provides industry-specific cost-of-equity estimates using analysts' forecasts in a growth model.

V. RISK ADJUSTMENTS TO WACC

Finance theory is clear that a single WACC is appropriate only for investments of broadly comparable risk: A firm's overall WACC is a suitable benchmark for a firm's average risk investments. Finance theory goes on to say that such a company-specific figure should be adjusted for departures from such an average risk profile. Attracting capital requires payment of a premium that depends on risk.

We probed whether firms use a discount rate appropriate to the risks of the flows being valued in questions on types of investment (strategic vs. operational), terminal values, synergies, and multidivisional companies. Responses to these questions displayed in Exhibit 3 do not display much apparent alignment of practice. When financial advisers were asked how they value parts of multidivision firms, all 10 firms surveyed reported that they use different discount rates for component parts (item 17). However, only 26 percent of companies always adjust the cost of capital to reflect the risk of individual investment opportunities (item 12). Earlier studies (summarized in Gitman and Mercurio (1982) reported that between a third and a half of firms surveyed did *not* adjust for risk differences among capital projects. These practices stand in stark contrast to the recommendations of textbooks and trade books: The books did not explicitly address all subjects, but when they did, they were uniform in their advocacy of risk-adjusted discount rates.

A closer look at specific responses reveals the tensions as theory based on traded financial assets is adapted to decisions on investments in real assets. Inevitably, a fine line is drawn between use of financial market data versus managerial judgments. Responses from financial advisers illustrate this. As shown in Exhibit 2, all advisers use different capital costs for valuing parts (e.g., divisions) of a firm (item 17); only half ever select different rates for synergies or strategic opportunities (item 18); only 1 in 10 state any inclination to use different discount rates for terminal values and interim cash flows (item 16). Two simplistic interpretations are that (1) advisers ignore important risk differences or (2) material risk differences are rare in assessing factors such as terminal values. Neither of these fits; our conversations with advisers reveal that they recognize important risk differences but deal with them in a multitude of ways. Consider comments from two prominent investment banks who use different capital costs for valuing parts of multidivision firms. When asked about risk adjustments for prospective merger synergies, these same firms responded as follows:

- "We make these adjustments in cash flows and multiples rather than in discount rates."
- "Risk factors may be different for realizations of synergies, but we make adjustments to cash flows rather than the discount rate."

While financial advisers typically value existing companies, corporations face further challenges. They routinely must evaluate investments in new products and technologies. Moreover, they deal in an administrative setting that melds centralized (e.g., calculating a WACC) and decentralized (e.g., specific project appraisal) processes. As the next box of comments illustrates, these complexities lead to a blend of approaches for dealing with risk. A number of respondents mentioned specific rate adjustments to distinguish between divisional capital costs, international versus domestic investments, and leasing versus nonleasing situations. In other instances, however, these same respondents favored cash-flow adjustments to deal with risks.

Why do practitioners risk-adjust discount rates in one case and work with cash-flow adjustments in another? Our interpretation is that risk-adjusted discount rates are more likely used when the analyst can establish relatively objective financial market benchmarks for what rate adjustments should be. At the business (division) level, data on comparable companies provide cost-of-capital estimates. Debt markets provide surrogates for the risks in leasing cash flows. International financial markets shed insights on cross-country differences. When no such market benchmarks are available, practitioners look to other methods for dealing with risks. Lacking a good market analog from which to glean investor opinion (in the form of differing capital costs), the analyst is forced to rely more on internal focus. Practical implementation of risk-adjusted discount rates thus appears to depend on the ability to find traded financial assets that are comparable in risk to the cash flows being valued and then to have financial data on these traded assets.

Comments Regarding Adjustments for Project Risk

When asked whether they adjusted discount rates for project risk, companies provided a wide range of responses:

- "No, it's difficult to draw lines between the various businesses we invest in, and we also try as best we can to make adjustments for risk in cash-flow projections rather than in cost of capital factors. . . . We advocate minimizing adjustments to cost of capital calculations and maximizing understanding of all relevant issues (e.g., commodity costs and international/ political risks)." At another point the same firm noted that "for lease analysis only the cost of debt is used."
- "No [we don't risk adjust cost of capital]. We believe there are two basic components: (1) projected cash flows, which should incorporate investment risk, and (2) discount rate." The same firm noted, however, "For international investments, the discount rate is adjusted for country risk." and "For large acquisitions, the company takes significantly greater care to estimate an accurate cost of capital."
- "No, but use divisional costs of capital to calculate a weighted average company cost of capital . . . for comparison and possible adjustment."
- "Yes, we have calculated a cost of capital for divisions based on pure play betas and also suggest subjective adjustments based on each project. Our feeling is that use of divisional costs is the most frequent distinction in the company."
- "Rarely, but at least on one occasion we have, for a whole new line of business."
- "We do sensitivity analysis on every project."
- "For the most part we make risk adjustments qualitatively; i.e., we use the corporate WACC to evaluate a project, but then interpret the result according to the risk of the proposal being studied. This could mean that a risky project will be rejected even though it meets the corporate hurdle rate objectives."
- "No domestically; yes internationally—we assess a risk premium per country and adjust the cost of capital accordingly."

The pragmatic bent of application also comes to the fore when companies are asked how often they reestimate capital costs (item 13, Exhibit 2). Even for those firms that reestimate relatively frequently, the next box of comments shows that they draw an important distinction between estimating capital costs and policy changes about the capital cost figure used in the firm's decision making.

Firms consider administrative costs in structuring their policies on capital costs. For a very large venture (e.g., an acquisition), capital costs may be revisited each time. On the other hand, only large material changes in costs may be fed into more formal project evaluation systems. Firms also recognize a certain ambiguity in any cost number and are willing to live with approximations. While the bond market reacts to minute basis-point changes in investor return requirements, investments in real assets, where the decision process itself is time-consuming and often decentralized, involve much less precision. To paraphrase one of our sample companies, we use capital costs as a rough yardstick rather than the last word in project evaluation.

Our interpretation is that the mixed responses to questions about risk adjusting and reestimating discount rates reflect an often sophisticated set of practical trade-offs; these involve the size of risk differences, the quality of information from financial markets, and the realities of administrative costs and processes. In cases where there are material differences in perceived risk, a sufficient scale of investment to justify the effort, no large scale administrative complexities, and readily identifiable information from financial markets, practitioners employ risk adjustments to rates quite routinely. Acquisitions, valuing divisions of companies, analysis of foreign versus domestic investments, and leasing versus nonleasing decisions were frequently cited examples. In contrast, when one or more of these factors is not present, practitioners are more likely to employ other means to deal with risks.

Comments Regarding Reestimating WACC

How frequently do you reestimate your company's cost of capital? Here are responses from best-practice companies:

- "We usually review it quarterly but would review more frequently if market rates changed enough to warrant the review. We would only announce a change in the rate if the recomputed number was materially different than the one currently being used."
- "We reestimate it once or twice a year, but we rarely change the number that the business units use for decision and planning purposes. We expect the actual rate to vary over time, but we also expect that average to be fairly constant over the business cycle. Thus, we tend to maintain a steady discount rate within the company over time."
- "Usually every six months, except in case of very large investments, in which it is reestimated for each analysis."
- "Whenever we need to, such as for an acquisition or big investment proposal."
- "Reevaluate as needed (e.g., for major tax changes), but unless the cost of capital change is significant (a jump to 21 percent, for instance), our cutoff rate is not changed; it is used as a *yardstick* rather than the last word in project evaluation."
- "Probably need a 100-basis-point change to publish a change. We report only to the nearest percent."

VI. CONCLUSIONS

Our research sought to identify the "best practice" in cost-of-capital estimation through interviews of leading corporations and financial advisers. Given the huge annual expenditure on capital projects and corporate acquisitions each year, the wise selection of discount rates is of material importance to senior corporate managers.

The survey revealed broad acceptance of the WACC as the basis for setting discount rates. In addition, the survey revealed general alignment in many aspects of the estimation of WACC. The main area of notable disagreement was in the details of implementing the capital asset pricing model (CAPM) to estimate the cost of equity. This paper outlined the varieties of practice in CAPM use, the arguments in favor of different approaches, and the practical implications.

In summary, we believe that the following elements represent "best current practice" in the estimation of WACC:

- Weights should be based on *market-value* mixes of debt and equity.
- The after-tax cost of debt should be estimated from *marginal* pretax costs, combined with *marginal* or *statutory* tax rates.
- CAPM is currently the preferred model for estimating the cost of equity.
- Betas are drawn substantially from published sources, preferring those betas using a long interval of equity returns. Where a number of statistical publishers disagree, best practice often involves judgment to estimate a beta.
- Risk-free rate should match the tenor of the cash flows being valued. For most capital projects and corporate acquisitions, the yield on the U.S. government Treasury bond of 10 or more years in maturity would be appropriate.
- Choice of an equity market risk premium is the subject of considerable controversy both as to its value and method of estimation. Most of our best-practice companies use a premium of 6 percent or lower, while many texts and financial advisers use higher figures.
- Monitoring for changes in WACC should be keyed to major changes in financial market conditions, but should be done at least annually. Actually flowing a change through a corporate system of project valuation and compensation targets must be done gingerly and only when there are material changes.
- WACC should be risk adjusted to reflect substantive differences among different businesses in a corporation. For instance, financial advisers generally find the corporate WACC to be inappropriate for valuing different parts of a corporation. Given publicly traded companies in different businesses, such risk adjustment involves only modest revision in the WACC and CAPM approaches already used. Corporations also cite the need to adjust capital costs across national boundaries. In situations where market proxies for a particular type of risk class are not available, best practice involves finding other means to account for risk differences.

Best practice is largely consistent with finance theory. Despite broad agreement at the theoretical level, however, there remain several problems in application that can lead to wide divergence in estimated capital costs. Based on these remaining problems, we believe that further applied research on two principal topics is warranted. First, practitioners need additional tools for sharpening their assessment of relative risk. The variation in company-specific beta estimates from different published sources can create large differences in capital cost estimates. Moreover, use of risk-adjusted discount rates appears limited by lack of good market proxies for different risk profiles. We believe that appropriate use of averages across industry or other risk categories is an avenue worth exploration. Second, practitioners could benefit from further research on estimating equity market risk premiums. Current practice displays large variations and focuses primarily on averaging past data. Use of expectational data appears to be a fruitful approach. As the next generation of theories gradually sharpen our insights, we feel that research attention to implementation of existing theory can make for real improvements in practice.

Finally, our research is a reminder of the old saying that too often in business we measure with a micrometer, mark with a pencil, and cut with an ax. Despite the many advances in finance theory, the particular "ax" available for estimating company capital costs remains a blunt one. Best-practice companies can expect to estimate their weighted-average cost of capital with an accuracy of no more than plus or minus 100 to 150 basis points. This has important implications for how managers use the cost of capital in decision making. First, do not mistake capital budgeting for bond pricing. Despite the tools available, effective capital appraisal continues to require thorough knowledge of the business and wise business judgment. Second, be careful not to throw out the baby with the bath water. Do not reject the cost of capital and attendant advances in financial management because your finance people are not able to give you a precise number. When in need, even a blunt ax is better than nothing.

REFERENCES

Aggarwal, Raj. "Corporate Use of Sophisticated Capital Budgeting Techniques: A Strategic Perspective and a Critique of Survey Results." *Interfaces* 10, no. 2 (April 1980), pp. 31–34.

Bierman, Harold J. "Capital Budgeting in 1992: A Survey." *Financial Management* 22, no. 3 (Autumn 1993), p. 24.

Brealey, Richard, and Stewart Myers. *Principles of Corporate Finance*. 4th ed. New York: McGraw-Hill, 1991.

Brigham, Eugene, and Louis Gapenski. *Financial Management, Theory and Practice*. 6th ed. Chicago: Dryden Press, 1991.

Carleton, Willard T., and Josef Lakonishok. "Risk and Return on Equity: The Use and Misuse of Historical Estimates." *Financial Analysts Journal* 4, no. 1 (January–February 1985), pp. 38–48.

Copeland, Tom; Tim Koller; and Jack Murrin. *Valuation: Measuring and Managing the Value of Companies*. 2nd ed. New York: John Wiley & Sons, 1994.

Dixit, Avinash K., and Robert S. Pindyck. *Investment under Uncertainty*. Princeton, NJ: Princeton University Press, 1993.

———. "The Options Approach to Capital Investment." *Harvard Business Review* 73, no. 3 (May–June 1995), pp. 105–15.

Ehrhardt, Michael. *The Search for Value: Measuring the Company's Cost of Capital*. Boston: HBS Press, 1994.

Fama, Eugene F., and Kenneth R. French. "Dividend Yields and Expected Stock Returns." *Journal of Financial Economics* 22, no. 1 (October 1986), pp. 3–25.

Gitman, Lawrence J. *Principles of Managerial Finance*. 6th ed. New York: HarperCollins, 1991.

Gitman, Lawrence J., and John R. Forrester, Jr. "A Survey of Capital Budgeting Techniques Used by Major U.S. Firms." *Financial Management* 6, no. 3 (Fall 1977), pp. 66–71.

Gitman, Lawrence J., and Vincent Mercurio. "Cost of Capital Techniques Used by Major U.S. Firms: Survey and Analysis of Fortune's 1000." *Financial Management* 11, no. 4 (Winter 1982), pp. 21–29.

Harris, Robert S., and Felicia C. Marston. "Estimating Shareholder Risk Premia Using Analysts' Growth Forecasts." *Financial Management* 21, no. 2 (Summer 1992), pp. 63–70.

Ibbotson Associates. *1995 Yearbook: Stocks, Bonds, Bills, and Inflation.* Chicago: Author, 1995.

———. *1994 Yearbook: Cost of Capital Quarterly.* Chicago: Author, October 1994.

Jagannathan, Ravi, and Ellen R. McGrattan. "The CAPM Debate." *The Federal Reserve Bank of Minneapolis Quarterly Review* 19, no. 4 (Fall 1995), pp. 2–17.

Kaplan, Steven N., and Richard S. Ruback. "The Valuation of Cash Flow Forecasts: An Empirical Analysis." *Journal of Finance* 50, no. 4 (September 1995), pp. 1059–93.

Kritzman, Mark. "What Practitioners Need to Know . . . About Future Value." *Financial Analysts Journal* 50, no. 3 (May–June 1994), pp. 12–15.

Lo, Andrew W., and A. Craig MacKinlay. "Stock Market Prices Do Not Follow Random Walks: Evidence from a Simple Specification Test." *Review of Financial Studies* 1, no. 1 (Spring 1988), pp. 41–46.

Moore, James S., and Alan K. Reichert. "An Analysis of the Financial Management Techniques Currently Employed by Large U.S. Companies." *Journal of Business Finance and Accounting* 10, no. 4 (Winter 1983), pp. 623–45.

Poterba, James M., and Lawrence H. Summers. "A CEO Survey of U.S. Companies' Time Horizons and Hurdle Rates." *Sloan Management Review* 37, no. 1 (Fall 1995), pp. 43–53.

———. "Mean Reversion in Stock Prices: Evidence and Implications." *Journal of Financial Economics* 22, no. 1 (October 1988), pp. 27–59.

Ross, Stephen; Randolph Westerfield; and Jeffrey Jaffe. *Corporate Finance* 4th ed. Chicago: Irwin, 1996.

Schall, Lawrence D.; Gary L. Sundem; and William R. Geijsbeek, Jr. "Survey and Analysis of Capital Budgeting Methods." *Journal of Finance* 33, no. 1 (March 1978), pp. 281–92.

Siegel, Jeremy J. "The Equity Premium: Stock and Bond Returns Since 1802." *Financial Analysts Journal* 48, no. 1 (January–February 1992), pp. 28–46.

Trahan, Emery A., and Lawrence J. Gitman. "Bridging the Theory-Practice Gap in Corporate Finance: A Survey of Chief Financial Officers." *Quarterly Review of Economics & Finance* 35, no. 1 (Spring 1995), pp. 73–87.

EXHIBIT 1
Three Survey Samples

Company Sample	Adviser Sample	Textbook/Trade Book Sample
Advanced Micro Devices	CS First Boston	Textbooks
Allergan	Dillon, Read	Brealey and Myers
Black & Decker	Donaldson, Lufkin, Jenrette	Brigham and Gapenski
Cellular One	J. P. Morgan	Gitman
Chevron	Lehman Brothers	Ross, Westerfield & Jaffe
Colgate-Palmolive	Merrill Lynch	Trade Books
Comdisco	Morgan Stanley	Copeland, Koller & Murrin
Compaq	Salomon	Ehrhardt
Eastman Kodak	Smith Barney	Ibbotson Associates
Gillette	Wasserstein Perella	
Guardian Industries		
Henkel		
Hewlett-Packard		
Kanthal		
Lawson Mardon		
McDonald's		
Merck		
Monsanto		
PepsiCo		
Quaker Oats		
Schering-Plough		
Tandem		
Union Carbide		
U.S. West		
Walt Disney		
Weyerhauser		
Whirlpool		

Note: For the full titles of textbooks and trade books, please see the preceding list of references.

EXHIBIT 2
General Survey Results

	Corporations	Financial Advisers	Textbooks/Trade Books
1. Do you use DCF techniques to evaluate investment opportunities?	89% Yes, as a primary tool 7% Yes, only as a secondary tool 4% No	100% rely on DCF, comparable companies multiples, comparable transactions multiples. Of these, 10% DCF is primary tool. 10% DCF is used mainly "as a check." 80% Weight the three approaches depending on purpose and type of analysis.	100% Yes
2. Do you use any form of a cost of capital as your discount rate in your DCF analysis?	89% Yes 7% Sometimes 4% N/A	100% Yes	100% Yes
3. For your cost of capital, do you form any combination of capital cost to determine a WACC?	85% Yes 4% Sometimes 4% No 7% N/A	100% Yes	100% Yes

4. What weighting factors do you use?
a. target vs. current debt/equity?
b. market vs. book weights?
	Target/Current
	             Market/Book
	52% Target 59% Market
	15% Current 15% Book
	26% Uncertain 19% Uncertain
	7% N/A 7% N/A
		Target/Current
		             Market/Book
		90% Target 90% Market
		10% Current 10% Book
			Target/Current
			             Market/Book
			86% Target
			           100% Market
			14% Current/Target

5. How do you estimate your before tax cost of debt?	52% Marginal cost 37% Current average 4% Uncertain 7% N/A	60% Marginal cost 40% Current average	71% Marginal cost 29% No explicit recommendation
6. What tax rate do you use?	52% Marginal or statutory 37% Average historical 4% Uncertain 7% N/A	60% Marginal or statutory 30% Average historical 10% Uncertain	71% Marginal or statutory 29% No explicit recommendation
7. How do you estimate your cost of equity? (If you do not use CAPM, skip to question 12).	81% CAPM 4% Modified CAPM 15% N/A	80% CAPM 20% Other (including modified CAPM)	100% Primarily CAPM Other methods mentioned: dividend-growth model arbitrage pricing model
8. As usually written, the CAPM version of the cost of equity has three terms: a risk-free rate, a volatility or beta factor, and a market risk premium. Is this consistent with your company's approach?	85% Yes 0% No 15% N/A	90% Yes 10% N/A	100% Yes

EXHIBIT 2 *(continued)*

	Corporations	Financial Advisers	Textbooks/Trade Books
9. What do you use for the risk-free rate?	4% 90-day T-bill 7% 3–7 year Treasuries 33% 10-year Treasuries 4% 20-year Treasuries 33% 10–30 year Treasuries 4% 10 yrs. or 90-day; depends 15% N/A (Many said they match the term of the risk-free rate to the tenor of the investment)	10% 90-day T-bill 10% 5–10 year Treasuries 30% 10–30 year Treasuries 40% 30-year Treasuries 10% N/A	43% T-bills 29% LT Treasuries 14% Match tenor of investment 14% Don't say
10. What do you use as your volatility or beta factor?	52% Published source 3% Financial adviser's estimate 30% Self-calculated 15% N/A	30% Fundamental beta (e.g., BARRA) 40% Published source 20% Self-calculated 10% N/A	100% mention availability of published sources
11. What do you use as your market risk premium?	11% Use fixed rate of 4–4.5% 37% Use fixed rate of 5–6% 4% Use geometric mean 4% Use arithmetic mean 4% Use average of historical and implied 15% Use financial adviser's estimate 7% Use premium over Treasuries 3% Use Value Line estimate 15% N/A	10% Use fixed rate of 5% 50% Use 7–7.4% (Similar to arithmetic) 10% LT arithmetic mean 10% Both LT arithmetic and geometric mean 10% spread above Treasuries 10% N/A	71% Arithmetic historical mean 15% Geometric historical mean 14% Don't say
12. Having estimated your company's cost of capital, do you make any further adjustments to reflect the risk of individual investment opportunities?	26% Yes 33% Sometimes 41% No	Not asked	86% Adjust beta for investment risk 14% Don't say
13. How frequently do you reestimate your company's cost of capital?	4% Monthly 19% Quarterly 11% Semiannually 37% Annually 7% Continually/every investment 19% Infrequently 4% N/A (Generally, many said that in addition to scheduled reviews, they reestimate as needed for significant events such as acquisitions and high-impact economic events)	Not asked	100% No explicit recommendation
14. Is the cost of capital used for purposes other than project analysis in your	51% Yes 44% No 4% N/A	Not asked	100% No explicit discussion

EXHIBIT 2 *(concluded)*

	Corporations	Financial Advisers	Textbooks/Trade Books
company? (For example, to evaluate divisional performance?)			
15. Do you distinguish between strategic and operational investments? Is cost of capital used differently in these two categories?	48% Yes 48% No 4% N/A	Not asked	29% Yes 71% No explicit discussion
16. What methods do you use to estimate terminal value? Do you use the same discount rate for the terminal value as for the interim cash flows?	Not asked	30% Exit multiples only 70% Both multiples and perpetuity DCF model 70% Use same WACC for TV 20% No response 10% Rarely change	71% Perpetuity DCF model 29% No explicit discussion 100% No explicit discussion of separate WACC for terminal value
17. In valuing a multidivisional company, do you aggregate the values of the individual divisions, or just value the firm as a whole? If you value each division separately, do you use a different cost of capital for each one?	Not asked	100% Value the parts 100% Use different WACCs for separate valuations	100%: Use distinct WACC for each division
18. In your valuations do you use any different methods to value synergies or strategic opportunities (e.g., higher or lower discount rates, options valuation)?	Not asked	30% Yes 50% No 20% Rarely	29%: Use distinct WACC for synergies 71% No explicit discussion
19. Do you make any adjustments to the risk premium for changes in market conditions?	Not asked	20% Yes 70% No 10% N/A	14% Yes 86% No explicit discussion
20. How long have you been with the company? What is your job title?	Mean: 10 years All senior, except one	Mean: 7.3 years 4 MDs, 2 VPs, 4 associates	N/A

EXHIBIT 3
Betas for Corporate Survey Respondents

	Bloomberg Betas		Value Line Betas	S&P Betas	Range Maximum–Minimum
	Raw	Adjusted			
Advanced Micro	1.20	1.13	1.70	1.47	0.57
Allergan	0.94	0.96	1.30	1.36	0.42
Black & Decker	1.06	1.04	1.65	1.78	0.74
Cellular One			Not listed		
Chevron	0.70	0.80	0.70	0.68	0.12
Colgate-Palmolive	1.11	1.07	1.20	0.87	0.33
Comdisco	1.50	1.34	1.35	1.20	0.30
Compaq Computer	1.26	1.18	1.50	1.55	0.37
Eastman Kodak	0.54	0.69	NMF	0.37	0.32
Gillette	0.93	0.95	1.25	1.30	0.37
Guardian Industries			Not listed		
Henkel			Not listed		
Hewlett-Packard	1.34	1.22	1.40	1.96	0.74
Kanthal			Not listed		
Lawson Mardon			Not listed		
McDonald's	0.93	0.96	1.05	1.09	0.16
Merck	0.73	0.82	1.10	1.15	0.42
Monsanto	0.89	0.93	1.10	1.36	0.47
PepsiCo	1.12	1.08	1.10	1.19	0.11
Quaker Oats	1.38	1.26	0.90	0.67	0.71
Schering-Plough	0.51	0.67	1.00	0.82	0.49
Tandem Computers	1.35	1.23	1.75	1.59	0.52
Union Carbide	1.51	1.34	1.30	0.94	0.57
U.S. West	0.61	0.74	0.75	0.53	0.22
Walt Disney	1.42	1.28	1.15	1.22	0.27
Weyerhauser	0.78	0.85	1.20	1.21	0.43
Whirlpool	0.90	0.93	1.55	1.58	0.68
Mean	1.03	1.02	1.24	1.18	0.42
Median	1.00	1.00	1.20	1.21	0.42
Standard deviation	0.31	0.21	0.29	0.41	0.19

Note:
1. Bloomberg's adjusted beta is $\beta_{adj} = (.66)\beta_{raw} + (.33)1.00$

EXHIBIT 4

Variations in Cost-of-Capital (WACC) Estimates for Black & Decker Using Different Methods of Implementing the Capital Asset Pricing Model[*]

1. Short-term rate plus arithmetic average historical risk premium (recommended by some texts)
   R_f = 5.36%, 90-day T-bills
   $R_m - R_f$ = 8.50%, Ibbotson arithmetic average since 1926

Beta Service	Cost of Equity (K_e)	Cost of Capital (WACC)
Bloomberg, β = 1.06	14.40%	9.70%
Value Line, β = 1.65	19.40%	12.20%
S&P, β = 1.78	20.50%	12.80%

2. Long-term rate plus risk premium of 7.20% ("modal" practice of financial advisers surveyed)
   R_f = 6.26%, 30-year T-bonds
   $R_m - R_f$ = 7.20%, modal response of financial advisers

Beta Service	Cost of Equity (K_e)	Cost of Capital (WACC)
Bloomberg, β = 1.06	13.90%	9.40%
Value Line, β = 1.65	18.10%	11.60%
S&P, β = 1.78	19.10%	12.10%

3. Long-term rate plus risk premium of 5.50% ("modal" practice of corporations surveyed)
   R_f = 6.26%, 30-year T-bonds
   $R_m - R_f$ = 5.50%, modal response of corporations

Beta Service	Cost of Equity (K_e)	Cost of Capital (WACC)
Bloomberg, β = 1.06	12.10%	8.50%
Value Line, β = 1.65	15.30%	10.20%
S&P, β = 1.78	16.10%	10.50%

[*]In all cases the CAPM is used to estimate the cost of equity, the cost of debt is assumed to be 7.81 percent based on a Baa rating, the tax rate is assumed to be 38 percent, and debt is assumed to represent 49 percent of capital.

Nike, Inc.: Cost of Capital

On July 5, 2001, Kimi Ford, a portfolio manager at NorthPoint Group, a mutual-fund-management firm, pored over analysts' write-ups of Nike, Inc., the athletic-shoe manufacturer. Nike's share price had declined significantly from the start of the year. Ford was considering buying some shares for the fund she managed, the NorthPoint Large-Cap Fund, which invested mostly in Fortune 500 companies, with an emphasis on value investing. Its top holdings included ExxonMobil, General Motors, McDonald's, 3M, and other large-cap, generally old-economy stocks. While the stock market had declined over the last 18 months, NorthPoint Large-Cap had performed extremely well. In 2000, the fund earned a return of 20.7 percent even as the S&P 500 fell 10.1 percent. The fund's year-to-date returns at the end of June 2001 stood at 6.4 percent versus the S&P 500's −7.3 percent.

Only a week ago, on June 28, 2001, Nike held an analysts' meeting to disclose its fiscal-year 2001 results.[1] The meeting, however, had another purpose: Nike management wanted to communicate a strategy for revitalizing the company. Since 1997, Nike's revenues had plateaued at around $9 billion, while net income had fallen from almost $800 million to $580 million (see **Exhibit 1**). Nike's market share in U.S. athletic shoes had fallen from 48 percent in 1997 to 42 percent in 2000.[2] In addition, recent supply-chain issues and the adverse effect of a strong dollar had negatively affected revenue.

---

[1]Nike's fiscal year ended in May.

[2]Douglas Robson, "Just Do . . . Something: Nike's Insularity and Foot-Dragging Have It Running in Place," *Business Week,* July 2, 2001.

At the meeting, management revealed plans to address both top-line growth and operating performance. To boost revenue, the company would develop more athletic-shoe products in the midpriced segment[3]—a segment that it had overlooked in recent years. Nike also planned to push its apparel line, which, under the recent leadership of industry veteran Mindy Grossman[4] had performed extremely well. On the cost side, Nike would exert more effort on expense control. Finally, company executives reiterated their long-term revenue-growth targets of 8–10 percent and earnings-growth targets of above 15 percent.

Analysts' reactions were mixed. Some thought the financial targets too aggressive; others saw significant growth opportunities in apparel and in Nike's international businesses.

Ford read all the analysts' reports that she could find about the June 28 meeting, but the reports gave her no clear guidance: a Lehman Brothers report recommended a "Strong Buy," while UBS Warburg and CSFB analysts expressed misgivings about the company and recommended a "Hold." Ford decided instead to develop her own discounted-cash-flow forecast to come to a clearer conclusion.

Her forecast showed that, at a discount rate of 10 percent, Nike was overvalued at its current share price of $42.09 (see **Exhibit 2**). She had, however, done a quick sensitivity analysis that revealed Nike was *under* valued at discount rates below 9.4 percent. As she was about to go into a meeting, she asked her new assistant, Joanna Cohen, to estimate Nike's cost of capital.

Cohen immediately gathered all the data she thought she might need **(Exhibits 1, 2, 3, and 4)** and began to work on her analysis. At the end of the day, she submitted her cost-of-capital estimate and a memo **(Exhibit 5)** explaining her assumptions to Ford.

---

[3]Sneakers in this segment sold for $70–$90 a pair.
[4]Mindy Grossman joined Nike in September 2000. She was the former president and chief executive of Jones Apparel Group's Polo Jeans Division.

EXHIBIT 1
Consolidated Income Statements

Year Ended May 31 (in millions except per share data)	1995	1996	1997	1998	1999	2000	2001
Revenues	4,760.8	6,470.6	9,186.5	9,553.1	8,776.9	8,995.1	9,488.8
Cost of goods sold	2,865.3	3,906.7	5,503.0	6,065.5	5,493.5	5,403.8	5,784.9
Gross profit	**1,895.6**	**2,563.9**	**3,683.5**	**3,487.6**	**3,283.4**	**3,591.3**	**3,703.9**
Selling and administrative	1,209.8	1,588.6	2,303.7	2,623.8	2,426.6	2,606.4	2,689.7
Operating income	**685.8**	**975.3**	**1,379.8**	**863.8**	**856.8**	**984.9**	**1,014.2**
Interest expense	24.2	39.5	52.3	60.0	44.1	45.0	58.7
Other expense, net	11.7	36.7	32.3	20.9	21.5	23.2	34.1
Restructuring charge, net	—	—	—	129.9	45.1	(2.5)	—
Income before income taxes	**649.9**	**899.1**	**1,295.2**	**653.0**	**746.1**	**919.2**	**921.4**
Income taxes	250.2	345.9	499.4	253.4	294.7	340.1	331.7
Net income	**399.7**	**553.2**	**795.8**	**399.6**	**451.4**	**579.1**	**589.7**
Diluted earnings per common share	1.36	1.88	2.68	1.35	1.57	2.07	2.16
Average shares outstanding (diluted)	294.0	293.6	297.0	296.0	287.5	279.8	273.3
Growth (%)							
Revenue		35.9	42.0	4.0	(8.1)	2.5	5.5
Operating income		42.2	41.5	(37.4)	(0.8)	15.0	3.0
Net income		38.4	43.9	(49.8)	13.0	28.3	1.8
Margins (%)							
Gross margin		39.6	40.1	36.5	37.4	39.9	39.0
Operating margin		15.1	15.0	9.0	9.8	10.9	10.7
Net margin		8.5	8.7	4.2	5.1	6.4	6.2
Effective tax rate (%)[*]		38.5	38.6	38.8	39.5	37.0	36.0

[*]The U.S. statutory tax rate was 35%. The state tax varied yearly from 2.5% to 3.5%.
Source: Company's 10-K SEC filing, UBS Warburg.

EXHIBIT 2
Discounted-Cash-Flow Analysis

	2002	2003	2004	2005	2006	2007	2008	2009	2010	2011
Assumptions:										
Revenue growth (%)	7.0	6.5	6.5	6.5	6.0	6.0	6.0	6.0	6.0	6.0
COGS/Sales (%)	60.0	60.0	59.5	59.5	59.0	59.0	58.5	58.5	58.0	58.0
S&A/Sales (%)	28.0	27.5	27.0	26.5	26.0	25.5	25.0	25.0	25.0	25.0
Tax rate (%)	38.0	38.0	38.0	38.0	38.0	38.0	38.0	38.0	38.0	38.0
Current assets/Sales (%)	38.0	38.0	38.0	38.0	38.0	38.0	38.0	38.0	38.0	38.0
Current liabilities/Sales (%)	11.5	11.5	11.5	11.5	11.5	11.5	11.5	11.5	11.5	11.5
Yearly depreciation equals capex.										
Cost of capital (%)	10.0									
Terminal growth rate (%)	5.0									
Discounted Cash Flow										
Operating income	1,218.4	1,351.6	1,554.6	1,717.0	1,950.0	2,135.9	2,410.2	2,554.8	2,790.1	2,957.5
Taxes	463.0	513.6	590.8	652.5	741.0	811.7	915.9	970.8	1,060.2	1,123.9
NOPAT	755.4	838.0	963.9	1,064.5	1,209.0	1,324.3	1,494.3	1,584.0	1,729.9	1,833.7
Capex, net of depreciation	—	—	—	—	—	—	—	—	—	—
Change in NWC	8.8	(174.9)	(186.3)	(198.4)	(195.0)	(206.7)	(219.1)	(232.3)	(246.2)	(261.0)
Free cash flow	764.1	663.1	777.6	866.2	1,014.0	1,117.6	1,275.2	1,351.7	1,483.7	1,572.7
Terminal value										12,733.3
Total flows	764.1	663.1	777.6	866.2	1,014.0	1,117.6	1,275.2	1,351.7	1,483.7	14,306.0
Present value of flows	694.7	548.0	584.2	591.6	629.6	630.8	654.4	630.6	629.2	5,515.6

Enterprise value	11,108.8
Less: current outstanding debt	1,296.6
Equity value	9,812.2
Current shares outstanding	271.5
Equity value per share	$ 36.14

Current share price: $ 42.09

Sensitivity of equity value to discount rate:	
Discount rate	**Equity value**
8.00%	$ 64.02
8.50	53.87
9.00	46.38
9.36	**42.09**
9.50	40.65
10.00	36.14
10.50	32.51
11.00	29.53
11.50	27.04
12.00	24.93

EXHIBIT 3
Consolidated Balance Sheets (in millions)

	May 31,	
	2000	2001
Assets		
Current assets:		
Cash and equivalents	$ 254.3	$ 304.0
Accounts receivable	1,569.4	1,621.4
Inventories	1,446.0	1,424.1
Deferred income taxes	111.5	113.3
Prepaid expenses	215.2	162.5
Total current assets	3,596.4	3,625.3
Property, plant and equipment, net	1,583.4	1,618.8
Identifiable intangible assets and goodwill, net	410.9	397.3
Deferred income taxes and other assets	266.2	178.2
Total assets	**$ 5,856.9**	**$ 5,819.6**
Liabilities and shareholders' equity		
Current Liabilities:		
Current portion of long-term debt	$ 50.1	$ 5.4
Notes payable	924.2	855.3₁
Accounts payable	543.8	432.0
Accrued liabilities	621.9	472.1
Income taxes payable	—	21.9
Total current liabilities	2,140.0	1,786.7
Long-term debt	470.3	435.9₁
Deferred income taxes and other liabilities	110.3	102.2
Redeemable preferred stock	0.3	0.3
Shareholders' equity:		
Common stock, par	2.8	2.8
Capital in excess of stated value	369.0	459.4
Unearned stock compensation	(11.7)	(9.9)
Accumulated other comprehensive income	(111.1)	(152.1)
Retained earnings	2,887.0	3,194.3
Total shareholders' equity	3,136.0	3,494.5
Total liabilities and shareholders' equity	**$ 5,856.9**	**$ 5,819.6**

Source: Company 10-K SEC filing.

EXHIBIT 4
Capital Market and Financial Information on or around July 5, 2001

Nike Share Price Performance Relative to S&P500:
January 2000 to July 5, 2001

Legend: —— Nike ········· S&P 500

Current yields on U.S. Treasuries

3-month	3.59%
6-month	3.59
1-year	3.59
5-year	4.88
10-year	5.39
20-year	5.74

Historical Equity Risk Premiums (1926–1999)

Geometric mean	5.90%
Arithmetic mean	7.50%

Current Yield on Publicly Traded Nike Debt*

Coupon	6.75% paid semiannually
Issued	07/15/96
Maturity	07/15/21
Current Price	$ 95.60

Nike Historic Betas

1996	0.98
1997	0.84
1998	0.84
1999	0.63
2000	0.83
YTD 06/30/00	0.69
Average	0.80

Consensus EPS estimates:

FY 2002	FY 2003
$2.32	$2.67

Nike share price on July 5, 2001: $ 42.09

Dividend History and Forecasts

Payment Dates	31-Mar	30-Jun	30-Sep	31-Dec	Total
1997	0.10	0.10	0.10	0.10	0.40
1998	0.12	0.12	0.12	0.12	0.48
1999	0.12	0.12	0.12	0.12	0.48
2000	0.12	0.12	0.12	0.12	0.48
2001	0.12				

Value Line Forecast of Dividend Growth from 1998–00 to 2004–06:
5.50%

*Data have been modified for teaching purposes.

Sources of data: Bloomberg Financial Services, Ibbotson Associates Yearbook 1999, Value Line Investment Survey, IBES.

EXHIBIT 5
Joanna Cohen's Analysis

TO: Kimi Ford
FROM: Joanna Cohen
DATE: July 6, 2001

SUBJECT: Nike's Cost of Capital

Based on the following assumptions, my estimate of Nike's cost of capital is 8.3 percent:

I. Single or Multiple Costs of Capital?

The first question I considered was whether to use single or multiple costs of capital given that Nike has multiple business segments. Aside from footwear, which makes up 62 percent of revenue, Nike also sells apparel (30 percent of revenue) that complement its footwear products. In addition, Nike sells sport balls, timepieces, eyewear, skates, bats, and other equipment designed for sports activities. Equipment products account for 3.6 percent of revenue. Finally, Nike also sells some non-Nike branded products such as Cole-Haan dress and casual footwear, and ice skates, skate blades, hockey sticks, hockey jerseys and other products under the Bauer trademark. Non-Nike brands account for 4.5 percent of revenue.

I asked myself whether Nike's business segments had different enough risks from each other to warrant different costs of capital. Were their profiles really different? I concluded that it was only the Cole-Haan line that was somewhat different; the rest were all sports-related businesses. However, since Cole-Haan makes up only a tiny fraction of revenues, I did not think it necessary to compute a separate cost of capital. As for the apparel and footwear lines, they are sold through the same marketing and distribution channels and are often marketed in "collections" of similar design. I believe they face the same risk factors, as such, I decided to compute only one cost of capital for the whole company.

II. Methodology for Calculating the Cost of Capital: WACC

Since Nike is funded with both debt and equity, I used the Weighted Average Cost of Capital (WACC) method. Based on the latest available balance sheet, debt as a proportion of total capital makes up 27.0 percent and equity accounts for 73.0 percent:

Capital sources	Book Values	
Debt		
Notes payable	$ 855.3	
Long-term debt	435.9	
	$1,291.2	→ 27.0% of total capital
Equity	$3,494.5	→ 72.0% of total capital

III. Cost of Debt

My estimate of Nike's cost of debt is 4.3 percent. I arrived at this estimate by taking total interest expense for the year 2001 and dividing it by the company's average debt balance.[1] The rate is lower than Treasury

---

[1]Debt balances as of May 31, 2000, and 2001, were $1,444.6 and $1,291.2, respectively.

yields but that is because Nike raised a portion of its funding needs through Japanese yen notes, which carry rates between 2.0 percent to 4.3 percent.

After adjusting for tax, the cost of debt comes out to 2.7 percent. I used a tax rate of 38 percent, which I obtained by adding state taxes of 3 percent to the U.S. statutory tax rate. Historically, Nike's state taxes have ranged from 2.5 percent to 3.5 percent.

IV. Cost of Equity

I estimated the cost of equity using the Capital Asset Pricing Model (CAPM). Other methods such as the Dividend Discount Model (DDM) and the Earnings Capitalization Ratio can be used to estimate the cost of equity. However, in my opinion, the CAPM is the superior method.

My estimate of Nike's cost of equity is 10.5 percent. I used the current yield on 20-year Treasury bonds as my risk-free rate, and the compound average premium of the market over Treasury bonds (5.9 percent) as my risk premium. For beta, I took the average of Nike's beta from 1996 to the present.

V. Putting it All Together

Inputting all my assumptions into the WACC formula, my estimate of Nike's cost of capital is 8.3 percent.

$$
\begin{aligned}
\text{WACC} &= K_d\,(1 - t) * D/(D + E) + K_e \quad * E/(D + E) \\
&= 2.7\% \qquad * 27.0\% \qquad + 10.5\% * 72.0\% \\
&= 8.3\%
\end{aligned}
$$

Coke versus Pepsi, 2001

On December 4, 2000, PepsiCo, Inc., and the Quaker Oats Company issued a joint press release announcing their merger. The terms of the merger stated that PepsiCo would acquire Quaker Oats in a stock-for-stock deal valuing Quaker at around $14 billion.

Judging by the share-price reactions to the announcement, observers viewed the deal as yet another setback for Coca-Cola. By acquiring Quaker Oats, PepsiCo would gain access to Gatorade and control *83.6 percent* of the sports-drink market. PepsiCo already pos-

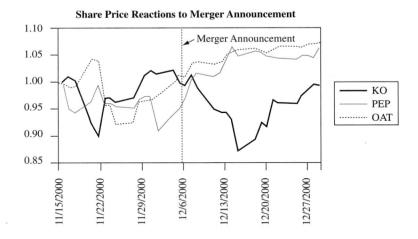

Share Price Reactions to Merger Announcement

This case was prepared by Jessica Chan under the supervision of Professor Robert F. Bruner. It was written as a basis for class discussion rather than to illustrate effective or ineffective handling of an administrative situation. The financial support of the Batten Institute is gratefully acknowledged. Copyright © 2001 by the University of Virginia Darden School Foundation, Charlottesville, VA. All rights reserved. *To order copies, send an e-mail to* dardencases@virginia.edu. *No part of this publication may be reproduced, stored in a retrieval system, used in a spreadsheet, or transmitted in any form or by any means—electronic, mechanical, photocopying, recording, or otherwise—without the permission of the Darden School Foundation.* Version 4.0.

sessed extremely strong brands in the noncarbonated-beverages segment, such as Aquafina, Tropicana, and Lipton. Now through Gatorade, PepsiCo would consolidate its lead even further. Analysts estimated that PepsiCo would control around 33 percent of the U.S. noncarbonated-beverage market after the Gatorade acquisition, far ahead of Coca-Cola's 21 percent.[1] A report by UBS Warburg stated,

> Given PEP's [PepsiCo's] #1 rank in the faster-growth segment and its improving competitive position in CSDs [carbonated soft drinks], we believe PEP could, over the long term, threaten Coca-Cola's lead in the domestic beverage category in all channels except fountain.[2]

Carolyn Keene, consumer analyst at the mutual fund firm Siegel, Parker and Lauck (SPL), wondered how this latest announcement would affect the two companies' prospects for value creation. Historically, Coca-Cola had trounced PepsiCo in terms of value created as measured by "EVA,"™ or Economic Value-Added (see **Exhibit 1**). She wondered if the trend would be reversed given recent developments. To develop a view, she decided to perform an EVA analysis for Coca-Cola and PepsiCo for 2001–03. She hoped this would reveal which of the two companies would be the more attractive investment over the next few years.

COMPANY BACKGROUND: THE COCA-COLA COMPANY

In 2000, the Coca-Cola Company's (ticker symbol: KO) annual sales were $20.5 billion, and its market value reached $110.1 billion. The company was the largest manufacturer, distributor, and marketer of soft-drink concentrates and syrups[3] in the world, and also marketed and distributed a variety of noncarbonated-beverage products, which included Minute Maid orange juice, Fruitopia, Dasani bottled water, and Nestea, among others.

From 1993 to 1998, the Coca-Cola Company had consistently garnered the first or second spot in *Fortune*'s annual ranking of the top wealth creators. One of the main reasons for this was the company's strategy of spinning off its bottling operations in order to avoid consolidation on its balance sheet. This move, implemented in 1985, contributed to a dramatic rise in returns on equity from 23 percent to as much as 57 percent over the last two decades (see **Exhibit 2**).

Recently however, the company had run into difficulties. The Asian financial crisis, South America's difficulties, and Russia's devaluation of the ruble all hurt KO. But business mistakes by Doug Ivester, CEO from 1997 to 1999, aggravated the situation.

---

[1]"Deal Ensures Pepsi Outdistancing Coke on the Flat," *South China Morning Post,* December 6, 2000.

[2]Caroline Levy, David Palmer, and Elyse Sakowitz, "PepsiCo, Inc.—Strong Buy," UBS Warburg, December 5, 2000.

[3]The Coca-Cola Company did not actually bottle and distribute its soft-drink products. Rather, the company manufactured concentrate and syrups that were then sold to authorized bottlers that were either majority or minority owned by KO or completely independent. These bottlers then combined the syrup or concentrate with carbonated water and sweetener, packaged the finished drinks in authorized containers bearing the Coca-Cola trademark, and sold these to retailers and wholesalers. Thus, KO's main source of profit was from the syrup.

An example of one such mistake occurred in November 1999, when Ivester instituted a 7.7 percent price hike on syrup, a rate that was double that of usual increases. The Coca-Cola Company's bottlers were infuriated, and felt that Ivester was gouging them in order to increase KO's profits. In response, the bottlers raised prices for the first time in years in order to improve profitability, resulting in a decrease in volume (see **Exhibit 3**). During Ivester's approximately two-year term, net income fell by 41 percent. The company's board of directors eased Ivester out in December 2000.

Douglas Daft, head of Coca-Cola's Middle and Far East and Africa groups, was chosen to succeed Ivester. Upon taking over, he immediately instituted major organizational changes such as cutting staff and reducing bureaucracy. But perhaps the most important change was his acknowledgment that KO needed to be a dominant player in the noncarbonated-beverages market. In contrast to Ivester, who had insisted on pushing the company's core soft-drink brands—Coca-Cola, Fanta, Sprite, and Diet Coke—Daft and his executives worked hard to come up with new noncarbonated products.

Some analysts were optimistic that the change in management would return the Coca-Cola Company to its glory days. Perhaps through improved relations with bottlers and acquisitions of noncarbonated beverages, KO would return to the pre-1998 profit margins. Other analysts were less enthusiastic. One thing was certain, however: with PepsiCo's invigorated management, KO would need to get back on its feet as quickly as it could.

COMPANY BACKGROUND: PEPSICO, INC.

In 2000, PepsiCo, Inc., was a $20-billion company involved in the snack-food, soft-drink, and noncarbonated-beverage businesses. The company sold and distributed salty and sweet snacks under the Frito-Lay trademark, and manufactured concentrates of Pepsi, Mountain Dew, and other brands for sale to franchised bottlers. The company also produced and distributed juices and other noncarbonated beverages.[4] Snack foods accounted for roughly two-thirds of PepsiCo's sales and operating income, while beverages accounted for the remainder.

PepsiCo as a focused snack-and-beverage company in 2000 was due mostly to the efforts of Roger Enrico, CEO from 1996 to 2000. During his tenure, Enrico instituted a massive overhaul at PepsiCo. In 1997, he sold off the fast-food chains KFC, Taco Bell, and Pizza Hut, ridding PepsiCo of a business that had long been a drag on returns. In 1999, he spun off Pepsi's capital-intensive bottling operations into an independent public company. By spinning off the bottling operations, PepsiCo would be left with just the higher-margin business of selling concentrate to bottlers.[5] At the same time, independent PepsiCo bottlers would be able to raise capital on their own, freeing up cash flow within the parent company

---

[4]Yahoo Finance.

[5]In a price war, "it's the bottlers' margins that get flattened, while the 'parent' companies enjoy higher sales volume because of the low prices. The concentrate business . . . can have gross margins of 80%, compared with between 35% and 40% for bottling." Nikhil Deogun, "PepsiCo's Sale of Bottling-Business Stake Isn't Being Greeted with 'dotcom' Hype," *The Wall Street Journal,* March 26, 1999, C1.

for other uses. Enrico also took aggressive steps to make PepsiCo a "total beverage company." He brokered the acquisitions of Tropicana, the market leader in orange juice, and Quaker Oats, whose Gatorade brand dominated the energy-drink market.

During Enrico's term, PepsiCo's return on equity almost doubled, from 17 percent in 1996 to 30 percent in 2000. (See Exhibit 2 for historical returns and Exhibit 1 for a historical EVA analysis.) On Wall Street, analysts were upbeat about PepsiCo's prospects.

INDUSTRY OVERVIEW AND COMPETITIVE EVENTS

In 2000, the beverage industry was undergoing a rapid transformation: the noncarbonated-drinks segment, although still representing only a small fraction of the beverage market, had grown by 62 percent in volume over the last five years, while soft-drink-volume growth had been sluggish.[6] According to *Beverage Digest,* the share of the carbonated soft-drink industry fell from 71.3 percent in 1990 to 60.5 percent in 2000.

In soft-drink volume, PepsiCo still lagged behind Coke, although it seemed to have caught up somewhat in recent years (see Exhibit 3). In the fall of 1999, for instance, PepsiCo, for the first time in its history, occupied two of the top three places for U.S. soft-drink brands on store shelves as its Mountain Dew dislodged Diet Coke from third place.[7]

Recent developments at both companies signaled an aggressive new round of competition. Below is a summary of recent competitive moves by both companies in several beverage categories:

Soft Drinks

Over the last five years, Pepsi had launched aggressive and exciting marketing campaigns (e.g., "Generation Next," "Joy of Pepsi") that helped boost volumes and visibility. In addition, Pepsi launched the "Power of One" campaign—a strategy that entailed moving Pepsi drinks next to Frito-Lay chips on store shelves to entice shoppers to pick up a Pepsi when they bought chips. This strategy also helped boost both Frito Lay's and Pepsi's volumes. In response to the success of the Pepsi campaigns, Coca-Cola resorted to a number of tactics, such as veering away from its traditional feel-good ads and launching trendier ones in the summer of 2000. Unfortunately, the new ads were highly unpopular and elicited negative reactions from customers and bottlers.[8] Coca-Cola pulled the ads and replaced them with the "Life Tastes Good" series, which marked a return to Coke's traditional "feel-good" themes while being trendy at the same time.

---

[6]McCarthy, "Buffeted: Coke's Muddle over Quaker," *Economist,* November 25, 2000.
[7]John A. Byrne, "PepsiCo's New Formula: How Roger Enrico Is Remaking the Company," *Business Week,* April 10, 2000.
[8]The ads were produced by the Cliff Freeman Ad Agency, famous for its controversial dot-com ad in which gerbils were shown being shot out of a cannon. One Coke commercial featured a grandmother in a wheelchair who throws a tantrum when she discovers there is no Coke at a family reunion.

Noncarbonated Beverages

Coke and PepsiCo raced to position themselves in this important and fast-growing market segment:

> *Orange juice:* In 1998, PepsiCo acquired Tropicana, the clear market leader in orange juice. Tropicana held more than 40 percent of the total chilled-orange-juice market and 70 percent of the not-from-concentrate orange-juice segment in the United States. Coke's Minute Maid had less than 20 percent of the chilled-orange-juice market.
>
> *Bottled water:* PepsiCo test-marketed Aquafina as early as 1994, while Coke did not enter the bottled-water market until 1999, with its Dasani brand. Aquafina was the number-one bottled-water brand in the U.S market in 2000.
>
> *Iced tea:* PepsiCo's Lipton boasted a 16-point-share lead over Coca-Cola's Nestea.
>
> *Sports drinks:* Pending the Federal Trade Commission's approval of the PepsiCo–Quaker Oats deal, PepsiCo would own Gatorade, which held 83 percent of the U.S. sports-drink market. Coca-Cola's Powerade was a distant second at 11 percent.
>
> *Specialty drinks:* PepsiCo, in alliance with Starbucks, introduced the highly popular Starbucks Frappuccino in 1996. It took Coca-Cola until 2000 to announce that it was going to test-market a frozen coffee beverage. In October 2000, PepsiCo beat Coca-Cola in acquiring South Beach Beverage Company, maker of the SoBe brand of teas and fruit juices.

FINANCIAL COMPARISON

Analysts expected that the coming months would be among the most exciting in the Coke-Pepsi saga. It would be interesting to see how the revived "cola wars" would play out. In the meantime, a look at some performance measures might provide clues as to what the future held.

- Ratio analysis. **Exhibits 4 and 5** present a variety of analytical ratios computed from the financial statements of each firm.
- Economic Profit Analysis. Also known as Economic Value Added, EVA can be used to estimate the value created or destroyed by comparing a firm's cash operating profits or "Net Operating Profits After Tax" (NOPAT) against a capital charge:

$$EVA = NOPAT - (\text{Weighted Average Cost of Capital} \times \text{Invested Capital})$$

Alternatively, the formula could be written as:

$$EVA = (\text{Return on Invested Capital} - WACC) \times \text{Invested Capital}$$

Return on Invested Capital (ROIC), as the name suggests, could be calculated by dividing NOPAT by Invested Capital. The second formula highlights the idea that a "spread" earned beyond a company's cost of capital results in value creation.

CONCLUSION

Coke and Pepsi had created one of the strongest rivalries in business history. Carolyn Keene now wanted to develop a view about the two companies' future performances. She obtained pro forma projections for the two firms from reports prepared by analysts at Crédit Suisse First Boston[9] (see **Exhibits 6 and 7**), and gathered information about current capital-market conditions (**Exhibit 8**). She also took out her guidelines for estimating the components of EVA (**Exhibit 9**). It would be nice to finish her analysis before going off for Christmas break.

---

[9]KO forecasts were obtained from the report "Third Quarter Review of 10Q: Flat Revenue and Varied Operating Performance," by Andrew Conway, Chris O'Donnell, and Corey Horsch, Crédit Suisse First Boston Equity Research, November 19, 2001. PepsiCo forecasts were obtained from the report "A Balanced Formula for Growth," by Conway, O'Donnell, and Horsch, Crédit Suisse First Boston Equity Research, November 8, 2001.

EXHIBIT 1
Historical EVA™ Estimation and Return Comparisons for Coca-Cola Company and PepsiCo, Inc.

The Coca-Cola Company ($MM)

	1994	1995	1996	1997	1998	1999	2000
NOPAT	2,547	2,783	2,583	3,381	3,178	2,605	2,349
Invested capital	7,769	8,466	9,649	13,825	15,896	15,644	15,864
Return on invested capital	32.8%	32.9%	26.8%	24.5%	20.0%	16.6%	14.8%
WACC	12.2%	11.4%	13.4%	12.9%	11.1%	9.9%	8.4%
ROIC-WACC Spread	20.6%	21.4%	13.4%	11.6%	8.9%	6.8%	6.4%
EVA	1,602	1,814	1,292	1,601	1,422	1,063	1,016

PepsiCo, Inc. ($MM)

	1994	1995	1996	1997	1998	1999	2000
NOPAT	2,122	2,204	1,892	1,922	2,522	1,794	2,292
Invested capital	22,507	27,009	26,823	16,392	19,439	12,849	13,146
Return on invested capital	9.4%	8.2%	7.1%	11.7%	13.0%	14.0%	17.4%
WACC	11.5%	11.0%	10.5%	11.6%	10.8%	9.9%	8.3%
ROIC-WACC Spread	−2.1%	−2.8%	−3.4%	0.1%	2.2%	4.1%	9.1%
EVA	(464)	(760)	(916)	24	428	522	1,201

Source: Casewriter estimates.

EXHIBIT 2
Return on Equity and Return on Asset Comparisons, Coca-Cola Co. and PepsiCo, Inc.

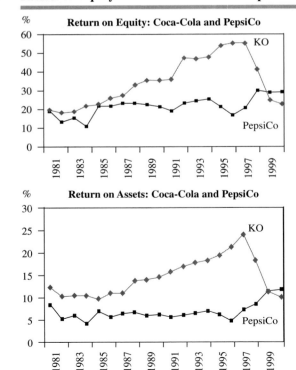

Source: Casewriter estimates.

EXHIBIT 3
U.S. Soft-Drink Market Shares and Volume, Coca-Cola and PepsiCo

	1990	1991	1992	1993	1994	1995	1996	1997	1998	1999	2000
Coca-Cola											
Gallonage (in millions)	4,915.5	5,038.4	5,108.9	5,310.0	5,580.8	5,915.4	6,223.9	6,473.0	6,764.4	6,730.5	6,737.2
Growth	4.0%	2.5%	1.4%	3.9%	5.1%	6.0%	5.2%	4.0%	4.5%	−0.5%	0.1%
Market share	41.0%	41.3%	41.3%	41.7%	42.0%	42.9%	43.8%	44.1%	44.6%	44.1%	44.0%
Market share gain/(loss)	0.6%	0.3%	0.0%	0.4%	0.3%	0.9%	0.9%	0.3%	0.5%	−0.5%	−0.1%
PepsiCo											
Gallonage (in millions)	3,970.5	4,010.2	3,827.6	3,899.0	4,070.6	4,201.8	4,370.2	4,500.2	4,704.1	4,732.3	4,736.1
Growth	3.0%	1.0%	−4.6%	1.9%	4.4%	3.2%	4.0%	3.0%	4.5%	0.6%	0.1%
Market share	33.1%	32.9%	30.9%	30.6%	30.7%	30.6%	30.8%	30.7%	31.0%	31.0%	30.9%
Market share gain/(loss)	0.1%	−0.2%	−2.0%	−0.3%	0.1%	−0.1%	0.2%	−0.1%	0.3%	0.0%	−0.1%
Soft Drink Industry											
Gallonage (in millions)	11,996.1	12,200.4	12,473.2	12,722.7	13,275.0	13,752.9	14,199.5	14,665.8	15,160.6	15,251.6	15,328.0
Growth	2.6%	1.7%	2.2%	2.0%	4.3%	3.6%	3.2%	3.3%	3.4%	0.6%	0.5%

Source: Compiled from Beverage World.

EXHIBIT 4
Analytical Financial Ratios for the Coca-Cola Company

	1994	1995	1996	1997	1998	1999	2000
Activity Analysis							
Average days outstanding	31.24	32.61	32.83	31.73	32.06	31.92	31.71
Working capital turnover	(16.33)	(11.27)	(10.62)	(8.90)	(6.14)	(5.49)	(6.52)
Fixed assets turnover	3.59	3.60	3.87	4.33	4.36	3.79	3.32
Total asset turnover	1.08	1.12	1.15	1.12	1.05	0.92	0.93
Liquidity Analysis							
Current ratio	0.64	0.59	0.80	0.75	0.87	0.90	0.87
Cash ratio	0.25	0.18	0.22	0.21	0.18	0.18	0.20
Cash from operations ratio	0.54	0.45	0.47	0.47	0.35	0.39	0.38
Long-Term Debt and Solvency Analysis							
Debt equity ratio	0.67	0.75	0.73	0.61	0.65	0.65	0.61
Times interest earned	18.63	14.80	13.69	19.38	17.93	11.82	8.26
Fixed charge coverage ratio	10.02	9.87	7.18	8.99	8.70	6.03	5.77
Capital expenditure ratio	3.83	3.55	3.50	3.69	3.98	3.63	4.89
Cash from operations-debt ratio	0.96	0.82	0.77	0.78	0.55	0.62	0.63
Profitability Analysis							
Operating margin	22.9%	22.3%	21.1%	26.5%	26.4%	20.1%	18.0%
Net profit margin	15.8%	16.6%	18.8%	21.9%	18.8%	12.3%	10.6%
ROA	16.8%	17.7%	19.1%	21.1%	22.9%	17.3%	11.5%
ROE	44.3%	48.1%	51.7%	48.0%	46.1%	37.1%	25.8%
Financial leverage effect	70.1%	68.9%	74.2%	89.2%	82.6%	71.1%	61.0%
Growth							
Sales	15.9%	11.4%	2.9%	1.7%	−0.3%	5.3%	3.3%
Book assets	15.4%	8.4%	7.4%	4.5%	13.4%	12.9%	−3.6%
Net income before unusual gain/loss	16.7%	16.9%	16.9%	18.2%	−14.4%	−31.2%	−10.4%
Adjusted NOPAT	19.5%	8.6%	−2.8%	27.7%	−0.7%	−19.8%	−7.3%
Net income	17.4%	16.9%	16.9%	18.2%	−14.4%	−31.2%	−10.4%
Operating income	19.5%	8.6%	−2.8%	27.7%	−0.7%	−19.8%	−7.3%

Source: Casewriters estimates.

EXHIBIT 5
Analytical Financial Ratios for PepsiCo, Inc.

	1994	1995	1996	1997	1998	1999	2000
Activity Analysis							
Average days outstanding	25.33	26.89	28.39	40.71	37.59	37.25	31.28
Working capital turnover	(34.07)	513.67	200.28	20.98	(28.69)	(12.86)	38.78
Fixed assets turnover	1.64	1.72	1.82	1.42	1.57	1.55	2.05
Total asset turnover	1.17	1.20	1.27	0.94	1.05	1.01	1.14
Liquidity Analysis							
Current ratio	0.96	1.06	1.00	1.47	0.55	1.10	1.17
Cash ratio	0.28	0.29	0.15	0.68	0.05	0.28	0.34
Cash from operations ratio	0.71	0.72	0.82	0.80	0.41	0.80	0.99
Long-Term Debt and Solvency Analysis							
Debt equity ratio	1.39	1.73	1.97	0.71	1.24	0.44	0.33
Times interest earned	4.96	4.38	4.24	5.57	6.54	7.76	14.59
Fixed charge coverage ratio	3.03	2.72	2.48	3.41	3.09	3.73	4.36
Capital expenditure ratio	1.65	1.78	1.83	2.27	2.29	2.71	3.67
Cash from operations-debt ratio	0.39	0.30	0.32	0.69	0.40	0.99	1.62
Profitability Analysis							
Operating margin	11.3%	9.9%	8.0%	12.7%	11.6%	13.8%	15.8%
Net profit margin	6.2%	5.3%	3.6%	10.2%	8.9%	10.1%	10.7%
ROA	7.2%	6.4%	4.6%	9.6%	9.3%	10.2%	12.2%
ROE	24.1%	24.7%	23.0%	16.9%	32.1%	30.0%	29.0%
Financial leverage effect	54.6%	54.7%	53.8%	45.1%	80.5%	77.1%	72.7%
Growth							
Sales	13.3%	6.7%	4.6%	−33.9%	6.8%	−8.9%	0.3%
Book assets	4.6%	2.6%	−3.6%	−18.0%	12.7%	−22.5%	4.5%
Net income before unusual gain/loss	12.3%	−10.0%	−28.5%	29.8%	33.7%	2.9%	6.5%
Adjusted NOPAT	10.1%	−6.7%	−14.8%	4.6%	−2.9%	9.1%	14.4%
Net income	10.3%	−8.3%	−28.5%	86.4%	−7.0%	2.9%	6.5%
Operating income	10.1%	−6.7%	−14.8%	4.6%	−2.9%	9.1%	14.4%

Source: Casewriters estimates.

EXHIBIT 6
Income-Statement and Balance-Sheet Forecasts for Coca-Cola Company

Income Statement	2001E	2002E	2003E
Net operating revenue	20,223	21,234	22,508
Cost of goods sold	6,092	6,285	6,617
Gross profit	14,131	14,949	15,891
Selling expense	7,508	7,569	7,985
General & admin.	1,224	1,248	1,273
	8,732	8,817	9,258
Operating income	5,399	6,132	6,633
Interest income	295	244	254
Interest expense	(310)	(280)	(264)
Equity income	197	227	261
Other income/			
(deductions), net	24	(10)	(10)
Pretax Income	5,605	6,313	6,874
Income Taxes	1,682	1,894	2,062
Net Income	3,923	4,419	4,812

Other projected items:			
Depreciation	489	542	597
Amortization	295	295	295
Cash taxes	1,738	1,957	2,131
Capital expenditures	700	750	750

Accumulated goodwill amortization at the end of 2000 was expected to be $192 million.

Balance Sheet	2001E	2002E	2003E
Cash & equivalents	2,238	2,406	2,432
A/R, Net	1,838	1,930	2,046
Inventories	1,015	1,048	1,103
Prepaid expenses & other	1,834	1,868	1,964
Total current assets	6,925	7,252	7,545
Investments in bottlers	5,962	6,189	6,449
Marketable securities	2,364	2,364	2,364
PP&E	7,334	8,084	8,834
Less: Acc. depreciation	(2,935)	(3,476)	(4,073)
Net PP&E	4,399	4,608	4,761
Goodwill & other	1,783	1,488	1,193
Total assets	21,433	21,901	22,312
A/P & accrued liabilities	3,796	3,868	4,066
Loans and notes payable	3,600	3,500	3,400.
Current portion of long-term debt	154	153	2
Accrued income taxes	643	724	788
Total current liabilities	8,193	8,245	8,256
Long-term debt	681	528	526
Other	991	991	991
Deferred income taxes	302	239	170
Total liabilities	10,167	10,003	9,943
Common stock	870	870	870
Additional paid-in capital	3,196	3,196	3,196
Retained earnings	23,466	26,097	29,067
Accumulated other			
comprehensive losses	(2,722)	(2,722)	(2,722)
Treasury stock	(13,543)	(15,543)	(18,043)
Total equity	11,267	11,898	12,368
Total liabilities and equity	21,434	21,901	22,311

Source (except for accum. goodwill amortization): "Third Quarter Review of 10Q: Flat Revenue and Varied Operating Performance," by Andrew Conway, Chris O'Donnell, and Corey Horsch, *Crédit Suisse First Boston* Equity Research, November 19, 2001.

EXHIBIT 7
Income-Statement and Balance-Sheet Forecasts for PepsiCo, Inc.

Income Statement	2001E	2002E	2003E	Balance Sheet	2001E	2002E	2003E
Revenues				Cash	1,775	3,677	2,457
Beverages	10,553	11,307	12,116	Investments	466	466	466
Frito-Lay	14,498	15,373	16,273	Cash and equivalents	2,241	4,143	2,923
Quaker Foods	2,042	2,109	2,179				
	27,093	28,789	30,568	A/R, Net	2,292	2,435	2,585
				Inventories	1,284	1,364	1,449
Operating Profit				Prepaid Exp. & Other	886	942	1,000
Beverages	1,667	1,818	1,976	Total current assets	4,462	4,741	5,034
Frito-Lay	2,675	2,955	3,239				
Quaker Foods	408	426	446	PP&E	7,449	8,021	8,493
Synergies	—	60	90	Intangibles	4,556	4,556	4,556
Corporate expense	(365)	(374)	(382)	Investments in unconsol, affiliated	3,095	3,235	3,414
	4,385	4,885	5,369	Other	952	1,019	1,090
Net interest expense	148	92	37	Total assets	16,052	16,831	17,553
Equity income	157	186	239				
				Short-term borrowings	202	—	—
Pretax income	4,394	4,979	5,571	Current portion of long term debt	281	444	64
				Accts payable & other current liabs	5,017	5,284	5,573
Provision for taxes	1,406	1,593	1,783	Total current liabilities	5,500	5,728	5,637
Net income	2,988	3,386	3,788				
				Long term debt	2,106	1,825	1,381
Other projected items:				Other liabilities	4,244	4,541	4,859
Depreciation	900	950	1,000	Deferred income taxes	1,625	1,974	2,252
Amortization	236	295	295	Total liabilities	13,475	14,068	14,129
Cash taxes	1,142	1,245	1,504	Preferred stock			
Capital expenditures	1,860	1,583	1,528	Common stock & add'l			
				paid-in capital	690	690	690
				Retained earnings	18,420	20,786	23,520
				Treasury stock	(8,434)	(8,434)	(11,434)
				Accumulated comprehensive loss	(1,394)	(1,394)	(1,394)
				Total equity	9,282	11,648	11,382
				Total liabilities and equity	22,757	25,716	25,511

Accumulated goodwill amortization at the end of 2000 was expected to be $751 million.

Source (except for depreciation, amortization, and accum. goodwill amortization): "A Balanced Formula for Growth," by Andrew Conway, Chris O'Donnell, and Corey Horsch, *Crédit Suisse First Boston Equity Research,* November 8, 2001.

EXHIBIT 8
Capital-Market Information on December 4, 2000

Current yields on U.S. Treasuries

3-month	6.15%
6-month	6.11
1-year	6.00
5-year	5.52
10-year	5.73
20-year	5.82

Historical Equity Risk Premiums (1926–1999)

Geometric mean	5.90%
Arithmetic mean	7.50%

Coca-Cola Co. and PepsiCo, Inc. Share Price Performance Relative to S&P500: January 1993 to December 4, 2000

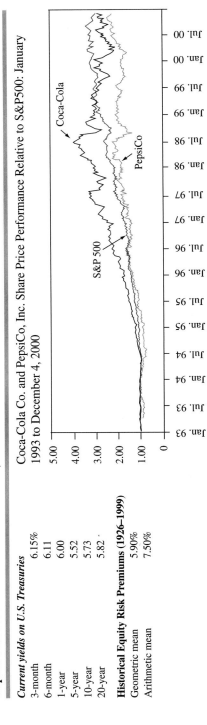

EXHIBIT 8 (*continued*)
Capital-Market Information on December 4, 2000

The Coca-Cola Company

Publicly Traded Debt

Coupon	5.75% paid semiannually
Maturity	4/30/2009
Current Price	91.54
Rating	A1

Historic Betas

1994	0.88
1995	0.83
1996	1.19
1997	1.11
1998	0.97
1999	0.71
2000	0.44
Average	0.88

Dividend History and Forecasts

Paymt Dates	31-Mar	30-Jun	30-Sep	31-Dec	Total
1996	—	0.125	0.125	0.25	0.50
1997	—	0.14	0.14	0.28	0.56
1998	—	0.15	0.15	0.30	0.60
1999	—	0.16	0.16	0.32	0.64
2000	—	0.17	0.17	0.34 E	0.68

E = estimate

Value Line Forecast of Dividend Growth from 1997–99 to 2003–05:	7.50%
Value Line EPS Estimate for FY 2001:	$ 1.75
Coke share price on December 4, 2000:	$ 62.75

Outstanding shares (in millions):

Basic	2,477
Diluted	2,487

PepsiCo, Inc.

Publicly Traded Debt

Coupon	5.75% paid semiannually
Maturity	1/15/2008
Current Price	93.26
Rating	A2

Historic Betas

1994	1.05
1995	1.07
1996	0.93
1997	0.96
1998	1.03
1999	0.73
2000	0.42
Average	0.88

Dividend History and Forecasts

Paymt Dates	31-Mar	30-Jun	30-Sep	31-Dec	Total
1996	0.20	0.115	0.115	-	0.43
1997	0.23	0.125	0.125	-	0.48
1998	0.25	0.13	0.13	-	0.51
1999	0.26	0.135	0.135	-	0.53
2000	0.27	0.14	0.14	-	0.55

Value Line Forecast of Dividend Growth from 1997–99 to 2003–05:	7.50%
Value Line EPS Estimate for FY 2001:	$ 1.63
PepsiCo share price on December 4, 2000:	$ 43.81

Outstanding shares (in millions):

Basic	1,446
Diluted	1,475

Sources of data: Bloomberg Financial Services, Ibbotson Associates 1999 *Yearbook*, Value Line *Investment Survey*, IBES.

EXHIBIT 9
Some Guidelines for Estimating Components of EVA

- **NOPAT.** "Net operating profit after taxes" (NOPAT) is calculated with the aim of arriving at the actual cash generated by the concern. Adjustments might include adding back goodwill amortization and other noncash expenses. Taxes must similarly be adjusted to reflect only actual cash taxes. Depreciation is not added back to NOPAT despite being a noncash expense, because of the assumption that depreciation represents a true economic cost (i.e., it is the amount that must be reinvested to maintain operations at the existing level). For consistency, invested capital is measured net of depreciation.
- **Invested Capital.** Invested capital means, simply, the amount of capital invested in the business. It may be calculated either from the asset side or from the liabilities + equity side of the balance sheet. The latter is the simpler method.
  Invested capital includes debt, equity, and other near-capital items that represent economic value employed on behalf of the firm, such as the present value of operating leases, write-offs and cumulative losses, and accumulated goodwill amortization. The rationale for including losses and write-offs in continuing capital is that these represent unproductive assets, or failed investment. Were they excluded from the capital equation, the sum would only count successful efforts and not accurately reflect the performance of the firm. Accumulated goodwill amortization likewise needs to be included in invested capital because it represents a true investment. Excess cash not needed for operations, such as marketable securities, may be deducted from the invested capital base.
- **Cost of capital.** The capital charge applied against NOPAT should be based on a blend of the costs of all the types of capital the firm employs, or the weighted-average cost of capital.

$$\text{WACC} = [K_d(1 - t)*D/(D+E)] + K_e*E/(D + E)$$

where: K_d = Cost of debt
T = Effective marginal tax rate
K_e = Cost of equity
D = Total debt
E = Total equity

The cost of debt (used for both debt and leases) is the annual rate consistent with each firm's bond rating. The cost of equity may be estimated in a variety of ways—a usual practice is to use the capital-asset-pricing model:[1]

$$K_e = R_f + \beta (R_m - R_f)$$

where: R_f = Risk-free rate, typically the yield on 10-year U.S. Treasury bonds
β = Beta, a measure of the volatility of a company's stock price with respect to market movements
$R_m - R_f$ = Market-risk premium, the additional return investors require over the risk-free rate to compensate them for investing in companies[2]

[1]Other ways of estimating the cost of equity include the dividend-growth and earnings-capitalization models.
[2]The two market premiums frequently used are 7.5 percent, which is an arithmetic average of annual market returns over the Treasury-bill rate from 1926 to 1998, and 5.9 percent, which is a compound or geometric average of market returns over Treasury bonds from 1926 to 1998. (Source: Ibbotson Associates 1999 *Yearbook.*)

Teletech Corporation, 1996

Margaret Weston, Teletech's chief financial officer, learned of Yossarian's letter late one evening in early January 1996. Quickly she organized a team of lawyers and finance staff to assess the threat. Maxwell Harper, the firm's CEO, scheduled a teleconference meeting of the firm's board of directors the next afternoon. Harper and Weston agreed that before the meeting they needed to fashion a response to Yossarian's assertions about the firm's returns.

Ironically, returns had been the subject of debate within the firm's circle of senior managers in recent months. A number of issues had been raised about the hurdle rate used by the company in evaluating performance, and in setting the annual capital budget. Since the company was expected to invest nearly $2 billion in capital projects in 1996, gaining closure and consensus on these issues had become an important priority for Margaret Weston. Now, Yossarian's letter lent urgency to the discussion. In the

This case was written by Robert F. Bruner and is dedicated to the memory of Professor Robert F. Vandell, a scholar in corporate finance and investment analysis and the author of an antecedent case upon which the present case draws. Teletech Corporation is a fictional company, reflecting the issues facing actual firms, and is used as a basis for class discussion rather than to illustrate effective or ineffective handling of an administrative situation. The financial support of the Batten Institute is gratefully acknowledged. Copyright © 1997 by the University of Virginia Darden School Foundation, Charlottesville, VA. All rights reserved. *To order copies, send an e-mail to dardencases@virginia.edu. No part of this publication may be reproduced, stored in a retrieval system, used in a spreadsheet, or transmitted in any form or by any means—electronic, mechanical, photocopying, recording, or otherwise—without the permission of the Darden School Foundation.* Rev. 12/01. Version 2.1.

short run, she needed to respond to Yossarian. In the long run, she needed to assess the competing viewpoints, and recommend new policies as necessary. What *should* be the hurdle rates for Teletech's two business segments? Was the Products and Systems segment really paying its way?

THE COMPANY

Teletech Corporation, headquartered in Dallas, Texas, defined itself as a "provider of integrated information movement and management." The firm had two main business segments: Telecommunications Services and Products and Systems, which manufactured computing and telecommunications equipment. In 1995, Telecommunications Services had earned a return on capital (ROC)[1] of 9.8 percent; Products and Systems had earned 12.0 percent. The firm's current book value of net assets was $16 billion, consisting of $11.4 billion allocated to Telecommunications Services, and $4.6 billion allocated to Products and Systems. An internal analysis suggested that Telecommunications Services accounted for 75 percent of the market value of Teletech, while Products and Systems accounted for 25 percent. The current capital expenditures proposed by Telecommunications Services offered prospective internal rates of return averaging of 9.8 percent; the IRR for prospective Products and Systems projects averaged 12.0 percent. Overall, it appeared that the firm's prospective return on capital would be 10.35 percent. Top management applied a hurdle rate of 10.41 percent to all capital projects, and in evaluating the performance of business units.

Over the past 12 months, the firm's shares had not kept pace with the overall stock market indices, or with industry indexes for telephone, equipment, or computer stocks. See Fig-

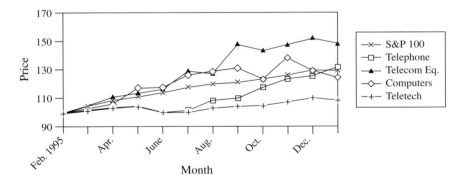

FIGURE 1
Teletech Share Price Performance Compared to Market and Industry Indexes

[1]Return on capital is calculated as the ratio of net operating profits after tax (NOPAT) to capital.

ure 1. Securities analysts had remarked on the firm's lackluster earnings growth, pointing especially to increasing competition in telecommunications, as well as disappointing performance in the Products and Systems segment. A prominent commentator on television opined that "there was no precedent for a hostile takeover of a telephone company, but in the case of Teletech, there is every reason to try."

Teletech's Telecommunications Services Segment

The Telecommunications Services segment provided long-distance, local, and cellular telephone service to more than 7 million customer lines throughout the Southwest and Midwest. Revenues in this segment grew at an average rate of 3 percent over the 1989–95 period. In 1995, segment revenues, net operating profit after tax (NOPAT), and net assets were $11 billion, $1.18 billion, and $11.4 billion, respectively. Since the court-ordered breakup of the Bell System telephone monopoly in 1983, Teletech had coped with gradual deregulation of its industry through aggressive expansion into new services and geographic regions. Most recently, the firm had been a leading bidder for cellular telephone operations, and for licenses to offer personal communications services (PCS). In addition, the firm had purchased a number of telephone operating companies in privatization auctions in Latin America. Finally, the firm had invested aggressively in new technology—primarily digital switches and optical-fiber cables—in an effort to enhance its service quality. All of these strategic moves had been costly: the capital budget in this segment had varied between $1.5 and $2 billion in each of the previous 10 years.

Unfortunately, profit margins in the telecommunications segment had been under pressure for several years. Government regulators had been slow to provide rate relief to Teletech for its capital investments. Other leading telecommunications providers had expanded into Teletech's geographic markets and invested in new technology and quality enhancing assets. Teletech's management noted that large cable TV companies might enter the telecommunications market and continue the pressure on margins.

On the other hand, Teletech was the dominant service provider in its geographic markets and product segments. Customer surveys revealed that the company was the leader in product quality and customer satisfaction. Teletech's management was confident that the company could command premium prices, however the industry might evolve.

Teletech's Products and Systems Segment

Before 1990, telecommunications had been the company's core business, supplemented by an equipment-manufacturing division that produced telecommunications components. In 1990, the company acquired a leading computer workstation manufacturer with the goal of applying state-of-the-art computing technology to the design of telecommunications equipment. The explosive growth in the microcomputer market and the increased use of telephone lines to connect home- and office-based computers with mainframes convinced Teletech management of the potential value of marrying telecommunications equipment and computing technology. Using Teletech's capital base, borrowing ability, and distribution network to catapult growth, the

Products and Systems segment increased its sales by nearly 40 percent in 1995. This segment's 1995 NOPAT and net assets were $480 million and $4.6 billion, respectively.

Products and Systems was acknowledged to be a technology leader in the industry. While this accounted for its rapid growth and pricing power, maintenance of that leadership position required sizable investments in R&D and fixed assets. The rate of technological change was increasing, as witnessed by sudden major write-offs by Teletech on products that until recently management had thought were still competitive. Major computer manufacturers were entering into the telecommunications-equipment industry. Foreign manufacturers were proving to be stiff competitors in bidding on major supply contracts.

FOCUS ON VALUE AT TELETECH

Teletech's mission statement said in part,

We will create value by pursuing business activities that earn premium rates of return.

Translating that statement into practice had been a challenge for Margaret Weston. First, it had been necessary to help managers of the segments and business units understand what "create value" meant for them. Because the segments and smaller business units did not issue securities into the capital market, the only objective measures of value were the securities prices of the whole corporation—but the activities of any particular manager might not be significant enough to drive Teletech's securities prices. Therefore, the company had adopted a measure of value creation for use at the segment and business unit level that would provide a proxy for the way investors would view each unit's performance. This measure, called "economic profit," multiplied the excess rate of return of the business unit times the capital it used:

$$\text{Economic Profit} = (\text{ROC} - \text{Hurdle rate}) \times \text{Capital employed}$$

where:

$$\text{ROC} = \text{Return on capital} = \frac{\text{NOPAT}}{\text{Capital}}$$

$$\text{NOPAT} = \text{Net operating profit after taxes}$$

Each year, the segment and business unit executives were measured on the basis of economic profit. This measure was an important consideration in strategic decisions about capital allocation, manager promotion, and the awarding of incentive compensation.

A second way in which the value creation perspective influenced managers was in the assessment of capital-investment proposals. For each investment, projected cash flows were discounted to the present using the firm's hurdle rate to give a measure of the net present value (or NPV) of each project. A positive (negative) NPV indicated the amount by which the value of the firm would increase (decrease) if the project were undertaken. The following equation shows how the hurdle rate was used in the familiar NPV equation:

$$\text{Net present value} = \sum_{t=1}^{n} \left[\frac{\text{Free cash flow}_t}{(1 + \text{hurdle rate})^t} \right] - \text{Initial investment}$$

HURDLE RATES

The hurdle rate used in the assessments of economic profit and NPV had been the focus of considerable debate in recent months. This rate was based on an estimate of Teletech's weighted average cost of capital (WACC). Management was completely satisfied with the intellectual relevance of a hurdle rate as an expression of the opportunity cost of money. The notion that the WACC represented this opportunity cost had been debated. Its measurement was never considered wholly scientific, but it had been accepted. For instance, Teletech was "split-rated" between AA$-$ and A$+$. An investment banker recently suggested that, at these ratings, new debt funds might cost Teletech 7.03 percent (about 4.22 percent after a 40 percent tax rate). With a beta of 1.041, the cost of equity might be about 11.77 percent. At market-value weights of 18 percent for debt and 82 percent for equity, the resulting WACC would be 10.41 percent. **Exhibit 1** summarizes the calculation. The hurdle rate of 10.41 percent was applied to all investment and performance-measurement analyses in the firm.

Arguments for Risk-Adjusted Hurdle Rates

How the rate should be used within the company in evaluating projects was another point of debate. Given the different natures of the two businesses and the risks each one faced, differences of opinion arose at the segment level over the appropriateness of measuring all projects against the corporate hurdle rate of 10.41 percent. The chief advocate of multiple rates was Rick Phillips, executive vice president of Telecommunications Services, who presented his views as follows:

> Each phase of our business is different, must compete differently, and must draw on capital differently. Until recently, telecommunications was a regulated industry, and the return on our total capital highly certain, given the stable nature of the industry. Because of the recognized safety of the investment, many telecommunications companies can raise large quantities of capital from the debt markets. In operations comparable to Telecommunications Services, 75 percent of the necessary capital is raised in the debt markets at interest rates reflecting solid AA quality, on average—this is better than the corporate bond rating of AA$-$/A$+$. Moreover, I have to believe that the cost of equity of Telecommunications Services is lower than for Products and Systems. I contrast this with the Products and Systems segment where, although sales growth and profitability are strong, risks are high. Independent equipment manufacturers are financed by higher yield BBB-rated debt and more equity with higher expected total returns.
>
> In my book, the hurdle rate for Products and Systems should reflect these higher costs of funds. Without the risk-adjusted system of hurdle rates, Telecommunications Services will gradually starve for capital, while Products and Systems will be force-fed—that's because our returns are less than the corporate hurdle rate, and theirs are greater. Telecommunications Services lowers the risk of the whole corporation, and should not be penalized.
>
> Here's a rough graph of what I think is going on. Telecommunications Services, which can earn 9.8 percent on capital, is actually profitable on a risk-adjusted basis, even though it is not profitable compared to the corporate hurdle rate. The triangle shape on the drawing shows about where Telecommunications Services is located. My hunch is that the reverse is true for Products and Systems, which promises to earn 12.0 percent on capital. P + S is located on the graph near the little circle.

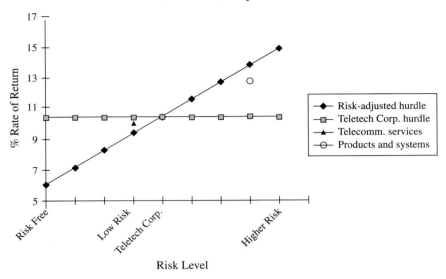

Constant vs. Risk-Adjusted Hurdle Rates

In deciding how much to loan us, lenders will consider the composition of risks. If money flows into safer investments, over time the cost of their loans to us will decrease.

Our stockholders are just as much concerned with risk. If they perceive our business as being more risky than other companies, they will not pay as high a price for our earnings. Perhaps this is why our price/earnings ratio is below the industry average most of the time. It is not a question of whether we adjust for risk—we already do informally. The only question in my mind is whether we make these adjustments systematically or not.

While multiple hurdle rates may not reflect capital-structure changes on a day-to-day basis, over time they will reflect prospects more realistically. At the moment, as I understand it, our real problem is an inadequate and very costly supply of equity funds. If we are really rationing equity capital, then we should be striving for the best returns on equity for the risk. Multiple hurdle rates achieve this objective.

Implicit in Phillips's argument, as Weston understood it, was the notion that if each segment in the company had a different hurdle rate, the costs of the various forms of capital would remain the same. However, the mix of capital used would change in the calculation. Low-risk operations would use leverage more extensively, while the high-risk divisions would have little or no debt funds. This lower-risk segment would have a lower hurdle rate.

Opposition to Risk-Adjusted Hurdle Rates

Phillips's views were supported by several others within Teletech; opposition was just as strong, however, particularly within the Products and Systems segment. Helen Buono, executive vice president for the segment, expressed her opinion as follows:

All money is green. Investors can't know as much about our operations as we do. To them the firm is an opaque box; they hire us to take care of what is inside the box, and judge us by the dividends coming out of the box. We can't say that one part of the box has a different hurdle rate than another part of the box, if our investors don't think that way. Like I say, all money is green: all investments at Teletech should be judged against one hurdle rate.

Multiple hurdle rates are illogical. Suppose that the hurdle rate for Telecommunications Services was much lower than the corporatewide hurdle rate. If we undertook investments that met the *segment* hurdle rate, we would be destroying shareholder value because we weren't meeting the *corporate* hurdle rate.

Our job as managers should be to put our money where the returns are best. A single hurdle rate may deprive an underprofitable division of investments in order to channel more funds into a more profitable division, but isn't that the aim of the process? Our challenge today is simple: we must earn the highest absolute rates of return we can get.

In reality, we don't finance each division separately. The corporation raises capital based on its overall prospects and record. The diversification of the company probably helps keep our capital costs down and enables us to borrow more in total than the sum of the capabilities of the divisions separately. As a result, developing separate hurdle rates is both unrealistic and misleading. All our stockholders want is for us to invest our funds wisely in order to increase the value of their stock. This happens when we pick the most promising projects, irrespective of their source.

MARGARET WESTON'S CONCERNS

As she listened to these arguments, presented over the course of several months, Weston became increasingly concerned with several related considerations. First, the corporate strategy directed the company toward integrating the two divisions. One effect of using multiple hurdle rates would be to make justifying high-technology research and application proposals more difficult, as the required rate of return would be increased. Perhaps, she thought, multiple hurdle rates were the right idea, but the notion that they should be based on capital costs rather than strategic considerations might be wrong. On the other hand, perhaps multiple rates based on capital costs should be used, but in allocating funds, some qualitative adjustment should be made for unquantifiable strategic considerations. In Weston's mind, theory was certainly not clear on how to achieve strategic objectives when allocating capital.

Second, using a single measure of the cost of money (the hurdle rate or discount factor) made the net present value results consistent, at least in economic terms. If Teletech adopted multiple rates for discounting cash flows, Weston was afraid the NPV and economic profit calculations would lose their meaning and comparability across business segments. To her, a performance criterion had to be consistent and understandable, or it would not be useful.

In addition, Weston was concerned with the problem of attributing capital structures to divisions. In Telecommunications Services, a major new switching station might be financed by mortgage bonds. But in Products and Systems, it was not possible for the division to borrow directly; indeed, any financing was feasible only because the corporation guaranteed the debt. Such projects were considered highly risky—perhaps, at best, warranting only a minimal debt structure. Also, Weston considered the debt-capacity decision difficult enough to make for the corporation as a whole, let alone for each division. Judgments could only be very crude.

In further discussions with those in the organization about the use of multiple hurdle rates, Weston ran across two predominant trains of thought. One argument held that the investment decision should never be mixed with the financing decision. A firm should decide what its investments should be and then how to finance them most efficiently. Adding leverage to a present-value calculation would distort the results. Use of multiple hurdle rates was simply a way of mixing financing with investment analysis. This argument also held that a single rate left the risk decision clear-cut: management could simply adjust its standard (NPV or economic profit) as risks increased.

The contrasting line of reasoning noted that the weighted-average cost of capital tended to represent an average market reaction to a mixture of risks. Lower-than-average-risk projects should probably be accepted even though they did not meet a weighted-average criterion. Higher-than-normal-risk projects should provide a return premium. While the multiple-hurdle-rate system was a crude way of achieving this end, it at least was a step in the right direction. Moreover, some argued that Teletech's objective should be to maximize return on equity funds, and because equity funds were and would remain a comparatively scarce resource, a multiple-rate system would tend to maximize returns to stockholders better than a single-rate system.

To help resolve these questions, Weston asked her assistant, Bernard Ingles, to summarize academic thinking about multiple hurdle rates. His memorandum is given in **Exhibit 2.** She also requested that he draw samples of comparable firms for Telecommunications Services and Products and Systems that might be used in deriving segment WACCs. The summary of data is given in **Exhibit 3.** Information on capital-market conditions in January 1996 is given in **Exhibit 4.**

CONCLUSION

Weston could not realistically hope that all the issues before her would be resolved in time to influence Victor Yossarian's attack on management. But the attack did dictate the need for an objective assessment of the performance of Teletech's two segments—the choice of hurdle rates would be very important in this analysis. However, she did want to institute a pragmatic system of appropriate hurdle rates (or one rate) that would facilitate judgments in the changing circumstances Teletech faced. What were the appropriate hurdle rates for the two segments? Was Products and Systems underperforming as Yossarian suggested? How should Teletech respond to the raider?

EXHIBIT 1

Summary of WACC Calculation for Teletech Corporation, and Segment Worksheet

	Corporate	Telecommunications Services	Products and Systems
MV asset weights	100%	75%	25%
Bond rating	AA−/A+	AA	BBB−
Pre-tax cost of debt	7.03%	7.00%	7.78%
Tax rate	40%	40%	40%
After-tax cost of debt	4.22%	4.20%	4.67%
Equity beta	1.04		
Rf	6.04%		
Rm-Rf	5.50%		
Cost of equity	11.77%		
Weight of debt	18.0%		
Weight of equity	82.0%		
WACC	**10.41%**		

EXHIBIT 2
Theoretical Overview of Multiple Hurdle Rates

To: Margaret Weston
From: Bernard Ingles
Subject: Theory of Segment Cost of Capital
Date: January 1996

You requested an overview of theories about multiple hurdle rates. Without getting into minutiae, the theories boil down to the following points:

1. The central idea is that required returns should be driven by risk. This is the dominant view in the field of investment management, and is based on a mountain of theory and empirical research stretching over several decades. The extension of this idea from investment management to corporate decision making is straightforward, at least in theory.

2. An underlying assumption is that the firm is transparent (i.e., that investors can see through the corporate veil and evaluate the activities going on inside). No one believes firms are *completely* transparent, or that investors are perfectly informed. But financial accounting standards have evolved toward making the firm more transparent. And the investment community has grown tougher and sharper in its analysis: Teletech now has 36 analysts publishing reports and forecasts on the firm. The reality is that for big publicly held firms, transparency is not a bad assumption.

3. Another underlying assumption is that the value of the whole enterprise is simply the sum of its parts—this is the concept of Value Additivity. We can define "parts" as either the business segments (on the left-hand side of the balance sheet) or the layers of the capital structure (on the right-hand side of the balance sheet). Market values (MVs) have to balance.

$$MV_{\text{Teletech}} = (MV_{\text{Telecommunications Services}} + MV_{\text{Products+Systems}}) = (MV_{\text{debt}} + MV_{\text{equity}})$$

If these equalities did not hold, then a raider could come along and exploit the inequality by buying or selling the whole and the parts. This is "arbitrage." By buying and selling, the actions of the raider would drive the MVs back into balance.

4. Investment theory tells us that the only risk that matters is nondiversifiable risk, which is measured by "beta." Beta indicates the risk that an asset will add to a portfolio. Because the investor is assumed to be diversified, she is assumed to seek a return for only that risk that she cannot shed, the nondiversifiable risk. Now, the important point here is that the beta of a portfolio is equal to a weighted average of the betas of the portfolio components. Extending this to the corporate environment, the "asset beta" for the firm will equal a weighted average of the components of the firm—again, the components of the firm can be defined in terms of either the right-hand side or the left-hand side of the balance sheet.

$$\beta_{\text{Teletech Assets}} = (w_{\text{Tel.Serv.}}\ \beta_{\text{Tel.Serv.}} + w_{\text{P+S}}\beta_{\text{P+S}}) = (w_{\text{debt}}\ \beta_{\text{debt}} + w_{\text{equity}}\ \beta_{\text{eqity}})$$

where: w = Percentage weights based on market values.

$\beta_{\text{Tel.Serv}}\ \beta_{\text{P+S}}$ = Asset betas for business segments.

β_{debt} = β for the firm's debt securities.

β_{equity} = β of firm's common stock (given by Bloomberg, etc.)

This is a very handy way to model the risk of the firm, for it means that we can use the Capital Asset Pricing Model to estimate the cost of capital for a segment (i.e., using segment asset betas).

5. Given all the previous points, it follows that the weighted average of the various costs of capital (K) for the firm (WACC), which is the theoretically correct hurdle rate, is simply a weighted average of segment WACCs:

$$\text{WACC}_{\text{Teletech}} = \left(w_{\text{Tel.Serv.}}\ \text{WACC}_{\text{Tel.Serv.}}\right) + \left(w_{\text{P+S}}\ \text{WACC}_{\text{P+S}}\right)$$

where: $w_{\text{Tel.Serv.}}\ w_{\text{P+S}} = $ market value weights.

$$\text{WACC}_{\text{Tel.Serv.}} = \left(w_{\text{debt.Tel.Serv.}}\ K_{\text{debt.Tel.Serv.}}\right) + \left(w_{\text{equity.Tel.Serv.}}\ K_{\text{equity.Tel.Serv.}}\right)$$

$$\text{WACC}_{\text{P+S}} = \left(w_{\text{debtP+S}}\ K_{\text{debtP+S}}\right) + \left(w_{\text{equityP+S}}\ K_{\text{equityP+S}}\right)$$

6. The notion in point 5 may not hold exactly in practice. First, most of the components in the WACC formula are estimated with some error. Second, because of taxes, information asymmetries, or other market imperfections, assets may not be priced strictly in line with the model—for a company like Teletech, it is reasonable to assume that any mispricings are just temporary. Third, the simple two-segment characterization ignores a hidden third segment: the corporate treasury department that hedges and aims to finance the whole corporation optimally—this acts as a "shock absorber" for the financial policies of the segments. Modeling the WACC of the corporate treasury department is quite difficult. Most companies assume that the impact of corporate treasury isn't very large, and simply assume it away. As a first cut, we could do this too, though it is an issue we should revisit.

Conclusions

- In theory, the corporate WACC for Teletech is appropriate *only* for evaluating an asset having the same risk as the whole company. It is not appropriate for assets having different risks than the whole company.
- Segment WACCs are computed similarly to corporate WACCs.
- In concept, the corporate WACC is a weighted average of the segment WACCs. In practice, the weighted-average concept may not hold, due to imperfections in the market and/or estimation errors.
- If we start computing segment WACCs, we must use the cost of debt, cost of equity, and weights *appropriate to that segment.* We need a lot of information to do this correctly, or else we really need to stretch to make assumptions.

EXHIBIT 3
Samples of Comparable Firms

	1995 Revenues	Equity Beta	Asset Beta	Bond Rating	Book Val. Debt/Cap.	Price/ Book	Mkt. Val. Debt/Cap.	Mkt. Val. Debt/Eq.	Price/ Earnings
Teletech Corporation	$16,000	1.041	0.92	AA−/A+	40%	3.01	18%	22%	12.9
Telecommunications Services Industry									
AT&T	$80,000	0.90	0.85	AA	39%	6.60	8.8%	9.7%	30.8
Alltel Corp.	3,160	0.75	0.63	A	49	2.99	24.3	32.2	16.0
Ameritech	13,325	0.75	0.67	AA	47	4.72	15.8	18.8	16.9
Bell Atlantic	13,500	0.80	0.68	AA	57	4.53	22.6	29.3	17.5
Bell South	17,780	0.75	0.72	AAA	44	11.90	6.2	6.6	19.0
Century Tel. Enterprs.	625	1.00	0.84	BBB+	46	2.63	24.5	32.4	15.8
Cincinnati Bell	1,350	0.80	0.69	AA	56	4.72	21.2	27.0	18.8
Citizens Utilities Co.	1,070	0.70	0.56	AA	42	1.68	30.1	43.1	15.8
Comsat	850	0.95	0.68	A	40	1.03	39.2	64.6	16.8
Frontier Corp.	1,750	0.80	0.74	A	42	5.50	11.6	13.2	28.3
GTE Corp.	20,250	0.80	0.66	BBB	69	6.52	25.4	34.1	16.9
MCI Communications	15,100	1.25	1.14	A	24	1.87	14.4	16.9	17.9
NYNEX Corp.	13,425	0.75	0.59	A−	62	3.75	30.3	43.6	15.6
Pacific Telesis	9,070	0.85	0.68	AA−	74	6.94	29.1	41.0	13.6
SBC Communications	12,560	0.90	0.80	A	54	5.59	17.3	21.0	18.0
Southern New England	1,840	0.75	0.58	AA	57	2.63	33.5	50.4	15.4
Sprint Corp.	13,550	1.05	0.87	BBB	52	3.13	25.7	34.7	15.0
U.S. West	9,450	0.65	0.52	AA−	66	4.67	29.4	41.6	14.3
Average		*0.84*	*0.72*		*51*	*4.52*	*22.8*	*31.1*	*17.9*
Telecommunications Equipment Industry									
ADC Telecomm. Inc.	$ 586	1.35	1.35	NR	0%	4.05	0.0%	0.0%	28.0
Acma-Cleveland	120	1.50	1.49	NR	1	1.51	0.7	0.7	12.8
Allen Group	325	1.60	1.55	NR	13	2.75	5.2	5.4	18.8
Andrew Corp.	626	1.25	1.23	NR	13	4.40	3.3	3.4	19.7
DSC Communications	1,450	1.30	1.26	NR	18	3.72	5.6	5.9	17.9
Newbridge Networks	675	1.55	1.55	NR	1	5.48	0.1	0.1	23.9
Qualcomm Inc.	386	1.55	1.52	NR	9	3.41	2.8	2.9	58.3
Tellabs Inc.	645	1.50	1.50	NR	1	7.96	0.1	0.1	26.6
Average		*1.45*	*1.43*		*7*	*4.16*	*2.2*	*2.3*	*25.8*
Computer and Network Equipment Industry									
Amdahl Corp.	$ 1,500	1.30	1.20	NR	12%	0.95	12.5%	14.3%	14.1
Bay Networks Inc.	1,342	1.75	1.74	NR	10	9.03	1.2	1.2	26.0
Cabletron Systems	1,060	1.60	1.60	NR	0	6.57	0.0	0.0	21.8
Cisco Systems	1,979	1.75	1.75	NR	0	13.83	0.0	0.0	26.9
Digital Equipment	13,813	1.10	1.04	NR	22	2.87	8.9	9.8	17.1
General Datacomm	221	1.85	1.79	NR	17	3.96	4.9	5.2	NMF
Hewlett-Packard	31,519	1.25	1.24	NR	6	3.33	1.9	1.9	14.6
SCI Systems	2,673	1.20	1.06	NR	32	2.20	17.6	21.4	12.7
Sequent Computer	535	1.95	1.92	NR	3	1.24	2.4	2.5	12.0
Standard Microsystems	345	1.60	1.52	NR	10	1.31	7.8	8.5	29.8
Stratus Computer	580	1.60	1.59	NR	2	1.36	1.5	1.5	13.3
Sun Microsystems	5,902	1.55	1.54	NR	3	4.18	0.7	0.7	17.6
Tandem Computers	2,285	1.55	1.50	NR	6	1.05	5.7	6.1	33.3
3Com Corp.	1,295	1.60	1.59	NR	12	11.90	1.1	1.1	25.8
Average		*1.55*	*1.51*		*10*	*4.56*	*4.7*	*5.3*	*20.4*

Sources: Bloomberg Financial Services and casewriter analysis.

EXHIBIT 4
Debt Capital Market Conditions, January 1996

Corporate Bond Yields, by Rating		U.S. Treasury Securities	
Industrials:			
AAA	6.50%	Short-term bills	5.20%
AA	7.00	Intermediate-term notes	5.43
A	7.64	Long-term bonds	6.04
BBB	7.78%		
BB	8.93		
B	10.49		
Utilities:			
AA	6.53%		
A	7.94		
BBB	8.06		

Source: Bloomburg Financial Services.

Paginas Amarelas

In July 1996, Brasil Investimentos retained J.P. Morgan & Company to advise it regarding a sale or restructuring of its subsidiary in the telephone-directory business, Paginas Amarelas. Juan Lopez, a new associate at J.P. Morgan's Latin America M&A group, was given the task of valuing the business. After several days of work and interaction with the client's management, Lopez was able to gain a better understanding of the business and the markets where they operated. He put together a forecast of the future cash flows (in U.S. dollars as requested by the client) for Paginas Amarelas' operations in the three countries in which it competed: Argentina, Brazil, and Chile. **Exhibit 1** presents the cash-flow forecasts in local currencies and U.S. dollars. **Exhibits 2, 3,** and **4** give the discounted-cash-flow (DCF) estimates using various discount rates and growth rates.

The next logical step was to estimate the weighted-average cost of capital (WACC) to serve as a target rate of return for each country operation. This WACC would permit him to determine from the estimates in Exhibits 2, 3, and 4 the DCF value of the three country operations. As he started to work on the task of estimating appropriate discount rates, Lopez realized that this would be much more challenging than calculating the cost of capital for companies operating in the United States.

This case was prepared from field research by Mario Wanderley under the direction of Professor Robert F. Bruner. The cooperation of P. B. Weymouth of J.P. Morgan & Co. is gratefully acknowledged, as are the helpful suggestions of Professor Bernard Dumas. The name, industry, and financial data of the client have been disguised. Copyright © 1998 by the University of Virginia Darden School Foundation, Charlottesville, VA. All rights reserved. *To order copies, send an e-mail to* dardencases@virginia.edu. *No part of this publication may be reproduced, stored in a retrieval system, used in a spreadsheet, or transmitted in any form or by any means—electronic, mechanical, photocopying, recording, or otherwise—without the permission of the Darden School Foundation.* Rev. 12/01. Version 2.0.

BRASIL INVESTIMENTOS

The client was a Brazilian industrial conglomerate with 1996 sales forecast at $1.5 billion. Paginas Amarelas had net annual turnover close to $140 million. Company executives were concerned about major changes taking place in the markets where Paginas Amarelas competed. The recent trend of substantial increases in the number of telephone lines in the region was anticipated to continue, and the Brazilian state-owned telephone companies were expected to be privatized throughout 1997 and 1998. New players were expected to enter the telephone-directory business in the region, as many of the local telephone companies being privatized would be bought by players that owned their own telephone-directory companies. These developments could soon result in a more competitive marketplace and in reduced margins. In light of this possible future scenario, management felt the need to evaluate quickly the prospective attractiveness of this business.

J.P. MORGAN & COMPANY

J.P. Morgan & Company was a global financial-services provider, ranking among the top four U.S. commercial banks and considered a major global player in the investment-banking industry. The new mandate from Brasil Investimentos to advise it regarding strategic alternatives for its telephone-directory business was important to J.P. Morgan. The mandate would help strengthen the relationship with Paginas Amarelas' parent company and strengthen Morgan's leadership position in Latin America. Among the alternatives contemplated by the J.P. Morgan team working on this mandate was the sale or spin-off of Paginas Amarelas.

In estimating the value of a company, J.P. Morgan generally made use of three methods—the DCF (Discounted Cash Flow) method, trading multiples, and transaction multiples. The DCF method consisted basically of projecting a company's free cash flows and discounting them by the weighted-average cost of capital, or WACC.[1] The cost of capital needed to reflect the operational and financial risks presented by the business, given an estimated long-term capital structure. The trading-multiples valuation "provides an estimate of value based on a public peer group,"[2] while the transaction-multiples valuation "provides a benchmark of value based on prices paid by strategic acquirers."[3]

THE TELEPHONE-DIRECTORY INDUSTRY IN LATIN AMERICA

Telephone-directory companies provided users with a listing of addresses and telephone numbers of essentially all local residential and commercial subscribers. Revenues were derived from advertising space on the listings, sold to businesses and professionals.

---

[1] WACC = [(After-tax cost of debt × Percentage of debt) + (Cost of equity × Percentage of equity)]
After-tax cost of debt = Cost of debt × (1 - Tax rate)
Cost of equity = Risk-free rate + (Beta × Equity market premium)
[2] J.P. Morgan & Co., client presentation.
[3] Ibid.

A telephone-directory enterprise shared characteristics with several other types of businesses. Similar to any publishing or printing company, it was affected by fluctuations in the cost of paper, printing, and distribution.[4] It provided information for its users, the telephone subscribers, just like information-service providers. It rendered its clients a channel to send messages to households, comparable to a direct-marketing company. The telephone-directory business also had a resemblance to newspapers and radio stations as it derived the vast majority of its revenues from advertising. Furthermore, the clientele of telephone-directory companies, newspapers, and radio stations was very similar—small and midsized local businesses and professionals.

In Latin America, each municipality typically had only one phone directory. Directory companies were bound by contracts between them and local telephone operators or local authorities to provide a given municipality with the telephone directory. These contracts were awarded through a competitive bid. The highest bidder won on a mix of technical and economic factors. Normally, the economic aspect carried a much higher weight than the technical aspect. Economics usually corresponded to what percentage of advertising revenues (generated through the sale of advertising space on the listings) the directory company was willing to share with the local telephone company or authority. The percentage of revenues shared generally ranged from 40 to 45 percent. The technical part pertained to previous experience in the business and proven publishing and distribution expertise.

These contracts had durations ranging from one to seven years. There were no guarantees that the current provider would be awarded the next contract, as all firms had to go through the same competitive process once the contract expired. In projecting the future cash flows, Lopez estimated the probability of renewal for each local contract, and built that into the model.

The telephone-directory business in Latin America had a cyclical nature, with its level of activities following economic cycles. In recessions, companies typically cut their promotional budgets, spending less money on telephone-directory advertising. A depressed economic environment led clients either to place smaller ads or forgo advertising. In a booming economy, companies increased their advertising expenditures. This cyclicality was not common in developed countries, where advertisers typically viewed telephone directories as a relatively cheap promotional channel and maintained advertising levels even in economic downturns.

The expenses associated with printing the telephone books represented a major portion of a telephone-directory company's costs (see **Exhibit 5**). As a result, an increase in the number of telephone lines and subscribers raised the company's costs because more books had to be printed and distributed. In developed countries, this additional expense was more than offset by increased advertising revenues, as the expanded audience would give telephone-directory companies the opportunity to command a higher price per square inch of advertising space sold.

---

[4]In general, telephone-directory companies that owned their own press facilities were not able to utilize 100 percent of their press lines' capacity just with their in-house jobs, and were forced to seek contracts to produce other printed matter. Even those telephone-directory companies that outsourced printing and distribution of books were still affected by these price fluctuations.

In Latin America, telephone-directory companies faced a different reality. Local advertisers were very price sensitive and typically had not adopted concepts such as *cost per thousand readers* in allocating their promotional budgets. Therefore, local clients were not willing to pay higher prices for advertising space. Increases in costs could not be passed on to clients. In general, advertisers would only recognize the benefits of a higher audience long after this surge had taken place.

PAGINAS AMARELAS COUNTRY OPERATIONS

Paginas Amarelas had operations in Argentina, Brazil, and Chile. In 1995, the Argentine subsidiary contributed 33 percent of Paginas Amarelas' total net revenues, while the Brazilian and Chilean units were responsible for 52 and 15 percent of total net revenues, respectively. In Argentina, Paginas Amarelas shared the market with two other telephone-directory companies. It had around 32 percent of the total market[5] and had enjoyed a healthy profit margin of around 17 percent. (See Exhibit 5 for a representative break-out of revenues and margins.) The telephone-directory business in Brazil had four major players. Paginas Amarelas had around 15 percent of the market and had enjoyed net margins of around 18 percent. In Chile, Paginas Amarelas was one of three telephone-directory companies and earned margins similar to those of the Brazilian unit.

The telephone market in the three countries where Paginas Amarelas operated had undergone significant development. Previously, telephone companies in the three countries were state-owned and enjoyed a monopoly (in 1996, this situation still existed in Brazil). The combination of these two factors—government control and no competition—contributed to the low level of services offered, the high prices charged, and the low telephone density in each of these countries.[6]

In Argentina and Chile, the privatization of state-owned carriers and the end of the monopoly resulted in superior service and lower service charges, which was followed by a significant increase in the number of lines. The privatization of the Brazilian telephone companies, anticipated to start in late 1997, was expected to yield similar results. Despite recent progress, the telephone density in these countries was still considerably lower than in developed countries (see **Table 1**), leaving a lot of room for growth.

The foreseen increase in the number of telephone lines in the three countries could lead to lower margins for Paginas Amarelas in the near term. The reduced margins would result from the incremental cost of printing more directories, combined with the inability to pass along the increased expenses to advertisers.

---

[5]Keep in mind that there was usually only one phone directory per municipality. Therefore, the directory company serving that market enjoyed a 100 percent market share in that city. The 32 percent market share referred to the percentage of telephone lines in the country served by Paginas Amarelas.

[6]In Brazil, this situation was even more acute as subscribers had to "buy" their telephone lines. In July 1996, a telephone line in Sao Paulo, Brazil, cost between $2,000 and $4,000, depending on the neighborhood, and would take up to 10 months to be connected after being purchased.

TABLE 1
Telephone Density under Selected Regional Carriers
(as of September 1996 for Latin America)

Carrier	Telefonica Argentina	Telecom Argentina	Telebras (Brazil)	CTC (Chile)	Average of G7 Countries
Lines/100 people	20.5	17.2	9.3	14.7	50.4

Source: J.P. Morgan & Co.—Equity Research, *Weekly Industry Update,* January 14, 1997;
The *Economist* Intelligence Unit, *Country Report,* Argentina, December 16, 1996.

Another aspect often associated with privatization and elimination of monopolies was the entrance of international players into the local market. With the American and European markets maturing, leading telecommunications companies (many of which had a telephone-directory subsidiary) and telephone-directory companies were looking toward high-growth markets abroad. This international expansion had been observed recently in several countries throughout Latin America, including Chile, and was expected to affect the Argentine and Brazilian market.

New players would bring increased competition and reduced margins. Municipalities that typically had only one telephone directory could have two or three in the near future. This would probably drive down the price of advertising in this medium.

MAJOR CHANGES IN LATIN AMERICA

Argentina, Brazil, and Chile had each, in the recent past, been under a military dictatorship. In the mid-to-late 1980s, democratic systems had replaced these military regimes. The current political situations in all three nations were stable, with the respective democratic systems well established.

The economies of Argentina, Brazil, and Chile had experienced major changes in the past five to ten years. High-inflationary environments, especially in Argentina and Brazil, gave way to more-stable economies, with recent annual inflation rates below 15 percent (see **Exhibit 6**). Closed markets, protected by high import tariffs, were rapidly being replaced by market economies. International trade had increased significantly since the process of deregulation started to take place and since the creation of Mercosur.[7]

The current governments of each nation had a firm commitment to free markets, privatization, trade liberalization, and low inflation. Such policies had prompted a sharp increase in foreign direct investment and moderate economic growth (see Exhibit 6).

---

[7]Mercosur was a free-trade bloc comprising Argentina, Brazil, Paraguay, and Uruguay. It represented a market with over 200 million people and GDP of close to $1 trillion.

At the end of 1994, the Mexican peso crisis[8] depressed investors' confidence in the region, and spread fears that similar problems would occur throughout Latin America. Foreign capital left the region, returning temporarily to the safe havens of developed countries' capital markets. As a result, the local equity markets and currencies of Latin American countries plummeted (see **Exhibit 7** for a comparison of stock-market performances).

RECENT DEVELOPMENTS IN EACH COUNTRY

Argentina

With 34 million people, Argentina was the second-largest country and economy in South America. It had the largest GDP per capita of the region. In 1983, the democratic regime was reestablished in the country. The Argentine economy reached stability in 1990 when Economy Minister Domingo Cavallo adopted the "Convertibility Plan," introducing a fixed 1:1 exchange rate between the peso and the U.S. dollar. The country enjoyed economic growth (and the president enjoyed great popularity) for almost four years, until the Mexican crisis. The Argentine economy was the hardest hit by the peso crisis after the Mexican economy. The country went into a deep recession with an economic contraction of 4.6 percent in 1995. Only recently did the Argentine economy show signs of recovery (see **Exhibit 8** for the Argentine peso–U.S. dollar exchange rate).

Notwithstanding recent improvements, unemployment remained at 17 percent. Unemployment rates and political scandals had reduced the popularity and power of President Menem. Concerns over a currency overvaluation also existed. The *Economist* Intelligence Unit projected real GDP growth in Argentina of 3 percent in 1996 and 4.2 percent in 1997.

Brazil

With a population in excess of 160 million people, Brazil was the largest country and economy in Latin America. It was also the most industrialized country in the region and its biggest market. Its democratic regime was reestablished in 1986. In 1994, after several unsuccessful plans aimed at reducing inflation, a new economic plan introduced by the current president and then finance minister, Fernando Henrique Cardoso, achieved the desired goal of price stabilization. The plan instituted a new currency, the real (the fifth new currency in a period of eight years). The value of the real was pegged to the dollar, being adjusted gradually within bands. Questions about the sustainability of the currency peg arose after the higher-than-expected fiscal deficit in 1996[9] and deterioration of the country's balance of foreign trade. (See **Exhibit 9** for the Brazilian real–U.S. dollar exchange rate.)

---

[8]The Mexican peso crisis was the result of currency mismanagement. The Mexican government kept the currency at an artificially high value. Subsequently, massive capital flight forced the government to accept a major devaluation.
[9]Government officials had set a target for 1996 fiscal deficit of 2.5 percent of GDP. It turned out to be 4.2 percent of GDP.

Chile

In 1996, this small country (with a population of close to 14 million people) was seen as an economic model for many Latin American nations. Under the dictatorship of General Augusto Pinochet, who ruled the nation for 18 years from 1973, the country started the change from a closed economy to a market economy. With the help of a group of Chilean economists, educated at the University of Chicago under Professor Milton Friedman, Pinochet cut government spending, reduced the civil service, and privatized several state-owned companies. The government also reduced import tariffs and started an effort to diminish the country's reliance on copper exports. By 1996, the national government had become a constitutional democracy.

The results of such drastic changes were reductions in unemployment, inflation, and interest rates. National savings rates increased to levels comparable to Asian markets, and the Chilean economy had been growing at a pace similar to the economies of the "Asian Tigers." Foreign investment was at its highest levels. In the mid-1990s, Chilean companies were actually exporting capital and investing overseas.

For the past decade, Chile had a much more stable economy than that of any other Latin American nation. The country's short-term outlook was also rosier, with the *Economist* Intelligence Unit projecting GDP growth of 6.7 percent in 1996 and average GDP growth of 5.5 percent in 1997–98. (See **Exhibit 10** for the Chilean peso-U.S. dollar exchange rate.)

INVESTMENTS IN LATIN AMERICAN SECURITIES

Fixed-income securities of issuers from Argentina, Brazil, and Chile had gained considerable attention from foreign investors. With the growth in investors' appetites for emerging markets' instruments came an increase in the liquidity of some securities, particularly of sovereign debt[10] and local blue-chip companies.

Foreign investors kept close track of social, economic, and political developments in emerging markets. Some observers believed that their expectations of the future economic and political conditions were reflected in the spread over U.S. Treasury bonds (of similar maturity) of local-government bonds and high-quality corporate instruments (see **Exhibits 11, 12,** and **13**). According to this view, yield spreads reflected investors' forward-looking assessment of the country's risk.[11]

---

[10]Sovereign debt refers to debt instruments issued by a foreign nation's government or state-owned institutions that are fully backed by the foreign nation's government.

[11]The spread over U.S. Treasury bonds that a given security trades at reflects not only the country risk (risk of expropriation, devaluation/inflation, inconvertibility of currency, political instability, etc.), but also the risk of default that the issuer presents (credit risk).

VALUATION ANALYSIS

In preparing the cash-flow forecasts in Exhibit 1, Lopez tried to factor in the future impact of the changes occurring in the telephone-directory business in the region. He also sought to take into account any type of synergies that could be enjoyed by a potential buyer. Lopez assumed that all three units would be sold to a single acquirer. Thus, Paginas Amarelas would continue to enjoy some of the synergies that it currently enjoyed, including increased bargaining power when buying paper, printing efficiencies,[12] and the network of contacts that management had throughout the region. One potential source of synergy that Lopez purposely left out was the ability that the single buyer would have to issue international debt on behalf of the three combined units. This added financial flexibility was not taken into account, given the fact that Paginas Amarelas' parent company had not taken advantage of it.

First, he discovered that the telephone-directory industry in Latin America had no local "pure-play" competitors,[13] making the determination of a beta for each country operation precarious at best. In addition, the efficiency of the local capital markets was questionable and so would be any estimate of the local market's equity premium. Finally, Lopez was not convinced he would be able to find a security from Argentina, Brazil, and Chile that offered no risk of default.

Determining the Cost of Debt

Lopez needed to estimate the WACC with which to discount free cash flows from Argentina, Brazil, and Chile. He decided to start with the easiest part, estimating the cost of debt.

Brasil Investimentos' executives had stated that the country operations had not borrowed money at the corporate level or as one entity (i.e., the three country operations together as the telephone-directory subsidiary), but only at the country level. Lopez's assessment was that all three local operations were relatively small to issue debt independently in the international markets. They would have to rely on the local markets for their borrowing needs. With that in mind, Lopez called J.P. Morgan bankers working at the credit department in offices located in the three countries. He was able to get from them an estimate of the U.S. dollar rates at which each country unit could expect to borrow (see **Exhibit 14** for estimated borrowing rates, tax rates, and long-term capital structure).

Determining the Cost of Equity

In pursuing the next step, calculating the cost of equity, Lopez could choose between two different approaches under the CAPM method (Capital Asset Pricing Model). One approach would be to use local markets' parameters (local risk-free rate, local-market premium and

---

[12]The Brazilian unit owned its own printing facility, which also served the Argentine and Chilean markets.
[13]Most of the players were subsidiaries of large, diversified companies.

beta). The other approach would be to use U.S. market parameters to come up with a cost of equity, which would then be adjusted to reflect the country risk.

The first path offered several difficulties. Lopez had problems in determining a risk-free rate for each country. He questioned whether there was such a thing as a risk-free rate for countries like Argentina, Brazil, and Chile. He knew that even sovereign bonds, like Brady bonds,[14] offered risk of default, because the governments of these countries had defaulted on debt and interest payments in the recent past.

Another challenge was estimating equity-risk premiums for each market. Lopez knew that there was little historical data on equity markets for most Latin American countries. He also realized that any available data usually covered short periods of time. Furthermore, most companies in Argentina, Brazil, and Chile were family owned, and many of them were not listed on stock exchanges. Of those companies listed, very few were heavily traded and had enough liquidity. Lopez realized that any equity-risk premium derived from the available data would not be a good estimate of the premium that investors required when undertaking equity investments in the respective countries.

In addition, he could not find any relevant pure-play competitor in the telephone-directory industry. Substantially all the companies operating in this industry owned other types of businesses. Those that did not were too small to provide a realistic comparison. Lopez then wondered how he could come up with a beta for Paginas Amarelas.

Given the difficulties and potential flaws posed by the first alternative, Lopez considered using either of two approaches. The first obtained a cost of equity using U.S. parameters but adjusted for country risks stemming from the local political and capital-market environments.[15] The second approach posed the challenge of estimating the "adjusting factors" that would correctly reflect the higher risk offered by equity investments in Argentina, Brazil, and Chile (while still leaving unanswered the question of which beta to use). Lopez sat back and started to think about the appropriate "adjusting factors."

Risk ratings by institutions like the *Economist* Intelligence Unit (EIU) and DRI/McGraw-Hill furnished some indication of country risk. Risk ratings (see **Table 2**) were estimated using several economic data and economic ratios—like the ratio of debt service to exports or foreign reserves—and tried to take into account the political situation in the country. Lopez debated whether these ratings were relevant to the valuation that he was conducting. Looking at the EIU risk ratings, he questioned whether they implied that making an investment in Brazil would be more than two times riskier than making the same investment in Chile.

The idea of calculating a WACC in U.S. dollars and adjusting it with an estimate of country risks brought additional questions to mind: Was this methodology theoretically sound? Should he use one "adjusting factor" for all Latin American countries or one for

---

[14]Brady bonds were U.S.-dollar-denominated bonds issued by governments of developing countries that were used as exchange for existing bank loans in default. The principal payments of these securities were collateralized (partly or in total) by U.S.-government zero-coupon bonds.

[15]One study had found that political-risk premiums and country betas were correlated 40 percent, suggesting that to use both terms in a CAPM might overstate country risk. One solution was to multiply the country beta by 0.60 to avoid double-counting country risk.

TABLE 2
EIU Risk Ratings by Country

	Argentina	Brazil	Chile
EIU risk rating	65	60	25

Source: J.P. Morgan & Co. document.

each country? Should the estimate of country risk used be the same, regardless of whether the investor is foreign or local? Should the discount rate be estimated using U.S.-market parameters even when one is dealing with a local prospective buyer?

CONCLUSION

Lopez returned to consider the DCF values in Exhibits 2, 3, and 4. Given an estimate of the investors' required rates of return on investments in Argentina, Brazil, and Chile, he could determine the value of each segment in U.S. dollars. The key issue, then, was to find the appropriate required rate of return for the telephone-directory business in each country.

EXHIBIT 1
Cash-Flow Forecasts in Local Currencies and U.S. Dollars (Currency values in thousands)

| | Free Cash Flows in Local Currency | | | | | | | |
	1997	1998	1999	2000	2001	2002	2003	2004
Argentina (pesos)	6,843	6,993	7,273	7,667	8,238	8,936	9,536	10,159
Brazil (reals)	11,469	12,122	12,850	13,740	14,833	16,167	17,335	18,553
Chile (pesos)	1,337,764	1,415,233	1,497,317	1,593,512	1,704,109	1,839,768	1,954,070	2,071,694

| | Inflation Forecast* | | | | | | | |
	1997	1998	1999	2000	2001	2002	2003	2004
Argentina	1.7%	2.5%	4.0%	4.5%	5.5%	5.5%	5.5%	5.5%
Brazil	6.9%	6.0%	6.0%	6.0%	6.0%	6.0%	6.0%	6.0%
Chile	6.5%	6.1%	5.8%	5.5%	5.0%	5.0%	5.0%	5.0%
United States	3.0%	3.0%	3.0%	3.0%	3.0%	3.0%	3.0%	3.0%

*(Casewriter's estimate)

| | Spot Exchange Rates and Forward Exchange Rates (Local Currency: U.S. Dollar) | | | | | | | | |
	Jul-96	1997	1998	1999	2000	2001	2002	2003	2004
Argentine peso	1.000	0.987	0.983	0.992	1.007	1.031	1.056	1.082	1.108
Brazilian real	1.012	1.050	1.081	1.112	1.145	1.178	1.212	1.248	1.284
Chilean peso	410.73	424.69	437.47	449.36	460.27	469.21	478.32	487.60	497.07

| | Free Cash Flows in U.S. Dollars | | | | | | | |
	1997	1998	1999	2000	2001	2002	2003	2004
Argentina	$ 6,930	$ 7,117	$ 7,331	$ 7,617	$ 7,990	$ 8,462	$ 8,816	$ 9,169
Brazil	10,920	11,215	11,551	12,002	12,591	13,334	13,893	14,448
Chile	3,150	3,235	3,332	3,462	3,632	3,846	4,007	4,168

Note on the estimation of U.S. dollar cash flows:
Cash flows were translated from local currency to U.S. dollars in the following manner:
1. Cash flows are projected in nominal local currency, taking inflation into account.
2. A forecast of the exchange rate (the forward rate) between the dollar and local currency was based on interest rate parity, which assumes that the exchange rate reflects differences in the inflation rate between the two countries.
3. Cash flows were then converted to U.S. dollars using the estimated exchange rate for each period.

EXHIBIT 2

Argentina

Sensitivity Analysis of DCF to Variations in WACC and Growth Rate in Perpetuity

Argentine Unit—Free Cash Flows and Sensitivity Analysis (in 000s USD)							
	1997	**1998**	**1999**	**2000**	**2001**	**2002**	**2003**	**2004**
FCF	$6,930	$7,117	$7,331	$7,617	$7,990	$8,462	$8,816	$9,169

Discounted Cash Flow Values by Growth and WACC
Nominal Growth Rate in Perpetuity

		1%	**3%**	**5%**	**6%**	**7%**	**9%**
	10.0%	$89,434	$104,371	$131,258	$154,785	$193,995	$507,677
	11.0	80,074	91,115	109,516	124,238	146,320	256,730
	12.0	72,435	80,814	93,981	103,856	117,682	172,984
	13.0	66,086	72,582	82,325	89,285	98,565	131,043
W	**14.0**	60,729	65,854	73,256	78,346	84,889	105,828
A	**15.0**	56,149	60,253	65,998	69,828	74,616	88,978
C	**16.0**	52,192	55,520	60,057	63,006	66,611	76,911
C	**17.0**	48,739	51,467	55,104	57,419	60,196	67,834
	18.0	45,701	47,959	50,911	52,756	54,937	60,752
	19.0	43,009	44,893	47,316	48,806	50,546	55,068
	20.0	40,606	42,191	44,198	45,417	46,823	50,401
	21.0	38,451	39,792	41,469	42,475	43,625	46,499
	22.0	36,506	37,648	39,060	39,898	40,847	43,185
	23.0	34,742	35,721	36,917	37,620	38,412	40,334
	24.0	33,137	33,979	34,999	35,594	36,259	37,854
	25.0	31,670	32,398	33,272	33,778	34,340	35,676

Casewriter's Note:

A terminal value for each business unit was calculated using the perpetuity growth formula:

$$\text{Terminal value} = \frac{\text{Last year's cash flow} \times (1 + \text{growth rate in perpetuity})}{\text{WACC} - \text{growth rate in perpetuity}}$$

The two-way tables give the DCF values of free cash flow and terminal value, where the terminal value is estimated using the constant growth valuation model with the indicated growth rates in perpetuity.

EXHIBIT 3
Brazil
Sensitivity Analysis of DCF to Variations in WACC and Growth Rate in Perpetuity

Brazilian Unit—Free Cash Flows and Sensitivity Analysis (in 000s USD)							
	1997	1998	1999	2000	2001	2002	2003	2004
FCF	$10,920	$11,215	$11,551	$12,002	$12,591	$13,334	$13,893	$14,448

Discounted Cash Flow Values by Growth and WACC
Nominal Growth Rate in Perpetuity

	1%	3%	5%	6%	7%	9%
10.0%	$140,927	$164,464	$206,831	$243,903	$305,689	$799,975
11.0	126,176	143,574	172,571	195,768	230,564	404,544
12.0	114,139	127,343	148,091	163,652	185,438	272,581
13.0	104,135	114,371	129,725	140,692	155,314	206,493
W 14.0	95,694	103,769	115,434	123,454	133,765	166,759
A 15.0	88,478	94,944	103,997	110,032	117,576	140,208
C 16.0	82,242	87,485	94,635	99,283	104,963	121,193
C 17.0	76,801	81,100	86,831	90,478	94,854	106,890
18.0	72,014	75,572	80,224	83,131	86,567	95,730
19.0	67,771	70,740	74,558	76,907	79,648	86,774
20.0	63,986	66,483	69,645	71,565	73,781	79,421
21.0	60,589	62,703	65,345	66,930	68,742	73,271
22.0	57,524	59,324	61,548	62,869	64,365	68,049
23.0	54,746	56,288	58,172	59,281	60,528	63,557
24.0	52,216	53,543	55,150	56,087	57,135	59,649
25.0	49,904	51,051	52,429	53,226	54,112	56,216

Casewriter's Note: A terminal value for each business unit was calculated using the perpetuity growth formula.

$$\text{Terminal value} = \frac{\text{Last year's cash flow} \times (1 + \text{growth rate in perpetuity})}{\text{WACC} - \text{growth rate in perpetuity}}$$

The two-way tables give the DCF values of free cash flow and terminal value, where the terminal value is estimated using the constant growth valuation model with the indicated growth rates in perpetuity.

EXHIBIT 4
Chile
Sensitivity Analysis of DCF to Variations in WACC and Growth Rate in Perpetuity

Chilean Unit—Free Cash Flows and Sensitivity Analysis (in 000s USD)							
	1997	**1998**	**1999**	**2000**	**2001**	**2002**	**2003**	**2004**
FCF	$3,150	$3,235	$3,332	$3,462	$3,632	$3,846	$4,007	$4,168

Discounted Cash Flow Values by Growth and WACC
Nominal Growth Rate in Perpetuity

		1%	**3%**	**4%**	**5%**	**6%**	**7%**
	8.0%	$52,855	$66,752	$78,911	$99,176	$139,708	$261,301
	9.0	45,984	55,483	63,083	74,483	93,482	131,481
	10.0	40,652	47,442	52,534	59,663	70,357	88,179
	11.0	36,397	41,416	45,000	49,780	56,472	66,509
W	**12.0**	32,925	36,734	39,352	42,719	47,207	53,492
A	**13.0**	30,039	32,992	34,960	37,421	40,584	44,802
C	**14.0**	27,604	29,933	31,448	33,298	35,612	38,586
C	**15.0**	25,522	27,388	28,575	29,999	31,740	33,916
	16.0	23,724	25,236	26,181	27,299	28,639	30,278
	17.0	22,154	23,394	24,157	25,047	26,099	27,362
	18.0	20,773	21,800	22,423	23,141	23,980	24,971
	19.0	19,549	20,406	20,920	21,507	22,185	22,975
	20.0	18,457	19,178	19,605	20,090	20,644	21,283
	21.0	17,478	18,087	18,446	18,849	19,307	19,829
	22.0	16,593	17,113	17,416	17,754	18,135	18,567
	23.0	15,792	16,237	16,494	16,780	17,100	17,460

Casewriter's Note: A terminal value for each business unit was calculated using the perpetuity growth formula.

$$\text{Terminal value} = \frac{\text{Last year's cash flow} \times (1 + \text{growth rate in perpetuity})}{\text{WACC} - \text{growth rate in perpetuity}}$$

The two-way tables give the DCF values of free cash flow and terminal value, where the terminal value is estimated using the constant growth valuation model with the indicated growth rates in perpetuity.

EXHIBIT 5
1995 Operating Ratios of Paginas Amarelas

	% of Gross revenues	% of Net Revenues
Revenues from Ads and Insertions		
– Refunds/ provisions for bad debt	1.6%	3.0%
Total revenues		
– Percent to local telephone co.	45.0	83.3
Net Revenues	54.0	100
Costs:		
Total printing costs	20.6	38.2
Layout costs	1.9	3.5
Distribution costs	0.4	0.8
Costs from information services	2.0	3.7
Variable costs	6.70	12.4
Fixed costs	5.08	9.4
Gross Profit	**17.2**	**31.9**
Depreciation	0.16	0.3
SG&A	3.94	7.3
Operating Income	**13.2**	**24.4**
Income taxes	4.6	8.5
Net Income	**8.5**	**15.8**

EXHIBIT 6
Historical and Forecast Economic Data for Argentina, Brazil, and Chile

	Nominal GDP in US$ billions						
	1992	1993	1994	1995	1996e	1997f	1998f
Argentina	$228.89	$257.85	$281.91	$275.43	$287.35	$305.87	$331.98
Brazil	364.28	423.53	564.82	717.42	748.61	772.43	798.04
Chile	42.75	45.64	52.18	67.30	75.27	79.46	85.79

Source: J.P. Morgan. *Emerging Markets: Economic Indicators,* January 10, 1997, 20.

	Real GDP growth						
	1992	1993	1994	1995	1996e	1997f	1998f
Argentina	8.70%	6.00%	7.40%	−4.40%	3.00%	4.20%	3.10%
Brazil	−0.90	4.70	5.80	4.20	3.20	3.40	3.40
Chile	11.00	6.30	4.20	8.50	6.70	4.80	6.20

Source: The *Economist* Intelligence Unit. Country Report on the three countries.

	Consumer prices—% Change from Previous Year						
	Dec 93	Dec 94	Dec 95	Jul 96	Nov 96	1997f	1998f
Argentina	7.4%	3.9%	1.6%	0.0%	0.4%	1.7%	2.5%
Brazil	2489.1	929.3	22.0	14.9	10.6	6.9	6.0
Chile	12.2	9.0	8.2	7.7	6.6	6.5	6.1

Source: J.P. Morgan. *Emerging Markets: Economic Indicators,* January 10, 1997, 7.

	Total external debt in US$ billions						
	1992	1993	1994	1995	1996e	1997f	1998f
Argentina	$ 71.90	$ 76.65	$ 90.71	$ 97.21	$ 99.91	$103.56	$107.91
Brazil	133.61	147.35	157.06	173.14	187.10	194.40	208.23
Chile	18.96	19.67	21.77	21.83	21.48	23.28	25.98

Source: J.P. Morgan, *Emerging Markets: Economic Indicators,* January 10, 1997, 18.

	Net foreign direct investment (in US$ millions)						
	1989	1990	1991	1992	1993	1994	1995
Argentina	$1,028	$1,836	$2,439	$2,562	$3,482	$ 477	$1,164
Brazil	608	324	89	1,924	801	2,035	3,475
Chile	1,279	582	400	321	375	848	1,008

Source: International Financial Statistics, January 10, 1997, 100, 150, 188.

	International Reserves (excluding gold, $ billions)				
	1994	1995	Jul 96	Sep 96e	Nov 96e
Argentina	$14.3	$14.3	$14.4	$15.2	$14.9
Brazil	38.8	51.8	59.5	58.8	60.5
Chile	13.1	14.1	14.6	14.6	15.0

Source: J.P. Morgan, *Emerging Markets: Economic Indicators,* January 10, 1997, 15.

(*Continued*)

EXHIBIT 6
Historical and Forecast Economic Data for Argentina, Brazil, and Chile—*Continued*

	Foreign currency debt ratings, July 1996		
	Argentina	**Brazil**	**Chile**
Moody's	B1	B1	Baa1
S&P	BB-	B+	A-
S&P Outlook	Stable	Positive	Stable

Source: J.P. Morgan, *Latin American Credit Ratings,* January 1997, 1, 2.

	Equity Markets					
Country / Index	**Dec-95**	**Aug-96**	**Sep-96**	**Oct-96**	**Nov-96e**	**Dec-96e**
Argentina / Merval	100	96.8	104.4	103.1	107.5	113.9
Brazil / Ibovespa	100	145.6	150.0	152.0	155.1	163.8
Chile / IGPA	100	92.4	94.3	93.8	88.3	85.4

Source: J.P. Morgan, *Emerging Markets: Economic Indicators,* January 10, 1997, 4.
Dec-95 = 100

e = estimate.
f = forecast.

EXHIBIT 7
Stock Market Performance

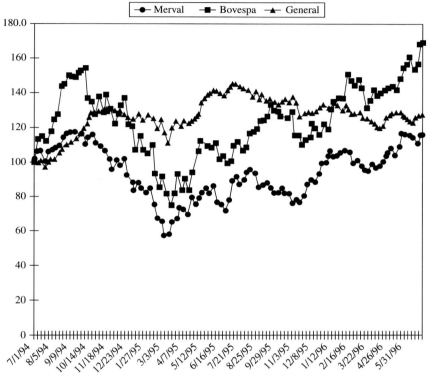

Stock Market Indexes – Comparative Performance
(Argentina - Merval, Brazil - Bovespa, Chile - General)

Figure by casewriter.

Source of data: J.P. Morgan & Company.

EXHIBIT 8
Spot Foreign-Exchange Rate: Argentine Peso to U.S. Dollar

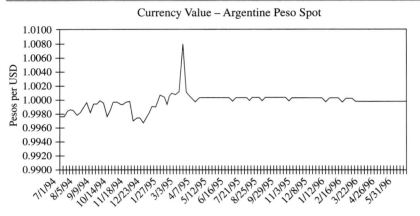

Figure by casewriter.

Source of data: J.P. Morgan & Company.

EXHIBIT 9
Spot Foreign-Exchange Rate: Brazilian Real to U.S. Dollar

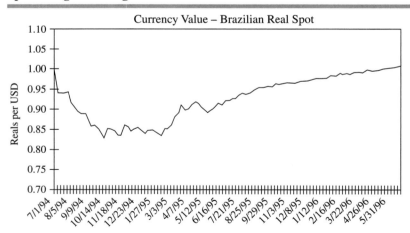

Figure by casewriter.

Source of data: J.P. Morgan & Company.

EXHIBIT 10
Spot Foreign-Exchange Rate: Chilean Peso to U.S. Dollar

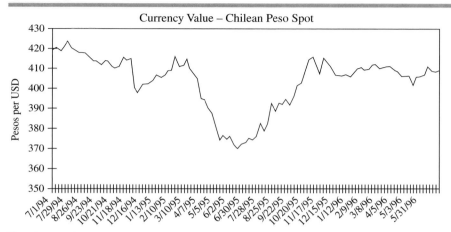

Figure by casewriter.

Source of data: J.P. Morgan & Company.

EXHIBIT 11
Spread over U.S. Treasuries: Argentine Government Bonds

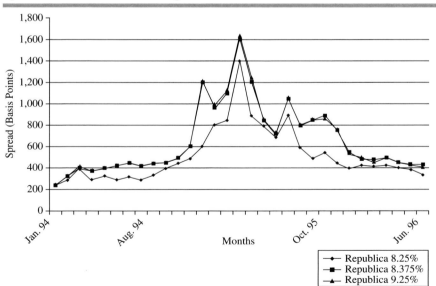

Figure by casewriter.

Source of data: J.P. Morgan & Company.

EXHIBIT 12
Spread over U.S. Treasuries: Brazilian Government Bonds

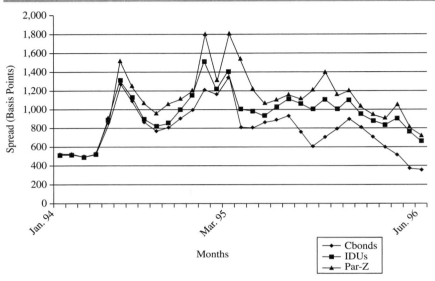

Figure by casewriter.

Source of data: J.P. Morgan & Company.

EXHIBIT 13
Spread over U.S. Treasuries: Chilean High-Grade Corporate Bonds

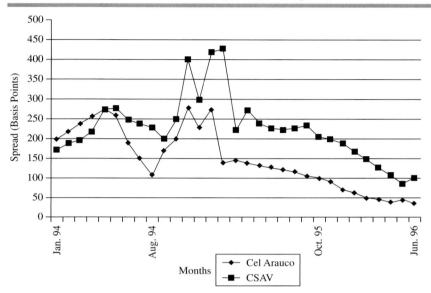

Figure by casewriter.

Source of data: J.P. Morgan & Company.

EXHIBIT 14
Capital-Market Conditions, July 1996

U.S. Treasury Yields

	Yield to Maturity
1 year T-bill	5.92%
2 year T-bond	6.21
5 year T-bond	6.57
10 year T-bond	6.80
30 year T-bond	7.00

Source: Bloomberg

Equity Market Risk Premiums

	Equity Market Risk Premium
U.S. (S&P500 Index)	5.5%
Global Equity Market Index (MSCI)	6.5

Estimated Local Borrowing Rates, Income Taxes, Capital Structure and Country Betas

	Argentina	Brazil	Chile	U.S.
Local risk free rate (2-year)	9.20%	11.99%	7.40%	6.57%
Local borrowing rate (1-year)	9.80%	12.40%	7.90%	7.25%
Income tax rate	35.0%	35.0%	15.0%	35.0%
Country beta (vs. U.S. S&P 500 Index)	1.96	2.42	0.65	1.00
Ratio of target market value of debt to sum of debt plus equity for telephone-directory business	20.0%	20.0%	20.0%	N/A
Volatility (standard deviation of local equity market index)	61.63%	60.86%	28.54%	10.08%
Correlation of local equity market index returns with returns on S&P 500 Index in the U.S.	0.32	0.40	0.23	1.00

Source: Casewriter estimates; J.P. Morgan & Co.; and International Finance Corporation, *1996 Emerging Stock Markets Factbook.*

Median Beta and Capital Structure Information for Certain U.S. Industries

	Direct Marketing	Information Services	Newspapers	Publishing/ Printing	Radio Stations
Unlevered beta, vs. MSCI Index	0.80	0.72	0.68	0.67	0.73
Unlevered beta, vs. S&P500 Index	0.86	0.79	0.74	0.76	0.77
Mean market value debt/capital ratio	20%	18%	17%	19%	21%

Source: Casewriter estimates and J.P. Morgan & Co.

Capital Budgeting and Resource Allocation

CASE 17

The Investment Detective

The essence of capital budgeting and resource allocation is a search for good investments in which to place the firm's capital. The process can be simple when viewed in purely mechanical terms, but a number of subtle issues can obscure the best investment choices. The capital-budgeting analyst is necessarily, therefore, a detective who must winnow good evidence from bad. Much of the challenge is knowing what quantitative analysis to generate in the first place.

Suppose you are a new capital-budgeting analyst for a company considering investments in the eight projects listed in **Exhibit 1.** The chief financial officer of your company has asked you to rank the projects and recommend the "four best" that the company should accept.

In this assignment, only the quantitative considerations are relevant. No other project characteristics are deciding factors in the selection, except that management has determined that projects 7 and 8 are mutually exclusive.

All the projects require the same initial investment, $2 million. Moreover, all are believed to be of the same risk class. The weighted-average cost of capital of the firm has never been estimated. In the past, analysts have simply assumed that 10 percent was an appropriate discount rate (although certain officers of the company have recently asserted that the discount rate should be much higher).

This case was prepared by Professor Robert F. Bruner with the permission of Professor Gordon Donaldson, the author of an antecedent case. It was written as a basis for class discussion rather than to illustrate effective or ineffective handling of an administrative situation. Copyright© 1988 by the University of Virginia Darden School Foundation, Charlottesville, VA. All rights reserved. *To order copies, send an e-mail to* dardencases@virginia.edu. *No part of this publication may be reproduced, stored in a retrieval system, used in a spreadsheet, or transmitted in any form or by any means—electronic, mechanical, photocopying, recording, or otherwise—without the permission of the Darden School Foundation.* Rev. 12/01. Version 2.1.

To stimulate your analysis, consider the following questions:

1. Can you rank the projects simply by inspecting the cash flows?
2. What criteria might you use to rank the projects? Which quantitative ranking methods are better? Why?
3. What is the ranking you found by using quantitative methods? Does this ranking differ from the ranking obtained by simple inspection of the cash flows?
4. What kinds of real investment projects have cash flows similar to those in Exhibit 1?

EXHIBIT 1
Project Free Cash Flows (dollars in thousands)

Project number:	1	2	3	4	5	6	7	8
Initial investment	$(2,000)	$(2,000)	$(2,000)	$(2,000)	$(2,000)	$(2,000)	$(2,000)	$(2,000)
Year 1	$ 330	$ 1,666		$ 160	$ 280	$ 2,200*	$ 1,200	$ (350)
2	330	334*		200	280		900*	(60)
3	330	165		350	280		300	60
4	330			395	280		90	350
5	330			432	280		70	700
6	330			440*	280			1,200
7	330*			442	280			2,250*
8	$ 1,000			444	280*			
9				446	280			
10				448	280			
11				450	280			
12				451	280			
13				451	280			
14				452	280			
15			10,000*	(2,000)	280			
Sum of cash-flow benefits	$ 3,310	$ 2,165	$10,000	$ 3,561	$4,200	$2,200	$ 2,560	$4,150
Excess of cash flow over initial investment	$ 1,310	$ 165	$ 8,000	$ 1,561	$2,200	$ 200	$ 560	$2,150

*Indicates year in which payback is accomplished.

Fonderia di Torino S.p.A.

In November 2000, Francesca Cerini, managing director of Fonderia di Torino S.p.A.,[1] was considering the purchase of a "Vulcan Mold-Maker" automated molding machine. This machine would prepare the sand molds into which molten iron was poured to obtain iron castings. The Vulcan Mold-Maker would replace an older machine and would offer improvements in quality and some additional capacity for expansion. Similar molding-machine proposals had been rejected by the board of directors for economic reasons on three previous occasions, most recently in 1999. This time, given the size of the proposed expenditure of about €1 million,[2] Cerini was seeking a careful estimate of the project's costs and benefits and, ultimately, a recommendation of whether to proceed with the investment.

THE COMPANY

Fonderia di Torino specialized in the production of precision metal castings for use in automotive, aerospace, and construction equipment. The company had acquired a reputation for quality products, particularly for safety parts (i.e., parts whose failure would result in

---

[1]S.p.A. stands for "Societa per Azioni," literally, a business under share ownership, like a public corporation in the United States.

[2]In November 2000, the exchange rate between the euro and the U.S. dollar was about €1.17:$1.00.

This case was prepared by Robert F. Bruner from field research and public information and draws its structure and some data from an antecedent case written by Brandt Allen. Fonderia di Torino is a fictional company representing the issues that faced actual firms. The author gratefully acknowledges the financial support of the Batten Institute. It was written as a basis for class discussion rather than to illustrate effective or ineffective handling of an administrative situation. Copyright © 2001 by the University of Virginia Darden School Foundation, Charlottesville, VA. All rights reserved. *To order copies, send an e-mail to* dardencases@virginia.edu. *No part of this publication may be reproduced, stored in a retrieval system, used in a spreadsheet, or transmitted in any form or by any means—electronic, mechanical, photocopying, recording, or otherwise—without the permission of the Darden School Foundation*, Rev. 12/01. Version 1.2.

loss of control for the operator). Its products included crankshafts, transmissions, brake calipers, axles, wheels, and various steering-assembly parts. Customers were original-equipment manufacturers (OEMs), mainly in Europe. OEMs were becoming increasingly insistent about product quality, and Fonderia di Torino's response had reduced the rejection rate of its castings by the OEMs to 70 parts per million.

This record had won the company coveted quality awards from BMW, Ferrari, and Peugeot, and had resulted in strategic alliances with those firms: Fonderia di Torino and the OEMs exchanged technical personnel and design tasks; in addition, the OEMs shared confidential market-demand information with Fonderia di Torino, which increased the precision of the latter's production scheduling. In certain instances, the OEMs had provided cheap loans to Fonderia di Torino to support capital expansion. Finally, the company received relatively long-term supply contracts from the OEMs and had a preferential position for bidding on new contracts.

Fonderia di Torino, located in Milan, Italy, had been founded in 1912 by Francesca Cerini's great-grandfather, Benito Cerini, a naval engineer, to produce castings for the armaments industry. In the 1920s and 1930s, the company expanded its customer base into the automotive industry. Although the company barely avoided financial collapse in the late 1940s, Benito Cerini predicted a postwar demand for precision metal casting and positioned the company to meet it. From that time, Fonderia di Torino grew slowly but steadily; its sales for calendar-year 2000 were expected to be €280 million. It was listed for trading on the Milan stock exchange in 1991, but the Cerini family owned 55 percent of the common shares of stock outstanding. (The company's beta was 1.25.)[3]

The company's traditional hurdle rate of return on capital deployed was 14 percent. (This rate had not been reviewed since 1984.) In addition, company policy sought payback of an entire investment within five years. At the time of the case, the market value of the company's capital was 33 percent debt and 67 percent equity. The debt consisted entirely of loans from Banco Nazionale di Milano bearing an interest rate of 6.8 percent. The company's effective tax rate was about 43 percent, which reflected the combination of national and local corporate income-tax rates.

Francesca Cerini, age 57, had assumed executive responsibility for the company 20 years earlier, upon the death of her father. She held a doctorate in metallurgy and was the matriarch of an extended family. Only a son and a niece worked at Fonderia di Torino, however. Over the years, the Cerini family had sought to earn a rate of return on its equity investment of about 18 percent—this goal had been established by Benito Cerini and had never once been questioned by management.

THE VULCAN MOLD-MAKER MACHINE

Sand molds used to make castings were prepared in a semiautomated process at Fonderia di Torino in 2000. Workers stamped impressions in a mixture of sand and adhesive under

---

[3]The rate of return on euro-denominated bonds issued by EU governments was 5.3 percent. Francesca Cerini assumed that the equity risk premium would be 6 percent. Also, she believed that current bond yields impounded an expected inflation rate of 3 percent for the foreseeable future.

heat and high pressure. The process was relatively labor intensive, required training and re-training to obtain consistency in mold quality, and demanded some heavy lifting from workers. Indeed, medical claims for back injuries in the molding shop had doubled since 1998 as the mix of Fonderia di Torino's casting products shifted toward heavy items. (Items averaged 25 kilograms in 2000.)

The new molding machine would replace six semiautomated stamping machines that, together, had originally cost €415,807. Cumulative depreciation of €130,682 had already been charged against this original cost; annual depreciation on these machines had been averaging €47,520 a year. Fonderia di Torino's management believed that these semiauto-mated machines would need to be replaced after six years. Cerini had received an offer of €130,000 for the six machines.

The current six machines required 12 workers per shift[4] (24 in total) at €7.33 per worker per hour, plus the equivalent of 3 maintenance workers, each of whom was paid €7.85 an hour, plus maintenance supplies of €4,000 a year. Cerini assumed that the semi-automated machines, if kept, would continue to consume electrical power at the rate of €12,300 a year.

The Vulcan Mold-Maker molding machine was produced by a company in Allentown, Pennsylvania. Fonderia di Torino had received a firm offering price of €850,000 from the Allentown firm. The estimate for modifications to the plant, including wiring for the ma-chine's power supply, was €155,000. Allowing for shipping, installation, and testing, the total cost of the Vulcan Mold-Maker machine was expected to be €1.01 million, all of which would be capitalized and depreciated for tax purposes over eight years. (Cerini assumed that, at a high and steady rate of machine utilization, the Vulcan Mold-Maker would need to be replaced after the eighth year.)

The new machine would require two skilled operators (one per shift), each receiving €11.36 an hour (including benefits), and contract maintenance of €59,500 a year, and would incur power costs of €26,850 yearly. In addition, the automatic machine was expected to save at least €5,200 yearly through improved labor efficiency in other areas of the foundry.

With the current machines, more than 30 percent of the foundry's floor space was needed for the wide galleries the machines required; raw materials and in-process invento-ries had to be staged near each machine in order to smooth the work flow. With the auto-mated machine, almost half of this space would be freed for other purposes (although at present there was no need for new space).

Certain aspects of the Vulcan Mold-Maker purchase decision were difficult to quantify. First, Cerini was unsure whether the tough collective-bargaining agreement her company had with the employees' union would allow her to lay off the 24 operators of the semiauto-mated machines. Reassigning the workers to other jobs might be easier, but the only posi-tions needing to be filled were those of janitors, who were paid €4.13 an hour. The extent of any labor savings would depend on negotiations with the union. Second, Cerini believed that the Vulcan Mold-Maker would result in even higher levels of product quality and lower

---

[4]The foundry operated two shifts a day. It did not operate on weekends or holidays. At maximum, the foundry would produce for 210 days a year.

scrap rates than the company was now boasting. In light of the ever-increasing competition, this outcome might prove to be of enormous, but currently unquantifiable, competitive importance. Finally, the Vulcan Mold-Maker had a theoretical maximum capacity that was 30 percent higher than that of the six semiautomated machines; but these machines were operating at only 90 percent of capacity, and Cerini was unsure when added capacity would be needed. The latest economic news suggested that the economies of Europe were headed for a slowdown.

Diamond Chemicals PLC (A): The Merseyside Project

Late one afternoon in January 2001, Frank Greystock told Lucy Morris, "No one seems satisfied with the analysis so far, but the suggested changes could kill the project. If solid projects like this can't swim past the corporate piranhas, the company will never modernize."

Morris was plant manager of Diamond Chemicals' Merseyside Works in Liverpool, England. Her controller, Frank Greystock, was discussing a capital project that she wanted to propose to senior management. The project consisted of a £9 million expenditure to renovate and rationalize the polypropylene production line at the Merseyside Plant in order to make up for deferred maintenance and exploit opportunities to achieve increased production efficiency.

Diamond Chemicals was under pressure from investors to improve its financial performance because of both the worldwide economic slowdown and the accumulation of the firm's common shares by a well-known corporate raider, Sir David Benjamin. Earnings per share had fallen to £30 at the end of 2000 from around £60 at the end of 1999. Morris thus believed that the time was ripe to obtain funding from corporate headquarters for a modernization program for the Merseyside Works—at least she had believed so until Greystock presented her with several questions that had only recently surfaced.

DIAMOND CHEMICALS AND POLYPROPYLENE

Diamond Chemicals, a major competitor in the worldwide chemicals industry, was a leading producer of polypropylene, a polymer used in an extremely wide variety of products

This case was prepared by Professor Robert F. Bruner as a basis for class discussion rather than to illustrate effective or ineffective handling of an administrative situation. Diamond Chemicals is a fictional company reflecting the issues facing actual firms. The author wishes to acknowledge the helpful comments of Dr. Frank H. McTigue, the literary color of Anthony Trollope, and the financial support of the Citicorp Global Scholars Program. Copyright © 2001 by the University of Virginia Darden School Foundation, Charlottesville, VA. All rights reserved. *To order copies, send an e-mail to* dardencases@virginia.edu. *No part of this publication may be reproduced, stored in a retrieval system, used in a spreadsheet, or transmitted in any form or by any means—electronic, mechanical, photocopying, recording, or otherwise—without the permission of the Darden School Foundation.* Version 1.4.

(ranging from medical products to packaging film, carpet fibers, and automobile components) and known for its strength and malleability. Polypropylene was essentially priced as a commodity.

The production of polypropylene pellets at Merseyside began with propylene, a refined gas received in tank cars. Propylene was purchased from four refineries in England that produced it in the course of refining crude oil into gasoline. In the first stage of the production process, polymerization, the propylene gas was combined with a diluent (or solvent) in a large pressure vessel. In a catalytic reaction, polypropylene precipitated to the bottom of the tank and was then concentrated in a centrifuge.

The second stage of the production process compounded the basic polypropylene with stabilizers, modifiers, fillers, and pigments to achieve the desired attributes for a particular customer. The finished plastic was extruded into pellets for shipment to the customer.

The Merseyside production process was old, semicontinuous at best, and, therefore, higher in labor content than competitors' newer plants. The Merseyside plant was constructed in 1967.

Diamond Chemicals produced polypropylene at Merseyside and in Rotterdam, Holland. The two plants were of identical scale, age, and design. The managers of both plants reported to James Fawn, executive vice president and manager of the Intermediate Chemicals Group (ICG) of Diamond Chemicals. The company positioned itself as a supplier to customers in Europe and the Middle East. The strategic-analysis staff estimated that, in addition to numerous small producers, seven major competitors manufactured polypropylene in Diamond Chemicals' market region. Their plants operated at various cost levels. **Exhibit 1** presents a comparison of plant sizes and indexed costs.

THE PROPOSED CAPITAL PROGRAM

Morris had assumed responsibility for the Merseyside Works only 12 months previously, following a rapid rise from an entry position of shift engineer nine years before. When she assumed responsibility, she undertook a detailed review of the operations and discovered significant opportunities for improvement in polypropylene production. Some of these opportunities stemmed from the deferral of maintenance over the preceding five years. In an effort to enhance the operating results of the Works, the previous manager had limited capital expenditures to only the most essential. Now, what had been routine and deferrable was becoming essential. Other opportunities stemmed from correcting the antiquated plant design in ways that would save energy and improve the process flow: (1) relocating and modernizing tank-car unloading areas, which would enable the process flow to be streamlined; (2) refurbishing the polymerization tank to achieve higher pressures and thus greater throughput; and (3) renovating the compounding plant to increase extrusion throughput and obtain energy savings.

Morris proposed the expenditure of £9 million on this program. The entire polymerization line would need to be shut down for 45 days, however, and because the Rotterdam plant was operating near capacity, Merseyside's customers would buy from competitors. Greystock believed the loss of customers would not be permanent. The benefits would be a lower energy requirement[1] as well as a 7 percent greater manufacturing throughput. In addition, the project was expected to improve gross margin (before depreciation and energy savings) from 11.5 percent to 12.5 percent. The engineering group at Merseyside was highly confident that the efficiencies would be realized.

Merseyside currently produced 250,000 metric tons of polypropylene pellets a year. Currently, the price of polypropylene averaged £541 per ton for Diamond Chemicals' product mix. The tax rate required in capital-expenditure analyses was 30 percent. Greystock discovered that any plant facilities to be replaced had been completely depreciated. New assets could be depreciated on an accelerated basis[2] over 15 years, the expected life of the assets. The increased throughput would necessitate a one-time increase of work-in-process inventory equal in value to 3 percent of cost of goods. Greystock included in the first year of his forecast "preliminary engineering costs" of £500,000, which had been spent over the preceding nine months on efficiency and design studies of the renovation. Finally, the corporate manual stipulated that overhead costs be reflected in project analyses at the rate of 3.5 percent times the book value of assets acquired in the project, per year.[3]

Greystock had produced the discounted-cash-flow summary given in **Exhibit 2**. It suggested that the capital program would easily hurdle Diamond Chemicals' required return of 10 percent for engineering projects.

CONCERNS OF THE TRANSPORT DIVISION

Diamond Chemicals owned the tank cars with which Merseyside received propylene gas from four petroleum refineries in England. The Transport Division, a cost center, oversaw the movement of all raw, intermediate, and finished materials throughout the company and was responsible for managing the tank cars. Because of the project's increased throughput, Transport would have to increase its allocation of tank cars to Merseyside. Currently, the Transport

---

[1]Greystock characterized the energy savings as a percentage of sales and assumed that the savings would be equal to 1.25 percent of sales in the first 5 years and 0.75 percent in years 6–10. Thereafter, without added aggressive "green" spending, the energy efficiency of the plant would revert to its old level, and the savings would be zero. He believed that the decision to make further environmentally oriented investments was a separate choice (and one that should be made much later) and, therefore, that to include such benefits (of a presumably later investment decision) in the project being considered today would be inappropriate.

[2]The company's capital-expenditure manual suggested the use of double-declining-balance (DDB) depreciation, even though other more aggressive procedures might be permitted by the tax code. The reason for this policy was to discourage jockeying for corporate approvals based on tax provisions that could apply differently for different projects and divisions. Prior to senior-management approval, the controller's staff would present an independent analysis of special tax effects that might apply. Division managers, however, were discouraged from relying heavily on these effects. In applying the DDB approach to a 15-year project, the formula for accelerated depreciation was used for the first 10 years, after which depreciation was calculated on a straight-line basis. This conversion to straight-line was commonly done so that the asset would depreciate fully within its economic life.

[3]The corporate policy manual stated that

> new projects should be able to sustain a reasonable proportion of corporate overhead expense. Projects that are so marginal as to be unable to sustain these expenses and also meet the other criteria of investment attractiveness should not be undertaken. Thus, all new capital projects should reflect an annual pretax charge amounting to 3.5 percent of the value of the initial asset investment for the project.

Division could make this allocation out of excess capacity, although doing so would accelerate from 2005 to 2003 the need to purchase new rolling stock to support anticipated growth of the firm in other areas. The purchase would cost £2 million. The rolling stock would have a depreciable life of 10 years,[4] but with proper maintenance, the cars could operate much longer. The rolling stock could not be used outside of Britain because of differences in track gauge.

A memorandum from the controller of the Transport Division suggested that the cost of these tank cars should be included in the initial outlay of Merseyside's capital program. But Greystock disagreed. He told Morris,

> The Transport Division isn't paying one pence of actual cash because of what we're doing at Merseyside. In fact, we're doing the company a favor in using its excess capacity. Even *if* an allocation has to be made somewhere, it should go on the Transport Division's books. The way we've always evaluated projects in this company has been with the philosophy of "every tub on its own bottom"—every division has to fend for itself. The Transport Division isn't part of our own Intermediate Chemicals Group, so they should carry the allocation of rolling stock.

Accordingly, Greystock had not reflected any charge for the use of excess rolling stock in his preliminary DCF analysis, given in Exhibit 2.

The Transport Division and Intermediate Chemicals Group reported to separate executive vice presidents, who reported to the chairman and chief executive officer of the company. The executive VPs received an annual incentive bonus pegged to the performance of their divisions.

CONCERNS OF THE ICG SALES AND MARKETING DEPARTMENT

Greystock's analysis had led to questions from the director of Sales. In a recent meeting, the director told Greystock,

> Your analysis assumes that we can sell the added output and thus obtain the full efficiencies from the project, but as you know, the market for polypropylene is extremely competitive. Right now, the industry is in a downturn and it looks like an oversupply is in the works. This means that we will probably have to shift capacity away from Rotterdam toward Merseyside in order to move the added volume. Is this really a gain for Diamond Chemicals? Why spend money just so one plant can cannibalize another?

The vice president of Marketing was less skeptical. He said that with lower costs at Merseyside, Diamond Chemicals might be able to take business from the plants of competitors such as Saône-Poulet or Vaysol. In the current severe recession, competitors would fight hard to keep customers, but sooner or later, the market would revive, and it would be reasonable to assume that any lost business volume would return at that time.

Greystock had listened to both the director and vice president and chose to reflect no charge for a loss of business at Rotterdam in his preliminary analysis of the Merseyside project. He told Morris,

---

[4]The Transport Division depreciated rolling stock using DDB depreciation for the first eight years, and straight-line depreciation for the last two years.

Cannibalization really isn't a cash flow; there is no check written in this instance. Anyway, if the company starts burdening its cost-reduction projects with fictitious charges like this, we'll never maintain our cost competitiveness. A cannibalization charge is rubbish!

CONCERNS OF THE ASSISTANT PLANT MANAGER

Griffin Tewitt, the assistant plant manager and direct subordinate of Morris, proposed an unusual modification to Greystock's analysis during a late-afternoon meeting with Greystock and Morris. Over the past few months, Tewitt had been absorbed with the development of a proposal to modernize a separate and independent part of the Merseyside Works, the production line for ethylene-propylene-copolymer rubber (EPC). This product, a variety of synthetic rubber, had been pioneered by Diamond Chemicals in the early 1960s and was sold in bulk to European tire manufacturers. Despite hopes that this oxidation-resistant rubber would dominate the market in synthetics, in fact, EPC remained a relatively small product in the European chemical industry. Diamond, the largest supplier of EPC, produced the entire volume at Merseyside. EPC had been only marginally profitable to Diamond because of entry by competitors and the development of competing synthetic-rubber compounds over the past five years.

Tewitt had proposed a renovation of the EPC production line for a cost of £1 million. The renovation would give Diamond the lowest EPC cost base in the world and improve cash flows by £25,000 ad infinitum. Even so, at current prices and volumes, the net present value (NPV) of this project was −£750,000. Tewitt and the EPC product manager had argued strenuously to the executive committee of the company that the negative NPV ignored strategic advantages from the project and increases in volume and prices when the recession ended. Nevertheless, the executive committee had rejected the project, mainly on economic grounds.

In a hushed voice, Tewitt said to Morris and Greystock,

Why don't you include the EPC project as part of the polypropylene line renovations? The positive NPV of the poly renovations can easily sustain the negative NPV of the EPC project. This is an extremely important project to the company, a point that senior management doesn't seem to get. If we invest now, we'll be ready to exploit the market when the recession ends. If we don't invest now, you can expect that we will have to exit the business altogether in three years. Do you look forward to more layoffs? Do you want to manage a shrinking plant? Recall that our annual bonuses are pegged to the size of this operation. Also remember that, in the last 20 years, no one from corporate has monitored renovation projects once the investment decision was made.

CONCERNS OF THE TREASURY STAFF

After a meeting on a different matter, Frank Greystock described his dilemmas to Andrew Gowan, who worked as an analyst on Diamond Chemicals' Treasury staff. Gowan scanned Greystock's analysis, and pointed out that cash flows and discount rate need to be consistent in their assumptions about inflation. The 10 percent hurdle rate you're using is a nominal target rate of return. The Treasury staff think this impounds a long-term inflation expectation of 3 percent per year. Thus, Diamond Chemicals' real (i.e., zero-inflation) target rate of return is 7 percent.

The conversation was interrupted before Greystock could gain a full understanding of Gowan's comment. For the time being, Greystock decided to continue to use a discount rate of 10 percent, because it was the figure promoted in the latest edition of Diamond Chemicals' capital-budgeting manual.

EVALUATING CAPITAL-EXPENDITURE PROPOSALS AT DIAMOND CHEMICALS

In submitting a project for senior-management approval, the project-initiators had to identify it as belonging to one of four possible categories: (1) new product or market, (2) product or market extension, (3) engineering efficiency, or (4) safety or environment. The first three categories of proposals were subject to a system of four performance "hurdles," of which at least three had to be met for the proposal to be considered. The Merseyside project would be in the engineering efficiency category.

1. *Impact on earnings per share.* For engineering-efficiency projects, the contribution to net income from contemplated projects had to be positive. This criterion was calculated as the average annual EPS contribution of the project over its entire economic life, using the number of outstanding shares at the most recent fiscal year-end as the basis for the calculation. (At FYE 2000, Diamond Chemicals had 92,891,240 shares outstanding.)
2. *Payback.* This criterion was defined as the number of years necessary for free cash flow of the project to amortize the initial project outlay completely. For engineering-efficiency projects, the maximum payback period was six years.
3. *Discounted cash flow.* DCF was defined as the present value of future cash flows of the project (at the hurdle rate of 10 percent for engineering-efficiency proposals), less the initial investment outlay. This net present value of free cash flows had to be positive.
4. *Internal rate of return.* IRR was defined as being that discount rate at which the present value of future free cash flows just equaled the initial outlay—in other words, the rate at which the NPV was 0. The IRR of engineering-efficiency projects had to be greater than 10 percent.

CONCLUSION

Morris wanted to review Greystock's analysis in detail and settle the questions surrounding the tank cars and potential loss of business volume at Rotterdam. As Greystock's analysis now stood, the Merseyside project met all four investment criteria:

1. Average annual addition to EPS	=	£0.018
2. Payback period	=	3.6 years

3. Net present value   =   £9.0 million
4. Internal rate of return   =   25.9 percent

Morris was concerned that further tinkering might seriously weaken the attractiveness of the project.

EXHIBIT 1
Comparative Information on the Seven Largest Polypropylene Plants in Europe

	Plant Location	Year Established	Plant Annual Output (metric tons)	Production Cost per ton (indexed to low-cost producer)
CBTG A.G.	Saarbrün	1981	350,000	1.00
Diamond Chem.	Liverpool	1967	250,000	1.09
Diamond Chem.	Rotterdam	1967	250,000	1.09
Hosche A.G.	Hamburg	1977	300,000	1.02
Montecassino SpA	Genoa	1961	120,000	1.11
Saône-Poulet S.A.	Marseille	1972	175,000	1.07
Vaysol S.A.	Antwerp	1976	220,000	1.06
Next 10 largest plants			450,000	1.19

Source: Casewriter's analysis.

EXHIBIT 2
Frank Greystock's DCF Analysis of Merseyside Project (financial values in millions of British pounds)

Assumptions

Annual output (metric tons)	250,000	Discount rate	10.0%
Output gain/Original output	7.0%	Depreciable life (years)	15
Price/ton (pounds sterling)	541	Overhead/Investment	3.5%
Inflation rate (prices and costs)	0.0%	Salvage value	0
Gross margin (ex. deprec.)	12.50%	WIP inventory/Cost of goods	3.0%
Old gross margin	11.5%	Months downtime, construction	1.5
Tax rate	30.0%	After-tax scrap proceeds	0
Investment outlay (mill.)	9.00	Preliminary engineering costs	0.5
Energy savings/Sales Yr. 1–5	1.25%		
Yr. 6–10	0.8%		
Yr. 11–15	0.0%		

Year	Now	1 2001	2 2002	3 2003	4 2004	5 2005	6 2006	7 2007	8 2008	9 2009	10 2010	11 2011	12 2012	13 2013	14 2014
1. Estimate of incremental gross profit															
New output (tons)		267,500	267,500	267,500	267,500	267,500	267,500	267,500	267,500	267,500	267,500	267,500	267,500	267,500	267,500
Lost output—construction		(33,438)													
New sales (millions)		126.63	144.72	144.72	144.72	144.72	144.72	144.72	144.72	144.72	144.72	144.72	144.72	144.72	144.72
New gross margin		13.8%	13.8%	13.8%	13.8%	13.8%	13.3%	13.3%	13.3%	13.3%	13.3%	12.5%	12.5%	12.5%	12.5%
New gross profit		17.41	19.90	19.90	19.90	19.90	19.18	19.18	19.18	19.18	19.18	18.09	18.09	18.09	18.09
Old output		250,000	250,000	250,000	250,000	250,000	250,000	250,000	250,000	250,000	250,000	250,000	250,000	250,000	250,000
Old sales		135.25	135.25	135.25	135.25	135.25	135.25	135.25	135.25	135.25	135.25	135.25	135.25	135.25	135.25
Old gross profit		15.55	15.55	15.55	15.55	15.55	15.55	15.55	15.55	15.55	15.55	15.55	15.55	15.55	15.55
Incremental gross profit		1.86	4.34	4.34	4.34	4.34	3.62	3.62	3.62	3.62	3.62	2.54	2.54	2.54	2.54
2. Estimate of incremental depreciation															
New depreciation		1.20	1.04	0.90	0.78	0.68	0.59	0.51	0.44	0.38	0.33	0.43	0.43	0.43	0.43
3. Overhead		0.32	0.32	0.32	0.32	0.32	0.32	0.32	0.32	0.32	0.32	0.32	0.32	0.32	0.32
4. Prelim. engineering costs		0.50													
5. Pretax incremental profit		−0.16	2.99	3.13	3.25	3.35	2.72	2.80	2.87	2.92	2.98	1.79	1.79	1.79	1.79
6. Tax expense		−0.05	0.90	0.94	0.97	1.01	0.82	0.84	0.86	0.88	0.89	0.54	0.54	0.54	0.54
7. After-tax profit		−0.11	2.09	2.19	2.27	2.35	1.90	1.96	2.01	2.05	2.08	1.25	1.25	1.25	1.25
8. Cash flow adjustments															
Less capital expenditure	−9.00														
Add back depreciation		1.20	1.04	0.90	0.78	0.68	0.59	0.51	0.44	0.38	0.33	0.43	0.43	0.43	0.43
Less added WIP inventory		0.31	−0.47	0.00	0.00	0.00	0.00	0.00	0.00	0.00	0.00	0.00	0.00	0.00	0.00
After-tax scrap proceeds		0.00													
9. Free cash flow	−9.00	1.40	2.66	3.09	3.06	3.02	2.49	2.47	2.45	2.43	2.41	1.68	1.68	1.68	1.68

NPV = 9.00
IRR = 25.9%

Diamond Chemicals PLC (B): Merseyside and Rotterdam Projects

James Fawn, executive vice president of the Intermediate Chemicals Group (ICG) of Diamond Chemicals, met with his financial analyst, John Camperdown, to review two mutually exclusive capital-expenditure proposals. The firm's capital budget would be submitted for approval to the board of directors early in February 2001, and any projects proposed by Fawn for the ICG had to be forwarded soon to the chief executive officer of Diamond Chemicals for his review. Plant managers in Liverpool and Rotterdam had independently submitted expenditure proposals, each of which would expand the polypropylene output of their respective plants by 7 percent.[1] Diamond Chemicals' strategic-analysis staff argued strenuously that a companywide increase in polypropylene output of 14 percent made no sense, but half that amount did. Thus, Fawn could not accept *both* projects; he could sponsor only one for approval by the board.

Corporate policy was to evaluate projects based on four criteria: (1) net present value (NPV), computed at the appropriate cost of capital, (2) internal rate of return (IRR), (3) payback, and (4) growth in earnings per share. In addition, the board of directors was receptive to "strategic factors"—considerations that might be difficult to quantify. The manager of the Rotterdam plant, Elizabeth Eustace, argued vociferously that her project easily hurdled all the relevant quantitative standards and that it had important strategic benefits. Indeed, Eustace had interjected these points in two recent meetings with senior management and at

---

[1]Background information on Diamond Chemicals and the polypropylene business is given in "Diamond Chemicals (A): The Merseyside Project" (Case 19).

This case was prepared by Professor Robert F. Bruner as a basis for class discussion rather than to illustrate effective or ineffective handling of an administrative situation. Diamond Chemicals is a fictional company, reflecting the issues facing actual firms. The author wishes to acknowledge the helpful comments of Dr. Frank H. McTigue, the literary color of Anthony Trollope, and the financial support of the Citicorp Global Scholars Program. Copyright © 2001 by the University of Virginia Darden School Foundation, Charlottesville, VA. All rights reserved. *To order copies, send an e-mail to dardencases@virginia.edu. No part of this publication may be reproduced, stored in a retrieval system, used in a spreadsheet, or transmitted in any form or by any means—electronic, mechanical, photocopying, recording, or otherwise—without the permission of the Darden School Foundation.* Version 1.4.

a cocktail reception for the board of directors. Fawn expected to review the proposal from Lucy Morris, manager of the Liverpool plant, at this meeting with Camperdown, but he suspected that neither proposal dominated the other on all four criteria. Fawn's choice would apparently not be straightforward.

THE PROPOSAL FROM MERSEYSIDE, LIVERPOOL

The project for the Merseyside plant entailed the enhancement of existing facilities and production process. Based on the type of project and the engineering studies, the potential benefits of the project were fairly certain (see "Diamond Chemicals [A]" for a detailed discussion of this project). To date, Morris, manager of the Merseyside Works, had limited her discussions about the project to conversations with Fawn and Camperdown. Camperdown had raised various exploratory questions about the project and had presented preliminary analyses of it to managers in Marketing and Transportation for their comments. The revised analysis emerging from these discussions would be the focus of discussion with Camperdown in the forthcoming meeting.

Camperdown had indicated that Morris's final memo on the project was short, only three pages. James wondered whether this memo would satisfy his remaining questions.

THE ROTTERDAM PROJECT

Elizabeth Eustace's proposal consisted of a 90-page document replete with detailed schematics, engineering comments, strategic analyses, and financial projections. The basic discounted-cash-flow (DCF) analysis is presented in **Exhibit 1** and shows that the project had an NPV of £14 million and an IRR of 17.9 percent. Accounting for a "worst-case" scenario, which assumed erosion of Merseyside's volume equal to the gain in Rotterdam's volume, the NPV was £11.6 million.

In essence, Eustace's proposal called for the expenditure of £8 million spread over three years to convert the plant's polymerization line from batch to continuous-flow technology and to install sophisticated state-of-the-art process controls throughout the polymerization and compounding operations. The heart of the new system would be an analog computer driven by advanced software written by a team of engineering professors at an institute in Japan. The three-year-old process-control technology had been used on a smaller polypropylene production facility in Japan and had produced significant improvements in cost and output. Other major producers were known to be evaluating this system for use in their plants.

Eustace explained that installing the sophisticated new system would not be feasible without also obtaining a continuous source of supply of propylene gas. She proposed to obtain this gas by pipeline from one refinery five kilometers away (rather than by railroad tank cars sourced from three refineries). Diamond Chemicals had an option to purchase a pipeline and its right-of-way for £3.5 million; then, for relatively little cost, the pipeline could be extended to the Rotterdam plant and the refinery at the other end. The option had been purchased several years earlier. A consultant had informed Eustace that to purchase a right-of-way at today's prices and to lay a comparable pipeline would cost approximately £6 million, a value at which the consultant believed the right-of-way could be sold today in an auction. The consultant also forecasted that in 15 years the value of the right-of-way would be £35 million.[2] This option was to expire in six months.

Some senior Diamond Chemicals executives believed firmly that if the Rotterdam project were not undertaken, the option on the right-of-way should be allowed to expire unexercised. The reasoning was summarized by Jeffrey Palliser, chairman of the executive committee:

> Our business is chemicals, not land speculation. Simply buying the right-of-way with an intention of reselling it for a profit takes us beyond our expertise. Who knows when we could sell it, and for how much? How distracting would this little side venture be for Elizabeth Eustace?

Younger members of senior management were more willing to consider a potential investment arbitrage on the right-of-way.

Eustace expected to realize benefits (such as increased output and gross margin) of this investment gradually over time as the new technology was installed and shaken down and as learning-curve effects were realized. She advocated a phased investment program (as opposed to all at once) in order to minimize disruption to plant operations and to allow the new technology to be calibrated and fine-tuned.

Given the complexity of the technology and the extent to which it would permeate the plant, the system would be very expensive to dismantle. Practically, there would be no going back once the decision had been made to install the new controls. Eustace's project would represent an irrevocable commitment to the analog technology at the Rotterdam plant.

Fawn recalled that the "strategic factors" to which Eustace referred had to do with the obvious cost and output improvements expected from the new system, as well as from an advantage from being the first major European producer to implement the new technology. Being the first to implement the technology probably meant a head start in moving down the learning curve toward reducing costs as the organization became familiar with the technology. Eustace argued,

> The Japanese, and now the Americans, exploit the learning-curve phenomenon aggressively. Fortunately, they aren't major players in European polypropylene, at least for now. This is a once-in-a-generation opportunity for Diamond Chemicals to leapfrog its competition through the exploitation of new technology.

In an oblique reference to the Merseyside proposal, Eustace went on to say,

> There are two alternatives to implementation of the analog process-control technology. One is a series of myopic enhancements to existing facilities, but this is nothing more than sticking one's

---

[2]The right-of-way had several alternate commercial uses. Most prominently, the Dutch government had expressed an interest in using the right-of-way for a new high-speed railroad line. However, the planning for this line had barely begun, which suggested that land-acquisition efforts were years away. Moreover, government budget deficits threatened the timely implementation of the rail project. Another potential user was Medusa Communications, an international telecommunications company that was looking for pathways along which to bury its new fiber-optical cables. Power companies and other chemical companies or refiners might also be interested in acquiring the right-of-way.

head in the sand, for it leaves us at the mercy of our competitors who *are* making choices for the long term. The other alternative is to exit the polypropylene business, but this amounts to walking away from the considerable know-how we've accumulated in this business and from what is basically a valuable activity. Our commitment to analog controls makes the right choice at the right time.

The analog process-control system seemed to be the most advanced on the market. There were rumors, however, that an engineering design team at Glüsingen University in Germany was testing a radically different process-control technology—based on lasers, spectral chromatography, and digital computing—and that it was outperforming the Japanese system on cost reduction and output improvement by a factor of 1.1:1. If these rumors were true, such a system might become commercially available within five years. While it would be possible to switch to the German technology in five years, doing so would mean writing off entirely the investment in the Japanese system.

Fawn wondered how to take the potential new technology into account in making his decision. Even if he recommended the Merseyside project today, the new controls (either Japanese, or German if successfully commercialized) could later be installed at Merseyside. Lucy Morris, the plant manager at Merseyside, told James Fawn that she preferred to "wait and see" how the German technology evolved before entertaining a technology upgrade at her plant. Fawn believed that the flexibility to change technologies differed between the Rotterdam and Merseyside proposals, and this difference might affect the value of the respective projects.[3]

CONCLUSION

James Fawn wanted to give this choice careful thought, because the plant managers at Merseyside and Rotterdam seemed to have so much invested in their own proposals. He wished that the capital-budgeting criteria would give a straightforward indication about the relative attractiveness of the two mutually exclusive projects. He wondered by what rational, analytical process he could extricate himself from the ambiguities of the present measures of investment attractiveness. Moreover, he wished he had a way to evaluate the primary technological difference between the two proposals: the Rotterdam project firmly committed Diamond Chemicals to the new process technology; the Merseyside project did not, but it retained the flexibility to allow the technology in the future.

---

[3]Using Monte Carlo simulation, Morris had estimated that the cash returns from both the German and Japanese technologies had standard deviations of 8 percent and that the correlation of the two returns was predictably high: 80 percent. The nominal risk-free rate of return was about 5.5 percent. The view of Diamond's engineers was that the German digital-based process-control system would emerge in the next five years or not emerge at all and that the probability of successful commercialization of the German technology was 50 percent.

EXHIBIT 1
Analysis of Rotterdam Project (values in British pounds)

Assumptions

Annual output (metric tons)	250,000	Setup and labor savings/Sales (yr. 1)	0.0%
Output gain per year/Prior year	2.0%	Discount rate	10.0%
Maximum possible output	267,500	Depreciable life (years)	15
Price/ton (pounds sterling)	541	Overhead/Investment	3.5%
Inflation (prices and costs)	0.0%	Salvage value	0
Gross margin growth rate/Year	0.80%	WIP inventory/Cost of goods sold	3.0%
Maximum possible gross margin	16.0%	Terminal value of right-of-way	35
Old gross margin	11.5%	Months downtime, construction 2001	5
Tax rate	30.0%	2002	4
Investment outlay (millions) Now	3.5	2003	3
End, 2001	2.5	2004	0
2002	1		
2003	1		

Year	Now	1 2001	2 2002	3 2003	4 2004	5 2005	6 2006	7 2007	8 2008	9 2009	10 2010	11 2011	12 2012	13 2013	14 2014	15 2015
1 Estimate of incremental gross profit																
New output		255,000	260,100	265,302	267,500	267,500	267,500	267,500	267,500	267,500	267,500	267,500	267,500	267,500	267,500	267,500
Lost output—construction		(106,250)	(86,700)	(66,326)	0											
New sales (millions)		80.47	93.81	107.65	144.72	144.72	144.72	144.72	144.72	144.72	144.72	144.72	144.72	144.72	144.72	144.72
New gross margin		11.6%	11.8%	12.1%	12.5%	13.0%	13.6%	14.4%	15.3%	16.0%	16.0%	16.0%	16.0%	16.0%	16.0%	16.0%
New gross profit		9.33	11.05	12.99	18.02	18.76	19.67	20.80	22.17	23.15	23.15	23.15	23.15	23.15	23.15	23.15
Old output		250,000	250,000	250,000	250,000	250,000	250,000	250,000	250,000	250,000	250,000	250,000	250,000	250,000	250,000	250,000
Old sales		135.25	135.25	135.25	135.25	135.25	135.25	135.25	135.25	135.25	135.25	135.25	135.25	135.25	135.25	135.25
Old gross profit		15.55	15.55	15.55	15.55	15.55	15.55	15.55	15.55	15.55	15.55	15.55	15.55	15.55	15.55	15.55
Incremental gross profit		−6.23	−4.50	−2.57	2.47	3.20	4.12	5.25	6.62	7.60	7.60	7.60	7.60	7.60	7.60	7.60
2. Estimate of incremental depreciation																
Yr. 1 outlays		0.33	0.29	0.25	0.22	0.19	0.16	0.14	0.12	0.11	0.09	0.12	0.12	0.12	0.12	0.12
Yr. 2 outlays			0.14	0.12	0.10	0.09	0.08	0.07	0.06	0.05	0.04	0.05	0.05	0.05	0.05	0.05
Yr. 3 outlays				0.15	0.13	0.11	0.09	0.08	0.07	0.06	0.05	0.05	0.05	0.05	0.05	0.05
Total, new depreciation		0.33	0.43	0.53	0.45	0.39	0.33	0.29	0.25	0.21	0.18	0.22	0.22	0.22	0.22	0.22
3. Overhead		0	0	0	0	0	0	0	0	0	0	0	0	0	0	0
4. Pretax incremental profit		−6.56	−4.94	−3.09	2.02	2.81	3.79	4.96	6.37	7.39	7.42	7.38	7.38	7.38	7.38	7.38
5. Tax expense		−1.97	−1.48	−0.93	0.61	0.84	1.14	1.49	1.91	2.22	2.23	2.21	2.21	2.21	2.21	2.21
6. After-tax profit		−4.59	−3.46	−2.17	1.41	1.97	2.65	3.47	4.46	5.17	5.19	5.17	5.17	5.17	5.17	5.17

(continued)

EXHIBIT 1 (continued)
Analysis of Rotterdam Project (values in British pounds)

Year	Now	1 2001	2 2002	3 2003	4 2004	5 2005	6 2006	7 2007	8 2008	9 2009	10 2010	11 2011	12 2012	13 2013	14 2014	15 2015
7. Cash flow adjustments																
Add back depreciation		0.33	0.43	0.53	0.45	0.39	0.33	0.29	0.25	0.21	0.18	0.22	0.22	0.22	0.22	0.22
Less added WIP inventory		1.46	−0.35	−0.36	−0.96	0.02	0.03	0.03	0.04	0.03	0.00	0.00	0.00	0.00	0.00	0.00
Capital spending		2.50	1.00	1.00												
Terminal value, land	3.50															35.00
8. Free cash flow	−3.50	−8.21	−3.68	−2.28	2.83	2.34	2.96	3.73	4.67	5.35	5.38	5.39	5.39	5.39	5.39	40.39
DCF Rotterdam = 14.01																
IRR, Rotterdam = 17.9%																
9. Adjustment for erosion in Merseyside volume:																
Lost Merseyside output		—	—	—	17,500	17,500	17,500	17,500	17,500	17,500	17,500	17,500	17,500	17,500	17,500	17,500
Lost Merseyside revenue		—	—	—	9.47	9.47	9.47	9.47	9.47	9.47	9.47	9.47	9.47	9.47	9.47	9.47
Lost Merseyside gross profits		—	—	—	1.09	1.09	1.09	1.09	1.09	1.09	1.09	1.09	1.09	1.09	1.09	1.09
Lost gross profits after taxes		—	—	—	0.76	0.76	0.76	0.76	0.76	0.76	0.76	0.76	0.76	0.76	0.76	0.76
Change in Merseyside inventory		—	—	—	0.28	0.28	0.28	0.28	0.28	0.28	0.28	0.28	0.28	0.28	0.28	0.28
Total effect on free cash flow		—	—	—	(0.48)	(0.48)	(0.48)	(0.48)	(0.48)	(0.48)	(0.48)	(0.48)	(0.48)	(0.48)	(0.48)	(0.48)
DCF, erosion Merseyside **(2.45)**																
DCF, Rotterdam adjusted for full erosion at Merseyside = **11.57**																
Cash flows after erosion	−3.50	−8.21	−3.68	−2.28	2.35	1.86	2.48	3.25	4.19	4.88	4.90	4.91	4.91	4.91	4.91	39.91
IRR 16.56%																

Genzyme/GelTex Pharmaceuticals Joint Venture

In early 1997, Greg Phelps, EVP of Genzyme Corporation, met with members of a joint-venture negotiating team to develop proposed terms of a joint-venture agreement. The venture would combine capabilities of Genzyme and GelTex Pharmaceuticals to market GelTex's first product, RenaGel. GelTex was an early-stage biotech research company with two products in its pipeline. GelTex had neither the capital nor the marketing organization to launch RenaGel. Therefore, the company had been looking for a partner that would contribute cash and marketing expertise in exchange for a share of profits in a joint venture.

Genzyme had revenues of $518 million in 1996, and had grown rapidly through the innovative use of joint ventures and alliances. The joint venture with GelTex was attractive to Genzyme for several reasons. In addition to the benefit of increasing earnings through the sale of RenaGel, the joint venture would represent an excellent fit for Genzyme's specialty therapeutics and allow the firm to tap new markets. Also, building a strong partnership with GelTex might enable Genzyme to strike the same kind of deal for GelTex's second product, CholestaGel, which was targeting a much larger segment, the multibillion-dollar market of anticholesterol drugs.

Greg Phelps was eager to conclude a deal and launch the venture with GelTex. Important questions, however, had to be addressed before consummating an agreement.

- *What was the likely enterprise value of the joint venture?* This estimate would need to reflect the risks inherent in investing in a drug not yet approved by the U.S. Food and Drug Administration (FDA). Also, the joint-venture team would need to determine the best way to value a business with no operating history and an uncertain future.

This case was prepared by Dr. Pierre Jacquet, M.D., Ph.D., MBA '98, and Professors Robert Bruner and Samuel E. Bodily. The cooperation of Genzyme is gratefully acknowledged. Certain financial data regarding the venture have been disguised. This case was written as a basis for class discussion rather than to illustrate effective or ineffective handling of an administrative situation. Copyright © 1999 by the University of Virginia Darden School Foundation, Charlottesville, VA. All rights reserved. *To order copies, send an e-mail to* dardencases@virginia.edu. *No part of this publication may be reproduced, stored in a retrieval system, used in a spreadsheet, or transmitted in any form or by any means—electronic, mechanical, photocopying, recording, or otherwise—without the permission of the Darden School Foundation.* Version 2.2.

- *How much of the venture should Genzyme acquire?* Typically, joint ventures between pharmaceutical firms and biotech companies featured an unequal division of interests (e.g., 80 percent pharma and 20 percent biotech). Phelps, however, wanted to consider the possible benefits of a 50-50 balance of interests.
- *How much should Genzyme pay for its interest?* Initial discussions had focused on a lump-sum payment of $27.5 million for a 50 percent interest. But the amount of any payment would depend on answers to the previous questions, on the assessment of risks, and on the impact on Genzyme's earnings. Accounting rules required that Genzyme expense investments that occurred before the venture received FDA approval; after approval, Genzyme could capitalize the investment and amortize it over the life of the venture.

Phelps turned to his team for analysis of these issues and proposals for GelTex.

GENZYME CORPORATION

Genzyme Corporation, headquartered in Cambridge, Massachusetts, was the fourth- largest biotech company in the United States. Unlike pharmaceutical companies that manufactured drugs through chemical processes, biotech companies used living organisms or their products to generate drugs. The company's sales reached $518 million in 1996 through researching, developing, manufacturing, and marketing products for human health care. Genzyme was founded as an enzyme-manufacturing company in 1981 by Henry Blair, a Tufts University scientist whose vision was to develop enzymes for use in diagnosis.[1] The first opportunity to turn Genzyme's expertise into a new therapeutic came with Ceredase, a treatment for Gaucher's disease. The drug was approved for sale in the United States in March 1991 to treat patients suffering moderate to severe symptoms of Gaucher's disease, a market of some 3,000 people.

Two years later, the company launched a recombinant form of Ceredase and started to enter new markets—surgical, pharmaceutical, diagnostic, and genomic products—through strategic alliances, joint ventures, and acquisitions. Such diversity allowed Genzyme to play a leadership role in a broad range of cutting-edge technologies and therapies, according to Genzyme's chairman, president, and CEO, Henri A. Termeer.[2] The company's diversity came from its three[a] divisions—Genzyme General; Genzyme Tissue Repair; and a subsidiary, Genzyme Transgenics—each with its own common stock traded on the NASDAQ (see **Exhibit 1**).

The wide array of technologies provided Genzyme with an excellent platform for achieving breakthroughs in major unmet medical needs. Rather than concentrate efforts on the next big hit, however, the company had decided to manage its R&D like a portfolio by outsourcing innovations through partnerships. Genzyme's strategy was to supplement its internal R&D with strategic alliances with external companies in order to access high-quality products in late-stage development.

---

[a]A fourth division, Genzyme Molecular Oncology, would be founded by the end of 1997.

THE GELTEX OPPORTUNITY

In early 1997, Genzyme was approached by GelTex's management team to form an alliance for launching RenaGel. Genzyme and GelTex had had a long-term relationship. Besides the fact that the boards of directors of both companies had common members, Henry Blair, the founder of Genzyme, had helped found GelTex in 1991.

History

GelTex was founded to develop ideas generated by George Whitesides, a professor of polymer chemistry at Harvard. Cofounder Dr. James Tananbaum, who worked with George Whitesides, developed the initial patents that composed GelTex's technology base. Tananbaum brought along two more founders with business expertise, Bob Carpenter and Henry Blair.

As Carpenter commented in an interview for the *Boston Business Journal:*[4]

> The company was set up very quickly. We invited 10 of our friends to dinner, all of whom were either scientists or biotech-company executives. And then Professor Whitesides and I pitched our idea to the invited guests. By the time dessert was served, $875,000 had been put on the table and GelTex was born.

The money lasted a year. In July 1993, another $6.8 million was raised from venture capitalists, and the company moved its makeshift lab from the North Shore of Boston to a 4,000-square-foot facility in Lexington. At the time, there were only four employees. In August 1994, another $10 million was raised in a third round of financing, and the company moved to its present location in Waltham, Massachusetts.

In November 1995, the company completed an initial public offering of its common stock, selling 2,875,000 common shares, with net proceeds to the company of $26.2 million after deducting offering costs. GelTex had 45 employees at the time of the joint-venture deal with Genzyme and had committed to a strategic alliance for RenaGel with two partners: Chugai Pharmaceuticals for marketing and distribution in Asia, and Dow Chemical for drug manufacturing. The possible joint venture between Genzyme and GelTex would concern only the U.S. and European markets.

Technology

Many drug-delivery companies had looked at polymers, which had the attractive features of being nonreactive in the body and able to store relatively large quantities of drug for slow release. GelTex had the innovative, reverse idea to find polymers that could soak up substances in the body. With this approach, GelTex set out to develop orally available polymers, or "hydrogels," that could absorb and eliminate, through their efficient binding surface areas, toxic substances from the human gastrointestinal tract.[3] During the digestive process, the intestinal tract delivered nutrients and water to the bloodstream and eliminated waste products and indigestible materials though the bowel. Absorption of nutrients, electrolytes, water, and certain digestive substances such as bile acid was controlled by the intestinal wall, which acted as a gateway from the intestines to the bloodstream. Once they entered the digestive tract, GelTex polymers absorbed water and expanded like a sponge, thereby increasing the surface area of available binding sites. The spongelike material helped trap the target substance and eliminated it from the intestinal tract, even at low dosage levels.

The target markets for GelTex's technology were patients with conditions treatable in the gastrointestinal tract, including the large markets of patients with elevated cholesterol, elevated phosphorus levels, certain infectious diseases, and inflammatory conditions of the intestine. The company's lead products were RenaGel (which bound dietary phosphates in patients with chronic kidney dysfunction) and CholestaGel (which bound bile acid to lower cholesterol absorption from the gastrointestinal tract).

Strategy

GelTex's overall strategy was to become a "virtual" company that took its products far enough into development to create value without building huge operating infrastructures. As stated by Mark Skaletsky, GelTex's CEO, the company's strategy was simple.[4] Instead of creating a big corporate infrastructure, the company minimized costs by hiring a handful of experts to oversee work in key areas and then outsourcing most of the actual work. By curtailing its expenses, GelTex had generally minimized its need for capital. When it did need money, the company, from the beginning, had been successful tapping private investors and venture-capital firms.

While GelTex farmed out a lot of work, it was still maintaining its own staff of 30 researchers and some support personnel, in addition to the core managers. The five areas that were being outsourced included preclinical testing, manufacturing, medical services, regulatory affairs, and business development. Depending on their area of supervision, all five individuals who oversaw the outsourcing and who also served as the company's management team were working with outside contractors, consultants, clinical-research organizations, and the FDA to get the work accomplished in their respective areas of responsibility.

RENAGEL

Healthy individuals' kidneys maintained a delicate balance between phosphorus and calcium levels in the blood by excreting excess phosphorus in the urine. In patients with chronic kidney failure, the kidneys were unable to remove enough phosphorus to maintain this critical balance. The resulting increased level of phosphorus, called hyperphosphatemia, resulted in the production of parathyroid hormone, which broke down bone to release calcium into the blood in an effort to reestablish the calcium-phosphorus balance. This process was responsible for bone demineralization, calcification of the circulatory system, and other serious complications.

When administered through the gastrointestinal tract, RenaGel was able to bind with phosphorus and decrease its absorption into the blood stream. The drug was expected to be effective in restoring the calcium-phosphorus balance in patients with chronic renal failure. Moreover, compared with other drugs available for this condition, RenaGel simplified administration of therapy for physicians and was associated with less-toxic effects.

Kidney-Failure Market

In 1997, there were nearly one million patients in the United States with chronic renal failure; of these, an estimated 210,000 required dialysis to survive. All of these patients had lost the ability to excrete phosphorus and were prescribed phosphate binders; hence, they were all candidates for RenaGel. The U.S. dialysis-patient population had grown at a compounded annual rate of 8 percent over the last 10 years, driven by multiple factors including the aging of the population, increases in the incidence of diabetes, and increased utilization of dialysis. Europe had roughly 165,000 dialysis patients, with the population growing at approximately 6 percent annually; the Japanese market had roughly a population of 130,000 dialysis patients, growing at the same rate as the European population.[3,5]

Current Treatment and Competition

The initial treatment in patients with chronic renal failure sought to maintain the level of phosphorus in the blood within normal limits by reducing the amount of phosphate in the diet. Sources of phosphates included eggs, dairy products, and meat products. This prevention therapy only worked in 10 percent of dialysis patients, leaving 90 percent to proceed to drug therapy.

There was only one drug approved by the FDA for lowering phosphate levels: Braintree Pharmaceuticals' PhosLo (calcium acetate), which required a prescription. Analysts estimated that PhosLo had about 50 percent of the market.[3] The rest of the market was filled by generic over-the-counter drugs: calcium carbonate and aluminum hydroxide. Both drugs created severe side effects and were not used chronically because of their high level of toxicity.[5]

There were also several drugs under development for the treatment of hyperphosphatemia. Most of these products were in an early stage of clinical development and were vitamin-D analogues that would act synergistically rather than compete with RenaGel.[5]

Patents and Stage of Clinical Development

GelTex had received a U.S. patent for RenaGel, as well as for a broader class of phosphate-binding agents. After having successfully completed phase I and phase II studies, GelTex announced, in early January 1997, positive preliminary results from a phase III study that encompassed 172 patients at 17 different medical centers. Two months later, GelTex reported positive results from a second phase III clinical trial on 82 patients and was planning to file for a new drug approval (NDA) with the Food and Drug Administration by the end of 1997.

DEVELOPMENT RISKS FOR DRUGS

Products in the biotech industry were characterized by many unique features, which made them difficult to value. Once a product was marketed, the revenues, costs, and product potential could be estimated with comparative ease. However, given the long time frame between idea inception, regulatory approval, and product marketing as well as the small number of ideas that ultimately resulted in a marketable product, biotech drugs were subject to numerous uncertainties.

There were three major risk factors in each pharmaceutical/biotech development project: the probability of clinical success or failure at progressive stages of development, delays in the development and approval process, and uncertainty of the future revenue stream (if any) of the resultant product.[6]

Clinical Risk

One feature of the biotechnology industry that made valuation so complex was the product life cycle. A biotech drug had two distinct life cycles, the development life cycle and the product life cycle. The development life cycle was critical to the value of a product because large capital resources were needed to sustain the significant levels of R&D. It was estimated that more than 80 percent of biotech projects failed during this cycle for economic and regulatory reasons.[7]

The development life cycle of a drug could be divided into six distinct stages through which any drug would have to progress in order to reach the marketplace:[1]

- *Preclinical research:* A drug that showed potential was tested in the laboratory and in animals to assess its safety and to analyze its biological effects. If the drug proved safe and demonstrated the desired biological effects, the firm filed a notice for an investigational new drug (IND) with the FDA. If the FDA did not object within 30 days, the company could proceed to conduct clinical testing with humans using the new compound. It was estimated that only 1 in 5,000 compounds that were considered under development entered the preclinical-testing phase.[8]
- *Phase I trial:* The phase I trial in clinical testing was designed to determine the safety and pharmacological properties of the drug. Each drug was typically tested in 20 or more healthy volunteers.
- *Phase II trial:* The phase II trials were designed to evaluate the effectiveness of the drug and to identify side effects. Tests were typically conducted with several hundred volunteers, some of whom received the drug and some of whom received a placebo.
- *Phase III trial:* The phase III trials measured the effect of the drug on a large sample of hundreds of patients over several years. These trials helped ascertain long-term side effects and provided information on the effectiveness of a range of doses administered to a mix of patients.
- *Registration:* Upon completion of the phase III trials, firms were required to file an NDA or a product-license application (PLA) with the FDA and submit documentation of all relevant data for review.

- *Regulatory review:* The FDA created a special advisory committee for each NDA and PLA that made the final recommendation as to whether the drug should be released for commercial sale. Safety monitoring continued even after approval.

To value the clinical risk of a biotech drug, one could consider its stage of clinical development and its probability to make it to market. As shown in **Exhibit 2,** a drug in phase III trial, such as RenaGel was in early 1997, had a 65 percent probability to move on through FDA filing to FDA approval and thus make it to market launch.

Development Time before Market Launch

As a drug progressed through the different clinical stages, the revenue stream generated through market launch drew closer. It took several years for a drug in phase III to reach the market. The uncertainty surrounding FDA approval was compounded by the impact of changing regulations and governmental policies as well as by the arrival of competing compounds. With regard to RenaGel, an expeditious response from the FDA would occur one year after filing, that is, in 1998. Because of the encouraging results of RenaGel's phase III studies, management believed that RenaGel would be launched in the United States at the beginning of 1999 and in Europe at the beginning of 2000. The team assumed a 20 percent probability of a one-year launch delay in the United States (and therefore in Europe) beyond those dates and a 10 percent probability of a two-year delay.

Market Success

Once a drug received FDA approval, uncertainties remained concerning its market success. Depending on market conditions (e.g., competition, health-care policies, and market need), the average life cycle of a biotech drug was estimated to be around 13 to 14 years, with the peak penetration rate reached within the first 5 years.[9] Drug sales generally peaked between years five and seven after market launch and started to decline by year nine because of the entrance of new or improved products. Currently, there was no serious competition for RenaGel in the hyperphosphatemia market, but many drugs were under development. For RenaGel, the team projected (conservatively) that the life cycle of the drug would be as low as 10 years and as high as 20 years, with the most likely outcome 13 years.

FINANCIAL PROJECTIONS FOR RENAGEL

Analysts on Genzyme's joint-venture team decided to use a discounted-cash-flow analysis to value the venture as an enterprise. As the analysts were building financial projections, however, they realized that there were many uncertainties associated with RenaGel. A typical discounted-cash-flow analysis would not unveil the different outcomes of the venture and their relative values. The team wondered whether running a Monte Carlo simulation for the different assumptions would be helpful to price the venture and design its term structure.

Forecast of Income Statement

Because many factors varied predictably with the volume of sales, the primary variable forecasted was RenaGel revenues. Once approved for the U.S. market, the drug was expected to enter the European market the following year. The Genzyme RenaGel joint venture would not supply the Asian market because GelTex had already licensed drug development and commercialization rights in those countries to Chugai Pharmaceuticals.

It was estimated that 90 percent of the U.S. market would be eligible for the drug, while this ratio might be lower (70 percent) for the European market. Many factors were expected to influence revenues.

- *Peak penetration rate in the market:* Based on different marketing analyses and analysts' reports, the best guess was a 50 percent peak penetration rate at year five, with a range from 20 percent to 59 percent (giving an average of 43 percent). Whatever the value of this peak rate, the analysts assumed that the pattern of penetration over time would be similar and thus the market penetration at any time would be proportional to the peak. The pattern of penetration over time assumed by the team is contained in the first complete line of **Exhibit 3.**
- *Compliance:* Not all patients who used the drug would do so faithfully, even with a doctor strongly recommending its use. The team believed that the most likely compliance rate would be 92 percent and was prepared for a number as low as 75 percent or as high as 94 percent. Based on these numbers, the average compliance would be 87 percent.
- *Price per patient:* The annual price of the drug per patient would depend on many things, including how many pills the patient used and competitive pressures on the price that could be charged for the pill. The joint-venture team had worked up a figure of $1,000 as the average annual price per patient. This figure was based on an estimate of $1,100 as the most likely outcome, with a range from $600 to $1,300.

Although the variable costs of the drug were hard to pinpoint, they were not the most critical variable in the success of the drug. The team members decided to use the average industry gross profit margin of 70 percent for their analysis. They also believed that a gross profit margin for RenaGel could not be pinpointed and that the standard deviation around that number would be about 5 percent.

The target market for RenaGel could reach 200,000 patients. Instead of targeting patients with chronic renal failure, however, the joint venture would market the drug to doctors with the largest patient populations. The analysts believed that a sales force of 45 people would be enough to serve the market. They prepared a schedule of the sales force and marketing costs as a percentage of sales revenue over time (Exhibit 3). Each member of the sales force would cost $200,000, rising at 5 percent a year.

The team realized that the marketing costs could turn out to be higher or lower than this schedule. The team assumed that the costs could be as low as 87 percent of the schedule or as much as 20 percent higher, and the most likely outcome was that they would be 93 percent of the schedule (which produced an average of exactly 100 percent). General and administrative costs were assumed to be 40 percent of the cost of the sales force.

Forecast of Free Cash Flows

Net working capital for the joint venture would comprise a 45-day collecting period for receivables, a 90-day period for RenaGel inventory, and a 45-day period for payables. The team forecasted capital expenditures of $14 million, split over the first three years of the venture (see **Exhibit 4**).

The last decision that had to be made by Genzyme's joint-venture team was choosing a cost of capital for discounting the cash flows of the joint venture. A common practice in the biotech industry was to use a 20–25 percent discount rate for products in advanced clinical trials. The weighted-average costs of capital for Genzyme and GelTex were, respectively, 14.75 percent and 23 percent on March 15, 1997.

CONCLUSION

Exhibit 4 shows the estimated value to Genzyme of a hypothetical 50 percent interest in the joint venture to be $44.896 million; subtracting a payment of $27.5 million gives a net present value (NPV) to Genzyme of $17.396 million. Phelps observed that this estimate hinged on many assumptions, which were uncertain. He wondered about the effect of this uncertainty on the expected value of the joint venture, and on the likelihood that the NPV would turn out to be negative. He wanted to revisit the impact of uncertainty, and then to develop its implications for the amount and timing of investment.

References

1. Elizabeth O. Teisberg. Genzyme Corporation: Strategic challenges with Ceredase. Harvard Business School, 1994. Case 9-793-120.
2. Annual Report: Top Biotechnology Companies. *MedAdNews* 1997; 16: 8–60.
3. Alex Zisson, Robert J. Olan. GelTex Pharmaceuticals, Inc.: Company Report. Hambrecht & Quist Institutional Research 1996, May 15.
4. Ellie McCormack. GelTex Pharmaceuticals stays ahead of the game. *Boston Business Journal,* 1995, June 9.
5   Barbara Dau Hoffman. GelTex Pharmaceuticals. Vector Securities International. March 10, 1997.
6. V. Walter Bratic, Patricia Tilton, Mira Balakrishnan. Navigating through a biotechnology valuation. *Journal of Biotechnology in Healthcare,* 1997; 4: 207–16.
7. Mark Edwards. A new approach to the evaluation of biopharmaceutical R&D projects and value creation by strategic alliances. *Recombinant Capital,* 1994.
8. J.F. Beary. *The drug development and approval process in the 90s.* Office of Research and Development, Pharmaceutical Research and Manufacturers of America, Washington, D.C.
9. D. Larry Smith. Valuation of life sciences companies: An empirical and theoretical approach. Hambrecht & Quist. January 4, 1994.

EXHIBIT 1
Ownership Structure of Genzyme Corporation and Affiliates

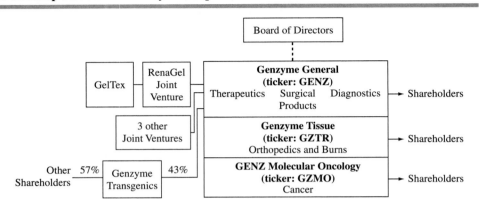

EXHIBIT 2
Transition Probability, Probability of Market Entrance,
and Development Periods for Biotech Drugs

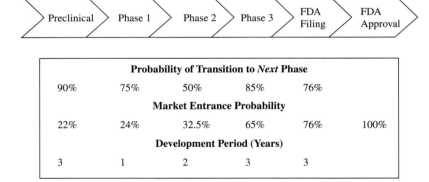

Probability of Transition to *Next* Phase					
90%	75%	50%	85%	76%	
Market Entrance Probability					
22%	24%	32.5%	65%	76%	100%
Development Period (Years)					
3	1	2	3	3	

EXHIBIT 3
Forecast of Income Statement ($000)

Genzyme Price for JV $27,500 **Genzyme Share of JV 50%**

Uncertainties

FDA Approval, Launch	1	Compliance (%)	87%
Launch delay (years)	0	Gross profit (%)	70%
Peak penetration rate	43%	Marketing Cost Multiplier	1
Price per patient ($)	1000	Life of Drug	14

Assumptions

	1	0
Market launch probability	65%	35%
U.S. Growth rate	8%	
Europe growth rate	6%	
Discount rate	20%	

Results

JV Enterprise Value	$89,793
Genzyme NPV	$17,396
GelTex NPV	$44,896

RenaGel market performance

performance	1997	1998	1999	2000	2001	2002	2003	2004	2005	2006	2007	2008	2009	2010	2011	2012
Market penetration, no launch delay	0%	0%	4%	9%	22%	34%	43%	43%	43%	43%	42%	41%	40%	39%	37%	34%
Actual penetration	0%	0%	4%	9%	22%	34%	43%	43%	43%	43%	42%	41%	40%	39%	37%	34%
U.S. patients	210,000	226,800	244,944	264,540	285,703	308,559	333,244	359,903	388,695	419,791	453,374	489,644	528,816	571,121	616,811	666,156
Eligibility	90%	90%	90%	90%	90%	90%	90%	90%	90%	90%	90%	90%	90%	90%	90%	90%
Total U.S. customers:	—	—	9,479	20,475	55,283	95,530	128,965	139,282	150,425	162,459	171,947	180,018	190,326	198,921	205,287	206,242
Europe patients	165,000	174,900	185,394	196,518	208,309	220,807	234,056	248,099	262,985	278,764	295,490	313,219	332,012	351,933	373,049	395,432
Europe eligibility	70%	70%	70%	70%	70%	70%	70%	70%	70%	70%	70%	70%	70%	70%	70%	70%
Total European customers:	—	—	—	5,915	12,540	33,231	56,361	74,678	79,158	83,908	88,942	92,393	94,939	98,517	101,059	102,362
Total customer base	—	—	9,479	26,391	67,824	128,761	185,326	213,960	229,584	246,367	260,889	272,411	285,265	297,438	306,346	308,603
Total revenues ($000s)	—	—	8,247	22,960	59,007	112,022	161,234	186,145	199,738	214,339	226,974	236,998	248,181	258,771	266,521	268,485
Gross Profit ($000) 70%	—	—	5,773	16,072	41,305	78,416	112,863	130,302	139,816	150,038	158,882	165,898	173,726	181,140	186,565	187,939
Expenses																
Sales force (number)	—	15	30	45	45	45	45	45	45	45	45	45	45	45	45	45
Sales force ($000s)	—	3,150	6,615	10,419	10,940	11,487	12,061	12,664	13,297	13,962	14,660	15,393	16,163	16,971	17,819	18,710
Marketing costs (% of sales)	—	—	65%	30%	15%	8%	5%	5%	5%	5%	5%	5%	5%	5%	5%	5%
Marketing costs ($000s)	—	—	5,361	6,888	8,851	8,962	8,062	9,307	9,987	10,717	11,349	11,850	12,409	12,939	13,326	13,424
G&A (% of sales force)	—	—	40%	40%	40%	40%	40%	40%	40%	40%	40%	40%	40%	40%	40%	40%
G&A ($000s)	800	800	2,646	4,167	4,376	4,595	4,824	5,066	5,319	5,585	5,864	6,157	6,465	6,788	7,128	7,484
R&D ($000)	4,000	3,000	3,000	3,000	3,000	3,000	3,000	3,000	3,000	3,000	3,000	3,000	3,000	3,000	3,000	3,000
Depreciation ($000)	400	400	950	950	950	950	950	950	950	950	950	950	950	950	950	950
Total expense ($000s)	5,200	7,350	18,572	25,424	28,116	28,993	28,897	30,987	32,553	34,214	35,823	37,350	38,987	40,648	42,223	43,569
EBIT ($000s)	(5,200)	(7,350)	(12,799)	(9,352)	13,188	49,423	83,967	99,315	107,264	115,824	123,059	128,548	134,740	140,492	144,341	144,371
Tax ($000s) @ 38%	(5,200)	(7,350)	(12,799)	(9,352)	5,012	18,781	31,907	37,740	40,760	44,013	46,762	48,848	51,201	53,387	54,850	54,861
Net income ($000s)	(5,200)	(7,350)	(12,799)	(9,352)	8,177	30,642	52,059	61,575	66,503	71,811	76,296	79,700	83,539	87,105	89,492	89,510

EXHIBIT 4
Forecast of Free Cash Flows ($000s)

		1997	1998	1999	2000	2001	2002	2003	2004	2005	2006	2007	2008	2009	2010	2011	2012
Net Income		(5,200)	(7,350)	(12,799)	(9,352)	8,177	30,642	52,059	61,575	66,503	71,811	76,296	79,700	83,539	87,105	89,492	89,510
Change in Net Working Capital																	
Receivables (days)	45	—	—	1,017	2,831	7,275	13,811	19,878	22,949	24,625	26,425	27,983	29,219	30,598	31,903	32,859	33,101
Inventories (days)	90	—	—	610	1,698	4,365	8,287	11,927	13,770	14,775	15,855	16,790	17,531	18,359	19,142	19,715	19,861
Payables (days)	45	—	—	(305)	(849)	(2,182)	(4,143)	(5,963)	(6,885)	(7,388)	(7,928)	(8,395)	(8,766)	(9,179)	(9,571)	(9,858)	(9,930)
Investment in working capital		—	—	1,322	3,680	9,457	17,954	25,842	29,834	32,013	34,353	36,378	37,985	39,777	41,474	42,716	43,031
Net change in working capital		—	—	(1,322)	(2,358)	(5,777)	(8,497)	(7,887)	(3,993)	(2,178)	(2,340)	(2,025)	(1,607)	(1,792)	(1,697)	(1,242)	(315)
Capital expenditure		(3,500)	(2,500)	(8,000)	—	—	—	—	—	—	—	—	—	—	—	—	—
Add back depreciation		400	400	950	950	950	950	950	950	950	950	950	950	950	950	950	950
Free Cash Flows		(8,300)	(9,450)	(21,170)	(10,760)	3,349	23,095	45,122	58,533	65,275	70,421	75,221	79,043	82,696	86,358	89,200	90,145
Terminal Value		—	—	—	—	—	—	—	—	—	—	—	—	—	—	—	43,031
Adjusted Free Cash Flows		(8,300)	(9,450)	(21,170)	(10,760)	3,349	23,095	45,122	58,533	65,275	70,421	75,221	79,043	82,696	86,358	89,200	133,176
Genzyme investment		$27,500															

	JV	Genzyme	GelTex
Enterprise value (000)	89,793	44,896	44,896
Genzyme investment NPV		$27,500	
Genzyme NPV		17,396	

Euroland Foods S.A.

In early January 2001, the senior-management committee of Euroland Foods was to meet to draw up the firm's capital budget for the new year. Up for consideration were 11 major projects that totaled more than €316 million. Unfortunately, the board of directors had imposed a spending limit on capital projects of only €120 million; even so, investment at that rate would represent a major increase in the firm's current asset base of €965 million. Thus, the challenge for the senior managers of Euroland Foods was to allocate funds among a range of compelling projects: new-product introduction, acquisition, market expansion, efficiency improvements, preventive maintenance, safety, and pollution control.

THE COMPANY

Euroland Foods, headquartered in Brussels, Belgium, was a multinational producer of high-quality ice cream, yogurt, bottled water, and fruit juices. Its products were sold throughout Scandinavia, Britain, Belgium, the Netherlands, Luxembourg, western Germany, and northern France. (See **Exhibit 1** for a map of the company's marketing region.)

The company was founded in 1924 by Theo Verdin, a Belgian farmer, as an offshoot of his dairy business. Through keen attention to product development and shrewd marketing, the business grew steadily over the years. The company went public in 1979, and, by 1993, was listed for trading on the London, Frankfurt, and Brussels exchanges. In 2000, Euroland Foods had sales of almost €1.6 billion.

This case was prepared by Casey Opitz and Robert F. Bruner and draws certain elements from an antecedent case by them. All names are fictitious. The financial support of the Batten Institute is gratefully acknowledged. The case was written as a basis for class discussion rather than to illustrate effective or ineffective handling of an administrative situation. Copyright © 2001 by the University of Virginia Darden School Foundation, Charlottesville, VA. All rights reserved. *To order copies, send an e-mail to* dardencases@virginia.edu. *No part of this publication may be reproduced, stored in a retrieval system, used in a spreadsheet, or transmitted in any form or by any means—electronic, mechanical, photocopying, recording, or otherwise—without the permission of the Darden School Foundation.* Version 1.1.

Ice cream accounted for 60 percent of the company's revenue; yogurt, which was introduced in 1982, contributed about 20 percent. The remaining 20 percent of sales was divided equally between bottled water and fruit juices. Euroland Foods' flagship brand name was "Rolly," which was represented by a fat dancing bear in farmer's clothing. Ice cream, the company's leading product, had a loyal base of customers who sought out its high-butterfat content, large chunks of chocolate, fruit, and nuts, and wide range of original flavors.

Euroland Foods' sales had been static since 1998 (see **Exhibit 2**), which management attributed to low population growth in northern Europe and market saturation in some areas. Outside observers, however, faulted recent failures in new-product introductions. Most members of management wanted to expand the company's market presence and introduce more new products to boost sales. These managers hoped that increased market presence and sales would improve the company's market value. Euroland Foods' stock was currently at 14 times earnings, just below book value. This price/earnings ratio was below the trading multiples of comparable companies, and it gave little value to the company's brands.

RESOURCE ALLOCATION

The capital budget at Euroland Foods was prepared annually by a committee of senior managers, who then presented it for approval to the board of directors. The committee consisted of five managing directors, the président directeur-général (PDG), and the finance director. Typically, the PDG solicited investment proposals from the managing directors. The proposals included a brief project description, a financial analysis, and a discussion of strategic or other qualitative considerations.

As a matter of policy, investment proposals at Euroland Foods were subject to two financial tests, payback and internal rate of return (IRR). The tests, or hurdles, had been established in 1999 by the management committee and varied according to the type of project:

Type of Project	Minimum Acceptable IRR	Maximum Acceptable Payback Years
1. New product or new markets	12%	6 years
2. Product or market extension	10%	5 years
3. Efficiency improvements	8%	4 years
4. Safety or environmental	No test	No test

In January 2001, the estimated weighted-average cost of capital (WACC) for Euroland Foods was 10.6 percent.

In describing the capital-budgeting process, the finance director, Trudi Lauf, said,

> We use the sliding scale of IRR tests as a way of recognizing differences in risk among the various types of projects. Where the company takes more risk, we should earn more return. The payback test signals that we are not prepared to wait for long to achieve that return.

OWNERSHIP AND THE SENTIMENT OF CREDITORS AND INVESTORS

Euroland Foods' 12-member board of directors included three members of the Verdin family, four members of management, and five outside directors who were prominent managers or public figures in northern Europe. Members of the Verdin family combined owned 20 percent of Euroland Foods' shares outstanding, and company executives combined owned 10 percent of the shares. Venus Asset Management, a mutual-fund management company in London, held 12 percent. Banque du Bruges et des Pays Bas held 9 percent and had one representative on the board of directors. The remaining 49 percent of the firm's shares were widely held. The firm's shares traded in Brussels and Frankfurt.

At a debt-to-equity ratio of 125 percent, Euroland Foods was leveraged much more highly than its peers in the European consumer-foods industry. Management had relied on debt financing significantly in the past few years to sustain the firm's capital spending and dividends during a period of price wars initiated by Euroland. Now, with the price wars finished, Euroland's bankers (led by Banque du Bruges) strongly urged an aggressive program of debt reduction. In any event, they were not prepared to finance increases in leverage beyond the current level. The president of Banque du Bruges had remarked at a recent board meeting,

> Restoring some strength to the right-hand side of the balance sheet should now be a first priority. Any expansion of assets should be financed from the cash flow after debt amortization until the debt ratio returns to a more prudent level. If there are crucial investments that cannot be funded this way, then we should cut the dividend!

At a price-to-earnings ratio of 14 times, shares of Euroland Foods common stock were priced below the average multiples of peer companies and the average multiples of all companies on the exchanges where Euroland Foods was traded. This was attributable to the recent price wars, which had suppressed the company's profitability, and to the well-known recent failure of the company to seize significant market share with a new product line of flavored mineral water. Since January 2000, all the major securities houses had been issuing "sell" recommendations to investors in Euroland Foods' shares. Venus Asset Management had quietly accumulated shares during this period, however, in the expectation of a turnaround in the firm's performance. At the most recent board meeting, the senior managing director of Venus gave a presentation in which he said,

> Cutting the dividend is unthinkable, as it would signal a lack of faith in your own future. Selling new shares of stock at this depressed price level is also unthinkable, as it would impose unacceptable dilution on your current shareholders. Your equity investors expect an improvement in performance. If that improvement is not forthcoming, or worse, if investors' hopes are dashed, your shares might fall into the hands of raiders like Carlo de Benedetti or the Flick brothers.[1]

At the conclusion of the most recent meeting of the directors, the board voted unanimously to limit capital spending in 2001 to €120 million.

---

[1] De Benedetti of Milan and the Flick brothers of Munich were leaders of prominent hostile-takeover attempts in recent years.

MEMBERS OF THE SENIOR-MANAGEMENT COMMITTEE

Seven senior managers of Euroland Foods would prepare the capital budget. For consideration, each project had to be sponsored by one of the managers present. Usually the decision process included a period of discussion followed by a vote on two to four alternative capital budgets. The various executives were well known to each other:

Wilhelmina Verdin (Belgian), PDG, age 57. Granddaughter of the founder and spokesperson on the board of directors for the Verdin family's interests. Worked for the company her entire career, with significant experience in brand management. Elected "European Marketer of the Year" in 1982 for successfully introducing low-fat yogurt and ice cream, the first major roll-out of this type of product. Eager to position the company for long-term growth but cautious in the wake of recent difficulties.

Trudi Lauf (Swiss), finance director, age 51. Hired from Nestlé in 1995 to modernize financial controls and systems. Had been a vocal proponent of reducing leverage on the balance sheet. Also had voiced the concerns and frustrations of stockholders.

Heinz Klink (German), managing director for Distribution, age 49. Oversaw the transportation, warehousing, and order-fulfillment activities in the company. Spoilage, transport costs, stock-outs, and control systems were perennial challenges.

Maarten Leyden (Dutch), managing director for Production and Purchasing, age 59. Managed production operations at the company's 14 plants. Engineer by training. Tough negotiator, especially with unions and suppliers. A fanatic about production-cost control. Had voiced doubts about the sincerity of creditors' and investors' commitment to the firm.

Marco Ponti (Italian), managing director for Sales, age 45. Oversaw the field sales force of 250 representatives and planned changes in geographical sales coverage. The most vocal proponent of rapid expansion on the senior-management committee. Saw several opportunities for ways to improve geographical positioning. Hired from Unilever in 1993 to revitalize the sales organization, which he successfully accomplished.

Fabienne Morin (French), managing director for Marketing, age 41. Responsible for marketing research, new-product development, advertising, and, in general, brand management. The primary advocate of the recent price war, which, although financially difficult, realized solid gains in market share. Perceived a "window of opportunity" for product and market expansion and tended to support growth-oriented projects.

Nigel Humbolt (British), managing director for Strategic Planning, age 47. Hired two years previously from a well-known consulting firm to set up a strategic-planning staff for Euroland Foods. Known for asking difficult and challenging questions about Euroland's core business, its maturity, and profitability. Supported initiatives aimed at growth and market share. Had presented the most aggressive proposals in 2000, none of which were accepted. Becoming frustrated with what he perceived to be his lack of influence in the organization.

THE EXPENDITURE PROPOSALS

The forthcoming meeting would entertain the following proposals:

Project	Expenditure (€ millions)	Sponsoring Manager
1. Replacement and expansion of the truck fleet	33	Klink, Distribution
2. A new plant	45	Leyden, Production
3. Expansion of a plant	15	Leyden, Production
4. Development and roll-out of snack foods	27	Morin, Marketing
5. Plant automation and conveyor systems	21	Leyden, Production
6. Effluent-water treatment at four plants	6	Leyden, Production
7. Market expansion southward	30	Ponti, Sales
8. Market expansion eastward	30	Ponti, Sales
9. Development and introduction of new artificially sweetened yogurt and ice cream	27	Morin, Marketing
10. Networked, computer-based inventory-control system for warehouses and field representatives	22.5	Klink, Distribution
11. Acquisition of a leading schnapps brand and associated facilities	60	Humbolt, Strategic Planning.

1. *Replacement and expansion of the truck fleet.* Heinz Klink proposed to purchase 100 new refrigerated tractor-trailer trucks, 50 each in 2001 and 2002. By doing so, the company could sell 60 old, fully depreciated trucks over the two years for a total of €4.05 million. The purchase would expand the fleet by 40 trucks within two years. Each of the new trailers would be larger than the old trailers and afford a 15 percent increase in cubic meters of goods hauled on each trip. The new tractors would also be more fuel and maintenance efficient. The increase in number of trucks would permit more flexible scheduling and more efficient routing and servicing of the fleet than at present and would cut delivery times and, therefore, possibly inventories. It would also allow more frequent deliveries to the company's major markets, which would reduce the loss of sales caused by stock-outs. Finally, expanding the fleet would support geographical expansion over the long term.

   As shown in **Exhibit 3,** the total net investment in trucks of €30 million and the increase in working capital to support added maintenance, fuel, payroll, and inventories of €3 million was expected to yield total cost savings and added sales potential of €11.6 million over the next seven years. The resulting IRR was estimated to be 7.8 percent, marginally below the minimum 8 percent required return on efficiency projects. Some of the managers wondered if this project would be more properly classified as "efficiency" than "expansion."

2. *A new plant.* Maarten Leyden noted that Euroland Foods' yogurt and ice-cream sales in the southeastern region of the company's market were about to exceed the capacity of its Melun, France, manufacturing and packaging plant. At present, some of the demand was being met by shipments from the company's newest, most efficient facility, located in Strasbourg, France. Shipping costs over that distance were high, however, and some sales were undoubtedly being lost when the marketing effort could not be supported by delivery. Leyden proposed that a new manufacturing and packaging plant be built in Dijon, France, just

at the current southern edge of Euroland Foods' marketing region, to take the burden off the Melun and Strasbourg plants.

The cost of this plant would be €37.5 million and would entail €7.5 million for working capital. The €21 million worth of equipment would be amortized over 7 years, and the plant over 10 years. Through an increase in sales and depreciation, and the decrease in delivery costs, the plant was expected to yield after-tax cash flows totaling €35.6 million and an IRR of 11.3 percent over the next 10 years. This project would be classified as a market extension.

3. *Expansion of a plant.* In addition to the need for greater production capacity in Euroland Foods' southeastern region, its Nuremberg, Germany, plant had reached full capacity. This situation made the scheduling of routine equipment maintenance difficult, which, in turn, created production scheduling and deadline problems. This plant was one of two highly automated facilities that produced Euroland Foods' entire line of bottled water, mineral water, and fruit juices. The Nuremberg plant supplied central and western Europe. (The other plant, near Copenhagen, Denmark, supplied Euroland Foods' northern European markets.)

The Nuremberg plant's capacity could be expanded by 20 percent for €15 million. The equipment (€10.5 million) would be depreciated over 7 years, and the plant over 10 years. The increased capacity was expected to result in additional production of up to €2.25 million a year, yielding an IRR of 11.2 percent. This project would be classified as a market extension.

4. *Development and roll-out of snack foods.* Fabienne Morin suggested that the company use the excess capacity at its Antwerp spice- and nut-processing facility to produce a line of dried fruits to be test-marketed in Belgium, Britain, and the Netherlands. She noted the strength of the Rolly brand in those countries and the success of other food and beverage companies that had expanded into snack-food production. She argued that Euroland Foods' reputation for wholesome, quality products would be enhanced by a line of dried fruits and that name association with the new product would probably even lead to increased sales of the company's other products among health-conscious consumers.

Equipment and working-capital investments were expected to total €22.5 million and €4.5 million, respectively, for this project. The equipment would be depreciated over seven years. Assuming the test market was successful, cash flows from the project would be able to support further plant expansions in other strategic locations. The IRR was expected to be 13.4 percent, slightly above the required return of 12 percent for new-product projects.

5. *Plant automation and conveyer systems.* Maarten Leyden also requested €21 million to increase automation of the production lines at six of the company's older plants. The result would be improved throughput speed and reduced accidents, spillage, and production tie-ups. The last two plants the company had built included conveyer systems that eliminated the need for any heavy lifting by employees. The systems reduced the chance of injury by employees; at the six older plants, the company had sustained an average of 223 missed-worker-days per year per plant in the last two years because of muscle injuries sustained in heavy lifting. At an average hourly total compensation rate of €14.00 an hour, more than €150,000 a year were thus lost, and the possibility always existed of more-serious injuries and lawsuits. Overall, cost savings and depreciation totaling €4.13 million a year for the project were expected to yield an IRR of 8.7 percent. This project would be classed in the efficiency category.

6. *Effluent-water treatment at four plants.* Euroland Foods preprocessed a variety of fresh fruits at its Melun and Strasbourg plants. One of the first stages of processing involved cleaning

the fruit to remove dirt and pesticides. The dirty water was simply sent down the drain and into the Seine or Rhine Rivers. Recent European Community directives called for any waste-water containing even slight traces of poisonous chemicals to be treated at the sources, and gave companies four years to comply. As an environmentally oriented project, this proposal fell outside the normal financial tests of project attractiveness. Leyden noted, however, that the water-treatment equipment could be purchased today for €6 million; he speculated that the same equipment would cost €15 million in four years when immediate conversion became mandatory. In the intervening time, the company would run the risks that European Community regulators would shorten the compliance time or that the company's pollution record would become public and impair the image of the company in the eyes of the consumer. This project would be classed in the environmental category.

7. and 8. *Market expansions southward and eastward.* Marco Ponti recommended that the company expand its market southward to include southern France, Switzerland, Italy, and Spain, and/or eastward to include eastern Germany, Poland, Czechoslovakia, and Austria. He believed the time was right to expand sales of ice cream, and perhaps yogurt, geographically. In theory, the company could sustain expansions in both directions simultaneously, but practically, Ponti doubted that the sales and distribution organizations could sustain both expansions at once.

Each alternative geographical expansion had its benefits and risks. If the company expanded eastward, it could reach a large population with a great appetite for frozen dairy products, but it would also face more competition from local and regional ice-cream manufacturers. Moreover, consumers in eastern Germany, Poland, and Czechoslovakia did not have the purchasing power that consumers did to the south. The eastward expansion would have to be supplied from plants in Nuremberg, Strasbourg, and Hamburg.

Looking southward, the tables were turned: more purchasing power and less competition but also a smaller consumer appetite for ice cream and yogurt. A southward expansion would require building consumer demand for premium-quality yogurt and ice cream. If neither of the plant proposals (i.e., proposals 2 and 3) was accepted, then the southward expansion would need to be supplied from plants in Melun, Strasbourg, and Rouen.

The initial cost of either proposal was €30 million of working capital. The bulk of costs would involve the financing of distributorships, but over the 10-year forecast period, the distributors would gradually take over the burden of carrying receivables and inventory. Both expansion proposals assumed the rental of suitable warehouse and distribution facilities. The after-tax cash flows were expected to total €56.3 million for southward expansion and €48.8 million for eastward expansion.

Marco Ponti pointed out that southward expansion meant a higher possible IRR but that moving eastward was a less risky proposition. The projected IRRs were 21.4 percent and 18.8 percent for southern and eastern expansion, respectively. These projects would be classed in the market-extension category.

9. *Development and introduction of new artificially sweetened yogurt and ice cream.* Fabienne Morin noted that recent developments in the synthesis of artificial sweeteners were showing promise of significant cost savings to food and beverage producers as well as stimulating growing demand for low-calorie products. The challenge was to create the right flavor to complement or enhance the other ingredients. For ice-cream manufacturers, the difficulty lay in creating a balance that would result in the same flavor as was obtained when using natural sweeteners; artificial sweeteners might, of course, create a superior taste.

In addition, €27 million would be needed to commercialize a yogurt line that had received promising results in laboratory tests. This cost included acquiring specialized production facilities, working capital, and the cost of the initial product introduction. The overall IRR was estimated to be 20.5 percent.

Morin stressed that the proposal, although highly uncertain in terms of actual results, could be viewed as a means of protecting present market share, because other high-quality-ice-cream producers carrying out the same research might introduce these products; if the Rolly brand did not carry an artificially sweetened line and its competitors did, the Rolly brand might suffer. Morin also noted the parallels between innovating with artificial sweeteners and the company's past success in introducing low-fat products. This project would be classed in the new-product category of investments.

10. *Networked, computer-based inventory-control system for warehouses and field representatives.* Heinz Klink had pressed unsuccessfully for three years for a state-of-the-art computer-based inventory-control system that would link field sales representatives, distributors, drivers, warehouses, and possibly even retailers. The benefits of such a system would be shorter delays in ordering and order processing, better control of inventory, reduction of spoilage, and faster recognition of changes in demand at the customer level. Klink was reluctant to quantify these benefits, because they could range between modest and quite large amounts. This year, for the first time, he presented a cash-flow forecast, however, that reflected an initial outlay of €18 million for the system, followed by €4.5 million in the next year for ancillary equipment. The inflows reflected depreciation tax shields, tax credits, cost reductions in warehousing, and reduced inventory. He forecast these benefits to last for only three years. Even so, the project's IRR was estimated to be 16.2 percent. This project would be classed in the efficiency category of proposals.

11. *Acquisition of a leading schnapps[2] brand and associated facilities.* Nigel Humbolt had advocated making diversifying acquisitions in an effort to move beyond the company's mature core business but doing so in a way that exploited the company's skills in brand management. He had explored six possible related industries in the general field of consumer packaged goods, and determined that cordials and liqueurs offered unusual opportunities for real growth and, at the same time, market protection through branding. He had identified four small producers of well-established brands of liqueurs as acquisition candidates. Following exploratory talks with each, he had determined that only one company could be purchased in the near future, namely, the leading private European manufacturer of schnapps, located in Munich.

The proposal was expensive: €25 million to buy the company and €30 million to renovate the company's facilities completely while simultaneously expanding distribution to new geographical markets. The expected returns were high: after-tax cash flows were projected to be €198.5 million, yielding an IRR of 27.5 percent. This project would be classed in the new-product category of proposals.

---

[2]Any of various strong dry liquors, such as a strong Dutch gin. Definition borrowed from *American Heritage Dictionary of the English Language,* 4th ed.

CONCLUSION

Each member of the management committee was expected to come to the meeting prepared to present and defend a proposal for the allocation of Euroland Foods' capital budget of €120 million. Exhibit 3 summarizes the various projects in terms of their free cash flows and the investment-performance criteria.

EXHIBIT 1
Nations Where Euroland Competed

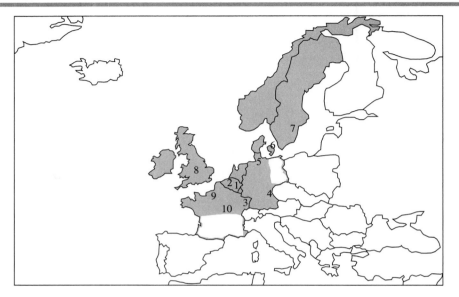

Note: The shaded area in this map reveals the principal distribution region of Euroland's products. Important facilities are indicated by the following figures:

1	Headquarters, Brussels, Belgium
2	Plant, Antwerp, Belgium
3	Plant, Strasbourg, France
4	Plant, Nuremberg, Germany
5	Plant, Hamburg, Germany
6	Plant, Copenhagen, Denmark
7	Plant, Svald, Sweden
8	Plant, Nelly-on-Mersey, England
9	Plant, Caen, France
10	Plant, Melun, France

EXHIBIT 2
Summary of Financial Results (all values in € millions, except per-share amounts)

	Fiscal Year Ending December		
	1998	**1999**	**2000**
Gross sales	1,614	1,608	1,611
Net income	77	74	56
Earnings per share	1.13	1.08	0.81
Dividends	30	30	30
Total assets	716	870	984
Shareholders' equity (book value)	559	640	697
Shareholders' equity (market value)	1,271	1,258	784

EXHIBIT 3

Free Cash Flows and Analysis of Proposed Projects[1] (all values in € millions)

Project	1	2	3	4	5	6	7	8	9	10
	Expand Truck Fleet (note 3)	New Plant (Dijon, France)	Expanded Plant (Nuremberg, Germany)	Snack Foods	Automation and Conveyer Systems	Southward Expansion (note 5)	Eastward Expansion (note 5)	Artificial Sweetener	Inventory-Control System	Strategic Acquisition (note 6)
Investment										
Property	30.00	37.50	15.00	22.50	21.00	0.00	0.00	22.50	22.50	45.00
Working capital	3.00	7.50	0.00	4.50	0.00	30.00	30.00	4.50	0.00	15.00
Year	**EXPECTED FREE CASH FLOWS (note 4)**									
0	−17.10	−45.00	−15.00	−9.00	−21.00	−30.00	−30.00	−27.00	−18.00	−25.00
1	−11.85	3.00	1.88	−9.00	4.13	5.25	4.50	4.50	8.25	−30.00
2	4.50	7.50	2.25	−9.00	4.13	6.00	5.25	6.00	8.25	7.50
3	5.25	8.25	2.63	4.50	4.13	6.75	6.00	6.75	7.50	13.50
4	6.00	9.00	3.00	4.50	4.13	7.50	6.75	7.50		16.50
5	6.75	9.38	3.38	6.00	4.13	8.25	7.50	7.50		19.50
6	7.50	9.75	3.75	6.75	4.13	9.00	8.25	7.50		22.50
7	10.50	10.13	2.25	7.50	4.13	9.75	9.00	7.50		25.50
8		7.50	2.25	8.25		10.50	9.75	7.50		28.50
9		7.88	2.25	9.00		11.25	10.50	7.50		31.50
10		8.25	2.25	9.75		12.00	11.25	7.50		88.50
Undiscounted Sum	11.55	35.63	10.88	29.25	7.88	56.25	48.75	42.75	6.00	198.50
Payback (years)	6	6	6	7	6	5	5	5	3	5
Maximum payback accepted	4	5	5	6	4	6	6	6	4	6
IRR	7.8%	11.3%	11.2%	13.4%	8.7%	21.4%	18.8%	20.5%	16.2%	27.5%
Minimum Accepted ROR	8.0%	10.0%	10.0%	12.0%	8.0%	12.0%	12.0%	12.0%	8.0%	12.0%
Spread	−0.2%	1.3%	1.2%	1.4%	0.7%	9.4%	6.8%	8.5%	8.2%	15.5%
NPV at Corp. WACC (10.6%)	−2.88	1.49	0.41	3.74	−1.31	17.99	13.49	13.43	1.75	69.45
NPV at Minimum ROR	−0.19	2.81	0.82	1.79	0.48	14.85	10.62	10.97	2.67	59.65
Equivalent Annuity (note 2)	−0.04	0.46	0.13	0.32	0.09	2.63	1.88	1.94	1.03	10.56

[1] The effluent treatment program is not included in this exhibit.

[2] The equivalent annuity of a project is that level annual payment that yields a net present value equal to the NPV at the minimum required rate of return for that project. Annuity corrects for differences in duration among various projects. In ranking projects on the basis of equivalent annuity, bigger annuities create more investor wealth than smaller annuities.

[3] This reflects €16.5 million spent both initially and at the end of year 1.

[4] Free cash flow = incremental profit or cost savings after taxes + depreciation − investment in fixed assets and working capital.

[5] Franchisees would gradually take over the burden of carrying receivables and inventory.

[6] €25 million would be spent in the first year, €30 million in the second, and €5 million in the third.

Star River 星河 Electronics LTD.

On July 5, 2001, her first day as chief executive officer (CEO) of Star River Electronics Ltd., Adeline Koh confronted a host of management problems. One week earlier, Star River's president and CEO had suddenly resigned to accept a CEO position with another firm. Koh had been appointed to fill the position—starting immediately. Several items in her in-box that first day were financial in nature, either requiring a financial decision or with outcomes that would have major financial implications for the firm. That evening, Koh asked to meet with her assistant, Andy Chin, to begin addressing the most prominent issues.

STAR RIVER ELECTRONICS AND THE OPTICAL-DISC-MANUFACTURING INDUSTRY

Star River Electronics had been founded as a joint venture between Starlight Electronics Ltd., U.K., and an Asian venture-capital firm, New Era Partners. Based in Singapore, Star River's sole business mission was to manufacture CD-ROMs as a supplier to major software companies. In no time, Star River had gained fame in the industry for producing high-quality discs.

The popularity of optical and multimedia products created rapid growth for the CD-ROM manufacturing industry in the mid-1990s. Accordingly, small manufacturers proliferated, creating an oversupply that pushed prices down by as much as 40 percent. Consolidation followed as less efficient producers began to feel the pinch.

This case is derived from materials originally prepared by Robert Bruner, Robert Conroy, and Kenneth Eades. The firms and individuals in the case are fictitious. The financial support of the Batten Institute is gratefully acknowledged. The case was written as a basis for class discussion rather than to illustrate effective or ineffective handling of an administrative situation. Copyright © 2001 by the University of Virginia Darden School Foundation, Charlottesville, VA. All rights reserved. *To order copies, send an e-mail to* dardencases@virginia.edu. *No part of this publication may be reproduced, stored in a retrieval system, used in a spreadsheet, or transmitted in any form or by any means—electronic, mechanical, photocopying, recording, or otherwise—without the permission of the Darden School Foundation.* Version 1.2.

Star River Electronics survived the shakeout thanks to its sterling reputation. While other CD-ROM manufacturers floundered, volume sales at the company grew at a robust rate in the past two years. Unit prices, however, had declined because of price competition and the growing popularity of substitute storage devices, particularly digital video discs (DVDs). The latter had 14 times more storage capacity and threatened to displace CD-ROMs. Although CD-ROM *disc drives* comprised 93 percent of all optical-disc-drive shipments in 1999, a study predicted that this number would fall to 41 percent by 2005, while the share of DVD drives would rise to 59 percent.[1] Star River had begun to experiment with DVD manufacturing, but DVDs still accounted for less than 5 percent of its sales at fiscal year-end 2001. With new installed capacity, however, the company hoped to increase the proportion of revenue from DVDs.

FINANCIAL QUESTIONS FACING ADELINE KOH

That evening, Koh met with Andy Chin, a promising new associate whom she had brought along from New Era Partners. Koh's brief discussion with Chin went as follows:

Koh: Back at New Era we looked at Star River as one of our most promising venture-capital investments. Now it seems that such optimism may not be warranted—at least until we get a solid understanding of the firm's past performance and its forecast performance. Did you have any success on this?

Chin: Yes, the bookkeeper gave me these: the historical-income statements **[Exhibit 1]** and balance sheets **[Exhibit 2]** for the last four years. The accounting system here is still pretty primitive. However, I checked a number of the accounts, and they look orderly. So I suspect that we can work with these figures. From these statements, I calculated a set of diagnostic ratios **[Exhibit 3]**.

Koh: I see you have been busy. Unfortunately, I can't study these right now. I need you to review the historical performance of Star River for me, and to give me any positive or negative insights that you think are significant.

Chin: When do you need this?

Koh: At 7:00 A.M. tomorrow. I want to call on our banker tomorrow morning and get an extension on Star River's loan.

Chin: The banker, Mr. Tan, said that Star River was "growing beyond its financial capabilities." What does that mean?

Koh: It probably means that he doesn't think we can repay the loan within a reasonable period. I would like you to build a simple financial forecast of our performance for the next two years (ignore seasonal effects), and show me what our debt requirements will be at the fiscal years ending 2002 and 2003. I think it is reasonable to expect that Star River's sales will grow at 15 percent each year. Also, you should assume capital expenditures of SGD54.6 million[2] for

---

[1]Global Industry Analysts, Inc., "TEAC—Facts, Figures and Forecasts," 5.
[2]SGD = Singaporean dollars.

DVD manufacturing equipment, spread out over the next two years and depreciated over seven years. Use whatever other assumptions seem appropriate to you based on your historical analysis of results. For this forecast, you should assume that any external funding is in the form of debt.

Chin: But what if the forecasts show that Star River cannot repay the loan?

Koh: Then we'll have to go back to Star River's owners, New Era Partners and Starlight Electronics U.K., for an injection of equity. Of course, New Era Partners would rather not invest more funds unless we can show that the returns on such an investment would be very attractive, and/or that the survival of the company depends on it. Thus, my third request is for you to examine what returns on book assets and book equity Star River will offer in the next two years and to identify the "key-driver" assumptions of those returns. Finally, let me have your recommendations about operating and financial changes I should make based on the historical analysis and the forecasts.

Chin: The plant manager revised his request for a new packaging machine and thinks these are the right numbers [see the plant manager's memorandum in **Exhibit 4**]. Essentially, the issue is whether to invest now or wait three years to buy the new packaging equipment. The new equipment can save significantly on labor costs but carries a price tag of SGD1.82 million. My hunch is that our preference between investing now versus waiting three years will hinge on the discount rate.

Koh: [laughing] The joke in business school was that the discount rate was always 10 percent.

Chin: That's not what my business school taught me! New Era always uses a 40 percent discount rate to value equity investments in risky start-up companies. But Star River is reasonably well established now and shouldn't require such a high-risk premium. I managed to pull together some data [see **Exhibit 5**] on other Singaporean electronics companies with which to estimate the required rate of return on equity.

Koh: Fine. Please estimate Star River's weighted-average cost of capital and assess the packaging-machine investment. I would like the results of your analysis tomorrow morning at 7:00.

EXHIBIT 1
Historical Income Statements for Fiscal Year Ended June 30 (SGD 000)

	1998	1999	2000	2001
Sales	71,924	80,115	92,613	106,042
Operating expenses:				
Production costs and expenses	33,703	38,393	46,492	53,445
Admin. and selling expenses	16,733	17,787	21,301	24,177
Depreciation	8,076	9,028	10,392	11,360
Total operating expenses	58,512	65,208	78,185	88,983
Operating profit	13,412	14,908	14,429	17,059
Interest expense	5,464	6,010	7,938	7,818
Earnings before taxes	7,949	8,897	6,491	9,241
Income taxes*	2,221	2,322	1,601	2,093
Net earnings	5,728	6,576	4,889	7,148
Dividends to all common shares	2,000	2,000	2,000	2,000
Retentions of earnings	3,728	4,576	2,889	5,148

*The expected corporate tax rate was 24.5%.

EXHIBIT 2
Historical Balance Sheets for Fiscal Year Ended June 30 (SGD 000)

	1998	1999	2000	2001
Assets:				
Cash	4,816	5,670	6,090	5,795
Accounts receivable	22,148	25,364	28,078	35,486
Inventories	23,301	27,662	53,828	63,778
Total current assets	50,265	58,697	87,996	105,059
Gross property, plant & equipment	64,611	80,153	97,899	115,153
Accumulated depreciation	(4,559)	(13,587)	(23,979)	(35,339)
Net property, plant & equipment	60,052	66,566	73,920	79,814
Total assets	110,317	125,262	161,916	184,873
Liabilities and Stockholders' Equity:				
Short-term borrowings (bank)[1]	29,002	37,160	73,089	84,981
Accounts payable	12,315	12,806	11,890	13,370
Other accrued liabilities	24,608	26,330	25,081	21,318
Total current liabilities	65,926	76,296	110,060	119,669
Long-term debt[2]	10,000	10,000	10,000	18,200
Shareholders' equity	34,391	38,967	41,856	47,004
Total liabilities and stockholders' equity	110,317	125,263	161,916	184,873

[1]Short-term debt was borrowed from City Bank at an interest rate equal to Singaporean prime lending rates + 1.5 percent. Current prime lending rates were 5.2 percent. The benchmark 10-year Singapore treasury bond currently yielded 3.6 percent.
[2]Two components made up the company's long term debt. One was a SGD10 million loan that had been issued privately in 1996 to New Era Partners and to Starlight Electronics Ltd., U.K. This debt was subordinate to any bank debt outstanding. The second component was a SGD8.2 million from a 5-year bond issued on a private placement basis last July 1, 2000 at a price of SGD97 and a coupon of 5.75% paid semiannually.

EXHIBIT 3
Ratio Analyses of Historical Financial Statements

	1998	1999	2000	2001
Profitability				
Operating margin (%)	18.6%	18.6%	15.6%	16.1%
Tax rate (%)	27.9	26.1	24.7	22.6
Return on sales (%)	8.0	8.2	5.3	6.7
Return on equity (%)	16.7	16.9	11.7	15.2
Return on assets (%)	5.2	5.2	3.0	3.9
Leverage				
Debt/equity ratio	1.13	1.21	1.99	2.20
Debt/total capital (%)	0.53	0.55	0.67	0.69
EBIT/interest (×)	2.45	2.48	1.82	2.18
Asset Utilization				
Sales/assets	65.2%	64.0%	57.2%	57.4%
Sales growth rate (%)	15.0%	11.4%	15.6%	14.5%
Assets growth rate (%)	8.0%	13.5%	29.3%	14.2%
Days in receivables	112.4	115.6	110.7	122.1
Payables to COGS	36.5%	33.4%	25.6%	25.0%
Inventories to COGS	69.1%	72.1%	115.8%	119.3%
Liquidity				
Current ratio	0.76	0.77	0.80	0.88
Quick ratio	0.41	0.41	0.31	0.34

EXHIBIT 4
Lim's Memo regarding New Packaging Equipment

MEMORANDUM

TO: Adeline Koh, President and CEO, Star River Electronics
FROM: Esmond Lim, Plant Manager
DATE: June 30, 2001
SUBJECT: New Packaging Equipment

Although our CD packaging equipment is adequate at current production levels, it is terribly inefficient. The new machinery on the market can give us significant labor savings as well as increased flexibility with respect to the type of packaging used. I recommend that we go with the new technology. Should we decide to do so, the new machine can be acquired immediately. The considerations relevant to the decision are included in this memo.

Our current packaging equipment was purchased five years ago as used equipment in a liquidation sale of a small company. Although the equipment was inexpensive, it is slow, requires constant monitoring and is frequently shut down for repairs. Since the packaging equipment is significantly slower than the production equipment, we routinely have to use overtime labor to allow packaging to catch up with production. When the packager is down for repairs, the problem is exacerbated and we may spend several two-shift days catching up with production. I cannot say that we have missed any deadlines because of packaging problems, but it is a constant concern around here and things would run a lot smoother with more reliable equipment. In 2002 we will pay about SGD15,470 per year for maintenance costs. The operator is paid SGD63,700 per year for his regular time, but he has been averaging SGD81,900 per year because of the overtime he has been working. The equipment is on the tax and reporting books at SGD218,400 and will be fully depreciated in three years time (we are currently using the straight-line depreciation method for both tax and reporting purposes and will continue to do so). Because of changes in packaging technology, the equipment has no market value other than its worth as scrap metal. But its scrap value is about equal to the cost of having it removed. In short, we believe the equipment has no salvage value at all.

The new packager offers many advantages over the current equipment. It is faster, more reliable, more flexible with respect to the types of packaging it can perform, and will provide enough capacity to cover all our packaging needs in the foreseeable future. With suitable maintenance, we believe the packager will operate indefinitely. Thus, for the purposes of our analysis, we can assume that this will be the last packaging equipment we will ever have to purchase. Because of the anticipated growth at Star River, the current equipment will not be able to handle our packaging needs by the end of 2004. Thus, if we do not buy new packaging equipment by this year's end, we will have to buy it after three years time anyway. Since the speed, capacity, and reliability of the new equipment will eliminate the need for overtime labor, we feel strongly that we should buy now rather than wait another three years.

The new equipment currently costs SGD1.82 million which we would depreciate over 10 years at SGD182,000 per year. It comes with a lifetime factory maintenance contract that covers all routine maintenance and repairs at a price of SGD3,640 for the initial year. The contract stipulates that the price after the first year will be increased by the same percentage as the rate of increase of the price of new equipment. Thus if the manufacturer continues to increase the price of new packaging equipment at 5 percent per annum as it has in the past, our maintenance costs will rise by 5 percent also. We believe that this sort of regular maintenance should ensure that the new equipment will keep operating in the foreseeable future without the need for a major overhaul.

Star River's labor and maintenance costs will continue to rise due to inflation at approximately 1.5 percent per year over the long term. Because the manufacturer of the packaging equipment has been increasing its prices at about 5 percent per year, we can expect to save SGD286,878 in the purchase price by buying now rather than waiting three years. The marginal tax rate for this investment would be 24.5 percent.

EXHIBIT 5
Data on Comparable Companies and Capital-Market Conditions

Name	% of Sales from CD-ROM and/or DVD Production	Price/ Earnings Ratio	Beta	Book D/E	Book Value per Share	Market Price per Share	Number of Shares Outstanding (millions)	Last Annual Dividend	5-Year Earnings Growth Forecast
Sing Studios, Inc.	20%	9.0	1.07	0.23	1.24	1.37	9.3	1.82	4.0%
Wintronics, Inc.	95	NMF	1.56	1.70	1.46	6.39	177.2	0.15	15.7
STOR-Max Corp.	90	18.2	1.67	1.30	7.06	27.48	89.3	none	21.3
Digital Media Corp.	30	34.6	1.18	0.00	17.75	75.22	48.3	none	38.2
Wymax, Inc.	60	NMF	1.52	0.40	6.95	22.19	371.2	1.57	11.3

Note: NMF means not a meaningful figure. This arises when a company's earnings or projected earnings are negative.

Singapore's equity market risk premium could be assumed to be close to the global equity market premium of 6 percent, given Singapore's high rate of integration into global markets.

Descriptions of companies

Sing Studios, Inc.
This company was founded 50 years ago. Its major business activities historically had been production of original-artist recordings, management and production of concert tours, and personal management of artists. It entered the CD-production market in the 1980s, and only recently branched out into the manufacture of CD-ROMs. Most of its business, however, related to the manufacture and sale of MIDI (Music Instrument Digital Interface) CDs.

Wintronics, Inc.
This company was a spin-off from a large technology-holding corporation in 1981. Although the company was a leader in the production of CD-ROMs and DVDs, it has recently suffered a decline in sales. Infighting among the principal owners has fed concerns about the firm's prospects.

STOR-Max Corp.
This company, founded only two years ago, had emerged as a very aggressive competitor in the area of CD-ROM and DVD production. It was Star River's major competitor and its sales level was about the same.

Digital Media Corp.
This company had recently been an innovator in the production of DVDs. Although DVD manufacturing was not a majority of its business (film production and digital animation were its main focus), the company was projected to be a major competitor within the next three years.

Wymax, Inc.
This company was an early pioneer in the CD-ROM and DVD industries. Recently, however, it had begun to invest in software programming and had been moving away from disc production as its main focus of business.

PART 5

Management of the Firm's Equity: Dividends, Repurchases, Initial Offerings

Eastboro Machine Tools Corporation

In mid-September of 2001, Jennifer Campbell, chief financial officer of Eastboro Machine Tools Corporation, paced the floor of her Minnesota office. She needed to submit a recommendation to Eastboro's board of directors regarding the company's dividend policy, which had been the subject of an ongoing debate among the firm's senior managers. Compounding her problem was the previous week's terrorist attacks on the World Trade Center and the Pentagon. The stock market had plummeted in response to the attacks, and along with it Eastboro's stock had fallen 18 percent, to $22.15. In response to the market collapse, a spate of companies had announced plans to buy back stock, some to signal confidence in their companies as well as in the U.S. financial markets, and others for opportunistic reasons. Now Jennifer Campbell's dividend-decision problem was compounded by the dilemma of whether to use company funds to pay out dividends or to buy back stock instead.

BACKGROUND ON THE DIVIDEND QUESTION

After years of traditionally strong earnings and predictable dividend growth, Eastboro had faltered in the past five years. In response, management implemented two extensive restructuring programs, both of which were accompanied by net losses. For three years in a row since 1996, dividends had exceeded earnings. Then, in 1999, dividends were decreased to a level below earnings. Despite extraordinary losses in 2000, the board of directors had

This case is dedicated to Professors Robert F. Vandell and Pearson Hunt, the authors of an antecedent case, long out of print, that provided the model of the economic problem for this case. "Eastboro" is a fictional firm, though it draws on dilemmas of contemporary companies. The financial support of the Batten Institute is gratefully acknowledged. Copyright © 2001 by the University of Virginia Darden School Foundation, Charlottesville, VA. All rights reserved. *To order copies, send an e-mail to* dardencases@virginia.edu. *No part of this publication may be reproduced, stored in a retrieval system, used in a spreadsheet, or transmitted in any form or by any means— electronic, mechanical, photocopying, recording, or otherwise—without the permission of the Darden School Foundation.* Version 1.1.

declared a small dividend. For the first two quarters of 2001, the board had declared no dividend. But in a special letter to shareholders, the board had committed itself to resuming the dividend as early as possible—ideally, in 2001.

In a related matter, senior management was considering embarking on a campaign of corporate-image advertising along with changing the name of the corporation to "Eastboro Advanced Systems International, Inc." Management felt that this would help improve the perception of the company in the investment community.

Overall, management's view was that Eastboro was a resurgent company that demonstrated great potential for growth and profitability. The restructurings had revitalized the company's operating divisions. In addition, newly developed machine tools designed on state-of-the-art computers showed signs of being well received in the market and promised to render competitors' products obsolete. Many within the company viewed 2001 as the dawning of a new era that, in spite of the company's recent performance, would turn Eastboro into a growth stock. The company had no Moody's or Standard & Poor's rating because it had no bonds outstanding, but *Value Line* rated it an "A" company.[1]

Out of this combination of a troubled past and a bright future arose Campbell's dilemma. Did the market view Eastboro as a company on the wane, a blue-chip stock, or a potential growth stock? How, if at all, could Eastboro affect that perception? Would a change of name help frame investors' views of the firm? Did the company's investors expect capital growth or steady dividends? Would a stock buyback instead of a dividend affect investors' perceptions of Eastboro in any way? And, if those questions could be answered, what were the implications for Eastboro's future dividend policy?

THE COMPANY

Eastboro Corporation was founded in 1923 in Concord, New Hampshire, by two mechanical engineers, James East and David Peterboro. The two men had gone to school together and were disenchanted with their prospects as mechanics at a farm-equipment manufacturer.

In its early years, Eastboro had designed and manufactured a number of machinery parts, including metal presses, dies, and molds. In the 1940s, the company's large manufacturing plant produced tank and armored-vehicle parts and miscellaneous equipment for the war effort, including riveters and welders. After the war, the company concentrated on the production of industrial presses and molds, for plastics as well as metals. By 1975, the company had developed a reputation as an innovative producer of industrial machinery and machine tools.

In the late 1970s, Eastboro entered the new field of computer-aided design and computer-aided manufacturing (CAD/CAM). Working with a small software company, it developed

---

[1] *Value Line*'s financial-strength ratings, from A++ to C, were a measure of a company's ability to withstand adverse business conditions and were based on leverage, liquidity, business risk, company size, and stock-price variability, as well as analysts' judgments.

a line of presses that would manufacture metal parts by responding to computer commands. Eastboro merged the software company into its operations and, over the next several years, perfected the CAM equipment. At the same time, it developed a superior line of CAD software and equipment that would allow an engineer to design a part to exacting specifications on a computer. The design could then be entered into the company's CAM equipment, and the parts would be manufactured without the use of blueprints or human interference. By year-end 2000, CAD/CAM equipment and software were responsible for about 45 percent of sales; presses, dies, and molds for 40 percent; and miscellaneous machine tools for 15 percent.

Most press and mold companies were small local or regional firms with limited clientele. For this reason, Eastboro stood out as a true industry leader. Within the CAD/CAM industry, however, a number of larger firms, including General Electric, Hewlett-Packard, and Digital Equipment, competed for dominance of the growing market.

Throughout the 1980s, Eastboro helped set the standard for CAD/CAM, but the aggressive entry of large foreign firms into CAD/CAM and the rise of the dollar dampened sales. In the mid-to-late 1990s, technological advances and aggressive venture capitalism fueled the entry of highly specialized, state-of-the-art CAD/CAM firms. Eastboro fell behind some of its competition in the development of user-friendly software and the integration of design and manufacturing. As a result, revenues declined from a high of $911 million in 1994 to $757 million in 2000.

To combat the decline in revenues and improve weak profit margins, Eastboro took a two-pronged approach. First, it devoted a greater share of its research-and-development budget to CAD/CAM in an effort to reestablish leadership in the field. Second, the company underwent two massive restructurings. In 1998, it sold two unprofitable lines of business with revenues of $51 million, sold two plants, eliminated five leased facilities, and reduced personnel. Restructuring costs totaled $65 million. Then, in 2000, the company began a second round of restructuring by altering its manufacturing strategy, refocusing its sales and marketing approach, and adopting administrative procedures that allowed for a further reduction in staff and facilities. The total cost of the operational restructuring in 2000 was $89 million.

The company's recent income statements and balance sheets are provided in **Exhibits 1 and 2.** Although the two restructurings produced losses totaling $202 million in 1998 and 2000, by 2001 the restructurings and the increased emphasis on CAD/CAM research appeared to have launched a turnaround. Not only was the company leaner, but also the CAD/CAM research led to the development of a system that Eastboro management believed would redefine the industry. Known as the Artificial Workforce, the system was an array of advanced control hardware, software, and applications that could distribute information throughout a plant.

Essentially, the Artificial Workforce allowed an engineer to design a part on the CAD software and input the data into a CAM that could control the mixing of chemicals or the molding of parts from any number of different materials on different machines. The system could also assemble and can, box, or shrink-wrap the finished product. The Artificial Workforce ran on complex circuitry and highly advanced software that allowed machines to communicate with each other electronically. Thus, no matter how intricate, a product could be designed, manufactured, and packaged solely by computer.

Eastboro had developed applications of the product for the oil-and-gas-refining and chemicals industries in 2000, and by the next year was developing applications for the trucking, automobile-parts, and airline industries.

By October 2000, when the first Artificial Workforce was shipped, Eastboro had orders totaling $75 million; by year-end, the backlog totaled $100 million. The future for the product looked bright. Several securities analysts were optimistic about the product's impact on the company. The following comments paraphrase their thoughts:

> The Artificial Workforce products have compelling advantages over competing entries and will enable Eastboro to increase its share of a market that, ignoring periodic growth spurts, will expand at a real annual rate of about 5 percent over the next several years.
>
> The company is producing the Artificial Workforce in a new automated facility which, when in full swing, will help restore margins to levels not seen for years.
>
> The important question now is how quickly Eastboro will be able to ship in volume. Manufacturing foul-ups and missing components have delayed production growth through May 2001, about six months beyond the original target date. And start-up costs, which were a significant factor in last year's deficits, have continued to penalize earnings. Our estimates assume that production will proceed smoothly from now on and that it will approach the optimum level by year's end.

Eastboro management expected domestic revenues from the Artificial Workforce series to total $90 million in 2001 and $150 million in 2002. Thereafter, growth in sales would depend on the development of more system applications and the creation of system improvements and add-on features. International sales through Eastboro's existing offices in Frankfurt, London, Milan, and Paris, and new offices in Hong Kong, Seoul, Manila, and Tokyo, were expected to provide additional revenues of $150 million as early as 2003. Currently, international sales accounted for about 15 percent of total corporate revenues.

Two factors that could affect sales were of some concern to Eastboro. First, although the company had successfully patented several of the processes used by the Artificial Workforce system, management had received hints through industry observers that two strong competitors were developing comparable products and would probably introduce them within the next 12 months. Second, sales of molds, presses, machine tools, and CAD/CAM equipment and software were highly cyclical, and current predictions about the strength of the U.S. economy were not encouraging. As shown in **Exhibit 3,** real GDP growth was expected to slow to 1.6 percent this year from around 4 percent over the past three years. Industrial production was expected to decline by 2.5 percent. Despite the macroeconomic environment, Eastboro management remained optimistic about the company's prospects because of the successful introduction of the Artificial Workforce.

CORPORATE GOALS

A number of corporate objectives had grown out of the restructurings and recent technological advances. First and foremost, management wanted and expected the firm to grow at an average annual compound rate of 15 percent. A great deal of corporate planning had been devoted to that goal over the past three years and, indeed, second-quarter financial data suggested that Eastboro would achieve revenues of about $870 million in 2001, as shown in Exhibit 1. If Eastboro achieved a 15 percent compound rate of growth through 2007, the company would reach $2.0 billion in sales and $160 million in net income.

In order to achieve this growth goal, Eastboro management proposed a strategy relying on three key points. First, the mix of production would shift substantially. CAD/CAM and peripheral products on the cutting edge of industry technology would account for three-quarters of sales; the company's traditional presses and molds would account for the remainder. Second, the company would expand aggressively internationally, where it hoped to obtain half of its sales and profits by 2007. This expansion would be achieved through opening new field sales offices around the world. Third, the company would expand through joint ventures and acquisitions of small software companies, which would provide one-half of the new products through 2007; internal research would provide the other half.

From its beginning, Eastboro had an aversion to debt. Management believed that small amounts of debt, primarily to meet working-capital needs, had its place, but that anything beyond a 40 percent debt-to-equity ratio was, in the oft-quoted words of cofounder David Peterboro, "unthinkable, indicative of sloppy management, and flirting with trouble." Senior management was aware that equity was typically more costly than debt, but took great satisfaction in the company's "doing it on its own." Eastboro's highest debt-to-capital ratio in the past 25 years—22 percent—occurred in 2000, and was still the subject of conversations among senior managers.

Although 11 members of the East and Peterboro families owned 30 percent of the company's stock and three were on the board of directors, management placed the interests of the public shareholders first. (Shareholder data are provided in **Exhibit 4.**) Stephen East, chairman of the board and grandson of the cofounder, sought to maximize the growth in the market value of the company's stock over time.

At the age of 61, East was actively involved in all aspects of the company's growth and future. He was conversant with a range of technical details of Eastboro's products and was especially interested in finding ways to improve the company's domestic-market share. His retirement was no more than four years into the future, and he wanted to leave a legacy of corporate financial strength and technological achievement. The Artificial Workforce, a project he had taken under his wing four years earlier, was beginning to bear fruit. He now wanted to ensure that the firm would also soon be able to pay a dividend.

East took particular pride in selecting and developing young managers with promise. Campbell had a bachelor's degree in electrical engineering and had been a systems analyst for Motorola before attending graduate school. She had been hired in 1991 out of a well-known MBA program. By 2000, she had risen to the position of chief financial officer.

DIVIDEND POLICY

Eastboro's dividend and stock-price histories are presented in **Exhibit 5.** Prior to 1995, both earnings and dividends per share had grown at a relatively steady pace, but Eastboro's troubles in the mid-to-late 1990s took their toll on earnings. As a consequence, dividends were pared back in 1999 to $0.25 a share—the lowest dividend since 1986. In 2000, the board of directors declared a payout of $0.25 a share despite reporting the largest per-share earnings loss in the firm's history, and, in effect, borrowing to pay the dividend. In the first two quarters of 2001, the directors had not declared a dividend. In a special letter to shareholders, however, the directors declared their intention to continue the annual payout later in 2001.

In August 2001, Campbell contemplated choosing among three possible dividend policies to recommend:

- *Zero-dividend payout.* This option could be justified in light of the firm's strategic emphasis on advanced technologies and CAD/CAM, and reflected the huge cash requirements of that move. The proponents of this policy argued that it would signal that the firm belonged in a class of high-growth and high-technology firms. Some securities analysts wondered whether the market still considered Eastboro a traditional electrical-equipment manufacturer or a more technologically advanced CAD/CAM company. The latter category would imply that the market was expecting strong capital appreciation but, perhaps, little in the way of dividends. Others cited Eastboro's recent performance problems. One questioned the "wisdom of ignoring the financial statements in favor of acting like a blue chip." Was a high dividend in the long-term interests of the company and its stockholders, or would the strategy backfire and make investors skittish?

  Campbell recalled a recently published study that found that firms were displaying a lower propensity to pay dividends. The study found that the percentage of firms paying cash dividends had dropped from 66.5 in 1978 to 20.8 in 1999.[2] In this light, perhaps the market would not react unkindly if Eastboro assumed a zero-dividend-payout policy.

- *40 percent dividend payout,* or a dividend of around $0.20 a share. This would restore the firm to an implied annual dividend payment of $0.80 a share, the highest since 1997. Proponents of this policy argued that there was undoubtedly some anticipation of such an announcement in the current stock price of $32 a share, and that this was justified by expected increases in orders and sales. Eastboro's investment banker suggested that the market might be expecting a strong dividend in order to bring the payout back in line with the 45 percent average within the electrical-industrial-equipment industry and with the 29 percent average in the machine-tool industry. Still others believed that it was important to send a strong signal to shareholders, and that a large dividend (on the order of a 40 percent payout) would suggest that the company had conquered its problems and that its directors were confident of future earnings. Supporters of this view argued that borrowing to pay dividends was not inconsistent with the behavior of most firms. Finally, some older members of management opined that a growth rate in the range of 10 to 20 percent should accompany a payout of 30 to 50 percent.

  Campbell remembered reading a *Wall Street Journal* article only a few days earlier in which the columnist had argued that with the recent collapse in technology and other growth stocks, investors were flocking to dividend-paying stocks. The article quoted Jeremy Siegel, a finance professor at the Wharton School: "A little more than a year ago, people laughed at dividends. . . . In the future, I believe that more attention will be paid to dividends and current earnings and less to growth."[3]

---

[2]Eugene Fama and Kenneth French, "Changing Firm Characteristics or Lower Propensity to Pay," *Journal of Financial Economics* 60 (April 2001): 3–43.

[3]Jonathan Clements, "Dividends, Not Growth, Is Wave of Future," *The Wall Street Journal,* August 21, 2001, C1.

- *Residual-dividend-payout policy.* A few members of the finance staff argued that Eastboro should pay dividends only after funding all projects offering positive net present values (NPVs). Their view was that investors were paying managers to deploy their funds at returns better than they could achieve otherwise, and that, by definition, such investments would yield positive NPVs. By deploying funds into these projects and otherwise returning unused funds to investors in the form of dividends, the firm would build trust with investors and be rewarded with higher valuation multiples. General Motors was the preeminent example of a firm that had followed such a policy, though few large publicly held firms followed its example.

  Another argument in support of this view was that dividend policy was "irrelevant" in a growing firm: any dividend paid today would be offset by dilution at some future date by the issue of shares necessary to make up for the dividend. This argument reflected the theory of dividends in a perfect market advanced by two finance professors, Merton Miller and Franco Modigliani.[4] The main disadvantage of this policy to Jennifer Campbell was that dividend payments would be unpredictable. In some years, dividends could be cut—even to zero—possibly imposing negative pressure on the firm's share price. Campbell was all too aware of Eastboro's own share-price collapse following its dividend cut. She recalled a study by another finance professor, John Lintner,[5] which found that firms' dividend payments tended to be "sticky" upward—that is, dividends would rise over time and rarely fall, and that mature slower-growth firms paid higher dividends, while high-growth firms paid lower dividends.

In response to this internal debate, Campbell's staff pulled together **Exhibits 6 and 7,** which present comparative information on companies in three industries—CAD/CAM, machine tools, and electrical-industrial equipment—and on a general sample of high- and low-payout companies. To test the feasibility of a 40 percent dividend payout rate, Campbell developed the projected sources and uses of cash provided in **Exhibit 8.** She took the boldest approach by assuming that the company would grow at a 15 percent compound rate, that margins would improve over the next few years to historical levels, and that the firm would pay a dividend of 40 percent of earnings every year. In particular, the forecast assumed that the firm's net margin would hover between 4 and 6 percent over the next six years, and then increase to 7.95 percent in 2007. The firm's operating executives believed that this increase in profitability was consistent with economies of scale to be achieved upon the attainment of higher operating output of the Artificial Workforce.

IMAGE ADVERTISING AND NAME CHANGE

As part of a general review of the firm's standing in the financial markets, Eastboro's director of Investor Relations, Cathy Williams, had concluded that investors misperceived the

---

[4]M.H. Miller and F. Modigliani, "Dividend Policy, Growth and the Valuation of Shares," *Journal of Business* 34 (October 1961): 411–33.
[5]J. Lintner, "Distribution of Incomes of Corporations among Dividends, Retained Earnings, and Taxes," *American Economic Review* 46 (May 1956): 97–113.

firm's prospects and that the firm's current name was more consistent with the firm's historical product mix and markets than with those expected in the future. Williams commissioned surveys of readers of financial magazines, which revealed a relatively low awareness of Eastboro or its business. Surveys of stockbrokers revealed higher awareness of the firm, but a low or mediocre outlook on Eastboro's likely returns to shareholders and growth prospects. Williams retained a consulting firm that recommended a program of corporate "image" advertising targeted toward opinion-leading institutional investors and individual investors. The objective was to enhance the awareness and image of Eastboro. Through focus groups, the consultants identified a name that appeared to suggest the firm's promising strategy: "Eastboro Advanced Systems International, Inc." Williams estimated that the image-advertising campaign and name change would cost approximately $10 million.

Stephen East was mildly skeptical. He said, "Do you mean to raise our stock price by 'marketing' our shares? This is a novel approach. Can you sell claims on a company the way Procter & Gamble markets soap?" The consultants could give no empirical evidence that stock prices responded favorably to corporate-image campaigns or name changes, though they did offer some favorable anecdotes.

CONCLUSION

Jennifer Campbell was caught in a difficult position. Members of the board and management disagreed on the very nature of Eastboro's future. Some managers saw the company as entering a new stage of rapid growth and thought that a large (or, in the minds of some, any) dividend would be inappropriate. Others thought that it was important to make a strong gesture to the public that management believed Eastboro had turned the corner and was about to return to the levels of growth and profitability seen in the 1970s and '80s. This action could only be accomplished through a dividend. Then there was the confounding question about the stock buyback: should Eastboro use funds to repurchase stocks instead of paying out a dividend? As she wrestled with the different points of view, she wondered whether management might be representative of the company's shareholders. Did the majority of public shareholders own stock for the same reason, or were their reasons just as diverse as those of management?

EXHIBIT 1
Consolidated Income Statements (dollars in thousands, except per-share data)

	For the Years Ended December 31,			
	1998	**1999**	**2000**	**Projected 2001**
Net sales	$858,263	$815,979	$ 756,638	$870,000
Cost of sales	540,747	501,458	498,879	549,750
Gross profit	317,516	314,522	257,759	320,250
Research & development	77,678	70,545	75,417	77,250
Selling, general, & administrative	229,971	223,634	231,008	211,500
Restructuring costs	65,448	0	89,411	0
Operating profit (loss)	(55,581)	20,343	(138,077)	31,500
Other income (expense)	(4,500)	1,065	(3,458)	(4,200)
Income (loss) before taxes	(60,081)	21,408	(141,534)	27,300
Income taxes (benefit)	1,241	8,415	(750)	9,282
Net income (loss)	$(61,322)	$ 12,993	$(140,784)	$ 18,018
Earnings (loss) per share	$ (3.25)	$ 0.69	$ (7.67)	$ 0.98
Dividends per share	$ 0.77	$ 0.25	$ 0.25	$ 0.39

Note: The dividends in 2001 assume a payout ratio of 40 percent.

EXHIBIT 2
Consolidated Balance Sheets (dollars in thousands)

	December 31st		
	1999	2000	Projected 2001
Cash & equivalents	$ 13,917	$ 22,230	$ 25,665
Accounts receivable	208,541	187,235	217,510
Inventories	230,342	203,888	217,221
Prepaid expenses	14,259	13,016	15,011
Other	22,184	20,714	21,000
Total Current Assets	489,242	447,082	496,407
Property, plant, & equipment	327,603	358,841	410,988
Less depreciation	167,414	183,486	205,530
Net property, plant, & equipment	160,190	175,355	205,458
Intangible assets	9,429	2,099	1,515
Other assets	15,723	17,688	17,969
Total assets	$674,583	$642,223	$721,350
Bank loans	$ 34,196	71,345	74,981
Accounts payable	36,449	34,239	37,527
Current portion of long-term debt	300	150	1,515
Accruals and other	129,374	161,633	183,014
Total Current Liabilities	200,318	267,367	297,037
Deferred taxes	16,986	13,769	16,526
Long-term debt	9,000	8,775	30,021
Deferred pension costs	44,790	64,329	70,134
Other liabilities	2,318	5,444	7,505
Total Liabilities	273,411	359,683	421,224
Common stock, $1 par value	18,855	18,855	18,835
Capital in excess of par	107,874	107,907	107,889
Cumulative translation adjustment	(6,566)	20,208	26,990
Retained earnings	291,498	146,065	156,875
Less treasury stock at cost:			
1986—256,151, 1987—255,506	(10,490)	(10,494)	(10,464)
Total shareholders' equity	401,172	282,541	300,126
Total liabilities & equity	$674,583	$642,223	$721,350

Note: Projections assume a dividend payout ratio of 40 percent.

EXHIBIT 3
Economic Indicators and Projections (all numbers are percentages)

	1998	1999	2000	August 2001	Projected 2002	Projected 2003
3-month Treasury bill rate (at auction)	4.8	4.6	5.8	3.9	3.8	4.5
10-year Treasury bond rate	5.26	5.64	6.03	5.17	5.7	7.2
AAA corporate bond rate	6.5	7.0	7.7	7.6	7.9	8.0
Change in:						
Real gross domestic product	4.4	4.2	5.0	1.6	2.6	3.4
Producer price index	−0.9	1.8	3.7	2.7	0.5	1.2
Industrial production	4.8	4.1	5.6	−2.5	2.6	5.9
Production of durable goods	9.1	8.2	10.0	−2.7	3.4	9.1
Consumption of durable goods	10.6	12.4	9.5	4.6	6.1	4.2
Consumer spending	4.7	5.3	5.3	3.0	3.0	3.1
Price deflator	1.3	1.5	2.0	2.3	2.2	2.6

Sources: U.S. Economic Outlook, WEFA Group, August 2001; *Value Line Investment Survey,* August 24, 2001.

EXHIBIT 4
Stockholder Comparative Data, 1990 and 2000 (thousands of shares)

	1990		2000	
	Shares	Percentage	Shares	Percentage
Founders' families	2,390	13	2,384	13
Employees and families	3,677	20	3,118	17
Institutional investors				
A. growth-oriented	2,390	13	1,101	6
B. value-oriented	1,471	8	2,384	13
Individual investors				
A. long-term; retirement	6,803	37	4,769	27
B. short-term; trading-oriented	919	5	2,384	13
C. other; unknown	735	4	2,201	12
	18,342	100	18,342	100

The investor-relations department identified these categories from company records. The type of institutional investor was identified from promotional materials stating the investment goals of the institutions. The type of individual investor was identified from a survey of subsamples of investors.

EXHIBIT 5
Per-Share Financial and Stock Data[1]

Year	Sales/ Share	EPS	DPS	CPS	Stock Price			Avg. P/E	Payout Ratio	Avg. Yield	Shares Outstanding (Millions)
					High	Low	Avg.				
1985	$14.52	$ 0.45	$0.18	$0.97	$20.37	$ 9.69	$14.48	32.4	40%	1.2%	15.49
1986	16.00	0.74	0.22	1.29	21.11	10.18	14.85	20.2	30%	1.5	15.58
1987	22.25	0.89	0.27	1.43	21.23	8.20	13.50	15.1	30%	2.0	16.04
1988	25.64	1.59	0.31	2.05	18.50	10.18	13.35	8.4	19%	2.3	17.87
1989	27.19	2.29	0.40	2.83	22.48	12.17	18.36	8.0	17%	2.2	18.08
1990	30.06	2.59	0.57	3.25	23.84	18.01	21.00	8.1	22%	2.7	18.39
1991	31.66	2.61	0.72	3.34	26.70	18.25	22.73	8.7	27%	3.1	18.76
1992	37.71	2.69	0.81	3.60	29.43	19.50	24.23	9.0	30%	3.4	18.76
1993	40.69	2.56	0.86	3.62	39.74	20.12	29.48	11.5	34%	2.9	18.78
1994	48.23	3.58	0.92	4.81	40.98	27.32	33.98	9.5	26%	2.7	18.88
1995	43.59	2.79	1.03	4.25	38.74	21.36	31.82	11.4	37%	3.2	18.66
1996	42.87	0.65	1.03	2.23	47.19	29.55	36.81	57.0	160%	2.8	18.66
1997	41.48	0.35	1.03	2.00	40.23	26.82	31.26	89.9	297%	3.3	18.66
1998	46.01	(3.29)	0.77	2.86	30.75	22.13	26.45	NMF	NMF	2.9	18.85
1999	43.88	0.70	0.25	1.99	71.88	50.74	61.33	88.2	35%	0.4	18.85
2000	41.26	(7.67)	0.25	−0.97	39.88	18.38	29.15	NMF	NMF	0.9	18.34

Note: NMF = not a meaningful figure.

[1] Adjusted for 3-for-2 stock split in January 1991 and 50 percent stock dividend in June 1995.

EXHIBIT 6
Comparative Industry Data (compiled from data available as of August 2001)

| | Sales ($MM) | Annual Growth Rate of Cash Flow (%) | | Current Payout Ratio (%) | Current Dividend Yield (%) | Debt/ Equity (%) | Insider Ownership (%) | P/E Ratio (x) |
		Last 10 Years	Next 3–5 Years					
Eastboro	$ 757	−15.8	+15	Nil	Nil	28	30	NMF
CAD/CAM Companies (software and hardware)								
Autodesk	936	10.5	15.5	12.8	0.6	0	5.0	17.5
Brooks Automation	321	NMF	30.0	Nil	Nil	0	7.7	NMF
Parametric Tech.	928	41.0	10.0	Nil	Nil	0	2.6	36.0
Intergraph	691	NMF	NMF	Nil	Nil	41.8	4.9	NMF
Mentor Graphics	590	−4.0	17.0	Nil	Nil	0.6	3.9	16.3
Moldflow Corp.	40	NA	21.0	Nil	Nil	0	14.9	32.5
Sun Microsystems	15,721	23.5	15.0	Nil	Nil	4.8	3.3	87.4
Gerber Scientific	554	3.0	3.0	Nil	Nil	68.0	16.9	33.4
Hewlett-Packard	9,601	29.5[1]	10.5	Nil	Nil	0.6	32.3	47.0
Electrical-Industrial- Equipment Manufacturers								
Emerson Electric	15,545	9.5	7.5	47.9	2.9	21.0	0.8	18.8
General Electric	63,807	11.5	10.5	43.3	1.4	37.3	< 1	30.8
Hubbell, Inc.	1,424	8.0	8.0	61.9	4.7	19.8	51.0	17.5
Honeywell	25,023	9.0	7.5	26.5	2.0	18.8	< 1	16.7
Esterline Tech.	491	7.5	11.5	Nil	Nil	29.3	6.2	10.5
Machine-Tool-Manufacturers								
Actuant Corp.	515	9.5	6.5	Nil	Nil	278.1	10.0	9.5
Lincoln Electric	1,059	8.0[1]	10.0	27.7	2.5	8.8	22.3	11.9
Milacron, Inc.	1,584	11.0	1.5	23.3	2.8	93.9	4.2	NMF
Snap-On Inc.	2,176	5.0	4.0	37.3	3.6	34.2	4.8	15.3

NMF = not a meaningful figure because of recent reported losses.
[1]Last five years only.

Source: Value Line Investment Survey, August 24, 2001.

EXHIBIT 7
Selected Healthy Companies with High- and Zero-Dividend Payouts (compiled from data available as of August 2001)

	Industry	Expected Return on Total Capital (next 3–5 years)	Expected Growth Rate of Dividends (next 3–5 years)	Current Dividend Payout	Current Dividend Yield	Expected Growth Rate of Sales (next 3–5 years)	Current P/E Ratio
High-Payout Companies							
Scudder High Income	Investment company	NA	NA	108	11.2	NA	NA
Hospitality Properties	Real estate inv. trust	9.0	NA	124	9.9	NA	12.2
New Plan Excel Realty	Real estate inv. trust	8.0	NA	145	10.1	NA	13.1
DQE	Electric utility	7.5	–4.5	122	7.9	5.0	19.7
Cedar Fair L. P.	Recreation	18.0	3.5	90	7.8	6.0	14.3
Plum Creek Timber	Paper and forest products	19.0	0.5	185	8.0	NMF	27.0
Puget Energy Inc.	Electric utility	7.5	0	85	7.7	13.0	12.0
National Presto Ind.	Home Appliances	7.0	1.5	97	7.0	12.5	18.1
Zero-Payout Companies							
Oracle Systems	Software	24.0	0	0	0	15.5	33.3
Novell	Software	15.5	0	0	0	9.5	NMF
AOL Time Warner	Media and entertainment	6.5	0	0	0	NMF	31.8
Broadcom Corp.	Telecommunications	7.5	0	0	0	NMF	NMF
Advanced Micro Devices	Semiconductor	15.5	0	0	0	12.5	35.2
Madden (Steven)	Retail	18.5	0	0	0	19.5	10.9
Lands' End	Retail	14.0	0	0	0	8.0	23.1
Enterasys Networks	Network systems	7.5	0	0	0	8.0	NMF
Cisco Systems	Network systems	13.5	0	0	0	18.0	NMF

Source: Value Line Investment Survey, August 24, 2001.

EXHIBIT 8
Projected-Sources-and-Uses Statement Assuming a 40 Percent Payout Ratio[1] (dollars in millions)

	2001	2002	2003	2004	2005	2006	2007	2001-07
Sales	$870	$1,001	$1,151	$1,323	$1,522	$1,750	$2,013	$9,630
Sources:								
Net income	18	40	58	73	91	98	160	538
Depreciation	23	26	30	35	41	47	53	252
	41	66	88	107	132	145	213	790
Uses:								
Capital expend.	44	50	58	66	68	79	91	456
Change in working capital	20	22	26	30	34	39	44	214
	63	73	83	96	102	117	135	670
Excess cash/(Borrowing needs)	(23)	(7)	4	12	29	27	78	120
Dividend	7	16	23	29	37	39	64	215
After dividend								
Excess cash/(Borrowing needs)	(30)	(23)	(19)	(18)	(7)	(12)	14	(95)

Note: Dividend calculated as 40 percent of net income.

[1]This analysis ignores the effects of borrowing on interest and amortization. It includes all increases in long-term liabilities and equity items other than retained earnings.

Donaldson, Lufkin & Jenrette, 1995 (Abridged)

On the afternoon of October 24, 1995, John Chalsty, president and CEO of the investment bank Donaldson, Lufkin & Jenrette ("DLJ") met with several colleagues to price the initial public offering (IPO) of 9.2 million shares of DLJ's stock. Also present, either in person or over the phone, were most of the board members of The Equitable Companies Incorporated ("Equitable"), DLJ's parent and 100 percent owner. For nearly six months, Mr. Chalsty had worked to prepare for an offering of DLJ shares to the public.

Equitable's chairman, Richard Jenrette, would watch while the firm he founded and which still bore his name, went public for the second time. The sale would mark another milestone of the successful restructuring of Equitable led by Mr. Jenrette. Investors could now see how much DLJ was worth on its own. Equitable had purchased DLJ in 1985 for $465 million. The filing range in the initial prospectus had been from $26 to $29 per share, placing a value on DLJ from $1.5 billion to $1.7 billion. Equitable would continue to own approximately 80 percent of DLJ after the offering.

The DLJ bankers who had worked with Mr. Chalsty and Equitable for six months, Pedro Galban, Bill Wheeler, Stephan Kiratsous, and Cameron Fleming, sat with the others. They had coordinated the offering and valued DLJ, primarily by comparing its results to those of other comparable publicly traded investment banks. However, DLJ proved to be a difficult comparison: its strategy was unlike that of larger investment banks. It focused on competing in higher margin business lines where it could be a leader. Traditionally, investors thought that the larger investment banks earned higher returns on capital, yet DLJ was smaller, and earned higher returns than most of the six largest firms in recent years.

This case was prepared by Douglas Fordyce under the direction of Professor Robert F. Bruner, and is a condensed version of two other cases prepared by Fordyce and Bruner, "Donaldson, Lufkin & Jenrette (A) and (B)" (UVA-F-1145, F-1146). Copyright © 1996 by the University of Virginia Darden School Foundation, Charlottesville, VA. All rights reserved. *To order copies, send an e-mail to* dardencases@virginia.edu. *No part of this publication may be reproduced, stored in a retrieval system, used in a spreadsheet, or transmitted in any form or by any means—electronic, mechanical, photocopying, recording, or otherwise—without the permission of the Darden School Foundation.* Rev. 12/01. Version 1.3.

Like other DLJ employees, the bankers were excited because DLJ would soon be able raise debt and equity on its own and aggressively pursue its strategy. They, too, would be able to own a part of DLJ. In fact, many employees would be exchanging their interests in long-term compensation plans for shares and options in DLJ after the offering.

Joining the bankers from DLJ was Duff Anderson, managing director of Equity Capital Markets. As lead manager of the offering, DLJ was responsible for marketing the stock and coordinating the efforts of the other underwriters. Mr. Anderson bore responsibility for working with other securities firms in explaining the investment opportunity the stock represented to investors and in gauging demand for the issue. He had to represent the investors who purchased shares from the underwriters, making sure they got a fair return. Yet, he wanted to ensure that Equitable and DLJ received a good price for the stock they sold. And finally, he had to represent the underwriters, who could be stuck with any shares that went unsold.

While the DLJ offering was oversubscribed by investors, some had questioned how successful DLJ would be in the future. Critics wondered if DLJ had sufficiently diverse businesses and enough of an international presence to compete in the ever-competitive securities industry. Others questioned if DLJ could maintain its enviable, collegial atmosphere in the face of public scrutiny. Pointing to the high prices for other securities firms, a few investors said that, while DLJ possessed one of the finest franchises on Wall Street, they worried that Equitable might be selling at the peak of the market. The stocks of investment banks had traded down 7.5 percent on average over the last week. Perhaps, the indications of interest given by investors would prove less firm than expected.

Now, after the lengthy process of due diligence, SEC filings, road-show presentations and meetings, all that remained for those present was setting the offering price of the stock.

THE SECURITIES INDUSTRY

Perhaps Wall Street had changed more in the last 20 years than it had since 1624 when Dutch traders erected what became the namesake wall on the southern tip of Manhattan. Before the mid-1970s, investment banks served as orderly financial intermediaries, underwriting "plain-vanilla" stocks and bonds, brokering securities for clients for a fixed fee and offering financial advice on mergers and acquisitions when asked. Investment banks maintained close relationships with a select group of corporations, acting as capital raiser and trusted advisor. The investment banks required little capital of their own, quickly moving securities from corporations to investors, rarely holding inventories of securities.

In this regulated environment, the function of investment banks was to bear capital market risks, in contrast to other firms. In an underwriting, investment banks purchased clients' securities at a fixed price to resell later in the market, at an uncertain price. Commercial banks accepted credit risk, the uncertainty of a borrower's ability to meet contractual interest and principal payments. Insurance companies underwrote event risk. Nonfinancial corporations accepted business risk, the operational risks inherent in their businesses.

Three regulatory changes threw this calm, profitable environment into turbulence. In 1974, the government enacted the Employee Retirement Income Security Act (ERISA), requiring pension managers to follow the "prudent man" rule when making investment decisions. Freed from investing just in bonds and blue chip stocks, pension managers diversified their portfolios into new markets, both domestically and abroad. The managers were compensated according to how they performed relative to the market. With competition, managers grew hungry for financial products that could enhance their performance and manage unwanted risks. They also demanded that securities firms be ready to buy or sell nearly any security to them, requiring brokers to establish large securities inventories.

A year later, the government hit the brokerage industry with May Day, when fixed brokerage commissions were eliminated. The new regulations dissolved the fixed commission structure and allowed investors to negotiate commissions with their brokers. Large institutions cut their commissions by up to 80 percent instantly.[1] Smaller brokerages combined with each other to rationalize their businesses, meet capital requirements, and take advantage of economies of scale in the "back office," the processing and record keeping side of the business. In the new environment, firms started to compete even more intensely with each other for clients.

Finally, in 1982 the SEC introduced Rule 415 which permitted "shelf registration" of securities. Under a shelf registration, a company filed one comprehensive registration statement to cover the issuance of a fixed amount of capital over a stated period, but left open the types of securities to be sold and when they would be brought to market. During that period, the company could quickly issue securities in two days, "pulling them off the shelf," to take advantage of favorable rates or conditions. Companies needed only to make quick updates to the initial registration statement. To win their underwriting business, issuers forced underwriters to bid more aggressively for their securities. This bidding cut the "gross spread," the percentage underwriters earned in the issuance process. Guy Moszkowski, the securities industry analyst at brokerage Sanford C. Bernstein, estimated that in 1982 underwriters earned 1.5 percent of the value of securities underwritten. By 1993 the gross spread had shrunk to just 0.67 percent.[2]

Technology, too, played a role in shaping the new financing arena. Computers supported the creation and pricing of more complex financial instruments, such as derivatives. In corporate finance, bankers could test multitudes of capital structures and their effects on a company through the use of spreadsheets. While margins eroded in the brokerage and underwriting businesses, blossoming fields like derivatives, junk bonds and mergers and acquisition (M&A) services for leveraged buyouts (LBOs') kept overall margins healthy. Innovation proved very profitable for those who could create the newest security or M&A tactic. Though temporarily very lucrative for their inventors, these innovations tended to be quickly duplicated by competitors.

Contemporaneously, governments deregulated interest rates and foreign exchange rates. Underwriters introduced products, like swaps and Yankee bonds, to take advantage of global capital markets. In most developed economies, deregulation and tighter monetary policies by reserve banks eventually led to a steady decline in interest rates from the early 1980s until 1994. This environment translated into an extended bull market, with a corresponding torrent of debt and equity issuances from companies. Investment banks received

---

[1] "Other People's Money," *The Economist,* April 15, 1995.
[2] Ibid.

less for their services but were more than compensated with higher volumes of transactions and increased trading activity.

Power shifted from individual investors to institutional investors during this period. With the rise of pension and mutual funds, institutional investors came to dominate the market. In 1980, individuals owned 60.9 percent of all equities, and institutions owned 29.1 percent. In 1994, individuals owned just 48.2 percent, and institutions 51.8 percent.[3] **Exhibit 1** details the growth of the financial markets. **Exhibit 2** documents the expansion of the securities industry.

In search of higher margins, investment banks moved into new areas, accepting new risks. They blurred the historical lines between financial institutions. They even moved into nonfinancial businesses. To compete with commercial banks, investment banking firms accepted credit risk by developing bridge loan funds and syndication departments. Investment bankers lent money to firms on a short-term basis to facilitate pending M&A transactions. These loans, called bridge loans, assisted acquirors in acquisitions by "bridging" the gap in financing until the companies could replace the bridge loan with more permanent capital. Separately, loan syndication departments in investment banks competed with commercial banks to take commercial loans, divide them into smaller loans and sell off the loans to a syndicate of banks. If they properly executed the transaction, syndicate managers could earn fees for the work, while never taking the loan onto their balance sheet. Syndication constituted one of the commercial banks' most profitable areas. They resented Wall Street invasion of their profit centers, even though the commercial banks were quickly moving into securities trading, advisory services and underwriting: Wall Street's businesses.

With the rise of derivatives, investment banks came to price and take on event risk. They insured against risks that corporations desired to shed. For example, an investment bank might offer to limit an airline's exposure to fluctuating jet fuel prices, allowing the airline to "lock-in" a set price for its fuel needs for the year. To accomplish this hedge, the bank would sell a series of forward contracts on jet fuel prices to the airline. The bank then might sell offsetting positions to another party who wanted exposure to jet fuel prices, or might keep the contract on its books. The derivative market soared to become a multitrillion-dollar market. As the derivatives market expanded, investment banks tailored generic contracts to meet companies' specific needs. The specialized use of derivatives played a large part in the development of the collateralized mortgage and asset backed debt markets.

With their knowledge of the markets and constant flow of information, investment banks moved into principal trading. They used their own capital, often leveraged, to bet on the directions of the markets. To varying degrees, firms established proprietary trading operations, with firms like Salomon Brothers and Goldman Sachs leading the pack. Profits could be quite high if the traders were right, but losses could be severe if their insights proved wrong. In 1994, Salomon Brothers lost $831 million pretax, largely due to misguided bets on the bond market. Many critics charged Wall Street with a conflict of interest in its principal trading because many of its clients were making similar market bets. In effect, critics charged, the banks competed against their own clients.

---

[3] "Equities, Corporate Bonds and Tax Exempt Securities," *Statistical Abstract of the United States 1995,* No. 825, p. 532.

Finally, many investment banks participated in merchant banking and venture capital investments. They risked their own funds to buy all or part of other companies outside the securities industry. Merchant banking deals often involved mature companies and took on large amounts of debt, while venture capital investments tended to be in growth stage companies. If the investment strategy proved correct, these investments could provide huge returns to the equity capital invested, garnering annual returns of 30 percent or greater. In the LBO field, investment banks competed for deals with LBO partnerships, like Kolberg, Kravis, Roberts & Co., Clayton Dubilier & Rice, and Saunders Karp & Co. In venture capital, they competed with other venture capitalists like Kleiner, Perkins, Caufield & Byers, and Welsh, Carson, Anderson & Stowe, as well as others.

Recently, many investment banks focused on trying to limit their exposure to U.S. interest rates. When rates increased almost 200 basis points from 1993 to 1994, firms were reminded of how much their businesses depended on low rates. Net profits for NYSE member firms declined from record-breaking heights in 1993 of $8.6 billion to $1.4 billion in 1994.[4] Underwritings dried up and bond portfolios plummeted. To dampen the effects of interest rate swings, firms have tried to increase their presence overseas and to develop fee-based asset management businesses.

In the 1970s and 80s, investment banks flocked to Europe and Japan as U.S. companies expanded abroad. The expansion required capital for equipment and for regulatory purposes. Many foreign regulatory bodies insisted that branch offices maintain regulatory capital on site. In the 1990s, investment banks built up trading and corporate finance operations in emerging markets, like Mexico, Brazil, Hong Kong and India. These markets often offered lower levels of competition from local securities firms, excellent growth and higher profits. Morgan Stanley placed great emphasis on growing abroad, allocating roughly one half of its capital overseas, generating 40 percent of its revenues.[5] Even with its strong presence abroad, Morgan made an attempt to merge with S. G. Warburg, one of the leading European investment banks, in 1995, though the merger fell through.

Many investment banks built or bought asset management businesses. Unlike other areas tied to interest rates, these businesses provided reliable revenue streams. They earned a fee based on a percentage of assets under management. Merrill Lynch created an asset management business that oversaw over $170 billion of assets. Annual management fees on the assets generated approximately $1.74 billion in revenues, roughly enough to cover the entire firm's fixed costs for a year. In 1995, Morgan Stanley paid $350 million for Miller Anderson & Sherrerd, an asset manager, to bulk up its business.

All of the changes in the industry necessitated capital—from holding more inventory for clients to building overseas operations to merchant banking investments. With so much capital at risk, earnings became more volatile. Profits could swing drastically with changes in underwriting volumes or interest rates.

In the future, many analysts expected further consolidation within the securities industry. They hypothesized that two factors would drive consolidation: globalization, and the

---

[4] "Securities Industry—Revenues and Expenses: 1980–1994," *Statistical Abstract of the United States 1995,* No. 833, p. 535.
[5] "Other People's Money," *The Economist,* April 15, 1995.

long-expected repeal of the Glass-Steagall regulations. They argued that firms needed a strong international presence to successfully compete for large underwriting assignments and to mitigate oscillations in U.S. interest rates.

The Glass-Steagall Act of 1933 separated investment banks and commercial banks after the Crash of 1929. Regulators assigned a portion of the blame for the Crash on the conflicts of interest in the two businesses. Commercial banks eventually earned the right to petition the Federal Reserve for underwriting powers. By 1995, J. P. Morgan, Chase Manhattan and Bankers Trust had successfully requested these powers. They competed with investment banks in trading, debt underwriting, and advisory services. They had limited success in their efforts to underwrite stock offerings. The repeal of Glass-Steagall, which many predicted to occur by the end of the decade, would undoubtedly bring more participants to the securities industry. More competition would put further pressure on margins as newcomers competed for market share on price.

Many expected that the European universal banks and U.S. money center banks would be acquirors of U.S. investment banks once the act was repealed. Conventional wisdom stated that three firms, Goldman Sachs, Merrill Lynch, and Morgan Stanley, were sufficiently global and well capitalized as to remain immune from being acquired. Some speculated that Lehman Brothers, PaineWebber, and Salomon Brothers were prime merger or takeover targets.

COMPANY HISTORY

In 1959, William Donaldson, Dan Lufkin, and Richard Jenrette set out with $100,000 to create an equity research firm that would serve institutional shareholders. Until that time, brokerage houses primarily catered to individual investors. The three Harvard Business School graduates saw that institutional investors were not adequately served.

The young firm prospered, offering sophisticated equity analysis to institutional investors in the hope of receiving their lucrative fixed-commission trading business. Gradually, the firm diversified in the face of competition and clients' demands for more services. As new businesses required more capital, the firm decided to go public in 1970. However, the New York Stock Exchange, of which DLJ was a member, prohibited members from having public shareholders. No NYSE member had ever offered shares to the public. *Business Week* reported on the controversial transactions, writing:

> Wall Street is, rather proudly, the home of the Big Risk and the Big Stake. Last week, three young men staked their 10-year old, $24 million firm in one of the most remarkable wagers in recent financial history. If they lose, they forfeit their membership in the nation's wealthiest club, the New York Stock Exchange. If they win, they can increase the value of their firm tenfold, literally overnight. Win or lose, they have already set in motion forces that in the coming decade will wrench the sinews of power in every quarter of the U.S. securities industry.[6]

---

[6] "Changing Wall Street's Rules," *Business Week,* May 31, 1969, pp. 70–74.

DLJ kept its NYSE membership, and in April of 1970, DLJ offered shares of itself to the public. At the time, DLJ had just over 400 employees with revenues of $21.9 million. The market valued the company at approximately $115 million.

DLJ continued its strategy of diversification during the seventies and early eighties. Faced with more capital requirements, DLJ chose to sell itself to Equitable in 1985 for $465 million. Equitable was then a mutual life insurance company, owned by policyholders. Richard Jenrette, head of DLJ, joined Equitable as chief investment officer shortly after the merger. He became chairman in 1990. Mr. Jenrette initiated a restructuring of Equitable in response to serious problems. In the restructuring, Mr. Jenrette cut $150 million in annual costs, and sold 49 percent of Equitable to AXA, a French holding company for a group of international insurance and financial services companies.[7] He also demutualized Equitable, raising $450 million in an initial public offering (IPO).[8] Equitable separated DLJ's original asset management operations, Alliance Capital Management ("Alliance"), from DLJ. Later Equitable sold part of Alliance to the public. In June of 1995, Alliance's market capitalization stood at approximately $2 billion. By 1995, AXA owned approximately 60 percent of Equitable.

Under Equitable, DLJ built industry and product groups as opportunity presented itself. DLJ focused on building higher margin businesses, like underwriting IPOs and high-yield ("junk") debt, creating specialized issues of mortgage-backed debt and merchant banking. It strove to be a leader in each market it selected. DLJ strategy was one of patience, keeping lean in the good times and taking chances when others saw gloom. For example, when many securities firms fired employees after the Black Monday, October 17, 1987, crash, DLJ actively hired select professionals. Similarly, after the junk bond market collapsed in 1990, DLJ sought out and hired a core group of junk bond specialists from fallen market leader Drexel Burnham Lambert.

DLJ's careful strategy excelled, pushing DLJ up the industry league tables, as shown in **Exhibit 3.** By the mid-1990s, DLJ required more capital to continue its growth. Together, DLJ and Equitable sought a solution.

DLJ BUSINESS GROUPS

The company was a leading investment and merchant bank that served institutional, corporate, government, and individual clients. In terms of capital, DLJ ranked as the 11th largest securities firm. DLJ's businesses included securities underwriting, sales and trading, merchant banking, venture capital, financial advisory services, investment research, correspondent brokerage services, and asset management. It operated through three principal groups: the Banking Group; the Capital Markets Group; and the Financial Services Group.

---

[7] "Equitable Chairman to Step Down," *Bloomberg Business News,* February 13, 1996.

[8] A mutual insurance company is owned by policyholders. In a demutualization, ownership is converted to common stock and distributed to policyholders. Often times, new shares are sold to the public.

DLJ Business Groups

Banking Group	Capital Markets Group	Financial Services Group
• Investment banking	• Institutional equities	• Pershing Division
• Merchant banking	• Taxable-fixed income	• Investment Services Group
• Emerging markets	• Equity derivatives	• Wood, Struthers & Winthrop
	• Sprout venture capital	

In 1995, DLJ employed 4,676 people, including 431 professionals in the Banking Group, 821 professionals in the Capital Markets Group, and 998 professionals in the Financial Services Group. Exhibit 4 shows the revenue growth by group from 1990 until 1995.

The Banking Group

The professionals in the Banking Group assisted clients in raising capital through the issuance of debt and equity securities in the public and private markets. The Investment Banking group also provided its clients with financial advice concerning mergers, acquisitions, restructurings and other transactions. Since 1990, the Investment Banking group had assisted its clients in raising over $150 billion in capital and completed over 300 M&A transactions, worth approximately $65 billion. While DLJ worked with clients from all industries, it focused on 17 sectors where it believed it had a competitive advantage. The firm also maintained successful groups in private placements, private fund raising (raising money for LBO funds, for example), structured finance, and restructurings.

The Merchant Banking group invested capital directly into companies, often in concert with the firm's clients. Institutional investors, DLJ itself, and DLJ employees provided the capital. DLJ utilized two investment funds with combined capital of $2.25 billion: DLJ Merchant Banking Partners L.P. and the DLJ Bridge Fund. These investments resulted in DLJ owning a minority or majority position in a company's equity and debt. Since its inception in 1985, the group had invested in 46 companies with an aggregate purchase price of over $18 billion. Since 1992, DLJ had placed $580 million in 20 companies and realized $610 million from seven partial or whole realizations. DLJ earned one of the highest returns among principal investors, with annual returns thought to be greater than 90 percent.[9] The bridge fund had completed 74 transactions totaling $12 billion of commitments to clients. The fund had $230 million of bridge loans outstanding as of June 30, 1995. The merchant banking activities earned money by charging a small fixed percentage for assets under management and keeping approximately 20 percent of the profits realized through the investments. The bridge operations earned money for committing to lend money and on interest on money it lent out.

Due to its success in merchant banking, DLJ planned to form four new funds in the near future: DLJ Investment Partners, to seek out lower risk investments in debt and

---

[9] Tom Pratt, "The Very Private World of Donaldson, Lufkin & Jenrette," *Investment Dealers Digest,* September 21, 1992.

equity mezzanine securities and joint ventures; the DLJ Real Estate Fund, which would participate in the real estate markets; the DLJ Senior Debt Fund, which would offer senior debt financing to the firm's clients, replacing traditional senior bank loans; and Global Retail Partners L.P. to invest in early-stage retailers. The Merchant Banking group utilized DLJ's underwriting, M&A and research resources in exploring and executing merchant banking transactions.

In February 1995, the firm founded the Emerging Markets group to provide a broad array of investment banking, merchant banking, sales, and trading services to clients in Latin America and Asia. Additionally, the Company agreed to invest $7 million in Pleiade Investments, a South African merchant bank.

The Banking Group produced high margins with lower levels of risk in favorable environments. Most of its costs were personnel-related. These costs were tied to the group's performance through year-end bonuses. So, if performance fell, bonuses and costs fell. Merchant Banking offered more risk as DLJ put its own capital in with its limited partners in purchasing securities in companies. While Merchant Banking had performed spectacularly in the past, its investments were subject to being totally lost at any time if the companies in which it invested had difficulties.

Capital Markets Group

The Capital Markets Group offered trading, research and sales services in fixed-income and equity securities. In these markets, DLJ focused on serving its clients and had not undertaken a large amount of proprietary trading.

The Taxable Fixed-Income division concentrated on serving institutional investors in high yield corporate, investment grade corporate, U.S. government (as a primary dealer) and mortgage-backed securities. The division employed 450 professionals, including 72 traders, 137 institutional salespeople, and 52 fixed-income research analysts.

The Institutional Equities division covered major U.S. institutions with 100 traders and salespeople. For listed equities, the company acted as principal and agent, often taking long and short positions to help clients quickly gain liquidity. Most trades were made in blocks of 10,000 shares or more. DLJ also made markets in approximately 350 securities traded on the National Association of Securities Dealers Automated Quotation System (NASDAQ). The division primarily made markets for stocks of companies that had been underwritten by Investment Banking or covered by the research department.

DLJ earned the moniker "The House that Research Built," referring to DLJ's founding as a research firm and continued strength in providing high quality research. While the firm offered a broad array of services, it still maintained one of the highest rated research departments on Wall Street. Approximately 90 investment analysts analyzed and made recommendations on nearly 1,000 companies in 75 industries. The firm was only one of two companies that had ranked in the top 10 in each of the 23 years of *Institutional Investor's* annual "All-America" research survey.

The company provided a limited amount of derivative products, mostly equity and index options through the Equity Derivatives division. Most of its products were tailored to meet a client's specific needs, in contrast to taking on trading risk or generating large volumes of generic derivatives. The Equity Derivatives division also participated in trading and distributing convertible securities.

Sprout, one of the oldest and largest venture capital operations, resided in the Capital Markets group. Sprout managed over $1 billion in capital, focusing on investments in business services, computer graphics and peripherals, health care, leveraged transactions, office automation, retailing, and telecommunications. The professionals in Sprout worked closely with those in research and Investment Banking.

To serve clients, the Capital Markets Group held large inventories of stocks and bonds. While these positions were hedged to varying extents, their values changed with changes in the overall market. Under U.S. GAAP, DLJ had to continuously mark its positions to market, creating losses and gains that appeared on the income statement. It financed much of its inventory through repurchase agreements with other financial institutions. These lenders would carefully watch DLJ and its financial condition in determining the rate they charged DLJ, which in turn, would impact DLJ's overall profitability.

Financial Services Group

The Financial Services Group (FSG) provided a broad array of services targeted to individual investors and the financial intermediaries who represented them. Approximately 1,000 professionals worked in FSG. In FSG, Pershing offered correspondent brokerage services, clearing transactions for over 500 U.S. brokerage firms and lending clients money for margin trades. Pershing's clients collectively managed over one million accounts with assets of $100 billion. In clearing trades for others, Pershing accounted for approximately 10 percent of the daily volume on the New York Stock Exchange. It earned its revenues on a fee-for-service basis and on the interest made on money it lent for margin trades. Pershing's Financial Network™ was the largest on-line discount broker in the United States, providing trading through several on-line services, like America On-Line, PRODIGY, and Reuters Money Network. Between 1990 and 1994, the average daily volume traded through this service soared at an annual rate of 128 percent.

The Investment Services Group (ISG) served high-net-worth investors and smaller institutions. ISG gave its clients access to DLJ's research and sales and trading capabilities. DLJ purchased Wood, Struthers & Winthrop in 1977 to provide investment management and trust services to its clients. Wood, Struthers & Winthrop managed $2.5 billion, and operated three U.S. equity funds and two fixed-income funds.

FSG required a significant commitment of people and equipment to cover its clients and clear trades. While tied to the overall market, it made money more through market volatility rather than market direction. DLJ earned interest income by lending to customers to purchase securities and by holding higher yielding inventory funded with lower cost capital. In this capacity, DLJ made money much like a bank did, on the spread between the rate at which it lent or invested money and the rate at which it borrowed money. In 1994, DLJ made $288.1 million in net interest income.

Separate to the above three groups, DLJ owned Autranet, a distributor of independent research. Approximately 450 independent research firms, who had no affiliation with underwriters, supplied Autranet with research. Autranet distributed the research to over 400 institutions.

DLJ'S PERFORMANCE AND OUTLOOK

Overall, the firm's growth outpaced most of the industry over the last five years, steadily advancing DLJ up the industry league tables. Its strategy to compete in several higher margin businesses seemed to be succeeding. Revenues and profits grew at rates consistent with its increased market share: from 1990 to 1994 revenues increased at a compound average rate of 21.9 percent while net income increased at 75.4 percent, generating an average annual pretax return on common equity of 33.6 percent. Each of the three operating groups expanded at roughly equal rates, though due to market conditions each experienced some fluctuation in year-to-year growth. **Exhibits 4, 5,** and **6** present DLJ's financial statements and pro forma capitalization.

Investors would soon have the opportunity to share in DLJ's success. Many securities industry analysts called DLJ one of the most desirable franchises on Wall Street. The analysts pointed to DLJ's focus on competing in select, high-margin businesses like initial public offerings, high-yield underwriting and trading, and merchant banking. Unlike some of its competitors, it did not commit large amounts of resources to the lower margin businesses of underwriting and trading of investment grade debt and municipal bonds. Investors who purchased DLJ's stock would be betting that DLJ could continue expanding its market share in its traditional areas and grow successfully in new areas with attractive profits. In many of its markets, however, if it wanted to continue gaining market share DLJ would have to increasingly compete against much larger firms, like Goldman Sachs, Merrill Lynch, and Morgan Stanley.

While recognizing DLJ's strengths, critics worried that DLJ did not have sufficient operations overseas or large, recurring-fee operations. DLJ maintained seven offices in Europe and Asia, though it had not stated that it planned on committing the necessary capital to develop its operations to compete around the world in all aspects of the securities industry with its competitors. DLJ seemed to choose foreign markets where it could obtain and maintain an advantage. And while DLJ's securities clearance division did generate significant recurring revenues, its profits were still tied to trading activity by its clients. It was not the steady, detached revenue stream that could come from an extensive asset management business. The critics were unsure that DLJ could find new business lines in which to grow that would maintain its growth rates and profit margins.

Writer Anne Schwimmer brought out some questions in a cover story about DLJ and the offering in *Investment Dealers' Digest (IDD)*. The article postulated that DLJ may have problems that could hinder post-IPO profits, such as an increasingly competitive high-yield market and a lack of diversified business lines. She questioned whether DLJ would maintain its culture with the increased scrutiny that public shareholders would bring.

In the high-yield market, she pointed to increasing competition where DLJ had enjoyed success and good margins. She speculated that the competition may have driven DLJ to underwrite some more speculative deals in high yield. She quoted a banker from a competing bank:

> Being a market leader, and in essence a firm that specializes in junk, they're not like a Goldman Sachs or Merrill Lynch or Morgan Stanley where you have a huge global business. Their mistake this year has been . . . (that) they saw so many competitors rushing into this market competing for mandates that they came down the credit quality spectrum, and started doing financings they wouldn't have done a year or two ago.

However, the banker continued, "To be honest with you, when we work with other firms, I like working with them the best."[10]

The article credited DLJ for building successful new businesses, like its institutional equities practice, but said that it needs further diversification. It also questioned whether or not DLJ's collegial atmosphere could survive in the face of public scrutiny. This atmosphere had been successful in nurturing professionals and keeping them at DLJ. Retaining key professionals was core to its mission. In the 1990s, DLJ had not suffered the talent drain and job-hopping that had plagued some firms. Employees strove to work hard, yet recognized the need to pursue interests outside of work. Indeed, DLJ's philosophy was that the best employees managed to maintain balance in their lives. While the firm endeavored to serve its clients and earn a fair return for shareholders, it also included in the last line of its statement of principles: "Have fun!"

Others were not as sure that the stock would be a good investment at the offering. In a *Wall Street Journal* article, James Gipson, manager of a $340 million equity fund that invested heavily in investment banking stocks, said that he didn't plan on buying DLJ stock at the offering. He stated, "DLJ has been more consistently profitable than the typical Wall Street firm . . . but stock offerings take place when the owners think it's a good time to sell."[11]

VALUING DLJ

DLJ organized a "road show" to present the company to investors. On the road show, John Chalsty, president and CEO, and Anthony Daddino, CFO, traveled to 16 cities in four countries making over 30 presentations in just 19 days. DLJ expected to sell the stock to investors who wanted exposure to the securities industry. These investors would examine DLJ and its prospects relative to other publicly traded securities firms.

Earnings and cash flows at these firms were difficult to predict. Many external factors beyond the industry's control dramatically affected business, such as interest rates in the United States and abroad, mergers and acquisition activity, domestic savings and investment rates, and the overall direction of the stock market. Additionally, analysts couldn't accurately predict how the firms would fare in their principal activities like trading, merchant banking and venture capital. On the trading side, strategies that succeeded in the past might fall flat or key traders might leave. Realization of profits from principal investments depended upon the opportunity to exit the investment through a public offering or a sale, and results fluctuated from year to year.

DLJ posed extra valuation challenges due to its concentration in several key areas that were especially difficult to forecast, like high-yield and IPO underwritings, and merchant banking. Picking comparable companies would be tenuous, as many of the other firms maintained large retail divisions, extensive principal trading activities and broad investment grade debt underwriting and trading operations.

---

[10] Anne Schwimmer, "Home Improvement?" *Investment Dealers' Digest,* October 30, 1995
[11] Michael Siconolfi, "DLJ Sets Sale of 20% Stake in Public Offering," *The Wall Street Journal,* August 30, 1995, A, 3:1.

The market tended to segregate the firms into four categories: bulge bracket, special bracket, regional and boutique firms, and discount brokers. The bulge brackets tended to compete for the business of large corporations, maintaining extensive staffs domestically and abroad in corporate finance and sales and trading. They were the largest firms, offering extensive services in almost every area of investment banking and brokerage. Special bracket firms often competed with the bulge brackets for business in selected industries and products, though kept smaller operations and focused primarily on U.S. clients. They generally possessed fewer people and less capital than the bulge bracket firms. Regional investment banks and boutiques catered to companies and investors in their regions or industry specialties. Most concentrated on covering a few key industries. Discount brokerages competed on price for retail investors' brokerage business, but generally didn't maintain underwriting or advisory departments. **Exhibit 7** presents a segmentation of the industry. **Exhibits 8–10** present market and financial information on other securities firms.

Certainly, investors would count on receiving dividends from DLJ. During the past five years investors in other brokerage stocks had fared well, as dividends from these firms had grown considerably and stock prices had increased. Beginning in the first quarter of 1996, DLJ's Board of Directors planned on instituting a $0.125 quarterly dividend per share, or $0.50 at an annual rate.

Securities industry analyst Guy Moszkowski of Sanford C. Bernstein & Company offered a separate valuation technique. He stated that he had observed an historical relationship between the current return on equity and the price to book ratio for capital markets firms like DLJ. Moszkowski noted that these firms often possessed a price to book ratio of 10 times the current return on equity in this part of the earnings cycle.[12]

In addition to its "fundamental" value, DLJ would have to contend with prevailing prices in the stock and bond markets and demand for IPOs in pricing the stock. If interest in IPOs dried up, DLJ might have to accept a lower price for its shares or postpone the offering. Generally, bankers priced IPOs 10 percent–15 percent below their estimated value (the so-called "IPO discount") in order to entice investors to purchase shares and to compensate them for buying stocks that lacked prior market prices. **Exhibit 11** presents data on the IPO market and the overall equity and credit markets.

THE OFFERING

As an underwriter, DLJ planned to offer 9.2 million shares of stock to public investors. Of these, 5.9 million shares consisted of secondary shares sold by Equitable and 3.3 million were primary shares offered by the company. The proceeds from secondary shares sold by Equitable would go to Equitable. Since these shares were already outstanding, they would

---

[12] Guy Moszkowski, "Donaldson, Lufkin & Jenrette—Company Report," Sanford C. Bernstein & Co, Inc., December 1, 1995.

not increase the number of shares outstanding. DLJ would receive the proceeds from the primary shares sold, which would increase the number of shares outstanding by 3.3 million. DLJ slated 7.36 million shares to be sold domestically and 1.84 million shares to be offered abroad.

Equitable also granted the underwriters a "green shoe." The green shoe was a 30-day option to purchase 1.38 million additional shares to cover any over-allotments made by the underwriters. DLJ anticipated that it would have 51.5 million shares outstanding after the offering. Equitable would own approximately 83 percent of DLJ's stock (80 percent if the green shoe were exercised.) In connection with the stock offering, DLJ registered with the SEC to sell $300 million of senior subordinated notes for general uses and to repay existing bank borrowings.

Technically, the shares offered by Equitable constituted an equity carve-out. In an equity carve-out, the parent company sold some of its interest in a subsidiary to the public. Many times, the parent sold less than 50 percent of its holdings in order to keep control of the subsidiary and to be able to consolidate the earnings and assets of the subsidiary on its own books. As long as the parent retained at least 50 percent of the equity of the subsidiary, it could consolidate its financial statements with those of its subsidiary under U.S. GAAP and thus be able to file a consolidated tax return.

Equity-carve outs and spin-offs (where a subsidiary's shares were distributed pro rata to existing investors) were very popular in the early 1990s as a way to increase shareholder value by unlocking hidden values, and creating "pure play" stocks that were easier for investors to value.

With the concurrent senior notes offering, DLJ obtained its own debt rating from Standard & Poor's of A- and Baa1 from Moody's. The credit markets could judge and lend to DLJ on its individual merits. If DLJ decided to increase its leverage, the ratings agencies would not penalize Equitable's debt ratings of A+ and A2. In return, Equitable still retained control of DLJ, and received cash from the sale of its shares. It got a "fair market value" for part of its investment in DLJ and established a public price for its remaining interest.

EMPLOYEE OWNERSHIP

In conjunction with the offering, DLJ offered approximately 500 employees the opportunity to exchange $100 million of their interests in compensation plans for approximately 5.2 million shares of restricted stock. This stock was subject to vesting and forfeiture in certain circumstances. Additionally, these employees could exchange $55.7 million of future compensation under these plans for options to purchase approximately 9.2 million shares of DLJ stock at the offering price. Employees who opted to not exchange their interests would receive cash instead. The number of shares and options issued would depend on the final offering price.

Additionally, DLJ asked the underwriters to reserve approximately 550,000 shares for sale to directors and current and former employees of DLJ and Equitable. These groups would have the opportunity to purchase the reserved shares at a price equal to the initial public offering price less underwriting discounts and commissions. If these parties purchased these shares, they would be prohibited from selling them for five months. The underwriters would sell any shares they did not buy to the general public.

Since DLJ was not a public firm in the past, it had to use various cash compensation plans to give employees long-term incentives and rewards. After it went public, DLJ could use options as many of its peers did.[13] The employees of Merrill Lynch, for example, owned roughly one quarter of the firm's stock and those of Morgan Stanley owned 39 percent. DLJ desired that its employees have their fortunes tied to those of the firm's other shareholders. If the employees gained control of the restricted stock and exercised the options gained under the exchange, they would own over 20 percent of DLJ's outstanding shares.

THE IPO PROCESS

Equitable and DLJ had selected the underwriters, choosing DLJ to serve as lead manager of the offering. They picked Goldman Sachs, Merrill Lynch, and Morgan Stanley to act as co-managers of the underwriting syndicate.[14] These four investment banks held responsibility for buying the shares from Equitable and DLJ and reselling them to investors. The four managers would receive the management fee, underwriting fee and selling concession for their services.

In addition, the co-managers invited 26 securities firms to participate in the underwriting syndicate. These firms would be allocated a certain number of shares to sell, receiving the underwriting fee and selling concession for compensation. The managers asked 73 firms to be in the selling group. Members of this group received the selling commission if they sold their allotted shares, but could return any unsold shares to the underwriters. This option reduced the risks borne by the selling group.

On October 24, 1995, Equitable and DLJ stood at the end of the IPO process, ready to price DLJ's shares. The process had begun months before, when Equitable decided to offer shares to the public. Equitable and DLJ had chosen the other co-managers. The co-managers then investigated DLJ and its operations, performing due diligence, trying to ascertain the nature and status of the company. The underwriters risked their reputations with every IPO they underwrote and had to ensure that the issuer fairly and accurately represented itself. Investors counted on the investment banks' due diligence as a blessing or sign of trust on the quality of the issuer.

After completing the due-diligence process, the co-managers, executives from DLJ, and their lawyers wrote the Form S-1 registration statement. Both DLJ and the underwriters had legal counsel assisting them through the entire process. In the S-1, DLJ offered extensive disclosures and descriptions of its business, history, risks, management, stock, and

---

[13] While the cash incentives DLJ used in the past counted as compensation expense, options granted as compensation did not count as an expense under GAAP.

[14] As a member of the NASD, DLJ complied with Schedule E, which stipulated that in an offering of a member firm's parent company's stock, the price could be no higher than the price recommended by a "qualified independent underwriter." Goldman Sachs served in this capacity for the offering.

performance, as prescribed by the regulations surrounding the issuance of securities established in the Securities Act of 1933.

The issuer included a preliminary filing range for the expected price of the stock in the S-1. For DLJ, the filing range was $26 to $29 per share. The range implied an offering size of $239.2 million to $266.8 million (if the underwriters exercised their over-allotment option the range increased to $275.1 million to $306.8 million.) Equitable and DLJ were not bound by this range, and could change the range with little effort. The S-1 also contained a copy of the preliminary prospectus to be used in the offering. On August 29th, DLJ filed the S-1 with the SEC, establishing the "registration date" and starting the official registration process.[15]

From the registration date, the SEC had a period of at least 20 business days to review and comment on the S-1. This task fell to the SEC's division of Corporation Finance. The SEC did not comment on the quality or future prospects of the issuer, but instead focused on compliance with the regulations and the level of disclosure in the registration statement. The SEC issued a letter of comment to the issuer, stating either that it found no problems with the registration or that the registration required further amendments. If the registration required refinements, the issuer made the changes and amended the registration. If the SEC found major problems in the statement, the issuer had to refile the registration with the SEC and issue a separate preliminary prospectus to potential investors.

While the SEC reviewed the registration statement, the issuer and managers were busy establishing the underwriting syndicate and marketing the security. The managers worked with the syndicate departments of other investment banks and brokerage firms to form the underwriting syndicate and selling group. These firms would ultimately sell the stock to investors.

The issuer and managers circulated the preliminary prospectus, known as a "red herring," and embarked upon a road show. During the road show, John Chalsty and Anthony Daddino made presentations to potential investors around the world. They met with investors in groups and in one-on-one sessions with large investors who requested these meetings. The first presentation was to the underwriters' sales forces to inform them of the particulars of the offering and issuing company. Sales people from the underwriters spoke with potential investors about their interest in purchasing the securities. The investors often indicated how willing they would be to purchase the securities at a given price. For example, an institutional investor might have said that she would consider buying 100,000 shares at $27 per share, 75,000 at $28 and 60,000 at $29. Other investors, particularly in issues with heavy demand, might offer to buy as much as they could within the filing range. These indications were not obligations to buy the security; the investors could back out and refuse to purchase the shares.

Duff Anderson and the rest of DLJ's Capital Markets group oversaw this process. They coordinated the information-gathering process. The lead manager was known as the "book manager" or "book runner" as that firm gathered and controlled the information concerning the potential orders from all of the underwriters. The book manager consolidated this information into a "book" that was utilized to gauge demand at different prices and to price

---

[15] For a more complete exploration of the offering process, see UVA F-1129, "The Issue Process for Public Securities."

the issue. The professional book manager had to use his expertise in deciphering the firmness of the indications and the intent of the investors in owning the security. Many times, investors tried to game the process, especially for "hot" issues. For example, investors might place orders for more shares than they actually desired, knowing that all orders would be scaled down to the available supply. Certain short-term investors might want to buy the stock at issuance then quickly sell the stock for a profit (a technique known as flipping.) Flipping added volatility to the after-market trading. Most issuers preferred to place their stock with longer-term investors. The book manager had to decide the depth and quality of the book.

When the underwriters and managers were satisfied with the level of indications and the conditions of the overall market, they negotiated the price of the security. After the issuer and underwriters agreed on the price, they filed an amendment to the registration statement that informed the SEC of the price of the security. The final prospectus then became effective. The issuer printed a final prospectus that included the price of the stock and circulated a copy of the prospectus to investors. After an issue went effective, the underwriters allocated and sold the shares to those who indicated their intent to purchase the securities.

The sale of the securities occurred on the public offering date, usually later in the day the issue went effective or the next morning. Underwriters tried to minimize the time between when the price was set—the price at which they committed to buy the securities—and the time when they sold the securities to the public. Three days after the offering date, the settlement occurred. Investors paid for and received their shares and the issuer received the net proceeds from the underwriters.

The pricing process before Equitable, DLJ and the other underwriters was one of negotiation. The underwriters and issuer faced conflicting pressures in pricing the security. The underwriters had to consider the interests of both of their clients—issuer and investor—while mitigating their own risks. If the price were too low, the issuer would not be content with the performance of the underwriters. The issuer might believe that the underwriter left too much money "on the table." Other prospective issuers took into account an underwriter's prior performance when selecting an underwriter. An underwriter who consistently underpriced securities would find that few companies wanted to use the firm. On the other hand, the investor would be happy to receive an underpriced security that would quickly appreciate in the aftermarket. However, underwriters received their remuneration as a percent of the offering price, directly tying their pay to the price they obtained for the securities.

Conversely, if the security were overpriced, the investor would be unhappy as the stock fell in trading after the initial issuance. The investor might try to cut her losses and sell the security, further driving down the price of the stock. The investor would be left with a "bad taste" from the loss and might reconsider purchasing shares from the underwriter and the issuer in the future. Future issuances from the underwriter and issuer might receive less demand. The issuer may have received more money than expected from the issuance, but the preexisting shareholders (perhaps founders and managers) were now probably "long" a declining stock. They, too, might be upset. In this offering, Equitable would still own 80 percent of DLJ's stock that it might want to sell in the future.

The underwriters faced additional problems when a security was overpriced. They had purchased the stock from the issuer at a set price, but might not be able to sell all of it at this price. In this case, the underwriters might "break syndicate" and sell the stock at whatever price they could get. Additionally, the underwriters might try to support a falling issue in the aftermarket by buying it to keep it from dropping further. The underwriters had then taken the stock and its risks on to their balance sheets with their own capital. Losses generated by these activities could quickly offset underwriting profits.

In the end, many capital market professionals said that, while there were many potential prices for any new issue, there was only one "right" price. The right price was a precarious balance of concerns for the issuer, for the investors, and for the investment banks themselves. Ideally, the price would satisfy all three constituents. The capital-markets bankers wanted to get the issuer the required money at a fair price without too much dilution. They strove to give each investor the stock he wanted, though many times the demand for shares was greater than the supply. They attempted to allocate the shares fairly, yet wanted an allocation that would move investors to purchase more shares in the aftermarket and in future offerings by the issuer. When investors didn't get all they wanted at the pricing, they would go out and buy more shares, driving the price up in the aftermarket. If the price went up, the underwriters wouldn't have to support the stock and the investors would be pleased. But if the stock went up too much, the issuer would feel that the underwriter left too much money on the table.

THE PRICING

Those sitting in the 49th-floor boardroom needed to make their decision. While each party might have different objectives in setting a price, they had to reach a consensus. Richard Jenrette and Equitable would receive cash and a marketable security for their investment in DLJ. Investors would get the chance to invest in a very profitable, fast-growing firm that might be on its way to becoming one of the largest firms in the industry. Yet, the firm would encounter many challenges in its drive to grow. Employees were eagerly awaiting the price to know how many shares and options they would obtain through the exchange. They were also anxious to see how the market would value what they had created under Equitable's ownership and guidance. The pricing decision would finish the IPO process, and set DLJ off on its new course, as a separate public company.

EXHIBIT 1
The Expansion of the Financial Markets 1986–1995 (dollars in billions)[1]

Indices	1986	1987	1988	1989	1990	1991	1992	1993	1994	09/95
Fed funds rate (%)	9.2	6.8	8.9	8.0	5.5	4.1	2.7	2.9	4.9	6.2
Treasury bonds (%)	7.8	9.1	9.1	8.0	8.3	7.4	7.4	6.4	7.9	6.5
DJ Industrial Average	1,896	1,939	2,169	2,753	2,633	3,168	2,201	3,754	3,834	4,789
NYSE Average daily										
Shares traded (million)	141	189	162	165	157	179	202	265	291	338
Underwriting Volumes										
Debt	$163	$131	$136	$149	$113	$195	$306	$452	$380	$568[2]
Common stock	43	42	30	23	19	56	71	102	62	91
IPOs	22	24	24	14	10	26	39	57	34	28
High-yield bonds	42	38	35	33	3	17	47	67	37	36
Mort. & asset backed	69	94	117	139	170	284	427	478	255	168
M&A and LBOs										
Value of transactions	$251	$221	$314	$314	$189	$124	$114	$179	$272	$406
No. of deals	2,619	2,723	3,171	3,846	3,615	3,354	3,697	4,822	5,704	6,572
LBOs as % of activity	18.3	18.1	17.0	22.8	1.8	4.4	5.5	5.2	2.7	1.5
Institutional Activity										
Total long-term funds	424	454	472	554	569	853	1,100	1,510	1,551	1,908[3]
Stock funds % of total	38	40	41	45	43	48	48	50	56	60
Bond funds % of total	62	60	59	55	57	52	52	50	44	40

[1]Smith Barney "Broker and Asset Managers-Industry Report," October 9, 1995.
[2]Underwriting and M&A data for September 30, 1995 is annualized.
[3]Data is through August and annualized.

EXHIBIT 2
Securities Industry Revenues and Expenses 1980 to 1993[1] (in millions of dollars)

	1980	1985	1988	1989	1990	1991	1992	1993
Revenues:								
Commissions	$ 6,777	$10,955	$11,932	$13,452	$12,032	$14,210	$16,249	$19,938
Trading & inv. gains	5,091	14,549	16,667	16,247	15,746	22,641	21,838	25,526
Underwriting profits	1,571	4,987	5,607	4,537	3,728	6,593	8,300	11,251
Mutual fund sales	278	2,754	2,644	3,038	3,242	4,176	5,950	8,116
Other	2,960	13,854	26,096	35,731	33,428	34,498	35,557	41,343
Non-interest revenue	17,677	47,099	62,946	73,005	68,176	82,118	87,894	106,174
Margin interest income	2,151	2,746	3,155	3,860	3,179	2,771	2,690	3,242
Total revenues	19,829	49,844	66,100	78,864	71,356	84,890	90,584	109,416
Expenses:								
Compensation	7,619	18,112	23,418	23,740	22,931	26,916	32,071	39,167
Exchange fees	1,055	2,314	2,804	3,057	2,959	3,200	3,722	5,364
Other expenses	4,119	11,446	16,899	17,422	16,583	18,605	21,908	24,766
Non-interest expenses	12,793	31,872	43,121	44,219	42,473	48,721	56,891	69,297
Interest expense	3,876	11,470	19,502	29,822	28,093	27,512	24,576	27,061
Total expenses	16,668	43,342	62,623	74,041	70,566	76,234	81,467	96,358
Pretax profits	$ 3,160	$ 6,502	$ 3,477	$ 2,823	$ 790	$ 8,656	$ 9,117	$13,058
Pretax margin	15.9%	13.0%	5.3%	3.6%	1.1%	10.2%	10.1%	11.9%
Margin excl. interest	27.6%	32.3%	31.5%	39.4%	37.7%	40.7%	35.3%	34.7%

[1] "Securities Industry—Revenues and Expenses: 1980–1994," *Statistical Abstract of the United States 1995,* No. 833, p. 535.

EXHIBIT 3
Selected Market-Share Information for DLJ 1990–1995[1]

U.S. M&A[2]	Years Ended December 31					Six Months	
	1990	1991	1992	1993	1994	1994	1995
No. of transactions	34	35	38	56	70	36	34
Rank based on value	12	12	9	11	11	7	7
Lead Managed Equity Offerings[3]							
All Common Stock							
No. of issues	2	17	26	48	22	15	21
Rank based on value	25	8	6	7	10	8	7
IPOs							
No. of issues	1	8	14	24	15	9	13
Rank based on value	17	13	6	7	7	8	3
Lead Managed High-Yield Issues[4]							
No. of issues	0	3	24	52	26	19	9
Rank based on value	—	4	3	1	2	2	1
Equity Research Rankings[5]							
"All-American" positions	35	37	43	45	44	NA	36
Overall rank	5	2	4	4	3	NA	2
"Completion percentage" rank[6]	1	1	1	1	2	NA	2
ISG Statistics							
Number of account executives	127	137	170	190	233	NA	236
Assets in accounts (billions)	$2.5	$3.2	$4.5	$6.0	$8.0	NA	$9.9

[1] *Source:* DLJ.
[2] *Source:* DLJ, from *Investment Dealers' Digest,* includes completed domestic deals.
[3] *Source:* DLJ, from *Investment Dealers' Digest,* includes domestic transactions and excludes closed-end funds.
[4] *Source:* DLJ, from *Investment Dealers' Digest,* includes domestic transactions and excludes split rated issues and private placements.
[5] *Source:* DLJ, from *Institutional Investor.*
[6] Completion percentage rank is based on the number of analysts divided by number of All-American placements.

EXHIBIT 4
DLJ's Revenue Growth by Operating Group 1990–1995[1]

Operating Group	Years Ended December 31 (Dollars in Millions)					4 Year CAGR	Six Months	
	1990	1991	1992	1993	1994		1994	1995
Banking	$152.4	$192.1	$ 428.4	$ 491.8	$ 390.0	26.5%	$178.2	$320.7
Capital markets	275.4	506.6	713.0	994.6	638.1	23.4%	345.4	344.5
Financial services	229.3	273.9	336.9	455.3	458.2	19.0%	233.6	284.9
Other	24.4	5.6	(26.5)	(38.1)	18.6	NM	2.9	1.7
Total	$681.8	$978.2	$1451.8	$1903.6	$1504.9	21.9%	$760.1	$974.8

[1] *Source:* DLJ.

EXHIBIT 5
Summary DLJ Historical Statements (dollars in millions)

Income Statement Data	Years Ended December 31					Six Months Ended June 30	
	1990	1991	1992	1993	1994	1994	1995
Revenues:							
Commissions	$228.9	$ 257.9	$ 289.7	$ 358.8	$ 376.1	$ 194.2	$ 225.0
Underwritings	150.3	170.9	350.3	574.6	261.1	139.5	171.2
Fees	88.9	166.2	158.1	211.3	281.3	112.9	173.5
Interest—net (a)	362.3	323.0	381.7	657.3	791.9	391.4	423.6
Principal transactions—net:							
Trading	98.9	264.2	272.0	381.5	165.7	99.2	154.9
Investment	37.9	17.3	195.9	79.9	97.6	28.8	99.1
Other	16.9	15.1	16.4	21.9	35.0	15.2	26.4
Total revenues	984.1	1,214.6	1,664.1	2,285.3	2,008.7	981.2	1,273.7
Cost and Expenses:							
Compensation and benefits	413.1	567.9	886.6	1,200.4	897.8	477.1	598.1
Interest	302.3	236.4	212.3	381.7	503.8	221.1	308.9
Other expenses	254.2	321.3	320.2	401.2	402.1	183.0	234.2
Total costs and expenses	969.6	1,125.6	1,419.1	1,983.3	1,803.7	881.2	1,141.2
Pretax income	14.5	89.0	245.0	302.0	205.0	100.0	132.5
Provision for income taxes	1.5	31.2	98.0	115.9	82.0	40.0	53.0
Net income before preferred dividends	$ 13.0	$ 57.8	$ 147.0	$ 186.1	$ 123.0	$ 60.0	$ 79.5
Dividends on preferred stock	—	—	—	—	21.0	13.0	9.9
Net income applicable to common shares	$ 13.0	$ 57.8	$ 147.0	$ 186.1	$ 102.0	$ 47.0	$ 69.6
Earnings per share					$1.98	$0.91	(c) $1.35
Dividends per share					$0.65	NA	(c) $0.33
Common shares outstanding (b)					51.5	51.5	(c) 51.5

Source: DLJ Prospectus.

(a) Interest is net of interest expense to finance U.S. government and agency instruments.

(b) Actual shares outstanding adjusted for the dilutive effect of the restricted stock units using the Treasury stock method.

(c) DLJ did not report earnings per share nor shares outstanding for these periods. These are estimated for illustrative purposes.

EXHIBIT 6
Summary Balance Sheets and Pro Forma Capitalization (dollars in millions)

Summary Balance Sheet Data	Years Ended December 31					Six Months Ended June 30	
	1990	1991	1992	1993	1994	1994	1995
Securities purchased under agreements to resell and securities borrowed	$ 6,405.3	$10,942.5	$ 14,378.4	$ 21,575.2	$19,166.9	$22,886.1	$26,750.8
Total assets	$13,997.1	$18,721.7	$ 24,436.2	$ 38,766.7	$33,161.1	$41,628.8	$42,417.1
Liabilities & Stockholders' Equity							
Securities sold under agreements to repurchase and securities loaned	$ 7,619.0	$11,200.8	$ 19.7	$ 24,116.7	$20,385.4	$25,705.6	$27,895.9
Long-term borrowings	270.5	268.1	478.6	549.0	539.9	544.9	723.1
Preferred stock	—	—	—	225.0	225.0	225.0	225.0
Stockholders' equity	$ 294.1	$ 340.3	$ 454.6	$ 750.3	$ 820.3	$ 775.9	$ 873.6
Other Financial Data (at end of period)							
Ratio of net assets to stockholders' equity	25.81 ×	22.86 ×	22.12 ×	22.91 ×	17.01 ×	24.16 ×	17.93 ×
Ratio of long-term borrowings to total cap	0.47	0.42	0.51	0.34	0.30	0.33	0.35
Pretax return on average equity	5.0%	28.1%	61.6%	50.1%	23.4%	23.3%	28.9%

Pro Forma Capitalization (In Thousands)	As of June 30, 1995		Percent of Total Capital	
	Actual	As Adjusted	Actual	As Adjusted
Short-term borrowings	$1,651,914	$1,523,881		
Notes		$ 300,000	0.0%	14.2%
Senior subordinated revolving credit	250,000	250,000	13.7%	11.9%
Term loan agreement	250,000	100,000	13.7%	4.7%
Swiss franc bonds	105,022	—	5.8%	0.0%
Medium-term notes	97,000	97,000	5.3%	4.6%
Other borrowings	21,067	21,067	1.2%	1.0%
Total long-term borrowings	723,089	768,067	39.7%	36.4%
Cumulative exchangeable preferred stock, at redemption value	225,000	225,000	12.4%	10.7%
Stockholders' equity:				
Common stock ($0.10 per value) 150,000,000 shares authorized: 50,000,000 Actual shares issued & outstanding; 53,300,000 as adjusted	1,000	5,330	0.1%	0.3%
Restricted stock units: no actual units issued and outstanding; 5,178,664 as adjusted units issued and outstanding	—	106,163	0.0%	5.0%
Paid-in capital	232,080	368,055	12.7%	17.4%
Retained earnings	640,855	637,157	35.2%	30.2%
Cumulative translation adjustment	(321)	(321)	0.0%	0.0%
Total stockholders' equity	873,614	1,116,384	48.0%	52.9%
Total capitalization (excl. short-term borrowings)	$1,821,703	$2,109,451	100.0%	100.0%

EXHIBIT 7
Groupings of Selected U.S. Investment Banks

Bulge Bracket	Special Bracket	Regional Firms
C. S. First Boston[1]	Alex. Brown & Sons	Advest Group
Goldman, Sachs (Private)	Bankers Trust (Comm. Bank)	Bowles, Hollowell (Private)
Lehman Brothers	Bear Stearns	Cowen & Co. (Private)
Merrill Lynch & Co.	Dean Witter Discover	Inter-Regional Financial[2]
Morgan Stanley	Dillon, Read (Private)	Interstate/Johnson Lane
Salomon Brothers	A. G. Edwards	Jefferies Group
	Hambrecht & Quist (Private)	Legg Mason
	Lazard Freres & Co. (Private)	Morgan Keegan
	Montgomery Sec. (Private)	Piper Jaffray Cos.
	J. P. Morgan (Comm. Bank)	Raymond James Financial
	PaineWebber Group	Scott & Stringfellow
	Prudential Securities[3]	Stephens Inc. (Private)
	Robertson, Stephens (Private)	Tucker Anthony[4]
	Smith Barney[5]	Wheat, First (Private)

[1] C. S. First Boston was owned by Crédit Suisse.
[2] Inter-Regional Financial Group owned Dain Bosworth and Rausher Pierce Resfnes.
[3] Prudential Securities was owned by The Prudential.
[4] Tucker, Anthony was owned by John Hancock.
[5] Smith Barney was owned by The Travelers.

EXHIBIT 8
Comparable Analysis of Selected Securities Firms (dollars in millions, except per share data)

	Alex. Brown	Bear Stearns	DLJ	A. G. Edwards	Lehman Brothers	Merrill Lynch	Morgan Stanley	Paine Webber	Salomon Brothers
Stock price as of October 23, 1995	$46.63	$ 20.00	NA	$ 25.13	$ 22.50	$ 56.98	$ 87.50	$ 21.50	$ 36.75
Shares outstanding (millions)	15.5	118.8	58.5	62.3	104.6	175.7	77.6	97.4	106.4
Market capitalization	$ 723	$ 2,376	NA	$ 1,565	$ 2,353	$10,011	$ 6,790	$ 2,095	$ 3,911
Long-term debt and preferred stock	173	4,792	993	0	13,605	16,775	9,929	2,710	14,353
Total market capitalization	$ 897	$ 7,168	NA	$ 1,565	$15,958	$26,787	$16,719	$ 4,805	$18,264
Last 12 months earnings per share	$ 5.39	$ 3.40	$ 2.42	$ 2.64	$1.59	$ 3.72	$ 4.06	$ (0.26)	$ 0.58
Last 12 months book value per share	29.53	16.59	19.72	15.80	27.95	31.06	52.34	15.04	34.64
Cal. yr. 1995 est. earnings per share (*Value Line*)	6.16	1.70	NA	2.58	2.25	5.44	6.66	0.52	3.50
Cal. yr. 1996 est. earnings per share (*Value Line*)	6.10	2.80	NA	2.80	2.45	5.85	8.00	2.40	3.75
Current implied dividend	0.80	0.60	0.50	0.56	0.20	1.00	1.28	0.48	0.64
Stock price/LTM earnings per share	8.7 ×	5.9 ×	NA ×	9.5 ×	14.2 ×	15.3 ×	21.6 ×	NMF ×	63.4
Stock price/Book value per share	1.6	1.2	NA	1.6	0.8	1.8	1.7	1.4	1.1
Stock price/Cal. yr. 1995 est. earnings per share	7.6	11.8	NA	9.7	10.0	10.5	13.1	41.3	10.5
Stock price/Cal. yr. 1996 est. earnings per share	7.6	7.1	NA	9.0	9.2	9.7	10.9	9.0	9.8
Current implied dividend yield	1.7%	3.0%	NA	2.2%	0.9%	1.8%	1.5%	2.2%	1.7%
Value Line's Estimated 1996–2000:									
Revenue growth	7.5%	12.0%	NA	9.5%	8.0%	13.0%	7.5%	9.0%	7.5%
Earnings	5.0%	10.0%	NA	9.5%	14.5%	8.0%	10.0%	10.5%	NMF
Dividends	10.5%	8.0%	NA	11.5%	19.0%	11.5%	9.0%	11.5%	2.0%
Book value	14.5%	14.0%	NA	13.0%	8.5%	14.5%	11.5%	9.0%	8.5%
Beta vs S&P 500	1.27	1.64	NA	1.41	1.20	1.79	1.66	1.67	1.13
Employees	2,300	7,500	4,676	10,741	7,771	46,023	9,236	16,025	6,400

Sources: Bloomberg Financial Services, *Value Line Investment Survey.*

EXHIBIT 8
Comparable Analysis of Selected Securities Firms
(dollars in millions, except per share data)—(*continued*)

Descriptions of Selected Publicly Traded Securities Firms

Alex. Brown & Sons: Founded in 1800, Alex. Brown was a Baltimore-based investment bank with traditional strengths in underwriting IPOs and common stock. Alex. Brown had focused on diversifying revenues into M&A and sales and trading. It maintained a strong banking and research presence in a selected number of industries where it could be a leader. Alex. Brown was perennially rumored to be a takeover target for someone wanting to enter the securities industry.

Bear Stearns & Co.: Bear Stearns traced its roots to 1923 and went public in 1985. Bear Stearns was one of the largest dealers in fixed-income products, especially mortgage-backed securities. It operated a large clearance business for smaller brokerage firms. It had recently experienced strong gains in its corporate finance and M&A practices. While it covered all types of clients, its primary focus was on middle market companies and selected products.

A. G. Edwards: St. Louis–based A. G. Edwards was founded in 1887 and went public in 1971. A. G. Edwards had 534 brokerage branches with 5,600 brokers, serving over 1 million clients. An estimated 95% of these were retail clients. A. G. Edwards maintained investment banking operations, focusing on regional clients. A. G. Edwards also offered other products targeted to individual investors.

Lehman Brothers: Lehman was a major global investment bank specializing in investment-grade debt and equity underwriting, and sales and trading (approximately 40% of revenues came from abroad). Founded in 1850, Lehman was acquired by American Express in 1983, then spun off to shareholders in 1994. It had undergone a major cost reduction program in recent years to increase profitability.

Merrill Lynch & Co: Merrill Lynch was the number one global underwriter for debt and equity in the 1990s. Its primary focus was on *Fortune* 500 clients in corporate finance. Recently, Merrill had strengthened its M&A and international businesses. It supplemented its investment banking operations with a massive asset management business. Merrill operated the largest retail brokerage network in the United States. Merrill had a large and excellent research staff. The firm actively participated in real estate, mortgage banking, cash management and insurance, as well. Its recent problems with an Orange County derivatives suit seemed to be lessening.

Morgan Stanley: Morgan Stanley was a major international investment bank, with particular strengths in global offerings, M&A, merchant banking and high-yield underwriting. Morgan Stanley had a reputation of being able to effectively handle the most complex transactions. It was building its asset management business. The firm was one of the first to expand overseas, and earned 40% of its revenues abroad. Its historical focus on Fortune 100 companies was expanding to cover emerging companies, especially in high technology.

PaineWebber: PaineWebber maintained the third largest brokerage force, with 6,025 brokers handling 2.5 million clients. Its corporate finance and research strengths were focused on covering middle-market companies. PaineWebber had embarked on a cost-cutting initiative to improve its profitability. It recently settled limited partnership claims against it for $200 million. In an effort to expand its trading and investment banking operations, PaineWebber purchased Kidder, Peabody in 1994.

Salomon Brothers: Salomon Inc. conducted business through Salomon Brothers and Phibro Energy. Phibro was a commodities trading and oil-refining company. Salomon was a traditional leader in fixed-income underwriting and trading. Recently, Salomon increased its emphasis on its corporate finance operations. It had a reputation as the premier proprietary trader. The firm was attempting to cut costs. The cost cutting efforts led to a new salary plan, that had caused many top professionals to leave. It had suffered through a trading scandal with the U.S. Treasury that had nearly caused the firm to collapse.

EXHIBIT 9
Inventory Holdings and Capital Structure Analysis of Selected Securities Firms (dollars in millions)

	Alex. Brown	Bear Stearns	DLJ	A. G. Edwards	Lehman Brothers	Merrill Lynch	Morgan Stanley	Paine Webber	Salomon Brothers
Securities-Inventory Analysis									
Government obligations	$ 3.3	$ 7,620.0	$ 7,336.4	$ 28.5	$24,162.0	$17,938.6	$23,582.0	$ 6,539.6	$66,959.0
Municipals	44.1	136.1	0.0	96.8	0.0	996.2	0.0	989.0	0.0
Mortgage-backed	1.7	2,497.4	411.2	0.0	6,014.0	2,923.7	0.0	3,734.0	1,616.0
Corporate debt	19.6	2,501.4	3,450.3	0.0	9,250.0	18,254.8	10,128.0	2,254.8	10,247.0
Corporate stock	29.0	6,182.2	392.0	25.2	5,950.0	9,875.2	7,980.0	835.5	4,385.0
CDs & money market instruments	0.0	0.0	0.0	0.0	2,799.0	1,551.5	0.0	820.4	0.0
Commodities & other	0.0	1,841.2	0.0	0.0	0.0	11,463.1	7,987.0	0.0	8,412.0
Total	$ 97.7	$20,778.3	$11,589.9	$150.5	$48,175.0	$63,003.1	$49,677.0	$15,173.3	$91,619.0
Percent of total inventory:									
Government obligations	3.4%	36.7%	63.3%	18.9%	50.2%	28.5%	47.5%	43.1%	73.1%
Municipals	45.1	0.7	0.0	64.3	0.0	1.6	0.0	6.5	0.0
Mortgage-backed	1.7	12.0	3.5	0.0	12.5	4.6	0.0	24.6	1.8
Corporate debt	20.1	12.0	29.8	0.0	19.2	29.0	20.4	14.9	11.2
Corporate stock	29.7	29.8	3.4	16.7	12.4	15.7	16.1	5.5	4.8
CDs & money market instruments	0.0	0.0	0.0	0.0	5.8	2.5	0.0	5.4	0.0
Commodities & other	0.0	8.9	0.0	0.0	0.0	18.2	16.1	0.0	9.2
Total assets	$1,915	$ 79,517	$ 42,417	$2,617	$117,518	$185,473	$132,264	$ 49,545	$ 162,586
Note: Resell agreements	$ 7	$ 24,741	$ 16,652	$ 114	$ 37,173	$ 45,502	$ 47,849	$ 27,622	$ 43,497
Capitalization Structure									
Short-term debt	$ 73	$ 9,230	$ 1,524	$ 0	$ 9,167	$ 31,762	$ 6,707	$ 1,673	$ 6,420
Repurchase agreements	0	31,907	25,076	0	57,887	54,274	62,322	29,540	77,817
Long-term debt	173	4,205	768	0	12,897	16,156	9,111	2,423	13,341
Preferred stock	0	588	225	0	708	619	818	287	1,012
Total common equity	458	1,971	1,116	985	2,923	5,459	4,062	1,466	3,687
Total equity	458	2,558	1,341	985	3,631	6,077	4,880	1,752	4,699
Total capital excluding repos	$ 705	$ 15,993	$ 3,633	$ 985	$ 25,695	$ 53,996	$ 20,698	$ 5,848	$ 24,460
Percent of total capital structure (excl. repos):									
Short-term debt	10.4%	57.7%	41.9%	0.0%	35.7%	58.8%	32.4%	28.6%	26.2%
Long-term debt	24.6	26.3	21.1	0.0	50.2	29.9	44.0	41.4	54.5
Preferred stock	0.0	3.7	6.2	0.0	2.8	1.1	4.0	4.9	4.1
Total common equity	65.0	12.3	30.7	100.0	11.4	10.1	19.6	25.1	15.1
Total debt/Total equity	53.8%	525.2%	170.9%	0.0%	607.7%	788.5%	324.1%	233.8%	420.5%
Long-term debt/Total equity	37.8	164.4	57.3	0.0	355.2	265.8	186.7	138.3	283.9
Total equity as % total assets	65.0	16.0	36.9	100.0	14.1	11.3	23.6	30.0	19.2
Senior debt rating (Moody's/S&P)	NR	A2/A	Baa1/A-	NR	Baa1/A	A1/A+	A1/A+	Baa1/BBB+	Baa1/BBB
Data as of	9/30/95	9/30/95	6/30/95	8/31/95	8/31/95	9/30/95	8/31/95	9/30/95	9/30/95

Source: D. P. Eberling, "Donaldson, Lufkin & Jenrette - Company Report," Prudential Securities, December 15, 1995 and company reports.

330

EXHIBIT 10
Revenue and Income Analysis of Selected Securities Firms (dollars in millions)

Income Statement Statistics	Alex. Brown	Bear Stearns	DLJ	A. G. Edwards	Lehman Brothers	Merrill Lynch	Morgan Stanley	Paine Webber	Salomon Brothers
1990–1994 Compound Average Growth Rates									
Gross revenues	22.2%	8.6%	17.7%	17.0%	NA	13.1%	12.4%	7.4%	–8.5%
Net revenues (a)	23.6	14.8	21.9	17.1	NA	13.6	12.9	9.9	–17.5
Commissions	19.8	12.5	13.1	20.3	NA	13.1	13.0	10.4	12.9
Investment banking revenues	21.4	17.0	22.7	15.2	NA	11.7	9.0	4.9	4.0
Principal transactions	40.3	14.9	17.8	11.4	NA	12.8	5.2	2.4	NM
Net income	74.2	21.1	75.4	24.7	NA	51.7	9.9	–1.1	NM
Earnings per share	74.2	37.0	NA	23.9	NA	56.1	5.5	NM	NM
Dividends per share	26.3	1.7	NA	17.9	NA	15.5	12.9	20.2	0.0
Last 12 Months Information									
Gross revenues	$716.5	$4,019.5	$3,818.6	$1,298.5	$11,040.0	$20,703.8	$10,391.0	$4,985.0	$8,086.0
Net revenues	686.2	2,258.9	1,904.8	1,294.6	2,781.0	9,744.8	3,862.0	3,077.1	2,421.0
Commissions	163.3	581.9	437.3	621.9	452.0	2,917.6	479.0	1,156.0	331.0
Investment banking revenues	241.0	377.8	767.5	97.0	652.0	1,165.2	1,076.0	295.3	413.0
Principal transaction revenues	125.9	944.4	421.6	216.0	1,227.0	2,406.3	1,366.0	814.5	493.0
Net income	82.4	298.9	159.0	148.6	202.0	1,061.5	532.0	2.7	132.0
Last 12 months earnings per share	$5.39	$3.40	$2.42	$2.64	$1.59	$3.72	$4.06	$(0.26)	$0.58
Current implied dividend per share	$0.80	$0.60	$0.50	$0.56	$0.20	$1.00	$1.28	$0.48	$0.64
Dividend payout (implied div./LTM EPS)	14.8%	17.6%	20.7%	21.2%	12.6%	26.9%	31.5%	NM	110.3%
Net margin (gross revenue)	11.5%	7.4%	4.2%	11.4%	1.8%	5.1%	5.1%	0.1%	1.6%
Net margin (net revenues)	15.3%	16.3%	10.6%	21.7%	13.6%	13.9%	24.6%	0.1%	5.7%
Percent Change in Line Items YTD 1994–YTD 1995									
Gross revenues	24.6%	28.8%	6.6%	15.1%	37.7%	18.0%	22.3%	34.9%	38.1%
Net revenues	23.6	20.9	36.5	15.4	3.0	1.6	20.0	28.2	80.2
Commissions	22.1	24.3	22.1	–17.2	3.0	2.1	13.0	25.0	–1.9
Investment banking revenues	28.1	18.3	63.2	–9.5	24.8	–7.3	33.3	4.9	–19.4
Principal transaction revenues	8.0	21.3	79.3	–1.7	–16.4	3.8	44.3	76.5	NM
Net income	22.6	40.9	42.1	26.6	207.1	5.5	57.6	–56.8	NM
Earnings per share	24.2	51.2	48.1	4.2	243.2	–25.9	–2.5	–100.0	NM
Dividend per share	15.0	0.0	NA	10.5	–40.0	13.6	8.0	0.0	0.0
Business Composition Analysis									
Revenue Source as a Percent of Net Revenues									
Commissions	23.8%	25.8%	23.0%	48.0%	16.3%	29.9%	12.4%	37.6%	13.7%
Investment banking revenues	35.1	16.7	40.3	7.5	23.4	12.0	27.9	9.6	17.1
Pricipal transactions	18.3	41.8	22.1	16.7	44.1	24.7	35.4	26.5	20.4
Other	22.7	15.7	14.6	27.8	16.2	33.4	24.4	26.4	48.9
Average ROE for previous three years	24.0%	24.4%	27.8	20.3%	NA	23.8%	17.7%	17.5%	11.0%

Source: D. P. Eberling, "Donaldson Lufkin & Jenrette—Company Report," Prudential Securities, December 15, 1995 and company reports.
(a) Net revenues are net of interest expense to finance U.S. government and agency instruments.

EXHIBIT 11
IPO and General Capital Market Data[1]
Number of IPO Transactions and Values

	1994		1995	
	Number	**Dollar Value**	**Number**	**Dollar Value**
January	40	$ 3,319.9	25	$ 1,422.6
February	77	5,101.1	46	1,541.3
March	75	5,822.9	36	1,741.8
April	54	3,154.9	47	2,951.0
May	78	2,359.8	42	1,908.7
June	66	4,089.7	69	3,379.8
July	47	3,521.6	60	2,729.5
August	54	2,540.4	55	2,861.0
September	41	2,400.1	38	2,362.0
October	65	4,556.6	—	—
November	49	3,235.8	—	—
December	38	2,014.1	—	—
Annual Total.	684	$42,116.9	—	—
Jan.–Sept.	*532*	*$32,310.0*	*418*	*$20,897.7*

General Credit and Equity Markets Data		
	October 23, 1994	**October 23, 1995**
Fixed Income Rates		
LIBOR (1 Month)	5.000%	5.875%
3-month Treasury	5.131	5.426
6-month Treasury	5.700	5.575
1-year Treasury	6.216	5.645
2-year Treasury	6.803	5.757
3-year Treasury	7.105	5.816
5-year Treasury	7.504	5.921
10-year Treasury	7.844	6.073
30-year Treasury	8.043	6.392
Equity Market Indices		
Dow Jones Industrial Avg.	3,891.30	4,755.48
S&P 500 Index	464.89	585.06
S&P Financials Index	42.92	59.69
S&P Investment Bank & Brokerage Index	120.80	172.09

[1]Bloomberg Business News.

eBay Inc. (A)

Gary Bengier, chief financial officer and vice president of operations at eBay, clicked on the send button as he e-mailed the week's financial update to Pierre Omidyar, the company's 31-year old chairman. It was September 15, 1998, and Wall Street was still reeling from a summer of severe market volatility. Much of the market's instability could be traced to bearish worries over a deepening and continuing economic crisis in Asia and other developing markets. Many investors feared that the U.S. economy would be unable to resist what was termed the "Asian Flu," and that economic recession was imminent. Although U.S. interest rates were still low at yields of 4.0 percent for Treasury Bills and 5.6 percent for 30-year Treasury bonds, the S&P 500 Index was down nearly 13 percent from its all time high set only two months earlier. After bottoming out at the end of August, the stock market had regained some upward momentum but with ongoing high volatility. Internet stocks, however, continued to decline in value. The Internet stock index (ISDEX) was off nearly 40 percent from its mid-July high. **Exhibit 1** shows the path of the S&P 500 index and the ISDEX for the past three months, while **Exhibit 2** presents the long-term trends in aggregate market volatility.

Two months earlier while stock valuations were at record levels, eBay had begun the registration process with the Securities and Exchange Commission (SEC) for its first public stock sale. Since the market correction, many other companies with initial public offerings (IPOs), such as Internet firms Barnes&Noble.com, uBid, and netValue, Inc., had either canceled or postponed their issues. In fact, the past few weeks had been the quietest month for IPOs since the mid-1970s. **Exhibit 3** provides the monthly number of canceled and postponed IPOs in 1998, relative to the number of offerings completed. Some investors speculated that eBay was likely to follow suit and either withdraw or postpone its offering.

eBAY

The demand for person-to-person trading was traditionally filled by consignment shops, collectible shows, flea markets, classified advertisements, and dealer shops. Sellers were generally required to pay for advertisements and selling space and to bear the full cost of transportation and marketing. These higher costs were passed on to buyers through higher prices. These conventional trading venues suffered from relatively high inventory management costs and restricted market coverage.

The idea for Internet consignment came to Pierre Omidyar when his girlfriend, an avid PEZ candy dispenser collector, expressed her displeasure over the lack of PEZ trading partners in the San Francisco Bay Area. Months later, in an effort to provide an Internet site where PEZ collectors could meet and make transactions, Pierre founded eBay. Through Internet consignment, Pierre was able to gain a much broader market without the high inventory management costs of regular consignment. Buyers and sellers could also access their trading forum 24 hours a day, while the cost of Internet consignment would be considerably less for both.

Traders argued that the time spent searching for items, and the social interaction involved in the process, were an important part of the collecting and trading experience. To attract collectors, Omidyar faced the challenge of recreating the environment and trading experience that buyers and sellers enjoyed. Omidyar added several clever ideas to eBay's web service to stimulate interest. First, he adopted an auctionlike trading format to not only create a sense of urgency, but also allow buyers to follow the bidding status for each item. Secondly, he provided sellers with opportunities to "spice up" their auction pages. Sellers were encouraged to upload pictures of their items or add music. Thirdly, Omidyar created the eBay Community, composed of registered traders sharing in common interests and passions for collectible and tradable goods. eBay listed all participants' e-mail addresses and provided chat rooms, such as the eBay café, where eBay community members could talk about sale items, hobbies, or other non-trading-related topics. Finally, eBay allowed users to discuss the relative quality of items, sellers, and buyers in the eBay community by providing a "Feedback Forum" for community members to interact.

eBay's first auction occurred on Labor Day 1995. Three years later, with over one thousand categories listed and 70,000 new sale items added daily, eBay had become the largest and most popular person-to-person trading community on the Internet. The goods traded on eBay's web site included: antiques, sports memorabilia, books, toys, cars, computers, dolls, coins, jewelry, electronics, photography, and music. The company neither received goods nor payments for goods, but simply provided an arena for buyers and sellers to interact. To generate revenue, eBay charged sellers a nominal posting fee ranging from $.25 to $2.00 an item and a completed transaction fee ranging from 1.25 percent to 5 percent of the final selling price. **Exhibit 4** provides the fee schedule. Auctions for posted items lasted from a couple of hours to a few weeks. Buyers were allowed to explore the site free of charge. At the close of an auction the seller and buyer were notified by eBay and the transaction was completed without eBay involvement.

eBay was one of the few profitable Internet companies in 1998. For the six months ended June 30, 1998, the company reported operating profit of $2.7 million on total revenues of $14.9 million, representing a 220 percent increase in profit and an 800 percent increase in revenue over the first half of the previous year. eBay's financial statements are provided in **Exhibits 5 and 6.**

COMPETITION

Having pioneered person-to-person trading forums on the Internet, eBay had grown its number of users from 340,000 to 850,000 over the first six months of 1998 and the number of simultaneous auctions had climbed from 200,000 to 500,000 over the same time frame. eBay saw the continuation of such market penetration to be vital to its continued success. eBay expected to expand its services to an international level by taking advantage of increasing worldwide access to the Internet. eBay's growth was currently supported by 76 employees.

Despite eBay's early lead, the market for person-to-person trading on the Internet was destined, however, to attract many of the new and up-and-coming Internet companies, as well as many large and well-established firms. Already the number of direct and indirect competitors was formidable. Currently, Yahoo! Auctions Powered by Onsale, Auction Universe (a subsidiary of Times-Mirror Company), uBid (a subsidiary of Creative Computers), and Excite, together with numerous other smaller specialized electronic-trading services, competed directly with eBay in the person-to-person trading market. In addition, First Auction, ZAuction, and Surplus Auction competed indirectly with eBay in the business-to-person market. Other large established companies, such as AOL, Microsoft, and Amazon.com, as well as QVC, Cendant Corporation, and large newspaper or media companies were expected to play more of a role in the industry in the future. A financial comparison of eBay's direct competitors is found in **Exhibit 7.**

The Internet industry had only recently emerged as a major medium of communication. International Data Corporation (IDC) estimated that the worldwide number of Internet users would grow from approximately 69 million in 1997 to 320 million in 2002. IDC also estimated that Internet commerce was to grow from approximately $32 billion worldwide in 1998 to $130 billion in 2000. Maintaining a competitive position in the surging Internet industry was particularly tenuous. Rapid technological advancements, capacity constraints, web/network infrastructure, and system security were some of the most important competitive issues. The need to provide reliable systems software and hardware was a considerable cost for Internet companies. The rapid pace of technological advancement required access to sufficient capital to implement swift change. System security issues posed the greatest danger for eBay. eBay's Web site relied heavily on systems support by Exodus Communications. A system failure by Exodus could severely damage eBay's own reputation. eBay was also exposed to the security risks of online commerce. If encrypted transmissions were decoded, customer transactions could potentially be altered or erased.

Two weeks ago, AOL had named eBay as its exclusive person-to-person auction service for a minimum of one year. Since the success of an Internet firm relied heavily on its ability to contract with search engines, bulletin board operators, and online access services, all of which provided users access to the firm's site, the AOL agreement substantially solidified eBay's competitive position.

eBAY'S PUBLIC OFFERING

eBay had considered a public equity offering to raise additional capital to repay outstanding debt and to invest in new technologies or businesses that could improve eBay's operations and service. To initiate the IPO process, eBay had selected Goldman Sachs as its lead underwriter, Fenwick & West as its legal counsel, and PricewaterhouseCoopers as its auditor. In the early summer of 1998, this team prepared a registration statement (Form S-1), submitting it to the SEC on July 15th. Over the following few weeks, the SEC examined the adherence to required disclosure requirements and registration compliance, but as required, made no comments on the quality of eBay's financial prospects. Discrepancies discovered by the SEC and cited in the letter of comment were addressed in subsequent eBay amendments to the registration, as is standard under SEC rules. During the SEC review, Goldman Sachs and eBay drew up the contract for distribution of the securities, agreeing to a firm-commitment, rather than a best-efforts offering.[1]

Goldman Sachs assembled the underwriting syndicate and issued the preliminary or "red herring" prospectus.[2] The syndicate members listed in **Exhibit 8** agreed to share the risk of selling their allotted portions of the offering. In return, the underwriters received 7 percent of the total offering proceeds through the underwriting discount. In addition to compensating the underwriters, eBay expected to incur approximately $1 million in direct offering expenses to cover the legal, auditing, printing, and registration fees. Historically, IPOs had been priced such that investors experienced strong positive returns on the first day (see **Exhibit 9**). Such underpricing provided an additional indirect cost to companies going public.

As is customary, the SEC restricted the type of information that eBay or the underwriting team could disclose. Company communication was limited to the preliminary prospectus, tombstone ads in major financial newspapers, and road-show presentations to institutional investors. Despite the market volatility, investor demand expressed at the road shows appeared to be strong.

CONCLUSION

eBay had reached a critical point. Bengier recognized the momentum generated by the IPO process, but was concerned about the implications of a failed offering. He worried that although the firm-commitment offering ensured receiving the contracted proceeds, an unsuccessful offering might have an important impact on access to new capital in the future.

---

[1]In a best-efforts offering the underwriter only agrees "to do their best" at placing an offering at the agreed upon price and number of shares. If after a period of "selling" the issue (usually 90 days), the minimum agreed upon number of shares had not been subscribed to; the underwriter would cancel the issue. In the more common firm-commitment offering, the underwriter guaranteed that an agreed-upon number of shares would be sold for a negotiated price. In some instances the underwriter might suggest beforehand that the number of shares be increased or decreased, depending on market demand.

[2]The preliminary prospectus is called a red herring because it must have "Preliminary Prospectus" written in red ink on the front cover.

So far in September no other company had dared bring an issue to market. Even Goldman, which had its own IPO in the works, was thinking of postponing its own offering. The last IPO had occurred on August 26, when the Tennessee bank, Bankfirst, had raised $19 million. The last Internet company to go public was the encryption firm, Entrust Technologies, which had raised $125 million over four weeks ago. Today Entrust stock was trading somewhat below its offering price and was not considered a successful issue. In fact, 88 percent of all IPOs for the year now traded below their original prices.[3] Delaying the offering for six months would cost the company less than $1 million in direct expenses, but potentially much more in delaying major investment initiatives.

If eBay went ahead with the offering, Bengier worried that the offering price would be strongly discounted. The emerging Internet stocks had experienced large declines in value recently. Internet stocks faced increased risks due to the uncertainty of the long-term viability of the industry. Fearing the increased uncertainty, investors had moved their capital to safer securities. Goldman had originally encouraged eBay to offer 3.5 million shares at between $14 and $18 per share. The underwriting syndicate continued to be cautious, yet encouraging. Typically IPOs were priced by applying industry market multiples like price-earnings, price-sales, or market-to-book ratios; however, this method had proved difficult in emerging industries like the Internet industry.

Bengier wished he had the opportunity to collect more data, but eBay's scheduled IPO date was only a week away. He felt that if eBay was going to pull the plug on the deal, it needed to make the decision now. If eBay were to go ahead with the offering, he needed to firm up the target price. Since the original agreement was to sell less than 9 percent of the company in the IPO (see **Exhibit 10**), a price of $16 would value the current owners' holdings at nearly $600 million—a tempting proposition.

---

[3]"Where Are All the IPOs?," CNNfn.

EXHIBIT 1
Equity Market Performance

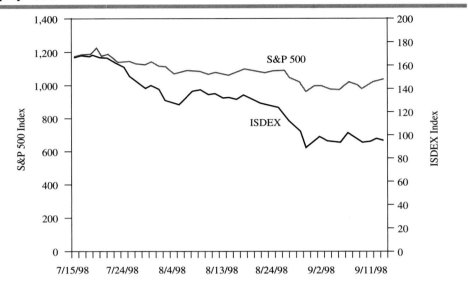

Source: Datastream, Internet.com.

EXHIBIT 2
Implied Equity Market Volatility
(CBOE 30-day Volatility Index for Optionable Stocks)

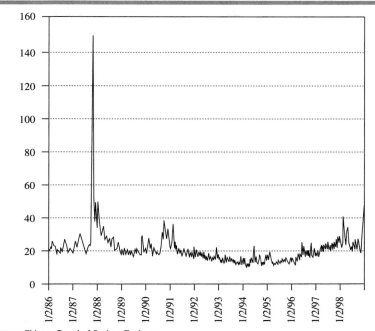

Source: Chicago Board of Options Exchange.

EXHIBIT 3
IPOs Issued, Postponed, and Withdrawn in 1998

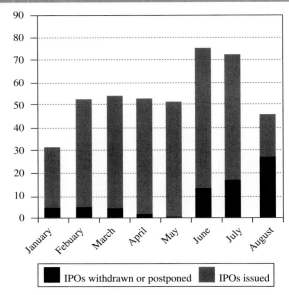

Source: IPO Data Systems.

EXHIBIT 4
eBay Transaction Fee Schedule

Posting Fees

Opening Value of Sale Item	Fee
$0.01 to $9.99	$0.25
$10.00 to $24.99	$0.50
$25.00 to $49.99	$1.00
Above $50.00	$2.00

Completed Transaction Fees*

Final Selling Price	Fee
$0.01 to $25.00	5.00 percent
$25.01 to $1,000	2.50 percent
Above $1,000	1.25 percent

* Completed transaction fees are calculated for each interval.
For example a $50 sale would generate fee revenue of $1.88
[$25.00 × 5% + $25.00 × 2.5%].

Source: Preliminary Prospectus.

EXHIBIT 5
Consolidated Balance Sheet for eBay Inc.

	Dec. 31, 1997	June 30, 1998
Assets		
Current assets:		
Cash and cash equivalents	$3,723,000	$10,716,000
Accounts receivable, net	1,024,000	2,846,000
Other current assets	220,000	453,000
Total current assets	4,967,000	14,015,000
Property and equipment, net	652,000	3,584,000
Intangible assets, net	0	2,216,000
Total assets	$5,619,000	$19,815,000
Total Liabilities and Stockholders' Equity		
Current liabilities:		
Debt and leases, current portion	$ 258,000	$ 314,000
Accounts payable	252,000	1,841,000
Customer advances	128,000	390,000
Income taxes payable	169,000	1,033,000
Other current liabilities	317,000	1,634,000
Total current liabilities	1,124,000	5,212,000
Debt and leases, long-term portion	305,000	167,000
Deferred tax liabilities	157,000	157,000
Total liabilities	1,586,000	5,536,000
Series B, mandatory convertible preferred stock	3,018,000	5,157,000
Series A, convertible preferred stock, $0.001 par value	4,000	4,000
Common stock, $0.001 par value	20,000	27,000
Additional paid-in capital	1,482,000	15,211,000
Notes receivable from stockholders	−68,000	−1,536,000
Unearned compensation	−1,399,000	−5,729,000
Retained earnings	976,000	1,145,000
Total stockholders' equity	1,015,000	9,122,000
Total liabilities and stockholders' equity	$5,619,000	$19,815,000

EXHIBIT 6
Consolidated Statement of Income for eBay Inc.

	Year Ended Dec. 31, 1997	Six Months Ended June 31, 1998
Net revenues	$5,744,000	$14,922,000
Cost of net revenues	746,000	1,736,000
Gross profit	4,998,000	13,186,000
Operating expenses:		
Sales and marketing	1,730,000	4,610,000
Product development	831,000	1,548,000
General and administrative	950,000	4,187,000
Acquired research and development	0	150
Total operating expenses	3,511,000	10,495,000
Income from operations	1,487,000	2,691,000
Interest and other income, net	59,000	101,000
Interest expense	−3,000	−25,000
Income before income taxes	1,543,000	2,767,000
Provision for income taxes	−669,000	−2,552,000
Net income	$ 874,000	$ 215,000
Net income per share	$0.11	$0.01

Source: Preliminary Prospectus.

EXHIBIT 7
Comparative Financial Information for Direct Competitors
(for six-months ended June 30, 1998, in millions except for per share and employee data)

	eBay	Onsale	uBid	Excite
Total revenues	$14.9	$91.0	$ 8.8	$ 56.0
Cost of revenues	1.7	82.8	8.1	12.1
Operating expenses	10.5	17.8	2.5	129.2
Net income	0.2	(8.2)	(1.9)	(87.1)
Earnings per share	$ 0.01	$ (0.44)	$(0.26)	$ (1.98)
Shares outstanding	34.2	18.8	7.3	44.0
Current assets	14.0	63.3	N.A.	82.9
Cash & short-term investments	10.7	51.9	N.A.	36.0
Total assets	19.8	66.9	2.7	125.6
Current liabilities	5.2	12.1	N.A.	41.9
Long-term debt	0.2	0.0	N.A.	5.0
Net worth	9.1	54.8	(2.2)	70.6
Recent stock price	N.A.	$ 20	Postponed	$31
IPO date		April 1997	Offering	April 1996
Employees	76	175	30	200

Source: SEC filings, casewriter estimates.

EXHIBIT 8
Participation in Underwriting Syndicate

Underwriter	Number of Shares[*]
Goldman, Sachs & Co	1,190,000
Donaldson, Lufkin & Jenrette	595,000
BancBoston Robertson Stephens	595,000
BT Alex Brown	595,000
Dain Rauscher Wessels	175,000
E*TRADE Securities	175,000
Volpe Brown Whelan & Company	175,000
Total	3,500,000

[*] Members of the underwriting syndicate maintain the option to purchase additional shares up to 15 percent of their allocation at the offer price, less the underwriters' discount of 7 percent.

Source: Preliminary Prospectus.

EXHIBIT 9
Average Initial-day Returns for All U.S. IPOs by Month (January 1988 to August 1998)

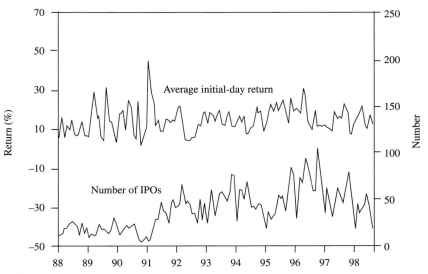

Source: Jay Ritter, University of Florida.

EXHIBIT 10
Current and Prospective Ownership Structure

Name of Beneficial Owner	Shares Beneficially Owned prior to Offering		Number of Shares Offered	Shares Beneficially Owned after Offering	
	Number	Percent		Number	Percent
Pierre M. Omidyar, Founder and Chairman	15,229,445	42.0%		15,229,445	38.3%
Jeffrey S. Skoll, VP Strategic Planning and Analysis	10,200,000	28.1		10,200,000	25.7
Robert C. Kagle, Benchmark Funds	8,791,836	24.3		8,791,836	22.1
Margaret C. Whitman, President and CEO	2,400,000	6.6		2,400,000	6.0
Scott D. Cook, Director and Founder of Intuit	257,250	*		257,250	*
Howard D. Schultz, Director and Founder of Starbucks	257,250	*		257,250	*
Community Foundation Silicon Valley**	107,250	*	10,725	96,525	*
All directors and executive officers	34,796,925	94.8		34,796,925	86.6
All existing stockholders	36,260,523	100.0		36,249,798	91.2
New investors			3,489,275	3,489,275	8.8

* Represents beneficial ownership of less than 1 percent.

** eBay had established a charitable fund, the eBay Foundation, to make donations to charitable organizations. The fund was capitalized through the company's donation of 107,250 shares of common stock to the Community Foundation Silicon Valley (CFCV). CFCV planned to sell 10,725 shares with the initial offering on behalf of the foundation. The eBay Foundation was expected to become an integral part of the eBay Community, with members helping to allocate charitable donations.

Source: Preliminary Prospectus. Assumes underwriters' over-allotment option to purchase additional shares is not exercised. Also does not include 7,564,500 existing stock options held by executives.

Planet *Cópias & Imagem*

In March 1996, the founders of Planet *Cópias & Imagem* reflected on their ambitious growth goals for the firm, and began to plan the financing program that would help them achieve those goals. Planet, which was headquartered in Lisbon, Portugal, had successfully established five document centers with a unique, "high-tech, high-touch" store concept that included complete document preparation services, the newest reproduction technology, 24-hour service, food service, musical entertainment, and a pleasant atmosphere.

The founding entrepreneurs of Planet, Michael Melloy, Pascal Monteiro de Barros, and Luis Quartin Bastos—who called themselves "the three amigos"—sought to position the firm as a "breakout growth, category-killer" retail chain in Europe and worldwide. They aimed to become the dominant retail document center chain. Luis expressed Planet's growth plans when he told Portugal's leading newspaper, "our goal is to have 100 megastores in 5 years."

The founders ideally wanted to take Planet public by 1999 (but no later than 2002) in an international initial public offering (IPO) on American and European exchanges. They hoped this would monetize and make liquid their sweat equity in the firm, and compensate them for the risks they had taken. Currently, most of the world's equity markets were receptive to IPOs (see **Exhibit 1**), though in the past, the IPO "window of opportunity" for young firms had opened and closed. Thus, the timing of an IPO would be uncertain, and depended on market opportunities.

The fundamental task of Luis, Michael, and Pascal was to craft a financial strategy that would accommodate Planet's cash needs in the near term while not sacrificing their long-term equity interest. The strategy would need to reflect expectations of Planet's capital requirements from now until the IPO. Also, the strategy needed to preserve the firm's financial flexibility, enhance the firm's value, expand its competitive position, and preserve the founders' control. Estimating the value of Planet would be an important element in deciding how much equity to surrender (i.e., sell) in order to raise capital. Finally, the strategy needed to indicate the types of capital to be issued, the amounts, timing, and bets implied in the sequencing of capital issues.

THE PLANET CONCEPT

Planet *Cópias & Imagem* focused on the creation, design, reproduction, and distribution of documents for students, businesses, and government agencies. The company owned five retail document services centers that integrated an extensive and technologically diverse design, copy, and finishing product mix. **Exhibit 2** gives a complete listing of Planet's services.

Planet stores were intended to be places to work, create, learn, mingle, and relax. The Planet document services center offered modern and clean architecture. The entire store was kept cool to aid the performance of modern technology workstations. The space was light and uncluttered, with ambient music sounding throughout the store. The store staff was young, energetic, bright, well-trained, and anxious to help. Someone working late on an urgent project could step over to the café for an espresso or pastry. Planet served food because Portuguese law prohibited any trade or business to remain open around the clock, unless it served food. The stores combined pleasing design, bright signage, unobtrusive music, friendly and knowledgeable staff, food and drink, 24-hour by 7-day availability, and highly visible locations. Equipment offered the latest technology in each field, and reflected strategic alliances with the main suppliers at the European headquarters level. **Exhibit 3** summarizes Planet's client base in Portugal and illustrates that the firm's business drew on a blend of corporate and retail customers. Michael Melloy said,

> Most of our competitors have small copy centers in the basements of buildings. Shops are crowded, dirty, and dark. They are using small capacity machines, many of which are 3–5 years old. They are not fun places to go. We want clients to make a favorable comparison of our stores with their former centers.

Planet currently operated in Lisbon only, and employed a "cluster" strategy combining a small store, two standard-size stores, a megastore, and a production center. This permitted Planet to exploit economies of scale in production and marketing, to provide service backups, and to be managed efficiently by a seasoned area manager. The Lisbon area model was the prototype for future Planet markets. This structure permitted a lower investment per market, as the area model could have a large product portfolio, without replicating the technological investment in every store.

Planet's core retail concept and its customer feedback mechanism permitted the product mix to evolve with the clients' changing needs. Likely additions to the Planet product line included Internet home page and CD-ROM design, specialized product sales (computing, engineering, design, arts, presentation), software sales, computer training and demonstrations, presentation and conference areas, and paging and cellular sales. New services would contribute to internal sales growth, and more rapid amortization of existing space and equipment investments.

Marketing was primarily in the form of heavily promoted store openings and the corporate sales force. Effective word-of-mouth advertising was an important reason for Planet's success. To build the word of mouth, Planet focused its marketing efforts on existing clients, and augmented its marketing with press coverage in leading business publications, publication of its own magazine, press conferences, and presentations at trade shows where potential customers could try Planet's innovative services. Planet gained a great deal of attention in the press and was featured in 12 different leading Portuguese business and computing publications in its first year.

The founders intended to enter multiple new markets with their specialty retail document centers. In order to take advantage of the unique window of opportunity presented by Planet's highly fragmented competition, the founders planned to replicate its concept in new, larger, and richer markets. Luis, Michael, and Pascal believed that Planet's concept had worldwide potential.

The success of the Planet store concept seemed confirmed by the pilot store's first-year sales, which were 241 million escudos, much greater than the average mature store sales for America's leading quick printing and reprographic chain. Within three years, the firm had grown to four retail locations, one production center, and 230 employees. But the costs and investments necessary to support the start-up and expansion produced the firm's net losses for 1994 and 1995. The operating cash flow for 1995 was also negative. **Exhibits 4, 5, 6,** and **7** present historical and forecast financial statements, and financial ratios—these are expressed in U.S. dollars[1] as the three founders were preparing to present a proposal for financing to a group of international banks and investment firms.

COMPANY HISTORY

In the summer of 1992, Luis Quartin Bastos evaluated strategic investment opportunities for a Portuguese holding company. This firm had been offered the opportunity to buy the franchise for Portugal of a chain of copying centers. Luis was the likely candidate to manage this new venture. To help him better evaluate the proposal, Luis asked a business school classmate, Michael Melloy, to prepare reviews of the industry, other possible franchisers, and the Portuguese market.

Melloy's final report was submitted in late February, 1993, and proved to be the genesis of Planet *Cópias.* Luis and the holding company disagreed with regard to the implementation of the report. Therefore Luis quit his job, and with Michael, enlisted a third classmate, Pascal, to found Planet. The three entrepreneurs gained the support of a leading Portuguese investor. Altogether they invested 60 million escudos to open a pilot store in the center of Lisbon. The three founders owned 51 percent and the silent partner retained the balance. After settling on the name, Planet *Cópias & Imagem,* they hired a design firm to create their corporate logo and image. For the initial site, they selected a 210-square-meter

---

[1]Assumes 150 escudos per US$1, the rate prevailing in March 1996.

location, in a busy area near two arts universities, in the Chiado section of Lisbon. Key vendors were chosen and construction began in November 1993. The pilot store (Planet Chiado) opened on January 4, 1994.

The first nine months were spent educating the market, training the workforce, and launching and testing the concept. The pilot store grew from one color copier to eight. Competitors quickly responded to Planet's initial success with similar product introductions and pricing. Planet's high-visibility entrance spawned four copycat firms in 1994. The three founders knew that they had a strong brand identity when unrelated businesses, such as a fast-food restaurant, began using their logo to attract customers.

Planet's board agreed to raise capital to open another four stores in Lisbon. The aim was to consolidate Lisbon, rather than spread out to different Portuguese cities. Lisbon represented over 70 percent of Portugal's GNP and an even higher percentage of Planet's corporate target clients—service companies. By clustering the stores in a small geographic region and pricing for share, Planet's intention was to achieve brand dominance. Spreading the locations out further might have extended the reach of the brand, but the spacing of the stores would have precluded shared asset investment. The three concurred that there was a temporary window of opportunity to expand aggressively and prevent against possible new entrants and would-be imitators. Luis said,

> Each store needs to be viewed as a distribution point. Imagine having an amazing product and only one location. The likely competitive behavior is to bring in imitations, which is happening with increasing frequency. The likely consumer behavior is to demand that we open new locations or look for approximate substitutes, which we also saw happening.

Banco Mello was retained to sell 1,200,000 new shares in Planet at 535 escudos per share, resulting in 1,600,000 shares after the offering. The offering closed in May 1995, was oversubscribed, and raised a total of 643 million escudos. The new shares were placed among 35 individuals and institutions in Portugal and abroad. When the offering was completed, Planet bought back 10 percent of the stock to be used as treasury stock for an ESOP for management. After the capital increase, in which founding investors also invested at the offering price, the "three amigos" controlled about 48 percent of the equity.

On June 1, Planet opened its second store, Planet Liberdade, in the heart of Lisbon's premier business district. After some initial delays due to a shortage of optimal real estate locations, Planet opened a large production center outside Lisbon in September. The megastore on Avenida da Republica, Lisbon's main avenue, opened in December and was the largest of its kind in Europe. Also in December, Planet opened in Carnaxide, a growing office park location on the outskirts of Lisbon. The following chart lists Planet's locations as of January 1996:

TABLE 1

Location	Type	Size (M^2)	Opening
Planet Chiado	Store	200	Jan. '94
Planet Liberdade	Store	220	June '95
Planet Meramar	Production center	450	Sep. '95
Planet Republica	Store	1,100	Dec. '95
Planet Carnaxide	Store	500	Dec. '95

Source: Company documents.

The four Planet stores and one production center met aggressive sales targets. There was no evidence of cannibalization. On the contrary, it appeared that each new store was reaching operating efficiency and higher sales levels increasingly earlier than expected due to growing brand identity.

PROFILE OF THE "BREAKOUT FIRM"

Conscious of having created a successful specialty retail concept, Luis, Michael, and Pascal identified and researched specialty retail firms which they called "breakout firms." Breakout firms demonstrated sustainable per-store growth and profitability with a rapid rate of expansion in number of stores. Kinko's (convenience documents), Barnes & Noble (books), Starbucks Coffee (specialty coffee), Blockbuster Video (video rental), and Boston Market (restaurants) were deemed illustrative breakout firms. The defining features of breakout growth specialty retailers were:

- Redefinition and professionalization of a fragmented sector. Barnes & Noble and Planet competed against the smaller "mom and pop" stores in their respective markets.
- Branding, and development of a store concept. Blockbuster and Planet took their businesses out of inadequate retail space and provided large, well lit, user-friendly environments.
- Use of state-of-the-art information systems. Blockbuster used its information technology to build a client profile to better manage content and build customer loyalty. Planet designed and was in the process of implementing a comprehensive management-information system.
- Infrastructure development and investment before growth. Infrastructure consisted of headquarters, information technology, training, store design and real estate functions. Though this led to operating losses in the early years of their histories, breakout firms were able to sustain much more rapid growth rates because of the infrastructure in place.
- Use of joint ventures and/or licensing. Boston Market and Planet both had well-defined partnering agreements.

Breakout firms aggressively expanded in target areas to gain large market share and name recognition. Expansion would begin with placement of a single store, followed by others in the region—the aim was market saturation. Such strategies were inherently *preemptive:* the goal was to create a strong market share ahead of potential competitors. Through branding and careful location of stores, breakout firms would raise barriers to entry. As the dominant firms in their respective segments, these firms came to be called "category killers" (i.e., killers of competition within the retail category). **Exhibit 8** presents financial and operating information on breakout growth firms.

The three founders believed that Planet's store economics compared favorably to these breakout firms. They pointed to a study by Hambrecht & Quist, an American investment bank, which suggested that in the current market environment, the highest valuation multiples were given to firms that offered both brand strength and distribution strength—Luis, Michael, and Pascal believed that Planet offered both.

EXPECTED TRENDS IN THE QUICK PRINTING AND REPROGRAPHICS INDUSTRY

Luis, Michael, and Pascal believed in several industry trends which would affect the outlook for their firm, and their plans. In an internal study, the three founders drew on their own knowledge and information of other sources to highlight these trends:[2]

- *Technological performance and customer convenience* will remain the two major critical success factors for firms in this industry.
- The significant *shift from printing to copying* will continue. Shorter product life cycles, price volatility, smaller target markets, and the need for speed, contribute to the economic efficiency of copying. Technological innovation in copying equipment will continue to improve image quality, computer connectivity, and speed.
- *Improvements in technology.* Use of color copiers will grow dramatically during the next five years. Copy speed will continue to increase. The variety of copier papers will continue to broaden. The cost per copy will continue to drop. Each of these factors improves the advantage of copying versus printing.
- *Payback periods for investments will continue to shorten.* One study of color servers indicated a total economic life of 18 months, with its greatest performance/price advantage in the first six months.
- Within retail communication service stores, *peripheral services offered will continue to grow.* Users want convenience and "one-stop shopping." With accelerating innovation and obsolescence of technology, consumers will increasingly be reluctant to invest in equipment that they can access at any time of day and need not purchase to use.
- The combination of customers wanting minimal costs, immediate access, equipment with advanced power and ease of use will contribute to the *growth of self-service concepts.* People do not want to wait. Self-service allows people to do their own work, when they want it, without paying extra for it. The pressures for disintermediation of non- or low-value-added intermediaries within retail services will accelerate.

KINKO'S: INDUSTRY LEADER IN RETAIL CONVENIENCE DOCUMENT COPYING

The leading competitor in the retail convenience document copying industry was Kinko's Service Corporation, a California-based chain of about 800 stores and annual per-store sales estimated to be in the neighborhood of $1 million.[3] Founded in September 1970 by Paul Orfalea, the company began with a 100-square-foot copy shop at a California college.

---

[2]The following points are quoted from a company document.
[3]Kinko's is a privately held corporation. The estimate was developed by the three founders from interviews with shop managers, employees, clients, and industry experts.

The three amigos attributed the growth and position of Kinko's to several factors:

- *Rapid adoption of substitute document technologies,* such as self-service computers linked to high-resolution printers.
- *Service speed and expansion of service.* By offering service 24 hours a day, 7 days a week, Kinko's achieved a 200 percent operating capacity advantage over their competitors. As businesses increasingly focused on smaller market segments and produced products with shorter life cycles and more volatile prices, they needed documents faster. The 24-hour operational strategy increased the speed advantage of copying, which increased the economic run size for firms that valued time.
- *Unique management and ownership structure.* Instead of using the franchise basis of organization, stores were operated as sub-chapter S corporations, with Kinko's holding a majority or total ownership position of a store. Minority positions were held by store manager/owners. Kinko's was a privately held company. All employees who had been with the firm for six months received benefits, including profit sharing. The incentive system promoted rapid growth with highly localized management focus.

By the late 1980s Kinko's had become a major resource for small and mid-size firms that wanted the advantages of a well-equipped large firm. By offering modern computing and copying equipment, self-service work areas, fax machines, and Federal Express services, Kinko's invented the virtual office before it became the popular business buzzword. However, Kinko's growth was almost entirely in North America. As of 1994, Kinko's had 11 international stores—eight in Canada, one in the Netherlands, and two in Japan.

In comparing Kinko's and Planet, Michael Melloy said,

> Kinko's does about 60 percent of what we do, the part (i.e., copying) that is low-margin and requires a lot of volume. The other 40 percent (graphic design, Internet, etc.) is beyond Kinko's current operational and technological capabilities, and serves as the platform for tomorrow's value-added office services. Nobody has a service mix that matches Planet's.

GROWTH OPPORTUNITIES

In December 1995, it became evident that the Planet concept was viable, even in Western Europe's second-poorest national market, Portugal. The three founders decided that the Planet concept should be exported to other, richer markets in order to grow the firm.

**Identified Target Store
Locations Possible for 1996**

Market	Stores
Northern Portugal	3–5
Greater Lisbon	3–5
Spain	10–20
United States	3–5

In 1996, Planet aimed to sign agreements with partners to open Planet stores in Portugal, Spain, and the United States. From 1997 to 2000, Planet would seek to grow as a specialized retail chain worldwide through numerous local joint ventures.

Historically, Planet had invested 125 million to 225 million escudos per store in Portugal. For the purposes of their own financial forecasting, the founders assumed a per-store investment of 137.7 million escudos ($900,000)—this assumed economies in purchasing and store opening expenses. Traditionally, 55 percent of the investment had been for equipment, 40 percent for leasehold improvements, and 5 percent for miscellaneous store-opening expenses (commissions, training, recruiting, etc.).

Planet had a geographically diverse existing shareholder base (distributed in the United States, Greece, Portugal, Brazil, Sweden, and the United Kingdom). The founders hoped to attract new investors looking for a successful concept with high growth through stock appreciation. After several years of aggressive geographic expansion into new markets, the company would seek a public listing, preferably in the United States.

ANALYSIS OF GROWTH AND FINANCING STRATEGY

Luis, Michael, and Pascal set forth an ambitious plan to grow the number of stores at the rate of 50 percent per year. They believed this target was the maximum rate their organization could handle at present. The three considered several possible sources of financing the growth of their firm:

- *Internal generation of cash.* The operating cash flow of the firm could be reinvested. This source of funds was the most attractive (of all sources) to the founders because it came without covenants, and it did not change the voting structure of the shareholders. The founders sought to interpret the forecast for the efficacy of a strategy focusing solely on internally generated cash.
- *Bank loans* were the next-most-preferred source of funds. Preliminary discussions with two institutions had indicated a willingness to consider a loan proposal that offered a minimum EBIT coverage ratio in the range of 3.0 times. And for both banks, that coverage ratio would be acceptable for only the first year. Thereafter, the minimum would rise to higher than three times. The contemplated interest rate would be 14 percent. Finally, the banks required personal guarantees of all debt by the founders.
- *Equity investment by the three founders.* If the preceding sources of funds fell short of requirements, equity investment would be indicated. The founders sought to preserve their equity interest and voting control in the firm. But practically, they had already invested their entire net worth in the firm, and provided guarantees for loans. Further acquisition of Planet shares by them would have to be earned (i.e., as "sweat equity") rather than purchased with cash.
- *Equity investment by Planet's "angel" investors.* Wealthy individuals who provided seed capital for the start-up of new ventures were called "angel" investors. These investors were known and trusted by the founders. Planet's angels had invested in the expectation that an IPO or buyout by an institutional investor would give them a profitable

exit from their investment in Planet. They would be surprised at the request for more equity. They might be induced to invest another $2 or $3 million, for another 20 percent of the shares. But they would probably not invest more than that. Investment by angels would dilute the interests of the three founders.

- *Equity investment by international private-equity groups.* One well-regarded group based in London had expressed an interest in the aggressive growth plans of Planet. This group had invested over 2 billion in private equity deals over the previous 20 years, and had achieved a compound rate of return for their investors of 40 percent. They sought to invest in situations offering equity returns (IRRs) of no less than 35 percent. The investment vehicle would be common shares or convertible preferred stock. For most of the situations in which this group invested, the returns would come not from dividends, but rather from the capital gain received upon exit. The target investment horizon was five to seven years. This group typically applied a multiple of six times EBITDA[4] to estimate the terminal exit value of their investments. In unusually mature "cash cow" situations, the exit multiple might be increased to 12 times. Generally, the more that the IRR of the investment depended on terminal value, the higher would be the target rate of return used by the private equity group. Ordinarily, private equity groups sought voting control of the firms in which they invested, and tended to intervene actively in management if there were any adverse variances from plan. Financing by a private equity group might enhance Planet's reputation and ability to go public. But Luis, Michael, and Pascal ranked this source of funds least because of its high cost and effect on control.

Exhibits 4, 5, 6, and 7 present the forecasts of Planet's financial statements consistent with the three founders' growth plans. **Exhibit 9** computes the DCF value of the firm using a weighted average cost of capital consistent with that DCF value.[5] **Exhibit 10** estimates the dilution of the founders' equity interest, and the EBIT coverage ratio consistent with assumptions about growth and equity financing. **Exhibit 11** presents a sensitivity analysis of dilution, EBIT coverage, founders' future wealth, and market/book ratio. These forecasts were expressed in U.S. dollars, to present the results in a currency most likely to appeal to a range of international investors and banks. Important assumptions of the forecast (see Exhibit 4) were:

- *Annual growth rate in number of stores: 50 percent.* The founders believed that the organization could sustain a growth rate of at most 50 percent per year. The reason they chose not to model a lower rate of growth was their sense that they faced an extraordinary window of opportunity in the marketplace which they wanted to exploit rapidly before another competitor (such as Kinko's) stepped in. The resulting number of stores each year is given in Exhibit 7, line 18. In this line, fractional amounts could be explained by partial expansions of existing stores. As one of the founders, Pascal, said:

  > The number of stores we open each year is the most important driver of the growth of our firm. Stores and sales per meter drive revenues. Stores drive capital spending. The number of stores

---

[4]"EBITDA" stands for earnings before interest, taxes, depreciation, and amortization, and is often used as one approximate measure of a firm's cash-operating income.

[5]The valuation in Exhibit 9 employs a circular reference so that the weights of debt and equity used in the valuation depend on the market value of equity that is estimated with the WACC.

drives EBITDA for determining exit values. Planet's creation of value derives from breakout growth.

- *Growth in sales per square meter: 4 percent.* For stores already in place, sales would increase each year due to inflation, currently 2.4 percent in Portugal (versus 2.7 percent in the United States), and due to an expansion of services. The founders believed that it was reasonable to assume that continual expansion of the product range would account for at least 1.6 percent real growth in sales per year. Pascal explained:

  > This is a conservative assumption. We think we can do better than 4 percent. But the forecast ignores the fact that each store does not leap into full-blown operation from the opening day. Usually, a store operates at less than capacity for a year or so until it establishes its franchise. The net impact is that the forecast is a little more optimistic in the early years when we are investing heavily and operating young stores at less than capacity, and a little pessimistic in the later years when we have a large portfolio of "cash cows" growing their sales per square meter each year at a healthy rate. The impact of these life cycle effects is something we can model later.

- *Sales per square meter in 1996: $2,000.* This compared to an estimate of $2,200 for Kinko's. Pascal believed $2,000 was a conservative assumption; since Planet had a broader product line than Kinko's, it should be possible to exceed the competitor's experience.

- *Capital investment per store in 1996: $900,000.* This compared to an estimate of $1 million per store for Kinko's. Pascal believed that with careful purchasing, supplier alliances, and special expertise in store development, it should be possible to lower the per-store investment.

- *Gross margin: 75 percent.* This was consistent with the founders' estimate for Kinko's. But it was significantly lower than Planet's gross margin achieved in 1994 (81 percent) and 1995 (80 percent).

- *Percent of financing need filled by equity: 0 percent.* As a starting point, the forecasts assumed that all external financial requirements would be funded by the issuance of debt securities. This assumption implied no dilution in the founders' interest in the firm, consistent with their strong desire to retain control.

The income statement projected in Exhibit 5 suggested that by 2002 the firm would grow to revenues of $97.3 million and earnings of $14.6 million. Also by that year, assets (see Exhibit 6) would grow to $149.6 million, for which debt would provide $98.6 million in financing. Shareholders' equity would amount to $31.2 million. Over the forecast period, the interest coverage ratio (see Exhibit 7, line 10) would fall to 1.2 times in 1996, and rise to 2.6 times by 2002. The three founders pondered the implications of this forecast for their growth and financing strategies.

An analyst had tested the sensitivity of the model results with a series of two-way tables. Exhibit 11 shows how variations in growth rate and equity mix affected EBIT coverage, market/book value, founders' wealth, and dilution. The "base case" model implicitly assumed that Planet would meet no significant competition to its "breakout growth" concept. **Exhibit 12** relaxed this assumption by varying margin and same-store growth rates to test their effects on financial performance—unlike Exhibit 11, Exhibit 12 assumed all of the external financing need was fulfilled with debt financing.

THE FOUNDERS' GOALS

Pascal summed up the strategic aims of the three amigos in the following words:

> We are builders, not caretakers. We want to implement our growth plan in order to realize our "breakout" vision for Planet and win recognition in the industry and the capital markets. We have invested our capital and our sweat. We look forward to earning a sizable return on our investment, to be realized through an initial public offering. Throughout the financing process, we want to resist diluting our economic and voting interest in the company.

THE MARKET FOR INITIAL PUBLIC OFFERINGS

Analysts observed that both Europe and the United States were in the midst of an impressive wave of initial public offerings (IPOs). Exhibit 1 presents information on offerings in recent years. Over long periods, the equity markets' interest in the shares of new public companies waxed and waned. During periods of high interest, many firms went public; during periods of low interest, few firms did. Thus, the ability of a firm to go public might depend both on the firm's readiness for a public offering, as well as the receptiveness of the equity markets. Analysts cautioned entrepreneurs to prepare their firms to be ready to exploit a capital market "window of opportunity."

In early 1996 the equity markets in Europe and the United States were near the highest levels in the past 10 years. Luis, Michael, and Pascal believed that if Planet were to sell equity to investors, the firm would realize higher prices in the current market environment, than if they waited and had to issue equity later in a less buoyant market.

CONCLUSION

In March of 1996, Portugal's leading business periodical nominated Luis, Michael, and Pascal as "Entrepreneurs of the Year." But the feeling of honor was matched with a sense of urgency to set a strategy that would prepare the firm for a successful international IPO. How could the firm finance itself in ways that would best meet the founders' goals and vision? How could the founders grow the firm rapidly, achieve their wealth aspirations, and yet minimize dilution and meet the requirements of the potential providers of capital? Luis, Michael, and Pascal settled in for yet another long night of work.

EXHIBIT 1
Information on Recent Initial Public Offerings

IPOs in Europe ($ billions)

	1991	1992	1993	1994	1995
France	$1.0	$0.7	$2.4	$ 3.7	$2.2
Denmark	0.2	0.0	0.0	2.9	0.3
Netherlands	0.6	0.0	0.4	2.8	0.5
Italy	0.1	0.5	0.4	2.1	2.5
Sweden	0.0	0.0	0.3	1.3	0.9
Germany	0.7	0.0	0.2	1.3	2.7
United Kingdom	1.9	0.0	3.7	1.0	1.4
Spain	0.1	0.2	1.4	0.8	0.6
Total	$4.6	$1.4	$8.8	$15.9	$11.1

N.B.: IPOs of equities in international offerings.
Source: OECD/DAF.

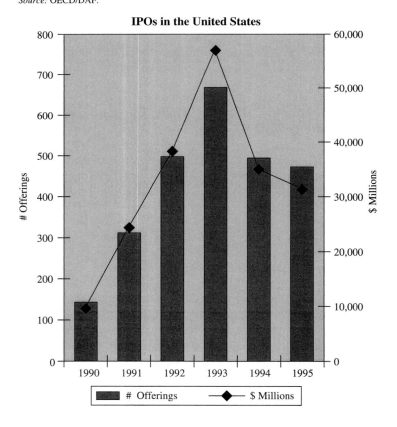

IPOs in the United States

EXHIBIT 2
Services Provided by the Company

Copying:
- Full-service black/white, color laser copies
- Rapid offset printing
- Binding and finishing
- Specialty papers, and materials
- Self-service black/white, color laser copies
- Oversize copies

Imaging:
- Rapid photo development
- Slide development
- Promotional gift items, T-shirts, mouse pads, puzzles, etc.

Postal:
- Mailbox rental
- DHL pickup and delivery
- Public fax

Self-Service Computing:
- Self-service PCs and Macs
- Self-service white printing (different levels)
- Self-service scanning
- Internet access[1]
- Database access
- CD-ROM rental
- Video-aided training
- Silicon graphics training center

Design:
- Operator-aided graphic design
- Desktop publishing
- Scanning
- Printing

Output:
- Full-color poster printing, mounting and laminating
- 35 MM slide output
- Color plotting and CAD output

Planet Café:
- Beverages
- Coffees
- Sandwiches, cookies, etc.
- Specialty newspaper and magazine sales

Supplies:
- Impulse purchase stationery products
- Design products
- Computer consumables

[1]In its attempts to provide quality self-service Internet access to its customers, Planet accidentally came across a unique opportunity to play an essential role in Internet access in Portugal. This could fit in with two other key strategic objectives: (1) electronically link all customers to Planet in an Internet-based IT system and (2) explore other ways to maximize the value of Planet's thousands of loyal customers. The Internet opportunities for Planet were to be studied on a market-by-market basis.

Source: Company documents.

EXHIBIT 3
Planet's Client Base in Portugal[1]

Walk-in Retail Clients

75% of total transactions
50% of total sales
Young (85% between 16 and 35 years old)
Computer literate, upwardly mobile
Mainly designers, artists, freelancers, students, and teachers

Corporate Service

25% of total transactions
50% of total sales
Popular services included graphic design, color output, presentations, and copying
Regular corporate clients include these firms:

ABN-Amro Bank	Eagle Star Vie	Opel Portugal
Afga Gevaert, Lba	El Corte Inglés	Pepsi-Cola International
Air France	EMI Songs	Petrogal
Alcatel-Comunicaçao	Entreposto Nissan	Philip Morris, Portugal
Aliança-UAP	Ernst & Young	Portucel
Amway	Esso	Portugal Telecom
Atlas Copco	Euro RSCG—Melorosa, Lda	Price Waterhouse
Banco Bilbao Vizcaya	Europ Assistance	Printemps
Banco Chemical	Europcar	Procter & Gamble
Banco Comercial Português	Rerrovial, S.A.	Repsol
Banco Espirito Santo	Filmes Castelo Lopes	Richard Ellis
Banco ESSI	Filmes Lusomundo, SA	Roche Farma
Banco Finantia	Glaxo Farmeutica, Lda	Royal Brands
Banco Fonsecas & Burnay	Grupo Argentaria	RTP
Banco Mello	Hay Consulting/Hay Group	Sanofi Beauté
Banco Santander	Healey & Baker	Securitas
Banco Totta & Açores	Hewlett Packard Portugal	SIC
Barclays Bank	Honeywell	SmithKline Beecham
Bates	J. Walter Thompson	Soci
British Airways	Johnson & Johnson	Tabaqueira
Bull Portuguesa	Kellogg's	Telecel
Caiza Geral de Depósitos	Lintas	Tetra Pak
Carrier Portugal	Marconi	Tranquilidade
Citibank	Mattel	Unisys
Colgate-Palmolive	McDonald's	United Distillery
Compaq Computer Portugal	McKinsey International	Valentim de Carvalho
Crédit Lyonnais	Merck Sharp & Dohme	Vista Alegre
Danone	Michelin	Walt Disney
DDB Needham	Miele	Warner Lambert Portugal
DHL	Nestlé	Willis Faber
Diário de Noticias	Novodesign	WundermanCato Johnson
Dun & Bradstreet	Ogilvy & Mather	Young & Rubicam

[1]*Source:* Company documents.

EXHIBIT 4
Summary of Forecast Assumptions

Description

Growth in number of stores, 1997+	50%
Growth in sales per square meter	4%
Sales per square meter, 1996	$ 2,000
Average square meters per store	450
Capital investment per store in 1996	$ 900,000
Gross margin	75%
Dividend payout	0%
Equipment rentals per store	$ 220,000
Employee costs per store	$ 130,000
Tax rate	35%
Percent of financing need met by equity issuance	0%
Interest rate	14%

	1994 (Actual)	1995 (Actual)	1996 (Proj'd)	1997 (Proj'd)	1998 (Proj'd)	1999 (Proj'd)	2000 (Proj'd)	2001 (Proj'd)	2002 (Proj'd)
Cash & invest. to sales	0.3%	0.4%	0.5%	0.5%	0.5%	0.5%	0.5%	0.5%	0.5%
Days in receivables	15.4	31.5	30.0	30.0	30.0	30.0	30.0	30.0	30.0
Days in payables	528.2	644.4	60.0	60.0	60.0	50.0	45.0	40.0	40.0
Days in inventory	21.5	161.6	90.0	60.0	60.0	50.0	40.0	30.0	30.0
Other current assets/sales	44.8%	207.4%	75.0%	50.0%	25.0%	15.0%	10.0%	10.0%	10.0%
Other current liabilities/sales	2.2%	59.4%	8.0%	6.0%	6.0%	6.0%	6.0%	6.0%	6.0%
Gross intangible assets/sales	48%	77%	60%	50%	50%	40%	30%	30%	30%
Annual depreciation/gross PP&E	N.A.	4.8%	3.2%	3.2%	3.2%	3.2%	3.2%	3.2%	3.2%

Source: Casewriter analysis.

EXHIBIT 5
Historical and Forecasted Income Statements (in U.S. dollars)

Years Elapsed from Present			1	2	3	4	5	6	7
Calendar Year	1994 (Actual)	1995 (Actual)	1996 (Proj'd)	1997 (Proj'd)	1998 (Proj'd)	1999 (Proj'd)	2000 (Proj'd)	2001 (Proj'd)	2002 (Proj'd)
1 Net sales	$1,577,390	$2,815,380	$6,750,000	$10,530,000	$16,426,800	$25,625,808	$39,976,260	$62,362,966	$97,286,228
2 Cost of goods sold	294,700	562,280	1,687,500	2,632,500	4,106,700	6,406,452	9,994,065	15,590,742	24,321,557
3 Gross profit	1,282,690	2,253,100	5,062,500	7,897,500	12,320,100	19,219,356	29,982,195	46,772,225	72,964,671
4 Operating expenses:									
5 Equipment rentals	916,170	2,384,650	1,650,000	2,475,000	3,712,500	5,568,750	8,353,125	12,529,688	18,794,531
6 Miscellaneous taxes	5,460	4,030	13,500	21,060	32,854	51,252	79,953	124,726	194,572
7 Employee costs	357,130	1,160,680	1,014,000	1,581,840	2,467,670	3,849,566	6,005,323	9,368,303	14,614,553
8 Other operating costs	0	6,350	13,500	21,060	32,854	51,252	79,953	124,726	194,572
9 Depreciation	136,720	408,630	228,282	340,602	515,821	789,163	1,215,577	1,880,781	2,918,501
10 Extraordinary	10	29,720	1,000	1,000	1,000	1,000	1,000	1,000	1,000
11 Total operating expenses	1,415,490	3,994,060	2,920,282	4,440,562	6,762,699	10,310,982	15,734,929	24,029,224	36,717,731
12 Operating income	(132,800)	(1,740,960)	2,142,218	3,456,938	5,557,401	8,908,374	14,247,266	22,743,001	36,246,940
13 Interest expense	(143,940)	(212,630)	(1,775,613)	(2,352,048)	(3,528,278)	(4,559,809)	(5,703,070)	(8,900,245)	(13,810,153)
14 Earnings before taxes	(276,740)	(1,953,590)	366,605	1,104,890	2,029,123	4,348,565	8,544,197	13,842,755	22,436,787
15 Income taxes	0	1,640	128,312	386,711	710,193	1,521,998	2,990,469	4,844,964	7,852,875
16 Net earnings	($276,740)	($1,955,230)	$238,293	$718,178	$1,318,930	$2,826,567	$5,553,728	$8,997,791	$14,583,911
17 Common shares & equivalents	400,000	1,600,000	1,600,000	1,600,000	1,600,000	1,600,000	1,600,000	1,600,000	1,600,000
18 E.P.S. (fully diluted)	($0.69)	($1.22)	$0.15	$0.45	$0.82	$1.77	$3.47	$5.62	$9.11
19 E.P.S. (primary)	($0.69)	($1.22)	$0.15	$0.45	$0.82	$1.77	$3.47	$5.62	$9.11
20 Primary no. shares	400,000	1,600,000	1,600,000	1,600,000	1,600,000	1,600,000	1,600,000	1,600,000	1,600,000
21 Dividends per share	$0.00	$0.00	$0.00	$0.00	$0.00	$0.00	$0.00	$1.00	$2.00

Source: Casewriter analysis.

360

EXHIBIT 6
Historical and Forecasted Balance Sheets (in U.S. dollars)

	1994 (Actual)	1995 (Actual)	1996 (Proj'd)	1997 (Proj'd)	1998 (Proj'd)	1999 (Proj'd)	2000 (Proj'd)	2001 (Proj'd)	2002 (Proj'd)
Assets									
1 Cash	$ 5,230	$ 10,980	$ 33,750	$ 52,650	$ 82,134	$ 128,129	$ 199,881	$ 311,815	$ 486,431
2 Accounts receivable	66,620	243,330	554,795	865,479	1,350,148	2,106,231	3,285,720	5,125,723	7,996,128
3 Merchandise inventories	17,330	248,990	416,096	432,740	675,074	877,596	1,095,240	1,281,431	1,999,032
4 Other current assets	132,107	1,166,060	1,265,625	1,316,250	1,026,675	960,968	999,407	1,559,074	2,432,156
5 Total current assets	221,287	1,669,360	2,270,265	2,667,119	3,134,031	4,072,924	5,580,248	8,278,043	12,913,747
6 Security deposits	0	0							
7 Gross property and equipment	1,061,040	4,883,810	7,133,810	10,643,810	16,119,410	24,661,346	37,986,766	58,774,422	91,203,164
8 Accumulated depreciation	74,710	310,820	539,102	879,704	1,395,525	2,184,688	3,400,265	5,281,046	8,199,547
9 Net property and equipment	986,330	4,572,990	6,594,708	9,764,106	14,723,885	22,476,658	34,586,502	53,493,376	83,003,617
10 Gross intangible assets	750,770	2,180,600	4,050,000	5,265,000	8,213,400	10,250,323	11,992,878	18,708,890	29,185,868
11 Amortization of intangible assets	62,020	234,860	545,150	1,012,500	1,316,250	2,053,350	2,562,581	2,998,220	4,677,222
12 Net intangible assets	688,750	1,945,740	3,504,850	4,252,500	6,897,150	8,196,973	9,430,297	15,710,670	24,508,646
13 Total assets	$1,896,367	$8,188,090	$16,419,823	$21,948,725	$32,968,466	$44,996,878	$61,589,925	$96,190,979	$149,611,878
Liabilities and Owners' Equity									
14 Accounts payable	$ 426,440	$ 992,620	$ 277,397	$ 432,740	$ 675,074	$ 877,596	$ 1,232,145	$ 1,708,574	$ 2,665,376
15 Notes payable	0	1,552,760	135,000	210,600	328,536	512,516	799,525	1,247,259	1,945,725
16 Sales and income taxes payable	34,350	77,240	11,915						
17 Other shareholder payables	0	43,020							
18 Other creditors	43,510	354,500	540,000	631,800	985,608	1,537,548	2,398,576	3,741,778	5,837,174
19 Accruals and deferrals	504,300	220,610	337,500	526,500	821,340	1,281,290	1,998,813	3,118,148	4,864,311
20 Total current liabilities	504,300	3,240,750	1,301,812	1,801,640	2,810,558	4,208,951	6,429,059	9,815,760	15,312,586
21 New debt issued (repur.) since 1995		–	12,682,948	16,800,344	25,201,986	32,570,063	40,736,211	63,573,179	98,643,951
22 Long-term debt	658,667	550,000	0	0	0	0	0	0	0
23 PV of leasing contracts	610,150	2,587,570	387,570	580,500	870,750	1,306,125	1,959,188	2,938,781	4,408,172
24 Total liabilities	1,773,117	6,378,320	14,371,780	19,182,483	28,883,294	38,085,139	49,124,458	76,327,721	118,364,708
25 Common stock	400,000	1,600,000	1,600,000	1,600,000	1,600,000	1,600,000	1,600,000	1,600,000	1,600,000
26 Paid-in capital	0	3,000,000	3,000,000	3,000,000	3,000,000	3,000,000	3,000,000	3,000,000	3,000,000
27 New equity issued (repur.) since 1995		–	0	(1,275,508)	0	0	0	0	0
28 Retained earnings	(276,750)	(2,231,980)	(1,993,887)	0	43,422	2,869,989	8,423,717	15,821,508	27,205,420
29 Less treasury stock	0	(558,250)	(558,250)	(558,250)	(558,250)	(558,250)	(558,250)	(558,250)	(558,250)
30 Total stockholders' equity	123,250	1,809,770	2,048,063	2,766,242	4,085,172	6,911,739	12,465,467	19,863,258	31,247,170
31 Total liabilities & stockholders' eq.	$1,896,367	$8,188,090	$16,419,823	$21,948,725	$32,968,466	$44,996,878	$61,589,925	$96,190,979	$149,611,878
Memo:									
32 Dividends		$ 0	$ 0	$ 0	$ 0	$ 0	$ 0	$ 1,600,000	$ 3,200,000
33 Capital expenditures		3,822,770	2,250,000	3,510,000	5,475,600	8,541,936	13,325,420	20,787,655	32,428,743
34 Depreciation expense		236,110	228,282	340,602	515,821	789,163	1,215,577	1,880,781	2,918,501
35 Additions to net wkg cap.		(1,288,377)	2,539,843	(102,974)	(542,007)	(459,500)	(712,784)	(688,906)	(861,122)
36 Incr. new external financing			12,682,948	4,117,396	8,401,642	7,368,077	8,166,149	22,836,968	35,070,771
37 Total new financing required			$12,682,948	$16,800,344	$25,201,986	$32,570,063	$40,736,211	$63,573,179	$98,643,951
38 New debt issued (repur.) since 1995			12,682,948	16,800,344	25,201,986	32,570,063	40,736,211	63,573,179	98,643,951
39 New equity issued (repur.) since 1995									
40 Check: total capital issued since 1995			12,682,948	16,800,344	25,201,986	32,570,063	40,736,211	63,573,179	98,643,951
41 New debt issued by year			10,580,188	4,117,396	8,401,642	7,368,077	8,166,149	22,836,968	35,070,771
42 New equity issued by year			0	0	0	0	0	0	0

Source: Casewriter analysis.

EXHIBIT 7
Financial Ratios

		1994 (Actual)	1995 (Actual)	1996 (Proj'd)	1997 (Proj'd)	1998 (Proj'd)	1999 (Proj'd)	2000 (Proj'd)	2001 (Proj'd)	2002 (Proj'd)
Profitability										
1	Gross margin (%)	81.3%	80.0%	75.0%	75.0%	75.0%	75.0%	75.0%	75.0%	75.0%
2	Opg. expenses to sales (%)	89.7	141.9	43.3	42.2	41.2	40.2	39.4	38.5	37.7
3	Cost of goods sold	−8.4	−61.8	31.7	32.8	33.8	34.8	35.6	36.5	37.3
4	Gross profit	0.0	−0.1	35.0	35.0	35.0	35.0	35.0	35.0	35.0
5	Return on sales (%)	−17.5	−69.4	3.5	6.8	8.0	11.0	13.9	14.4	15.0
6	Equipment rentals	−224.5	−108.0	11.6	26.0	32.3	40.9	44.6	45.3	46.7
7	Miscellaneous taxes	−14.6	−23.9	1.5	3.3	4.0	6.3	9.0	9.4	9.7
Leverage										
8	Debt/equity ratio (×)	10.29	2.59	6.19	6.07	6.17	4.71	3.27	3.20	3.16
9	Debt/total capital	91.1%	72.2%	86.5%	86.3%	86.5%	83.1%	77.4%	77.0%	76.7%
10	Ebit/interest (×)	0.9	8.2	1.2	1.5	1.6	2.0	2.5	2.6	2.6
Liquidity										
11	Quick ratio (×)	0.14	0.08	0.45	0.51	0.51	0.53	0.54	0.55	0.55
12	Current ratio (×)	0.44	0.52	1.74	1.48	1.12	0.97	0.87	0.84	0.84
Growth and Returns										
13	Primary earnings per share ($)	($0.69)	($1.22)	$0.15	$0.45	$0.82	$1.77	$3.47	$5.62	$9.11
14	Change in E.P.S. (%)	NMF	−76.6%	NMF	201.4%	83.6%	114.3%	96.5%	62.0%	62.1%
15	Dividends per share ($)	$0.00	$0.00	$0.00	$0.00	$0.00	$0.00	$0.00	$1.00	$2.00
16	Dividends to net income (%)	0.0%	0.0%	0.0%	0.0%	0.0%	0.0%	0.0%	17.8%	21.9%
17	Sales growth rate (%)	NMF	78.5%	139.8%	56.0%	56.0%	56.0%	56.0%	56.0%	56.0%
Store Numbers, Size and Sales										
18	Ending number of stores	1.00	5.00	7.50	11.25	16.88	25.31	37.97	56.95	85.43
19	New stores added	1.00	4.00	2.50	3.75	5.63	8.44	12.66	18.98	28.48
20	Unit growth (%)	23.0%	23.0%	50.0%	50.0%	50.0%	50.0%	50.0%	50.0%	50.0%
21	Ending square meters	200	2,270	3,375	5,063	7,594	11,391	17,086	25,629	38,443
22	Change in square meters (%)	NMF	1035.0%	48.7%	50.0%	50.0%	50.0%	50.0%	50.0%	50.0%
23	Avg. square meters per store	200	350	450	450	450	450	450	450	450
24	Avg. sales per square meter ($)	$7,887	$1,240	$2,000	$2,080	$2,163	$2,250	$2,340	$2,433	$2,531
25	Avg. sales per store ($)	1,577,390	563,076	900,000	936,000	973,440	1,012,378	1,052,873	1,094,988	1,138,787
26	Same store sales incrs (%)	NMF	−64.3%	59.8%	4.0%	4.0%	4.0%	4.0%	4.0%	4.0%
27	Capital investment per store ($)	$1,061,040	$976,762	$900,000	$936,000	$973,440	$1,012,378	$1,052,873	$1,094,988	$1,138,787

Notes:
1. "NMF" stands for "not a meaningful figure."
2. Average sales per square meter (line 24) and same store sales increase (line 26) declined in 1995 because new stores were not in operation for full year.

Source: Casewriter analysis.

EXHIBIT 8

Information on Breakout Firms as of January 1996 (all currency amounts are in $ millions)

Company Name	Business Description	Prior Year's Sales	EBIT	Net Income	Assets	Book Value of Equity	Market Value of Equity	Book Debt to Equity	Tax Rate	Beta	Five Year Annual Revenue Growth	EBIT Multiple	Market to Book Value Multiple	Price Earnings Multiple
Autozone	Auto Superstores	$1,808	$275	$139	$1,112	$685	$5,047	0.00	39%	1.25	30%	18.4	7.4	29.5
Baby Superstores	Infant CareProducts	175	14	7	92	58	874	0.03	38%	1.78	67%	64.3	15.1	68.9
Barnes & Noble	Books Superstores	1,623	107	24	1,026	358	1,154	0.73	47%	0.93	22%	18.7	3.2	38.9
Bed Bath & Beyond	Household Goods Stores	440	59	30	177	109	1,806	0.20	41%	1.19	38%	36.7	16.6	46.3
Benson Eyecare Corp	Optical Goods Stores	169	22	8	262	109	261	0.60	34%	0.88	343%	19.0	2.4	32.6
Best Buy Co	Consumer Electronics	5,080	122	48	1,507	379	758	0.60	39%	0.93	66%	9.9	2.0	15.8
Boston Chicken	Fast Food Stores	160	79	34	1,074	717	2,203	0.46	39%	1.38	167%	40.7	3.1	51.6
Circuit City Stores	Consumer Electronics	5,583	279	179	2,004	893	3,305	0.20	37%	0.67	25%	14.2	3.7	18.5
Gymboree	Child Amusement	188	38	22	127	93	642	0.07	43%	2.02	48%	18.1	6.9	24.8
Herltiz AG	Stationery/Office Supplies	940	72	24	1,205	950	629	0.26	34%	0.64	64%	11.0	0.7	30.1
Home Depot Inc	Building Materials	15,470	1,232	732	7,354	4,930	22,185	0.10	39%	1.24	33%	19.8	4.5	30.3
Just for Feet	Footware	56	5	3	90	73	497	0.06	46%	1.98	81%	105.4	6.8	72.6
Office Depot Inc	Office Supplies	5,313	266	132	2,531	1,022	3,578	0.38	40%	1.09	46%	18.5	3.5	27.1
Petco	Pet Food and Supplies	189	12	5	77	41	232	0.17	29%	0.47	27%	22.6	5.7	47.1
PetsMart	Pet Food and Supplies	818	27	(10)	448	259	1,782	0.30	11%	1.58	109%	85.8	6.9	NMF
Rio Hotel & Casino Inc	Coin Op Amusement	193	37	19	309	166	366	0.70	37%	1.01	25%	16.8	2.2	19.3
Staples	Office Supplies	2,000	110	40	1,009	385	2,465	0.71	33%	1.39	109%	38.3	6.4	45.0
Starbucks	Coffee and Supplies	465	65	26	468	312	1,656	0.27	45%	1.70	71%	32.4	5.3	53.0
Sunglass Hut	Sunglasses	290	45	17	154	72	1,605	0.59	38%	1.68	43%	56.7	22.3	83.6
Mean								0.34	37%	1.25	74%	34.1	6.6	40.8

Sources of data: Value Line Investment Survey and Bloomberg Financial Services.

EXHIBIT 9
Estimate of DCF Value, Free Cash Flows, and Weighted Average Cost of Capital

Assumptions

1 EBITDA Multiple at Exit	6
2 Tax Rates =	35%

	Jan. 1, 1996	1996	1997	1998	1999	2000	2001	2002
Estimation of Free Cash Flows								
3 Operating income		$2,142,218	$3,456,938	$5,557,401	$8,908,374	$14,247,266	$22,743,001	$36,246,940
4 Taxes		749,776	1,209,928	1,945,090	3,117,931	4,986,543	7,960,050	12,686,429
5 EBIAT		1,392,442	2,247,010	3,612,311	5,790,443	9,260,723	14,782,950	23,560,511
6 + Depreciation		228,282	340,602	515,821	789,163	1,215,577	1,880,781	2,918,501
7 − Capital expend		(2,250,000)	(3,510,000)	(5,475,600)	(8,541,936)	(13,325,420)	(20,787,655)	(32,428,743)
8 − Additions (reductions) to wkg. cap.		987,083	(102,974)	(542,007)	(459,500)	(712,784)	(688,906)	(861,122)
9 Free cash flow		357,807	(819,414)	(805,462)	(1,502,830)	(2,136,337)	(3,435,018)	(5,088,609)
10 Terminal value								234,992,647
11 Total FCF		$357,807	−$819,414	−$805,462	−$1,502,830	−$2,136,337	−$3,435,018	$229,904,038
DCF Value at End of Year	*Jan. 1, 1996*	*1996*	*1997*	*1998*	*1999*	*2000*	*2001*	*2002*
12 Annual discount rate	32.47%	29.53%	29.44%	28.56%	28.56%	28.77%	27.51%	
13 Value of enterprise	$48,047,886	$61,878,330	$80,912,505	$104,824,947	$135,267,064	$177,612,942	$229,904,038	$234,992,647
14 Value of debt	4,690,330	13,069,948	17,380,844	26,072,736	33,876,188	42,695,399	66,511,961	103,052,123
15 Value of equity	$43,357,556	$48,808,382	$63,531,661	$78,752,212	$102,390,876	$134,917,543	$163,392,078	$131,940,524
16 Market/book value of equity	23.96	23.83	22.97	19.28	14.81	10.82	8.23	4.22
Estimation of Annual Weighted Average Cost of Capital								
17 Book value of debt	$4,690,330	$13,069,948	$17,380,844	$26,072,736	$33,876,188	$42,695,399	$66,511,961	$103,052,123
18 Book value of equity	1,809,770	2,048,063	2,766,242	4,085,172	6,911,739	12,465,467	19,863,258	31,247,170
19 Book value of capital	6,500,100	15,118,012	20,147,086	30,157,908	40,787,927	55,160,866	86,375,219	134,299,292
20 Book value debt/Equity ratio	2.59	6.38	6.28	6.38	4.90	3.43	3.35	3.30
21 Market/Book value of equity	23.96	23.83	22.97	19.28	14.81	10.82	8.23	4.22
22 Market value debt/Equity ratio	0.11	0.27	0.27	0.33	0.33	0.32	0.41	0.78
23 Cost of equity	35.00%	35.00%	35.00%	35.00%	35.00%	35.00%	35.00%	35.00%
24 Cost of debt (pretax)	14%	14%	14%	14%	14%	14%	14%	14%
25 Tax rate on income	0.35	0.35	0.35	0.35	0.35	0.35	0.35	0.35
26 After-tax cost of debt	9.10%	9.10%	9.10%	9.10%	9.10%	9.10%	9.10%	9.10%
27 Weight of debt	9.8%	21.1%	21.5%	24.9%	24.9%	24.0%	28.9%	43.9%
28 Weight of equity	90.2%	78.9%	78.5%	75.1%	75.1%	76.0%	71.1%	56.1%
29 WACC	32.47%	29.53%	29.44%	28.56%	28.56%	28.77%	27.51%	23.64%

Notes: This discounted cash flow valuation of the firm employs the following features:

1. Terminal value (line 10, year 2002) is calculated as the multiple (line 1) times EBITDA (lines 3 plus 6) in the final year.
2. The weighted average cost of capital (line 29) is reestimated every year, to reflect changes in the financial leverage of the firm (lines 27 and 28).
3. The calculation intentionally models a circular reference so that the weights of capital (lines 27 and 28) are consistent with the DCF value of equity in each year (line 15).
4. The value of equity each year equals the value of the enterprise (line 13), less the value of debt outstanding (line 14).
5. The value of the enterprise each year equals the *following year's* value of the enterprise (line 13) plus free cash flow (line 13) discounted at the WACC for that year. For instance, to obtain the enterprise value at year-end 2001, the model "looks ahead" to the free cash flow for 2002 and the value of the enterprise at year-end 2002, and discounts the sum of those values back to year-end 2001 at 23.64 percent, the WACC for 2002.
6. The cost of equity of 35 percent (line 23) uses the private equity investors' required rate of return.

EXHIBIT 10
Analysis of Founders' Dilution and Wealth (values in U.S. dollars)

Assumptions

1 Percent of equity used to meet need	0%
2 Annual growth rate in number of stores	50%

	Jan. 1, 1996	1996	1997	1998	1999	2000	2001	2002
3 Incremental external financing need (from Exhibit 6, Line 35)		$12,682,948	$4,117,396	$8,401,642	$7,368,077	$8,166,149	$22,836,968	$35,070,771
4 Total value of equity raised (repurchased) (Exh. 6, L. 42)		—	—	—	—	—	—	—
5 Total market value of equity (Exh. 9, L. 15)	$43,357,556	$48,808,382	$63,531,661	$78,752,212	$102,390,876	$134,917,543	$163,392,078	$131,940,524
6 Shares outstanding at beginning of year		1,600,000	1,600,000	1,600,000	1,600,000	1,600,000	1,600,000	1,600,000
7 Sale price of new shares (Note 1)		$30.51	$39.71	$49.22	$63.99	$84.32	$102.12	$82.46
8 New shares sold (shares repurchased)	—	—	—	—	—	—	—	—
9 Ending shares outstanding		1,600,000	1,600,000	1,600,000	1,600,000	1,600,000	1,600,000	1,600,000
10 % voting control of founders (if no further outlays)		48.0%	48.0%	48.0%	48.0%	48.0%	48.0%	48.0%
11 Loss of voting % from present base of 48% (Note 2)		0.0%	0.0%	0.0%	0.0%	0.0%	0.0%	0.0%
12 EBIT coverage ratio (Exh. 7, L. 10)		1.21	1.47	1.58	1.95	2.50	2.56	2.62
13 Market/Book ratio (Exh. 9, L. 16)	23.96	23.83	22.97	19.28	14.81	10.82	8.23	4.22
14 Wealth of founders (Line 10 times Line 5)	$20,811,627	$23,428,023	$30,495,197	$37,801,062	$49,147,621	$64,760,421	$78,428,197	$63,331,452
15 Cumulative external financing need (Exh. 6, L. 21)	—	$12,682,948	$16,800,344	$25,201,986	$32,570,063	$40,736,211	$63,573,179	$98,643,951

Notes

1. The sale price of new shares is estimated as the current market value of equity less the cash to be raised through share issuance, divided by the shares outstanding at the beginning of the year.
2. Line 11 is a measure of the founders' voting dilution, and is calculated as the percentage of shares held by the founders, less 48 percent, their initial interest.

EXHIBIT 11
Sensitivity Analysis of Outcomes by Growth Rate of Stores, and Equity Issuance

1996 EBIT Coverage
% Equity Financing

		50%	60%	70%	80%	90%
	0%	2.81	3.55	4.78	7.24	14.63
	5%	2.77	3.50	4.71	7.13	14.41
	10%	2.73	3.45	4.65	7.04	14.21
	15%	2.70	3.41	4.59	6.95	14.04
Growth	20%	2.67	3.37	4.54	6.87	13.88
Rate in	25%	2.64	3.34	4.49	6.81	13.74
Stores	30%	2.62	3.31	4.45	6.74	13.62
	35%	2.60	3.28	4.41	6.69	13.50
	40%	2.58	3.25	4.38	6.63	13.40
	45%	2.56	3.23	4.35	6.59	13.30
	50%	2.54	3.21	4.32	6.54	13.21

1996 Market Value/Book Value Ratio
% Equity Financing

		50%	60%	70%	80%	90%
	0%	0.6	0.6	0.6	0.7	0.7
	5%	0.8	0.8	0.8	0.8	0.8
	10%	1.0	1.0	0.9	0.9	0.9
	15%	1.3	1.2	1.1	1.1	1.0
Growth	20%	1.6	1.5	1.4	1.3	1.2
Rate in	25%	2.0	1.8	1.7	1.6	1.5
Stores	30%	2.5	2.2	2.0	1.9	1.8
	35%	3.0	2.7	2.5	2.3	2.1
	40%	3.7	3.3	3.0	2.7	2.5
	45%	4.6	4.0	3.6	3.2	3.0
	50%	5.5	4.8	4.3	3.9	3.6

Founders' Wealth in 2002 ($ millions)
% Equity Financing

		50%	60%	70%	80%	90%
	0%	$0.2	$0.0	$0.0	$0.0	$0.0
	5%	$2.3	$1.9	$1.5	$1.2	$0.9
	10%	$4.8	$4.3	$3.8	$3.4	$3.0
	15%	$7.9	$7.3	$6.7	$6.2	$5.8
Growth	20%	$11.6	$11.0	$10.4	$9.8	$9.3
Rate in	25%	$16.3	$15.6	$14.9	$14.3	$13.7
Stores	30%	$22.0	$21.3	$20.6	$19.9	$19.3
	35%	$29.1	$28.4	$27.7	$27.0	$26.3
	40%	$37.9	$37.2	$36.5	$35.7	$35.0
	45%	$48.7	$48.0	$47.2	$46.5	$45.7
	50%	$61.9	$61.2	$60.5	$59.7	$58.9

Founders' Loss of Voting % from Present Base of 48%
% Equity Financing

		50%	60%	70%	80%	90%
	0%	−46.4%	−47.7%	−47.8%	−47.8%	−47.8%
	5%	−34.6%	−37.5%	−39.8%	−41.7%	−43.1%
	10%	−27.5%	−30.3%	−32.7%	−34.7%	−36.3%
	15%	−23.1%	−25.8%	−28.0%	−30.0%	−31.6%
Growth	20%	−20.4%	−22.8%	−24.9%	−26.8%	−28.4%
Rate in	25%	−18.6%	−20.9%	−22.9%	−24.6%	−26.2%
Stores	30%	−17.4%	−19.6%	−21.5%	−23.1%	−24.6%
	35%	−16.6%	−18.6%	−20.4%	−22.1%	−23.5%
	40%	−16.0%	−18.0%	−19.7%	−21.3%	−22.7%
	45%	−15.5%	−17.5%	−19.2%	−20.7%	−22.1%
	50%	−15.2%	−17.1%	−18.8%	−20.3%	−21.6%

Source: Casewriter analysis.

EXHIBIT 12
Sensitivity Analysis of Outcomes by Gross Margin and Growth in Sales per Square Meter

1996 Ebit Coverage

	% Gross Margin				
Growth in Sales/Meter	70%	72%	75%	77%	80%
0%	1.00	1.09	1.23	1.33	1.49
1%	0.99	1.08	1.23	1.32	1.48
2%	0.98	1.08	1.22	1.32	1.47
3%	0.98	1.07	1.21	1.31	1.47
4%	0.97	1.06	1.21	1.31	1.46
5%	0.97	1.06	1.20	1.30	1.46
6%	0.96	1.05	1.19	1.29	1.45
7%	0.96	1.05	1.19	1.29	1.44
8%	0.95	1.04	1.18	1.28	1.44

Founders' Wealth in 2002 ($ millions)

	% Gross Margin				
Growth in Sales/Meter	70%	72%	75%	77%	80%
0%	$19.5	$25.7	$35.1	$41.4	$50.8
1%	$25.2	$31.8	$41.7	$48.4	$58.3
2%	$31.1	$38.1	$48.6	$55.6	$66.1
3%	$37.4	$44.7	$55.8	$63.2	$74.3
4%	$43.9	$51.7	$63.3	$71.1	$82.8
5%	$50.7	$58.9	$71.2	$79.4	$91.7
6%	$57.8	$66.4	$79.4	$88.0	$101.0
7%	$65.2	$74.3	$88.0	$97.1	$110.7
8%	$72.9	$82.5	$96.9	$106.5	$120.9

1996 Market Value/Book Value Ratio

	% Gross Margin				
Growth in 0% Sales/Meter	70%	72%	75%	77%	80%
0%	14.0	14.6	15.3	15.8	16.4
1%	16.0	16.6	17.3	17.7	18.3
2%	18.1	18.7	19.4	19.8	20.3
3%	20.4	20.9	21.5	21.9	22.4
4%	22.8	23.2	23.8	24.2	24.6
5%	25.3	25.7	26.2	26.6	27.0
6%	27.9	28.3	28.8	29.0	29.4
7%	30.7	31.0	31.4	31.7	32.0
8%	33.6	33.8	34.2	34.4	34.7

Cumulative External Financing Need by 2002 ($millions)

	% Gross Margin				
Growth in Sales/Meter	70%	72%	75%	77%	80%
0%	$96.7	$92.9	$87.1	$83.3	$77.5
1%	$99.8	$95.8	$89.8	$85.8	$79.7
2%	$103.0	$98.8	$92.6	$88.4	$82.1
3%	$106.4	$102.1	$95.5	$91.2	$84.6
4%	$110.0	$105.5	$98.6	$94.1	$87.3
5%	$113.8	$109.0	$101.9	$97.2	$90.1
6%	$117.7	$112.8	$105.4	$100.5	$93.1
7%	$121.9	$116.7	$109.0	$103.9	$96.2
8%	$126.2	$120.9	$112.9	$107.5	$99.5

Source: Casewriter analysis.

PART 6

Management of the Corporate Capital Structure

An Introduction to Debt Policy and Value

Many factors determine how much debt a firm takes on. Chief among them ought to be the effect of the debt on the value of the firm. Does borrowing create value? If so, for whom? If not, then why do so many executives concern themselves with leverage?

If leverage affects value, then it should cause changes in either the discount rate of the firm (i.e., its weighted-average cost of capital) or the cash flows of the firm.

1. Please fill in the following:

	0% Debt/ 100% Equity	25% Debt/ 75% Equity	50% Debt/ 50% Equity
Book value of debt	0	$2,500	$5,000
Book value of equity	$10,000	$7,500	$5,000
Market value of debt	0	$2,500	$5,000
Market value of equity	$10,000	$8,350	$6,700
Pretax cost of debt	.07	.07	.07
After-tax cost of debt	.0462	.0462	.0462
Market value weights of:			
Debt	0	—	—
Equity	1.0	—	—
Unlevered beta	.8	.8	.8
Risk-free rate	.07	.07	.07
Market premium	.086	.086	.086
Cost of equity	—	—	—
Weighted average cost of capital	—	—	—
EBIT	$2,103	$2,103	$2,103
− Taxes (@ 34%)	—	—	—
EBIAT	—	—	—
+ Depreciation	$500	$500	$500
− Capital exp.	$(500)	$(500)	$(500)
Free cash flow	—	—	—
Value of assets (FCF/WACC)	—	—	—

Why does the value of assets change? Where, specifically, do the changes occur?

2. In finance, as in accounting, the two sides of the balance sheet must be equal. In the previous problem, we valued the asset side of the balance sheet. To value the other side, we must value the debt and the equity, and then add them together.

	0% Debt/ 100% Equity	25% Debt/ 75% Equity	50% Debt/ 50% Equity
Cash flow to creditors:			
Interest	0	$175	$350
Pretax cost of debt	.07	.07	.07
Value of debt:			
(CF/r_d)	—	—	—
Cash flow to shareholders:			
EBIT	$2,103	$2,103	$2,103
− Interest	—	$(175)	$(350)
Pretax profit	—	—	—
Taxes (@ 34%)	—	—	—
Net income	—	—	—
+ Depreciation	$500	$500	$500
− Capital exp.	$(500)	$(500)	$(500)
− Debt amortiz.	0	0	0
Residual cash flow	—	—	—
Cost of equity	—	—	—
Value of equity (CF/r_e)	—	—	—
Value of equity plus value of debt	—	—	—

As the firm levers up, how does the increase in value get apportioned between creditors and shareholders?

3. In the preceding problem, we divided the value of all the assets between two classes of investors—creditors and shareholders. This process tells us where the change in value is *going*, but it sheds little light on where the change is *coming from*. Let's divide the free cash flows of the firm into *pure business flows* and cash flows resulting from *financing effects*. Now, an axiom in finance is that you should discount cash flows at a rate consistent with the risk of those cash flows. Pure business flows should be discounted at the unlevered cost of equity (i.e., the cost of capital for the unlevered firm). Financing flows should be discounted at the rate of return required by the providers of debt.

	0% Debt/ 100% Equity	25% Debt/ 75% Equity	50% Debt/ 50% Equity
Pure business cash flows:			
EBIT	$2,103	$2,103	$2,103
Taxes (@ 34%)	$(715)	$(715)	$(715)
EBIAT	$1,388	$1,388	$1,388
+Depreciation	$500	$500	$500
− Capital exp.	$(500)	$(500)	$(500)
Cash flow	$1,388	$1,388	$1,388
Unlevered beta	.8	.8	.8
Risk-free rate	.07	.07	.07
Market premium	.086	.086	.086
Unlevered WACC	—	—	—

Value of pure business flows:			
(CF/Unlevered WACC)	—	—	—
Financing cash flows			
Interest	—	—	—
Tax Reduction	—	—	—
Pretax cost of debt	.07	.07	.07
Value of financing effect:			
(tax reduction/pretax cost of debt)	—	—	—
Total value (sum of values of pure			
business flows and financing effects)	—	—	—

The first three problems illustrate one of the most important theories in finance. This theory, developed by two professors, Franco Modigliani and Merton Miller, revolutionized the way we think about capital-structure policies. The M&M theory says:

$$\underset{\text{Problem 1}}{\underset{\wedge}{\substack{Value\ of \\ assets}}} = \underset{\text{Problem 2}}{\underset{\wedge}{\substack{Value\ of \\ debt}}} + \underset{\wedge}{\substack{Value\ of \\ equity}} = \substack{Value\ of \\ unlevered \\ firm} + \underset{\text{Problem 3}}{\underset{\wedge}{\substack{Value\ of \\ debt\ tax \\ shield^1}}}$$

4. What remains to be seen however, is whether shareholders are better or worse off with more leverage. Problem 2 does not tell us, because there we computed total value of equity, and shareholders care about value *per share*. Ordinarily, total value will be a good proxy for what is happening to the price per share, but in the case of a relevering firm, that may not be true. Implicitly we assumed that, as our firm in problems 1–3 levered up, it was repurchasing stock on the open market (you will note that EBIT did not change, so management was clearly not investing the proceeds from the loans in cash-generating assets). We held EBIT constant so that we could see clearly the effect of financial changes without getting them mixed up in the effects of investments. The point is that, as the firm borrows and repurchases shares, the total value of equity may decline, but the price per share may *rise*.

Now, solving for the price per share may seem impossible, because we are dealing with two unknowns—share price and change in the number of shares:

$$\text{Share price} = \frac{\text{Total market value of equity}}{\text{Original shares} \ - \ \text{Repurchased shares}}$$

But by rewriting the equation, we can put it in a form that can be solved:

$$\text{Share price} = \frac{\text{Total market value of equity} \ + \ \text{Cash paid out}}{\text{Number of original shares}}$$

Referring to the results of problem 2, let's assume that all the new debt is equal to the cash paid to repurchase shares. Please complete the following table:

---

[1]Debt tax shields can be valued by discounting the future annual tax savings at the pretax cost of debt. For debt that is assumed to be outstanding in perpetuity, the tax savings is the tax rate, t, times the interest payment, $r \times B$. The present value of this perpetual savings is $trB/r = tB$.

	0% Debt/ 100% Equity	25% Debt/ 75% Equity	50% Debt/ 50% Equity
Total market value of equity	—	—	—
Cash paid out	—	—	—
Number of original shares	1,000	1,000	1,000
Total value per share	—	—	—

5. In this set of problems, is leverage good for shareholders? Why? Is levering/unlevering the firm something shareholders can do for themselves? In what sense should shareholders pay a premium for shares of levered companies?

6. From a macroeconomic point of view, is society better off if firms use more than zero debt (up to some prudent limit)?

7. As a way of illustrating the usefulness of the M&M theory and consolidating your grasp of the mechanics, consider the following case and complete the worksheet. On March 3, 1988, Beazer Plc. (a British construction company) and Shearson Lehman Hutton, Inc. (an investment-banking firm) commenced a hostile tender offer to purchase all the outstanding stock of Koppers Company, Inc., a producer of construction materials, chemicals, and building products. Originally, the raiders offered $45 a share; subsequently, the offer was raised to $56 and then finally to $61 a share. The Koppers board generally asserted that the offers were inadequate and its management was reviewing the possibility of a major recapitalization.

To test the valuation effects of the recapitalization alternative, assume that Koppers could borrow a maximum of $1,738,095,000 at a pretax cost of debt of 10.5 percent and that the aggregate amount of debt will remain constant in perpetuity. Thus, Koppers will take on additional debt of $1,565,686,000 (i.e., $1,738,095,000 minus $172,409,000). Also assume that the proceeds of the loan would be paid as an extraordinary dividend to shareholders. **Exhibit 1** presents Koppers' book- and market-value balance sheets, assuming the capital structure before recapitalization. Please complete the work sheet for the recapitalization alternative.

EXHIBIT 1
Koppers Company, Inc. (values are in thousands)

	Before Recapitalization	After Recapitalization
Book-Value Balance Sheets		
Net working capital	$ 212,453	
Fixed assets	601,446	
Total assets	$ 813,899	
Long-term debt	172,409	
Deferred taxes, etc.	195,616	
Preferred stock	15,000	
Common equity	430,874	
Total capital	$ 813,899	
Market-Value Balance Sheets		
Net working capital	$ 212,453	
Fixed assets	1,618,081	
PV debt tax shield	58,619	
Total assets	$1,889,153	
Long-term debt	172,409	
Deferred taxes, etc.	0	
Preferred stock	15,000	
Common equity	1,701,744	
Total capital	$1,889,153	
Number of shares	28,128	
Price per share	$ 60.50	
Value to Public Shareholders		
Cash received	0	
Value of shares	$1,701,744	
Total	1,701,744	
Total per share	$ 60.50	

Structuring Corporate Financial Policy: Diagnosis of Problems and Evaluation of Strategies

This note outlines a diagnostic and prescriptive way of thinking about corporate financial policy. Successful diagnosis and prescription depend heavily on thoughtful creativity and careful judgment, so the note presents no "cookbook" solutions. Rather, it discusses the elements of good *process* and offers three basic stages in that process:

Description: The ability to describe a firm's financial policies (which have been chosen either explicitly or by default) is an essential foundation of diagnosis and prescription. Part I defines "financial structure" and discusses the design elements by which a senior financial officer must make choices. This section illustrates the complexity of a firm's financial policies.

Diagnosis: One derives a "good" financial structure by triangulating from benchmark perspectives. Then one compares the idealized and actual financial structures, looking for opportunities for improvement. Part II presents an overview of three benchmarks by which the analyst can diagnose problems and opportunities: (1) the expectations of investors; (2) the policies and behavior of competitors; and (3) the internal goals and motivations of corporate management itself. Other perspectives may also exist. Parts III, IV, and V discuss in detail the estimation and application of the three benchmarks. These sections emphasize artful homework and economy of effort by focusing on key considerations, questions, and information. The goal is to derive insights unique to each benchmark, rather than to churn data endlessly.

Prescription: Action recommendations should spring from the insights gained in description and diagnosis. Rarely, however, do unique solutions or ideas exist; rather,

This note was prepared by Professor Robert F. Bruner and draws on collaborative work with Katherine L. Updike.

the typical chief financial officer (CFO) must have a *view* about competing suggestions. Part VI addresses the task of comparing competing proposals. Part VII presents the conclusion.

PART I: IDENTIFYING CORPORATE FINANCIAL POLICY: THE ELEMENTS OF ITS DESIGN

You can observe a lot just by watching.
—Yogi Berra

The first task for financial advisors and decision makers is to understand the firm's *current* financial policy. Doing so is a necessary foundation for diagnosing problems and prescribing remedies. This section presents an approach for identifying the firm's financial policy, based on careful analysis of the *tactics* by which that policy is implemented.

The Concept of Corporate Financial Policy

The notion that firms *have* a distinct financial policy is startling to some analysts and executives. Occasionally, a chief financial officer will say, "All I do is get the best deal I can whenever we need funds." Almost no CFO would admit otherwise. In all probability, however, the firm has a more substantive policy than the CFO admits to. Even a style of myopia or opportunism is, after all, a policy.

Some executives will argue that calling financing a "policy" is too fancy. They say that financing is reactive: it happens after all investment and operational decisions have been made. How can reaction be a policy? At other times, one hears an executive say, "Our financial policy is simple. . . ." Attempts to characterize a financial structure as reactive or simplistic overlook the considerable richness of choice that confronts the financial manager.

Finally, some analysts make the mistake of "one-size-fits-all" thinking; that is, they assume that financial policy is mainly driven by the economics of a certain industry and they overlook the firm-specific nature of financial policy. Firms in the same, well-defined industry can have very different financial policies. The reason is that financial policy is a matter of *managerial choice.*

"Corporate financial policy" is a set of broad *guidelines* or a preferred *style* to guide the raising of capital and distribution of value. Policies should be set to support the mission and strategy of the firm. As the environment changes, policies should adapt.

The analyst of financial policy must come to terms with its ambiguity. Policies are guidelines; they are imprecise. Policies are products of managerial choice rather than dictates of an economic model. Policies change over time. Nevertheless, the framework in this note can help the analyst define a firm's corporate financial policy with enough focus to identify potential problems, prescribe remedies, and make decisions.

The Elements of Financial Policy

Every financial structure reveals underlying financial policies through the following seven elements of financial-structure design:[1]

1. *Mix* of classes of capital (such as debt versus equity, or common stock versus retained earnings): *How heavily does the firm rely on different classes of capital? Is the reliance on debt reasonable in light of the risks the firm faces and the nature of its industry and technology?* Mix may be analyzed through capitalization ratios, debt-service coverage ratios, and the firm's sources-and-uses-of-funds statement (where the analyst should look for the origins of the new additions to capital in the recent past). Many firms exhibit a pecking order of financing: they seek to fill their funds needs, through retentions of profits, then through debt, and, finally, through the issuance of new shares. *Does the firm observe a particular pecking order in its acquisition of new capital?*

2. *Maturity structure of the firm's capital:* To describe the choices made about the maturity of outstanding securities is to be able to infer the judgments the firm made about its priorities—for example, future financing requirements and opportunities or relative preference for refinancing[2] risk versus reinvestment[3] risk. A risk-neutral position with respect to maturity would be where the life of the firm's assets equals the life of the firm's liabilities. Most firms accept an inequality in one direction or the other. This might be due to ignorance, or to sophistication: managers might have a strong internal "view" about their ability to reinvest or refinance. Ultimately, we want managers to maximize value, not minimize risk. The absence of a perfect maturity hedge might reflect managers' better-informed bets about the future of the firm and markets. Measuring the maturity structure of the firm's capital can yield insights into the bets that managers are apparently making. The standard measures of maturity are term to maturity, average life, and duration. *Are the lives of the firm's assets and liabilities roughly matched? If not, what gamble is the firm taking (i.e., is it showing an appetite for refunding risk or interest-rate risk)?*

3. *Basis of the firm's coupon and dividend payments:* In simplest terms, basis addresses the firm's preference for fixed or floating rates of payment and is a useful tool in fathoming management's judgment regarding the future course of interest rates. Interest-rate derivatives provide the financial officer with choices conditioned by caps, floors, and other

---

[1] For parsimony, this note will restrict its scope to these seven items. One can, however, imagine other dimensions than those listed here.

[2] Refinancing risk exists where the life of the firm's assets is *more* than the life of the firm's liabilities. In other words, the firm will need to replace (or "roll over") the capital originally obtained to buy the asset. The risk of refinancing is the chance that the firm will not be able to obtain funds on advantageous terms (or at all) at the roll-over date.

[3] Reinvestment risk exists where the life of the firm's assets is *less* than the life of the firm's liabilities. In other words, the firm will need to replace (or "roll over") the investment which the capital originally financed. The risk of reinvestment is the chance that the firm will not be able to reinvest the capital on advantageous terms at the roll-over date.

structured options. Understanding the basis choices of management can reveal some of the fundamental "bets" management is placing, even when it has decided to "do nothing." *What is the firm's relative preference for fixed or floating interest rates? Are the firm's operating returns fixed or floating?*

4. *Currency* addresses the global aspect of a firm's financial opportunities. These opportunities are expressed in two ways: (a) management of the firm's exposure to foreign exchange rate fluctuations, and (b) exploitation of unusual financing possibilities in global capital markets. Exchange rate exposure arises when a firm earns income (or pays expenses) in a range of currencies. Whether and how a firm hedges this exposure can reveal "bets" that management is making about the future movement of exchange rates and the future currency mix of the firm's cash flows. The financial policy analyst should look for foreign-denominated securities in the firm's capital and for swap, option, futures, and forward contracts—all of these can be used to manage the firm's foreign exchange exposure. The other way that currency matters to the financial policy analyst is as an indication of the willingness of management to source its capital "offshore." This is an indication of sophistication and of "having a view" about the parity of exchange rates with security returns around the world. In a perfectly integrated global capital market, the theory of interest rate parity would posit the futility of finding "bargain financing" offshore. But global capital markets are not perfectly integrated, and interest rate parity rarely holds everywhere. Experience suggests that financing bargains may exist temporarily. Offshore financing may suggest an interest in finding and exploiting such bargains. *Is the currency denomination of the firm's capital consistent with the currency denomination of the firm's operating cash flows? Do the balance sheet footnotes show evidence of foreign exchange hedging? Also, is the company in effect sourcing capital on a global basis or is it focusing narrowly on domestic capital markets?*

5. *Exotica:* Every firm faces a spectrum of financing alternatives, ranging from "plain vanilla" bonds and stocks to hybrids and one-of-a-kind, highly tailored securities.[4] This element considers management's relative preference for financial innovation. Where a firm positions itself on this spectrum can shed light on management's openness to new ideas, intellectual originality, and, possibly, opportunistic tendencies. As a general matter, option-linked securities often appear in corporate finance where there is some disagreement between issuers and investors about a firm's prospects. For instance, managers of high-growth firms will foresee rapid expansion and vaulting stock prices; bond investors, not having the benefit of inside information, might only see high risk— issuing a convertible bond might be a way to allow the bond investors to capitalize the risk[5] and enjoy the creation of value through growth, in return for accepting a lower current

---

[4] Examples of highly tailored securities include exchangeable and convertible bonds (such as those issued by Chubb Company), hybrid classes of common stock (such as General Motors' class E and H shares), and contingent-securities (such as Eli Lilly's contingent payment unit, a dividend-paying equity issued in connection with an acquisition).

[5] In general, the call options embedded in a convertible bond will be more valuable the greater the volatility of the underlying asset.

yield. Also, the circumstances under which exotic securities were issued are often fascinating episodes in a company's history. *Based on past financings, what is the firm's appetite for issuing exotic securities? Why have the firm's exotic securities been tailored as they are?*

6. *External control:* Any management team probably prefers little outside control. One must recognize that, in any financial structure, management has made choices about subtle control trade-offs, including *who* might exercise control (e.g., creditors, existing shareholders, new shareholders, or a raider) and the control *trigger* (e.g., default on a loan covenant, passing a preferred stock dividend, a shareholder vote). How management structures control triggers (e.g., the tightness of loan covenants) or forestalls discipline (e.g., through the adoption of poison pills and other takeover defenses) can reveal insights about management's fears and expectations. Clues about external-control choices may be found in credit covenants, collateral pledges, the terms of preferred shares, the profile of the firm's equity holders, the voting rights of common stock, corporate bylaws, and antitakeover defenses. *In what ways has management defended against or yielded to external control?*

7. *Distribution* seeks to determine any patterns in (a) the way the firm markets its securities (i.e., acquires capital) and (b) the way the firm delivers value to its investors (i.e., returns capital). Regarding marketing, insights emerge from knowing where a firm's securities are listed for trading, how often shares are sold, and who advises the sale of securities (the advisor a firm attracts is one indication of its sophistication). Regarding delivery of value, the two generic strategies involve dividends or capital gains. Some companies will pay low or no dividends and force their shareholders to take returns in the form of capital gains. Other companies will pay material dividends, even borrowing to do so. Still others will repurchase shares, split shares, and declare extraordinary dividends. Managers' choices about delivering value yield clues about management's beliefs about investors and about the company's ability to satisfy investor needs. *How have managers chosen to deliver value to shareholders, and with whose assistance have they issued securities?*

A Comparative Illustration

The value of looking at a firm's financial structure through these seven design elements is that the insights they provide can become a basis for developing a broad, detailed picture of the firm's financial policies. Also, the seven elements become an organizational framework for the wealth of financial information that is typically available on publicly owned companies.

Consider the examples of Reebok International Ltd., which manufactures high-quality footwear, and The Limited, Inc., a women's clothing retailer. Sources such as *Moody's Industrial Manual* distill information from annual reports and regulatory filings and permit the analyst to draw conclusions about the seven elements of each firm's financial policy. Drawing on the financial results for 1990, analysts may glean the following insights about the policies of Reebok and The Limited:

Elements of Financial Policy	Reebok International Ltd.	The Limited, Inc.
Mix	**Equity Orientation** • Debt/assets = 0.096. • Sold equity 1986, 1987 • Huge cash balance • Debt rating A3 • Acquisitions financed by stock swap or cash from stock sale	**Moderate Debt** • Debt/assets = 0.18 • Debt rating A1 • No equity sold since initial public offering in 1971 • Finances acquisitions with stock swaps • Unused bank lines equal $800 million
Maturity	**Medium to Long** • Avg. life = 7.5 years	**Barbell**[6] • Avg. life = 3.7 years • 78% @ 1 year • 22% @ 9 years • Long-term debt funds finance subsidiary
Basis	**Fixed Rates** • 7% of debt is floating rate • Replaces floating-rate bank debt with equity and fixed-rate debt	**Mixed** • 44% of debt is floating rate
Currency	**Exclusively US$**	**Exclusively US$**
Exotica	**No Exotics** • Modest use of leases	**No Exotics, but . . .** • Uses commercial paper as source of long-term capital • Bonds sold in book-entry form to reduce administrative costs[7] • A retailer with no large lease obligations! • Apparently prefers to borrow and buy
Control	**Favors Large Stockholders** • Noncumulative voting for directors • Debt unsecured and callable	**Debt** is unsecured but noncallable **Significant investors** • Two Wexner family members on board (Wexner is CEO) • Cumulative voting[8] for directors
Distribution	**Steady Dividends** • Raised dividends when earnings fell in 1988 • Payout 13–24%	**Capital Gains** • Rapid growth • Many stock splits • Declining dividend-payout trend: 19%, 17.5%, 16.6%
	Some International • Sold shares abroad in 1987 • See name	**Some International** • Listed for trading in New York, London, Tokyo
	Loyal to Advisor • Kidder underwrote all equity and debt • Agents: Citibank and Bank of Boston	**Various Advisors** • Bear Stearns, Salomon, Morgan Stanley • Agents: BONY, First Chicago

---

[6] A "barbell" maturity structure is bimodal, with debt coming due mainly in both the near term and the far term. Some experts believe that such a maturity structure hedges against future interest-rate movements: if rates fall, the short-term debt will exploit the trend; if rates rise, the long-term debt mitigates the impact.

[7] The Moody's citation reveals that the bonds will be represented by a single "global security" deposited with the Depository Trust Co., a subsidiary of the New York Stock Exchange that settles "paperless" securities transactions. Under "book-entry" registration, investors receive no securities, only an acknowledgment that securities are held for them on account at intermediaries such as Depository Trust. Book-entry registration may lower administrative costs for the issuer.

[8] Cumulative voting is a scheme of shareholder elections of directors whereby shareholders may cast all their votes, cumulatively, for one person. Thus, if four directors' seats are to be filled, the shareholder may cast as many as four votes for one candidate. Cumulative voting is viewed as a means of protecting the representation of minority or dissident blocs of shareholders.

As the table shows, standard information available on public companies such as these yields important contrasts in the financial policies of the two firms. Note that the insights are *informed guesses:* neither of these firms explicitly describes its financial policies. Nonetheless, with practice and good information, the validity of the guesses can be high.

Reebok and The Limited present distinctly different policy profiles. Reebok's is a conservative policy in almost every dimension. The Limited's is sophisticated and slightly more aggressive. Two such firms would warrant very different sets of questions by a director or outside financial advisor. The key idea is that financial policies can be characterized by the tracks they leave. Good strategic assessment begins with good "tracking" of current or past policy.

PART II: GENERAL FRAMEWORK FOR DIAGNOSING FINANCIAL POLICY OPPORTUNITIES AND PROBLEMS

Having parsed the choices embedded in the firm's financial structure, one must ask, "Were these the *right* choices?" What is "right" is a matter of the context and the clienteles to which management must respond. A firm has many potential claimants.[9] The discussion that follows will focus on the perspectives of competitors, investors, and senior corporate managers.

1. *Does the financial policy create value?*

   From the standpoint of investors, the best financial structure will (a) maximize shareholder wealth, (b) maximize the value of the entire firm (i.e., the market value of assets), and (c) minimize the firm's weighted-average cost of capital. When these conditions occur, the firm makes the best trade-offs among choices on each of the seven dimensions of financial policy. This analysis is all within the context of the *market* conditions.

2. *Does the financial policy create competitive advantage?*

   Competitors should matter in the design of corporate financial policy. Financial structure can enhance or constrain competitive advantage mainly by opening or foreclosing avenues of competitive response over time. Thus, a manager should critically assess the strategic options created or destroyed by a particular financial structure. Also, assuming that they are reasonably well managed, competitors' financial structures are probably an indicator of good financial policy in a particular industry. Thus, a manager should want

---

[9] With a moment's reflection, the analyst will call up a number of claimants, or "stakeholders," or clienteles, whose interests the company might serve. Managers, customers, and investors are often the first to come to mind. Creditors (e.g., bankers) often have interests that are different from equity investors. Workers (and unions) often make tangible claims on the firm. Governments, through their taxing and regulatory powers, do so as well. One might extend the list to environmentalists and other social activists. The possibilities are almost limitless. For parsimony, this discussion treats only the three perspectives that yield the most insight about financial policy.

to know how his or her firm's financial structure compares to the peer group. In short, this line of thinking seeks to evaluate the relative position of the firm in its competitive environment on the basis of financial structure.

3. *Does the financial policy sustain the vision of senior management?*

The internal perspective tests the appropriateness of a capital structure from the standpoint of the expectations and capacities of the corporate organization itself. The analyst begins with an assessment of corporate strategy and the resulting stream of cash requirements and resources anticipated in the future. The realism of the plan should be tested against expected macroeconomic variations, as well as against possible but unexpected financial strains. A good financial structure meets the classic maxim of corporate finance, "Don't run out of cash": in other words, the ideal financial structure adequately funds the growth goals and dividend payouts of the firm without severely diluting the firm's current equity owners. The concept of self-sustainable growth provides a straightforward test of this ideal.

The next three sections will discuss these perspectives in more detail.

All three perspectives are not likely to offer a completely congruent assessment of financial structure. The investor's view looks at the *economic* consequences of a financial structure; the competitor's view considers *strategic* consequences; the internal view addresses the *survival and ambitions* of the firm. The three views ask entirely different questions; an analyst should not be surprised when the answers diverge.

Rather like estimating the height of a distant mountain through the haze, the analyst develops a concept of the best financial structure by a process of *triangulation.* Triangulation involves weighing the importance of each of the perspectives as *complements* rather than as substitutes, identifying points of consistency, and making artful judgments where the perspectives diverge.

The goal of this analysis should be to articulate concretely the design of the firm's financial structure, preferably in terms of the seven elements discussed in Section I. This exercise entails developing notes, comments, and calculations for every one of the cells of this analytical grid:

Elements of Financial Structure	Current Structure	Investor View	Competitor View	Internal View	Evaluation/ Comments
1. Mix					
2. Maturity					
3. Basis					
4. Currency					
5. Exotica					
6. External Control					
7. Distribution					

No chart can completely anticipate the difficulties, quirks, and exceptions that the analyst will undoubtedly encounter. What matters most, however, is a way of thinking about the financial-structure design problem that encourages both critical thinking and organized, efficient digestion of information.

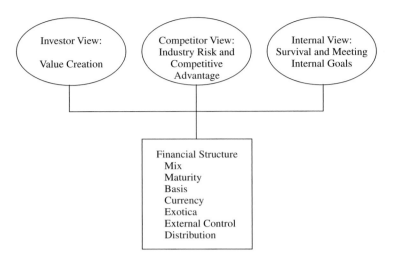

FIGURE 1
Overview of Financial-Structure Analysis

Figure 1 summarizes the approach presented in this section. Good financial-structure analysis develops three complementary perspectives on financial structure, then blends those perspectives into prescription.

PART III: ANALYZING FINANCIAL POLICY FROM THE INVESTORS' VIEWPOINT[10]

In finance theory, the investors' expectations should influence all managerial decisions. This theory follows the legal doctrine that firms should be managed in the interests of their owners. It also recognizes the economic idea that, if investors' needs are satisfied after all other claims on the firm are settled, then the firm must be "healthy." The investors' view also confronts the reality of capital-market discipline: the best defense against a hostile takeover (or other type of intrusion) is a high stock price. The threat of capital-market discipline has done more in the 1980s and 1990s to rivet the attention of management on *value creation* than any academic theories.

Academic theory, however, is extremely useful in identifying value-creating strategies. Economic value is held to be the present value of expected future cash flows discounted at a rate consistent with the risk of those cash flows. Considerable care must be given to the

---

[10] Excellent summaries of the investors' orientation are found in Tom Copeland, Tim Koller, and Jack Murrin, *Valuation: Measuring and Managing the Value of Companies,* 2nd ed. (New York: Wiley, 1994); and Alfred Rappaport, *Creating Shareholder Value,* 2nd ed. (New York: Free Press, 1997).

estimation of cash flows and discount rates (a review of discounted-cash-flow [DCF] valuation is beyond the scope of this note). Theory suggests that leverage can create value through the *benefits of debt-tax shields* and can destroy value through the *costs of financial distress.* The balance of these costs and benefits depends on specific capital-market conditions, which are conveyed by the debt and equity costs that capital providers impose on the firm. Academic theory's bottom line is:

> An efficient (i.e., value-optimizing) financial structure is one that simultaneously minimizes the weighted-average cost of capital and maximizes the share price and value of the enterprise.

The investors' perspective is a rigorous approach to evaluating financial structures: valuation analysis of the firm and its common stock under existing and alternative financial structures. The "best" structure will be one that creates the most value.

The phrase "alternative financial structures" is necessarily ambiguous but should be interpreted to include a wide range of alternatives, including leveraged buyout, leveraged recapitalization, spinoffs, carve-outs, and even liquidation. However radical the latter alternatives may seem, the analyst must understand that investment bankers and corporate raiders routinely consider these alternatives. To anticipate the thinking of these agents of change, the analyst must replicate their homework.

Careful analysis does not rest with a final number, but rather considers a range of elements:

Cost of debt: The analysis focuses on yields to maturity and the spreads of those yields over the Treasury yield curve. Floating rates are always effective rates of interest.

Cost of equity: The assessment uses as many approaches as possible, including the capital-asset pricing model, the dividend-discount model, the financial-leverage equation, the earnings/price model, and any other avenues that seem appropriate. Though it is fallible, the capital-asset pricing model has the most rigor.

Debt/Equity Mix: The relative proportions of types of capital in the capital structure are important factors in computing the weighted-average cost of capital. All capital should be estimated on a *market-value* basis.

Price/Earnings Ratio, Market/Book Ratio EBIT Multiple: Comparing these values to average levels of the entire capital market or an industry group can provide an alternative check on the valuation of the firm.

Bond Rating: The creditors' view of the firm is important. S&P and Moody's publish average financial ratios for bond-rating groups. Even for a firm with no publicly rated debt outstanding, simple ratio analysis can reveal a firm's likely rating category and its current cost of debt.

Ownership: The relative mix of individual and institutional owners and the presence of block holders with potentially hostile intentions can help shed light on the current pricing of a firm's securities.

Short Position: A large, short-sale position on the firm's stock can indicate that some traders believe a decline in share price is imminent.

To conclude, the first rule of financial policy analysis is *Think like an investor.* The investors' view assesses the value of a firm's shares under alternative financial structures and the existence of any strongly positive or negative perceptions in the capital markets about the firm's securities.

PART IV: ANALYZING FINANCIAL POLICY FROM A COMPETITIVE PERSPECTIVE

The competitive perspective matters to senior executives for two important reasons. First, it gives an indication about (1) "standard practice" in the industry and (2) the strategic position of the firm relative to the competition. Second, it implies rightly that finance can be a strategic competitive instrument.[11]

The competitive perspective may be the hardest of the three benchmarks to assess: there are few clear signposts in industry dynamics, and, as most industries become increasingly global, the comparisons become even more difficult to make. Despite the difficulty of this analysis, however, senior executives give inordinate attention to it. The well-versed analyst must, therefore, be able to assess the ability of current policy (and its alternatives) to maintain or improve its competitive position.

This analysis does not proceed scientifically, but rather evolves iteratively toward an accurate assessment of the situation.[12] The steps might be defined as follows:

1. Define the universe of competitors.
2. "Spread" the data and financial ratios on the firm and its competitors in comparative fashion.
3. Identify similarities and, more importantly, differences. Probe into anomalies. Question the data and the peer sample.
4. Add information needed, such as a foreign competitor, another ratio, and historical normalization, etc.
5. Discuss or clarify the information with the CFO or industry expert.

As the information grows, the questions will become more probing. What is the historical growth pattern? Why did the XYZ company suddenly increase leverage or keep a large cash balance? Did the acquisition of a new line actually provide access to new markets? Are changes in dividend policy or debt mix and maturity related to new products and markets?

Economy of effort demands that the analyst begin with a few ratios and data that can be easily obtained (e.g., from *Value Line,* 10Ks, etc.) If a company is in several industries and does not have pure competitors, choose group-divisional competitors and, to the extent possible, use segment information to devise ratios that will be valid (i.e., operating income to sales, rather than an after-tax equivalent). Do not forget information that may be outside the financial statements and may be critical to competitive survival, such as geographic diversification, research and development expenditures, and union activity. For some industries, other key ratios are available through trade groups, such as same-store sales and capacity analyses. Whatever the inadequacy of the data, the comparisons will provide direction for subsequent analysis.

---

[11] For a discussion of finance as a competitive instrument, see the classic work, *Financial Strategy: Studies in the Creation, Transfer, and Destruction of Shareholder Value,* William E. Fruhan, Jr., (Homewood: Irwin, 1979).

[12] A good overview of industry and competitor analysis may be found in Michael Porter, *Competitive Analysis* (New York: Free Press, 1979). An excellent survey of possible information sources on firms is in Leonard M. Fuld, *Competitor Intelligence* (New York: Wiley, 1985).

The ratios and data to be used will depend on the course of analysis. An analyst could start with the following general types of measures with which to compare a competitor group:

1. Size: sales, market value, number of employees or countries, market share.
2. Asset productivity: return on assets (ROA), return on invested capital, market to book value.
3. Shareholder wealth: price/earnings (P/E), return on market value.
4. Predictability: Beta, historical trends.
5. Growth: 1–10 year compound growth of sales, profits, assets, and market value of equity.
6. Financial flexibility: debt-to-capital, debt ratings, cash-flow coverage, estimates of cost of capital.
7. Other significant industry issues: unfunded pension liabilities, post-retirement medical-benefit obligations, environmental liabilities, capacity, research and development expense to sales, percentage of insider control, etc.

One of the key issues to resolve in analyzing the comparative data is whether all the peer-group members display the same results and trends. Inevitably, they will not—which begs the question, why not? Trends in asset productivity and globalization are affecting competitors differently and eliciting a range of strategic responses. This phenomenon should stimulate further research.

The analyst should augment personal research efforts with the work of industry analysts. Securities analysts, consultants, academicians, and journalists, both through their written work and via telephone conversations, can provide valuable insights based on extensive personal contacts in the industry.[13]

Analyzing competitors develops insights into the range of financial structures in the industry and the appropriateness of your firm's structure in comparison. Developing these insights is more a matter of qualitative judgment rather than letting numbers speak for themselves. For instance:

1. Suppose your firm is a highly leveraged computer manufacturer with an uneven record of financial performance. Should it unlever? You discover that the peer group of computer manufacturers is substantially equity financed, owing largely to the rapid rate of technological innovation and the predation of a few large players in the industry. The *strategic rationale* for low leverage is to survive the business and short-product-life cycles. Yes, it might be good to unlever.
2. Suppose your firm is an airline and finances its equipment purchases with flotations of commercial paper. The average life of the firm's liabilities is four years, while the average life of the firm's assets is 15 years. Should the airline refinance its debt using securities with longer maturity? You discover that the peer group of airlines finances its assets with leases, equipment-trust certificates, and project-finance deals that almost exactly match the economic lives of assets and liabilities. The *strategic rationale* for lengthening the maturity structure of liabilities is to hedge against yield-curve changes that might

---

[13] See, for instance, *Nelson's Guide to Securities Research* for a directory of securities analysts. The indexes to *The Wall Street Journal,* and the Frost & Sullivan *Predicast* can give quick overviews of industry trends.

adversely affect your firm's ability to refinance, yet leave its peer competitors relatively unaffected.

3. Here's a trickier example: your firm is the last nationwide supermarket chain that is publicly held; all other major supermarket chains have gone private in LBOs. Should your firm lever up through a leveraged-share repurchase? Competitor analysis reveals that other firms are struggling to meet debt-service payments on already thin margins and that a major shift in customer patronage may be under way. You conclude that price competition in selected markets would trigger a realignment in market shares in your firm's favor because the competitors have little pricing flexibility. In this case, adjusting to the industry-average leverage would not be appropriate.

PART V: DIAGNOSING FINANCIAL POLICY FROM AN INTERNAL PERSPECTIVE[14]

Internal analysis is the third major screen of a firm's financial structure. It accounts for the expected cash requirements and resources of a firm, and tests the consistency of the firm's financial structure with the profitability, growth, and dividend goals of the firm. The classic tools of internal analysis are the forecast cash flow, financial statements, and sources-and-uses-of-funds statements. The standard banker's credit analysis is consistent with this approach.

The essence of this approach is a concern for (a) the preservation of the firm's *financial flexibility,* (b) the *sustainability* of the firm's financial policies and (c) the *feasibility* of the firm's strategic goals. For instance, the long-term goals may call for a doubling of sales in five years. The business plan for achieving this goal may call for the construction of a greenfield plant in year one, then regional-distribution systems in years two and three. Substantial working-capital investments will be necessary in years two through five. How this growth is to be financed has huge implications for your firm's financial structure *today.* Typically, an analyst addresses this problem by forecasting the financial performance of the firm, experimenting with different financing sequences and choosing the best one, then determining the structure that makes the best foundation for that financing sequence. This analysis implies the need to maintain future financial flexibility.

Financial Flexibility

Financial flexibility is easily measured as the excess cash and unused debt capacity on which the firm might call. In addition, there may be other reserves such as unused land or excess stocks of raw materials which could be liquidated. All reserves that could be mobi-

---

[14] An excellent overview of the "internal" view of a firm's financial policies may be found in Gordon Donaldson, *Managing Corporate Wealth: The Operation of a Comprehensive Financial Goals System* (New York: Praeger, 1984).

lized should be reflected in an analysis of financial flexibility. Illustrating with the narrower definition (cash and unused debt capacity), one can measure financial flexibility as follows:

1. Select a target minimum debt rating acceptable to the firm. Many CFOs will have in mind a target minimum, such as a BBB/Baa rating.
2. Determine the book[15] value debt/equity mix consistent with the minimum rating. Standard & Poor's, for instance, publishes average financial ratios (including debt/equity) that are associated with each debt-rating category.[16]
3. Determine the book value of debt consistent with the debt/equity ratio from step 2. This gives the amount of debt that would be outstanding if the firm moved to the minimum acceptable bond rating.
4. Estimate financial flexibility using the following formula:

Financial flexibility = Excess cash + (Debt at minimum rating - Current debt outstanding)

The amount estimated by this formula indicates the financial reserves on which the firm can call to exploit unusual surprising opportunities (such as the chance to acquire a competitor) or to defend against unusual threats (such as a price war, sudden product obsolescence, or a labor strike).

Self-sustainable Growth

A shorthand test for sustainability and internal consistency is the self-sustainable growth model. This model is based on one key assumption: over the forecast period, the firm sells no new shares of stock (this assumption is entirely consistent with the actual behavior of firms over the long run).[17] As long as the firm does not change its mix of debt and equity, the self-sustainable model implies that assets can grow only as fast as equity grows. Thus the issue of sustainability is significantly determined by the firm's return on equity (ROE) and dividend payout ratio (DPO):

$$\text{Self-sustainable growth rate of assets} = \text{ROE} \times (1 - \text{DPO})$$

The test of feasibility of any long-term plan involves comparing the growth rate implied by this formula and the *targeted* growth rate dictated by a management plan. If the targeted growth rate equals the implied rate, then the firm's financial policies are just in balance. If the implied rate exceeds the targeted rate, the firm will gradually become more liquid, creating an asset-deployment opportunity. If the targeted rate exceeds the implied rate, the firm must raise more capital, either by selling stock, levering up, or reducing the dividend payout.

---

[15] Ideally one would work with market values rather than book values. But the rating agencies compute their financial ratios only on a book-value basis. Since this analysis in effect mimics the perspective of the rating agencies, the analyst must work with book values.

[16] See *CreditWeek,* published by Standard & Poor's.

[17] From 1950 to 1989, only 5 percent of the growth of the U.S. economy's business sector was financed by the sale of new common stock. The most significant sources were short-term liabilities, long-term liabilities, and retained earnings, in that order.

Management policies can be modeled finely by recognizing that ROE can be decomposed into various factors using two classic formulas:

DuPont System of Ratios: ROE = P/S × S/A × A/E

P/S = profit dividend by sales or net margin, a measure of profitability

S/A = sales divided by assets, a measure of asset productivity

A/E = assets divided by equity, a measure of financial leverage

Financial-Leverage Equation:[18] $ROE = ROTC + ((ROTC - K_d) \times (D/E))$

$ROTC$ = return on total capital

K_d = cost of debt

D/E = debt divided by equity, a measure of leverage

Inserting either of these formulas into the self-sustainable growth rate equation gives a richer model of the drivers of self-sustainability—one sees, in particular, the importance of internal operations. The self-sustainable growth model can be expanded to reflect explicitly measures of a firm's operating and financial policies.

The self-sustainable growth rate model tests the internal consistency of a firm's operating and financial policies. *This model, however, provides no guarantee that a strategy will maximize value.* Value creation does not begin with growth targets; growth per se does not necessarily lead to value creation, as the growth-by-acquisition strategies of the 1960s and 1970s abundantly illustrate. Also, the adoption of growth targets may foreclose other, more profitable strategies—these targets may invite managers to undertake investments yielding less than the cost of capital. Meeting sales or assets-growth targets can destroy value. Thus, any sustainable-growth analysis must be augmented by questions about the value-creation potential of a given set of corporate policies. These questions include: (1) What are the magnitude and duration of investment returns as compared to the firm's cost of capital? (2) With what alternative set of policies is the firm's share price maximized? With questions such as these, the investor orientation discussed in Part III is turned inward to double-check the appropriateness of any inferences derived from financial forecasts of sources-and-uses of funds statement and from the analysis of the self-sustainable growth model.

PART VI: WHAT IS BEST?

Any financial structure evaluated against the perspectives of investors, competitors, and the internal goals will probably show opportunities for improvement. Most often, CFOs choose to make changes at the margin rather than tinker radically with a financial structure. For

---

[18] This is the classic expression for the cost of equity, as originally presented in the work of Nobel Prize winners Franco Modigliani and Merton Miller.

changes large and small, however, the analyst must develop a framework for judgment and prescription.

The following framework is a way of identifying the tradeoffs among "goods" and "bads" rather than finding the right answer. Having identified the trade-offs implicit in any alternative structure, it remains for the CFO and adviser to choose the structure with the most attractive trade-offs.

The key elements of evaluation are:

Flexibility: the ability to meet unforeseen financing requirements as they arise—these requirements may be favorable (e.g., a sudden acquisition opportunity) or unfavorable (e.g., Source Perrier and the benzene scare). Flexibility may involve liquidating assets or tapping the capital markets in adverse market environments or both. Flexibility can be measured by bond ratings, coverage ratios, capitalization ratios, liquidity ratios, and the identification of salable assets.

Risk: the predictable variability in the firm's business. Such variability may be due to both macroeconomic factors (e.g., consumer demand) and industry- or firm-specific factors (e.g., product life cycles, biannual strikes in advance of wage negotiations). To some extent, past experience may indicate the future range of variability in earnings before interest and taxes (EBIT) and cash flow. High leverage tends to amplify these predictable business swings. The risk associated with any given financial structure can be assessed by EBIT-EPS (earnings per share) analysis, break-even analysis, the standard deviation of EBIT, and beta. In theory, beta should vary directly with leverage.[19]

Income: this compares financial structures on the basis of value creation. Measures such as DCF value, projected ROE, EPS, and cost of capital indicate the comparative value effects of alternative financial structures.

Control: alternative financial structures may imply changes in control or different control constraints on the firm as indicated by the percentage distribution of share ownership and by the structure of debt covenants.

Timing: asks the question of whether the current capital market environment is the right moment to implement any alternative financial structure, and what the implications for future financings will be if the proposed structure is adopted. The current market environment can be assessed by examining the Treasury yield curve, the trend in the movement of interest rates, the existence of any "windows" in the market for new issues of securities, P/E multiple trends, etc. Sequencing considerations are implicitly captured in the assumptions underlying alternative DCF value estimates and can be explicitly examined by looking at annual EPS and ROE streams under alternative financing sequences.

---

[19] This relationship is illustrated by the formula for estimating a firm's levered beta:

$$B_l = B_u \times [1 + (1 - t) \times D/E]$$

B_l = levered beta
B_u = unlevered beta
t = firm's marginal tax rate
D/E = the firm's market-value, debt-to-equity ratio.

This flexibility, risk, income, control, and timing (FRICT) framework can be used to indicate the relative strengths and weaknesses of alternative financing plans. To use a simple example, suppose that your firm is considering two financial structures: (1) 60 percent debt and 40 percent equity (i.e., debt will be issued); and (2) 40 percent debt and 60 percent equity (i.e., equity will be issued). Also, suppose that your analysis of the two structures under the investor, competitor, and internal-analysis screens leads you to make this basic comparison:

	60 Percent Debt	40 Percent Debt
Flexibility	"Lowish," not bad	High
	BBB debt rating	AA debt rating
	$50 million reserves	$300 million reserves
Risk	High	Medium
	EBIT coverage = 1.5	EBIT coverage = 3.0
Income	Good-to-high	Mediocre
	DCF Value = $20/share	DCF Value = $12 per share (dilutive)
Control	Covenants tight	Covenants not restrictive
	No voting dilution	10% voting dilution
Timing	Interest rates low today	Equity multiples are low today
	Risky sequence	Low risk sequence for future

The 60 percent debt structure is favored on the grounds of income, control, and today's market conditions. The 40 percent debt structure is favored on the grounds of flexibility, risk, and the long-term financial sequencing. This example boils down to a decision between "eat well" and "sleep well." It remains up to senior management to make the difficult choice between the two alternatives, giving careful attention to the views of the investor, competitors, and managers.

PART VII: CONCLUSION

Description, diagnosis, and prescription in financial structuring form an iterative process. It is quite likely that the CFO in the eat well/sleep well example would send the analyst back for more research and testing of alternative structures. Figure 2 presents an expanded view of the basic cycle of analysis and suggests more about the complexity of the financial structuring problem. With time and experience, the analyst develops an intuition for efficient information sources and modes of analysis. In the long run, this intuition makes the cycle of analysis manageable.

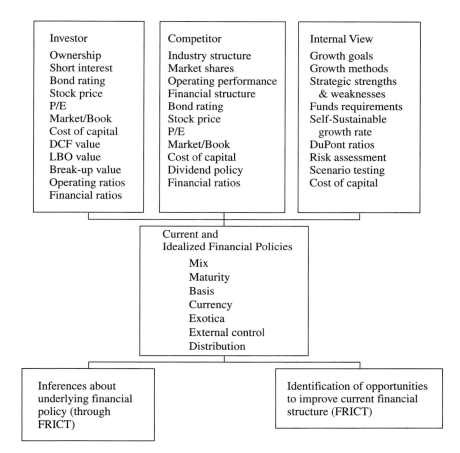

FIGURE 2
Expanded Illustration of Process of Developing a Financial Policy

MCI Communications, Corp.: Capital Structure Theory

On a cold winter morning in February 1996, Katzu Mizuno stood admiring the panoramic view of New York Harbor from the nineteenth floor of the World Trade Center. In his first five months in New York as a first-year associate for Lynch Investments, Katzu had been pleasantly surprised to have some free time to explore the Big Apple. During this period, he had found an apartment, been to Madison Square Garden for a Knicks game, attended the symphony at Lincoln Center, and had made frequent trips to a sushi bar in his neighborhood. The tranquility of the moment ended, however, with an urgent phone call from his boss, Anna Curti.

Earlier that morning, MCI Communications, Corp., a long-time client of the firm, had called seeking advice about establishing a program to repurchase some of its outstanding common stock. As **Exhibit 1** shows, throughout most of 1995 MCI's stock had been a sluggish performer in an otherwise buoyant market, and management sensed a growing restlessness on the part of shareholders. At a recent meeting of the board of directors, discussions had centered on repurchasing some of company's stock as a means to enhance shareholder value. One longtime director, Gavin Philips, pushed hard to finance the repurchase by increasing MCI's debt financing. He argued that this action would send a bold signal to the market about the future prospects of the firm. To be effective as a signal, Philips suggested that the company would need to increase its debt-equity ratio from its current level of around 40 percent to "more or less twice that." He said, "Even at that debt level, MCI's debt-to-cap would be moderate relative to the industry." He estimated that such action would require MCI to issue approximately $2 billion in additional debt. Other direc-

This case was prepared by Susan Chaplinsky, Associate Professor of Business Administration, and Robert S. Harris, Professor of Business Administration, University of Virginia. Support for this work came from funds provided by both the Darden School Foundation and the TVA: This case is drawn entirely from public data. All persons and events recounted are fictionalized to facilitate the teaching objectives of the day. Copyright © 1997 by the University of Virginia Darden School Foundation, Charlottesville, VA. All rights reserved. *To order copies, send an e-mail to* dardencases@virginia.edu. *No part of this publication may be reproduced, stored in a retrieval system, used in a spreadsheet, or transmitted in any form or by any means—electronic, mechanical, photocopying, recording, or otherwise—without the permission of the Darden School Foundation.* Rev. 3/00.

tors, concerned that the increased debt burden might impede the company's current capital-expansion program, argued for a less extreme approach. They favored an open-market purchase program instead. Under this option, the company would announce its intentions to repurchase its stock from "time to time" but only as corporate funds allowed. This course of action, therefore, did not call for any increase in debt.

On hearing the directors' concerns, a senior vice president of MCI, William Duran, called Curti to seek advice on the repurchase and particularly whether debt financing would be advisable. Duran also indicated that since the board hoped to disclose the details of its plan to improve shareholder value by the end of next week, it would be necessary to get back to him as soon as possible. Curti responded quickly: she assigned a second-year associate, Lance Alton, to gauge the possible interest in any debt securities MCI might choose to issue, and she asked Mizuno to examine the consequences of substantially increasing the firm's use of debt. She instructed both of them to report their initial findings to her the following day.

Mizuno decided to compare MCI with its major competitors in long-distance telecommunications. However, he grew somewhat alarmed when his initial screen of peer companies produced approximately 40 firms in long-distance communications.[1] He knew that all of these firms could not be considered comparable to MCI based on their business risk, the markets they operated in, and their tax and regulatory environments. After comparing them to MCI on these dimensions, he narrowed his list to certain companies. (See Table 1.)

Exhibit 2 contains financial data for the peer companies. In assembling the data, Mizuno made several assumptions to help ensure consistency across the peer firms. First, although he was not certain of the tax status of each firm, he decided to initially assume that all companies faced a 40 percent tax rate. Second, it was the usual practice at Lynch to use a market-risk premium of 7 percent, the latest estimate of the arithmetic mean return of stocks over Treasury bonds.

Mizuno recalled from his finance classes that the maximum value of the firm corresponded to the lowest overall cost of capital. Thus, he intended to estimate what the cost of equity and the weighted average cost of capital (WACC) might be if MCI pursued this capital-structure change. After discussions with other personnel at the bank, he concluded that the higher debt equity ratio would increase MCI's borrowing costs from its current level of 6.3 percent. **Exhibit 3** contains the latest capital market rates from which an estimate of the revised borrowing costs could be obtained. But what would the cost of equity (K_E) be? Mizuno decided that one approach was through "levering" and "unlevering" betas using the following equation:

$$\beta_{E,L} = \beta_U (1 + D(1 - T)/E)$$

where $\beta_{E,L}$ and β_U are the betas for levered and unlevered equity, respectively, D and E are the market values of debt and equity, respectively, and T is the corporate tax rate.[2]

---

[1]The domestic companies competing with MCI in telecommunication services were Ameritech, Bell Atlantic, BellSouth, NYNEX, Pacific Telesis, SBC Communications, US West, AT&T, Sprint, Worldcom, Frontier Communication, GTE, So. New England, IntelCom, and MFS Communications. In addition, there were 25 international telecommunication services companies.

[2]See "The Effects of Debt-Equity Policy on Shareholder Return Requirements and Beta" (UVA-F-1168) for a discussion of the underlying principles and the rationale for the equations developed here.

TABLE 1
Description of Industry Comparables

Company	Description
Ameritech	Ameritech is a holding company for Illinois, Indiana, Michigan, Ohio, and Washington State Bells and other subsidiaries, providing communications services directly to 75 percent of the population in these states. In 10/83 Ameritech became the first regional holding company to offer cellular phone service (21 million POPS). 1994 revenue breakdown: local service, 42 percent; long-distance, 12 percent; network access, 23 percent; other, 23 percent. Purchased 49.9 percent stake in Telecom Corporation of New Zealand on 9/90 (now 25 percent after additional equity offerings). Ameritech will be among the first of the Baby Bells to offer long-distance telephone services. Bond rating AA2.
AT&T	AT&T Corporation is the world's largest long-distance telephone company. Formerly American Telephone and Telegraph, AT&T resulted from a court-ordered breakup of the Bell System in 1983, when it received about 23 percent of the former company's assets. AT&T operates in global information management, financial services, and leasing. 1994 revenue breakdown: telecommunication services, 59 percent; product and system sales, 28 percent; rentals and other, 10 percent; financial services and leases, 3 percent. Acquired McCaw Cellular in '94, NCR in '91; LIN Broadcasting in '95. Bond rating AA3.
MCI Communications	MCI Communications Corporation, the second-largest long-distance carrier, offers long-distance services domestically and internationally. Primary business is U.S. voice, using MCI's 3,556 million circuit-mile microwave and fiber network. Offers 800 Service, operator assistance, worldwide direct dialing, fax, and 900 Service. British Telecom holds 100 percent of Class A common stock representing a 20 percent voting interest. Bond rating A2.
Sprint Corporation	Sprint Corporation operates the second-largest independent-telephone system in the United States. Merged with Centel Corporation in a pooling-of-interests in March 1993. Provides long-distance services through US Sprint and local telecommunication services to 6.65 million access lines. Cellular business serves a market of 20.2 million POPs. Also has directory publishing and supply distribution operations. 1994 revenue breakdown: long distance, 53 percent; local phone, 34 percent; other, 13 percent. Bond rating BBB-.
Worldcom, Inc.	Worldcom, Inc. (formerly LDDS Communications, Inc.) is the fourth-largest long-distance carrier in the nation. The company offers long-distance service through its 15,000-mile owned-and-leased network. Serves the entire United States and points to 230 countries. The company derives a predominant share of its total revenues from sales to commercial customers. Products include: switched and dedicated lines for voice and data. Acquired IDB Communications, 12/94; WiTel Network Services, 1/95. Bond rating BBB-.

In addition to the information on peer firms, **Exhibits 4** and **5** contain the latest income statement and balance sheet for MCI. This information could be used to estimate the expected changes in earnings per share that would occur at different levels of operating income (EBIT) with a debt-financed stock repurchase. The beginnings of an EBIT/EPS analysis are formulated in **Exhibit 6.** Mizuno knew that this analysis and its implications would be of great interest to MCI's senior management.

As Mizuno prepared to tackle the analysis, he was concerned that his approach might not capture all the complexities of the decision. While shareholders' required returns typically increase as a firm uses more debt financing, he knew that the theoretical predictions of the cost of equity were only approximations. Mizuno had prepared a "to do" list from his readings on capital costs (**Exhibit 7**) and thought these might help guide him through the analysis. To be sure no issues had been ignored, he would pursue a three-pronged approach: (1) examine the effects of debt on the firm's future coverage ratios under both expected and downside cash flow projections, (2) check with Lance on the reactions gathered from potential creditors (i.e., would severe covenants be required?), and (3) review the company's need for future flexibility and consider how this financial strategy might affect business decisions.[3]

It would be a long night ahead. However, before he pursued these additional issues, Mizuno decided to start with the guidance theory offered.

---

[3]A useful framework for analysis is the FRICTO framework in which the analyst looks at Flexibility, Risk, Income, Control, Timing, and Other factors.

EXHIBIT 1

Telecommunications Industry Stock-Price Performance (value of $1,000 investment made January 22, 1993, as of December 29, 1995)

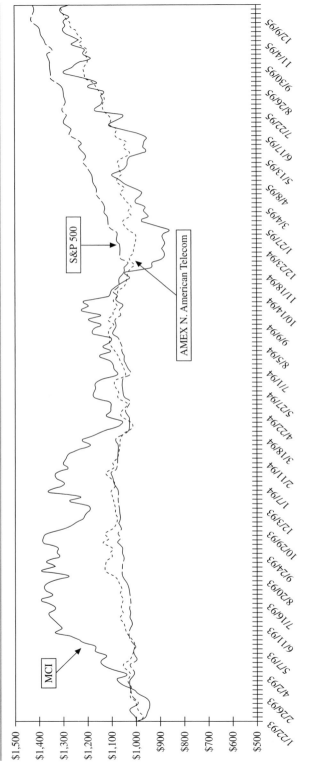

Stock/Index	Total Return
MCI Communications	25.53%
S&P 500	41.23
AMEX N. American Telecom	30.25

EXHIBIT 2
Financial Characteristics for Long-Distance Telecommunications Firms

Company	Recent Share Price	Number of Shares (millions)	Market Capitalization (millions)	Long-Term Debt Incl. Current Portion + Capitalized Leases (LTD)	Total Interest Coverage (EBIT/ Interest)	LTD/(LTD + Book Value of Equity)	LTD/(LTD + Market Value of Equity)	LTD/Book Value of Equity	LTD/Market Value of Equity
Ameritech	$ 59.50	554	$ 32,963	$ 4,547	7.1	0.392	0.121	0.645	0.138
AT&T	66.88	1,592	106,473	13,073	9.6	0.392	0.109	0.645	0.123
MCI Communications	27.75	681	18,898	3,944	6.2	0.292	0.173	0.412	0.209
Sprint	40.00	351	14,040	5,474	4.7	0.573	0.281	1.342	0.390
WorldCom (LDDS)	35.25	193	6,803	3,392	2.9	0.632	0.333	1.717	0.499
S&P500	**608.24**								

Company	Stock Beta[1]	Estimated Year-End EPS[2]	Price/ Earnings Ratio[3]	Annual Dividend	Dividend Payout (%)	Dividend Yield (%)	Historic 5-Year Growth EPS (%)[4]	Projected 5-Year Growth EPS (%)[4]	Firm Value[5]/96 EBITDA
Ameritech	1.06	$ 3.75	15.9	$2.12	56.6%	3.6%	4.5	8.5	6.7
AT&T	1.11	4.00	16.7	1.32	33.0	2.0%	7.0	11.5	8.9
MCI Communications	1	1.75	15.9	0.05	2.9	0.2%	14.5	11.5	5.4
Sprint	1.05	2.90	15.8	1.88	64.9	4.7%	17.5	13.5	6.1
WorldCom (LDDS)	1.77	1.75	20.1	0	0	0.0%	35.0	NA	9
S&P500	**1**	**39.00**	**15.6**	**13.9**	**35.6**	**2.3%**	**7.0**		

Source: February 1996 Salomon Brothers Global Equities Report and *Value Line*. Financial statement data are from year-end 1995.

[1]Stock betas are from Bloomberg, Inc., and *Value Line*.
[2]Estimated 1996 Year End EPS.
[3]Based on 1996 estimated EPS.
[4]Growth rates in EPS are from *Value Line*.
[5]Firm Value is the sum of long-term debt (LTD) and the market value of equity.

EXHIBIT 3
Capital-Market Conditions, February 15, 1996

U.S. Treasury Obligations	Yield
3-month bills	4.898%
6-month bills	4.894
1-year notes	4.832
2-year notes	4.872
3-year notes	4.977
5-year notes	5.235
10-year notes	5.697
30-year notes	6.168%

Corporate Debt Obligations (10-year)	Yield
AAA	6.030%
AA1	6.160
A1	6.190
BBB1	6.470
BB1	7.090
BB2	8.260
B1	9.420
AAA Phones	6.090
AA1 Phones	6.150
A1 Phones	6.260
BBB1 Phones	6.460%

Other Instruments	
Federal Reserve Bank Discount Rate	5.125%
Certificates of Deposit (6-month)	4.633
Commercial Paper (6-month)	4.840%

U.S. Treasury Yield Curve

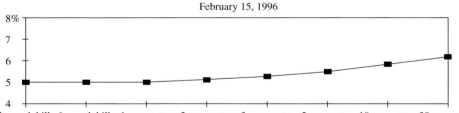

February 15, 1996

Data Source: Bloomberg.

EXHIBIT 4
Income Statement Year ended December 31, 1995
(in millions, except per share amounts)

REVENUE	$15,265
OPERATING EXPENSES	
Telecommunications	7,813
Sales, operations and general	4,506
Depreciation	1,308
Asset write-down	520
Total operating expenses	14,147
INCOME FROM OPERATIONS	1,118
Interest expense	181
INCOME BEFORE INCOME TAXES AND EXTRAORDINARY ITEMS	937
Income tax provision	364
Income before extraordinary item	573
NET INCOME	$ 573
Earnings applicable to common stockholders	$ 573
EARNINGS PER COMMON AND COMMON EQUIVALENT SHARES	
Income before extraordinary item	$0.84
Total	$0.84
Weighted average number of common shares	681

EXHIBIT 5
Balance Sheet December 31, 1995 (in millions)

ASSETS
CURRENT ASSETS

Cash and cash equivalents	$ 471
Marketable securities	373
Receivables	2,954
Other current assets	749
TOTAL CURRENT ASSETS	4,547
PROPERTY AND EQUIPMENT	14,243
Accumulated depreciation	(5,238)
Construction in progress	1,304
TOTAL PROPERTY AND EQUIPMENT, NET	10,309
OTHER ASSETS	4,445
TOTAL ASSETS	$19,301

LIABILITIES AND STOCKHOLDERS' EQUITY
CURRENT LIABILITIES

Accrued telecommunications expense	$ 706
	1,936
Other accrued liabilities	1,728
Long-term debt due within one year	500
TOTAL CURRENT LIABILITIES	4,870
Long-term debt	3,444
Deferred taxes and other	1,385
TOTAL NONCURRENT LIABILITIES	4,829
STOCKHOLDERS' EQUITY	9,602
TOTAL LIABILITIES AND STOCKHOLDERS' EQUITY	$19,301

EXHIBIT 6
EPS vs. EBIT

Interest rate on old debt
Pre recap debt
Tax rate

Interest rate on new debt
Added debt
Tax rate

Status Quo

	Worst Case	Most Likely	Best Case
Operating income (EBIT)			
Interest expense			
Taxable income			
Taxes			
Net income			
Shares outstanding			
EPS (status quo)			

Additional Debt

	Worst Case	Most Likely	Best Case
Operating income (EBIT)			
Interest expense (old + new)			
Taxable income			
Taxes			
Net income			
Shares outstanding			
EPS (w/new debt)			

EPS

EBIT

EXHIBIT 7
Analysts' Checklist for Cost-of-Capital Estimates

Principle	Why	Specific Implications
Think like an investor and be forward looking.	You are estimating investor-required returns for the future.	Avoid using historical costs such as the historical interest rate.
Use financial market data.	Use market values and other financial market data because that's what investors deal with.	Use market value weights and forward-looking estimates of debt costs, equity costs, and tax rates.
Find comparable companies with similar business risk.	Different levels of risks carry different required rates of return.	Try to find companies that are comparable on important risk dimensions. These may include lines of business, international activity, competitive position, and strategic plans.
Be sensitive to trade-offs in looking for the best comparable versus using many companies.	If you focus on the one "best" comparable you have higher chances of large estimation errors in statistical estimates you may be using (e.g., betas). If you include a wide range of comparables, estimation errors may average out but you may not have as good a match on risk.	Look at both industry averages and specific comparables. If they differ, think about why.
Cost of equity must reflect not only business risk but also financial risk.	Shareholder required returns (and betas) are based on both business risk and financial risk introduced by the use of debt.	The cost of equity (and cost of debt) used in a WACC calculation must be consistent with the weights used. If looking at comparable companies, check to see if they have similar capital structures. One technique is to compute WACCs for each company. Another approach tries to unlever costs of equity to adjust for financial risk. The first approach assures numbers are consistent but doesn't directly address differences in debt policy. The second requires use of theoretical approximations.
Look to yields in debt markets for cost of debt.	In bond markets, yields to maturity and quotes on new issues (e.g. from banks or investment banks) provide forward-looking costs of debt.	Know your banker and debt markets well.
Use a number of models and approaches to triangulate your estimate.	Theoretical models are useful but not perfect in their application. Assumptions and comparables are sometimes hard to specify exactly. See if your results are very sensitive to what appears to be reasonable alternatives.	Try different methods to estimate cost of equity. Look at how sensitive your results are to these and your choice of comparables.
Be wary of false precision.	Estimating costs of equity and weighted average costs of capital involve many judgments and approximations. Your final estimate is subject to these approximations.	Cost of capital estimates are approximate. Narrow your range but don't think you've got it exactly right.
Match cash flows and discount rates in terms of currencies.	Increasingly, companies operate in many countries. If you are analyzing cash flows denominated in a currency (say DM), one must make sure that the cost of capital estimate reflects investor perceptions of investments in that specific currency.	There are two basic approaches. One is to estimate a cost of capital for each different currency, making sure to adjust for differential inflation among currencies. The second is to translate cash flows to a common currency using forecasted exchange rates and then use the common currency for cost of capital.

Polaroid Corporation, 1996

In late March 1996, Ralph Norwood, the recently appointed treasurer of Polaroid Corporation, reflected on several matters of concern about the firm's debt policy that would require his attention in the coming months. One immediate concern was Polaroid's outstanding $150 million, 7.25 percent notes, which were due to mature in January 1997. Investment bankers, keenly interested in garnering advisory and underwriting business from Polaroid, had sought to present proposals for refunding the issue. However, Norwood felt that any refunding decision should be part of a larger review of the firm's financial policies. Accordingly he undertook a review of the firm's overall debt policy, focusing primarily on the mix of debt and equity and on the maturity structure of the debt. He also sought to consider issues of control, the establishment of any special advisory relationships, and the use of new financial instruments.

In recent years Polaroid's share price had traded in a narrow range, reflecting small sales and earnings growth. However, a new plan to exploit aggressively the existing Polaroid brand, introduce product extensions, and enter new emerging markets (such as Russia) had been proposed to spur the firm's performance. The restructuring plan was spearheaded by Gary T. DiCamillo, the first outsider appointed chief executive officer (CEO) in the firm's history. DiCamillo had only recently joined the firm in November 1995. Norwood believed the plan would reinvigorate the company without materially increasing its operating risk. With important changes in the works, Norwood felt it essential that his financial policies afford Polaroid the necessary funding and flexibility to pursue the initiatives of the new CEO.

THE EARLY YEARS

Polaroid Corporation was founded in 1937 by Edwin Land, who had dropped out of Harvard College to pursue ideas on the polarization of light. The early years of Polaroid reflected the characteristics of Land: inventive, determined, and single-minded. The first instant camera was produced in 1948 and from that moment 90 percent of the company's efforts were dedicated to the development of the field. Within four decades, sales of the firm grew from $142,000 to over $1 billion, largely on the basis of Land's interest and oversight of the research effort in instant photography. Significant breakthroughs included instant black-and-white film (1954), instant color film (1960), and the SX-70 camera and film (1972) which freed the user from having to coat the developing picture.

In 1977 the firm's sales exceeded $1 billion for the first time, though this achievement was offset by increasing pressures from the sales force for new sources of growth, in the form of cheaper products. Internally there had been major efforts to develop products beyond instant photography: document copiers, and an instant movie camera and film. The movie project debuted in 1977 as Polavision, an instant motion picture technology. Unfortunately, sales languished largely because of the advent of video-camera technology. In 1979, the directors wrote off the inventory of Polavision products and effectively exited from the business. In 1980, Edwin Land stepped down as CEO of the firm; he retired from the board in 1982 and a year later sold his Polaroid stock in a public offering.

RECENT FINANCIAL PERFORMANCE

The two most notable events of the past decade were prompted by the actions of others. In 1976 Eastman Kodak Company introduced an instant camera and film product that threatened Polaroid's dominance of the instant-photography field. Polaroid sued Kodak for patent infringement, and 10 years later in 1986 was awarded the largest patent judgment in history, some $900 million. Meanwhile, few significant new products were developed during this time. In 1988, with no large shareholder like Edwin Land to protect the firm and expecting the proceeds from the Kodak patent judgment, Polaroid received an unsolicited tender offer from Shamrock Holdings. Shamrock proposed to pay the shareholders an extraordinary dividend from the Kodak proceeds, and to manage the company more tightly. Polaroid's management wanted to reinvest the proceeds in the business. To fend off the takeover threat, the firm conducted a leveraged recapitalization which involved the innovative use of an employee stock ownership plan (ESOP). The leveraged recap dramatically increased the firm's debt to capital ratio from zero in 1988 to 56 percent in 1989. Shortly thereafter, the firm began a program of steady share repurchases. Despite the repurchase program, long-term debt to capital fell to 42 percent by 1995. **Exhibit 1** gives a 10-year summary of the financial characteristics of the firm.

Over the past 10 years, the firm's share price growth had lagged the growth in the broad market indexes. From 1986 to 1995, Polaroid's compound annual sales growth rate was 3.6 percent in nominal terms, and after adjusting for inflation, virtually zero. Earnings losses appeared in 1988, 1993, and 1995, and were associated with both declines in operating profit, and restructuring costs (consisting of both severance payments and write-offs). The sales and earnings results reflected the growing maturity of the instant photography market in the United States and the absence of major new-product introductions. Consistent with the perceived maturity of their market segment, Polaroid's price-earnings (P/E) ratio of 12.1 fell well below the market's P/E of 15.2 in 1995.

The concerns over profitability and the lack of strong sales growth in cameras and film were also echoed in the comments of analysts following the firm. One analyst described Polaroid's challenge:

> Instant photography is a razor blade business. Cameras are sold at low margins to encourage film sales. The company's instant film sales are its primary margin product. Expanding the "installed base" of camera enhances the opportunities to sell film. The "burn rate" of film on newly purchased cameras, as might be expected, is highest and trails off in a reasonable predictable pattern thereafter. This correlation allows the company to make reasonable estimates of film unit sales volume. It also, obviously, means that there is a strong emphasis on selling cameras.[1]

The patents the company held protected it from any significant competition domestically in the field of instant photography. In international markets, Polaroid's only competitor was Fuji, who had a film and instant-camera product it marketed in Europe and Japan. However, even in Japan, Polaroid enjoyed a dominant market share. Thus, in the consumer market, Polaroid's strength for instant photography was unrivaled. In the commercial market, Polaroid's sales derived primarily from the use of instant photography for identification purposes (e.g., ID badges), and other applications in medicine and law enforcement. Increasingly the expansion of digital imaging threatened to erode the firm's base of users, as customers shifted from instant photography to digital solutions. In recent years, Polaroid's Commercial Group accounted for approximately half of its total sales and one-third of instant-film sales.[2] In the digital area, Polaroid faced stiff competition from many well-capitalized technology companies, such as Xerox, 3M, and Sony. To date, Polaroid's development efforts in digital imaging had entailed heavy start-up costs.

Norwood acknowledged many of the same concerns, but felt that the analyst community had taken a shortsighted view of Polaroid's potential. Echoing its past, the firm continued to be "engaged primarily in one line of business, the design, manufacture, and sale of instant photographic imaging products worldwide,"[3] with photographic products accounting for 90 percent of the firm's revenues in 1995. Norwood said, "The basic business is low growth; but it's an incredible annuity." Second, sales to international markets had strong growth potential. In many emerging-market countries, no infrastructure existed to develop 35-mm film. With rising standards of living worldwide, there was a large untapped market for instant photography, and Polaroid's cameras were in high demand. **Exhibit 2** illuminates the growth in international revenues. The percentage mix of U.S. versus international sales had almost precisely reversed from 1993 to 1995. This reversal reflected steady growth in the international segment of between 3 and 8 percent per year. In contrast, sales

---

[1]*Duff & Phelps Credit Rating Report, Polaroid Corporation,* Duff & Phelps, Inc., November 18, 1996, page 2.
[2]*Polaroid—Company Report,* Prudential Securities, December, 4, 1996, page 4.
[3]*Polaroid Annual Report 1995,* page 44.

in the United States had fallen 2 percent in 1994 and 12 percent in 1995. Sales to Russia alone accounted for 9 percent of total sales in 1995.

Exhibits 3 and 4 give the latest year's income statement and balance sheet for Polaroid.

CURRENT FINANCING AND FUTURE OUTLOOK

Against this backdrop, Norwood assessed the current and future financing requirements of the firm. One important issue for consideration was the extent to which the financing of the firm would be impacted by the plans of the new CEO. Gary DiCamillo was appointed Polaroid's chairman and CEO following a successful term as president of Black & Decker's PowerTools unit. At Black & Decker, DiCamillo was viewed as an energetic leader, whose efforts were instrumental in developing a line of new products that helped to revive Black & Decker's brand name. DiCamillo brought similar energy and plans to Polaroid. Shortly after his arrival, he announced a major restructuring of the firm, to reduce the workforce by some 2,500 positions (roughly 20 percent), and to reduce expenses by more than $150 million annually. In particular, he terminated the production of the Captiva camera, and curtailed several major research and engineering programs, emphasizing instead projects having the greatest potential for commercialization. Finally, he sharply reduced corporate overhead costs. The effect of this restructuring was to trigger a special charge to earnings in 1995 of $247 million caused by the severance and early retirement programs, and by the write-down of equipment and inventory. As a result, Polaroid reported a net loss of $140.2 million, compared with 1994 earnings of $117.2 million.

In February 1996, DiCamillo announced a new management structure built around three core areas: Consumer, Commercial, and New Business. The purpose of the new structure was to focus the organization more effectively on customers' imaging needs, and to integrate product development responsibilities within each group. DiCamillo wrote:

> Both the restructuring and reorganization reflect my conviction that we can grow our core photographic and emerging electronic imaging businesses. I believe we can leverage our considerable brand power, technological expertise, and global distribution reach to create new growth opportunities and revitalize our instant photography business.[4]

To meet its various financing needs, Polaroid maintained a five-year $150 million working capital line of credit to be used for general purposes. This line was to expire in 1999. In 1994 and 1995 there had been no borrowings under this line. The company maintained international lines of credit to support the firm's foreign currency balance sheet exposure. At the end of 1995, borrowings outside the United States were $160.4 million. Additional unused borrowings under these lines of credit were $160 million.

Polaroid's long-term debt outstanding consisted of three issues:

- **Notes:** $150 million, 7.25 percent notes due January 15, 1997, had been issued at a discount (to yield 7.42 percent); $200 million, 8 percent notes were due March 15, 1999,

---

[4]Quoted from Letter to Shareholders, *Polaroid Annual Report 1995,* page 3.

and had been issued with a discount to yield 8.18 percent. Both issues of notes were non-callable.

- **ESOP Loan:** The loan had been drawn in 1988 to establish Polaroid's leveraged employee stock ownership plan (ESOP), as part of the leveraged recapitalization of the firm. Scheduled principal payments were made semiannually through 1997 when a final payment of $37.7 million was due. The weighted average interest rate on the loan was 5.2 percent, 4.4 percent, and 3.6 percent during 1995, 1994, and 1993 respectively. Special tax benefits to providers of ESOP loans accounted for the unusually low interest rates.
- **Convertible Subordinated Debentures:** $140 million, 8 percent convertibles due in 2001. These carried an annual interest rate of 8 percent, and were convertible to common stock at $32.50 per share. These were redeemable by the company after September 30, 1998, or sooner if the stock price exceeded $48.75 per share for 20 of 30 consecutive trading days. All of the debentures were held by Corporate Partners.[5]

Virtually all of the firm's debt was due within six years. As Ralph Norwood commented, "The weighted average maturity structure of our debt was about four years. All our borrowings would need to be repaid or refinanced in a relatively short time." **Exhibit 5** illustrates the estimation of Polaroid's weighted average maturity of its debt.

In addition to the scheduled debt repayments, Ralph Norwood reviewed other possible demands on the firm's resources. He believed that capital expenditures would about equal depreciation for the next few years. Also, though sales might grow, working capital turns should decline, resulting in a reduction in net working capital in the first year, followed by increases later. Both of these effects reflected the tight asset management under the new CEO. While cash dividends would be held constant for the foreseeable future, the firm would continue with its program of opportunistic share repurchases, which had varied between $20 and $60 million per year. Exhibit 1 summarizes the firm's share repurchase activity in recent years.

Exhibit 6 gives a five-year forecast of Polaroid's income statement and balance sheet. This forecast was consistent with the lower end of analysts' projections for revenue growth and realization of the benefits of DiCamillo's restructuring program. It assumed that the existing debt would be refinanced with similar debt. Major share repurchases were not presumed in the forecast. The forecast would need to be revised to reflect the impact of any recommended changes in financial policy.

CONSIDERATIONS IN ASSESSING FINANCIAL POLICY

In addition to assessing the firm's internal financing requirements, Norwood also recognized that his policy recommendation would have an important role in shaping the perceptions of the firm by the bond-rating agencies and investors.

---

[5]If the rights were fully exercised, the resulting stock would represent approximately a 9 percent stake in Polaroid. The company was currently attempting to negotiate the repurchase of the conversion rights from Corporate Partners. On March 29, 1996, Polaroid's share price closed at $44.00. The annualized volatility or "sigma" of returns on Polaroid's shares over the previous 100 days was 17.7 percent. The yield on six-year U.S. Treasury Notes was 6.05 percent.

- **Bond Rating.** Polaroid currently had a "split" rating where Standard & Poor's rated the firm's senior[6] long-term debt BBB and Moody's rated it Baa3, (roughly equivalent to a BBB− in the Standard & Poor's system). **Exhibit 7** presents the bond-rating definitions for this and other rating categories. BBB/Baa3 was an "investment-grade" rating, whereas the next rating grade lower (BB/Ba) was "noninvestment grade" and often referred to as "high yield or junk debt." Some large investors (such as pension funds and charitable trusts) were barred from investing in noninvestment-grade debt. Many individual investors shunned it as well. For that reason, the yields on noninvestment-grade debt over U.S. Treasury securities (i.e., spreads) were typically considerably higher than the spreads for investment-grade issues. Also, the ability to issue noninvestment-grade debt depended to a much greater degree on the strength of the economy, and on favorable credit market conditions than did investment-grade debt. Norwood said:

  > You don't pay much of a penalty in yield as you go from A to BBB. There's a range over which the risk you take for more leverage is de minimus. But you pay a big penalty as you go from BBB to BB. The penalty is not only in the form of higher costs, but also in the form of possible damage to the Polaroid brand. We don't want the brand to be sullied by the association with junk debt.

  For these reasons, Ralph Norwood sought to preserve an investment-grade rating for Polaroid. But where in the investment grade range should Polaroid be positioned? **Exhibit 8** summarizes the bond ratings for a sample of Polaroid's peer firms, which Norwood described as "large global consumer technology products companies," and for a large sample of firms in general. **Exhibit 9** gives financial ratios associated with the various rating categories. Although Norwood knew the ratings agencies looked closely at the debt to capital ratio ("debt capitalization"), he believed that the EBIT Coverage ratio was also a good measure of credit quality. **Exhibit 10** gives Polaroid's EBIT coverage ratios for the past 10 years. Norwood's decision would require him to first choose a target bond rating. Thereafter, he would have to determine the minimum and maximum amounts of debt that Polaroid could carry to achieve the desired rating.

- **Flexibility.** Norwood was also aware that choosing a target debt level based on an analysis of industry peers might not fully capture the flexibility Polaroid would need to meet its own possible future adversities. Norwood said:

  > Flexibility is how much debt you can issue before you lose the investment-grade bond rating. I want flexibility, and yet I want to take advantage of the fact that with more debt, you have lower cost capital. I am very comfortable with our strategy and internal financial forecasts for our business; if anything, I believe the forecasts probably underestimate, rather than overestimate our cash flows. But let's suppose that a two-sigma adverse outcome would be an EBIT equal to $150 million—I can't imagine in the worst of times an EBIT less than that.

Accordingly, Norwood's final decision on the target bond rating would have to be one that maintained reasonable reserves against Polaroid's worst-case scenario.

---

[6]The convention in finance is that the "firm's bond rating" refers to the rating on the firm's *senior* debt, with the understanding that any subordinated debt issued by the firm will ordinarily have a lower bond rating. For instance, Polaroid's senior debt had the split BBB/Baa3 rating, while its subordinated convertible bonds were rated BB/Ba.

- **Cost of Capital.** Consistent with management's emphasis on value creation, Norwood believed that choosing a financial policy that minimized the cost of capital was important. He understood that exploitation of debt tax shields could create value for shareholders—up to a reasonable limit, and that beyond the limit, costs of financial distress would become material, and cause the cost of capital to rise. One investment bank, Hudson Guaranty, presented Norwood with estimates of the pretax cost of debt and cost of equity by rating category. These estimates are given in **Exhibit 11.** The cost of debt was estimated by averaging the current yield-to-maturity of bonds within each rating category. The cost of equity (k_e) was estimated by Hudson Guaranty using the Capital Asset Pricing Model. The cost of equity was computed for each firm using its beta and other capital market data. The individual estimates of k_e were then averaged within each bond-rating category. Norwood remarked on the relatively flat trend in the cost of equity within the investment-grade range. Hudson Guaranty replied that "changes in leverage within the investment-grade range are not regarded as material to investors." It remained for Norwood to determine which rating category provided the lowest costs of capital.
- **Current Capital-Market Conditions.** Any policy recommendations would need to acknowledge the feasibility of implementing those policies today as well as in the future. **Exhibit 12** presents information about current yields in the U.S. debt markets. The current situation in the debt markets was favorable as the U.S. economy continued in its fifth year of economic expansion. The equity markets seemed to be pausing after a phenomenal advance in prices in 1995. The outlook for interest rates was stable, though any sign of inflation might cause the Federal Reserve Board to lift interest rates. Major changes in taxes and regulations were in abeyance, at least until the outcome of the presidential elections to be held in November 1996.

CONCLUSION

Ralph Norwood leafed through the analyses and financial data he had gathered for his recommendations. He reflected on the competing goals of value creation, flexibility, and bond rating. His plan would have to afford Polaroid low costs and continued access to capital under a variety of operating scenarios. This would require him to test the possible effect of downside scenarios on Polaroid's coverage and capitalization ratios under alternative debt policies. He aimed to recommend a financial policy that would balance these goals and provide guidance to the directors and the financial staff regarding the target mix of capital and the maturity structure of the company's debt. With so many competing factors to weigh, Norwood felt it unlikely that his plan would be a "perfect plan." But then he remembered one of Gary DiCamillo's favorite sayings: "If you wait until you have a 99 percent solution, you'll never act; go with an 80 percent solution."

EXHIBIT 1
Ten-Year Financial Summary (in U.S. $ millions except per-share values and numbers of shares)

At fiscal year ended December 31	1995	1994	1993	1992	1991	1990	1989	1988	1987	1986
Selected Income Statement Information										
Net sales U.S.	$1,019.0	$1,160.3	$1,178.8	$1,145.7	$1,113.6	$1,058.3	$1,091.8	$1,048.3	$1,009.3	$964.3
International	1,217.9	1,152.2	1,066.1	1,006.6	957.0	913.4	812.9	814.6	754.6	664.9
Total	2,236.9	2,312.5	2,244.9	2,152.3	2,070.6	1,971.7	1,904.7	1,862.9	1,763.9	1,629.2
Operating expenses	2,147.7	2,112.2	2,059.5	1,938.5	1,824.0	1,687.4	1,600.5	1,689.1	1,610.1	1,493.5
Profit from opns. before restructuring exp.	89.2	200.3	185.4	213.8	246.6	284.3	304.2	173.8	153.8	135.7
Restructuring expense	247.0	0.0	44.0	0.0	0.0	0.0	40.5	151.9	0.0	0.0
Interest expense	52.1	46.6	47.9	58.5	58.4	81.3	86.2	29.0	15.0	18.6
Net earnings	-140.2	117.2	-51.3	99.0	683.7	151.0	145.0	-22.6	125.2	108.2
Common shares, end of year (000s)	45,533	45,998	46,806	46,668	48,919	50,070	52,110	71,635	61,918	61,918
Common shares repurchased (000s)	1,218	941	0	2,258	1,151	2,040	19,525	0	0	0
Repurchase outlay ($ millions)	$40.2	$30.6	$0.0	$63.4	$30.6	$55.6	$950.6	$0.0	$0.0	$0.0
Common shares issued (000s)	753	133	138	7	0	0	0	9,717	0	0
Earnings per share	-$3.09	$2.49	-$1.10	$2.06	$12.54	$2.20	$1.96	-$0.34	$2.02	$1.75
Dividend per share	$0.60	$0.60	$0.60	$0.60	$0.60	$0.60	$0.60	$0.60	$0.60	$0.50
Selected Balance Sheet Information										
Working capital	$ 738.5	$ 886.8	$ 833.6	$ 789.0	$ 695.3	$ 609.1	$ 642.0	$ 980.0	$ 652.6	$ 602.4
Net property, plant & equipment	691.0	747.3	718.2	657.3	549.4	461.0	430.9	433.8	359.6	357.7
Total assets	2,261.8	2,316.7	2,212.3	2,008.1	1,889.3	1,701.3	1,776.7	1,957.2	1,599.4	1,444.6
Long-term debt (LTD)	526.7	566.0	602.3	637.4	471.8	513.8	602.2	402.3	0.0	0.0
Redeemable preferred stock	0.0	0.0	0.0	0.0	0.0	348.6	321.9	0.0	0.0	0.0
Common stockholders' equity	717.7	864.4	767.3	808.9	772.9	207.7	148.8	1,011.5	1,048.2	960.1
Addns. to property plant and equip.	167.9	146.7	165.6	201.5	175.8	120.9	94.5	127.0	116.6	82.9
Depreciation	$132.7	$118.2	$100.3	$89.1	$85.5	$87.2	$87.4	$81.9	$75.7	$71.2
Book value LT debt/capital	42.3%	39.6%	44.0%	44.1%	37.9%	48.0%	56.1%	28.5%	0.0%	0.0%
Market value LT debt/capital	19.6%	27.5%	27.8%	30.5%	26.6%	25.3%	28.5%	23.4%	0.0%	0.0%
Selected Valuation Information (at years' ends)										
Polaroid stock price	$47.38	$32.50	$33.50	$31.13	$26.63	$23.38	$22.88	$18.38	$11.88	$33.25
S&P 500 Index	615.93	459.27	466.25	435.71	417.09	330.22	353.40	277.72	247.08	242.17
Polaroid average P/E (1)	12.1	13.3	15.6	14.2	12.2	15.6	21.8	NMF	14.7	16.6
S&P Industrials Average P/E (1)	15.2	15.5	18.4	19.8	19	14.4	12.6	10.8	15.3	17.5
Polaroid market/book ratio	3.01	1.73	2.04	1.80	1.69	5.63	8.01	1.30	0.70	2.14
Polaroid beta	1.05	1.05	1.15	1.15	1.20	1.25	1.25	1.25	1.20	1.10
Yield on 30-Year T-bonds	6.88%	7.37%	6.59%	7.67%	8.14%	8.61%	8.45%	8.96%	8.59%	7.80%
Yield on 90-day T-bills	5.49%	4.25%	3.00%	3.43%	5.38%	7.50%	8.11%	6.67%	5.78%	5.97%
Total annual return on large co. stocks	33.00%	1.30%	9.90%	7.67%	30.55%	-3.17%	31.49%	18.81%	5.23%	18.47%

Notes: 1. P/E ratios are computed on earnings before restructuring charges, litigation award, and other extraordinary items.

Sources: *Polaroid Annual Report 1995*, *Value Line Investment Survey*, Federal Reserve *Bulletin*, Standard & Poor's *Current Statistics*, Ibbotson Associates *Stocks, Bonds Bills, Inflation 1995*.

EXHIBIT 2
Information on International Revenues

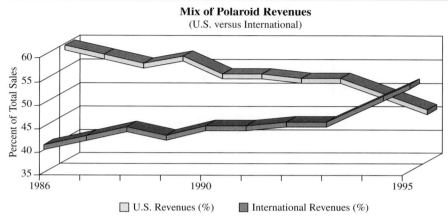

Mix of Polaroid Revenues
(U.S. versus International)

□ U.S. Revenues (%) ■ International Revenues (%)

Source of graph data: *Polaroid Annual Report 1995,* pp. 48–49.

Estimated Quarterly Polaroid Sales to Russia

($ millions)	1993	1994	1995
1st Quarter	0	$22 m	$38 m
2nd Quarter	0	24	35
3rd Quarter	$10 m	51	74
4th Quarter	10	57	49
Full Year	$20 m	$154 m	$196 m

Source: B. L. Landry, "Polaroid—Company Report" Morgan Stanley
& Co. October 25, 1996

Performance by Geographic Segment ($ millions, eliminations of interregional amounts not shown)

	1993	1994	1995
Sales: U.S.	$1,609.6	$1,656.6	$1,498.4
Europe	945.2	1,051.7	1,106.9
Asia Pacific, Canada, Latin and South America	524.7	531.1	602.4
Profits/(loss): U.S.	$ 44.1	$ 100.8	$ (179.4)
Europe	43.7	81.8	20.6
Asia Pacific, Canada, Latin and South America	56.8	45.2	24.4
Assets: U.S.	$1,532.7	$1,480.5	$1,526.1
Europe	556.0	613.8	669.9
Asia Pacific, Canada, Latin and South America	216.9	248.1	258.4

Source: *Polaroid Annual Report 1995,* page 45.

EXHIBIT 3
Income Statement:
Consolidated Statement of Earnings (in $ millions)

	Years Ended December 31	
	1995	**1994**
Net sales		
United States	$1,019.0	$1,160.3
International	1,217.9	1,152.2
Total net sales	2,236.9	2,312.5
Cost of goods sold	1,298.6	1,324.2
Marketing, research, & admin.	849.1	788.0
Restructuring & other.	247.0	0.0
Total costs	2,394.7	2,122.2
Profit/(loss) from operations	(157.8)	200.3
Interest income	8.7	9.7
Other income	(0.2)	(2.7)
Interest expense	52.1	46.6
Earnings/(loss) before taxes	(201.4)	160.7
Tax expense	(61.2)	43.5
Net earnings/(loss)	(140.2)	117.2

Source: *Polaroid Annual Report 1995.*

EXHIBIT 4
Balance Sheet (in $ millions)

	1995	1994
Assets		
Current assets		
Cash and cash equivalents	$ 73.3	$ 143.3
Short-term investments	9.8	85.6
Receivables, less allowances	550.4	541.0
Inventories	615.5	577.4
Prepaid expenses and other	208.5	141.4
Total current assets	1,457.5	1,488.7
Gross property, plant, and equipment	2,164.4	2,043.4
Less accumulated depreciation	1,473.4	1,296.1
Net property, plant, and equipment	691.0	747.3
Prepaid taxes—non-current	113.3	80.7
Total assets	$2,261.8	$2,316.7
Liabilities and Stockholders' Equity		
Current liabilities		
Short-term debt	$ 160.4	$ 117.1
Current portion of long-term debt	39.7	35.9
Payables and acrruals	274.9	275.7
Compensation & benefits	197.4	121.4
Taxes payable	46.6	51.8
Total current liabilities	719.0	601.9
Long-term debt	526.7	566.0
Accrued postretirement benefits	257.2	247.2
Accrued postemployment benefits	41.2	37.2
Total liabilities	$1,544.1	$1,452.3
Preferred stock	0.0	0.0
Common stockholders' equity		
Common Stock	$ 75.4	$ 75.4
Additional paid-in capital	401.9	387.2
Retained earnings	1,525.8	1,692.1
Less treasury stock, at cost	1,205.4	1,174.5
Less deferred compensation	80.0	115.8
Total common stockholders equity	717.7	864.4
Total liabilities and stockholders' equity	$2,261.8	$2,316.7

Source: Polaroid Annual Report 1995.

EXHIBIT 5
Maturity Structure of Debt

	Debt Repayment ($ millions)	Debt Repayment (% of total)	Maturity (years)	Weighted maturity (years)
1996	$ 39.7	7.0%	1	0.07
1997	187.8	33.0	2	0.66
1998	0	0	3	0
1999	200.0	35.0	4	1.41
2000	0	0	5	0
2001	140.0	25.0	6	1.48
Total	$567.5	100%		3.62 years

Note: For simplicity, this table assumes all debt payments are made on an annual basis. Any semiannual or quarterly principal payments would reduce slightly the estimated weighted maturity.
Source: Casewriters' analysis.

EXHIBIT 6
Financial Forecast, 1996–2000 (values in U.S. $ millions)

	Actual		Projected			
	1995	1996	1997	1998	1999	2000
Annual increase in sales	−3.2%	2.0%	5.0%	6.0%	6.0%	7.0%
Opng. profit/sales	4.0%	8.0%	9.5%	10.0%	10.0%	10.0%
Tax rate		40.0%				
Wkg. capital/sales		37.0%				
Income Statement						
Net sales	$2,236.9	$2,281.6	$2,395.7	$2,539.5	$2,691.8	$2,880.3
Operating profit	89.2	182.5	227.6	253.9	269.2	288.0
Interest income	8.5	5.0	5.0	5.0	5.0	5.0
Interest expense	−52.1	(52.1)	(52.1)	(52.1)	(52.1)	(52.1)
Pretax income	45.6	135.4	180.5	206.8	222.1	240.9
Tax expense	−61.2	(54.2)	(72.2)	(82.7)	(88.8)	(96.4)
Net income	−15.6	81.3	108.3	124.1	133.2	144.6
Dividends	27.3	27.3	27.3	27.3	27.3	27.3
Retentions to earnings	$ (42.9)	$ 53.9	$ 81.0	$ 96.8	$ 105.9	$ 117.2
Balance Sheet						
Cash	$ 83.1	$ 148.3	$ 187.1	$ 230.7	$ 280.3	$ 327.8
Working capital (without debt)	855.5	844.2	886	939.6	996.0	1,065.7
Prepaid tax	113.3	113.3	113.3	113.3	113.3	113.3
Net fixed assets	691.0	691.0	691.0	691.0	691.0	691.0
Total assets	1,742.9	1,796.8	1,877.8	1,974.6	2,080.5	2,197.8
Debt (long and short term)	726.8	726.8	726.8	726.8	726.8	726.8
Other long term liablilities	298.4	298.4	298.4	298.4	298.4	298.4
Stockholders' equity	717.7	771.6	852.6	949.4	1,055.3	1,172.6
Total liabilities & stockholders' equity	$1,742.9	$1,796.8	$1,877.8	$1,974.6	$2,080.5	$2,197.8
Free Cash Flow						
EBIT		$ 182.5	$ 227.6	$ 253.9	$ 269.2	$ 288.0
Less taxes on EBIT		(73.0)	(91.0)	(101.6)	(107.7)	(115.2)
Plus depreciation		140.0	140.0	140.0	140.0	140.0
Less capital expenditures		(140.0)	(140.0)	(140.0)	(140.0)	(140.0)
Less additions/plus reductions in wkg. cap.		11.3	(42.2)	(53.2)	(56.4)	(69.7)
Free Cash Flow		$ 120.8	$ 94.3	$ 99.2	$ 105.1	$ 103.1

Source: Casewriter analysis, consistent with forecast expectations of securities analysts.

EXHIBIT 7
Moody's Bond-Rating Definitions

Aaa	Bonds which are rated **Aaa** are judged to be of the best quality. They carry the smallest degree of investment risk and are generally referred to as "gilt edge." Interest payments are protected by a large or by an exceptionally stable margin and principal is secure. While the various protective elements are likely to change, such changes as can be visualized are most unlikely to impair the fundamentally strong position of such issues.
Aa	Bonds which are rated **Aa** are judged to be of high quality by all standards. Together with the **Aaa** group they comprise what are generally known as high grade bonds. They are rated lower than the best bonds because margins of protection may not be as large as in Aaa securities or fluctuations of protective elements may be of greater amplitude or there may be other elements present which make the long term risks appear somewhat larger than in Aaa securities.
A	Bonds which are rated **A** possess many favorable investment attributes and are to be considered as upper medium grade obligations. Factors giving security to principal and interest are considered adequate but elements may be present which suggest a susceptibility to impairment sometime in the future.
Baa	Bonds which are rated **Baa** are considered as medium grade obligations, i.e., they are neither highly protected nor poorly secured. Interest payment and principal security appear adequate for the present but certain protective elements may be lacking or may be characteristically unreliable over any great length of time. Such bonds lack outstanding investment characteristics and in fact have speculative characteristics as well.
Ba	Bonds which are rated **Ba** are judged to have speculative elements; their future cannot be considered as well assured. Often the protection of interest and principal payments may be very moderate and thereby not well safeguarded during both good and bad times over the future. Uncertainty of position characterizes bonds in this class.
B	Bonds which are rated **B** generally lack characteristics of the desirable investment. Assurance of interest and principal payments or of maintenance of other terms of the contract over any long period of time may be small.
Caa	Bonds which are rated **Caa** are of poor standing. Such issues may be in default or there may be present elements of danger with respect to principal or interest.
Ca	Bonds which are rated **Ca** represent obligations which are speculative in a high degree. Such issues are often in default or have other marked shortcomings.
C	Bonds which are rated **C** are the lowest rated class of bonds, and issues so rated can be regarded as having extremely poor prospects of ever attaining any real investment standing.

Source: *Moody's Industrial Manual 1995,* page vi.

EXHIBIT 8
Distribution of Peer Firms' Bond Ratings

Peers	Moody's Rating	S&P's Rating
Minnesota, Mining and Manufacturing	Aaa	AAA
Eastman Kodak Hewlett-Packard Fuji	Aa	AA
Xerox Sony	A	A
Black & Decker Polaroid Tektronix	Baa	BBB
Digital Equipment	Ba	BB

Source: Company document.

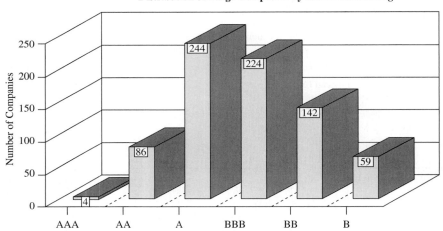

Distribution of Large Companies by Senior Debt Rating

Source of graph: Company documents, and Hudson Guaranty analysis reflecting all rated firms with market value between $250 million and $10 billion at year-end 1995.

EXHIBIT 9
Key Industrial Financial Ratios by Rating Categories: Median Values for the Three Years 1993–95

	AAA	AA	A	BBB	BB	B
Pretax interest coverage (x)[1]	13.50	9.67	5.76	3.94	2.14	1.17
EBITDA[2] Interest coverage (x)	17.08	12.80	8.18	6.00	3.49	2.16
Funds from operations total debt (%)	98.20	69.10	45.50	33.30	17.70	12.80
Free operating cash flow/total debt (%)	60.00	26.80	20.90	7.20	1.40	−0.90
Pretax return on permanent capital (%)	29.30	21.40	19.10	13.90	12.00	9.00
Operating income/sales (%)	22.60	17.80	15.70	13.50	13.50	12.30
Long-term debt/capital (%)[3]	13.30	21.10	31.60	42.70	55.60	65.50
Total debt/capital incl. short-term debt (%)[4]	25.90	33.60	39.70	47.80	59.40	69.50

Standard and Poor's defined these ratios based on the book value of these items as follows:

[1]Pretax interest coverage is EBIT/interest expense.
[2]EBIT plus depreciation and amortization/interest expense.
[3]Long-term debt/capital = long-term debt/(long-term debt + stockholders equity)
[4]Total debt/capital incl. short-term debt = (short-term debt + long-term debt)/(short-term debt + long-term debt + stockholders equity)

Source: Standard & Poor's *CreditWeek,* October 30, 1996, p. 26.

EXHIBIT 10
Polaroid's EBIT Coverage Ratios by Year (1987 to 1995)

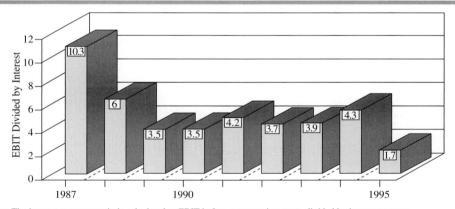

Note: The interest coverage ratio is calculated as EBIT before restructuring costs, divided by interest expense.

Source: Company document.

EXHIBIT 11
Capital Costs by Rating Category

	AAA	AA	A	BBB	BB	B
Cost of Debt (Pretax)	6.70%	6.90%	7.00%	7.40%	9.00%	10.60%
Cost of Equity	10.25	10.3	10.4	10.5	11.75	13.00

Source: Company documents and analysis by Hudson Guaranty using August 1995 data calculated for 314 publicly rated industrial firms, and adjusted to reflect capital market conditions in March 1996.

EXHIBIT 12
Capital-Market Conditions, March 26, 1996

U.S. Treasury Obligations	Yield
90-day bills	5.08%
1-year notes	5.37
5-year notes	6.00
10-year bonds	6.24
15-year bonds	6.42
20-year bonds	6.72
25-year bonds	6.77

Corporate Debt Obligations (10-year)	
AAA	6.73%
AA	6.87
A	7.04
BBB	7.40
BB	9.10
B	10.52

Other Instruments	
Prime rate loans	8.25%
Federal reserve bank discount rate	5.00
Certificates of deposit (90 day)	5.29
Commercial paper (6 months)	5.26

U.S. Treasury Yield Curve

At March 26, 1996   At January 1, 1996

CASE 32

Rosario Acero S.A.

In March 1997, Pablo Este sat in a comfortable chair in the living room of his home in Buenos Aires, reflecting on the future of the small steel mill he owned. The initial years of Rosario Acero S.A., the former Rosario Works of Giganto Acero S.A., had been one challenge after another—the divestiture of Rosario from Giganto, downsizing the operations and workforce, searching for new customers during the six-month Giganto Acero strike at a time when sales to Giganto Acero accounted for nearly one-half the company's total sales, and arguing with local bankers over the value of receivables due from customers facing possible bankruptcy.[1]

Now, after six profitable quarters, the company was preparing to issue its first long-term securities since its incorporation in 1993. The concern Pablo Este faced in March 1997 was the type of capital to acquire. The company's size—revenues were below $35 million pesos[2]—definitely limited options, but Sr. Este, as majority shareholder and chairman of Rosario Acero S.A.'s board of directors, wanted to consider all the options available at the time.

He had engaged Raul Martinez, an independent financial consultant, to investigate a private placement of eight-year senior notes with warrants. Sr. Martinez's initial report stated that Rosario Acero S.A. could raise its required $7.5 million at a coupon rate of 13 percent. Another option Sr. Este was interested in evaluating was an initial public offering

---

[1] *Acero* is Spanish for "steel." "S.A." stands for *"sociedad anonimo,"* the equivalent of a corporation.

[2] The Argentine peso was fixed at a 1:1 exchange rate with the U.S. dollar. Local convention was to indicate the currency with the dollar sign.

This case adapts an earlier study written by Renee Weaver and revised by Casey Optiz under the direction of Professor Robert F. Bruner. It was written as a basis for class discussion rather than to illustrate effective or ineffective handling of an administrative situation. All names and financial data have been disguised. Copyright © 1998 by the University of Virginia Darden School Foundation, Charlottesville, VA. All rights reserved. *To order copies, send an e-mail to* dardencases@virginia.edu. *No part of this publication may be reproduced, stored in a retrieval system, used in a spreadsheet, or transmitted in any form or by any means—electronic, mechanical, photocopying, recording, or otherwise—without the permission of the Darden School Foundation.* Rev. 12/01. Version 1.2.

of Rosario Acero S.A.'s stock through a local investment bank. And perhaps now was the time to sell the entire company to another firm.

THE COMPANY

History

Just two days after Christmas 1992, Giganto Acero announced the closing of 15 unprofitable business units, among which was the Rosario, Argentina, plant operated by Giganto Acero since 1932. In April 1993, Pablo Este, a Rosario native, Harvard Business School graduate, and successful small business entrepreneur, was introduced by Rosario civic leaders to members of the plant's top management. After reviewing the situation, Sr. Este agreed to commit the necessary capital, time, and managerial expertise to save the operation and make the mill a viable company in Rosario. Giganto Acero would remain an important customer. After brief negotiations, Sr. Este and a group of investment partners purchased the assets of the plant for $14 million, the bulk of which was financed by seller notes from Giganto Acero—Este and his partners invested only $250,000 in the equity of the firm. The plant began operating as Rosario Acero S.A. in July 1993.

Product Lines and Sales

Taking advantage of existing facilities and numerous opportunities to cut costs, Rosario management positioned the company as a niche player in the industry. Rosario Acero S.A. sold a variety of cast and fabricated steel products to over 35 steel and other heavy industry customers. The percentage of sales in each major product category for the years 1994–1996 is shown in **Exhibit 1.** Six product managers located in Rosario oversaw each of six product categories: rolling-mill rolls, steel castings, staves, mill liners, continuous caster rolls, and miscellaneous products. The company employed five outside salespersons on straight salary in Buenos Aires and Rosario, Argentina; Montevideo, Uruguay; São Paulo, Brazil; and Santiago, Chile.

The vast majority of the company's sales were to integrated steel producers (Giganto Acero and Brasilia Metal together accounted for 65 percent of sales in 1994; 49 percent in 1995; and 42 percent in 1996) and minimills. These buyers were very different types of customers. The integrated producers tended to multisource orders, which made them less price-sensitive consumers than minimills; they also tended to place more value on their long-standing supplier relationships. Minimills tended to be price sensitive, and though they relied on a single supplier, they were more likely to consider purchasing from suppliers outside of Mercosur.[3]

The company's chief product was rolling-mill rolls, which were like rolling pins found in a kitchen. These rolls were sold in pairs, and were used to squeeze moving slabs of hot

---

[3]Mercosur was the South American free trade association formed by treaty among Argentina, Brazil, and Uruguay.

or cold steel into a certain shape and thickness. Rolling-mill rolls accounted for nearly half of the firm's net sales in 1996. The company estimated its gross margins on this product at 32 percent. The company ranked itself second in the Mercosur market for rolling-mill rolls, with a 17 percent share.

Continuous caster rolls were used to channel molten steel as it was cooled during the casting process.[4] Repair and remachining of caster rolls was required on a regular basis. Rosario Acero S.A. provided this refurbishment, in addition to preparation of new rolls, to its customers who did not have the in-house capability to refurbish rolls. Company officials estimated gross margins on continuous caster rolls at 12 percent. The market for new rolls in Mercosur was approximately $25 million in 1996, so Rosario's sales gave it about a 13 percent share.

Rosario Acero S.A. produced both machined[5] (finished) and nonmachined (rough) steel castings in a variety of sizes from 1,500 to 45,000 kilograms for a diverse group of customers, including steel makers, cement producers, shipbuilders, automotive manufacturers, extrusion-press operators, and rock and coal crushers. One example of steel castings was the slag pot, a steel vessel used to receive the impurities thrown off from blast furnaces and reheating furnaces. The company estimated the total potential slag pot market in Mercosur at $5 million, of which its share in the manufacture of small pots (those under 30,000 kilograms) was 80 percent. Overall, gross margins on rough castings were approximately 18 percent; gross margins on finished castings were just 2 percent.

Mill liner was a rolled steel liner plate and lift bar used in industrial grinding machines for grinding cement, pulverizing coal, and grinding high-silica sand for glass production. Rosario Acero S.A. produced mill liners from purchased parts at gross margins of 40 percent.

Facilities and Operations

All of Rosario Acero S.A.'s production took place at the company's sole facility in Rosario, Argentina. The plant housed two electric furnaces used to melt scrap metal for production (for a total melting capacity of 61,000 kilograms). All melting and pouring was done from 17:00 to 9:00 on weekdays, or on weekends, to minimize energy costs. This practice saved an estimated $50,000 in monthly electricity costs. Factory overhead accounted for 63 percent of Rosario Acero S.A.'s cost of goods sold.

Plant equipment and facilities had been well maintained under Giganto Acero ownership, with capital spending totaling over $25 million from 1976–89. Capital spending by Rosario Acero S.A. totaled $3 million from 1993 to March 1997, with additional spending planned from a portion of the long-term capital to be raised.

Rosario Acero S.A. relied on one primary source, located in Buenos Aires, for the scrap metal used in its production of rolls and castings. **Exhibit 2** lists scrap prices during the recent

---

[4]Molten steel would be poured into rectangular boxes where it would harden into steel ingots. This process was known as "casting" the steel. More generally, there were two ways to shape steel: (1) bend, stretch, cut, drill, or squeeze it under pressure, or (2) pour it into a preformed mold where it would harden into the desired shape—the latter was casting.

[5]Machining was a process of shaping the steel through cutting or drilling.

year. Within the structure of Rosario Acero S.A.'s costs, direct materials including scrap accounted for 26 percent of the cost of goods sold in 1996.

The company's plant operated seven days a week on three shifts as of the end of 1996, with an hourly work force of 816. The unionized work force, (40 percent semiskilled, 60 percent skilled), earned an average hourly wage of $3.75 during 1996. Direct labor accounted for 11 percent of Rosario Acero S.A.'s cost of goods sold in 1996. All hourly employees were represented by the Union de Obreros Metalurgicos (Metalworkers' Union) under a contract that expired in June 1998. The hourly wage rate for comparable work was $4.25. Union leaders had told Pablo Este that the hourly employees would demand a better-than-competitive contract at the expiration of the current contract—this was to compensate the employees for staying with the firm through its difficulties.[6]

The company also operated with 118 administrative employees, and a new CEO, Enrique Salazar, was appointed in May 1996 to assume operational responsibility under Pablo Este. Other members of senior management under Giganto Acero ownership held the same positions now, with the exception of the former company president, who had resigned in February 1997.

Six top managers other than Pablo Este held 25 percent of the stock outstanding at the end of 1996. Sr. Este held 58 percent. Este's investment partners held the balance of the shares outstanding.

THE STEEL INDUSTRY IN 1997

In 1996 the Argentine steel industry enjoyed a moderately profitable year. Several factors accounted for this turnaround in the industry. First, capacity cutbacks and modernization programs of the past half decade paid off; the industry reached 80 percent capacity in 1996, with utilization for high-demand items near 100 percent. In addition, the birth of the Mercosur trade group promoted more trade by Argentine firms with customers in Brazil and Uruguay.

Forecasts for 1997 and the next three to five years were favorable but contingent on producers continuing their recent efforts to remain competitive in the industry. Domestic steel shipments were estimated to be 70 million metric tons, slightly below 1996 because of cutbacks in inventories rather than lower consumption. Imports were expected to continue their decline from the 1996 level of 20 million metric tons to less than 19 million tons in 1997.

ROSARIO ACERO S.A.'S OUTLOOK

Rosario Acero S.A.'s revenues and earnings had grown since the company began operations in July 1993. The company's balance sheets and income statements for this period are provided in **Exhibits 3** and **4.** Management predicted continued growth into the new century,

---

[6]The financial forecasts by Pablo Este assumed modest increases in wage rates, consistent with expectations for competitive market conditions.

with different product lines growing at different rates. Annualized rates of growth from 1996 to 2002 were projected by product line as follows:

Product Line	1996 Sales (in millions)	1996–2002 Projected Growth Rate
Rolling-mill rolls	$16.0	13.9%
Castings	9.0	1.4
Slag pots	1.4	19.6
Mill liner	1.6	14.5
Continuous caster rolls	3.3	5.7
Fabricated and other	3.5	6.8
Total	$34.8	Average 10.32%

In addition to continuing to serve present customers, Sr. Este wanted the company to pursue customers outside Mercosur. As yet, management had taken no action to investigate external markets, largely because of capital constraints on the firm.

ROSARIO ACERO S.A.'S FINANCING ALTERNATIVES

Management was seeking $7.5 million in long-term capital for three purposes in early 1997: (1) $4.8 million to pay down the company's present working-capital line of credit, (2) $975,000 to repay long-term debt that would mature in mid-1997, and (3) the remaining $1,725,000 for capital improvements and general purposes. The company would retain its recently negotiated $5 million working-capital line of credit with Banco de Sol of Buenos Aires. This line, at 2 percent above the local lending base rate, was not secured by any collateral,[7] though Pablo Este had given a personal guarantee backed by certain commercial real estate he owned. The banker had stated emphatically that an increase in the line of credit and release of Pablo Este from his guarantee would be out of the question without more long-term capital supporting the loan and a longer record of successful financial performance.

The private placement of eight-year notes recommended by Raul Martinez would have the terms set forth in **Exhibit 5.** The potential purchasers were two Spanish investment funds. The fee associated with issuing the placement through Sr. Martinez would be $52,000. The prospective investors demanded warrants with the debt, because of the firm's small size, relatively high leverage, and absence of a long history of operating profitability. Sr. Martinez explained that the warrants were a "kicker" that increased the effective return to the investors. The covenants associated with this placement were yet to be negotiated. The Spanish investors told Martinez that the minimum acceptable EBIT coverage ratio (i.e., EBIT divided by interest expense) would be 2.0. As a foundation for

---

[7]The custom of extending working-capital loans "clean" (i.e., unsecured by the firm's receivables and inventory) was due to the difficulties in Argentina of getting a perfected lien, and filing new paperwork to keep up the lien as the inventory and receivables rolled over.

valuing the warrants, Sr. Martinez estimated the average volatility of peer steel companies' shares at 0.35. Martinez had also determined that in several recent comparable private placements of debt, the effective annual cost of the financing to the issuer had been between 14 and 16 percent, representing a huge premium over the Argentine base lending rate of 8.5 percent.

A second financing alternative that Pablo Este considered was an initial public offering (IPO) of the company's stock. While the 233,000 shares of stock currently outstanding were not presently traded, six senior managers had been offered (and had accepted) a chance to invest three times since the company's inception at prices as follows:[8]

December 1994:	15,480 shares at $3.00/share
January 1995:	14,220 shares at $4.00/share
December 1996:	28,550 shares at $9.00/share

These purchases accounted for management's 25 percent equity interest in the firm.

Fees associated with an IPO were expected to be about 8 percent, but they could be reduced to 2 percent if a "best efforts" placement was selected rather than a guaranteed underwriting. Public trading of the stock would have implications for the shares held by top management and Sr. Este. For instance, Sr. Este wanted to see the issue open at a price higher than the $9 that managers had most recently paid for their shares of Rosario Acero S.A. For this reason, he had concluded that the size of the issue would have to be determined after a market value had been placed on the company.

The IPO market had recovered modestly since the Mexican peso crash of November 1994. By March 1997, the stock market had rebounded from the "tequila effect" of the peso crash. The Merval index had risen over the previous three years, suggesting a growing optimism among equity investors in Argentina. The market for IPOs was following this same recovery route, although the volume of IPOs was still relatively light.

The success of IPOs in recent months had depended a great deal on the quality of the offering; issues in more stable and mature industries that appealed to the knowledgeable investors were faring better than media and communications issues. A number of the recent IPOs involved privatizations of state-owned enterprises. Other IPOs were spin-offs from larger industrial groups seeking to rationalize their operations. One recent example was a spin-off of a subsidiary involved in a commodity fertilizer business that brought $22 a share on 11 million shares, surpassing expectations of $17 to $20 a share set for the issue prior to the November crash. In contrast was a retailer's first issue that had been planned for the end of November 1996. The company had expected to issue $9 million in equity, but it was forced to look elsewhere for funds when it could not locate another underwriter after its first banker withdrew.

Pablo Este had recently entertained the idea of selling Rosario Acero to another concern, although no specific price had been estimated for the company at that time. This option could be considered in more detail, this time as a means of obtaining funds or issuing stock to the public.

To value Rosario Acero S.A., Sr. Este had forecasted the financial performance of the firm under either financing option, the debt-and-warrants issue (see **Exhibits 6, 7,** and **8**)

---

[8]The number of shares currently outstanding, 233,000, included these recent share sales.

or the equity issue (see **Exhibit 9, 10,** and **11**). Also, he obtained average valuation multiples for minimills from a recent investment report; these indicated an average equity value of 1.5 times book value, 21 times 1996 earnings, and 18 times estimated 1997 earnings. Sr. Este had also gathered information on several publicly held steel producers in Mercosur that were somewhat similar to Rosario Acero S.A. This information is contained in **Exhibit 12.** He wondered whether to simply average the results of all the peers given in that exhibit, or to exclude any; Picasso Acero, for instance, had experienced a turbulent year due to a strike and vandalism at its plant. Based on his own experience with leveraged buyouts, Sr. Este believed that a potential LBO purchaser might place a value on the company's equity by using a multiple of 4 times EBIT and then subtracting total debt.

Interest rates over the past few years are provided in **Exhibits 13** and **14.** Research by Raul Martinez revealed that economists and financial institutions were forecasting annual rates of inflation between 2.5 and 4.0 percent, and real GNP growth at 1.5 to 6.0 percent.

Pablo Este was 66 years old and the patriarch of a large extended family. While he had no intention of retiring from Rosario's board of directors soon, he was concerned about the liquidity of his valuable investment in the firm. It was important to him and the other equity investors to increase the marketability of Rosario's common stock. However, tempering any momentum to choose the IPO was the cautious sentiment among senior management regarding the impact of any securities issuance on their administrative control of the firm.

Sr. Este realized that, as chairman of the board, he could easily rely on someone else to explore the various options that might be available to Rosario Acero S.A. As the key framer of the company's success so far, however, he had an interest in seeing the board select the alternative that would best assure a continuation of that financial and employment success. With much information in front of him and all of his knowledge of Rosario Acero S.A. in his head, Pablo Este sat down to determine which long-term financing option he would support.

EXHIBIT 1
Percentage of Company Sales by Product Line[1]

	1994	1995	1996	Feb. 1997[2]	Recent Gross Profit Margins
Rolls	40%	46%	46%	68%	32%
Castings	29	27	29	20	18 (rough)
					2 (finished)
Continuous caster rolls	4	6	9	6	12
Mill liners	8	5	5	2	40
Staves	0	3	1	1	
Other products	17	8	5	4	80 (small pots)
Services	2	4	4	0	
Total	100%	100%	100%	100%	

[1]Columns may not add to 100 because of rounding.
[2]1997 percentages based on bookings as of February 1997.
Source: Company records.

EXHIBIT 2
Scrap Prices of Dealer Bundles
(price per metric ton delivered
from Buenos Aires)

Date of Estimate	Price Range
12/95	$ 96–97
1/96	99–100
2/96	104–105
3/96	98–99
4/96	93–94
5/96	103–104
6/96	114–115
7/96	115–116
8/96	119–120
9/96	131–132
10/96	159–160
11/96	159–160
12/96	144–145
1/97	139–140

Source: Company records.

EXHIBIT 3
Balance Sheets (pesos in thousands)

	As of December 31		
	1994	**1995**	**1996**
Cash	$ 119	$ 0	$ 245
Accounts receivable	3,077	3,845	6,846
Inventories	5,186	4,786	4,682
Other current assets	865	168	381
Total current assets	9,247	8,799	12,154
Property, plant, & equipment	13,938	14,054	14,210
Other	193	187	116
Total assets	$23,378	$23,040	$26,480
Working capital notes payable	$ 4,650	$ 4,998	$ 4,821
Current portion long-term debt	1,706	1,171	1,335
Accounts payable	3,313	3,048	4,663
Other current liabilities	804	1,993	2,315
Total current liabilities	10,473	11,210	13,134
Long-term debt	11,804	8,847	8,467
Deferred taxes & leases	312	1,258	1,282
Total liabilities	22,589	21,315	22,883
Common stock (Par = $1/sh)	210	202	233
Additional paid-in capital	71	114	191
Retained earnings	508	1,409	3,173
Total owners' equity	789	1,725	3,597
Total liabilities & equity	$23,378	$23,040	$26,480

Source: Company financial statements.

EXHIBIT 4
Income Statements (in thousands of pesos, except per-share data)

| | As of December 31 | | |
	1994	1995[1]	1996
Revenues	$25,084	$26,605	$34,836
Cost of goods sold (including depreciation)[2]	18,138	21,784	27,654
Selling, general, & administrative	3,598	3,767	3,959
Interest	1,586	1,461	1,098
Restructuring expenses	445	142	537
Profit before tax	1,317	(549)	1,588
Tax provision (benefit)	577	(285)	4
Income (loss) before extraordinary item	740	(264)	1,584
Extraordinary item[3]	265	1,165	179
Net income	$ 1,005	$ 901	$ 1,763
Earnings per share	$4.79	$4.46	$7.57

[1]Company loss in 1995 was attributed to sales lost as a result of a six-month strike against Giganto Acero, a major account for Rosario.
[2]COGS includes depreciation of $736,000 in 1994, $876,000 in 1995, and $935,000 in 1996.
[3]Extraordinary income resulted from refunding of debt, net of applicable income taxes in 1995 and 1996. Credits on income taxes due to net operating loss carryovers resulted in extraordinary income in 1994.

Source: Company financial statements.

EXHIBIT 5
Summary of Terms of Proposed Private Placement

Amount	$7,500,000
Issue	Senior notes with warrants
Maturity	8 years due 2004
Takedown	Second quarter 1997
Interest Rate	13% per annum, payable semiannually
Amortization	Interest only for the first six years. Mandatory principal payments of $1,875,000 in the seventh year, and $5,625,000 in the eighth year.
Optional Redemption	None for the first six years. Callable thereafter at the following redemption prices as a whole or in part:

Year 7	105%
Year 8	100% (no premium)

Warrants The notes will be accompanied by an 8-year nondetachable warrant entitling the holder to purchase 40,000 shares of common stock at an exercise price of $1 per share. The warrant shares will be subject to antidilution provisions and be adjusted for stock splits, stock dividends, recapitalizations, mergers, and the sale of stock, issuance of options, or securities or warrants convertible or issuable into common stock, all at a price in excess of $1 per share.

The number of warrant shares will be adjusted on a one-time basis based on the average of net operating income for the years 1997 and 1998. Such adjustment will occur in the first quarter of 1999.

Net Operating Income	Number of Shares	Percent of Ownership
$6,000,000 or greater	40,000	15.0%
5,999,999–5,000,000	47,725	17.5
4,999,999–4,000,000	56,250	20.0
3,999,999–3,000,000	65,325	22.5
less than 3,000,000	75,000	25.0

Net operating income will be defined as stated in the company's audited financials, before interest and provision for income taxes, and will conform with generally accepted definitions of operating income.

Optional Put The warrant shares can be put to the company, starting at the end of the fifth year by the holder of the warrant at a price per share equivalent to the then "appraised market value per share." Such value shall be calculated by taking operating income before taxes and interest for the latest four quarters and multiplying the sum by six, adding cash and marketable securities, and deducting short-term and long-term debt. This sum will be divided by fully diluted shares outstanding to arrive at an "appraised market value per share." The warrant holder may not put in excess of 25% of his warrant shares to the company in any one year.

Provision for Early Redemption Redemption of the senior notes before maturity would not be permitted.

Registration Rights The warrant shares will be subject to one free right of registration after the company's initial public offering and unlimited rights to piggyback other public offerings of the stock, subject to consent of underwriters.

Restrictive Covenants on the Notes To be negotiated.

Source: Raul Martinez, second draft of Private Placement Memorandum.

EXHIBIT 6

Forecast of Income Statement: Growth Financed with the Privately Placed Debt-and-Warrants Issue (in millions of pesos, except per-share data)

Common Assumptions

Revenue growth rate=	10.30%	Inventory/Revenues=	13.00%
COGS/Revenues=	78.00%	Other curr. assets/Revenues=	1.00%
SG&A/Revenues=	13.00%	Gross fixed assets/Revenues=	48.00%
Tax rate=	34.00%	Accts. payable/Revenues=	14.00%
Depreciation/Gross fixed assets=	5.60%	Other. curr. liabs/Revenues=	7.00%
Cash/Revenues=	1.00%	Interest rate=	10.00%
Accts. receivable/Revenues=	20.00%	Change in defd tax/Taxes=	25.00%
Base lending rate=	8.50%	Primary shares=	233,000
		Fully-diluted shares=	273,000

	Actual	Projected					
	1996	**1997**	**1998**	**1999**	**2000**	**2001**	**2002**
Income Statement							
Revenues	$ 34.80	$ 38.38	$ 42.34	$ 46.70	$ 51.51	$ 56.81	$ 62.67
Cost of goods sold	(27.65)	(29.94)	(33.02)	(36.43)	(40.18)	(44.32)	(48.88)
Selling, gen'l, & admin.	(3.96)	(4.99)	(5.50)	(6.07)	(6.70)	(7.39)	(8.15)
Earnings before interest and taxes	3.19	3.45	3.81	4.20	4.64	5.11	5.64
Interest (notes and old loans) (1)	(1.10)	(0.73)	(0.70)	(0.65)	(0.59)	(0.51)	(0.41)
Interest (new loan @ 13%)		(0.98)	(0.98)	(0.98)	(0.98)	(0.98)	(0.98)
Profit before taxes	2.09	1.75	2.13	2.57	3.07	3.63	4.26
Taxes	0.00	(0.59)	(0.72)	(0.88)	(1.04)	(1.23)	(1.45)
Profit after taxes	$ 2.09	$ 1.15	$ 1.41	$ 1.70	$ 2.03	$ 2.40	$ 2.81
Profit with extraord. item	1.76						
Earnings per share	$ 7.57	$ 4.96	$ 6.04	$ 7.29	$ 8.70	$ 10.28	$ 12.06

Note 1: The firm is assumed to borrow at base rate plus 2 percent, and lend at base rate less 2 percent.

EXHIBIT 7
Forecast of Balance Sheets: Growth Financed with the Private Placement of Debt and Warrants (pesos in millions, except per-share data)

	Actual	Projected					
	1996	1997	1998	1999	2000	2001	2002
Balance Sheet							
Cash	$ 0.20	$ 0.38	$ 0.42	$ 0.47	$ 0.52	$ 0.57	$ 0.63
Accounts receivable	6.80	7.68	8.47	9.34	10.30	11.36	12.53
Inventory	4.70	4.99	5.50	6.07	6.70	7.39	8.15
Other current assets	0.40	0.38	0.42	0.47	0.52	0.57	0.63
Total current assets	12.10	13.43	14.82	16.34	18.03	19.88	21.93
Gross fixed assets	16.70	18.42	20.32	22.42	24.72	27.27	30.08
Accumulated depreciation	(2.50)	(3.53)	(4.67)	(5.93)	(7.31)	(8.84)	(10.52)
Net fixed assets	14.20	14.89	15.65	16.49	17.41	18.43	19.56
Other assets	0.10	0.10	0.10	0.10	0.10	0.10	0.10
Total assets	$ 26.40	$ 28.43	$ 30.57	$ 32.93	$ 35.54	$ 38.42	$ 41.59
Notes payable (or excess cash)	$ 4.80	$ (0.76)	$ (0.84)	$ (0.81)	$ (1.00)	$ (1.44)	$ (2.17)
Accounts payable	4.60	5.37	5.93	6.54	7.21	7.95	8.77
Other current liabilities	2.30	2.69	2.96	3.27	3.61	3.98	4.39
Total current liabilities	11.70	7.30	8.05	9.00	9.82	10.49	10.99
Old long term debt	9.80	7.43	7.23	6.73	6.23	5.73	5.23
New long term debt		7.50	7.50	7.50	7.50	7.50	7.50
Deferred taxes	1.30	1.45	1.63	1.85	2.11	2.42	2.78
Total liabilities	22.80	23.67	24.41	25.07	25.66	26.14	26.50
Common stock	0.20	0.20	0.20	0.20	0.20	0.20	0.20
Paid-in surplus	0.20	0.20	0.20	0.20	0.20	0.20	0.20
Retained earnings	3.20	4.35	5.76	7.46	9.49	11.88	14.69
Total liabilities and equity	$ 26.40	$ 28.43	$ 30.57	$ 32.93	$ 35.54	$ 38.42	$ 41.59
Comparative Ratios							
EBIT/Interest	2.90	2.03	2.27	2.58	2.96	3.45	4.08
EBIT/(Interest + Amort.)	1.93	0.36	1.95	2.00	2.06	2.11	2.16
Liabilities/Equity	6.33	4.98	3.96	3.19	2.59	2.13	1.76
(Debt+Notes)/Equity	4.06	2.98	2.25	1.71	1.29	0.96	0.70
Profit/Revenues	5.1%	3.0%	3.3%	3.6%	3.9%	4.2%	4.5%
Profit/Equity	49.0%	24.3%	22.8%	21.6%	20.5%	19.5%	18.6%

EXHIBIT 8
Forecast of Free Cash Flow: Growth Financed with Debt and Warrants (pesos in millions)

	Projected					
	1997	1998	1999	2000	2001	2002
Earnings before interest and taxes	3.45	3.81	4.20	4.64	5.11	5.64
Taxes	(1.17)	(1.30)	(1.43)	(1.58)	(1.74)	(1.92)
Earnings before interest and after taxes	2.28	2.51	2.77	3.06	3.37	3.72
Plus depreciation	1.03	1.14	1.26	1.38	1.53	1.68
Less capital expenditures	(1.72)	(1.90)	(2.09)	(2.31)	(2.55)	(2.81)
Less additions to net working capital	(0.17)	(0.55)	(0.61)	(0.67)	(0.74)	(0.82)
Free cash flow	1.41	1.20	1.33	1.46	1.61	1.78

EXHIBIT 9
Forecast of Income Statements: Growth Financed with Equity, Shares Sold at $9.00 Each (pesos in millions, except per-share data)

Common Assumptions

Revenue growth rate=	10.30%	Inventory/Revenues=	13.00%
COGS/Revenues=	78.00%	Other curr. assets/Revenues=	1.00%
SG&A/Revenues=	13.00%	Gross fixed assets/Revenues=	48.00%
Tax rate=	34.00%	Accts. payable/Revenues=	14.00%
Depreciation/Gross fixed assets=	5.60%	Other. curr. liabs/Revenues=	7.00%
Cash/Revenues=	1.00%	Interest rate=	10.00%
Accts. receivable/Revenues=	20.00%	Change in defd tax/Taxes=	25.00%
Base lending rate=	8.50%	1996 primary shares=	233,000
		1997 + primary shares=	1,066,333

	Actual	Projected					
	1996	1997	1998	1999	2000	2001	2002
Income Statement							
Revenues	$ 34.80	$ 38.38	$ 42.34	$ 46.70	$ 51.51	$ 56.81	$ 62.67
Cost of goods sold	(27.65)	(29.94)	(33.02)	(36.43)	(40.18)	(44.32)	(48.88)
Selling, gen'l, & admin.	(3.96)	(4.99)	(5.50)	(6.07)	(6.70)	(7.39)	(8.15)
Earnings before interest and taxes	3.19	3.45	3.81	4.20	4.64	5.11	5.64
Interest (on notes and old loans) (1)	(1.10)	(0.68)	(0.60)	(0.50)	(0.37)	(0.23)	(0.07)
Interest (new loan @ 13%)		0.00	0.00	0.00	0.00	0.00	0.00
Profit before taxes	2.09	2.77	3.21	3.71	4.26	4.88	5.57
Taxes	0.00	(0.94)	(1.09)	(1.26)	(1.45)	(1.66)	(1.89)
Profit after taxes	$ 2.09	$ 1.83	$ 2.12	$ 2.45	$ 2.81	$ 3.22	$ 3.68
Profit with extraord item	1.76						
Earnings per share	$ 7.57	$ 1.72	$ 1.99	$ 2.29	$ 2.64	$ 3.02	$ 3.45

Note 1. The firm is assumed to borrow at base rate plus 2 percent, and lend at base rate less 2 percent.

EXHIBIT 10
Forecast of Balance Sheets: Growth Financed with Equity, Shares Sold at $9.00 Each (in millions of pesos, except per-share data)

	Actual	Projected					
	1996	1997	1998	1999	2000	2001	2002
Balance Sheet							
Cash	$ 0.20	$ 0.38	$0.42	$ 0.47	$ 0.52	$ 0.57	$ 0.63
Accounts receivable	6.80	7.68	8.47	9.34	10.30	11.36	12.53
Inventory	4.70	4.99	5.50	6.07	6.70	7.39	8.15
Other current assets	0.40	0.38	0.42	0.47	0.52	0.57	0.63
Total current assets	12.10	13.43	14.82	16.34	18.03	19.88	21.93
Gross fixed assets	16.70	18.42	20.32	22.42	24.72	27.27	30.08
Accumulated depreciation	(2.50)	(3.53)	(4.67)	(5.93)	(7.31)	(8.84)	(10.52)
Net fixed assets	14.20	14.89	15.65	16.49	17.41	18.43	19.56
Other assets	0.10	0.10	0.10	0.10	0.10	0.10	0.10
Total assets	$26.40	$28.43	$30.57	$32.93	$35.54	$38.42	$41.59
Notes payable (or excess cash)	4.80	(1.53)	(2.40)	(3.21)	(4.29)	(5.66)	(7.37)
Accounts payable	4.60	5.37	5.93	6.54	7.21	7.95	8.77
Other current liabilities	2.30	2.69	2.96	3.27	3.61	3.98	4.39
Total current liabilities	11.70	6.54	6.49	6.59	6.53	6.27	5.79
Old long-term debt	9.80	7.43	7.23	6.73	6.23	5.73	5.23
New long-term debt		0.00	0.00	0.00	0.00	0.00	0.00
Deferred taxes	1.30	1.54	1.81	2.12	2.49	2.90	3.37
Total liabilities	22.80	15.50	15.52	15.44	15.24	14.89	14.39
Common stock	0.20	1.20	1.20	1.20	1.20	1.20	1.20
Paid-in surplus	0.20	6.70	6.70	6.70	6.70	6.70	6.70
Retained earnings	3.20	5.03	7.15	9.59	12.41	15.63	19.30
Total liabilities and equity	$26.40	$28.43	$30.57	$32.93	$35.54	$38.42	$41.59
Comparative Ratios							
EBIT/Interest	2.90	5.08	6.32	8.45	12.37	21.95	81.14
EBIT/(Interest + Amort.)	1.93	0.37	2.27	2.32	2.38	2.43	2.48
Liabilities/Equity	6.33	1.20	1.03	0.88	0.75	0.63	0.53
(Debt+Notes)/Equity	4.06	0.46	0.32	0.20	0.10	0.00	-0.08
Profit/Revenues	5.1%	4.8%	5.0%	5.2%	5.5%	5.7%	5.9%
Profit/Equity	49.0%	14.2%	14.1%	14.0%	13.8%	13.7%	13.5%

EXHIBIT 11
Forecast of Free Cash Flow: Growth Financed with Equity, Shares Sold at $9.00 Each
(in millions of pesos)

	Projected					
	1997	**1998**	**1999**	**2000**	**2001**	**2002**
Earnings before interest and taxes	3.45	3.81	4.20	4.64	5.11	5.64
Taxes	(1.17)	(1.30)	(1.43)	(1.58)	(1.74)	(1.92)
Earnings before interest and after taxes	2.28	2.51	2.77	3.06	3.37	3.72
Plus depreciation	1.03	1.14	1.26	1.38	1.53	1.68
Less capital expenditures	(1.72)	(1.90)	(2.09)	(2.31)	(2.55)	(2.81)
Less additions to net working capital	(0.17)	(0.55)	(0.61)	(0.67)	(0.74)	(0.82)
Free cash flow	1.41	1.20	1.33	1.46	1.61	1.78

EXHIBIT 12
Selected 1996 Data on Publicly Listed Peer Firms

Description of Business

Acero Dali S.A. (AD)	Production and fabrication of steel reinforcing and merchant bars. Principal customers: building, road, and bridge contractors; municipal, county, and state agencies; concrete manufacturers; railroad, utility, and industrial companies. Marketing areas: Argentina, Uruguay, Brazil, and the Caribbean. Directors own 3% of stock.
Colon S.A. (CSA)	Makes and distributes furnace lining materials (69% of sales), mainly to the steel industry. Produces filter media, filters, and oil control products. Mines a variety of ores and clays (14%). Insiders control about 55% of stock.
Greco Acero (GA)	Produces carbon-steel products exclusively by the electric furnace method. Steel scrap is a major raw material. Makes 75% of sales in Argentina to steel service centers, fabricators, and hardware jobbers. Main markets: agriculture and construction. Escobar family owns about 45% of stock.
Velasguez S.A. (VAZ)	Manufactures steel and steel joists (holds 30% of regional market for joists). Major markets: construction, energy, rail, agriculture.
Picasso Acero S.A. (PI)	Leading processor of ferrous scrap (75% of sales) and nonferrous scrap (10%). Picasso family holds about 25% of stock; Tiger group about 15%. Sustained losses in the most recent year due to a strike and strike-related vandalism at its plant.

Operating Information[1]	AD	CSA	GA	VAZ	PI
Sales	$381.0	$362.8	$397.4	$755.2	$117.1
Operating margin	55.6	11.7	26.0	144.9	(1.1)
Net income	16.9	7.5	10.3	46.4	(5.1)
Operating margin/Sales	14.6%	3.2%	6.5%	19.2%	(0.9%)
Net income/Sales	4.4	2.1	2.6	6.1	(4.4%)
LT debt/Capital (book)	40%	56%	22%	33%	42%
Total debt/Capital (book)	57%	66%	40%	37%	65%
Total debt/Equity (book)	1.33	1.94	0.67	0.59	1.86
Market equity/Book equity	1.85	1.25	1.50	2.10	0.90
Total debt/Equity (market)	0.72	1.55	0.44	0.28	2.06
Dividend payout ratio (3-yr. avg.)	27%	0%	15%[2]	12%	0%
Dividend yield	3.0%	0%	3.3%	1.0%	0%
P/E ratio	9.5	15.9	11.3	15.0	7.3
Beta	1.35	1.05	1.00	1.15	2.50
Stock price range (52 weeks)	$44 1/2 – 18 1/4	$20 1/4 – 13 1/2	$24 1/4 – 11 1/8	$49 1/2 – 29 1/2	$54 – 18 3/4
Close Mar. 1, 1997	$32 3/4	$18 5/8	$19 1/2	$42 1/2	$33
5-year annualized per-share growth projections					
Sales	10%		9%	10%	5%
Earnings	17%			12%	
Dividends	14%			12%	8%

[1]All operating information for most recent fiscal year as of March 1997 and in millions of pesos. Other information current as of March 1997 unless noted.
[2]Payout based on 1996 only. No dividends paid previously.
(All data are disguised.)

EXHIBIT 13
Debt-Market Conditions

	March 1997
Average corporate bond yield	9.86%
Base lending rate	8.50
10-year Argentine T-bond	8.50
3-month Argentine T-bill	5.70%

Interest Rate Trends

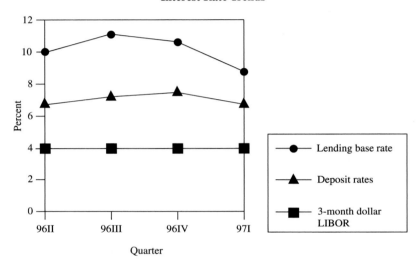

EXHIBIT 14
Current Yields on Selected Debt Issues in South America

Company	Rating[1]	Form of Debt	Coupon	Mat. Date	Current Yield	Yield to Maturity
Sola S.A.	BBB	Notes	8.625	2005	9.02	9.41
HABASA	BBB-	Subordinated notes	9.300	2003	10.35	10.49
Mercado S.A.	CCC+	Subordinated debent.	11.990	2005	16.89	13.05
Orientar S.A.	BBB-	Notes	10.500	2004	10.47	10.45
Serenidad S.A.	CCC-	Sen. sf. debent.	7.750	2004	12.86	17.42
Turismo S.A.	CCC+	Senior subord. notes	13.250	2003	13.25	13.25
Util S.A.	CCC	Sub. sf. debent.	5.000	2003	15.25	16.10
Tulipan S.A.	CCC-	Sinking fund debent.	8.100	2005	15.88	19.08

[1]According to a well-known international debt rating agency, "Debt rated BBB is believed to have a satisfactory capacity to pay interest and repay principal, though that capacity would decline readily if adverse economic conditions or changing circumstances should arise. . . . Debt rated . . . CCC . . . is predominantly speculative."

Recent Private Placement Yields, BBB- Issues

	Company	Form of Debt	Maturity Date	Coupon
January	Grua S.A.	Fixed rate notes	2005	11.25%
	Globo S.A.	Sr. notes	2001	11.35
	Disquete S.A.	Sr. notes	2001	11.40
February	EnergaS.A.	Sr. notes	2006	11.20
	EnergaS.A.	Sr. notes	2002	11.60
	VemcoS.A.	Sub. secured notes	2001	11.50
March	Luza Solaro S.A.	Sec. non-recourse notes	2001	10.90
	Dorar S.A.	Sec. notes	1999	10.80
	Contrahacer S.A.	Sr. sec. notes	2002	10.85
	Coronar S.A.	Sr. notes	2001	10.20

(Data have been disguised.)

Threshold Sports, LLC

Carl Frischkorn closed the door and walked to his desk. As he sat down, he began to reflect on the meeting he had just attended in the conference room of Threshold Sports, LLC. There, Frischkorn had listened as company founders David Chauner and Jerry Casale discussed the company's growth plans. Among the most critical challenges before Threshold was financing. The firm's founders were certain they would need outside financing of $500,000 to grow according to their plans, but they were unsure what type of financing would best fit their needs, how to value the firm, and how to communicate that value to outsiders. Their task over the next few days would be to find answers. For help in the matter, they had sought the input of Frischkorn, a management consultant, angel investor, and chairman of Threshold Sports.

Founded three months earlier in March 2000, Threshold Sports, LLC, was a sports marketing and event production company focusing on the U.S. cycling market. Partners Gerard Casale Jr. and David Chauner had formed the limited liability corporation to buy the cycling assets of Octagon Worldwide, the sports division of advertising and marketing firm The Interpublic Group (IPG). Through the newly formed Threshold, Casale and Chauner sought to market and produce in the United States competitive cycling events like those found throughout Europe.

THE CYCLING MARKET

Part of the Olympic Games since 1896, bicycle racing was popular as both an amateur and professional sport throughout the world. In Europe, indoor and outdoor racing were extremely popular among both amateurs and professionals. The professional circuit in Europe ran from February through October and included the world's largest and most famous annual competitive cycling event, the prestigious Tour de France. The Tour, which covered about 2,256 miles over a four-week period, commanded a worldwide television audience of 1 billion viewers.

In the United States, the popularity of cycling was undeniable. In 1999, U.S. retailers sold a record 7.4 million bicycles. As of 2000, approximately 73 million Americans rode bicycles—outnumbering the ranks of skiers, golfers, and tennis players combined.

Despite the popularity of cycling in the United States and the existence of a national cycling association (USA Cycling, known as USAC), both amateur and professional cycling in the United States lagged in development when compared to other sports. Often regarded simply as a pastime or method of transportation, amateur cycling lacked the community support and organization associated with other amateur sports such as Little League baseball, YMCA soccer, or youth tennis. Likewise, professional cycling in the United States had yet to offer the level of competition and organization available in other sports such as football, baseball, basketball, or hockey, each of which had grown into a multibillion-dollar business (see **Exhibit 1**). Although interest in cycling as a competitive sport had grown with the notable successes of American cyclists Greg LeMond and Lance Armstrong, professional U.S. cycling had yet to develop a signature competitive series such as the PGA Tour or offer an equivalent to the Tour de France.[1]

THRESHOLD SPORTS

Threshold sought to fill the void in U.S. cycling by managing and producing European-style competitive cycling events. Threshold felt confident it could fill this small but attractive niche because of management's experience with event planning and relationships within the cycling world. For 15 years Chief Operating Officer Casale, 52, had staged cycling events including national championship races as well as the cycling events of the 1996 Olympic Games. President and CEO Chauner, 62, was a former Olympic cyclist and a member of the U.S. Bicycling Hall of Fame. In their collective careers as sports promoters, Chauner and Casale had been responsible for producing more than 100 professional cycling events.

On April 1, 2000, Threshold Sports obtained multiyear contracts from Octagon Marketing to host three major cycling events for the USAC: the First Union Cycling Series, BMC Software Grand Prix, and the Saturn U.S. PRO Cycling Tour. According to the terms of the deal, Threshold would pay Octagon an annual lease for the life of the First Union Series Title Sponsorship Agreement while the Saturn and BMC contracts were assigned to Threshold at no cost.

---

[1]LeMond was the first American to win the Tour de France and went on to win the competition three times (1986, 1989, and 1990). Armstrong made headlines by winning the 1999 Tour less than three years after recovering from cancer. Armstrong was chosen to lead the 2002 Olympic Torch Relay in preparation for the 2002 Winter Olympic Games in Salt Lake City.

The First Union Series consisted of a four-event road race series in the Philadelphia area. The crown jewel of the series was the popular First Union US Pro Cycling Championship founded in 1985 by Threshold principals Chauner and Casale. The race attracted 700,000 spectators annually. First Union Bank had already committed to sponsoring the event for $1,150,000 per year for the duration of the five-year contract. Threshold management expected the series to generate annual revenues of approximately $2 million based on sponsorships and merchandising. Threshold would earn a management fee that started at $420,000 and increased to $510,000 and would pay annual lease payments of $200,000 in 2001 increasing to $260,000 in 2005. Profits generated after operating costs, lease payments, and management fees would be split 0.75/0.25 between Threshold and Octagon Marketing respectively.

The BMC Software Grand Prix was a four-event road racing series held in Austin, Houston, San Jose, and Boston. The Lance Armstrong Foundation managed the Austin event while Threshold managed the other three events. According to the contract, which ran through 2003, Threshold's annual revenue for the series would be a minimum of $1,150,000 plus a 50 percent profit share with USAC.

Threshold also obtained an exclusive five-year license to develop and manage the US PRO Cycling Tour (P.C.T), a 17-event series that included both the First Union and BMC races. The Saturn automobile company had contracted to be title sponsor for both 1999 and 2000 with commitments of $700,000 for each year. For the 2000 Tour, Threshold already attracted an additional $300,000 in sponsorships.

In addition to the contracts, Threshold purchased event-staging equipment from Octagon for $65,000—less than one-third its replacement value. Prior to its purchase by Octagon, the equipment had been the principal asset of Special Events Suppliers (SES), an equipment-leasing business operated by Jerry Casale. SES leased the equipment for concerts, city festivals, and parades (including the 1992 presidential inauguration parade). One of its highest profile and lucrative leases was a seven-figure contract staging the 1996 Olympic Cycling events in Atlanta.

GROWTH PROSPECTS AND PLANS

In considering Threshold's long-term prospects, the founders reflected on the success of established sports such as the National Football League (NFL), Major League Baseball (MLB), or the National Basketball Association (NBA) with television and merchandising contracts in the billions of dollars. The key, it seemed, was branding. According to Mark Holtzman, senior vice president for consumer products of NFL Properties, the league's marketing arm, "We see ourselves, like Disney or Tommy Hilfiger, as a brand that has extensions 365 days a year."[2]

Threshold's founders knew that problems in established sports—including strikes and lockouts—had created an opening for relative upstart sports such as the National Associa-

---

[2]Richard Alm, "National Football League Revamps Marketing Strategy," *Dallas Morning News,* September 9, 2001.

tion for Stock Car Racing (NASCAR) and so-called "extreme sports." Monday Night Football audiences were down 10 percent in 1998, in part perhaps, because people were watching alternative sports on Disney's sports network ESPN. ESPN's household audiences of "extreme sports" such as skateboarding, snowboarding, skysurfing, and street luge increased 119 percent from 1994 through 1998.[3] During the same period, sponsorship revenue for extreme sports had increased from $24 million to $135 million. NASCAR's growth was also impressive. NASCAR's television audience had increased each year since 1990 and by 1999, when it reached 250 million fans, was second only to the NFL. Sales, meanwhile, had grown from $80 million in 1990 to $1.13 billion in 1999.[4] Threshold's owners hoped that they could grow their niche in a similar fashion.

In the near-term, Threshold's founders believed that they could double revenues within three years by developing additional USAC racing events and leasing the company's staging equipment for noncompany events. The profit/loss projections for events and projects for the next five years are shown in **Exhibit 2.** The projected profit/loss statement for the firm is shown in **Exhibit 3.**

To reach its near-term goal, Threshold sought to stage at least one new major racing event and one lesser race in 2001. The following two years they planned to do the same for a total of six new races in three years. As of June 2000, the firm was in the process of developing races in Atlanta, New York, San Francisco, and Valley Forge:

San Francisco, CA	Threshold was negotiating with Tailwind Sports, manager of the U.S. Postal Service Cycling Team, to produce an event in San Francisco. Threshold expected to receive approximately $1,100,000 in corporate sponsorships from the event scheduled for September 9, 2001.
New York, NY	The New York City Sports Commission had endorsed Threshold to develop the New York City Cycling Championship.
Atlanta, GA	Threshold had formed a joint venture with Ivory Communications to develop a cycling event with organizations involved in the 1996 Olympic Games.
Valley Forge, PA	The Valley Forge Convention and Visitors Bureau retained Threshold to plan and organize a weekend festival in October 2001. Called the American Cycling Jamboree, the festival would feature competitions, exhibitions, concerts, and demonstrations.

FINANCING NEEDS AND ALTERNATIVES

Given Threshold's growth plans and its current balance sheet (shown in **Exhibit 4**), the founders agreed that the company needed additional financing to support the first growth phase. According to management's estimates, financing the development of the additional

---

[3]Karl Taro Greenfeld, "A Wider World of Sports," *Time,* November 9, 1998.
[4]National Association for Stock Car Racing and industry estimates.

races would require approximately $500,000 in working capital. Because of their limited experience in finance, the principals approached Frischkorn for help in arranging the deal.

Frischkorn faced three significant challenges with regard to Threshold's financing needs. First, he needed to determine the type of securities to be issued that would best suit the company's needs; most importantly, he needed to determine the value of the company and thus the appropriate pricing of the offering; and finally, he needed to identify potential investors he might approach with the offering.

Frischkorn believed that the size, history, and character of the company favored a private placement rather than a public issue. Among the financing alternatives Threshold was considering were a common stock offering, a convertible preferred stock offering, and debt financing.

Common Stock

To raise the needed capital, Threshold could issue additional common stock to new investors. Issuing common stock to other investors would dilute the voting interests of the current equity holders, and possibly dilute the stream of reported earnings per share.[5] The extent of any EPS dilution would depend on the profitability of projects funded by the new capital. Ultimately, the owners wondered whether any new equity financing would dilute the *market value* of their interest in Threshold.

Convertible Preferred Stock

Another option open to Threshold was to issue convertible preferred stock, which under preestablished terms could be converted into the common stock of the company. Preferred stock carried no voting rights. Dividends could be suspended, but all preferred dividends would have to be paid in full before dividends could be paid to holders of common shares. (See the Appendix to this case for a structure under which Frischkorn believed convertible preferred stock might be issued.)

Debt Financing

Threshold would not qualify for investment-grade debt and would therefore have to entice investors by offering high-yield debt if it were to issue a bond offering. Paying the interest associated with high-yield debt would seriously constrain Threshold's cash flow and thus its growth. A more likely, albeit short-term, source of debt financing would be a traditional revolving credit loan from Threshold's bank. According to Threshold's management, the firm's banker was willing to loan the company the necessary funds as long as principals Chauner and

---

[5]In corporate finance terms, "dilution" means reduction. Its opposite is "accretion." Dilution may refer to any of three effects: (1) reduction in voting power, (2) reduction in financial results such as EPS, and (3), reduction in market value of the firm—these three are known respectively as control, accounting, and economic dilution.

Casale personally guaranteed the loans. (See **Exhibit 5** for the terms under which Frischkorn believed a loan might be obtained.) Both founders had bristled at the idea of personal guarantees and argued that the revolving credit could provide Threshold with the cash they needed in the short term, but was not a long-term solution to Threshold's need for capital.

As an angel investor, Frischkorn had garnered experience with each type of financing that Threshold was considering, but in those circumstances he had to weigh the advantages and disadvantages only from the investor's perspective. In the case of Threshold, he had to weigh the advantages and disadvantages of each type of financing from the *company's perspective.* He also had to consider the effects of dilution any deal would have on the voting control of the current owners (**Exhibit 6**).

Frischkorn thought about some of the other private placements in which he had been involved. He recalled that the more mature companies in which he had invested had frequently chosen debt offerings because of the tax advantages of paying interest over paying dividends. Many of the younger companies, meanwhile, had elected to issue common stock because it provided flexibility in terms of paying (or not paying) a dividend. Still, he recalled a number of deals in which the issuing company had chosen to offer preferred stock because it conveyed no voting rights and allowed some flexibility regarding the timing of dividends.

PLACEMENT

Placing the offering presented a challenge for Frischkorn. In Frischkorn's experience, risk-tolerant individual investors had usually provided the necessary capital for these deals even though the deals offered a relatively low yield compared to other investments. The individuals, interested in early-stage financing, found preferred stock attractive due to its liquidation preference. Most corporate investors Frischkorn had contacted were uninterested in providing such early-stage seed capital regardless of the tax advantage offered by preferred shares.[6]

Generally, Frischkorn had been successful in attracting investors for a number of the companies in which he was involved. Yet Threshold was different from Frischkorn's other investments, which included both old economy start-ups as well as new economy Internet plays. He believed that Threshold would appeal primarily to investors who were cycling enthusiasts and people with a personal knowledge of the key management members. He knew that he would have to screen potential investors carefully.[7]

---

[6]Individual investors report all dividends from preferred issues as ordinary income while corporate investors may, for tax-reporting purposes, exclude from income 70 percent of the dividends received from preferred issues.

[7]As a private placement, all investors in the offering had to qualify as "accredited investors" as defined under Regulation D of the Securities Act of 1933. Under Regulation D, an accredited investor was generally defined as:

(i) an individual who is a director or officer of the Company; or

(ii) an individual who has individual income in excess of $200,000 in each of the two most recent years, or joint income with that of his or her spouse in excess of $300,000 in each of such years, and who reasonably expects income in excess of such amounts in the current year; or

(iii) an individual who has an individual net worth, or a joint net worth with that of his or her spouse, in excess of $1,000,000.

Regardless of their individual circumstances or identities, all new and current Threshold investors would be interested in potential exit strategies. Frischkorn himself was keenly aware of at least two potential means of exit: the possible sale of the business to a large advertising agency or an initial public offering. In the near-term, the former seemed more likely than the latter. IPG, Omnicom Group, and WPP Group were all public companies that acted as holding companies of individual marketing firms and were actively acquiring small branded firms. A future sale to one of these umbrella organizations could provide an exit strategy for investors, provide Threshold with certain scale economies, and still allow Threshold to maintain its own brand identity as well as some level of independence. Given Threshold's relationship with Octagon, a sale such as this seemed the most likely outcome for now. A future public offering, while still a possibility, seemed a less likely exit strategy at this time.

VALUATION

A significant aspect of Frischkorn's advisory problem was estimating the value of Threshold. Based on his experience, Frischkorn knew that some investors would argue that the company was worth only what was visible on the balance sheet and therefore would suggest a traditional asset valuation approach. In conversations, Chauner and Casale had argued vehemently that the firm was worth much more than what appeared on the balance sheet and should be valued based on its growth prospects. They favored valuing Threshold using a discounted cash flow approach. Unconvinced which valuation method would prevail, Frischkorn pointed out that any preferred stock investor in Threshold would require at least a 20 percent rate of return and a common stock investor would probably seek returns in excess of 30 percent.

Complicating Frischkorn's appraisal was the changing investment environment and its impact on valuations. As seen in **Exhibit 7,** the NASDAQ had endured a dramatic correction in the three months since March 2000. Internet stocks were hit particularly hard, but the decline affected even nontech stocks. The abrupt change in public valuations had closed the IPO window for many companies and that, in turn, had impacted private valuations. According to venture capitalists, valuations dropped significantly from March through May. Noting the change in climate, Rick Kroon, head of Donaldson Lufkin & Jenrette Securities' venture-capital arm, Sprout, said, "The market will start to be more selective, and [VCs will] wait until their companies are more mature before taking them public. . . . That's healthier for everyone in the long run."[8] Other VCs concurred: "We're walking away from a lot of deals today that we wouldn't have only a few weeks ago. . . . These companies just aren't going to get funded, particularly by anyone involved in late-stage or expansion capital at all," says Matthew Cowan, general partner at Bowman Capital.[9] Given the changing environment, Frischkorn concluded that angel investors buying common stock in such an immature company would require a return in excess of 30 percent.

---

[8]Suzanne McGee, "Deals & Deal Makers: Sky Is No Longer the Limit for Venture-Capital Firms," *The Wall Street Journal,* May 9, 2000, C1.
[9]Ibid.

While Frischkorn had been in his meeting, his associate Phil Peterson had performed some preliminary research for the Threshold deal. The report included information about current yields as shown in **Exhibits 8** and **9.** It also included some analytical information about outstanding debt, preferred, and convertible preferred securities **(Exhibits 10, 11,** and **12).**

An interesting aspect of the report revolved around Peterson's search for "comparables." Initially, Peterson had encountered great difficulty finding firms, particularly U.S. firms, that matched Threshold's niche. Undeterred, he had collected information on a number of publicly traded companies including sports marketing companies such as Magnum Sports and Entertainment, entertainment companies such as Disney, and advertising agencies such as Cordiant Communications Group (CRI) in London, Omnicrom Group Inc. (OMC), WPP Group Plc (WPP) also in London, and Interpublic Group of Companies (IPG), the parent company of Octagon.

With the help of an investment banking friend, Petersen had broadened his search and discovered two other companies that could be described as sports marketing events managers: Sports and Outdoor Media International PLC in London (SOR), and Tow Co. Ltd in Tokyo. According to the information available through Bloomberg Financial, SOR traded on the London Exchange. Tow was a privately held Japanese company that was currently preparing for a public offering. Fortunately, Petersen's friend provided him with a copy of Tow's red herring prospectus, which included basic financial information about the company as well as information about its market and growth prospects.

In an effort to estimate Threshold's growth prospects, Petersen gathered information from Multex Data Group. According to Multex, as a group, advertising agencies including Cordiant, IPG, Omnicom, and WPP were expected to show profit growth of 31.17 percent in 2001 and 15.47 percent in 2002 while earnings of the S&P 500 were expected to climb 1.41 percent in 2001 and decline 9.95 percent in 2002. These estimates were significantly higher than the 11 percent growth estimated for both Tow and its market in the company's red herring.

Petersen included summary information about all the companies, their businesses, and their financials in his report. (See **Exhibits 13** and **14.**) Attached to the report Petersen added a note dated June 15, 2000:

> Carl—Here's the information you requested on current market conditions and comparables. In our discussion this week you asked about EBIT multiples for private companies. Although I am unable to provide the exact reference, I recently read in one of the financial journals that the EBIT multiple for private companies is six. Let me know if you need anything else.—Phil

CONCLUSION

Frischkorn sat back and wondered, How does one value an entity whose primary asset is goodwill and the leases (or rights) to produce events? How does one create and then attribute value to a "brand" such as the Pro Cycling Tour? More specifically, how much was Threshold worth based on either an asset valuation or a DCF valuation? Was one type of financing more suitable than another for Threshold? Which was most appropriate? And what type of investors would be interested in this deal?

EXHIBIT 1
Major U.S. Sports Organizations

Sports Organization	2000 Sales (in millions)	1-Yr. Sales Growth	Employees	Revenue/ Employee
Major League Baseball (MLB)	$3,177.0	12.00%	200	$15,888,000.00
National Basketball Association (NBA)	2,164.0	126.50	800	2,705,000.00
National Football Association (NFL)	3,602.2	10.10	450	8,004,888.89
National Hockey League (NHL)	1,697.2	15.00	289	5,872,664.36

Source: Industry Standard.

EXHIBIT 2
Estimated Event Income and Loss, 2001–05 (in thousands)

Projected Event Income	2001	2002	2003	2004	2005
First Union Series	$1,700	$1,800	$1,910	$2,125	$ 2,525
US PRO Tour	1,200	1,350	1,525	1,700	2,300
BMC Grand Prix	1,300	1,425	1,540	1,725	2,350
Pre-Event Consulting	15	25	35	50	70
New Event 1	500	575	660	750	900
New Event 2	300	350	410	490	625
New Event 3	—	500	580	675	850
New Event 4	—	250	325	475	550
New Event 5	—	—	500	565	725
New Event 6	—	—	250	325	475
Total Event Income	**$5,015**	**$6,275**	**$7,735**	**$8,880**	**$10,170**

Operations Cost	2001	2002	2003	2004	2005
First Union Series	$1,650	$1,700	$1,785	$1,925	$ 1,985
US PRO Tour	1,100	1,200	1,260	1,325	1,350
BMC Grand Prix	1,200	1,250	1,315	1,385	1,400
Octagon Lease	200	225	236	248	260
New Event 1	450	475	500	550	555
New Event 2	275	300	330	365	380
New Event 3	—	475	500	525	555
New Event 4	—	225	245	255	265
New Event 5	—	—	475	510	535
New Event 6	—	—	225	250	260
Profit Share	50	88	113	220	610
Total Operations Cost	**$4,925**	**$5,938**	**$6,984**	**$7,558**	**$ 8,155**
Net Event Income (Loss)	**$90**	**$338**	**$752**	**$1,322**	**$ 2,015**

Note: Pre-event consulting income refers to fees generated from consulting work performed to research a new event for a municipality. Operations Cost for each contracted project includes a management fee to Threshold Sports.

EXHIBIT 3
Estimated Fee Income and Loss, 2001–05 (in thousands)

	2001	2002	2003	2004	2005
Income					
Management fee income	$1,150	$1,525	1,750	2,100	2,240
Special projects income	80	80	90	105	110
Profit (loss) from racing events	90	337	752	1,322	2,015
Misc. income	2	3	3	4	3
Total Income	$1,322	$1,945	$2,595	$3,531	$4,368
Expenses					
Salaries & overhead	$1,104	$1,296	$1,495	$1,719	$1,977
Special projects	35	55	60	72	85
Depreciation	11	16	22	28	34
Capital expenditures	50	50	60	60	60
Expansion expense	40	55	100	200	225
New business	24	30	60	100	200
Total Expenses	$1,264	$1,502	$1,797	$2,179	$2,581
Net Profit (Loss)	**$58**	**$443**	**$798**	**$1,351**	**$1,787**

EXHIBIT 4
Balance Sheet, Fiscal Year Ended May 31, 2000

Assets

Current Assets

Cash	$379,349
Accounts receivable	363,084
Other current assets	2,900
Total Current Assets	**$745,333**
Staging equipment	65,000
Total Assets	**$810,333**

Liabilities & Equity

Liabilities

Accounts payable	$133,590
Other current liabilities	9,937
Accrued expenses	322,000
Total Liabilities	**$465,527**

Equity

Net Income and Capital	344,806
Total Equity	$344,806
Total Liabilities & Equity	**$810,333**

EXHIBIT 5
Terms of Revolving Credit Loan

Type of loan	Revolving credit line
Principal amount	Up to $500,000
Term	36 months
Annual interest rate	Prime + 4%
Current prime rate	9.10%
Security	Business equipment plus personal guarantee
Purpose of loan	Working capital
Payment due date	The fourth day of each month
Prepayment penalty	None

EXHIBIT 6
Current Ownership Structure

	Holdings	Current Ownership
Class A Units		
David Chauner	12.0 units	40%
Jerry Casale	9.0 units	30
Robin Morton	3.0 units	10
Carl Frischkorn	3.0 units	10
Loren Smith	1.5 units	5
Frank Chauner	1.5 units	5
	30.0 units	100%

EXHIBIT 7
Equity-Market Conditions: Closing Values and Trendlines

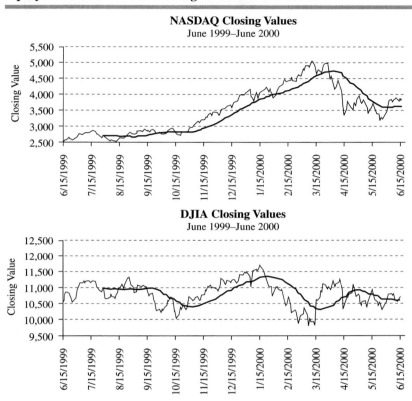

Source: Financial Forecast Center (www.forecasts.org).

EXHIBIT 8
Capital-Market Conditions: Selected Interest Rates for Week Ending June 2, 2000

	Yield
Fed funds	6.53%
U.S. Treasury securities	
3 month	5.78%
1 year	6.30
3 year	6.60
5 year	6.49
30 year	6.00
Corporate bonds	
Aaa	7.83%
Baa	8.76

Source: Federal Reserve Statistical Release H.15, June 5, 2000.

Corporate Bond Yields According to Bond Rating and Maturity

Maturity	AAA	AA	A	BBB	BB+	BB/BB-	B
1	6.77	6.85	7.19	7.79	11.26	10.29	11.04
5	7.67	7.98	8.25	8.93	10.50	11.05	12.20
10	7.62	7.98	8.27	8.99	9.74	10.94	12.26
15	7.92	8.32	8.61	9.35	9.62	NA	NA
20	7.94	8.36	8.65	9.47	NA	NA	NA
25	7.92	8.36	8.66	NA	NA	NA	NA

Note: Data as of May 30, 2000. U.S. Industrials include Yankee bond issues. Minimum $100 million outstanding.

Source: Standard & Poor's *CreditWeek,* June 7, 2000, 46, from Standard & Poor's Fixed Income Research-Bond Corp.

EXHIBIT 9
Market Conditions

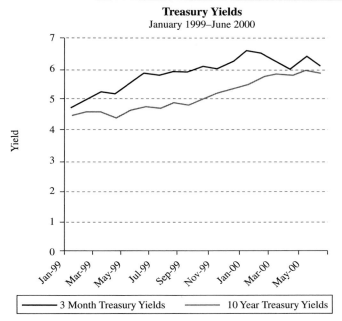

Treasury Yields
January 1999–June 2000

Source: The Federal Reserve Board of Governors Release H.15.

EXHIBIT 10
Key Industrial Financial Ratios by Rating Categories: Median Three-Year Ratios for 1996–98

Industrial long-term debt	AAA	AA	A	BBB	BB	B	CCC
Pretax interest coverage (×)	12.9	9.2	7.2	4.1	2.5	1.2	(0.9)
EBITDA interest coverage (×)	18.7	14.0	10.0	6.3	3.9	2.3	0.2
Funds from operations/total debt (%)	89.7	67.0	49.5	32.2	20.1	10.5	7.4
Free operating cash flow/total debt (%)	40.5	21.6	17.4	6.3	1.0	(4.0)	(25.4)
Return on capital (%)	30.6	25.1	19.6	15.4	12.6	9.2	(8.8)
Operating income/sales (%)	30.9	25.2	17.9	15.8	14.4	11.2	5.0
Long-term debt/capital (%)	21.4	29.3	33.3	40.8	55.3	68.8	71.5
Total debt/capital (incl. STD) (%)	31.8	37.0	39.2	46.4	58.5	71.4	79.4

Source: Wesley E. Chinn, Standard & Poor's Research, "Adjusted Key U.S. Financial Ratios," July 7, 1999.

EXHIBIT 11
Sample of Dividend Yields for Preferred Stocks, June 2000

Security	S&P Rating	Maturity Date	Dividend Yield
ABN AMRO Cap. Fd. II 7.125%	A+	3/31/04	9.0%
HSBC USA $2.8575	A+	9/30/07	7.2
Australia & New Zealand Bank 9.125%	A	2/24/03	9.3
NB Capital 8.35% Sr. A Dep.	A-	9/2/07	9.6
LaSalle RE Holding 8.75%	BB+	3/26/07	12.5
SEMCO Cap Tr I 10.25%	BB+	4/18/05	10.3
AICI Cap Trust 9%	B+	9/29/02	19.0
Host Marriott 10% B	B	4/28/05	12.1
United Dominion Realty 8.60% B	BBB	5/28/07	10.8
FelCor Lodging Trust 9% Dep	BB-	5/6/03	12.9
ONB Cap. Tr. I 9.50% Tru PS	BBB-	3/14/05	9.2

Source: Standard & Poor's *Stock Guide,* June 2000.

EXHIBIT 12

Analytical Ratios on a Sample of Convertible Preferred Securities

Security	Apache $2.015 C Cv Pfd	Chiquita Brands $3.75 cm CV B Pfd	Sealed Air $2.00 CV Pfd A	Standard Automotive 8.50% Sr CV Pfd	Superior Telecom 8.50% TR 1 cm CV Pfd	USX-US Steel Group 6.50% cm CV Pfd
S&P rating	BBB-	B-	BB	NR	CCC+	BB
Dividend yield	4.03%	18.11%	3.88%	11.64%	17.36%	8.80%
Conversion ratio	0.8197	3.3333	0.8846	1.0000	1.1496	1.0840
Price of convertible pfd	$50.06	$21.00	$51.50	$9.00	$27.00	$37.06
Price of underlying stock	57.25	4.00	54.00	6.69	11.13	21.06
Parity (CV ratio * Stock price)	46.93	13.33	47.77	6.69	12.79	22.83
Premium ([CV Price/parity]−1)	6.67%	57.54%	7.81%	34.53%	111.10%	62.33%

Source: Bloomberg Financial and Standard & Poor's.

Notes: Financial data and calculations as of 6/15/00.

Conversion ratio reflects the number of common shares to be received in exchange for one share of convertible preferred.

Parity (also known as conversion parity price) is the common stock price at which immediate conversion would make sense.

The *premium* reflects the mark-up of the convertible over parity. It is the percentage difference between the two.

EXHIBIT 13
Selected Marketing and Entertainment Companies

Name	Symbol[1]	Business	Description
Cordiant Communications Group	CRI (LN) ADR:CDA	Advertising services	A holding company whose subsidiaries operate in more than 70 countries. Businesses encompass advertising, merchandising, market research, direct marketing, public relations, and media services. Also provides services in television and multimedia production, as well as live conferences and exhibitions.
The Walt Disney Co.	DIS	Multimedia	Conducts operations in media networks, studio entertainment, theme parks and resorts, consumer products, and Internet and direct marketing. Produces motion pictures, television programs, and musical recordings as well as publishes books and magazines. Also operates ABC radio and television and theme parks.
Interpublic Group of Companies	IPG	Advertising services	An organization of advertising agencies and marketing service companies. Operates globally in sectors of advertising, independent media buying, direct marketing, health-care communications, interactive consulting services, marketing research, promotions, experiential marketing, public relations, and sports marketing.
Magnum Sports & Entertainment Inc.[2]	MAGZ	Advertising services	Provides management, marketing, and commercial endorsement agency services to various sports entities.
Omnicom Group Inc.	OMC	Advertising services	Provides marketing communications and advertising services through global, national, and regional independent agencies in public relations, specialty advertising, and direct response and promotional marketing. Holds minority interests in other businesses.
Sports & Outdoor Media International Plc	SOR (LN)	Advertising services	Acts as a sports stadia advertising agent to major sports rights holders in UK and Australia, selling ground signage and other forms of advertising at cricket and rugby grounds. Also has a sports marketing and sponsorship consultancy business.
Tow Co., Ltd.[3]	N/A	Advertising services	Plans, advertises, produces, and manages various types of events. Primarily manages exhibitions, ceremonies, festivals, product promotion campaigns, public service announcements, sporting events, and expositions. The company was privately held but was preparing to make its initial public offering in 7/00.
WPP Group Plc	WPP (LN) ADR:WPPGY	Advertising services	Operates a communications services group with 1,300 offices in 102 countries. Operations encompass advertising, media investment management, information and consultancy, public relations and public affairs, health care and specialist communications, and branding and identity services.

[1]LN indicates the stock trades on the London Exchange. ADRs are available where noted.
[2]Formerly Worldwide Entertainment & Sports.
[3]Initial public offering of 1 million shares expected in July 2000, to be traded on the Tokyo Exchange (JP).

EXHIBIT 14
Selected Financial Information on Comparable Companies, Fiscal Year 1999

Symbol	FY 1999 Sales (millions)	Shares Outstanding (millions)	FYE Share Price	Equity Market Value (millions)	Book Value (millions)	Total Debt (millions)	Total Debt to Equity	Total Debt to Equity Market Value	Price to Book	Price to Earnings	EBITDA Multiplier	100 Day Volatility (percent)	Beta	Unlevered Beta
CRI (LN)	£335.80	228.80	£2.93	£670.38	(£40.20)	£84.00	NM	0.13	NM	35.73	15.09	47.9	1.10	NM
DIS	$23,435.00	2,069.00	$26.00	$53,794.00	$21,323.00	$11,693.00	0.55	0.22	2.63	44.32	10	41.6	0.86	0.65
IPG	$4,977.82	307.01	$57.69	$17,710.64	$1,846.08	$1,311.09	0.71	0.07	10.19	44.04	17.89	43.7	1.07	0.77
MAGZ	$1.12	3.49	$2.00	$6.98	$6.08	$0.12	0.02	0.02	5.73	N/A	N/A	N/A	0.37	0.37
OMC	$5,130.55	177.49	$100.00	$17,749.00	$1,676.02	$842.00	0.50	0.05	11.43	49.75	19.65	41.3	1.02	0.78
SOR (LN)	£14.56	33.77	£0.83	£28.03	£12.48	£15.18	1.22	0.54	0.37	92.17	N/A	53.1	0.33	0.19
TOW (JP)	¥5,396.00	N/A	N/A	N/A	¥1,002.00	¥1.95	0.95	N/A	N/A	N/A	N/A	N/A	N/A	NM
WPP (LN)	£9,345.90	774.54	£9.50	£7,358.13	£195.80	£515.10	1.58	0.07	23.88	42.84	24.1	50.8	0.86	0.44

Source: Bloomberg Financial.

Notes: NM=Not Meaningful. N/A=Not Available. Volatility reflects most recent 100 days prior to 6/1/00. Volatility and beta values for foreign securities reflect those of ADRs.

APPENDIX
SUMMARY OF TERMS OF HYPOTHETICAL CONVERTIBLE-PREFERRED-STOCK OFFERING

Amount:	$500,000 (maximum)
Securities:	A maximum of 10 convertible preferred units.
Price per Unit:	$50,000 (original purchase price).
Cumulative Preferred Return:	To be determined. Initial proposal: 10 percent dividend on par value which shall accrue and be payable on a cumulative and noncompounding basis. If there are insufficient funds to pay the cumulative preferred return in full, payment shall be made on a pro-rata basis. The cumulative preferred return shall accrue annually commencing on the closing date of this offering and shall terminate on December 31, 2005.
Liquidation Preference:	In the event of any liquidation, dissolution, or winding up of the company, the holders of these units will be entitled to receive (in preference to the holders of other interests) the initial investment less any capital distributions that may have previously been made plus all unpaid portions, if any, of the cumulative preferred return.
Conversion Privilege:	To be determined. Initial proposal for units to be convertible at any time into shares of common stock at a strike price of 1.5 times most recent book value per share of common.
Holder Redemption Right:	Beginning March 31, 2005, and each anniversary thereof, holders of these convertible preferred units shall have the right to require the company to redeem the convertible preferred units.
Company Redemption Right:	The company may redeem any convertible preferred units, annually, by notice within 90 days following the end of each calendar year. The redemption price will be at par value.
Mandatory Tax Distribution:	For each calendar year unit holders will receive a special cash distribution in an amount equal to 35 percent of the income allocated to such holders.
Voting Rights:	Holders of convertible preferred units shall not have voting rights.
Right of First Refusal:	In the event that a holder wishes to sell or otherwise transfer its investment interest pursuant to a bona-fide offer from a third party, the holder shall first offer the investment interest to (i) the company, and (ii) then to the nonselling holders, upon the same terms and conditions of the bona-fide offer.
Co-Sale Rights:	If any holder owning more than 25 percent of the company intends to sell its interest pursuant to a third party offer, the nonselling holders may include their membership interests in the sale on a pro-rata basis.

Drag Along Rights:

If holders of membership interests which in the aggregate represent 50 percent or more of the company elect to sell the company pursuant to a sale of assets, sale of membership interests, merger or otherwise, such members may compel the remaining members to consent to, and participate in, such sale.

Preemptive Right:

All holders of membership interests shall have a pro-rata right to participate in subsequent equity financings of the company subject to customary exclusions.

Analysis of Financing Tactics: Leases, Options, and Foreign Currency

Merton Electronics Corporation

Patricia Merton, president and majority shareholder of Merton Electronics, was dissatisfied with her company's results over the past year (see **Exhibits 1 and 2**). Sales had risen by over 12 percent compared to the previous year, very close to budget, but at a considerably slower pace than what had been enjoyed during the previous three years. At the same time, 1997 earnings fell by more than 40 percent, reflecting increasingly difficult market conditions. Margins had been flat or falling for the past three years, but 1997 was the worst. Operational improvements had been maintained, keeping working capital and cash needs under control. Also, Merton had secured additional long-term financing and an increase in the company's credit line. Although continued growth would require additional investment in new computer and office equipment and other fixed assets, she expected this could be largely financed out of cash flow—if margins did not deteriorate further and working capital could be kept in line with sales.

Since its founding in 1950 by Thomas Merton, Merton Electronics had been a distributor for GEC, a large manufacturer of electrical and electronics products for consumer and institutional markets. Over the years, in addition to the GEC products, the company had added noncompeting lines of electrical appliances, records, compact discs, and cassettes. In 1980, it began to broaden its product lines by importing Japanese consumer electronics. Four years later, it entered into an exclusive import agreement with the Goldstone Corporation of Taiwan, a major producer of television and other electronic equipment. These products were distributed to retail firms and dealers throughout a broad geographical area.

By the beginning of the 1990s, the company had entered into the personal computer (PC) market, distributing both hardware and software products. It became the national distributor for Fuji Electronics, a major Japanese manufacturer of PCs and related products, in September 1993. This market had proven to be fast growing, accounting for more than half of total sales, although only about a third of profits, in 1997; this part of the business was becoming more and more competitive, as price-cutting had become rampant from mail-order and computer-discount houses.

This case was written by Professor Lee Remmers. Copyright© 1998 by Lee Remmers.

Patricia Merton had been working in the company for two years when her father, Thomas Merton, died in the spring of 1991. As the only family member with experience in the company, she succeeded him as president. Together with her mother, she controlled 65 percent of the share capital of the firm. The remaining shares were held by her father's brother and sister, their families, and a few long-service employees.

During the first weeks of 1998, Merton had been taking advantage of the relative calm that usually marked that time of the year. This was when they took the semiannual inventory, tended to various small problems that had been pushed aside during the past few months, and thought about the future.

One of the things that continued to disturb her was the volatility of the yen, and more recently, the Taiwanese dollar (see **Exhibit 3**). Over half of the equipment sold in the PC, TV and VCR, and hi-fi product lines was imported from Japanese suppliers. From a volume of about $20 million two years earlier, yen-denominated purchases had approached $27 million during the past 12 months. Annual purchases totaling another $4 million were from Taiwanese suppliers. With the volume expected in the consumer electronics and PC product lines, Patricia Merton foresaw purchases from Fuji Electronics, the company's principal supplier, and other Asian manufacturers to increase in the future.

Typical of Merton's Japanese suppliers, Fuji Electronics had always insisted on invoicing in yen. In contrast, at the beginning of their agreement, Goldstone Corporation had invoiced in U.S. dollars. This changed in 1989, when the company was informed that from then on, the Taiwanese dollar would be used for billing.

Once an order was placed, the Asian suppliers shipped by airfreight, normally within 60 days. Payment terms were 30 days from the end of the delivery month; hence the ¥284 million value of goods delivered in January 1998 would be paid at the end of February (**Exhibit 4**). With few exceptions, the spot price on the last day of the month in which the order was placed was used for the invoice. This meant that Merton had on average a 90-day currency exposure for each order.

Two years earlier, toward the end of January 1996, concerned that the falling margins were at least partially due to the impact of a rising exchange rate, Patricia Merton had asked her general manager, Charles Brown, to gather some data on the monthly volume of purchases from Japanese suppliers as well as the yen–dollar exchange rates. The data gathered by Brown at the time astonished her. The effect of the yen's more or less continual appreciation against the dollar until the summer of 1995 meant that purchases during that period appeared to have cost the company significantly more—in dollar terms—than if the exchange rate had been stable. Fortunately, thanks to the popularity of the Fuji products, they had been able until 1995 to increase prices to partially offset their higher dollar costs. Also, the Japanese suppliers had absorbed some of the yen's rise by cutting prices significantly. But as the dollar fell through the ¥100 "barrier," it became more and more difficult to maintain margins. During the first four months of 1995, the rising yen translated into an almost $1.1 million higher cost of purchases. Although Brown did not prepare a detailed analysis of purchases before 1995, he estimated that "losses" were, if anything, considerably larger. On the other hand, his data had shown that between July and December 1995, a strengthening dollar produced "gains" of over $1.4 million. As a result of this analysis, they had sought the advice of their banker in January 1996.

Listening to his clients' story, the banker agreed that Merton did face significant currency risk. Further, he reminded them that since Merton Electronics imported a higher portion of its products from Japan than some of its principal competitors, its profit margins were much more sensitive to the value of the yen than theirs were. In view of this, he advised them to hedge their yen purchases. The bank would arrange hedges to cover the orders placed during the month. They agreed that this would be on a monthly basis to obtain the better rates relatively large transactions would provide. The hedges would, he explained, fix in advance the dollar cost of each month's orders. This would effectively remove the currency problem from their everyday concerns and allow them to concentrate on running the business. As for purchases from the Taiwanese suppliers, the banker told them the Taiwanese authorities managed their currency so that it stayed more or less fixed to the U.S. dollar, that even if it were to move it was likely to depreciate and, for these reasons, hedging would not be worthwhile. This advice was taken. Since 1996, Merton had systematically hedged each yen purchase order; purchases from Taiwanese suppliers were not hedged.

Now, after two years, Patricia Merton thought it was time to review this policy. Once again she asked Brown to look at their experience over the past year, going back to January 1997. What this showed was completely different from the previous analysis. Although the yen was still volatile, it had mainly weakened against the dollar during this period. By hedging, the dollar cost of yen purchases had been about $25.5 million during 1997. If the purchases had not been hedged, but the yen bought on the spot market when the invoices came due, the dollar cost would have been about $24.6 million—an almost $900,000 difference! This was almost exactly the pretax earnings for 1997. Extremely disturbed by what Brown told her, Patricia Merton immediately contacted the firm's banker and arranged to see him later in the day.

Merton's meeting with her banker was strained at the beginning. Somewhat defensive, he maintained that since neither he nor anyone else could have accurately predicted how the yen–dollar exchange rate would have moved during the past two years, hedging the exposures was the most prudent policy for Merton. Furthermore, with so much economic and political uncertainty in Japan and the rest of Asia at the present time, he could not recommend in good conscience a better solution to managing the yen risk. When Patricia Merton asked him why he had not encouraged them earlier to hedge the Taiwanese dollar payments, he recalled his advice at the time was that it had been basically pegged to the U.S. dollar for several years and anyway was difficult to hedge satisfactorily because of exchange controls imposed by the Taiwan authorities. He reckoned that by following his recommendation not to hedge the Taiwanese dollar purchases, the U.S. dollar costs had been lower in 1997 by some $125,000 compared to what they would have been if hedged. Not entirely satisfied by his explanation, Merton asked him what he thought they should do now.

The issue boiled down to whether the company should take on currency risk or not, and, if so, how much. With over 60 percent of its purchases subject to currency fluctuations, the banker stuck to his earlier view that the firm could not afford to ignore this risk. He admitted that, with hindsight, not hedging would have been the best policy over the past one to two years. This meant that Merton would have bought the foreign currency on the spot market each time payments to the Asian suppliers were made. This, he said, was essentially a bet on a stronger dollar, which turned out to be the case. Quickly checking the numbers, he noted that if the ¥880 million worth of goods on order or already invoiced at the end of

January were to be settled at the current spot rate of ¥127, this would cost Merton about $6.93 million. As it stood, the company was already committed to pay $7.04 million since these purchases had been hedged when the goods were ordered. In other words, hedging appeared to have cost them some $110,000 at the present time. This lost opportunity would be larger or smaller depending on what the yen would do between now and when the invoices were settled. Nevertheless, he still would not advise the company to "do nothing" and expose itself to large possible currency losses in the future. Patricia Merton, as president and major shareholder of the company, would have to decide.

Accepting his arguments that it would be unwise to "do nothing," she thought it would be useful to review the alternative courses that the company might follow. Although the company had been using forward contracts for some 18 months to hedge the yen purchases, Merton felt she needed to have her memory refreshed and asked the banker to outline once again how the different hedges worked.

According to the banker, there were two basic choices when hedging. It could "lock in" today an exchange rate that would be close to the current spot rate; the forward contracts they had been using provided this type of hedge. Or they could enter into an option contract that would set an upper bound on the cost of yen but allow them to take advantage of cheaper yen if that should happen by the time the invoices had to be paid. The option would provide some of the advantages of not hedging and limit the disadvantages—but at a cost.

To lock in an exchange rate, the banker went on, meant that the future price of a foreign currency—the *future spot rate*—would in effect be set today; in other words, the hedge was a bet on a stronger yen. This type of hedge ensured that whatever the future spot rate might turn out to be, the *effective* price paid for yen would still be that which was agreed today. There were three ways to lock in an exchange rate: a forward contract, a money-market transaction, and a currency futures contract. Each of these carried precisely defined terms with regard to price, maturity, and certain other performance measures. Any modifications in the terms of the contract, such as changing its maturity, would have to be negotiated and agreed with the party providing the hedge, possibly resulting in additional cost.

The *forward contract hedge,* which the company had used for the past 18 months, was an arrangement by which it bought from the bank a specified quantity of yen to be delivered at a specified date in the future—normally when the invoice had to be settled. The exchange rate was fixed at the outset. At ¥125.50, the 90-day forward rate was at present nearly 1.5 percent more "expensive" than the spot rate. With this hedge, Merton would receive yen from the bank on the agreed maturity date, pay the bank the amount of dollars at the forward exchange rate set earlier (¥125.50), and then use the yen to pay the Japanese suppliers.

The *money market hedge* was also an arrangement with the bank. Merton would buy yen today on the spot market and place it in a yen time deposit or some other yen asset until needed to pay the suppliers. The purchase of yen would be financed in dollars by a short-term loan or by using cash reserves if they were available. The cost of this hedge would be the difference between the interest paid on the dollar loan and that received from the yen deposit. The banker reminded them that Merton could borrow dollars at 25 *basis points*[1]

---

[1]A basis point is 1/100 of a percent, i.e., 0.0001. Basis points are generally used in pricing loans and certain other financial instruments. Rates are usually quoted on an annual basis.

over the current *prime* rate (8.50 percent); but they would only earn at present ⅜ percent on a three-month Euroyen time deposit, Japanese rates being at an all-time low (see **Exhibit 5** for rates).

The *yen futures hedge* was provided by an instrument traded on the Chicago Mercantile Exchange (CME).[2] Quotations for yen futures on January 22 appear on **Exhibit 6.** As protection against loss from currency fluctuations, this hedge was very similar to the forward contract provided by the bank. Merton would *buy* a sufficient number of futures to create the hedge. It could then wait until the futures contracts came to maturity and take delivery of the yen. Alternatively, if Merton decided the hedge was no longer needed *before* the futures contracts reached maturity, they could be sold. If a rise in the value of the yen meant it cost more dollars to settle the purchase account with the Japanese suppliers, it also meant that the futures would be sold at a profit, thereby providing an offset. However, the mechanics of futures contracts differ considerably from forwards. The contracts are made through a member of the futures exchange, usually a broker. Currency futures come in standard contract sizes (for the yen ¥12.5 million) and standard maturity dates (the third Wednesday of March, June, September, December). They are revalued daily (marked-to-market) with any profit or loss immediately settled between broker and client. To trade on the futures market, the client must open and maintain collateral (a margin account) with the broker. This changes from time to time but at present is a minimum of $1,500 per contract. In addition, the broker will charge a small commission.

The *currency option contract* was available from either banks or exchanges. Option contracts give the *right but not the obligation* to buy (a *call*) or to sell (a *put*) currency or some other asset within a specified period and at a predetermined price known as the *strike* or *exercise price.*

Bank or OTC[3] options can be tailored to meet the client's precise needs for maturity, amount, or currency. They are usually European-type options; that is, they may only be exercised at expiration. Most bank options are on spot currency. Merton's banker pointed out that besides dealing in "plain vanilla" (standard) call and put options, he could also offer them *synthetic* or *exotic* instruments. Synthetics were combinations of calls, puts, and sometimes forward contracts that were designed to meet particular risk/return objectives of a client. A so-called *zero-cost option* is one of the more widely used of these. Exotics were options that had some particular feature that gave the buyer a lower premium at the price of a more risky payoff.[4]

Like futures, *exchange traded* options have standardized maturities and amounts. The expiration dates are similar to those for futures: March, June, September, and December. In addition, the American exchanges offer some "nearby" expiration dates (see Exhibit 6). For example, at the end of January, contracts were offered for February and April expiration as well as for the March and June standard months. Only a few major currencies are available. Most are priced in U.S. dollars, even those traded on European or Asian exchanges. They are usually so-called American-type options; in other words, they may be exercised at any time

---

[2]Currency futures are also traded on exchanges in London (LIFFE), Singapore (SIMEX), Sidney, and elsewhere in the world.

[3]OTC: over the counter.

[4]Among the most popular were average rate and barrier or knockout options.

before expiration. Recently, European-style options have been introduced on some exchanges—they can only be exercised at maturity. Those traded on the Philadelphia exchange are on spot currency. Chicago's CME and London's LIFFE contracts are on currency futures. To buy an option on an exchange, the full premium[5] must be paid in advance. To sell (or write) an option requires a specified margin to be maintained with the broker.

Besides going over the hedging instruments, the banker raised a number of other issues for Merton to consider. The company imported goods from its Japanese suppliers on a continuous basis throughout the year. If they did decide to continue hedging these purchases, should it be when the orders were placed as they have been doing up to now? Or should they wait until the time when the purchase invoice was actually received? What about hedging periodically for a longer period of 6 to 12 months once operating plans and budgets were agreed? Finally, if they do continue to hedge, should it be for the entire amount at risk—however it was measured—or only some portion of it?

Merton's banker concluded by stressing that there was no "correct" hedging approach. It depended on the particular needs and financial position of the company, and the attitudes of its management and shareholders towards risk. Whether or not the hedge was profitable would only be known ex post, when the supplier was paid. In the case of Merton Electronics, hedging yen during the past months turned out to be the wrong decision; in contrast, it was the correct decision for the Taiwanese dollar. If instead yen had strengthened against the dollar, locking in the rate would have been the correct decision. Further, he cautioned that under some competitive situations, hedging could actually increase risk rather than decrease it.

The discussion left Merton nearly as baffled as when she arrived at the bank. On leaving, she told the banker that she needed a few days to decide what to do. Back at the office, Merton told Brown that she was pretty much convinced that they should begin to devote a bit more time and thought to managing their currency position. Although they had "lost" some $900,000 on yen purchases during the past few months from a rather simplistic "hedge everything" policy, there was clearly too much uncertainty for a "do nothing" policy to be justified. The problem was to decide quickly what to do.

Anxious to resolve this matter quickly, Patricia Merton asked Brown to prepare a brief report on how their company's currency risk should be managed. In particular, she asked him to set out the relative advantages in terms of cost and risk for each of the alternatives that had been described to them by the banker. To provide a practical example, he could use the ¥300 million exposure arising from the goods that were ordered in January and which would be due for payment in April, 90 days from then. She suggested that Brown use the January 22 market rates which they had picked up at the bank (Exhibit 5) and, for the purpose of the analysis, assume that the suppliers would be paid and the hedges lifted on April 22. She also asked him to check out whether they would have been better off hedging with options over the past months than with forwards. She herself intended to give some thought to broader policy issues, including whether they should hedge at all and, if so, how much, when, and under what circumstances?

---

[5]The LIFFE exchange uses a margin system similar to that for futures trading. Hence, a specified minimum margin is maintained with the broker rather than paying a cash premium up front.

EXHIBIT 1
Comparative Income Statements (dollars in thousands)

	Year Ending December 31, 1996	Year Ending December 31, 1997
Sales revenue	53,682	60,392
Cost of goods sold	44,336	51,228
Gross margin	9,346	9,164
Variable expenses	3,277	3,687
Fixed expenses	3,652	4,009
Depreciation	171	207
Operating earnings (EBIT)	2,246	1,261
Interest expense	565	348
Earnings before taxes	1,681	913
Corporate taxes	581	301
Earnings after taxes	1,100	612

EXHIBIT 2
Comparative Balance Sheets (dollars in thousands)

	December 31, 1996	December 31, 1997
Assets		
Current assets		
Cash and deposits	95	115
Prepaid expenses	96	70
Accounts receivable	7,816	8,794
Inventories	8,880	9,350
	16,887	18,329
Fixed assets (net)	1,290	1,585
Goodwill	150	150
Total assets	18,327	20,064
Capital and liabilities		
Current liabilities		
Bank credit	4,257	2,237
Mortgage—current	150	150
Accrued expenses	392	359
Accounts payable		
Domestic	2,215	2,497
Foreign (yen)	3,312	3,670[*]
	10,826	8,913
Mortgage loan	750	600
Subordinated loan	—	500
Capital stock	1,500	1,500
Retained earnings	5,751	6,313
Owners' equity	7,251	7,813
Total capital and liabilities	18,327	20,064

[*]Dollar value of foreign currency accounts payable (¥375.2 million at spot rate of ¥130.5/U.S.$; Taiwan $25.9 million at spot rate of TWD 32.6/U.S.$).

EXHIBIT 3
Foreign Exhange Data

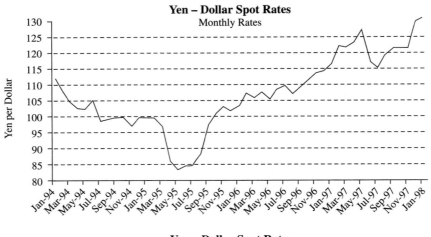

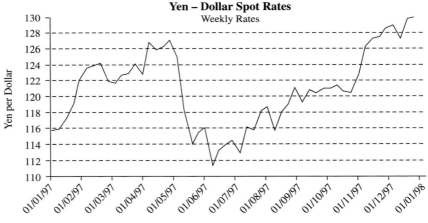

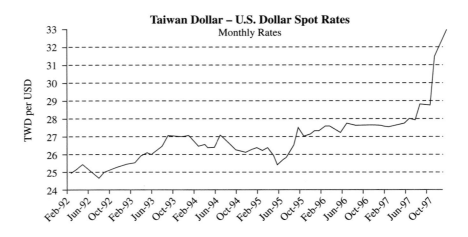

EXHIBIT 4
Actual and Forecasted Purchases from Japanese Suppliers, January 1997–April 1998

Purchase Amount ¥ Million	Order Date	Average ¥/$ Spot	Delivery and Invoice Date	Payment Date	Average ¥/$ Spot	Change in Order Value in $ 000
224.7	January 97	116	March 97	April 97	123	+110.2
261.1	February 97	122	April 97	May 97	127	+84.3
276.6	March 97	121	May 97	June 97	117	−78.2
271.1	April 97	123	June 97	July 97	115	−153.3
237.6	May 97	127	July 97	August 97	118	−142.7
192.2	June 97	117	August 97	September 97	121	+54.3
253.5	July 97	115	September 97	October 97	121	+109.3
294.5	August 97	118	October 97	November 97	121	+61.9
395.3	September 97	121	November 97	December 97	129	+202.6
330.8	October 97	121	December 97	January 98	130	+189.3
284.6	November 97	121	January 98	February 98	?	?
295.5	December 97	129	February 98	March 98	?	?
300.0	January 98	130	March 98	April 98	?	?
325.0	February 98	?	April 98	May 98	?	?
375.0	March 98	?	May 98	June 98	?	?
340.0	April 98	?	June 98	July 98	?	?

EXHIBIT 5
Currency and Other Financial Market Data, January 22, 1998

Spot yen: 127.35–127.40 per $; $0.7849–$0.7852 per ¥100
90-day forward yen: 125.50–125.75 per $; $0.7952–$0.7968 per ¥100
90-day Euroyen interest rates: 3/8%–1/2% per annum
Japanese 10-year government bond yield: 1 3/4%
90-day Eurodollar interest rates: 5 1/2%–5 5/8% per annum
Merton short-term borrowing rate: Prime (8 1/2%) + 25 basis points
March 1998 yen futures (CME): $0.7928; June 1998 yen futures (CME): $0.8031
90-day yen call options [OTC]: $0.7852 strike—$0.0249 per 100 yen
                                  $0.7968 strike—$0.0188 per 100 yen

EXHIBIT 6
Interest Rates

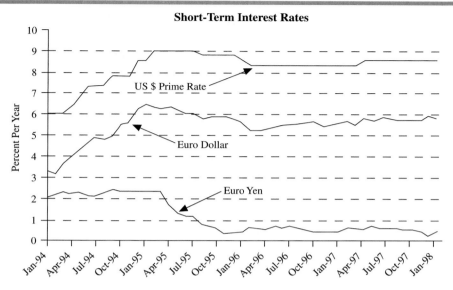

Short-Term Interest Rates

US $ Prime Rate

Euro Dollar

Euro Yen

Futures Prices

Japan Yen (CME)—12.5 million yen; $ per yen (.00)

	Open	High	Low	Settle	Change	Lifetime High	Lifetime Low	Open Interest
Mar	.7928	.7970	.7890	.7917	−.0024	.9375	.7512	88,937
Jun	.8046	.8046	.7950	.8017	−.0024	.9090	.7637	2,293
Sept	—	—	—	.8117	−.0024	.8695	.7735	413

Est. vol. 20,416; vol Th 36,578; open int. 91,647, +608.

Source: *The Wall Street Journal,* January 23–24, 1998.

Futures Option Prices

Japanese Yen (CME)—12.5 million yen; cents per 100 yen

Strike Price	Calls—Settle February	Calls—Settle March	Calls—Settle April	Puts—Settle February	Puts—Settle March	Puts—Settle April
7,800	1.66	2.21		0.49	1.05	1.12
7,850	1.32	1.92		0.65	1.25	1.30
7,900	1.03	1.65		0.86	1.48	
7,950	0.80	1.42		1.12	—	—
8,000	0.62	1.21	2.08	1.45	2.02	
8,050	0.48	1.03	1.84	1.81	—	—

Est. vol. 4,445; Wed. 6,552 calls 4,970 puts
Op. int. Wed. 49,854 calls 65,330 puts

Source: The Wall Street Journal, January 23–24, 1998.

473

National Railroad Passenger Corporation ("Amtrak"): Acela Financing

On April 30, 1999, Arlene Friner, CFO of Amtrak, instructed her Treasury staff to review a leveraged lease proposal from BNY Capital Funding LLC ("BNYCF"). Several weeks prior, Amtrak and its adviser, Babcock & Brown Financial Corporation, had invited financial institutions to submit lease-financing proposals for Amtrak's planned purchase of locomotives and high-speed train sets.[1] The equipment would be utilized on the "Acela" line, Amtrak's new brand that was designed to differentiate Amtrak passenger trains and service in the Northeast corridor from the existing service.[2] Acela, scheduled to begin service in late 1999, promised to offer faster trip times and premium service (see **Exhibit 1**).

Friner and her staff had gone over the proposals and agreed that BNYCF was among those that offered the best terms. Now she had to decide whether Amtrak should finance the equipment purchases using BNYCF's leveraged lease proposal or, instead, borrow money and purchase the equipment on its own.

COMPANY BACKGROUND

In 1970, the United States Congress created The National Railroad Passenger Corporation (Amtrak) to ensure that "modern, efficient intercity passenger rail service would remain an

---

[1]A train set consisted of one first-class coach car, one bistro car, three coach cars, one end coach car, and two power cars.
[2]Babcock and Brown memorandum, 1.

This case was prepared by Jessica Chan under the supervision of Professor Robert F. Bruner. The author wishes to thank Lisa Levine of the Equipment Leasing and Finance Foundation, Dennis Neumann and Barbara Dering of BNY Capital Funding LLC, and Raj Srinath of Amtrak. The financial support of the Batten Institute is gratefully acknowledged. The case was written as a basis for class discussion rather than to illustrate effective or ineffective handling of an administrative situation. Copyright © 2001 by the University of Virginia Darden School Foundation, Charlottesville, VA. All rights reserved. *To order copies, send an e-mail to* dardencases@virginia.edu. *No part of this publication may be reproduced, stored in a retrieval system, used in a spreadsheet, or transmitted in any form or by any means—electronic, mechanical, photocopying, recording, or otherwise—without the permission of the Darden School Foundation.* Version 1.5.

integral part of the national transportation system."[3] The government mandated Amtrak to take over the rail passenger operations of private railroads. Since then, Amtrak had become the primary provider of passenger rail service in the United States. Amtrak's national network provided service to more than 20 million intercity passengers, and operated 516 stations in 44 states.

Historically, Amtrak had received annual subsidies from the federal government. In 1997, however, Congress passed the Amtrak Reform and Accountability Act (ARAA), which stipulated that Amtrak eliminate its reliance on federal subsidies by 2002. After 2002, no federal funds could be used for Amtrak's operating expenses. This represented a formidable challenge, as Amtrak had never been profitable in its 30-year history. (See **Exhibits 2 and 3** for Amtrak's historical income statements and latest balance sheet.) Thus, to meet Congress's goal of operating self-sufficiency by 2002, Amtrak developed a radical new business plan, the centerpiece of which was a high-speed rail service that was projected to bring in net annual revenues of $180 million by fiscal-year 2002.[4]

ACELA

In its Northeast Corridor, which served routes from Virginia to Maine,[5] Amtrak branded this new high-speed rail service "Acela":

> Acela is designed to be more than high-speed trains—it is a brand representing a new way of doing business. Acela was designed to bring high speed and high quality to Northeast Corridor passengers. The Acela service will offer faster trip times, comfortable amenities, and highly personalized service. Acela is the latest and boldest step by Amtrak to change its rail service into a more customer-focused, commercially driven, premium transportation service.[6]

The Acela trains, designed to operate as fast as 150 miles per hour (241.35 kilometers per hour), promised to reduce travel time significantly. For instance, the trip from Washington, D.C., to Boston, which currently took 7 hours and 30 minutes, would take 5 hours and 50 minutes on the high-speed trains.[7] The first high-speed trains, the Acela Express, were scheduled to begin service between New York City and Boston in late 1999, while the New York to Washington leg would be added within a year. The full high-speed service was expected to be in place by the fall of 2000.

---

[3]Executive Summary: 1999 Assessment of Amtrak's Financial Needs through 2002.

[4]Amtrak's fiscal year ended September 30.

[5]Amtrak was organized along three Strategic Business Units (SBUs): Amtrak Northeast Corridor, Amtrak Intercity, and Amtrak West. The Northeast Corridor included all the routes in the Northeast from Virginia to Maine; Amtrak West included the West Coast routes in California and the Pacific Northwest, and extended to Vancouver, British Columbia. Amtrak Intercity was the remainder of the system across the middle of the country.

[6]Babcock and Brown memorandum, 3.

[7]Information provided by Raj Srinath, senior director of Corporate Finance, Amtrak.

THE EQUIPMENT

To operate the Acela Regional Service as planned, Amtrak needed to purchase 15 dual-cab, high-horsepower electric locomotives, and 20 high-speed train sets. Each train set consisted of one first-class coach car, one bistro car, three coach cars, one end coach car, and two power cars. The estimated total cost for all the equipment was around $750 million:

	Number	Cost	Aggregate Cost
High-speed locomotives	15	$ 7,161,300	$107,419,500
Train sets	20	32,129,050	642,581,000
Total			$750,000,500

The train sets and locomotives had estimated useful lives of 25 years, and residual values equivalent to approximately 15 percent of the original equipment cost. Amtrak used straight-line depreciation for accounting purposes, and seven-year MACRS[8] for tax purposes. Amtrak was subject to the corporate income tax rate of 35 percent.

Friner had already been able to arrange financing for all the equipment save for six locomotives and seven train sets, which totaled $267.9 million in value. This was the amount (not $750 million) for which she was considering the BNYCF leveraged-lease proposal.

FINANCING OPTIONS

Three options were available for Amtrak to gain use of the equipment: (1) borrow money to fund the purchase, (2) lease the equipment from a financial institution such as BNYCF, or (3) rely on federal sources for funding.

Borrow and Buy

A major bank had offered to underwrite a bond issuance for Amtrak with a 20-year term at 6.75 percent per annum. This arrangement would call for Amtrak to make semiannual payments of $12.303 million, beginning in December 1999. The locomotives and train sets would serve as collateral for the loan. A member of the Treasury staff suggested that one drawback to this alternative was that Amtrak had recently issued debt—as such, the public market might already be saturated with Amtrak paper.

Lease

BNYCF had proposed a leveraged lease[9] structure for this transaction (see diagram in **Exhibit 4**). BNY Capital Funding LLC, a wholly owned subsidiary of The Bank of New York,

---

[8]Modified Accelerated Cost Recovery System. See **Exhibit 5** for a seven-year MACRS schedule.
[9]There were three common types of financial leases. Direct leases were those in which the lessor purchased the equipment or asset and rented this out to the lessee. In sale-and-leaseback arrangements, the lessee already owned the asset but sold it to a lessor and leased it back. Leveraged leases were those in which the lessor borrowed money to fund part of the purchase of assets, pledging the lease contract as security for the loan.

would act as lessor. It would provide the equity funds needed to finance the purchase. On the other hand, The Export Development Corporation (EDC) of Canada would be the sole lender and debt provider, agreeing to provide 80 percent of the required funds. The equity investor, BNY Capital Funding LLC, provided the remaining 20 percent, and would receive lease payments only after the debtor had been paid.

The equity and debt funds on closing would flow through Wilmington Trust, an independent third party to the transaction that acted as owner-trustee. The rent payments on rental dates would also flow through Wilmington Trust, which would then distribute the payments to either EDC or BNY Capital Funding LLC.

Under the lease proposal, Amtrak would need to make semiannual payments according to the schedule provided in **Exhibit 6**. At the end of the lease term, Amtrak could buy the equipment from BNY Capital Funding LLC at the higher of terminal or fair market value.[10] Amtrak also had an early-buyout option in which it could acquire the equipment from BNY Capital Funding LLC in 2017 for $126.6 million.

Rely on Federal Sources

Theoretically, Amtrak could use federal monies to fund the Acela equipment purchases. Although Congress had mandated that Amtrak could not use federal subsidies for operating expenses, it had agreed to continue funding Amtrak for capital appropriations. Purchase of the Acela equipment would be considered a capital-asset acquisition and, as such, federal grant monies could be used. However, federal grants were considered by Friner and her staff to be a "premium and precious" commodity; thus, Amtrak preferred to use the grant money to fund capital projects that could not be easily and cost-effectively financed, such as safety, right-of-way and infrastructure-related projects, and major overhauls. On the other hand, Acela train sets and other rolling stock could be very efficiently financed through the capital markets.

CONCLUSION

Arlene Friner needed to make a decision soon. The timely commencement of the Acela service was crucial to Amtrak's prospects for self-sufficiency. She needed to arrange financing immediately so the equipment would be delivered on time.

---

[10]Using historical data, the Treasury staff estimated that the standard deviation of the market-value fluctuations of train sets and locomotives was 25 percent. The 17-year risk-free rate currently stood at 5.78 percent. The Treasury staff also calculated Amtrak's WACC to be 11.8 percent.

EXHIBIT 1
About Acela

Northeast Travel

New World-Class Service From Amtrak®.

Acela,^{SM} A blend of "acceleration" and "excellence." Acela^{SM} (pronounced ah-CELL-ah) represents the Amtrak® commitment to excel. To make your journey the best it can be at every stage — from faster, more efficient reservation systems to striking new and renovated stations to premium on-board services. Acela Express^{SM} is the name of the sleek new high-speed trains you'll see in the Northeast this year.

But Acela means more than fast trains. It stands for leading technology, superior comfort and modern amenities. With three levels of service — Express, Regional and Commuter — Acela offers an unparalleled standard of travel for every guest on every train. A standard that includes consistently professional, highly personalized service; new and refurbished trains with a contemporary interior design; convenient connections to a wide variety of destinations across the U.S. and thoughtful touches for your pleasure and comfort. Simply stated, Acela puts top priority on your time and provides a pleasant travel experience. It's Amtrak's commitment to the way you choose to travel.

At 150 MPH, This is Not Your Ordinary Train Trip.

If your life is on the fast track, **Acela Express**^{SM} is Amtrak's top-of-the-line ride to business or pleasure in the Northeast. The new 150-mph Acela Express trains will replace Metroliner® this year. These trains are designed to offer state-of-the-art equipment and premium service to travelers who expect nothing but the best. We're even improving our station locations — we've added a new Route 128 station near Boston and updated Penn Station in New York.

Reserved First class and Business class seating accommodate your busy agenda with comfort, upscale business amenities and polished professional service.

Plush seats with foot-rests and adjustable head cushions invite you to relax and recharge. Listen to music, enjoy a gourmet-to-go snack or sandwich. When there's work to do, you have an electrical outlet at your seat, adjustable lighting and a large tray table for your laptop. You can hold a meeting at one of our 32 conference tables located throughout the train. Or take a break in the bistro-like atmosphere of the Cafe car, where there's beer on tap and news on the TV screen. Aboard Acela Express, it's all about how you use your time.

Source: http://amtrak.com/savings/acela.html. Note: Image has been modified to fit page.

EXHIBIT 2
Income Statement (in millions of dollars)

	Fiscal Year Ending September 30				
	1994	1995	1996	1997	1998
Revenues					
Passenger related and other	$1,152	$1,177	$1,213	$1,341	$1,392
Commuter	184	213	234	242	260
Reimbursable	77	107	108	91	91
Federal payments	—	—	—	—	542
Total revenues	**$1,413**	**$1,497**	**$1,555**	**$1,674**	**$2,285**
Expenses					
Salaries, wages, and benefits	$1,330	1,241	1,236	1,299	1,448
Train operations	358	321	321	365	356
Facility and office related	153	172	181	187	190
Maintenance of way goods and services	45	73	59	46	52
Advertising and sales	91	90	109	98	102
Interest	185	144	149	160	181
Depreciation and amortization	245	230	238	242	294
Other	83	34	25	39	15
One time charges/(gains)	(244)	—	—	—	—
Total expenses	**$2,246**	**$2,305**	**$2,318**	**$2,436**	**$2,638**
Operating income/(loss)	**(833)**	**(808)**	**(763)**	**(762)**	**(353)**
Exclude federal payments and related interest					577
Operating loss restated	**$ (833)**	**$ (808)**	**$ (763)**	**$ (762)**	**$ (930)**
Federal Grants:					
Federal operating grant	$ 352	392	285	223	202
Excess railroad retirement taxes	150	150	120	142	142
Federal capital—interest	—	—	—	42	—
Federal capital—progressive overhaul & other	—	—	36	37	82
Total federal grants	**$ 502**	**$ 542**	**$ 441**	**$ 444**	**$ 426**
Net loss	**$ (331)**	**$ (266)**	**$ (322)**	**$ (318)**	**$ (504)**

Source: Amtrak annual report.

EXHIBIT 3
Balance Sheet (in millions of dollars)

	FY Ending Sept. 30, 1998
ASSETS	
Current assets	
Cash and equivalents	$ 274.7
Temporary cash investments	409.7
Accounts receivable, net	88.7
Materials and supplies	91.6
Other current assets	3.4
Total current assets	**868.1**
Property and equipment	9,456.4
Less accumulated depreciation	(3,106.9)
Net PPE	6,349.5
Other assets and deferred charges	87.6
Total assets	**$ 7,305.3**
LIABILITIES AND CAPITALIZATION	
Current liabilities	
Accounts payable	$ 270.8
Accrued expenses and other current liabilities	186.7
Deferred ticket revenue	61.4
Current maturities of long term debt and capital lease obligations	102.2
Total current liabilities	**621.1**
Long-term debt and capital lease obligations	
Capital lease obligations	1,213.1
Equipment and other debt	322.5
	1,535.6
Other liabilities and deferred credit	
Deferred federal payments	457.0
Casualty reserves	136.2
Postretirement employee benefits obligation	118.4
Environmental reserve	35.4
Advances from railroads and commuter agencies	20.6
Other	1.5
	769.1
Total liabilities	**2,925.8**
Capitalization	
Preferred stock	10,939.7
Common stock	93.9
Other paid-in capital	6,471.3
Accumulated comprehensive loss	(13,125.4)
	$ 4,379.5
Total liabilities and capitalization	**$ 7,305.3**

Source: Amtrak annual report.

EXHIBIT 4
BNY Capital Funding LLC's Proposed Leveraged-Lease Structure

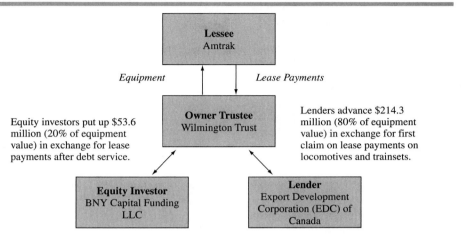

Note: Diagram based on illustration in *Principles of Corporate Finance* by Richard Brealey and Stewart Myers, 5th ed., p. 755.

EXHIBIT 5
Seven-Year MACRS
Depreciation Schedule[1]
(in percentages of
depreciable investment)

Year	% Depreciated
1	14.29%
2	24.49
3	17.49
4	12.49
5	8.93
6	8.93
7	8.93
8	4.45

[1]Because of the half-year
convention, seven-year MACRS
involved eight years of
depreciation expenses.

EXHIBIT 6
BNY Capital Funding LLC's
Proposed Lease-Payment
Schedule (in dollars)

Date Due		Amount
1999	June	$ —
	Dec.	200,102
2000	June	3,761,228
	Dec.	7,965,652
2001	June	10,022,594
	Dec.	10,316,948
2002	June	8,617,634
	Dec.	10,360,645
2003	June	9,828,570
	Dec.	10,367,985
2004	June	8,607,823
	Dec.	10,418,573
2005	June	9,683,063
	Dec.	10,435,186
2006	June	8,580,151
	Dec.	11,599,993
2007	June	7,338,339
	Dec.	11,468,211
2008	June	9,475,208
	Dec.	15,792,709
2009	June	7,765,741
	Dec.	20,224,322
2010	June	5,067,035
	Dec.	15,872,556
2011	June	4,121,823
	Dec.	22,807,129
2012	June	3,336,587
	Dec.	23,645,133
2013	June	2,662,913
	Dec.	24,055,367
2014	June	1,957,919
	Dec.	20,017,608
2015	June	6,067,613
	Dec.	6,287,652
2016	June	12,292,315
	Dec.	21,394,788
2017	June	6,551,924
	Dec.	18,107,167
2018	June	8,612,133
	Dec.	13,469,295
2019	June	8,864,543
	Dec.	6,654,238
2020	June	2,035,748
	Dec.	1

Corning, Inc.: Zero-Coupon Convertible Debentures Due November 8, 2015 (A)

On November 8, 2000, Corning announced that it would issue $2.7 billion in zero-coupon convertible debentures priced at $741.923 per $1,000 principal amount. The initial public offering price yielded 2.00 percent per annum to maturity, compounded semiannually. A summary of terms is given in **Exhibit 1.** Concurrent with the offering, Corning was also conducting a separate public offering of 30 million shares of its common stock at $71.25 a share.[1] Neither offering was contingent upon completion of the other. The entire financing would raise around $4.8 billion.

Corning planned to use the proceeds of both offerings to fund its acquisition of Pirelli S.p.A.'s 90 percent interest in Optical Technologies USA, Pirelli's optical components and devices business. The total acquisition consideration was approximately $3.6 billion in cash. The acquisition agreement had been announced on September 27, 2000, and was still pending regulatory approval. However, observers agreed that the acquisition was likely to be completed.

The issue of the Corning zero-coupon convertibles came to the attention of Julianna Coopers, an investment analyst at the Paradigm Group of mutual funds. The Paradigm Group offered 36 different funds and managed over $50 billion in assets. Coopers and her group handled Paradigm's Convertible Securities Fund, which sought "high returns through a combination of current income and capital appreciation."

Coopers had been tasked with assessing the new issue of Corning convertibles. She needed to decide that day whether to recommend purchasing some of these bonds for the

---

[1] www.ipo.com

This case was prepared by Jessica Chan under the supervision of Professor Robert F. Bruner. It was written as a basis for class discussion rather than to illustrate effective or ineffective handling of an administrative situation. Copyright © 2001 by the University of Virginia Darden School Foundation, Charlottesville, VA. All rights reserved. *To order copies, send an e-mail to dardencases@virginia.edu. No part of this publication may be reproduced, stored in a retrieval system, used in a spreadsheet, or transmitted in any form or by any means—electronic, mechanical, photocopying, recording, or otherwise—without the permission of the Darden School Foundation.* Version 2.6.

Convertible Securities Fund. Her task was to assess the risk of the bond issue, and judge the adequacy of the yield, offering price, and conversion terms.

THE COMPANY

Corning, Inc., competed in three broadly defined operating segments: Telecommunications, Advanced Materials, and Information Display. The Telecommunications division accounted for roughly 70 percent of company revenue. **Exhibit 2** contains a breakdown of sales and net income by operating segment while **Exhibit 3** provides a detailed breakdown of the products within each operating segment.

Corning was the world's largest manufacturer of optical fiber and amplifiers, with a 50 percent share of the optical-fiber market, twice that of its nearest competitor, Lucent. At the time of the offering, the market for fiber was in a sold-out state, and Corning had presold the next 18 months of its entire fiber-manufacturing capacity.[2] Worldwide demand for fiber had grown by 40 percent in 1999, and management expected the same robust growth rate for 2000. Going forward, industry analysts expected the annual growth rate for fiber to be between 20 and 25 percent through 2002, although there was some debate about a potential fiber glut.

Within the company's Telecommunications division, its Photonics business was growing at a triple-digit annual rate. The Photonics business manufactured products that enhanced the flexibility and performance of communications networks. These were products that boosted, combined, separated, and connected optical signals transmitted over fiber-optic networks. Because of strong demand, Corning was expanding capacity for Photonics sixfold over the next 18 months.[3]

The nontelecommunications businesses of Corning were also performing impressively. The company was the number-one supplier of flat panel glass for LCDs (liquid crystal displays) used in PC screens, televisions, digital cameras, and other devices, and commanded roughly a 60 percent world-market share. Demand for flat panel displays was growing at around 40 percent per annum, amid stable pricing. The flat panel business was expected to reach roughly $500 million in 2000 and to hit $1 billion in a few years.[4] In addition, Corning's biotechnology-related products were experiencing healthy demand. This segment was expected to grow by 30 to 35 percent annually, led by DNA analysis products.[5]

A rich valuation for Corning shares testified to the rosy outlook for the company. Corning's average P/E ratio for the past month had been roughly 94 × estimated 2000 earnings and 75 × estimated 2001 earnings, compared with an average of around 30 × for the S&P 500. (**Exhibit 4** contains a history of Corning's share-price performance and P/E ratios.)

---

[2]Gavin Duffy and T. Peter Andrew, "Corning: Charging Ahead at the Speed of Light," A.G. Edwards report, November 6, 2000.

[3]Timothy Anderson and B. Alexander Henderson, "Corning, Inc.: Initiating Coverage with a Buy," Salomon Smith Barney, September 20, 2000.

[4]Ibid.

[5]Ibid.

However, Corning's future was also fraught with risks. The most pressing concerns related to the following:[6]

Dependence on service providers. Service providers required huge investments for network expansion and capacity building. There was a risk that, as investors became more aware of the capital-intensive nature of the business, funding for service providers would dry up, in turn affecting demand for Corning's products.

Potential supply glut in fiber market. Some industry analysts suggested that excess fiber capacity was beginning to emerge. They argued that if all the fiber in the ground were lit, it would be more than enough to support all bandwidth needs for some time. In contrast, other analysts expressed the view that there was currently not enough equipment to light and connect all the fiber in the ground. Corning did not think that an oversupply was approaching.

The end of major long-haul carriers' fiber build-outs. In the past few years, Corning had benefited as major U.S. long-haul carriers like MCI, Sprint, and AT&T had deployed fiber rapidly. Now after the ramp-ups, build-outs by major U.S. carriers were likely to slow down, just as Corning was increasing its fiber-manufacturing capacity. This meant that Corning would have to shift its reliance to overseas and metro carrier markets. While overseas growth was expected to be strong, foreign service providers were also smaller and seen as more risky.

Technological change. The market for Corning's products was characterized by rapidly changing technologies, evolving industry standards and frequent new product introductions. Corning's success would depend heavily on timely and successful introduction of new products and on its ability to address competing technologies.[7]

ANALYZING THE CONVERTIBLE BOND OFFERING

After reading the prospectus for the convertible bond offering, Coopers began her analysis by putting together a table of metrics that convertible bond traders traditionally used for evaluating converts. **Exhibit 5** shows the results of her work.

After studying Exhibit 5, Coopers decided to value the converts directly. She believed that doing so would be better than relying on traditional ratios in arriving at an independent judgment. In valuing the converts directly, she relied on the idea that converts were actually hybrid securities composed of a straight bond and one or more embedded options, such as the right to convert the bond to common stock. The value (V) of a convertible bond was therefore just the sum of the straight bond value, and the values of the embedded options:

$$V_{CV\ Bond} = V_{Straight\ Bond} + V_{Option\ 1} + V_{Option\ 2} + \cdots + V_{Option\ n}$$

[6]Ibid.
[7]Corning prospectus for zero-coupon convertible debentures due November 8, 2015.

By valuing each component directly, she could arrive at an appropriate price for the convert. She began with the straight bond portion, which was easier to value. Straight bonds were usually evaluated on the adequacy of their yield to maturity relative to the risk and maturity of the bond. If Coopers used the offering price of $741.923 and principal repayment of $1,000, the yield to maturity would come out to 2.00 percent.[8] However, she knew that this did not properly reflect all the elements of the convert as the price of $741.923 should contain both the value of the bond and the embedded options. Instead, the true value of the "straight bond" portion could be estimated by using yields on similar-rated corporate bonds. She reviewed Corning's recent ratings (**Exhibit 6**), computed its debt and coverage ratios pro forma for the convertible bond and equity issuances, and compared her results against statistics for different bond-rating categories (**Exhibit 7**). She then put together a sample of straight-debt issuances of similar-rated companies (**Exhibit 8**) and proceeded to value the bond portion of the converts.

Valuing the Conversion Option

Next Coopers attempted to value the conversion option: "The right to convert is effectively an American call option that allows me to buy Corning shares at $89.062 per share anytime between now and the next 15 years. Right now the stock is trading at $71.25 per share, so I wouldn't convert at this time. But there is a value to my owning an option to convert when conversion becomes favorable. I can use the Black-Scholes option pricing model to value that option."[9]

"The most important assumption I need to feed into the model is the volatility of Corning stock, since the value of my call option depends to a large extent on the stock price. The more volatile the stock, the more valuable my call option is because the distribution of potential stock prices is wider." She gathered data on Corning's dividend history (**Exhibit 9**), as well as data on historical volatilities of Corning, its peer firms, and the main stock indices (Exhibit 10). She also gathered data for computing the implied volatilities of Corning using recently traded Corning options (**Exhibit 11**).

"Another important assumption is the risk-free rate. The Black-Scholes model uses this rate to obtain the present value of the expected payoff[10] from the option." Coopers went to check the current yields on U.S. Treasuries (**Exhibit 12**).

As she entered her assumptions into the model, she reminded herself that after obtaining the value of the conversion option, she would need to adjust for dilution in order to account for the conversion of the bond into shares, and for the issuance of new common stock in connection with the company's concurrent stock offering.

---

[8]$741.923 today would grow to $1,000 in 15 years if it earned 2.0 percent compounded semiannually.

[9]Strictly speaking, the Black-Scholes model should be used to value only European options. But because American options were usually held to maturity in order to preserve the "time value" of the option, they could essentially be thought of as European options. The exception was when a stock underlying an American call option paid a large-enough dividend. In that case, an investor might exercise the call option well before maturity in order to obtain the dividend. In such instances, it was not appropriate to use the Black-Scholes model.

[10]The payoff was the difference between the stock price and the exercise price, if the difference was positive. If negative, the payoff was zero.

Valuing the Redemption Option

After valuing the conversion option, Coopers observed that the terms of the bond offering allowed Corning to "call," or redeem, the bond issue anytime after November 8, 2005. Thus, the redemption provision gave Corning flexibility to repay the bond early. Effectively, the company was "long" a call on the convert, and the bondholder was "short" a call.

Coopers thought more carefully about the redemption option and tried to visualize the circumstances in which Corning might redeem the convertible bond. If interest rates declined, bond prices should theoretically go up. But Corning could, by virtue of its redemption option, call in the bonds at prices well below their market value. Coopers thought out loud, "With a noncallable bond, as yields decline, the bond value rises. But with callable bonds, the increase in price 'tops out' because of the expectation that the issuer will exercise the option to refund the bond with cheaper debt."

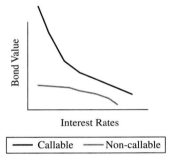

However, Coopers noted that in the case of most convertible bonds, refunding the bond with cheaper debt almost never made sense because convertibles usually carried very low coupons. With a low coupon rate, interest rates would have to fall dramatically before it became economically attractive to refund the bond with another, even lower-coupon issue, or to use interest-generating cash to repay the bond. Instead, redemption provisions had a different purpose: to permit the issuer to force conversion of the bonds into common stock.[11] Of course, this only occurred when the conversion option was "in the money."

"Without being forced to convert to stock by some threat of redemption, I might continue to hold the convertible bond even if the option is in the money.[12] But with this redemption option, Corning could force me to make the conversion. From my standpoint, being forced to do anything is a negative. Therefore, this redemption provision has to reduce the value of the bond."

---

[11]Rapidly growing companies often forced conversion in order to expand their base of equity capital as a foundation for greater debt financing. Creditors usually made lending decisions on the basis of conventional definitions of debt and equity. The conventional definitions might ignore economic reality. An in-the-money convertible bond traded like, and was economically similar to, common equity. From this standpoint, forced conversion to expand the borrowing capacity of the firm was unnecessary window dressing. Nevertheless, very few issuers of convertible bonds permitted them to run their full term as debt.

[12]Investors tended to hold convertible bonds until just before maturity in order to preserve the "time value" of the option.

Valuing redemption provisions was so complicated, however, because the likelihood that the firm would call the bond early depended on two key drivers: interest rates and stock prices.[13] Coopers could not simulate this using the Black-Scholes model that she had. Rather, she would have to build a spreadsheet that accurately modeled this complexity. Because Coopers was in a hurry, she asked one of the derivatives experts within the firm to help her. He came back an hour later with the following values for the redemption option based on different volatility assumptions:

Volatility	.25	.75	1.25
Redemption option value (per bond)[14]	$103.18	$284.98	$336.66

Other Embedded Options

Coopers reviewed the term sheet to see if there were any other embedded options that she had not accounted for. She noticed another option that allowed investors to "sell" back the debentures to Corning on two specified dates: November 8, 2005, and November 8, 2010. She thought, "Effectively, this is a put option. In fact, these are actually two put options. But the interrelatedness of the two puts makes this option difficult to value. The existence of the 2010 option depends on whether or not I exercise the 2005 option, and that, in turn, depends on whether redemption is favorable at that point."

Given the complexity of valuing the put options, Coopers asked the derivatives expert for help once more. He came back with the following estimates:

Volatility	.25	.75	1.25
Put option value (per bond)[15]	$96.9	$166.25	$273.1

Finally, Coopers noticed the change in control provision that gave bondholders the right to require Corning to repurchase the converts if the company became the subject of a merger or acquisition. "This option is favorable for me because it protects me against the possibility of someone buying the company and loading it up with debt. But Corning is a large firm with a large equity base and good operating history; I think it is very unlikely that the company would be bought. Therefore, I will assign no value to this option."

A FURTHER TEST OF REALITY

Before she could make her final decision on whether to invest in the Corning bonds, Coopers needed to think carefully about several things. First was the stock price performance of Corning. The stock currently traded at $71.25, but only a year ago it was at less than half

---

[13]It was rational for the issuer to call the bond if the redemption price of the bond was less than either its "bond equivalent value" (i.e., present value of principal and interest) or its "equity equivalent value" (current stock price times conversion ratio of the bond).

[14]Estimated using a binomial option-pricing model.

[15]Estimated using a binomial option-pricing model.

that amount. Much of the run-up had to do with what investors saw as a "white-hot" market for optical-fiber technology. At its current price, Corning's P/E ratio was very high. But then again, Corning's stock had hit $113 earlier in the year. "Perhaps the conversion option, which effectively allows me to buy stock at $89, is not so bad considering the high that the stock has reached," Coopers thought. "I have to consider this very carefully. If the share price falls, I will be left holding a bond that has a yield to maturity of only 2 percent."

She decided to analyze how valuable the firm would need to be in order to put the conversion option "in the money." She reviewed the prospectus, which illustrated both the company's actual capitalization at September 30, 2000, and its capitalization as adjusted to give effect to the convertible bond offering and the concurrent offering of common stock (see **Exhibit 13**).

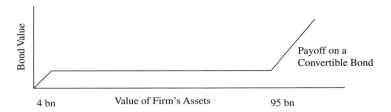

"The company's total debt is around $4 billion. As long as the total value of its assets does not fall below $4 billion, the convertible bonds are worth at least their aggregate principal amount of $2.71 billion. Now what will the value of the assets need to be in order for the bond to be worth more as equity? Well, my breakeven price for equity is the exercise price of $89.0625 per share. There are going to be 988.7 million shares outstanding after the concurrent equity offering. In addition, the company has issued stock options in connection with recent acquisitions totaling 30 million shares. If all options are exercised, including those embedded in the convertible bond offering, there will be another 53 million shares all in all.[16] Thus, the total number of shares will be 1.0413 billion. If I multiply this by my breakeven price, I get a total equity value of $92.7 billion. Adding the company's existing long-term debt of around $2 billion, my calculations tell me that the market value of Corning's assets must be around $95 billion for my bond to be worth more as equity. As it stands right now, the market value of Corning's assets stands at around $65 billion."

Coopers wondered whether the market value of Corning's assets would reach $95 billion before 2015. She also thought about potential further dilution. Corning had been on an acquisition "roll" in recent months and might continue to acquire more companies given its current capacity constraints. If so, how would it affect the holders of the convertible bonds?

Coopers pondered these questions as she prepared her final report to the portfolio manager of her fund.

---

[16]If call options were exercised, shares from the convertible bond offering were calculated as follows: total principal amount of $2,712,546,000 divided by $1,000 principal per debenture = 2,712,546 debentures. Each debenture was convertible into 8.3304 shares, for a total of 22,596,593 shares.

EXHIBIT 1
Summary of Terms of the Offering

Securities Offered	$2,712,546,000 aggregate principal amount at maturity of our zero-coupon convertible debentures due November 8, 2015. The debentures are senior unsecured obligations of Corning.
Offering Price	$741.923 per $1,000 principal amount at maturity.
Interest	We will not pay interest on the debentures prior to maturity.
Maturity Date	November 8, 2015.
Conversion Right	You may convert the debentures into shares of our common stock initially at a conversion rate of 8.3304 shares for each debenture at any time before the close of business on November 8, 2015, unless we have previously redeemed or repurchased the debentures. The initial conversion rate is equivalent to an initial conversion price of approximately $89.0625 per share, which is based on the initial public offering price of the debentures. The conversion rate may be adjusted in certain circumstances.
Original Issue Discount	For U.S. federal income tax purposes we are offering each debenture at an original issue discount equal to the principal amount at maturity of each debenture less the initial public offering price. You should be aware that, although we will not pay interest on the debentures until maturity, U.S. investors must include original issue discount as the discount accrues in their gross income for U.S. federal income tax purposes prior to the conversion, redemption, sale, or maturity of the debentures (even if such debentures are ultimately not converted, redeemed, sold, or paid at maturity).
Use of Proceeds	We plan to use a portion of the net proceeds from this offering and our concurrent common stock offering to fund the Pirelli acquisition. If the Pirelli acquisition is not completed, or if we receive proceeds from these offerings in excess of what we require to fund the Pirelli acquisition, we will use these proceeds for general corporate purposes.
Optional Redemption by Corning	We may redeem some or all of the debentures at our option at any time on or after November 8, 2005, at a redemption price equal to the initial public offering price plus accrued original issue discount through the redemption date.
Repurchase at Option of Holders	You may require us to repurchase some or all of your debentures on November 8, 2005, and November 8, 2010, at repurchase prices specified in this prospectus supplement.
Repurchase at Option of Holders upon a Change in Control	If we are the subject of a change in control, you may require us to repurchase some or all of your debentures at a price equal to the initial public offering price plus accrued original issue discount through the repurchase date.

Source: Corning prospectus. Note: This exhibit has been modified from its original form for instructional purposes.

EXHIBIT 2
Sales and Net Income Breakdown by Operating Segment

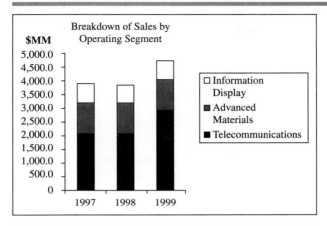

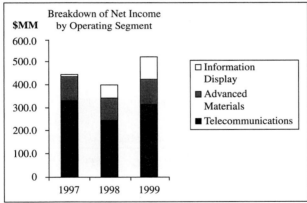

Source: Company offering memorandum.

EXHIBIT 3
Products within the Three Major Business Segments

Telecommunications

- Optical Fiber (Single-Mode and Multi-Mode)
    Long Haul, Submarine, Metro Area and Premise Networks
- Corning Cable Systems (Formerly Siecor, Siemens Communications Cables)
    Fiberoptic and Copper Cabling
    Related Hardware including: Assemblies, Interconnects, Splicers, and Test Equipment
    Submarine, Cable TV and Private Networks
- Photonics
    Products for the Routing, Switching, and Amplification of Optical Signals
    Dense Wave Division Multiplexing (DWDM) Modules
    Optical Amplifier Modules
    Components such as Thin-Film Filters, Multiclad Couplers and Fiber Bragg Gratings
    Optical Cross Connects
    Pump and Transmission Lasers

Information display

- Glass for Flat-Panel and Active Matrix Liquid Crystal Displays (AMLCDs)
    Flat-Panel Glass for Notebook Computer Screens, Desktop Monitors, Digital Cameras, PDA's and Automotive
    Navigational Displays
- Glass Panels and Funnels for Televisions and CRTs (Conventional Video Components) and Projection Video Lens Assemblies

Advanced materials

- Environmental Products
    Component parts for Catalytic Converters
- Semiconductor Materials
    Fused Silica Lens Assemblies used by semiconductor manufacturers in Microlithography Techniques for Etching
    Transistor Lines onto Silicon Wafers
- Science Products
    Various Materials used to enhance Drug Discovery Process by enabling High-Speed Drug Testing

Source: Gavin Duffy and T. Peter Andrew, "Corning: Charging Ahead at the Speed of Light," A.G. Edwards report, November 6, 2000.

EXHIBIT 4
Historical Stock-Price Information

	1995	1996	1997	1998	1999	2000[*]
Stock price						
High	10.4	13.0	21.7	15.0	43.0	113.3
Low	7.1	8.1	11.3	7.8	15.2	74.0
Average	8.8	10.3	15.6	12.1	22.6	34.6
Beta (average)	0.87	0.81	0.95	0.83	1.06	1.53
Corning P/E[**]						
High	27.69	30.83	31.97	31.69	64.47	169.92
Low	23.67	25.61	20.74	17.84	34.33	77.13
Average	25.22	27.55	27.68	24.09	41.21	114.17
S&P 500 P/E						
High	17.60	21.15	24.82	32.27	35.82	32.37
Low	15.96	16.89	19.32	22.77	28.91	26.20
Average	16.61	19.21	22.34	26.75	32.46	29.52
P/E premium/(discount)						
High	57.3%	45.8%	28.8%	−1.8%	80.0%	424.9%
Low	48.3	51.6	7.3	−21.6	18.8	194.4
Average	51.9	43.4	23.9	−9.9	27.0	286.8

52-week hi-lo from November 8, 2000	
High	113.33
Low	27.35
Average	68.16

[*]Through November 8, 2000.
[**]Based on monthly data.

Source of data: Bloomberg Financial Services, S&P's Research Insight Database.

EXHIBIT 5
Convertible Debt Comparables

		(a)	(b)	(c)	(d)		(e)	(f)	(g)	(h)	(i)
	Bond Rating	Yield to Maturity	Bond Price (for $1,000 par value)	Conversion Ratio	Conversion Price per Share	Current Stock Price	Conversion Premium per Share	Interest Income per Bond	Dividend Income per Bond	Income Spread per Bond	Premium Payback Period
Corning 2015	A2	2.00%	$ 741.9	$ 8.33	$89.06	$71.25	25.0%	—	$ 2.00	$ (2.00)	(74.2)
Baker Hughes (Sr.) (Zero) 2008	A2	Flat	792.5	18.60	42.61	34.38	23.9	—	8.56	(8.56)	(17.9)
Deere & Co. 5 1/2s 2001	A		3,372.5	91.58	36.83	36.81	0.0	55.0	80.59	(25.59)	(0.1)
E'town Corp 6 3/4s 2012	A–	0.49%	1,685.0	25.00	67.40	67.38	0.0	63.4	51.00	12.40	0.0
Hewlett Packard (Zero) 2017	A+	Flat	693.7	15.09	45.97	46.50	–1.1	—	4.83	(4.83)	1.7
Loews Corp. 3 1/2s 2010	A+	6.35%	822.5	15.38	53.48	34.56	54.7	35.0	7.69	27.31	10.7
Magna Int'l 5s 2002	A–	6.66%	970.0	13.38	72.49	44.88	61.5	50.0	15.39	34.61	10.7
Motorola Inc (Zero) 2013	A	Flat	800.0	21.36	37.45	24.94	50.2	—	3.42	(3.42)	(78.2)
Oak Industries 4 7/8s 2008	A–		4,930.0	64.43	76.52	76.50	0.0	47.8	15.46	32.34	0.0
Omnicom Group 2 1/4s 2013	A		1,852.5	20.07	92.30	92.25	0.1	22.5	14.05	8.45	0.1
Potomac Elec Pwr (Sr) 5s 2002	A–		960.0	29.50	32.54	22.88	42.2	50.0	48.97	1.03	276.7
Times Mirror (Zero) 2017	A–		587.5	14.57	40.32	37.06	8.8	—	5.83	(5.83)	(8.2)
USF&G Corp (Zero) 2009	A	Flat	865.0	16.64	51.98	51.25	1.4	—	17.97	(17.97)	(0.7)
Young & Rubicam 3s 2005	A–	2.94%	1,000.3	11.38	87.90	66.88	31.4	30.0	2.73	27.27	8.8

Definitions of terms:

(a) Return from principal and interest only.

(b) Current quote

(c) Number of shares to be received in exchange for $1,000 par value of bond.

(d) Obtained by dividing the *bond price* by the *conversion ratio*. This is effectively the price that an investor pays for the common stock and is also known as the exercise price.

(e) The premium of the exercise price over the current stock price.

(f) Annual interest income per $1,000 bond.

(g) The annual dividend income that would be received by converting into the underlying common stock. Calculated by multiplying the annual dividend per common share by the conversion ratio.

(h) The difference between interest income and dividend income per bond. In effect this represents the income differential between converting and not converting.

(i) Obtained by dividing the dollar conversion premium per share by the income spread per share. The higher the ratio, the less favorable it is to convert.

Source of data: Standard and Poor's Bond Guide, November 2000

All issues cited are convertible bond debentures outstanding in November 2000.

494

EXHIBIT 6
Credit-Rating History for Selected Corning Offerings

Rating History for Senior Unsecured Debt—Moody's		Rating History for LT Local Issuer Credit—S&P	
Rating	Effective	Rating	Effective
A2	2/2/2000	A*−	9/27/2000
A3	12/24/1996	A	5/14/1996
A2	1/21/1992	A+	3/21/1991
A1	11/29/1982	AA−	3/10/1982
Aa3	4/26/1982	AA−	11/9/1973

*-Denotes a negative outlook.

Rating Scale Comparison

Moody's	S&P
Aaa	AAA
Aa1	AA+
Aa2	AA
Aa3	AA−
A1	A+
A2	A
A3	A−
Baa1	BBB+
Baa2	BBB
Baa3	BBB−
Ba1	BB+
Ba2	BB
Ba3	BB−
B1	B+
B2	B
B3	B−
Caa1	CCC+
Caa2	CCC+
Caa3	CCC−

Ratings Definitions:

Moody's Investors Service: Long-Term Debt Ratings

A   Bonds which are rated A possess many favorable investment attributes and are to be considered as upper medium-grade obligations. Factors giving security to principal and interest are considered adequate, but elements may be present which suggest a susceptibility to impairment sometime in the future.

Standard & Poor's Long-Term Issuer Credit Ratings

A   An obligor rated 'A' has STRONG capacity to meet its financial commitments but is somewhat more susceptible to the adverse effects of changes in circumstances and economic conditions than obligors in higher-rated categories.

Source: Bloomberg Financial Services.

EXHIBIT 7
Key Industrial Financial Ratios by Rating Categories: Median Three-Year Ratios for 1996–98

Industrial long-term debt	AAA	AA	A	BBB	BB	B	CCC	Corning Pro-Forma for Convertible Bond and Equity Offerings
Pretax interest coverage (×)	12.9	9.2	7.2	4.1	2.5	1.2	−0.9	5.02
EBITDA interest coverage (×)	18.7	14	10	6.3	3.9	2.3	0.2	8.05
Funds from operations/total debt (%)	89.7	67	49.5	32.2	20.1	10.5	7.4	20.9
Free operating cash flow/total debt (%)	40.5	21.6	17.4	6.3	1	−4	−25.4	−2.1
Return on capital (%)	30.6	25.1	19.6	15.4	12.6	9.2	−8.8	3.67
Operating income/sales (%)	30.9	25.2	17.9	15.8	14.4	11.2	5	14
Long-term debt/capital (%)	21.4	29.3	33.3	40.8	55.3	68.8	71.5	28.2
Total debt/capital (incl. STD) (%)	31.8	37	39.2	46.4	58.5	71.4	79.4	29

Sources: Chinn, Wesley E., "Adjusted Key U.S. Financial Ratios," *Standard & Poor's Research,* July 7, 1999; Casewriter estimates.

EXHIBIT 8
Sample of Comparable Straight Current Coupon Bonds

Issuer	S&P Rating	Maturity	Yield to Maturity
AirTouch Communications	A	2008	7.56%
American Stores	A−	2017	7.99
Bell Atlantic	A+	2012	7.73
Coca-Cola Enterprises	A	2017	7.81
Corning Inc	A	2013	7.50
Walt Disney Co.	A	2015	7.90
Enron Oil and Gas	A−	2008	7.70
IBM	A+	2019	7.65
Lucent Technologies	A	2028	7.87
New York Tel. Co.	A+	2013	7.47
Nordstrom, Inc.	A	2009	8.11
Southwest Airlines	A−	2027	7.95
WorldCom Inc.	A−	2010	7.45
Mean			7.75%
Median			7.73%
Standard Deviation			0.21%

Source: Standard and Poor's Bond Guide, October 2000.

EXHIBIT 9
Corning's Dividend History (in dollars per share)

Payment Dates	31-Mar	30-Jun	30-Sep	31-Dec	Full Year
1997	0.06	0.06	0.06	0.06	0.24
1998	0.06	0.06	0.06	0.06	0.24
1999	0.06	0.06	0.06	0.06	0.24
2000	0.06	0.06	0.06		

Source: Bloomberg; Value Line Investment Survey.

EXHIBIT 10
Estimates of Historical Volatilities as of November 8, 2000

	1 Month	3 Months	6 Months	1 Year
Corning	123.56	85.74	77.63	79.67
JDS Uniphase	140.07	90.14	91.56	95.42
Lucent	159.76	100.95	83.01	77.88
Ciena	144.15	102.11	98.64	110.26
Average	**141.89**	**94.74**	**87.71**	**90.81**
Dow Jones Industrial Average	22.36	16.24	16.57	19.93
S&P 500 Index	25.81	17.98	18.63	20.92
Nasdaq 100 Index	66.45	47.72	51.31	51.51

Source: Bloomberg Financial Services.

EXHIBIT 11
Premiums for Corning Options on the Chicago Board Options Exchange: Closing Prices as of November 7, 2000

Option & NY Close	Strike Price	Calls: Last		Puts: Last	
		November	May	November	May
$ 68.50	$70.00	$3.25	No option	4.75	No option
68.50	70.00	No option	15.50	No option	14.50
68.50	80.00	0.75	No option	12.63	No option
68.50	83.38	0.44	No option	16.13	No option
Days to maturity		17	193	17	193

Source: The Wall Street Journal, November 8, 2000.

EXHIBIT 12
Capital-Market Conditions around November 8, 2000

Yields on U.S. Treasuries

3-month	6.34%
1-year	6.14
3-year	5.79
5-year	5.68
7-year	5.78
10-year	5.70
30-year	5.76

Yields on Corporates, by Rating

Aaa	7.53%
Baa	8.35

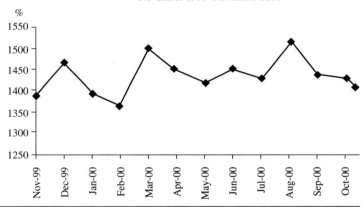

Trend in 10-Year Treasury Yields:
November 1999–November 2000

Trend in S&P 500 Index:
November 1999–November 2000

Source: Bloomberg Financial Services; Federal Reserve Board releases.

EXHIBIT 13
Actual and Pro Forma Balance Sheet (in millions)

	September 30, 2000	
	Actual	**As Adjusted**
Cash and short-term investments	1,237.5	5,286.9
Current maturities of long-term debt and short-term notes payable	111.4	111.4
Loans payable beyond one year	1,946.3	1,946.3
Zero coupon convertible debentures	—	2,012.5
Minority interest in subsidiary companies	138.7	138.7
Convertible preferred stock	8.9	8.9
Common shareholders' equity		
Common stock, issued: 958.7 million actual and 988.7 million as adjusted	6,600.0	8,678.0
Retained earnings	2,113.7	2,113.7
Treasury stock	(746.9)	(746.9)
Accumulated other comprehensive loss	(114.6)	(114.6)
Total common shareholders' equity	7,852.2	9,930.2
Total capitalization	9,946.1	14,036.6
Debt to equity ratio	26.2%	41.0%
Debt to capitalization	20.8%	29.1%

Source: Corning prospectus.

Enron Corporation's Weather Derivatives (A)

Everybody talks about the weather, but nobody does anything about it.[1]

In October 2000, Mary Watts, the chief financial officer of Pacific Northwest Electric (PNW), a utility servicing the Pacific Northwest Region of the United States, reviewed the financial plan for PNW's 2000–2001 forthcoming winter season. Winter temperatures affected the firm's revenues: the colder the season, the greater the electricity usage. She recalled that the last few years had offered a warmer-than-average winter climate, resulting in adverse financial results for PNW. The weather, combined with rapid deregulation in PNW's market area, meant that the firm reported substantially no EPS growth from 1995 to 1999, in an otherwise buoyant economic setting. PNW's stock price had suffered accordingly. On her desk was a report from a weather advisory service predicting another unseasonably warm winter.

Watts remembered a recent conversation with Mike James, a representative of Enron Corporation. Mike had presented a new "weather derivative" product from Enron that he claimed could minimize PNW's weather-related volume risk. Watts wondered how these derivatives worked, and how they might be used to help restore PNW's credibility in the

---

[1]Charles Dudley Warner, in an editorial in *Hartford Courant,* 1897.

This case was prepared from field research by Mari Capestany and Professors Robert Bruner and Samuel Bodily. It is intended to serve as a basis for classroom discussion rather than to illustrate effective or ineffective managerial decision making. Certain names, facts, and financial data have been disguised to preserve confidential information and/or sharpen the managerial issues in the case. The resulting presentation, however, reasonably reflects the actual managerial setting. The assistance and cooperation of Enron Corporation is gratefully acknowledged. Copyright © 2000 by the University of Virginia Darden School Foundation, Charlottesville, VA. All rights reserved. *To order copies, send an e-mail to* dardencases@virginia.edu. *No part of this publication may be reproduced, stored in a retrieval system, used in a spreadsheet, or transmitted in any form or by any means—electronic, mechanical, photocopying, recording, or otherwise—without the permission of the Darden School Foundation. Version 1.2.*

capital markets. Should she consider purchasing Enron's weather protection products for the upcoming winter season? She would need to decide soon about the use of these derivatives if she wanted to put in place a hedge for the winter months ahead.

PACIFIC NORTHWEST ELECTRIC

PNW was a significant producer of electric power, with primary coverage in parts of Oregon, Washington, Northern California, Idaho, and Montana. Its revenues in 1999 were $11 billion; net income was $800 million. Earnings per share were $1.04 in 1999, up from $1.03 in 1995. Noting the basically flat EPS trend for PNW and expressing concern for the firm's dividend coverage, securities analysts were reluctant to advocate holding PNW's shares. Thus, the utility's share price underperformed broad market indexes, and indexes of the utility industry. Mary Watts estimated that the warmer-than-usual weather of the past four years had accounted for about two-thirds of the firm's underperformance in earnings.

PNW was a capital-intensive firm, spending about $1 billion per year in capital projects. The firm's recent record of financial performance held important implications for PNW's ability to finance its capital spending. First, it contributed to a higher cost of capital for PNW. The firm's share prices had been more volatile than usual for a public utility, yielding a higher beta and cost of equity. Similarly, the firm's debt rating had slipped from A- to BBB+, producing a cost of debt higher by 75 basis points at the margin. In the former environment of return regulation, it might have been possible for PNW to recover the higher capital costs from consumers. But in the current deregulating environment, where consumers could purchase power from a variety of producers on the power grid, cost disadvantages would lead to a loss of market share. Second, slippage in financial performance might restrict the firm's access to capital in a restrictive financial climate.

WEATHER RISK

The U.S. Department of Commerce estimated that at least $1 trillion of the total U.S. gross national product (about $7 trillion) was sensitive to variations in weather. This reflected economic sectors as disparate as agriculture, apparel retailing, and ski resorts that depended on *appropriate* variations in weather. "Weather" subsumed a variety of specific conditions such as temperature, wind, precipitation, type of precipitation, storms and hurricanes, haze, and "misery" (i.e., the combination of heat and humidity)—adverse changes in any of these could correlate with lost demand, lost workdays, or generally lost ability to fill demand. Theoretically, any of these forms of weather risk could be the focus of risk hedging by firms. Indeed, it was possible to purchase insurance from catastrophic loss due to extreme events such as tornadoes, tsunamis, and floods. But only since 1997 could companies purchase protection from the more normal variations in weather.

Of paramount concern to the U.S. public utility industry was variation in temperatures. "Weather risk is the biggest independent variable in the power business," noted an industry publication.[2] Customer demand for power was highly correlated with seasonal temperatures. Unexpected decreases in demand (e.g., from a warm winter or cool summer) could have a detrimental impact on a company's earnings. One analyst noted that over a "recent 15-year period . . . temperature variations in 10 major population centers in the U.S. caused the cost of energy consumed for space heating and cooling to vary by an average of $3.6 billion per year."[3] Utilities typically determined their seasonal budgets from historical averages of temperature and demand. However, if winter temperatures, for example, were warmer than average, customers used less heat—therefore utilities' revenues fell below budget. Historically, utilities and Wall Street had discounted weather-related earnings' volatility because weather was seen as an uncertainty that could not be hedged. Weather risk was therefore a company's exposure to volume changes as a result of variability in temperature.

The utility industry measured weather conditions in terms of heating or cooling degree-days (HDD, CDD). Degree-days were determined by the deviation of the average daily temperature from an established benchmark of 65 degrees Fahrenheit. It was assumed that, at 65 degrees, customers used neither heat nor air conditioning. Therefore, a mean temperature of 55° on February 1, 2000, would equal 10 heating degree-days ($65° - 55°$) for that day. Weather conditions for a particular season were stated in terms of degree days accumulated across the entire period.

The *risk* associated with temperature lay in the uncertainty surrounding the mean temperature for a season. Effects such as El Niño[4] and La Niña[5] created cyclical variations in temperature. And over the past 100 years, there had been an unmistakable increase in temperature—this was attributed, variously, to global warming and "heat island" effects.[6] Compounding matters were possible asymmetries in risk exposure across competitors in an industry. Competitors might be fully exposed, partially hedged, or fully hedged regarding weather risk—these differences in exposure might elicit different competitive reactions to variations in weather. For instance, the fully hedged firm might seek to exploit adversity imposed on the unhedged firm.

---

[2]*Energy & Power Risk Management* 2, no. 8 (December 1997/January 1998).

[3]Ibid.

[4]The El Niño effect is a cyclical warming of the tropic region of the Pacific Ocean associated with increased rainfall in the southern United States, and drought in the western Pacific region, warmer winters in the north-central United States, and cooler winters in the Southeast and Southwest of the United States. The name means "little boy" in Spanish, and derives from the arrival of this effect around Christmas. El Niño occurs on an approximate seven-year cycle.

[5]La Niña is a countervailing cooling of the tropic Pacific Ocean that tends to occur after El Niños, and is associated with warmer-than-normal winter temperatures in the southeastern United States and cooler temperatures in the Northwest.

[6]A "heat island" reflected the increased retention of radiant energy from the sun, associated with the increased mass of cities, paved roads, use of concrete construction, etc. Cities such as Orlando, Florida, and Phoenix, Arizona, which had grown rapidly in the preceding 30 years, reported significant increases in mean temperature, associated with the heat-island effect.

MOTIVES AND INSTRUMENTS FOR HEDGING WEATHER RISK

Firms might seek to manage their exposure to weather risk for a variety of reasons:[7]

- **Smooth revenues** or compensate for the loss of demand. An ice cream manufacturer might seek insurance against an unseasonably cool summer.
- **Cover excess costs.** An unexpected frost could destroy crops and raise the costs to a consumer foods manufacturer. Industrial consumers of energy might seek to hedge against "spikes" in the cost of purchased electricity associated with peak load demand in the summer.
- **Reimburse lost opportunity costs.** Ideally, manufacturers would produce, and retailers would stock, the exact quantity of product that customers would buy. Weather introduced uncertainty into estimates of customer demand. In the event of stock-outs, businesses lost the opportunity to sell their products. Firms might seek to hedge this risk, e.g., the ice cream manufacturer might seek weather insurance against stock-outs in an unseasonably hot summer.
- **Stimulate sales.** Customers may delay their purchase decision until a seasonal trend in weather becomes apparent. Cruise lines, resorts, and ski lift operators witness this behavior annually. Firms might use weather derivatives to back up their "money back guarantee" of consumer satisfaction.
- **Diversify investment portfolios.** Financial investors might seek to exploit the low correlation between returns associated with weather and returns from other financial instruments. Weather derivatives could potentially reduce risk and/or increase returns in a portfolio.

The first weather protection contract was arranged in August 1997 between Enron Capital and Trade Resources (ECT) and an eastern U.S. electric utility. Enron Corporation was the world's leading integrated natural gas and electricity company. The company delivered physical commodities, risk management, and financial services to provide energy solutions to customers around the world. By the year 2000 Enron had been named "most innovative company" by *Fortune* magazine for five years in a row.

Upon discovering a methodology for hedging its own weather risk, Enron believed that this innovation could be useful for its customers as well, and set out to create customized products to help customers manage their own weather risk. Enron's weather protection products were targeted at power producers and utilities or any company that was exposed to volume risk as a result of changes in weather. A big challenge facing Enron and other marketers of weather protection products was that utilities were very slow, conservative, and resistant to the use of derivative financial instruments.

Although historically utilities only hedged price risk (through the use of futures), the introduction of weather protection products now allowed "companies to protect against weather conditions adversely affecting volume-related revenues."[8]

Specifically, weather derivatives provided protection against the deviation of actual cumulative degree-days from an established threshold. Degree-days were calculated using the average temperature readings for a predetermined geographic location (usually the closest

---

[7]The following points draw upon *Managing Weather* (Enron Corporation, 1999).

[8]*Hedging Weather Risk* (Enron Corporation, 1998).

airport) as measured by the National Weather Service. Depending on the sensitivity of demand to cumulative degree-days, the utility was able to determine how much margin it would lose if seasonal temperatures deviated from the average. The degree-day threshold was determined by the utility's level of risk tolerance—how much income it is willing to lose as a result of weather variability. (Most weather derivative contracts were short term, with an average transaction period equal to five months.)

If, at the end of the transaction period, the actual cumulative degree-days were below the established threshold, the utility would receive a payment to offset the loss in income associated with lost demand (volume).

Weather protection products could take on several structures:[9]

- A **floor** provides the customer with downside protection when the underlying variable, such as degree-days, *falls below* the established threshold. The upside opportunity remains unconstrained. The payout for the floor is equal to the degree-day differential times a $/dd. Most sellers of weather derivatives, however, were unwilling to accept all of the downside risk associated with a floor and therefore set a payout limit.

- A **ceiling cap** provides the customer with compensation if the underlying weather variable goes *above* a predetermined level. The seller of the ceiling cap pays this compensation to the buyer. A midwestern state might buy a snowfall ceiling cap that would compensate it if snowfall exceeded a certain level—this payment would help to reimburse the state for excessive snow removal expenses. Temperature ceiling caps could be stated in degree-days or payout limits.

- A **collar** is a two-part transaction in which a customer buys a cap or a floor to provide financial protection against adverse weather conditions, and simultaneously sells a floor or a cap at a different strike price that limits its financial upside if weather is favorable. The second part (the sale) helps to finance the first part (the purchase of the insurance.)

- A **swap** allows the customer to generate a fixed revenue stream. If actual degree-days were less (greater) than the threshold, the utility receives a payment equal to the degree-day differential times an agreed upon price per degree-day ($/dd.) If actual degree-days were greater (less) than the threshold, the utility pays the seller. A swap was generally similar to the collar in its economic effect, except that it offered a single trigger level, whereas the collar offered two. For instance, a utility might enter into a 30-day HDD swap with a reference temperature of 65 degrees Fahrenheit. If the actual average temperature turns out to be 55 degrees, the utility is due 300 degree-days $[30 \times (65 - 55)]$ multiplied by the amount of money agreed for each degree-day.

- **Futures contracts** can be purchased on the Chicago Mercantile Exchange, and were introduced for trading in 1999. Generally, a futures contract is a legal agreement to deliver or accept a commodity at a specified time and an agreed price. The CME contracts are specifically designed around temperature variations, i.e., HDD or CDD. The buyer and seller agree upon a price for a contract tailored to a specific month, one of 12 city locations, and a HDD/CDD index level. Variations in temperature above or below the value lead to a daily cash settlement between the buyer and seller.

- **Option on a futures contract.** The CME also permitted trading in options on futures.

---

[9]The description of instruments paraphrases a discussion in *Managing Weather.*

An important difference between the exchange-traded contracts on one hand and the insurance and tailored weather protection contracts on the other hand lay in their accounting treatment. Under the new FAS Rule 133, risk hedges of all sorts would need to be marked-to-market frequently *as long as the hedge was pegged to a market index.* One prominent auditor remarked that most weather derivatives would not require this accounting treatment since inches of rainfall or heating degree-days would be outside of the scope of the rule.[10]

THE MARKET FOR WEATHER PROTECTION

Several markets converged in weather protection instruments:

- **Insurance.** The insurance industry provided weather-related protection, typically for catastrophic events such as hurricanes, floods, and tornadoes. Players in this market sought to pool risks across a large number of insured parties. As long as the insured events were independent, cross-sectionally and over time, pooling would pay. Typically, coverage arranged through insurance companies was tailored and dealt with catastrophic events.
- **Capital and commodities markets.** In 1997, Enron had originated standardized contracts in weather protection that were relatively liquid securities and dealt with standard variations in weather. In 1999, the CME began trading in weather futures and options, which also were standardized contracts. The rise of this market as a second source for weather protection reflected the growing trend of *securitization* of assets through capital markets. Market makers in weather derivatives included Enron, Koch Energy Trading, Aquila Energy, Southern Company Energy Marketing, and Duke Power—firms with a historical basis in the energy industry.

One participant observed that "The truth is that the convergence of these two industries is well under way . . . the question isn't which industry wins the battle for business, but what these institutions, whatever their background, will look like, and who will best be able to meet customer demands."[11]

Potential users of weather protection were widely distributed through the U.S. economy. Some of the most active players were heating oil distributors and local gas distribution companies, firms that, because of their deregulated markets, could not pass along the costs of weather variation to customers. Public utilities were significantly exposed to weather risk, but slow to come into the weather protection market because of regulations which did permit them to pass along costs to consumers.

Enron's objective was to balance the market for weather protection through aggregation of contracts.

---

[10]Based on a remark by Deirdre Schiela, partner at PricewaterhouseCoopers, quoted in "No Hedging for Weather Derivatives?" *American Banker and Bond Buyer CFO Alert* (October 12, 1998).

[11]Quotation of William Jewett, senior vice president and chief underwriting officer of Centre Re, division of Zurich Reinsurance, in "New Kids on the Capital Markets Block; Reinsurers Want Not Only to Securitize Every Insurance Risk Imaginable, But to Go Head-to-Head with Wall Street in Other Key Areas Too," *Investment Dealer's Digest* (August 3, 1998).

DETERMINING PNW'S NEED FOR WEATHER PROTECTION

PNW's winter season lasted from November through March. Mary Watts would need to make a decision soon about hedging PNW's weather risk. The first step in her analysis was to determine how sensitive PNW's earnings are to changes in weather. She gathered historical weather information and calculated the correlation of PNW's winter demand to historical seasonal heating degree-days. Watts remembered hearing that the average temperature of metropolitan areas was increasing due to increased population, automobiles and other demographic trends. Watts's weather data would have to be adjusted for this historical trend or she may run the risk of undervaluing the cost of protection. The load data should also be trend adjusted to eliminate the impact of increased overall demand due to new customers. Watts's analysis revealed that seasonal demand has a 91.7 percent correlation with a 1 percent change in cumulative seasonal heating degree-days.

Using PNW's residential tariffs and its cost to generate the power to supply demand, Watts could calculate the gross margin per heating degree-day and the loss in income for a corresponding loss in volume. She could then translate that loss in income to a $/HDD. On average, PNW received $60.30/MWH for power sold to residential customers and paid $20/MWH to generate or purchase power to supply its demand.

Because PNW was exposed to volume risk if weather were warmer than average, PNW would want protection from winter heating degree-days falling significantly below the average. Watts believed that PNW would accept no more than a 5 percent variability in HDD.

HYPOTHETICAL WEATHER DERIVATIVE CONTRACT FOR PNW

Exhibit 1 presents a hypothetical contract of the sort that Enron would negotiate with PNW to cover its weather exposure for the forthcoming winter. The contract specified that in return for the initial purchase of the contract, PNW would receive a one-time payment at the expiration of the contract determined by the extent of the adverse deviation from the HDD target. (See **Exhibit 2** for a glossary of terms.)

THE DECISION

Mary Watts knew that PNW was a very conservative company that would not be persuaded easily to use derivative hedging products. Although PNW's revenues were extremely sensitive to weather conditions, weather protection required a rather sizable up-front premium. But because 2000–2001 was expected to be an unseasonably warm winter, the impact on earnings could be devastating. Given the unpredictability of weather, however, PNW might not want to hedge all of its weather exposure; this would also minimize the cost of protection by effectively reducing the $/HDD. Additionally, the cost of protection could be reduced if she chose a lower HDD threshold.

QUESTIONS

1. Why do they call these contracts derivatives? Where is the optionality in these contracts?

2. Please draw a diagram of payoffs at the end of the life for the contract presented in **Exhibit 1**.

3. Please deconstruct the options embedded in the contract given in **Exhibit 1**. (Are they puts or calls? Are the positions long or short from PNW's standpoint?)

4. What are the pros and cons of weather protection from PNW's perspective?

5. Why is Enron in this situation? What does Enron stand to gain?

6. How should Mary Watts proceed to assess, and decide upon, the use of weather protection for PNW? What criteria should she use to make her decision?

EXHIBIT 1
Sample Contract

[Date]

[Counterparty Name – ABC Co]
[Address]
[Address]
Attention: [Name]

Fax No.:
Telephone No.:

Re: FLOOR TRANSACTION Contract No. WR[ ]

Reference is made to the Master Agreement dated as of [ ] (the "Agreement") between ABC Co and XYZ Co pursuant to which this Confirmation is delivered and to which the Transaction contemplated herein is subject.

This is confirmation of the following Transaction:

Option Type:	HDD Weather Floor
Notional Amount:	$20,000 Per Heating Degree Day
Trade Date:	October 23, 2000
Effective Date:	November 1, 2000
Termination Date:	March 31, 2001
Premium Payment Details:	ABC Co shall pay XYZ $[premium] two Business Days after the Trade Date.
Determination Period:	The period from and including the Effective Date to and including the Termination Date.
Payment Date(s):	The fifth Business Day after the Floating Amount for the Determination Period is determinable, **provided, however,** that a one time adjustment in the amount paid will be made by the appropriate party, if applicable, if the National Climatic Data Center ("NCDC") makes any correction or adjustment to the reported daily high and low temperatures within 95 days of the end of the Determination Period for any day within the Determination Period.
Fixed Amount Payer: (Buyer of the Floor)	ABC Co
Floating Amount Payer: (Seller of the Floor)	XYZ Co
Strike Amount:	400 HDD
Floating Amount:	The sum of the Heating Degree Days ("HDD") for each day during the applicable Determination Period.

HDD for each day is equal to the greater of (i) 65 minus the non-rounded average of the daily high and daily low temperatures in degrees Fahrenheit from and including 12:01 AM on that day to and including 12:00 AM on the next day local time as measured by the National Weather Service ("NWS"), and reported by the NCDC, for the Reference Weather Station or (ii) zero. The daily high and low temperatures measured by the NWS and reported by the NCDC shall be rounded to whole numbers prior to the calculation of HDDs as follows: if the first number after the decimal point is five (5) or greater then the whole number shall be increased by one (1), and if the first number after the decimal point is less than five (5) then the whole number shall remain unchanged (the "Rounding Convention").

Reference Weather Station: Seattle-Tacoma International Airport, Washington.

Fallback Reference
Weather Station:

If for any day during the Determination Period a daily high or daily low temperature is unavailable for the Reference Weather Station then the missing temperature(s) for that day at such Reference Weather Station shall be calculated in accordance with the following procedure: (i) the daily high (if the missing temperature is a daily high) or daily low (if the missing temperature is a daily low) temperature for the corresponding day of each of the previous 30 years at such Reference Weather Station shall be identified as reported in Fahrenheit by the NCDC (which numbers as reported by the NCDC shall not be rounded by the parties) and an average temperature shall be determined, which average temperature shall be determined to and including four decimal points; (ii) in accordance with the above procedures, the daily high or daily low temperature as appropriate shall be determined for the corresponding day of each of the previous 30 years at the Weather Station at Portland, Oregon Airport (the "Fallback Reference Weather Station") as reported in Fahrenheit by the NCDC (which numbers as reported by the NCDC shall not be rounded by the parties), and an average temperature shall be determined, which average temperature shall be determined to and including four decimal points; (iii) the average temperature generated in (ii) above shall be subtracted from the average temperature generated in (i) above (with the resulting number (whether positive or negative) referred to as the "Average Temperature Difference Number"); (iv) the daily high or daily low temperature as appropriate for the corresponding Fallback Reference Station for the day for which the daily high or daily low temperature is missing for the Reference Weather Station shall be identified as reported in Fahrenheit by the NCDC (which number as reported by the NCDC shall not be rounded); and (v) the temperature determined in (iv) shall be adjusted by adding the Average Temperature Difference Number if it is a positive number and subtracting the absolute value of the Average Temperature Difference Number if it is a negative number, with the resulting number being rounded in accordance with the Rounding Convention. The final rounded whole number determined in (v) shall be deemed the daily high or daily low temperature as appropriate for the Reference Weather Station for the relevant day and shall be the number used to make the calculations as required pursuant to the procedures set forth in the "Floating Amount" above.

Data Sources:

The data used to determine the Floating Amount (and to the extent required, data for any Fallback Reference Weather Station) shall be obtained from the NCDC's official website located at http://www.nndc.noaa.gov/cgi-bin/nndc/ph2_lcd_v2.cgi, or any successor thereto; provided, however, if data is not reported for any particular day at such website, then the data for such day shall be obtained from the website for the appropriate Regional Climate Data Center located at http://www.nws.noaa.gov/regions.shtml, or any successor thereto; and provided further to the extent that (i) the NCDC data is corrected or adjusted within 95 days of the end of the Determination Period or (ii) the data is temporarily sourced from the Regional Climate Data Center, then the data for such new, adjusted or corrected number(s) shall be obtained from the NCDC's official website located at http://www4.ncdc.noaa.gov/cgi-win/wwcgi.dll?WWNolos~Product~PB-078. Notwithstanding the foregoing, if neither the Regional Climate Data Center nor the NCDC issues data for the Reference Weather Station, then the procedures set forth under "Fallback Reference Weather Station(s)" shall be utilized to determine the missing data.

| Strike Amount Differential: | The amount equal to the excess (if a positive number) of (i) the Strike Amount over (ii) the Floating Amount |
| Payment Amount: | Notwithstanding any provision of the Agreement to the contrary, if the Strike Amount is greater than the Floating Amount, the Floating Amount Payer shall pay the Fixed Amount Payer an amount in US Dollars equal to the product of (i) the Notional Amount and (ii) the Strike Amount Differential, which amount shall be due and payable on the applicable Payment Date, **provided, however,** that the maximum amount payable by the Floating Amount Payer shall not exceed $800,000. |

EXHIBIT 2
Glossary of Terms

Demand: The rate at which power is being used by consumers.

Energy: Actual electrical flow, sold on an hourly, monthly, or similar basis.

IPP: The passing of PURPA (1978) gave rise to Qualified Facilities, which were cogeneration facilities selling surplus power to the utilities. Since EPAct of 1992 IPPs are now also often referred to as EWGs.

Kilowatt (KW): One thousand watts.

Kilowatt-hour (KWh): One kilowatt of power supplied for a continuous period of one hour. This is the principal unit used for pricing retail electrical energy.

Load: The electric current being transmitted or demanded.

Megawatt (MW): One million watts or one thousand kilowatts.

Megawatt-hours (MWh): One thousand kilowatt-hours.

Power Marketer: A company that buys and resells electricity, and therefore assumes economic risk in the transactions. Power marketers are usually independent entities, although some electric utilities have set up their own marketing operations. Power marketers are responsible for arranging the transmission of power to the purchaser.

Public Utility Regulatory Policies Act, 1978 (PURPA): PURPA was passed as part of the National Energy Act. It set out to create incentives for the development of cogeneration facilities. Qualifying Facilities (QFs) had to produce electric and thermal power and could sell all, or only their excess electric power to utilities. Utilities were required to purchase this power at their full avoided cost.

Tick Size: Notational amount of a contract—the dollars per HDD to be paid out.

Watt: The standard measure of electricity's capacity to do work. It is the voltage (pressure) multiplied by the amperage (or speed).

PART 8

Valuing the Enterprise: Acquisitions and Buyouts

Rocky Mountain Advanced Genome Inc.

In January 1996, negotiations neared conclusion for a private equity investment by Big Sur Capital Management Company in Rocky Mountain Advanced Genome (RMAG). The owners of RMAG, who were also its senior managers, proposed to sell a 90 percent equity interest to Big Sur for $46 million. The proceeds of the equity sale would be used to finance the growth of the firm. Big Sur's due-diligence study of RMAG had revealed a highly promising high-risk investment opportunity. It remained for Kate McGraw, a managing director with Big Sur, to negotiate the specific price and terms of investment. McGraw aimed to base her negotiating strategy on an assessment of RMAG's economic value, and to structure the interests of Big Sur and the managers of RMAG to create the best incentives for value creation.

McGraw's analysis so far had focused on financial forecasting of equity cash flows. The final steps would be to estimate a terminal value for the company (also called "continuing value") and to discount the cash flows and terminal value to the present. She also sought an assessment of forecast assumptions. In this regard, she requested help from Janice Kelley, a new associate with Big Sur.

BIG SUR CAPITAL MANAGEMENT COMPANY

Big Sur, located in San Francisco, California, had been organized in 1968 as a hedge fund, though over the years it proved more successful in a variety of "private equity" investments and had gradually shifted its activities to this area. The firm had $2 billion under management.

The firm's portfolio consisted of 64 investments, about evenly split between venture capital investments and participations in leveraged buyouts.

ROCKY MOUNTAIN ADVANCED GENOME

RMAG, headquartered in Colorado Springs, Colorado, had been founded 15 months earlier by seven research scientists who had taken leaves of absence from major universities and pharmaceutical companies to establish the firm. The company used gene-sequencing techniques with a computer-driven search algorithm to identify genes in human DNA. In the firm's short life span, it had uncoded about 60 percent of all human genes, and was using that information to design treatments for diseases. RMAG and its pharmaceutical partners had identified 97 possible drug therapies. But given that it typically took 15 years and $350 million to take a drug from the lab bench to the drugstore, it would be years before the company determined whether any of these therapies would be effective.

The company's business consisted of three segments:

- **Diagnostic test kits** would afford low-cost and virtually error-free detection of a wide range of medical conditions. Development of the kit technologies was finished; the products were moving rapidly through the Food and Drug Administration (FDA) approval process and because of their noninvasive and nontherapeutic nature, might be available for sale within 12 months. After the conclusion of the genome mapping process more test kit applications were expected to emerge.
- **Agricultural biogenetic engineering.** Management believed that applying the same gene-mapping technology to corn and other commodity plants would permit the realization of truly disease-resistant, high-growth varieties. RMAG worked with two hybrid seed producers in a joint venture. RMAG's development costs were underwritten by the producers, and RMAG would receive a royalty on sales of new varieties produced by the joint venture. Management believed that revenues in this segment could begin within 24–36 months.
- **Human therapeutics.** The search for vaccines and antibiotics with which to fight incurable diseases was potentially the most economically attractive segment. Most of the activity in this segment was funded by major pharmaceutical companies under joint venture/royalty arrangements similar to the agricultural segment. RMAG also conducted proprietary research in this area. Management's long-term strategy was to use external funding (through joint venture arrangements) to the fullest extent possible, as a means of carrying the firm until its first major proprietary breakthrough. But despite external funding, RMAG still faced significant capital requirements stemming from investment in infrastructure, staffing, and its own proprietary research program.

RMAG's management believed that the genome-mapping activity would pay off dramatically and quickly: by the year 2003 they believed that the revenues of the firm (consisting of underwritten research, royalties, and sales of proprietary products) would top $1 billion. Kate McGraw was less optimistic, believing that the FDA approval process would slow down the commercialization of RMAG's new products. The cash flow forecasts of management and of Kate McGraw are given in **Exhibits 1** and **2**. Kate assumed that the firm would not finance itself with debt; thus, the forecasted free cash flows were identical with equity cash flows.

In assessing RMAG, Kate McGraw could look toward two small publicly held companies in this general field.

- **Human Genome Sciences, Inc.** of Rockville, Maryland. This firm was the leader in the field, and had uncoded 90 percent of the human genome. The firm claimed to have developed over 150 new therapies. On January 18, 1996, the firm announced that it had cracked the genetic code to the *staphylococcus aureus* bacterium, the most common cause of infections in hospitals, and the major cause of toxic shock syndrome and wound infection. At the announcement, Human Genome's stock price rose 21 percent. Over the previous 12 months, the firm's stock price had risen 220 percent. CEO William Haseltine said that the stock price was "based on people's perception of how many product opportunities there are going to be. It's a projection of what the future value is going to be, based on what the present value is."[1] The firm's beta was 0.82; price/expected earnings ratio was 87.77; price/book ratio was 11.71; price/sales was 15.61; and price/free cash flow was 88.67. The firm had no debt outstanding. The firm's sales had grown from zero in 1992, to $22 million in 1993, $41 million in 1994, and an expected $76.5 million in 1995. The company paid no dividend.
- **Myriad Genetics Inc.** of Salt Lake City, Utah, used the well-documented family trees of Utah families as a tool to help identify genetic defects and possible remedies—this was a much more targeted research strategy than Human Genome's approach of mechanistically sequencing thousands of unknown genes. Myriad concentrated on cancers and cardiovascular diseases. In December 1995, the firm filed a patent for the full gene sequence of a tumor suppressor gene that produced susceptibility to breast cancer—this would permit the company to commercialize tests and therapeutics exploiting the gene sequence. The firm went public on October 6, 1995, at $18 per share; in January 1996, the firm's shares traded around $31. With negative historical and expected earnings, the firm's price/earnings ratio was meaningless. However, the firm traded at 4.55 times book value. Revenues were $600,000 in 1994, and were expected to be $1,300,000 in 1995.

Securities analysts were cautious about the fledgling gene-sequencing industry. The widespread belief was that gene sequencing would deliver *some* breakthrough. One analyst said, "nearly everyone is into genomics. Everyone is a believer."[2] Yet there was almost no consensus on how soon the breakthroughs would occur, or how significant they would be. Filing for patents on gene sequences was at the edge of the legal envelope. The field was being flooded with entrepreneurial research scientists. The FDA approval process was at best uncertain in this area. And established firms witnessed internal clashes over direction.

---

[1]"Bloomberg Forum: Human Genome has 150 Potential Drugs, CEO Says," *Bloomberg Financial News Service,* February 13, 1996.

[2]David T. Molowa, analyst with Bear, Stearns & Co., quoted in "The Gene Kings," *Business Week,* May 8, 1995, p. 78.

THE IDEA OF TERMINAL VALUE

To assist her in the final stages of preparing for the negotiations, Kate McGraw called in Janice Kelley, who had just joined the firm after completing an undergraduate degree. To lay the groundwork for the assignment, Kate began by describing the concept of terminal value:

Kate: Terminal value is the lump-sum of cash flow at the *end* of a stream of cash flows; that's why we call it "terminal." The lump-sum represents either (a) the proceeds to us from exiting the investment, or (b) the present value (at that future date) of all cash flows beyond the forecast horizon.

Jan: Since they are way off in the future, terminal values really can't be worth worrying about, can they? I don't believe most investors even think about them.

Kate: Terminal values are worth worrying about for two reasons. First, they are present in the valuation of just about every asset. For instance, in valuing a U.S. Treasury bond, the terminal value is the return of your principal at the maturity of the bond.

Jan: Some investors might hold to maturity, but the traders who really set the prices in the bond markets almost never hold to maturity.

Kate: For traders, terminal value equals the proceeds from selling the bonds when you exit from each position. You can say the same thing about stocks, currencies, and all sorts of hard assets.. Now, the second main reason we worry about terminal value is that in the valuation of stocks and whole companies terminal value is *usually a very big value driver.*

Jan: I don't believe it. Terminal value is a distant future value. The only thing traders care about is dividends.

> Jan's first task:
> Present and explain
> the data
> in **Exhibit 3**.

Kate: I'll bet you that if you took a random sample of stocks—I'll let you throw darts at the financial pages to choose them—and looked at the percentage of today's share price *not* explained by the present value of dividends for the next five years, you would find that the unexplained part would dominate today's value. I believe that the unexplained part is largely[3] due to terminal value.

Jan: I'll throw the darts, but I still don't believe it—I'll show you what I find.

VARIETIES OF TERMINAL VALUES

Kate: We can't really foresee terminal value, we can only *estimate* it. For that reason, I like to draw on a wide range of estimators as a way of trying to home in on a best guess of terminal value. The estimators include (a) accounting book value, (b) liquidation value, (c) multiples of income, and (d) constant growth perpetuity value. Each of these has advantages and disadvantages, as my chart here shows (see **Exhibit 4**). I like the constant growth model best and the book value least, but they all give information, so I look at them all.

---

[3]The unexplained part could also be due to option values that are not readily captured in a discounted cash flow valuation.

Jan: Do they all agree?

Kate: They rarely agree. Remember that these are imperfect estimates. It's like picking the point of central tendency out of a scatter diagram or triangulating in on the height of a tree, using many different points of observation from the ground. It takes a lot of careful judgment because some of the varieties of terminal value are inherently more trustworthy than others. And from one situation to the next, the different estimators have varying degrees of appropriateness. In fact, even though I usually disregard book value, there are a few situations in which it might be a fair estimate of terminal value.

Jan: Like when?

Kate: Give it some thought; you can probably figure it out. Give me some examples of where the various estimators would be very appropriate and rather inappropriate. But remember that no single estimator will give us Truth. Wherever possible, we want to use a variety of approaches.

> Jan's second task:
> Draw on Exhibit 4.

TAXES

Jan: What about taxes in terminal values? Shouldn't I impose a tax on the gain inherent in any terminal value?

Kate: Sure, if you are a taxpaying investor and if it is actually your intent to exit the investment at the forecast horizon. But lots of big investors in the capital markets (such as pension funds and university endowments) do not pay taxes. And other investors really do not have much tax exposure because of careful tax planning. Finally, in M&A analysis and most kinds of capital budgeting analysis, the most reasonable assumption is *buy and hold,* in perpetuity. Overall, the usual assumption is *not* to tax terminal values. But we all need to ask the basic question at the start of our analysis, is the investor likely to pay taxes?

LIQUIDATION VS. GOING CONCERN VALUES

Jan: Now I'm starting to get confused. I thought "terminal" meant the end . . . and now you're talking about value in perpetuity. If terminal value is really the ending value, shouldn't we be talking about a *liquidation value?* Liquidation values are easy to estimate: we simply take the face value of net working capital, add the proceeds of selling any fixed assets, and subtract the long-term debt of the company.

Kate: *Easy* isn't the point. We have to do what's economically sensible. For instance, you wouldn't want to assume that you would liquidate Microsoft in three years just because that's as far into the future as you can forecast. Microsoft's key assets are software, people, and ideas. The value of those will never get captured in a liquidator's auction. The real value of Microsoft is in a stream of future cash flows. When we come to a case like Microsoft, we see the subtlety of "terminal value"—in the case of *most* companies it means "continuing value" derived from the going concern of the business. Indeed, many assets live well beyond the forecast horizon. Terminal value is just a summary (or present value) of the cash flows beyond the horizon.

Jan: So when would you use liquidation value?

Kate: I've seen it a lot in corporate capital budgeting, cases like machines, plants, natural resources projects, etc. The assets in those cases have definite lives. But companies and *businesses* are potentially very long-lived and should be valued on a going concern basis. But I still look at liquidation value because I might find some interesting situations where liquidation value is higher than going concern value. Examples would be companies subject to oppressive regulation or taxation and firms experiencing weird market conditions—in the late 1970s and early 1980s, most oil companies had a market value *less* than the value of their oil reserves. You don't see those situations very often, but still it's worth a look.

MARKET MULTIPLES AND CONSTANT GROWTH VALUATION

Jan: Aren't multiples the best terminal value estimators? They are certainly the easiest approach.

Kate: I use them, but they've got disadvantages, as my chart (Exhibit 4) shows. They're easy to use, but too abstract for my analytical work. I want to get real close to the assumptions about value, and for that reason, I use this version of the constant growth valuation model to value a firm's assets:

$$TV_{Firm} = \frac{FCF\ (1 + g_{FCF}^{\infty})}{WACC - g_{FCF}^{\infty}}$$

"FCF" is free cash flow. "WACC" is weighted average cost of capital. And "g"[4] is the constant growth rate of free cash flows to infinity. This model was derived from an infinitely long DCF valuation formula.

$$PV_{Firm} = \frac{FCF_0\ (1 + g_{FCF}^{\infty})}{(1 + WACC)} + \frac{FCF_0\ (1 + g_{FCF}^{\infty})^2}{(1 + WACC)^2} + \frac{FCF_0\ (1 + g_{FCF}^{\infty})^3}{(1 + WACC)^3} + \cdots + \frac{FCF_0\ (1 + g_{FCF}^{\infty})^n}{(1 + WACC)^n}$$

If the growth rate is constant over time, this infinitely-long model can be condensed into the easy-to-use constant growth model.

---

[4]This is a sensible assumption for healthy firms, under the axiom of the limited liability of investors: investors cannot be held liable for claims against the firm beyond the amount of their investment in the firm. However, in the cases of punitive government regulations or an active torts system, investors may be compelled to "invest" further in a losing business. Examples would include liabilities for clean-up of toxic waste, remediation of defective breast implants, and assumption of medical costs of nicotine addiction. In these instances, the value of the firm to investors could be negative.

When I'm valuing equity instead of assets, I use the constant-growth valuation formula, but with equity-oriented inputs:

$$TV_{Equity} = \frac{Residual\ cash\ flow\ -\ (1\ +\ g^\infty_{RCF})}{Cost\ of\ equity\ -\ g^\infty_{RCF}}$$

Residual cash flow (RCF) is the cash flow which equityholders can look forward to receiving—a common name for RCF is dividends. A key point here is that the growth rate used in this model should be the growth rate appropriate for the type of cash flow being valued; and the capital cost should be appropriate for that cash flow as well.

You may have seen the simplest version of the constant growth model—the one that assumes zero growth—which reduces to dividing the annual cash flow by a discount rate.

Jan: Sure, I have used a model like that to price perpetual preferred stocks. In the numerator, I inserted the annual dividend; in the denominator I inserted whatever we thought the going required rate of return will be for that stream.

Kate: If you insert some positive growth rate into the model, the resulting value gets bigger. In a growing economy, the assumption of growing free cash flows is quite reasonable. Sellers of companies always want to persuade you of their great growth prospects. If you buy the optimistic growth assumptions, you'll have to pay a higher price for the company. But the assumption of growth can get unreasonable if pushed too far. Many of the abuses of this model have to do with the little infinity symbol, ∞: the model assumes *constant growth at the rate,* g, *to infinity.*

"PETER PAN" GROWTH: WACC < g

Jan: Indeed, if you assume a growth rate greater than WACC, you'll get a *negative* terminal value.

Kate: That's one instance in which you cannot use the constant growth model. But think about it: WACC less than g *can't* happen; a company cannot grow to infinity at a rate greater than its cost of capital. To illustrate why, let's rearrange the constant growth formula to solve for WACC:

$$WACC = \frac{FCF_{Next\ Period}}{Value\ of\ firm_{Current\ Period}} + g^\infty_{FCF}$$

If WACC is less than g, then the ratio of FCF divided by value of the firm would have to be *negative.* Since the value of the healthy firm to the investors cannot be less than zero,[4] the source of negativity must be FCF—that means the firm is absorbing rather than throwing off cash. Recall that in the familiar constant growth terminal value formula, FCF is the flow that compounds to infinity at the rate g. Thus, if FCF is negative, then the entire stream of FCFs must be negative—the company is like Peter Pan: *it never grows up;* it never matures to the point where it throws off positive cash flow. This is a crazy implication, for investors would not buy securities in a firm that never paid a cash return. In short, you cannot use the constant growth model where WACC is less than *g,* nor would you want to because of the unbelievable implications of that assumption.

USING HISTORICAL GROWTH RATES; SETTING FORECAST HORIZONS

Kate: A more common form of abuse of this model is to assume a very high growth rate, simply by extrapolating the past rate of growth of the company.

Jan: Why isn't the past growth rate a good one?

Kate: Companies typically go through life cycles. A period of explosive growth is usually followed by a period of maturity and/or decline. Take a look at the three deals in this chart (see **Exhibit 5**): a start-up of an animation movie studio in Burbank; a bottling plant in Mexico City, and a highspeed private toll road in Los Angeles.

- **Movie studio.** The studio has a TV production unit with small but steadily growing revenues and a full feature-length film production unit with big but uncertain cash flows. The studio does not reach stability until the 27th year. The stability is largely due to the firm's film library which should be sizable by then. After year 27, exploiting the library through videos and re-releases will act as a shock absorber, dampening swings in cash flow due to the production side of the business. Also, at about that time, one can assume that the studio reaches production capacity.
- **Bottling plant.** The bottler must establish a plant and an American soda brand in Mexico, which accounts for the initial negative cash flows and slow growth. Then, as the brand takes hold, the cash flows increase steeply. Finally, in year 12, the plant reaches capacity. After that, cash flows grow mainly at the rate of inflation.
- **Toll road.** This will take 18 months to build, and will operate at capacity almost immediately. The toll rates are government regulated, but the company will be allowed to raise prices at the rate of inflation. The cash flows reach stability in year 3.

A key point of judgment in valuation analysis is to *set the forecast horizon at that point in the future where stability or stable growth begins.* You can't use past rates of growth of cash flows in each of these three projects because the explosive growth of the past will not be repeated. Frankly, over long periods of time, it is difficult to sustain cash flow growth much in excess of the economy. If you did, you would wind up owning everything!

> Jan's third task: Set the forecast horizon for the three projects. See Exhibit 5.

Jan: So at what year in the future will you set the horizon and estimate a terminal value for these three projects? And what growth rate will you use in your constant growth formula for them? Uh-Oh. I know, "Figure it out for yourself . . ."

GROWTH RATE ASSUMPTION

Kate: There are two classic approaches for estimating a growth rate to use in the constant-growth formula. The first is to use the self-sustainable growth rate formula,

$$g \cdot^{\infty} = ROE - (1 - DPO)$$

This assumes that the firm can only grow as fast as it adds to its equity capital base (through the return on equity, or "ROE," less any dividends paid-out, indicated through the dividend payout ratio, or "DPO"). I'm not a big fan of this approach because most naive analysts simply extrapolate *past* ROE and DPO without really thinking about the future. Also it relies on accounting ROE and can give some pretty crazy results.[5]

The second approach assumes that nominal growth of a business is the sum of *real growth* and *inflation*. In more proper mathematical notation the formula is:

$$g_{Nominal}^{\infty} = \left[\left(1 + g_{Units}^{\infty} \right) - \left(1 + g_{Inflation}^{\infty} \right) \right] - 1$$

This formula uses the economist's[6] notion that the nominal rate of growth is the product of the rate of inflation and the "real" rate of growth. We commonly think of real growth as a percentage increase in units shipped. But in rare instances, real growth could come from price increases due, for instance, to a monopolist's power over the market. For simplicity, I just use a short version of the model (less precise, though the difference in precision is not material):

$$g_{Nominal}^{\infty} = g_{Unit}^{\infty} + g_{Inflation}^{\infty}$$

Now, this formula focuses you on two really interesting issues: the real growth rate in the business, and the ability of the business to pass along the effects of inflation. The consensus inflation outlook in the United States today calls for about a 3 percent inflation rate indefinitely. We probably have not got the political consensus to drive inflation to zero, and the Fed has shown strong resistance to letting inflation rise much higher. Well, if inflation is given, then the analyst can really focus her thinking on the more interesting issue of the real growth rate of the business.

The real growth rate is bound to vary by industry. Growth in unit demand of consumer staple products (like Band-Aids) is probably determined by growth rate of the population—less than 1 percent in the United States. Growth in demand for luxury goods is probably driven by growth of real disposable income—maybe 2 percent today. Growth in demand for industrial commodities like steel is probably about equal to the real rate of growth of GNP—about 2.5 percent on average through time. In any event, all of these are small numbers.

---

[5]For a full discussion of the self-sustainable growth rate model, see "A Critical Look at the Self-Sustainable Growth Rate Concept," a technical note published by Darden Educational Materials Services (UVA-F-0951).
[6]The economist Irving Fisher derived this model of economic growth. Its common name is the Fisher Formula.

When you add these real growth rates to the expected inflation rate today, you get a small number—this is intuitively appealing since over the very long run, the increasing maturity of a company will tend to drive its growth rate downward.

TERMINAL VALUE FOR ROCKY MOUNTAIN ADVANCED GENOME

Kate: We're negotiating to structure an equity investment in RMAG. We and management disagree on the size of the cash flows to be realized over the next 10 years (see Exhibits 1 and 2). I'm willing to invest cash on the basis of *my* expectations, but I'm also willing to agree to give RMAG's management a contingent payment if they achieve *their* forecast. To begin the structuring process, I needed valuations of RMAG under their and our forecasts. We have the cash flow forecasts, and we both agree that the weighted average cost of capital (WACC) should be 20 per-

> Jan's fourth task:
> Interpret Exhibit 6.

cent—that's low for a typical venture capital investment, but given that RMAG's R&D partners are bearing so much of the technical risk in this venture, I think it's justified. All I needed to finish the valuation was a sensible terminal value assumption— I've already run a sensitivity analysis using growth rates to infinity ranging from 2 to 7 percent (see **Exhibit 6**). The rate at which the firm grows will place different demands on the need for physical capital and net working capital—the higher the growth rate, the greater the capital requirements. So, in computing the terminal value using the constant growth model, I adjusted the free cash flow for these different capital requirements. Here are the scenarios I ran:

Nominal Growth Rate to Infinity	Capital Expenditures in Terminal Year, Net of Depreciation	Net Working Capital Investment in Terminal Year
2%	$0 million	$0 million
3	−$5	−$3
4	−$12	−$5
5	−$15	−$7
6	−$20	−$8
7	−$28	−$9

RMAG's management believes that they can grow at 7 percent to infinity, assuming a strong patent position on breakthrough therapeutics. I believe that a lower growth

> Jan's fifth task:
> What drives g^∞?

rate is justified, though I would like to have your recommendation on what that rate should be. Should we be looking at the population growth rate in the United States (about 0.5 percent per year), or the real growth rate in the economy (about 2.5 percent per year), or the historical real growth rate in pharmaceutical industry revenues (5 percent per year)? Are there other growth rates we should be considering?

We ought to test the reasonableness of the DCF valuations against estimates afforded by other approaches. Estimates of book and liquidation values of the company are not very helpful in this case, but multiples estimates would help. Price/Earnings multiples for RMAG are expected to be 15–20 times at the forecast horizon—this is considerably below the P/Es for comparable companies today, but around the P/Es for established pharmaceutical companies today. Price to book ratios for comparable companies today are between 4 and 12 times—RMAG's book value of equity is $3.5 million. Please draw on any other multiples you might know about. We do not foresee RMAG paying a dividend for a long time.

> Jan's sixth task: Estimate terminal values using multiples and prepare present value estimates using them.

Jan: This makes me skeptical about the whole concept. Terminal value for a high-tech company will be an awfully mushy estimate. How do you estimate growth? How sensitive is terminal value to variations in assumed growth rates? And with several terminal value estimates, how do you pick a "best guess" figure necessary to complete the DCF analysis? And once you've done all that, how far apart are the two valuations?

Kate: You need to help me find intelligent answers to those questions. Please let me have your recommendations about terminal values, their assumptions, and ultimately, about what you believe is a sensible value range today for RMAG, from our standpoint and management's. By "value range," I mean high and low estimates of value for the equity of RMAG that represent the bounds within which we will start negotiating (the low value), and above which we will abandon the negotiations.

> Jan's seventh task: Triangulate in on value ranges and recommend a deal structure.

CONCLUSION

Later, Kate McGraw reflected on the investment opportunity in RMAG. It looked as if management's asking price was highly optimistic; $46 million would barely cover the projected cash deficit for 1996. This implied that further rounds of financing would be needed for 1997 and beyond. But buying into RMAG now was like buying an option on future opportunities to invest—the price of this option was high, but the potential payoff could be immense if the examples of Human Genome Sciences and Myriad Genetics were accurate reflections of the potential value creation in this field. Indeed, it was reasonable to assume that RMAG could go public in an initial public offering (IPO) shortly after the first major breakthrough was announced. An IPO would accelerate the exit from this investment. If an IPO occurred, Big Sur would not sell its shares in RMAG, but instead would distribute the RMAG shares tax-free to clients for whom Big Sur was managing investments. Kate wondered how large the exit value might be, and what impact an early exit would have on the investment decision.

> Kate's task: Assess early exit values, and impact on decision.

EXHIBIT 1
Cash Flow Forecast, by RMAG Management (values in millions of dollars)

Income Statement	Actual 1995	1996	1997	1998	1999	2000	2001	2002	2003	2004	2005
Sales											
Cancer diagnostics	$ 0	$ 1	$ 15	$ 56	$ 107	$ 181	$ 249	$ 274	$282	$285	$289
Other diagnostics	2	12	28	45	75	110	135	165	190	210	225
Agriculture	0	0	2	13	52	106	146	166	174	186	189
Human therapeutics	0	0	0	0	8	57	171	250	330	352	362
Total sales	2	13	45	114	242	454	701	855	976	1,033	1,065
Cost of sales	7	10	21	41	84	159	246	322	335	350	361
Gross profits	(5)	3	24	73	158	295	455	533	641	683	704
Contract revenue	16	21	23	15	12	4	3	3	3	3	3
Operating expenses											
R&D	14	20	24	18	21	21	32	43	51	52	50
SG&A	12	15	24	45	93	176	259	323	369	372	349
Total expenses	26	35	48	63	114	197	291	366	420	424	399
Other income	3	2	2	0	(3)	(10)	(25)	(38)	(43)	(37)	(20)
Income before taxes	(12)	(9)	1	25	53	92	142	132	181	225	288
Taxes	0	0	5	9	19	32	57	76	89	90	85
Net income	**(12)**	**(9)**	**(4)**	**16**	**35**	**60**	**85**	**56**	**92**	**135**	**203**
Free Cash Flow											
Net income	(12)	(9)	(4)	16	35	60	85	56	92	135	203
Noncash items	0	1	2	2	6	10	18	19	15	8	(1)
Working capital	(4)	(8)	(12)	(22)	(63)	(101)	(118)	(100)	(61)	1	39
Capital expenditures	(15)	(6)	(5)	(23)	(53)	(93)	(111)	(98)	(66)	(10)	(10)
Free cash flow	**$(31)**	**$(22)**	**$(19)**	**$(27)**	**$(76)**	**$(124)**	**$(126)**	**$(123)**	**$(20)**	**$134**	**$231**

Source: Casewriter analysis.

EXHIBIT 2
Cash Flow Forecast, by Big Sur Analysts (values in millions of dollars)

Income Statement	Actual 1995	1996	1997	1998	1999	2000	2001	2002	2003	2004	2005	2006
Sales												
Cancer diagnostics	$ 0	$ 0	$ 2	$ 11	$ 22	$ 36	$ 56	$ 71	$85	$95	$106	$114
Other diagnostics	2	4	11	22	40	59	89	135	145	160	185	199
Agriculture	0	1	4	7	12	15	25	50	60	75	91	105
Human therapeutics	0	0	0	0	0	0	0	14	56	80	110	140
Total sales	2	5	17	40	74	110	170	270	346	410	492	558
Cost of sales	7	17	20	25	39	54	72	96	124	142	154	160
Gross profits	(5)	(12)	(3)	15	35	56	98	174	222	268	338	398
Contract revenue	16	22	22	15	12	4	4	4	4	4	4	4
Operating expenses												
R&D	14	23	25	27	29	33	37	44	52	53	54	58
SG&A	12	21	25	32	44	64	87	104	127	138	136	136
Total expenses	26	44	50	59	73	96	124	147	179	191	191	194
Other income	3	0	0	1	(1)	(2)	(2)	(3)	(2)	0	0	3
Income before taxes	(12)	(34)	(31)	(29)	(27)	(38)	(24)	28	45	80	152	210
Taxes	0	0	0	1	4	(13)	4	11	15	27	39	48
Net income	**(12)**	**(34)**	**(31)**	**(30)**	**(31)**	**(25)**	**(28)**	**17**	**30**	**53**	**112**	**162**
Free Cash Flow												
Net income	(12)	(34)	(31)	(30)	(31)	(25)	(28)	17	30	53	112	162
Noncash items	2	3	3	3	4	6	8	10	14	18	20	23
Working capital	(6)	(6)	(6)	(7)	(14)	(17)	(19)	(20)	(28)	(16)	(6)	(6)
Capital expenditures	(15)	(9)	(9)	(9)	(10)	(11)	(15)	(18)	(24)	(27)	(28)	(30)
Free cash flow	**$(31)**	**$(46)**	**$(43)**	**$(43)**	**$(51)**	**$(47)**	**$(54)**	**$(11)**	**$(8)**	**$28**	**$ 98**	**$149**

Source: Casewriter analysis.

EXHIBIT 3
Jan Kelley's Dart-Selected Sample of Firms with Analysis of Five-Year Dividends as a Percent of Stock Price

	Recent Price	Annual Dividend	Five-Year Dividend Growth %	Beta	Equity Cost	Present Value of Five Years = Dividends	Percent of Market Price Not Attributable to Dividends
Signal	$42.00	$ 0.78	14.5%	1.15	12.3%	$ 4.14	90%
Burlington Northern	78.00	1.20	0.0	1.15	12.3	4.30	94
Caterpillar	57.00	1.20	30.0	1.25	12.8	9.37	84
Cooper Inds.	34.00	1.32	2.5	1.15	12.3	5.06	85
Cummins Engine	35.00	1.00	26.0	1.10	12.0	7.22	79
Delux Corp.	28.00	1.48	1.5	0.90	10.9	5.71	80
Donnelley R.R.	39.00	0.68	16.0	1.05	11.7	3.81	90
Dun & Bradstreet	62.00	2.63	4.0	1.00	11.5	10.73	83
Eaton Corp.	51.00	1.50	6.5	1.05	11.7	6.51	87
Emerson Electric	71.00	1.75	9.5	1.05	11.7	8.24	88
Equifax	20.00	0.32	6.5	1.25	12.8	1.35	93
Federal Express	82.00	0.00	0.0	1.35	13.4	0.00	100
Fluor Corp.	58.00	0.60	11.5	1.25	12.8	2.90	95
Honeywell	44.00	1.01	11.5	1.10	12.0	4.98	89
Illinois Tool Works	59.00	0.62	10.5	1.10	12.0	2.98	95
Kelly Services	28.00	0.78	11.0	1.10	12.0	3.80	86
Owens-Corning	44.00	0.00	0.0	1.50	14.2	0.00	100
Raychem	57.00	0.32	4.5	1.30	13.1	1.27	98
ServiceMaster	30.00	0.95	2.5	0.80	10.4	3.82	87
Sherwin-Williams	40.00	0.64	6.5	1.10	12.0	2.76	93
Stone Container	18.00	0.15	7.0	2.25	18.2	0.56	97
Tenneco	47.00	1.60	6.0	1.15	12.3	6.75	86
WMX Technologies	30.00	0.60	5.5	1.20	12.6	2.48	92
Westinghouse	$16.00	0.20	0.0	1.15	12.3	0.72	96
						Average	90%

N.B.. To illustrate the estimate of 90 percent for AlliedSignal, the annual dividend of $0.78 was projected to grow at 14.5% per year to $0.89 in 1997, $1.02 in 1998, $1.17 in 1999, $1.34 in 2000, and $1.54 in 2001. The present value of these dividends discounted at 12.3 percent is $4.14. This equals about 10 percent of AlliedSignal's stock price, $42.00. The complement, 90 percent, is the portion of market price not attributable to dividends.

Source of data: Value Line Investment Survey for prices, dividends, growth rates, and betas. Other items calculated by casewriter.

EXHIBIT 4
Key Terminal Value Estimators

Approach	Advantages	Disadvantages
Book value	- Simple - Authoritative	- Ignores some assets and liabilities - Historical costs: backward-looking - Subject to accounting manipulation
Liquidation value	- Conservative	- Ignores "going concern" value - (Dis)orderly sale?
Replacement value	- Current	- Replace *what?* - Subjective estimates
Multiples, Earnings capitalization - Price/Earnings - Value/EBIT - Price/Book	- Simple - Widely used	- "Earnings" subject to accounting manipulation - Snapshot estimate: may ignore cyclical, secular changes - Depends on comparable firms: ultimately just a measure of relative, not absolute value
Discounted cash flow	- Theoretically based - Rigorous - Affords many analytical insights - Cash focus - Multiperiod - Reflects time value of money	- Time-consuming - Risks "analysis paralysis" - Easy to abuse, misuse - Tough to explain to novices

Source: Casewriter.

EXHIBIT 5
Cash Flows of Three Deals with Differing Rates of Development (values in millions of dollars)

Year	Movie Studio	Bottling Plant	Toll Road
1	$(20)	$(20)	$(20)
2	(40)	(60)	90
3	(60)	(100)	169
4	(20)	5	172
5	0	10	176
6	20	20	179
7	30	40	183
8	50	65	187
9	75	115	190
10	100	150	194
11	90	180	198
12	80	190	202
13	60	200	206
14	55	204	210
15	70	208	214
16	85	212	219
17	95	216	223
18	105	221	227
19	130	225	232
20	150	230	237
21	140	234	241
22	160	239	246
23	190	244	251
24	225	249	256
25	240	254	261
26	230	259	266
27	255	264	272
28	260	269	277
29	265	275	283
30	270	280	288
31+	Steady growth to infinity.		

Projected Cash Flows by Investment

— Movie Studio —■— Bottling Plant —△— Toll Road

Source: Casewriter analysis.

EXHIBIT 6

Sensitivity Analysis of RMAG Terminal Value and Present Value by Variations in Terminal Value Scenarios (values in millions of dollars)

			RMAG's View			
Annual growth rate to infinity	**2%**	**3%**	**4%**	**5%**	**6%**	**7%**
WACC	20%	20%	20%	20%	20%	20%
Annual capex (net of depr'n.) 2006	$0	$(5)	$(12)	$(15)	$(20)	$(28)
Annual addition to NWC 2006	—	(3)	(5)	(7)	(8)	(9)
Adjusted free cash flow 2006	202	194	185	180	174	165
Terminal value 2005	1,142	1,173	1,200	1,257	1,314	1,355
PV of terminal value 2005	185	189	194	203	212	219
PV free cash flows 1996–2005	$(151)	$(151)	$(151)	$(151)	$(151)	$(151)
Total Present Value	**$ 33**	**$ 38**	**$ 43**	**$ 52**	**$ 61**	**$ 68**
			Big Sur's View			
Annual growth rate to infinity	**2%**	**3%**	**4%**	**5%**	**6%**	**7%**
WACC	20%	20%	20%	20%	20%	20%
Annual capex (net of depr'n.) 2007	$0	$(5)	$(12)	$(15)	$(20)	$(28)
Annual addition to NWC 2007	—	(3)	(5)	(7)	(8)	(9)
Adjusted free cash flow 2007	185	177	168	163	157	148
Terminal value 2006	1,049	1,073	1,093	1,142	1,189	1,219
PV of terminal value 2006	141	144	147	154	160	164
PV free cash flows 1996–2006	$(118)	$(118)	$(118)	$(118)	$(118)	$(118)
Total Present Value	**$ 23**	**$ 26**	**$ 29**	**$ 35**	**$ 42**	**$ 46**

Source: Casewriter analysis.

Yeats Valves and Controls Inc.

In early May 2000, W. B. "Bill" Yeats, chairman, CEO, and founder of Yeats Valves and Controls Inc., met with his good friend Edna Millay, an investment banker and member of Yeats Valves' board of directors, to discuss the proposed acquisition of Yeats Valves by TSE International Corporation. Serious negotiations for combining the two companies had started in March, following casual conversations dating back to late 1999. These initial talks focused on broad motives for each side to do a deal, and on the "social issues" (such as management and compensation in the new firm). The negotiations had reached a point where the only major problem remaining was to determine a basis on which shares of Yeats Valves common stock would be exchanged for those of TSE International.

Before entering final negotiations with Tom Eliot, CEO of TSE International Corporation, Yeats wanted to hear Edna Millay's opinion of the TSE International proposition and obtain her advice about price and negotiating strategy. "From my point of view, if the price is right, the TSE International deal will be a good one," Yeats told Millay. "I've been assured that I can still run my own show after the merger. Yeats Valves and Controls Inc. will become an independent operating division at TSE International. All my top management team and employees will be retained, and they'll probably have a richer array of opportunities for bonuses and advancement than at a small independent company like ours. I'll get five-year options to purchase 80,000 shares of TSE International stock at 90 percent of its market price at the close of the acquisition and an incentive bonus that will increase my pay between $50,000 and $200,000 per year. (Bill Yeats' salary at the firm was $300,000 per year.) And I will be placed on the board of directors at TSE International."

Yeats had never thought seriously about a possible sellout before last November, when he had his 62nd birthday. "I began to wonder what would happen to the company after I retired or died," he reminded Edna Millay. "I've got a darn good top-management team here, but they are all specialists. I don't think any one of them could step in and run the show alone. It's a tough business to learn, and I don't think I could find a successor very easily nor train him quickly. There's stability in the TSE International combination that's worth something personally to me.

"As you can see, there are lots of reasons for me to want to see the acquisition take place. However, I want to make sure it's also going to be good for our shareholders. They've put a lot of faith in me at very critical times in the company's history, and I wouldn't want to sell them down the river accidentally."

YEATS VALVES AND CONTROLS INC.

Yeats Valves and Controls Inc., headquartered at Innisfree, California, was principally engaged in the manufacture of specialty valves and heat exchangers. The firm had many standard items, but nearly 40 percent of its volume and more than 50 percent of its profits derived from special applications for the defense and aerospace industries. Such products required extensive engineering work of a kind only a few firms were capable of matching. Yeats had a reputation for engineering excellence in the most complex phases of the business, and as a result, often did prime contract work on highly technical devices for the government.

The company was an outgrowth of a small company organized in 1980 for engineering and developmental work on an experimental heat exchanger product. In 1987, as soon as the product was brought to the commercial stage, Yeats Valves and Controls Inc. was organized to acquire the patents and properties, both owned and leased, of the engineering corporation. Bill Yeats, who founded the engineering firm, founded Yeats Valves and continued as CEO.

The raw materials used by the company were obtainable in ample supply from a number of competitive suppliers. Marketing arrangements presented no problems; sales to machinery manufacturers were made directly by a staff of skilled sales engineers. Auden Company, a large company in a related field, was an important foreign channel of distribution under a nonexclusive distributor arrangement. About 15 percent of Yeats Valves' sales came from Auden. Foreign sales through Auden and direct through Yeats Valves' own staff accounted for 30 percent of sales. Half of the foreign sales originated in emerging economies, mainly Brazil, Korea, and Mexico. The other half originated in the United Kingdom, Italy, and Germany.

Although the foreign-currency crises in the mid-1990s had temporarily interrupted Yeats Valves' sales growth, better economic conditions in the markets of developed countries, together with Yeats Valves' recent introduction of new products for the aerospace and defense industries offered the company excellent prospects for improved performance. As such, sales in the first quarter of 2000 grew 20–25 percent over the corresponding period in 1999, whereas many of Yeats Valves' competitors were experiencing limited growth. **Exhibits 1** and **2** show the most recent balance sheet for Yeats Valves and Controls Inc. and income statements from 1995 onward. **Exhibit 3** presents five years of projected sales, earnings, and other data for Yeats Valves.

The Yeats Valves plants, all of modern construction, were organized for efficient handling of small production orders. The main plant was served by switch tracks in a 15-car dock area of a leading railroad and also by a truck area for the company's own fleet of trucks. From 1997 to 1999, net additions to property had totaled $7,600,000. Yeats, outstanding in research in his own right, had always stressed research and development of improved products, with patent protection, although the company's leadership was believed to be based on its head start in the field and its practical experience.

The success of Yeats Valves and Controls Inc. had brought numerous overtures from companies looking for diversification, plant capacity, management efficiency, financial resources, or an offset to cyclical business. For instance, when Yeats Valves was taken public in 1986, Auden Company, which later became a holder of 20 percent of Yeats Valves common stock, advanced a merger proposal. Word of the proposal reached the financial commentators, who reported possible action by the Department of Justice in antitrust proceedings. Although lawyers for Yeats Valves were confident that they had a ready defense in an antitrust suit, the practical question was one of whether such a legal victory on principle would offset perhaps two or more years of litigation, possibly through to the Supreme Court. Lawsuits notably do not build volume, as Yeats noted at the time, and they use up time and energy that management should devote to operating problems. Hence, the idea was not developed further.

However, as Yeats neared retirement, the idea of selling Yeats Valves to a bigger firm seemed almost necessary. Compelling reasons existed besides his impending retirement[1] and the problem of management succession. First, Yeats Valves needed a deep-pocketed partner to expand, and to bankroll more research and development projects. Conducting research to continue developing leading-edge products for aerospace and defense required sizable investments. Second, Yeats believed that Yeats Valves would benefit from gaining access to a large marketing and distribution network. Yeats Valves was highly successful in its own niche, but Yeats concluded that more segments could be tapped if Yeats Valves' products were more aggressively marketed and widely available. Third, as the company continued to grow, it would need to gain production know-how for high-volume manufacturing. Yeats Valves did not have this kind of expertise. Finally, there had been an increasing trend of consolidation in Yeats Valves' industry over the last year. Yeats feared that without a strong-muscled partner, Yeats Valves would be swamped by competition. Thus, when the opportunity with TSE International Corporation came along in 1999, Yeats determined to make it work as best as he could. Yeats believed that Rockheed-Marlin Corporation, a large defense contractor, could be induced to make an offer for Yeats Valves, though he preferred TSE International Corporation as a merger partner.

Bill Yeats and Tom Eliot had known each other for four years, having been introduced at an industry conference where they were both speakers. As founders and significant stockholders of their respective firms, they liked and respected each other. Talks of a possible combination seemed to gain momentum following the announcement by Yeats Valves of a U.S. government contract to develop an advanced hydraulic controls system code-named "widening gyre" for use in the much-discussed anti-ballistic missile defense shield. Bill

---

[1] For Yeats's estate planning purposes, selling his shares in Yeats Valves would also work to his advantage better.

Yeats believed that the "widening gyre" R&D program would generate valuable patents, numerous options for ongoing R&D, and commercial applications in nautical, aerospace, and automotive products. Bill Yeats and his team were most interested in the R&D aspects of the program, and hoped that TSE or some other partner would assume the work on commercialization, and numerous possible product extensions. Yeats insisted that the financial forecasts for his firm were conservative, and included only the most predictable benefits of "widening gyre." He told Edna Millay, "I hope TSE will recognize the intellectual capital we have built up for the 'widening gyre' program. We're all very excited about it; it could be really big. We have one high-profile government contract. But right now the forecasts don't show its promise. And the stock price doesn't reflect our growth prospects. How should we build it into our negotiations?"

TSE INTERNATIONAL CORPORATION

TSE International Corporation was incorporated in 1970. In 2000, the company manufactured products ranging from advanced industrial components to chains, cables, nuts and bolts, castings and forgings, and other similar products and sold them, mostly indirectly, to various industrial users. One division produced parts for aerospace propulsion and control systems with a broad line of intermediate products. A second division produced a wide range of nautical navigation assemblies and allied products. The third division manufactured a line of components for missile and fire-control systems. These products were all well regarded by its customers, and each was a significant factor in its natural market. Financial statements for TSE International are provided in **Exhibits 4** and **5**—the firm's debt was currently rated Baa.

The company's raw material supply, in the form of sheets, plates, and coils of various metals came from various producers. The TSE International plants were modern, ample, equipped with substantially new machinery, and adequately served by railroad sidings. The firm was considered a low-cost producer, made possible by unusual production know-how. TSE International was also known as a tough competitor.

THE CURRENT SITUATION

During the early part of 2000, a series of group meetings had taken place between Yeats and Eliot and their respective company counsel. From the very start of the negotiations for combining the two companies, the merits of alternative methods had been considered by counsel for both parties. A straight common-for-common exchange was expected to be the most likely outcome, although Yeats was willing to consider an assets-for-stock exchange. Both methods would be structured to provide a deferment of the tax liability. Whatever terms were finally worked out, the agreement would be subject to the approval of the stockholders of both companies.

There were 560 stockholders of Yeats Valves and Controls Inc., and roughly 70 percent of the stock was held within the board of directors and their families, including 20 percent owned by Auden Company and 40 percent owned by Bill Yeats. Yeats had kept the board of directors fully informed throughout the discussions with TSE International. The proposed merger was discussed with the president of Auden Company, whose approval obviously was necessary because of his company's 20 percent interest. Although the Auden executives were not convinced that the proposal had strict business merit, they decided not to object but, instead, gave notice that they would sell their company's holdings of Yeats Valves stock. Auden Company was about to undertake new expansion of its own, and its executives were not disposed to keep minority interests in a company like TSE International Corporation. However, they saw no reason for not maintaining their satisfactory relationships with the Yeats Valves enterprise when it should become a TSE International division.

Edna Millay, as a director of Yeats Valves, had been kept fully informed about all the merger discussions. She was intrigued with the possibility that Yeats Valves might be more fully valued if it were part of a larger, more diversified enterprise. As a smaller, unlisted firm, Yeats Valves had recently traded at a price-earnings ratio of 10.3 times, perhaps reflecting the risks associated with a small, concentrated enterprise, possibly vulnerable to competition from larger firms. The New York Stock Exchange listing of TSE International would be attractive to some shareholders, although Edna Millay's firm had earned significant commissions specializing in handling Yeats Valves' NASDAQ trading. TSE International's recent price-earnings ratio was 11.0 times. **Exhibit 6** shows recent market prices of Yeats Valves and TSE International shares.[2] **Exhibit 7** provides valuation information on exchange-listed possible peer firms of Yeats Valves and TSE International. **Exhibit 8** presents information on recent acquisitions within Yeats Valves' industry. **Exhibit 9** presents money market and stock return data for recent years.

"Edna, what do you think of the merger?" Yeats asked his friend as they sat down to analyze the deal. "It looks good to me, yet maybe I've gotten too close to the situation to uncover all the things I should be seeing. I also worry that our people, who have gotten used to an independent, entrepreneurial culture here at Yeats Valves, would have trouble adjusting at a big firm like TSE International. Do you think that the merger will benefit Yeats Valves, and if so what is the minimum price we should ask to ensure that our stockholders profit from this merger?"

Bill Yeats continued, "April 2000 was pretty cruel to those dot.com companies. Our firm is different. We've got a great growth outlook, but our valuation is still low. Is this merger a move that will help fetch a better multiple? Or, should we wait to see if our efforts are better rewarded?" With that comment, Yeats passed the following clipping to Edna Millay:

> *Modest Valuations*—In light of currently modest share prices, we believe that the number of acquisitions will increase in the future. Some valuations are so low, in fact, managers are considering leveraged buyouts of their individual companies. . . . We advise most investors to delay additional commitments until the stock market settles.[3]

---

[2]Value Line had assigned a beta of .85 to TSE International's stock. Because it was a smaller unlisted firm, no rating organization had calculated a beta for Yeats Valves and Controls Inc.

[3]*Value Line Investment Survey,* May 5, 2000, p. 1301.

EXHIBIT 1
Balance Sheet as of December 31, 1999 (dollar figures in thousands)

Assets

Cash		$ 1,884
U.S. Treasury tax notes and other Treasury obligations		9,328
Due from U.S. government		868
Accounts receivable net[*]		2,316
Inventories, at lower of cost or market[**]		6,888
Other current assets		116
Total current assets		$21,400
Investments		1,768
Plant, property, and equipment, at cost		
Land[***]	$ 92	
Buildings	6,240	
Equipment[***]	18,904	
Less: allowance for depreciation	7,056	
	$18,180	
Construction in process	88	
Total plant, property, and equipment, net		$18,268
Patents		156
Cash value of life insurance		376
Deferred assets		156
Total assets		$42,124

Liabilities and Stockholders' Equity

Accounts payable		$ 2,016
Wages and salaries accrued		504
Employees' pension cost accrued		208
Tax accrued		72
Dividends payable		560
Provision for federal income tax		1,200
Total current liabilities		$ 4,560
Deferred federal income tax		800
Common stock, par 50 cents, authorized and outstanding 1,440,000 shares		720
Capital surplus		7,680
Earned surplus		28,364
Total equity		$36,764
Total liabilities and stockholders' equity		$42,124
Current ratio		4.69
Quick ratio		3.16

[*]Allowance for doubtful accounts—$190,392 (probably conservative)

[**]Obsolete inventories were written off semiannually.

[***]Equivalent land in the area had a market value of $320,000, and the building had an estimated market worth of $16,800,000. Equipment had a replacement cost of approximately $24,000,000 but a market value of about $16,000,000 in an orderly liquidation.

EXHIBIT 2
Summary of Earnings and Dividends, Years Ended December 31, 1995–1999 (dollar figures in thousands, except per share figures)

	1995	1996	1997	1998	1999	(Unaudited) Three months ended 3/30	
						1999	2000
Sales	$ 36,312	$ 34,984	$ 35,252	$ 45,116	$ 49,364	$ 11,728	$ 14,162
Cost of goods sold	25,924	24,200	24,300	31,580	37,044	8,730	10,190
Gross profit	10,388	10,784	10,952	13,536	12,320	2,998	3,972
Selling, general, admin.	2,020	2,100	2,252	2,628	2,936	668	896
Other income, net	92	572	108	72	228	14	198
Income before taxes	8,460	9,256	8,808	10,980	9,612	2,344	3,274
Taxes	3,276	3,981	3,620	4,721	4,037	1,009	1,391
Net income	5,184	5,275	5,188	6,259	5,575	1,335	1,883
Depreciation	784	924	1,088	1,280	1,508	364	394
Cash dividends	1,680	2,008	2,016	2,304	2,304	576	753
Earnings per common share	3.74	3.61	3.60	4.35	3.87	0.93	1.31
Cash dividends declared:							
Per preferred share	5.00	1.25					
Per common share	1.00	1.40	1.40	1.60	1.60	0.40	0.52
Capital expenditures	-	1,826	2,011	2,213	2,433	2,675	2,675
Working capital needs	-	3,492	3,867	4,289	4,757	5,273	5,273
Percent payout to common stock	27.8%	38.2%	38.9%	36.8%	41.3%	43.1%	40.0%
Ratio analysis							
Sales	100.0	100.0	100.0	100.0	100.0	100.0	100.0
Cost of goods sold	71.4	69.2	68.9	70.0	75.0	74.4	72.0
Gross profit	28.6	30.8	31.1	30.0	25.0	25.6	28.0
Selling, general, and admin.	5.6	6.0	6.4	5.8	5.9	5.7	6.3
Other income, net	0.3	1.6	0.3	0.2	0.5	0.1	1.4
Income before fed. taxes	23.3	26.5	25.0	24.3	19.5	20.0	23.1
Net income	14.3	15.1	14.7	13.9	11.3	11.4	13.3

EXHIBIT 3

Forecast of Sales, Earnings and Other Items for Years Ending December 31, 2000–2004
(dollar figures in thousands except per share figures)

	Actual	Projected				
	1999	2000	2001	2002	2003	2004
Sales	$ 49,364	$ 59,600	$ 66,000	$ 73,200	$ 81,200	$ 90,000
Cost of goods sold	37,044	42,316	47,850	52,704	58,058	63,900
Gross profit	12,320	17,284	18,150	20,496	23,142	26,100
Selling, general, admin.	2,936	3,612	4,024	4,464	4,952	5,492
Other income, net	228	240	264	288	320	352
Income before taxes	9,612	13,912	14,390	16,320	18,510	20,960
Taxes	4,037	5,565	5,756	6,528	7,404	8,384
Net income	5,575	8,347	8,634	9,792	11,106	12,576
Depreciation	1,508	1,660	1,828	2,012	2,212	2,432
Cash dividends	2,304	2,304	2,880	3,456	4,320	5,184
Earnings per share	3.87	5.80	6.00	6.80	7.71	8.73
Dividends per share	1.60	1.60	2.00	2.40	3.00	3.60
Capital expenditures	—	1,826	2,011	2,213	2,433	2,675
Working capital needs	—	3,492	3,867	4,289	4,757	5,273
Ratio analysis						
Sales	100.0	100.0	100.0	100.0	100.0	100.0
Cost of goods sold	75.0	71.0	72.5	72.0	71.5	71.0
Gross profit	25.0	29.0	27.5	28.0	28.5	29.0
Selling, general, and admin.	5.9	6.1	6.1	6.1	6.1	6.1
Other income, net	0.5	0.4	0.4	0.4	0.4	0.4
Income before fed. taxes	19.5	23.3	21.8	22.3	22.8	23.3
Net income	11.3	14.0	13.1	13.4	13.7	14.0

EXHIBIT 4
TSE International Corporation Consolidated Balance Sheet as of December 31, 1999
(dollar figures in thousands)

Assets

Cash		$ 46,480
U.S. government securities, at cost		117,260
Trade accounts receivable		241,761
Inventories, at lower of cost or market		179,601
Prepaid taxes and insurance		2,120
Total current assets		$ 587,222
Investment in wholly owned Canadian subsidiary		158,081
Investment in supplier corporation		104,000
Cash value of life insurance		3,920
Miscellaneous assets		2,160
Property, plant and equipment, at cost:		
Buildings, machinery, equipment	$ 671,402	
Less: allowances for depreciation and amortization	260,001	
Property, plant and equipment, net	$ 411,402	
Land	22,080	
Property, plant, equipment, and land, net		389,321
Patents, at cost, less amortization		1,120
Total assets		$1,245,825

Liabilities and Stockholders' Equity

Notes payable to bank		$ 5,795
Accounts payable and accrued expenses		90,512
Payrolls and other compensation		38,399
Taxes other than taxes on income		3,052
Provision for federal taxes on income refund—estimated		32,662
Current maturities of long-term debt		30,900
Total current liabilities		$ 201,320
Note payable to bank[1]		119,100
Deferred federal income taxes		29,668
2 % cum. Conv. Preferred stock, $20 par, 1,389,160 shares outstanding[2]		27,783
Common stock, $2 par; 96,000,000 shares authorized; 62,694,361 shares issued		125,389
Capital surplus[3]		21,904
Retained earnings		720,661
Total equity		$ 895,737
Total liabilities and stockholders' equity		$1,245,825

[1]$150,000,000 note, payable semiannually beginning June 30, 2000; $30,900,000 due within one year, shown in current liabilities. One covenant required company not to pay cash dividends, except on preferred stock, or to make other distribution on its shares or acquire any stock, after December 31, 1999, in excess of net earnings after that date.
[2]Issued in January 1999; convertible at rate of 1.24 common share to one preferred share; redeemable beginning in 2004; sinking fund beginning in 2004.
[3]Resulting principally from the excess of par value of 827,800 shares of preferred stock over the pay value of common share issues in conversion in 1999.

EXHIBIT 5
TSE International Corporation Summary of Consolidated Earnings and Dividends for Years Ended December 31, 1995–1999 (dollars in thousands except per share figures)

	1995	1996	1997	1998	1999
Net sales	$1,623,963	$1,477,402	$1,498,645	$1,980,801	$2,187,208
Cost of products sold	1,271,563	1,180,444	1,140,469	1,642,084	1,793,511
Gross profit	352,400	296,958	358,176	338,717	393,697
Selling, admin, general expenses	58,463	69,438	74,932	87,155	120,296
Earnings before federal income taxes	293,937	227,520	283,244	251,562	273,401
Tax expense	126,393	95,558	116,130	101,882	109,360
Net earnings	167,544	131,962	167,114	149,679	164,041
Depreciation	19,160	20,000	21,480	24,200	26,800
Cash dividends declared	85,754	77,052	53,116	77,340	92,238
Net earnings per common share	2.55	1.86	2.01	1.92	2.23
Cash dividends declared					
Per common share	1.39	1.25	0.86	1.25	1.49
Per preferred share	—	—	—	—	0.40
Cash payout	51.2%	58.4%	31.8%	51.7%	56.2%
Ratio analysis					
Sales	100.0%	100.0%	100.0%	100.0%	100.0%
Cost of goods sold	78.3	79.9	76.1	82.9	82.0
Gross profit	21.7	20.1	23.9	17.1	18.0
Selling, admin, general expenses	3.6	4.7	5.0	4.4	5.5
Income before fed. taxes	18.1	15.4	18.9	12.7	12.5
Net income	10.3	8.9	11.2	7.6	7.5

EXHIBIT 6
Market Prices of Yeats Valves and Controls Inc. and TSE International Corporation Common Stock, 1995–YTD 2000 (in dollars per share)

| | Yeats Valves and Controls | | | TSE International Corporation | | | | |
| | Common Stock | | | Common Stock | | | Preferred Stock | |
	High	Low	Close	High	Low	Close	High	Low
1995	16.3	8.8	15.0	12.3	10.1	11.9		
1996	24.8	14.0	22.6	14.4	11.8	13.2		
1997	25.0	20.0	22.3	12.8	9.3	11.1		
1998 Quarter Ended:								
March 31	24.4	20.8	21.5	14.1	12.8	14.0		
June 30	22.8	20.4	21.0	13.7	12.0	11.8		
September 30	22.8	20.4	21.5	12.8	10.5	11.3		
December 31	24.4	20.1	21.0	12.4	11.3	11.9		
1999 Quarter Ended:								
March 31	23.5	20.0	21.8	11.6	10.2	10.7	13.61	12.22
June 30	23.6	19.9	22.0	11.6	10.9	10.9	13.15	12.05
September 30	22.8	20.0	22.5	13.6	11.1	13.6	14.23	12.37
December 31	30.0	22.3	28.5	17.0	13.3	16.8	17.32	13.77
2000 Quarter Ended:								
March 31	32.1	26.0	31.5	20.7	15.1	20.7	17.32	13.99
Current Quotation	34.3	31.5	39.8	22.6	18.3	22.0	17.63	15.36

EXHIBIT 7
Information on Peer Firms in the Industrial Machinery Sector

	Price/ Earnings Ratio	Beta	Dividend Yield	Expected Growth Rate of to 2005	Debt/ Capital
CASCADE CORP. Designs, manufactures and markets hydraulically actuated products.	8.2×	0.85	4.0%	12.5%	49%
CURTISS-WRIGHT CORPORATION Manufactures precision components in motion (42%) and flow (36%) control; metal treatment (36% of sales).	10.3	0.65	1.4	10.0	8
FLOWSERVE CORP. Makes, designs, and markets fluid-handling equipment (pumps, valves, and mechanical seals).	11.0	0.80	Nil	6.5	39
IDEX CORP. Designs, manufactures, and markets industrial pumps, compressors, and a wide range of industrial products.	14.6	1.10	1.9	9.0	42
ROPER INDS. Operates in three segments: industrial controls, fluid handling, and analytical instrumentation.	16.3	0.75	0.9	15.5	39
TECUMSEH PRODUCTS Manufactures compressors, condensers, pumps for commercial, industrial, and agricultural applications. Foreign sales and exports totaled 43% of 1999 sales.	7.0	0.65	3.0	8.5	1
THOMAS INDS. Leading manufacturer of compressors and vacuum pumps.	10.7	0.85	1.6	9.5	16
WATTS INDUSTRIES Designs, manufactures, and sells an extensive line of valves for the plumbing & heating and water-quality markets.	10.4	NMF	2.9	14.0	36

Source: Value Line Investment Survey, May 5, 2000.

EXHIBIT 8
Information on Selected Recent M&A Transactions in the Industrial Machinery and Aerospace Sectors

Acquiror	Business	Target	Business	Effective Date
General Electric Co	Electrical, construction prod	Honeywell International Inc	Mnfr aerospace, automotive prod	10/20/2000
United Technologies Corp	Mnfr aircraft engines, defense	Sundstrand Corp	Mnfr aerospace, indl equip	06/11/1999
AlliedSignal Inc	Mnfr aircraft engines, radar	Tristar Aerospace Co	Mnfr aerospace hardware	12/15/1999
Meritor Automotive Inc	Whl car, truck equip and parts	Arvin Industries Inc	Mnfr auto parts, accessories	07/10/2000
DaimlerChrysler AG	Automobiles & trucks	Detroit Diesel	Manufacture diesel, alt engines	10/12/2000
Goldman Industrial Group	Mnfr metal working machinery	Bridgeport Machines	Mnfr metal cutting mach tools	08/19/1999
Siemens Energy & Automation	Mnfr, whl electronic parts	Moore Products Co	Mnfr control instruments	02/24/2000
TI Group PLC	Mnfr engineered metal prods	Walbro Corp	Mnfr fuel system components	06/17/1999
Ingersoll-Rand Co	Mnfr industrial machinery	Hussmann International Inc	Mnfr refrigeration systems	06/19/2000

EXHIBIT 9
Capital Market Interest Rates and Stock Price Indexes (averages percent per annum except for May 1, 2000, which offers closing prices)

	1997	1998	1999	May 1, 2000
U.S. Treasury Yields				
3-month bills	5.06%	4.78%	4.64%	6.60%
30-year bonds	6.61	5.58	5.87	5.98
Corporate Bond Yields by Rating				
Aaa	7.27	6.53	7.05	8.67
Aa	7.48	6.80	7.36	9.15
A	7.54	6.93	7.53	9.35
Baa	7.87	7.22	7.88	9.60
Stock Market				
S&P500 Index	873	1,085	1,327	1,481
Price/earnings ratio	15.9×	17.4×	19.4×	18.8×
Industrial Machinery Stocks				
Price/earnings ratio	12.9×	13.9×	14.9×	15.0×
Dividend yield	1.8%	1.5%	1.6%	1.6%

N.B.: The geometric average equity market risk premium for the period 1926–1999 was about 5.5 percent. The arithmetic average equity market risk premium for that period was about 7.2 percent.

Sources: Value Line Investment Survey, May 5, 2000; *Federal Reserve Bulletin,* April 2000; *The Wall Street Journal,* May 2, 2000.

Transaction Size ($ MM)	Target Net Sales Last 12 Months ($MM)	Equity Value/ Target Net Income	Equity Value/ Target Book Value	Enterprise Value/Target Net Sales	Enterprise Value/Target Operating Income	Enterprise Value/ Target Cash Flow	Enterprise Value/Net Income	Premium (Discount) 4 Weeks Prior to Announcement Date
45,204.7	31,052.0	24.7	4.8	1.61	16.85	11.98	27.36	54.63
4,408.3	2,024.0	16.7	6.8	2.13	11.40	9.37	18.66	54.08
269.8	205.1	10.0	2.7	1.37	7.92	7.49	15.52	65.22
1,138.4	3,010.3	7.5	1.1	0.38	8.99	4.84	14.37	22.2
581.2	2,256.2	12.2	1.3	0.29	8.48	5.22	14.78	77.78
57.0	197.0	29.0	0.8	0.37	11.40	9.37	18.66	53.85
168.6	168.9	63.0	2.5	0.96	26.76	15.53	62.08	79.38
630.3	697.4	19.8	4.0	0.79	13.44	7.14	44.87	NA
1,837.2	1,306.8	27.3	7.2	1.448	15.243	12.478	33.013	109.95

Chrysler Corporation: Negotiations between Daimler and Chrysler

In January 1998, Jürgen Schrempp, CEO of Daimler-Benz A.G., approached Chrysler Corporation chairman and CEO Robert Eaton about a possible merger, acquisition, or deep strategic alliance between their two firms. Schrempp argued that:

> The two companies are a perfect fit of two leaders in their respective markets. Both companies have dedicated and skilled work forces and successful products, but in different markets and different parts of the world. By combining and utilizing each other's strengths, we will have a preeminent strategic position in the global marketplace for the benefit of our customers. We will be able to exploit new markets, and we will improve return and value for our shareholders.[1]

Schrempp recounted,

> I just presented the case, and I was out again. The meeting lasted about 17 minutes. I don't want to create the impression that he was surprised. When the meeting was over, I said, "If you think I'm naïve, this is nonsense I'm talking, just tell me." He smiled and said, "Just give me a chance. We have done some evaluation as well, and I will phone you in the next two weeks." I think he phoned me in a week or so.[2]

Independently Eaton had concluded that some type of combination of Chrysler with another major automobile firm was needed: the firm was currently financially healthy, but indus-

---

[1]Press release, Daimler-Benz A.G., May 6, 1998.
[2]"Gentlemen Start Your Engines," *Fortune,* June 8, 1998, p. 140.

This case was prepared from public information by Professors Robert Bruner, Petra Christmann, and Robert Spekman and by Assistants Brian Kannry and Melinda Davies. This case is intended to be used in a negotiation exercise with "Daimler-Benz A.G.: Negotiations Between Daimler and Chrysler" (UVA-F-1241). The financial support of the Darden Partnership Program, and the Darden School Foundation are gratefully acknowledged. Copyright © 1998 by the University of Virginia Darden School Foundation, Charlottesville, VA. All rights reserved. *To order copies, send an e-mail to* dardencases@virginia.edu. *No part of this publication may be reproduced, stored in a retrieval system, used in a spreadsheet, or transmitted in any form or by any means—electronic, mechanical, photocopying, recording, or otherwise—without the permission of the Darden School Foundation.* Rev. 12/01. Version 2.2.

try overcapacity and huge prospective investment outlays called for an even larger type of global competitor. Before seeing Schrempp, Eaton had polled investment bankers for their ideas about a major automotive merger, and had spoken with executives from BMW on this topic.

Eaton replied positively to Schrempp's idea of an industrial combination. Now lay ahead the task of forging the details of the agreement to combine. Robert Eaton appointed a small task force of business executives and lawyers to represent Chrysler in the detailed negotiations. Eaton challenged this team on several counts: exploit the benefits of combination; preserve and strengthen the Chrysler brands; minimize the adverse effects of combination on employees and executives; and maximize shareholder value. Eaton reflected on the varieties of terms the Chrysler team might seek, and immediately convened a meeting to begin planning the team's negotiation strategy. Eaton said,

> My number one criteria is that [any deal] has got to be a long-term upside with no negative short-term impact. It's got to be good for the shareholders. That's my—and my board's—fiduciary responsibility.[3]

CHRYSLER CORPORATION

In 1920, Walter P. Chrysler, a multimillionaire and the president of Buick at age 45, stormed out of the head office of General Motors with the prospect of starting his own car company. The Chrysler Corporation was officially launched in 1924 with the introduction of the Chrysler Six and rapidly grew to become the third largest automaker in America. While Chrysler managed to survive the Great Depression intact, labor problems and rampant mismanagement brought the company to the brink of financial ruin multiple times (e.g., 1956, 1965, and 1993), but most notably in 1980. Under the leadership of Lee Iacocca, and with the support of federal loan guarantees, Chrysler managed to turn itself around one more time, returning to profitability in 1982. While the late 1980s proved tough for the industry as a whole, the introduction and meteoric rise of the family minivan (a market controlled 47 percent by Chrysler as of 1996) coupled with the 1987 acquisition and subsequent exploitation of the Jeep brand name left Chrysler the envy of the U.S. auto market by the mid-1990s. As *Fortune* magazine stated in late 1996, "If a vehicle is in demand and generates high profit margins, you can bet Chrysler's making it."[4] While Chrysler's success and relatively conservative management style attracted praise from industry observers, it also attracted the attention of Las Vegas billionaire Kirk Kerkorian, who with the help of retired Lee Iacocca, mounted a hostile bid for Chrysler in 1995. The $55 per share ($27.50 today following a 2-for-1 stock split in 1996) not only failed to win approval of Chrysler's board, but turned out to be largely unfinanced, leaving Chrysler to continue under current management.

---

[3]John Pepper, "Why Eaton Cut the Deal," *Detroit News,* May 7, 1998, detnews.com.
[4]Susan E. Kuhn, "Auto Stocks: Today's Big Steal," *Fortune,* November 25, 1996, pp 204–205.

CHRYSLER PRODUCTS

Chrysler focused heavily on trucks in its product offering. In 1997 trucks (including mini-vans) accounted for about two-thirds of Chrysler's vehicle sales in the United States and cars for about one-third. Chrysler's trucks include sport utility vehicles, such as the Jeep Wrangler, Jeep Cherokee, and the Dodge Durango, pick-up trucks, such as the Dodge Ram, and minivans such as the Plymouth Voyager.

One of Chrysler's most successful products was the minivan, which Chrysler invented in 1983. Dodge Caravan/Plymouth Voyager, the world's most successful minivan, was first introduced in 1984. Chrysler dominated the segment ever since. In 1997, minivans accounted for about one-third of Chrysler's truck sales; see **Exhibit 1**. Chrysler's profitability was high in the sport/utility market despite of increased competition from new products, especially at the top end and at the bottom end of the market.

Chrysler's cars were sold under the Chrysler, Dodge, and Plymouth brand names. Chrysler's larger cars (such as the Stratus) were priced similar to those of Mercedes-Benz's lower-middle-class cars (in size), namely the C-Class. While Chrysler's cars were much larger and more powerful than Mercedes of comparable price, they lacked Mercedes' attention to detail in manufacturing and brand image. At the bottom end of the range, Chrysler offered the Dodge/Plymouth Neon.

CHRYSLER PRODUCT DEVELOPMENT AND MANUFACTURING STRATEGY

Chrysler was known for a short cycle of concept-to-market for new products, low development costs, efficient plants, good supplier relations, and creative styling. Vehicle development time for Chrysler declined to 24 months in 1996 from 60 months in 1988. The efficiency in the product development process could be mainly attributed to platform teams—autonomous groups that consisted of all the professionals required to design and produce a new car, which were introduced by Chrysler in 1989. Chrysler's innovation was to put all the engineers and designers assigned to a specific project together on a single floor, along with representatives of marketing, finance, purchasing, and even outside suppliers, and grant them considerable autonomy. Close contact kept the teams fast and efficient. The teams used target pricing, in which the cost of the car was determined at the beginning of the process, not the end, Chrysler had consistently performed better than its target time and budget goals. The system worked so well that in 1991 Chrysler dissolved most of its functional groups and reassigned its members to four platform teams—small car, large car, minivan, and Jeep/truck. Harbour & Associates, a consulting firm in Troy, Michigan, estimated that Chrysler's R&D costs per vehicle were $550, compared to over $2,000 per vehicle for Mercedes.

Since 1989 Chrysler narrowed its supplier base from 2,500 companies to 1,140 and had fundamentally changed the way it worked with those that remained. Suppliers were offered long-term contracts, were involved in the design process for new cars, and were encouraged to make cost-saving suggestions through an initiative called SCORE (Supplier Cost Reduction Effort) introduced in 1989. This initiative yielded $2.5 billion in savings since its inception.[5] As a result, Chrysler was the least vertically integrated of the big three U.S automakers. It purchased 75 percent of its components, (versus 50 percent at Ford and 30 percent at GM in early 1998).[6]

Unlike other U.S. auto manufacturers, which had improved the bottom line almost entirely by cutting costs, Chrysler's profits surged by introducing new models. Its vehicle lineup was known as one of the most innovative in the industry. The LH series (Chrysler Concorde, Dodge Intrepid, and Eagle Vision) introduced in the 1993 model year was Chrysler's first new car platform in a decade. These cars were very well received in the marketplace and have been largely accredited as a major factor contributing to Chrysler's latest turnaround.

CHRYSLER INTERNATIONAL STRATEGY

In the 1990s Chrysler substantially internationalized its sales. International vehicle sales (i.e. sales outside North America) rose from less than 50,000 units in 1990 to 237,060 units in 1997, but were still accounting for less than 10 percent of Chrysler's total unit sales. The Jeep name was invaluable to Chrysler's gradual international spread due to the appeal and name recognition the Jeep enjoyed in large parts of the world. Chrysler's American Motors acquisition in 1987 came with Jeep.

Latin America was a focus of the geographic expansion of Chrysler. Sales of its products increased by more than 100 percent in this region from 1996 to 1997. Venezuela with retail sales of 20,716 units was the number one Latin American market for Chrysler, making Chrysler fourth in market share in that country behind Toyota, GM, and Ford. The automaker produced the Jeep Grand Cherokee and Cherokee sport utility vehicles and the Neon passenger car at its Carabobo Assembly Plant in Valencia, Venezuela, for local distribution and export to Colombia and Ecuador. In 1998, Chrysler planned to open a new 950,000-square-meter manufacturing facility in Curitiba, Brazil, to assemble the Dodge Dakota pickup truck, adding Jeep Cherokee production to the Cordoba plant in Argentina, opening a parts warehouse/technical training center in Buenos Aires, Argentina, and breaking ground on a $500 million joint venture engine plant with BMW in Brazil. (The 40,000-square-meter engine plant will be an adjacent facility to the Dodge Dakota assembly plant.) Because Venezuela, Argentina, and Brazil's import duties ranged between 60 and 70 percent, Chrysler had opted to produce vehicles in those countries, contrasting with a general preference to establish an international presence via importing its domestic-produced vehicles.

Chrysler had been completely absent from Europe for many years. Since it came back in 1990, it was very successful with the Voyager, which was built in Graz, Austria, for the European market. However, Chrysler was far from the leadership position it had in the U.S.

---

[5]Debra Walker, "Supply Chain Collaboration Saved Chrysler $2.5 Billion and Counting," *Supply Chain Management,* August 1998, p. 60.

[6]These data are drawn from a table titled, "Estimated Levels of Integration and Production Parts Purchasing," *Automotive News Europe,* January 19, 1998.

minivan market. Leading minivan manufacturers in Europe were Ford and Volkswagen, that accounted for about one-third of European minivan sales in 1997, and Renault, which surpassed Ford and Volkswagen in 1998 by adding the stretched Grand Espace to its product line. Ford and Volkswagen were selling three basically identical models—Ford Galaxy, VW Sharan, and Seat Alhambra—produced in a joint venture factory in Portugal. Chrysler's overall market share in Europe was still only 0.7 percent in 1997, which was partly due to the lack of car models for the European market. The Vision/Concorde/Intrepid was too large for Europe, the Stratus had attracted mainly buyers for the four- to five-passenger convertible, and the Neon had too many popular European competitors. Another primary reason for Chrysler's comparatively modest impact on the European market was its still rather thin sales network.

DAIMLER-BENZ A.G.

Gottlieb Daimler and Karl Benz were rival German car makers at the turn of the century. While both Daimler and Benz achieved individual success in the early 1900s, the challenge of rebuilding Germany after World War I, as well as competing with the burgeoning Ford Motor Company, led the two companies to merge in 1926 to form Daimler-Benz. While the company shifted to military production during World War II, Daimler began manufacturing cars again in 1947. By the 1980s, Daimler and its Mercedes brand had become synonymous with premier quality and craftsmanship. Flush with success, Daimler began a program of diversification in the mid-1980s, intending to transform the company into a self-described "integrated technology group" with product lines ranging from transportation to aerospace to microelectronics to white goods. Unfortunately, a string of largely unprofitable acquisitions in the late 1980s left Daimler unfocused and inefficient, culminating in a staggering DM5.7 billion loss for 1995 (the largest peacetime loss ever by a German company). Under the direction of new chief executive Jürgen Schrempp, Daimler began to shed unprofitable business units, return the company to its core business of making high-quality automobiles, and move toward a more "American-style" management designed to enhance shareholder value. By 1997, the company had returned to profitability on record sales.

DAIMLER-BENZ DIVERSIFICATION UNDER REUTER

Under Chairman Edzard Reuter, who took office in 1987, Daimler undertook a series of acquisitions amounting to an estimated $6.2 billion that turned Daimler-Benz into one of the world's biggest industrial conglomerates. Reuter reorganized the company into a holding structure with four separate companies in 1989: Mercedes for cars and trucks, DASA for Aerospace, Daimler-Benz InterServices (Debis) for financial and computer services, and AEG for engineering. To refocus the company from defense to civilian aircraft, DASA under the leadership of Jürgen Schrempp acquired 51 percent of the money-losing Dutch Fokker Company, a maker of short- and intermediate-range propeller and jet passenger planes, in 1993.

During Reuter's chairmanship, Gerhard Liener, Daimler's chief financial officer, pushed for a listing of the company on the New York Stock Exchange, which necessitated publishing the company's returns under American accounting rules. These accounting rules required Daimler to report on current operations, which revealed a huge operating loss of $3.3 billion in 1993. Of the four holding companies only Debis reported a profit. Reuter faced a barrage of criticism, especially as the new companies remained the loss-makers while Mercedes-Benz swung back to big profits in 1994. Jürgen Schrempp replaced Reuter as chairman in 1995.

JÜRGEN SCHREMPP

Jürgen Schrempp was born in the western German city of Freiburg in 1944. Following his school education he joined Daimler as a motor mechanic apprentice at the Mercedes-Benz Freiburg branch in 1967. He later went to university to train as an engineer and returned to Daimler-Benz. From 1967 Schrempp worked in a number of different areas at the Daimler-Benz A.G. In 1974 he was appointed to the management of the South African subsidiary, Mercedes-Benz of South Africa, initially in the Service Division and after 1980 as the board member responsible for engineering. In 1982 Schrempp took over as president of Euclid Inc., of Cleveland, Ohio, at the time a 100 percent subsidiary of Daimler-Benz A.G. and manufacturer of extremely heavy-duty trucks. Schrempp told the headquarters that it would cost too much to fix the unit and recommended its sale. The board took his advice and after Schrempp successfully divested the unit he returned as vice president to Mercedes-Benz of South Africa in 1984. In 1985 he was appointed president of the South African subsidiary. Two years later he was called back to Stuttgart to join the Daimler-Benz management board and head the Daimler-Benz Aerospace subsidiary. He orchestrated the purchase of the Dutch aircraft maker Fokker, which was part of Reuter's diversification program, a move that turned out to be a mistake later on.

DAIMLER-BENZ RESTRUCTURING UNDER SCHREMPP

When Schrempp took charge, cuts in defense spending were hurting the aerospace unit's military operations, while cancellations of commercial aircraft orders resulting from spending cuts by airlines in order to be competitive in the deregulated airline market were pinching the Airbus operation. More than 300 supposedly firm orders were cancelled in late 1994 and early 1995. This represented more than half of the company's backlog and the equivalent of about 30 months' production. The worldwide truck business was slumping and the Mercedes auto operations had not yet recovered from the early 1990s onslaughts of Lexus and Infiniti.

During his tenure as chairman Schrempp proved to be a master of boardroom politics with the ability to make decisions quickly and the willingness to take risks. Schrempp focused on shareholder value, something that was not typically done by European companies. Despite Daimler's listing on the NYSE and the increase in transparency of Daimler-Benz's accounts resulting from accounting changes, Daimler's top executives were not in the habit

TABLE 1
Daimler-Benz Operating Profits and Revenues by Division (in million DM)

	1997		1996	
	Operating Profit	**Revenues**	**Operating Profit**	**Revenues**
Passenger cars	3,132	53,892	3,090	46,652
Commercial vehicles	481	39,140	(354)	32,152
Aerospace	432	15,286	(196)	13,053
Services	457	15,498	288	13,143
Directly managed businesses	(129)	7,555	(585)	8,014

of putting stockholders first. To sell the idea of shareholder value, Schrempp started calling colleagues at random and asking them for Daimler's current stock price. At first, he says, "seven did not know and three were wrong. Nowadays they can tell me." Schrempp instituted the rule that every single business at Daimler had to achieve a 12 percent return on capital, or be capable of achieving a 12 percent return on capital in the foreseeable future. If it could not, it would be sold. Such a rule was very uncommon for German companies. This rule resulted in a reduction of the total number of businesses from 35 to 23. Major divestitures were the sale of the company's unprofitable electrical engineering business (AEG), and the closure of the aircraft maker Fokker. In addition, Schrempp demanded superior performance from the rest of the company's units. Against the resistance of the strong German unions he reduced the workforce by 10 percent.

Schrempp reorganized Daimler-Benz into five divisions that contained 23 business units in the beginning of 1997. The divisions were passenger cars, commercial vehicles, aerospace, services, and directly managed businesses (rail systems, automotive electronics, MTU/Diesel engines); see **Table 1**.

Critics in Germany said that Schrempp was a renegade supporter of "Anglo-Saxon" corporate ethics, who put Daimler-Benz share price before the welfare of workers and disrupted the long-standing social contract between employers and labor by destroying thousands of jobs and squeezing pay and benefits. Schrempp's relations with labor were difficult. His most famous clash with employees came over their sick benefits, which he attempted to cut back in 1996. The decision, not followed by other companies, triggered such an uproar he was forced to back down. On the other hand Schrempp has won praise from investors. So far the results of the restructuring have been impressive. After a record net loss in 1995 of $3.17 billion, one of the biggest annual losses in European corporate history, Daimler posted profits of about $1.6 billion for 1996 and $1.8 billion before a tax credit in 1997.

DAIMLER-BENZ AEROSPACE SEGMENT

In the aerospace business Daimler became more productive and efficient. Three of 10 plants were closed and new production methods helped to reduce cycle time between plane order and delivery by 50 percent. Schrempp also decided to stop financing the company's struggling Dutch airline maker, NV Fokker, and write off the entire investment. In the process Schrempp proved to be a master of boardroom politics. He acknowledged his role in buying the company a few years earlier and asked for a vote of confidence from the board. The board backed him in full. "I am the first top man who has blown out 2.3 billion marks (by investing in 51 percent of Fokker) and to say without a doubt, this was my fault. While other managers have been fired for 50 million marks, I'm still here. And I think I'm not even arrogant—just very self assured."[7]

In addition, Airbus started a new effort to capture market share from the world leader Boeing. Key to this plan was to enlarge the Airbus family of planes, bringing out new models that ate into categories where Boeing had an effective monopoly. This new strategy combined with strong airline orders and the weak German mark resulted in Airbus's recovery. In 1997 orders rose nearly 50 percent to an all-time high of 460 planes, valued at nearly $30 billion, giving Airbus 45 percent of the world market. As a result Daimler's Benz's aerospace division (DASA) reported 1997 operating profits of DM432 million on revenues of DM 15,286 million after posting losses in 1995 and 1996.

DAIMLER-BENZ COMMERCIAL VEHICLE SEGMENT

When Schrempp took over, the truck business had been hurt by a combination of weak European markets, fierce price competition from Volvo and Scania, Daimler's outmoded truck and bus design, and the company's high-cost production methods. In Europe, Daimler addressed these problems through production of a series of new heavy-duty trucks, lighter trucks, and vans. In addition, the company went face-to-face with its unions, stretching the boundaries of Germany's collective bargaining agreements to the limit to negotiate productivity agreements plant by plant.

Many truck operations were relocated to places like Turkey and Brazil so that roughly half of all Daimler truck production was outside Germany. Daimler's U.S. truck operation, Freightliner, was in a different position. The company had been boosting market share since the early 1990s. Freightliner's share in the North American market in heavy-duty Class 8 tractor-trailer cabs rose from 23 percent in 1995 to 29 percent in 1996, and 30 percent in 1997. The aim was to increase the share to more than 40 percent by 2000. The effort was helped by the 1997 purchase of Ford Heavy Trucks. The decision to buy Ford's heavy-duty truck operations took only two weeks. "Under the previous system it would have taken six to eight months," said Schrempp.[8]

DAIMLER-BENZ PASSENGER CAR SEGMENT

The automotive division was hurt in the early 1990s by the new luxury cars introduced by Toyota's Lexus, Honda's Acura, and Nissan's Infiniti. These cars compared in quality, comfort,

[7]Andrea Rothman, and Rupert Spiegelberg, "Flamboyant Daimler Executive Is Famous for His Risk-Taking," *Seattle Times,* May 7, 1998, p. D1.

[8]Greg Steinmetz and Brandon Mitchener, "Under Schrempp, Daimler Switches Focus to Cars, Profit," *The Wall Street Journal,* May 7, 1998, p. B1.

and styling to Mercedes cars, but they cost much less. Part of the price difference was due to exchange rates, which gave the Japanese a temporary advantage. Germany's high labor costs hurt Daimler too. At more than $30 an hour plus benefits the labor cost was the world's highest. Daimler also suffered from antiquated and inefficient production methods. By one account, while it took 20 man-hours to build a Lexus, it took between 60 and 80 hours to make a Mercedes. The wakeup call from Japan was not ignored by Mercedes, but there was considerable resistance to change at the top and progress was slow. One of Schrempp's first moves after being appointed chairman was, as with the truck operations, to face down the powerful unions and hammer out new plant contracts that would boost productivity and cut costs.

Car Segment Growth Strategy and Models

Mercedes-Benz specialized in top-quality luxury vehicles, and even the company's middle-class cars were choice models costing more than comparably sized competitors. Schrempp was convinced that, to survive, Mercedes had to grow. Growth, he figured, meant expanding down market. The basic aim was to lessen the company's dependence on pricey models like the S-class. Mercedes' strategy was not to enter the mass market, but rather to establish premium niches within every part of it—a niche for people who will pay premium for prestige and perceived quality. In essence, Mercedes was trying to enter the mass market without becoming part of it, a feat Mercedes managed to pull off with its C-Class, unveiled in 1982. With that example in mind, Schrempp put his authority behind the M-class sport utility vehicle, the A-class town car, and the Smart car joint venture with Swatch. In addition to that he extended the existing product lines in the E-class, the C-class, and the S-Class by introducing new models. As Schrempp saw things, the common factor of all these cars is that they serve not a mass market but a niche of people who are prepared to pay extra for perceived quality and the Mercedes name. That, he figured, offered some protection from down auto cycles.

The M-class sport utility vehicle, built in Mercedes' facility in Tuscaloosa, Alabama, opened in 1997, had a list price starting at about $35,000, and competed with the likes of the Ford Explorer and the Jeep Grand Cherokee. This facility was Mercedes' first major foray into car making outside Germany. The M-class was very successful since its launch in late 1997. In early 1998 a potential buyer had to wait up to eight months for delivery. There were plans to increase the production capacity of the Alabama plant by 20 percent in 1999 from 65,000 to 80,000 units a year, with some designated for export to Europe.

The A-class, a small commuter car that so far had only been marketed in Europe, had been surrounded by controversy from the beginning. It was the least expensive Mercedes to sell to date (at about $14,000), it was small, and had only an 82-horsepower engine. Most of the controversy stemmed from the fact that the car failed to pass the so-called "Elk test" performed by Swedish auto journalists, a no-brakes, high-speed violent swerve to simulate avoiding a large animal that had wandered out on the highway. The front-wheel-drive car flipped over, threatening Daimler with a huge marketing disaster. Daimler's stock dropped on the news by 25 percent to a low of $63, and the company was forced to back down from blaming the journalists. Schrempp put together a task force of what he called "our most brilliant people" to come up with a solution. Nineteen days later, they released a plan that included a halt on all A-class sales and a change in the car design to lower the chassis, put on wider tires and install "electronic stabilizing runners" on the inside of the wheel, at a cost of $200 million. By January 1998, after the changes had been made the car passed the test and sales resumed. Daimler estimated that it could sell the 150,000 A-class cars that it could make in a year. After fixing the problems with the A-class and posting healthy 1997 results, the shares recovered and resumed their ascent. Schrempp knew he was walking a tightrope: "If we make a mistake, it would not only affect the profitability of the A-class, it would have a negative impact on Mercedes generally."[9] By 1999 Mercedes hoped to be producing 200,000 A-Class vehicles in Germany and another 70,000 in a new $400 million plant in Brazil.

The Smart car—which was being built by Daimler but was not a Mercedes—was the product of a 81/19 percent joint venture of Daimler-Benz and SMH AG, the Swiss maker of Swatch watches. The car was a tiny two-seater designed for city use. It was not expected to sell in the United States. This car would be built in a new factory in France (annual capacity of 200,000 units).

Daimler had also introduced a stream of new models including the new E-Class, wagons for the C-Class, and the new SLK, a small roadster, which had a steel roof that retracted into the trunk. This car, which was selling at $40,000, followed BMW's Z3 and Porsche's Boxster to open up a completely new sports car niche in the United States—somewhere between the $20,000 Mazda Miata and a $70,000 Porsche 911. The SLK pursued a more youthful image for Mercedes. Waiting lists for this car were as long as two years in the middle of 1997. In 1997 Daimler introduced its CLK coupe, followed by a CLK convertible. In 1998 Daimler was expected to introduce an all-new luxury S-class model, followed perhaps in 2001 or 2002 by the Maybach, an even more luxurious car which (the prototype suggested) could come with such features as a hot-and-cold drink bar, an in-car personal computer, and a large-screen TV.

Passenger car sales by model and by geographic area are shown in **Table 2**.

In 1997, global automotive sales increased by only 3 percent; however, Daimler sales increased by 11 percent, one of the biggest increases of any major automaker. This success was primarily due to the market success of the new vehicles and favorable exchange rates.

Daimler-Benz Car Segment Design and Production

To achieve its goal of producing cheaper cars without penalizing profitability, Daimler was breaking the rules on how to succeed in the auto business. Conventional wisdom suggested that automakers should reduce the number of different platforms on which they build different chassis. That was what Toyota, Chrysler, and VW had done. But Mercedes was producing a new platform for each of its new car lines and expected money on each at a production level that was below the breakeven point for the bigger full line manufacturers. By sharing platforms "it is certainly cost effective, but I don't think it's the way to do it. If you just put a different

---

[9]Paul Klebnikov, "Mercedes-Benz' Bold Niche Strategy," *Forbes,* September 8, 1997, p. 68.

TABLE 2
Daimler-Benz Passenger Car Sales 1997

	Units ('000)	% Change from 1996	Price Category
World	715	11	
A-Class	7		$14,000
C-Class	349	24	$35,000
CLK	22		$40,000
SLK	47		
E-Class	277	−5	
S-/SL-Class	63	−8	$65,000
M-Class	16		$34,000
G-Class	3	−23	
Europe	477	8	
Western Europe (w/o Germany)	194	11	
Germany	277	5	
North America	130	40	
USA (retail sales)	122	35	
Latin America	7	11	
Far East (excl. Japan)	28	−7	
Japan (new registrations)	42	2	
Middle East	9	1	
Republic of South Africa	12	−18	

TABLE 3
Vehicle Operations by Geographic Area

	Production Locations	Sales Organization Locations	Revenues (mill. DM)	Personnel
Europe	21	3,435	55,966	171,778
North America	10	655	19,190	15,321
South America	4	468	4,683	13,128
Africa	3	272	3,077	3,815
Australia/Oceania	1	186	1,044	682
Asia	7	931	7,672	2,618

body on the same base, all you are doing is fooling customers. That's not the way to win sales," said Schrempp.[10] Daimler-Benz reduced its level of vertical integration, but at 40 percent Daimler was still more vertically integrated than Chrysler at 25 percent.

Daimler-Benz Car Segment International Strategy

Daimler sold its cars worldwide and had a global distribution network. Daimler was also increasingly locating automotive production outside Germany, as shown in **Table 3**. More

---

[10]Jay Palmer, "Shake-Up Artist: Daimler-Benz Chairman Juergen Schrempp Has Knocked the Dust Off Mercedes, Restoring Hope for European Manufacturers," *Barron's,* March 23, 1998, p. 35.

than two-thirds of Daimler's total revenues originated outside Germany, and more than one-third of its stock was held internationally.

OWNERSHIP OF DAIMLER-BENZ EQUITY

Deutsche Bank had cut its interest in Daimler from 28 percent to 21.7 percent. Deutsche Bank had at times taken the lead in strategic decisions at Daimler. It engineered the appointment of Edzard Reuter as chairman of Daimler's management board in 1987 and supported Daimler's diversification strategy in the 1980s. German institutional investors held about 48 percent of Daimler's shares. The Emirate of Kuwait owned about 13 percent.

Unlike the single boards found in the United States, German companies had a management board (Vorstand), composed solely of executives charged with a company's day-to-day operations, and a supervisory board (Aufsichtsrat), which represented a company's largest shareholders and its workers and oversaw the management board. The system gave each board certain checks and balances so that neither dominated the firm.

DAIMLER-BENZ LABOR UNIONS

Germany had a dual system of worker representation. At the company level, workers had the right to participate in management decisions. Under the German system of codetermination, almost half of the seats of the supervisory board (Aufsichtsrat) had to be filled with labor representatives in large enterprises. While they could be outvoted in the supervisory board, their access to information and decision making gave them a stronger hand in labor negotiations. Worker councils (Betriebsräte) also represented the interests of the workers at the company level. They had a voice in social and personnel matters.

At the national level, 17 large labor unions, which were organized on an industry basis, were primarily responsible for industrywide collective bargaining of wages and salaries, and other matters, such as shortening of the workweek and vacation time. IG Metall, the powerful metalworkers union, which had 2.7 million members, represented automobile industry workers.

Compared to other countries the collective bargaining process for wages was accompanied by relatively few strikes in Germany. Reasons contributing to this low strike rate were the existing conflict resolution mechanism as well as German labor law that obliged management and labor groups to seek peaceful solutions to conflicts, as well as generally cooperative relationships between capital and labor.

EXECUTIVE COMPENSATION

Compensation for German executives was significantly lower than for their American counterparts. Executive pay in German firms had to be reviewed by the supervisory board of a company. In addition, German companies were not required to disclose executive pay to the same extent as U.S companies were required by the U.S. Securities and Exchange Commission. Daimler disclosed pay only on an aggregate basis and reported that in 1997 the 10 executives on the management board received total remuneration of DM20 million,[11] or $11.3 million at a recent exchange rate of DM 1.77 to the dollar. Schrempp currently made about $2.5 million a year. In comparison, Chrysler chairman and CEO Robert Eaton made $16 million in 1997.

Under Schrempp, Daimler was the first German company to offer stock options to its executives. The union members on the supervisory board opposed Schrempp's decision to offer stock options to management but he prevailed on an 11–9 vote within the board. Another proposal, to create an incentive pay plan that rewarded employees based on their contribution to overall profits, passed more easily. All 150,000 Mercedes workers would qualify for a bonus.

TRENDS IN THE GLOBAL AUTOMOBILE INDUSTRY

As of early 1998, recent events suggested that the competitive landscape of the automobile industry had changed permanently. While the announcement of alliances and mergers was a steady occurrence over the years, the nature and frequency of these deals had become more intense. Price Waterhouse estimated that worldwide in 1997, auto firms struck 750 mergers or alliances with a total value of $28 billion. Consistent with both the airlines and the telecommunications industries, there was a more assertive attempt to consolidate players in the industry, thereby creating a new form of competition—the truly global car company. Presently, only a small number of automakers, like Toyota, VW, Ford, and GM, had the capability to go global without major acquisitions. These first-tier firms could pursue a worldwide strategy by buying smaller producers with recognized name brands. The mantra became "if you wish to succeed, you have to be worldwide." Standard & Poor's DRI predicted that over the next 10 years there would be a reduction in the number of international producers with the current 39 being reduced to about 20 major companies.

Car manufacturers had been operating internationally for many years. They had exported models to other countries, assembled and engineered cars and trucks for foreign markets, and sourced from non-U.S. suppliers for years. In addition, these firms had taken equity stakes in numerous foreign partners. The list included, for example, Ford and Jaguar, Ford and Mazda, GM and Saab, GM and Suzuki, and BMW and Rover. Yet, efforts to form truly global companies were different. Simply, there were few successes at building and distributing a *global car*. The motivations driving Chrysler and Daimler-Benz extended beyond the development of a global car. Typically, consolidation was driven by a series of factors.

These factors were all responses to the pressures of a dynamic, changing industry. It was too simple to say that the world was changing. There were relentless cost and time pres-

---

[11]Daimler-Benz 1997 Annual Report, p. 80.

sures where the design and introduction of new and innovative models must be completed in shorter time periods and less expensively. Adding to the complexity was the fact that consumer tastes were changing, the Internet lowered barriers to information transfer, product introduction, and commonality among processes and products became the path to the bottom line.[12] At the extreme, there was talk about the era of the virtual customer who was integrated into a manufacturing process that was fed by global suppliers and that fed into worldwide distribution. However, there were a number of recent trends that appeared to lie at the heart of the recent consolidation wave.

Overcapacity

The industry was plagued by excess capacity. Through consolidation, assembly plants could be rationalized. Car makers in Western Europe already had the capacity to produce 30 percent more cars than they could sell.[13] The result was idle equipment, wasted investments, underutilized workers, and subnormal returns. The tension around these decisions was the political pressure against shutting domestic plants, laying off workers, and searching for lower cost labor and manufacturing sites in developing countries. Ironically, this movement of manufacturing to developing countries partly exacerbated the problem of excess capacity. Many of the plants, for example, in Asia had been built with government blessing as an attempt to promote manufacturing and create fairly high-paying jobs, not to mention that a home-grown auto industry was a matter of national pride. Emerging economies like Brazil saw an automotive industry as a means to increase its ability to export product and stimulate internal growth. Yet, a number of the smaller companies in Asia particularly were at risk, like Kia and Hyundai. While not acquisition targets per se, both were likely to be sought as joint venture partners. Many believed that the consolidation would take out capacity, which would reduce the pricing pressures that were being caused by the worldwide excess production capacity.

Development Costs

The costs associated with all aspects of new model development made it very difficult for a small manufacturer to survive since these costs were allocated over a smaller volume of cars. Development costs included design and tooling, emissions engineering, electronics, and manufacturing process design. Other nonproduction costs associated with manufacturing included the expense of linking suppliers and dealers electronically and on a global basis. Attempts to shorten the production and the design cycles would pay off over time but also require a substantial initial investment. A dramatic redesign of a car could include the use of lighter weight materials, the use of alternative fuel sources, and changes to both the engine and the braking system. The price tag for these changes would make even the largest companies worried.

---

[12]David Smith, "US Automakers Take a New Spin; the World Has Changed and So Have They," *Ward's Auto World* 3, vol. 34, p. 38.

[13]"Anne Swardson, European Carmakers' Traffic Jam," *Washington Post,* September 10, 1998, section C1.

Sourcing and Supply Chain Costs

In part the consolidation in the industry was driven by a desire to lower the costs of purchased materials by combining purchasing functions and exercising greater power as a result. Typically, firms attempted to reap price concessions from suppliers based on sheer volume. Beyond the savings that accrued through volume, there were gains to be made in the use of common parts. When Chrysler began purchasing the same air-bag part from Robert Bosch, who previously supplied Mercedes, the cost to both fell 40 percent, since Bosch could now justify dedicated production in Mexico. Smart sourcing also had a component that affected the revenue side of the equation in that by working more closely with key suppliers, car makers could leverage their suppliers' expertise and other sources of competitive advantages. Honda, for example, attributed significant gains in its ability to design and produce new models at lower costs to the input and expertise of its key suppliers.

Market Access and Product Diversity

The ability of niche manufacturers to survive over the long term was limited both by geography and the narrow focus of their product line. At the core of merger discussions in the automotive industry of the 1990s was the notion of complementarity and the potential partners' ability to fill gaps in both markets and products. One assumption was that only full product line, global producers would survive. Market access was affected both by existing distribution networks and the national policy dictating the manner in which a foreign automaker could enter the host country. In some instances, local production might be required, or there might be rules regarding a certain percentage of local content in the cars sold. Although the merger failed, part of the rationale for the Volvo-Renault marriage was a complementarity in market presence. In addition, the product lines did not overlap much and on the surface seemed to fill gaps in the other's offerings. BMW was attracted to Rover because its products broadened its product offering without diluting the up-market BMW image with smaller cars and sports utility vehicles. BMW's strategy was to encourage Rover's *Britishness* with big investments in the United Kingdom while sharing parts and improving quality and distribution.[14]

Legal and Financial Considerations

It was likely that the consolidation among companies would provide access to capital and capital markets that might have been limited either because of regional biases or size considerations. To be global in scope and size not only bestowed more favorable rates on the issuance of stock or debt, but broadened the range of available financial markets. For instance, as a benefit of consolidation a foreign-based company might trade in the United States as a global stock rather than through the use of ADRs that carried both complex regulatory issues and often added expense. The point was that such global firms set the pace for the globalization of the equity markets. In addition, a second-order effect was the governance structure of the newly consolidated company and the question of which country's laws took precedence. There might be less governmental control and say in how the newly

---

[14]Brandon Mitchener, "BMW-Rover Deal Offers Clues to Future Daimler-Benz," *The Wall Street Journal Interactive,* May 29, 1998.

TABLE 4
Potential Benefits to both Chrysler and Daimler-Benz

Benefits to Chrysler	Shared Benefits	Benefits to Daimler-Benz
• Boost nonexistent position in Europe • Improved quality from D-B engineering • Gives a European manufacturing base • Might gain from luster of Mercedes nameplate • Broadens line to luxury end • Use some production capacity around the world • Improve technical capability, lower warranty costs • Improved safety features available	• $1.4 billion in pretax cost savings, expected in 1999; expected to grow to $3.0 billion in 2001 and to grow at rate of inflation thereafter • Purchasing power • Better capacity utilization • Technology transfer	• Expand manufacturing and dealership operations in United States • Create opportunity for joint development, at lower costs • Expand U.S. production ability • Combine with trucks, the lighter lines from Chrysler • Helps align cost structure • Borrow creative styling • Jeep adds to the image for SUV (urban and rugged)

formed global firm could behave as compared to when the individual companies were separate entities. To some extent, competing on the world scene might reduce the regulatory power/influence of local national governments.

For Chrysler and Daimler-Benz, there were a number of gains to be achieved through their merger. **Table 4** summarizes the advantages to both. The question remained whether each gained equally. Although Schrempp and Eaton contemplated a "merger of equals," creating the third largest automaker in the world, Daimler-Benz might appear to be the more senior partner because of its size.

STRATEGIC ALTERNATIVES

As companies examined the options available to them to join forces and attempted to accomplish goals that would be difficult to achieve alone, there were a number of alternatives to consider. The automotive industry had, in recent years, witnessed a number of alliances (some in which equity stakes were taken and others where there was no exchange of ownership), joint ventures, mergers, and acquisitions.

Merger In a merger, companies (such as Chrysler and Daimler-Benz) agreed to an exchange of stock that resulted in the joint ownership of a new company. Typically, the two companies, in a friendly exchange of stock, combined to achieve cost savings through the elimination of redundant facilities and other mechanisms through which cost savings were gained. In addition, they often pursued opportunities that would be hard to achieve alone. Schrempp and Eaton expected, for example, to realize pretax cost savings of $1.4 billion in 1999 through the exchange of components and technology, combined purchasing, and shared distribution networks. Eaton's staff believed that these synergies would grow to $3.0 billion by 2001, and grow at the rate of inflation in the U.S. dollar thereafter. (These synergies are *not* reflected in the exhibits which accompany this case.) There were also a number of other benefits that resulted as both partners learned from each other, and incorporated the best practices of both in the merged company.

Alliances Unlike a merger, an alliance combined separate companies for the purposes of the collaborative efforts delineated by the partners. However, the separate organizations remained autonomous businesses, each retaining its own governance structure and operating processes and principles. Joint activities, shared decision making, coordination of activities, open lines of communications, and so forth were all part of the glue that held the alliance together. An alliance was a quasi-organizational form in which separate and distinct firms joined to accomplish goals that would be difficult to achieve alone. The challenge was to develop a management process to encourage the joint cooperative efforts of the partners. To the extent that one entered an alliance with a traditional "command and control" mentality, one would find that it could be difficult to accomplish one's ends. One could not control what one did not own. Alliances, if properly formed and nurtured, could accomplish the same goals as one might in a vertically integrated firm without the added cost burden. Alliances were collaborative ventures in which companies acknowledged their interdependence and acted in the interest of the alliance. Unlike a merged, or acquired entity, there remained the possibility of opportunistic behavior whereby one partner acted in its own self-interest to the detriment of the other. That is, alliance partners had multiple tasks: they worked together to accomplish joint goals but also maintained individual agendas and objectives. When these different goals conflicted, the alliance suffered and the proposed advantages were lost. In this regard alliances were quite fragile and were subject to pressures and tensions not found in ventures where two or more firms relinquished their sovereignty to become one centrally managed and controlled organization with one set of goals. Although alliance contracts were likely to be used to formalize the terms and conditions of the relationship, alliances were held together by trust and commitment to the shared vision of the alliance partners.

Joint ventures Joint ventures (JV) were another form of alliance in which partners joined selected assets and formed a separate entity which became jointly owned by the partners. One primary difference between JV alliances and the alliance forms discussed above was the degree of embeddedness between the partners. JV partners had committed resources (e.g., people, factories, dollars, technology) and these assets became comingled in the joint venture, and their ability to exit the relationship was often more tedious. Also, joint ventures tended to have more formal agreements between partners based mainly on the fact that partners have formally comingled assets in this newly formed separate entity. There was a joint governance structure for the JV that is jointly administered by the partners depending on their equity-sharing agreement. While most managers believed they would prefer to be the dominant shareholder (e.g., equity interest in excess of 50 percent), there was a compelling argument for equal equity sharing joint ventures. This argument was based on the belief that equal share in the JV led to greater commitment and a willingness on the part of the partners to work hard to overcome problems in the JV. Again, the elements of trust and commitment were important and served to complement the joint venture agreement that nominally set the structure of the relationships.

Joint venture partners sometimes struggled in their ability to equitably determine the value of each partner's contribution to the alliance. For example, one partner might bring hard assets to the JV and the other might bring intellectual capability (e.g., innovations, technology, knowledge of markets). The problem would then become how to determine a fair exchange rate. Simply, the question might arise how many new ideas equaled a factory worth $5 million to convert to the needs of the joint venture.

Preferred Relationships Of the four relationship types discussed here, preferred relationships were the least formal and therefore the most volatile in the sense that they were viewed as more transactional in nature and more subject to the whims of the partners. Ties and linkages tended to be loose and viewed as less long term in nature. For instance, parties might decide to trade with each other, and to do so for many years. However, the level of communications and the content of information shared never went beyond the transaction at hand. In an alliance, as opposed to these more arms-length dealings, partners tended to exchange information germane to longer-term plans and strategic requirements over time. Preferred relationships suggested that all things being equal, partners would continue to interact but there was a much less episodic nature to the relationship. Commitment to the relationship tended to be lower than in any of the other relationships mentioned above. These kinds of relationships were often found between buyers and suppliers where one was given the status of a preferred supplier by virtue of certain standards being met (e.g., certification and ISO9002). In addition, there might exist a long-term relationship through which both parties shared a degree of comfort and trust. At the same time, the ability to disengage was relatively easy to do both because of the nature of the linkages and the fact that the psychological bonds between partners was relatively low.

Table 5 compares the various relationship types discussed here.

Chrysler's negotiation team would need to assess these alternative forms of combination, giving particular attention to the relative attractiveness of the outright acquisition of Chrysler by Daimler versus the other types of deals. Schrempp had specifically mentioned an acquisition; it was Robert Eaton's expectation that the negotiating team would seriously

TABLE 5
An Array of Relationships

	← Low	Ownership	High →		
Commitment HIGH **Long-term focus**	Strategic Sourcing		Joint Ventures	Joint Venture	Acquisition Merger
	Evergreen contracts	Just-in-time and standard outsourcing	R&D partnerships to co-develop	Co-manufacturing/ production	
			Shared info about mkts/R&D		
	Preferred suppliers	Reseller relationships			
Commitment LOW **Short-term focus**	Commodity purchasing order	Collaborative advertising			
Degree of Commitment					Wholly owned
	Loose linkages	Standard resources	Shared funds	Shared equity	

explore this path as a first course of action. But ultimately, Chrysler's Board of Directors would want some justification for why outright acquisition dominated other types of deals as a way to exploit the benefits of combination.

HISTORY OF THE MERGER DISCUSSIONS[15]

At the Detroit International Auto Show in mid-January 1998, Jürgen Schrempp, CEO of Daimler-Benz, visited with Robert Eaton, chairman and CEO of Chrysler. Schrempp discussed with Eaton some of his thoughts about the likelihood of consolidation in the worldwide automotive industry and suggested it might be mutually beneficial if Daimler-Benz and Chrysler were to consider a merger. Eaton indicated that Chrysler had been conducting its own studies of the industry and had similar views. Eaton said that he would telephone Schrempp within the next couple of weeks. Toward the end of January, Robert Eaton telephoned Jürgen Schrempp to suggest a meeting early in February. On February 5, 1998, the Chrysler board was briefed on the discussion between Schrempp and Eaton.

On February 12, 1998, Robert Eaton and Gary Valade, executive vice president and chief financial officer of Chrysler, met with Schrempp and Dr. Eckhard Cordes, the Daimler-Benz board member responsible for Corporate Development and Directly Managed Businesses, to discuss the possibility of combining the two companies. Following this discussion they decided to consult with their respective financial advisors and to meet again on February 18, 1998.

On February 17 and 18, 1998, Cordes and representatives of Goldman Sachs (the merger adviser to Daimler) met with Valade and representatives of Crédit Suisse First Boston (the merger adviser to Chrysler) to discuss various transaction structures. During the course of these discussions, Valade stated that it was important to Chrysler that any potential transaction maximize value for its stockholders, that it be tax-free to Chrysler's U.S. stockholders and tax efficient for DaimlerChrysler A.G, that it have the post-merger governance structure of a "merger-of-equals," that it have the optimal ability to be accounted for as a pooling-of-interests, that it result in the combination of the respective businesses of Daimler-Benz and Chrysler into one public company. Cordes indicated that it was important to Daimler-Benz that any potential transaction maximize value for its stockholders, that it be tax-free to Daimler-Benz's German stockholders and tax efficient for DaimlerChrysler A.G. and that the surviving entity of any combination be a German stock corporation, thereby enhancing the likelihood of acceptance of the transactions by all important constituencies of Daimler-Benz. During these meetings, various tax, corporate, and management issues were discussed with a view to developing a transaction structure that would accommodate the parties' objectives.

Valade and Cordes were scheduled to meet again in the first week of March to discuss the progress of their working teams. At this time, Valade requested that Daimler-Benz provide Chrysler with its preliminary thoughts on valuation.

---

[15]This section draws details from the F-4 Registration statement by Chrysler Corporation, submitted to the U.S. Securities and Exchange Commission.

TABLE 6
Key Valuation Results

	US$/Share	
Valuation of Chrysler's Equity		
Recent share price	$ 40.75	
Book value per share	$ 16.82	
DCF Estimates with Terminal Values using:	*Multiples (1)*	*Constant Growth (2)*
WACC approach	$ 64.53	$64.34
Equity residual approach	$ 60.71	$60.67
Adjusted present value	$ 70.34	$70.34
Multiples Estimates using Industry Averages (see Ex. 13)		
Price/Earnings times forward EPS	$ 76.76	
Price/Cash flow times forward CF opns.	$101.58	
Market/Book value times book value	$ 38.00	
Valuation of Daimler's Equity		
Recent share price	$ 99.63	
Book value per share	$ 68.03	
DCF Estimates with Terminal Values using:	*Multiples (1)*	*Constant Growth (2)*
WACC approach	$ 86.95	$86.12
Equity residual approach	$ 55.79	$57.20
Adjusted present value	$ 82.84	$82.84
Multiples Estimates using Industry Averages (see Ex. 13)		
Price/Earnings times forward EPS	$ 60.06	
Price/Cash flow times forward CF opns.	$ 85.21	
Market/Book value times book value	$153.71	

(1) Terminal value multiples for Chrysler are 4 times EBITDA for the WACC and APV approaches, and 8.5 times earnings for the P/E approach. For Daimler, the multiples are 6.5 and 16.
(2) Constant growth rates used in estimating terminal values are 3% for Chrysler, and 4% for Daimler.

VALUATION AND EPS ANALYSIS

Exhibits 2 through **9** present forecasts of financial statements for both companies, as well as discounted cash flow valuations using the free cash flow/WACC approach. The analysts' financial model actually estimated value using three DCF approaches (WACC, adjusted present value, and equity residual), and used two ways to estimate terminal values (constantly growing perpetuities, and multiples of earnings). Analysts could also consider the firms' current stock price, latest book value, and valuations based on various industry average multiples. **Table 6** summarizes the estimates of value of Chrysler and Daimler shares in U.S. dollars.

The Chrysler deal team would also need to consider the financial reporting impact of any deal structure. Merely for illustration, **Exhibit 10** summarizes the calculations of earnings per share dilution that might result from a share-for-share exchange. This illustration assumes an exchange ratio of one share of Daimler stock per one share of Chrysler stock, and reveals earnings dilution of 25.6 percent in 1997 for Daimler, followed by earnings accretion in subsequent years. In contrast, if the merger were accounted for as a purchase, Daimler's earnings dilution for 1997 would be 34.2 percent. **Exhibit 10** also shows that Chrysler would contribute 46.9 percent of Newco's revenues, and 60.8 percent of its EBITDA.

Exhibits 11 and **12** present the longer-term financial and stock price histories of both companies in the form of reports from *Value Line Investment Survey.* **Exhibit 13** gives information on peer firms in the automobile manufacturing industry. **Exhibit 14** gives the recent stock price history of both firms, as well as estimates of their betas, and sigmas, or percentage volatility of their stock prices, based on trading on the New York Stock Exchange. **Exhibit 15** presents details on the debt capitalization of both firms. **Exhibit 16** gives information on recent mergers and acquisitions activity; **Exhibit 17** offers details on a selection of acquisitions in the automobile industry. **Exhibit 18** presents data on recent macroeconomic trends in the United States and Germany. **Exhibit 19** gives information on capital market conditions prevailing in the United States and Germany at the end of February 1998.

NEGOTIATION OF DETAILED ACQUISITION TERMS

Gary Valade and the Chrysler negotiating team could contemplate a variety of dimensions for the deal:

- **Price or value.** How much value should Chrysler shareholders receive in consideration for the sale of their firm?
- **Form of payment.** Initially, Eaton and Schrempp had contemplated a stock-for-stock transaction. However, once the negotiators got into the detailed deal design, there was a possibility that the deal could be structured in terms of cash for stock or fixed income securities for stock. Indeed, some sort of contingent payment could be included in the consideration given for Chrysler's shares. If a stock-for-stock deal were proposed, the two sides would need to state an explicit *exchange ratio* indicating how many shares of Daimler were to be received for one share of Chrysler. A separate ratio might indicate the exchange of employee stock options for the buyer's shares, though ordinarily this was based on the assumption of the option into stock, and therefore was not necessarily required. A related issue was whether the exchange ratio was to be fixed, or could vary within limits as the stock prices of Daimler and Chrysler varied up to the date of closing. It might take six months to consummate an acquisition of this size, once the merger announcement was made. These limits, popularly called a *collar,* defined the range within which the stock prices of the two firms would be allowed to vary before any adjustment in the deal terms might be made. If the negotiators agreed to a collar, it would be necessary to specify the limits within which the stock prices could vary without triggering an adjustment in the exchange ratio, and the adjustments to be made if the stock prices exceeded those limits.
- **Merger or acquisition.** The transaction could be structured as a "merger of equals," or as an acquisition of one firm by another. The Chrysler side was mainly interested in a merger of equals. Shareholders might be influenced in their voting by the appearance of one firm dominating the other, regardless of the economic reality of the deal.
- **Need for shareholder vote.** Shareholder voting provisions influenced deal design in that they affected the speed with which the deal could be closed, and the possibility

for interference by large shareholder groups. In the United States, a vote of the share-holders required the distribution of a prospectus and proxy statement and the scheduling of a special shareholder meeting. The concern about interference was typically important for acquirers, who feared "second-guessing" by investors or outsiders. Two types of deals would require votes by Daimler shareholders. The first was where a large number of new shares would be created, as in a large stock-for-stock acquisition. The second was a "statutory" merger in which both firms would be extinguished and an entirely new firm ("Newco") would emerge—this would require a vote of both firms shareholders.

- **Accounting treatment.** In the United States, merging firms could account for the merger on a *purchase* basis, or a *pooling-of-interests* basis. Generally, pooling accounting resulted in higher earnings per share for the new firm, because it did not entail the creation of "goodwill" that had to be amortized under U.S. Generally Accepted Accounting Principles (GAAP). In order for the transaction to be accounted for on a pooling basis, it had to meet several tests, of which the primary ones were: (a) continuity of ownership interests (at least 80 percent of the previous shareholders of the acquired firm had to remain as shareholders of the new firm); (b) equal size of the two firms; (c) each entity must have been independent of the other for two years prior to the deal; (d) the combination must be effected in a single transaction—contingent payouts were not permitted in pooling transactions; (e) the acquiring firm must issue only common stock in exchange for substantially all the voting common stock of the other company (e.g., 90 percent); and (f) the new firm must not dispose of a significant portion of assets within two years after merger.

- **Treatment for major shareholders.** Deutsche Bank, the largest German financial institution, held a 21.7 percent interest in Daimler-Benz. Deutsche Bank held several seats on (and the chairmanship of) Daimler's board, and was instrumental in appointing Jürgen Schrempp as CEO in 1994 in a push for shareholder value maximization. Also the Emirate of Kuwait held 13 percent of Daimler's stock. Kirk Kerkorian held approximately 14 percent of Chrysler's stock through his holding company, Tracinda Corporation. In 1994 and 1995, Kerkorian had threatened Chrysler with a hostile takeover attempt, claiming the firm was underperforming and that it was sitting on too much cash ($8 billion). Chrysler fended off Kerkorian's advances with promises to increase the dividend, accelerate share repurchases, and relax the poison pill trigger from 10 to 15 percent of shares outstanding. While Kerkorian had agreed to a "standstill" on his attempts to take over the firm, his interest was large enough to influence other investors in any Chrysler shareholder vote on a deal. Kerkorian was known to be a sophisticated investor, who would probably favor a tax-deferred deal. Deutsche Bank, the Emirate of Kuwait, and Kerkorian would emerge from a stock-for-stock acquisition as significant shareholders in the new firm. Therefore, it would be advisable to obtain the advance support of these interested parties.

- **Tax treatment.** Some deal structures could trigger an immediate tax liability for the selling (Chrysler) shareholders, on the difference between the cost basis of their shares, and the consideration received. Other structures would defer this liability. Generally, the tax-deferred deals (or "tax-free" deals, as popularly called) entailed the acquisition of the target firm's stock with the stock of the buyer, or the buyer's subsidiary. Deals that entailed payment with cash or notes, or that entailed the purchase of assets, would trigger an immediate tax liability. An opinion of a tax advisor, and ultimately, a ruling (or "letter") from the United States Internal Revenue Service would confirm whether any contemplated structure was to be taxable or tax-free.

- **Applicable law.** The new corporation could be incorporated in Germany or the United States. If incorporated in Germany, it would be subject to German law. If incorporated in the United States, the U.S. law would apply.

- **Governance.** The merger agreement would need to specify the location of headquarters, treatment of workers (especially, the distribution of board seats to Daimler's principal labor union, IG Metall, or to the United Auto Workers), the election of directors generally, and the individual to be named CEO of the firm. Under the German Co-Determination Law of 1976, a firm of Daimler's size would have a supervisory board (much like an American Board of Directors) and a management board. German law required a supervisory board of 20 members, 10 of whom were appointed by shareholders, and the others by employees—German law specifically required that corporations must have 49 percent labor representation on their supervisory boards. The terms of the deal could specify in advance whether and how the Daimler and Chrysler sides were to divide up the 10 supervisory directors, as well as the size and composition (Daimler vs. Chrysler) of the management board.

- **Union recognition.** Daimler operated a nonunionized factory in Alabama. In a combination between Daimler and Chrysler, it was likely that Chrysler's union, the United Auto Workers, would require that the UAW be recognized as the bargaining agent for that plant.

- **Official language.** It was customary in cross-border mergers and acquisitions for the deal terms to specify the official language for the firm, post-consummation.

- **Executive compensation.** The contract might also specify any senior executive compensation for the foreseeable future. This would be important if the analysts sought to equalize the compensation across the newly merged firm.

- **Listing on stock exchanges.** Considering the combined shareholders of both companies, a stock-for-stock deal would leave American and German shareholders with a major interest in a multinational firm. If shares were listed outside the home country of the shareholders, it would make those shares somewhat less liquid, and less attractive. Agreeing in advance on where the shares were to be listed would influence the shareholders in their vote on any merger or acquisition.

EXHIBIT 1
Chrysler Corporation Unit Sales Trends

	1997	1996	Change
U.S. Retail Market:			
Car sales	736,530	832,633	(96,103)
Car market share	8.9%	9.7%	20.8%
Truck sales (including minivans)	1,567,258	1,618,193	(50,935)
Truck market share	21.7%	23.4%	21.7%
Combined car and truck sales	2,303,788	2,450,826	(147,038)
Combined car and truck market share	14.9%	15.9%	21.0%
Minivans only	518,445	—	N.A.
Minivan market share	44.4%	—	N.A.
U.S. and Canada Retail Market:			0.0%
Combined car and truck sales	2,559,950	2,690,340	(130,390)
Combined car and truck market share	15.1%	16.1%	21.0%
North America			
Combined car and truck sales	2,649,542	—	N.A.
Combined car and truck market share			
Worldwide			
Combined car and truck sales	2,886,981	2,958,800	(71,819)
International shipments (outside North America)	237,000	224,000	13,000

Source: Chrysler Corporation Annual Report.

EXHIBIT 2
Chrysler Corporation Income Statement

	1995	1996	1997	1998	1999	2000	2001	2002
					Projected			
Revenues	$53,195.0	$61,397.0	$61,147.0	$64,815.8	$68,704.8	$72,827.1	$77,196.7	$81,828.5
COGS (excluding depreciation)	41,304.0	45,842.0	46,743.0	49,547.6	52,520.4	55,671.7	59,012.0	62,552.7
Selling, general, & administrative	5,227.0	6,144.0	6,145.0	6,513.7	6,904.5	7,318.8	7,757.9	8,223.4
EBITDA	6,664.0	9,411.0	8,259.0	8,754.5	9,279.8	9,836.6	10,426.8	11,052.4
Depreciation	2,220.0	2,312.0	2,696.0	3,194.7	3,406.7	3,631.4	3,869.7	4,122.2
Amortization of goodwill & intangibles	0.0	0.0	0.0	39.3	38.3	37.4	36.4	35.5
Other expense (income)	0.0	0.0	0.0	0.0	0.0	0.0	0.0	0.0
EBIT	4,444.0	7,099.0	5,563.0	5,520.5	5,834.8	6,167.8	6,520.7	6,894.7
Interest (income)	0.0	0.0	0.0	(412.3)	(437.0)	(463.2)	(491.0)	(520.5)
Interest expense—straight debt	995.0	1,007.0	1,006.0	1,014.4	995.3	963.8	932.4	900.9
Interest expense—convertible debt	0.0	0.0	0.0	0.0	0.0	0.0	0.0	0.0
Interest expense—revolver	0.0	0.0	0.0	(11.7)	(66.2)	(147.9)	(225.6)	(305.6)
Pretax income	3,449.0	6,092.0	4,557.0	4,930.1	5,342.7	5,815.1	6,304.9	6,819.9
Income taxes	1,328.0	2,372.0	1,752.0	1,893.2	2,051.6	2,233.0	2,421.1	2,618.9
Minority interest	0.0	0.0	0.0	0.0	0.0	0.0	0.0	0.0
Extraordinary item (income)	96.0	191.0	0.0	0.0	0.0	0.0	0.0	0.0
Net income	2,025.0	3,529.0	2,805.0	3,037.0	3,291.1	3,582.1	3,883.8	4,201.1
Straight preferred dividends	0.0	0.0	0.0	0.0	0.0	0.0	0.0	0.0
Convertible preferred dividends	21.0	3.0	1.0	0.0	0.0	0.0	0.0	0.0
Net income to common	2,004.0	3,526.0	2,804.0	3,037.0	3,291.1	3,582.1	3,883.8	4,201.1
Earnings per share:								
Basic	$2.68	$4.83	$4.15	$5.02	$5.44	$5.92	$6.42	$6.95
Fully diluted	$2.56	$4.74	$4.09	$4.77	$5.17	$5.63	$6.10	$6.60

EXHIBIT 3
Chrysler Corporation Balance Sheets

	1995	1996	1997	1998	1999	2000	2001	2002
					Projected			
Cash and equivalents	8,125.0	7,752.0	7,848.0	8,318.9	8,818.0	9,347.1	9,907.9	10,502.4
Accounts receivable	2,003.0	2,126.0	1,646.0	1,744.8	1,849.4	1,960.4	2,078.0	2,202.7
Inventory	4,448.0	5,195.0	4,738.0	5,022.3	5,323.6	5,643.0	5,981.6	6,340.5
Other current assets	14,608.0	14,268.0	15,711.0	16,653.7	17,652.9	18,712.1	19,834.8	21,024.9
Total current assets	29,184.0	29,341.0	29,943.0	31,739.6	33,644.0	35,662.6	37,802.3	40,070.5
Property, plant, & equipment	20,468.0	23,052.0	27,082.0	31,082.3	35,322.6	39,817.3	44,581.7	49,632.0
Accumulated depreciation	7,873.0	8,147.0	9,114.0	12,308.7	15,715.4	19,346.8	23,216.5	27,338.6
Net property, plant, & equipment	12,595.0	14,905.0	17,968.0	18,773.6	19,607.2	20,470.5	21,365.2	22,293.3
Goodwill & other intangibles	2,082.0	1,995.0	1,573.0	1,533.7	1,495.3	1,457.9	1,421.5	1,386.0
Equity in income of affiliates	0.0	0.0	0.0	0.0	0.0	0.0	0.0	0.0
Other long-term assets	9,895.0	9,943.0	10,934.0	10,934.0	10,934.0	10,934.0	10,934.0	10,934.0
Total assets	53,756.0	56,184.0	60,418.0	62,980.9	65,680.5	68,525.0	71,523.1	74,683.8
Accounts payable	8,290.0	8,981.0	9,512.0	10,082.7	10,687.7	11,328.9	12,008.7	12,729.2
Other current liabilities (excl. S/T debt)	7,032.0	8,864.0	9,717.0	10,300.0	10,918.0	11,573.1	12,267.5	13,003.5
Total current liabilities	15,322.0	17,845.0	19,229.0	20,382.7	21,605.7	22,902.0	24,276.2	25,732.7
Straight debt	14,193.0	13,396.0	15,485.0	15,485.0	15,029.8	14,574.7	14,119.5	13,664.4
Convertible debt	0.0	0.0	0.0	0.0	0.0	0.0	0.0	0.0
Revolver				(377.9)	(1,759.2)	(3,013.1)	(4,263.2)	(5,595.9)
Total debt	14,193.0	13,396.0	15,485.0	15,107.1	13,270.6	11,561.5	9,856.3	8,068.5
Deferred taxes	0.0	0.0	0.0	1,537.2	2,566.2	3,268.4	3,761.4	4,120.8
Minority interest	0.0	0.0	0.0	0.0	0.0	0.0	0.0	0.0
Other long-term liabilities	13,282.0	13,372.0	14,342.0	14,342.0	14,342.0	14,342.0	14,342.0	14,342.0
Total liabilities	42,797.0	44,613.0	49,056.0	51,369.1	51,784.5	52,074.0	52,235.8	52,264.0
Straight preferred stock	0.0	0.0	0.0	0.0	0.0	0.0	0.0	0.0
Convertible preferred stock	0.0	0.0	0.0	0.0	0.0	0.0	0.0	0.0
Common stock (Par + APIC)	4,679.0	2,742.0	757.0	(1,043.0)	(1,043.0)	(1,043.0)	(1,043.0)	(1,043.0)
Retained earnings	6,280.0	8,829.0	10,605.0	12,654.8	14,939.0	17,494.0	20,330.3	23,462.8
Total liabilities & stockholders' equity	53,756.0	56,184.0	60,418.0	62,980.9	65,680.5	68,525.0	71,523.1	74,683.8

EXHIBIT 4
Chrysler Corporation Discounted Cash Flow Valuation (values in $ millions)

	Projected				
Discounted Cash Flow Analysis: WACC Method	1998	1999	2000	2001	2002
Net income	3,037.0	3,291.1	3,582.1	3,883.8	4,201.1
Interest expense	1,002.7	929.1	815.9	706.8	595.2
Tax effect of interest expense	(385.0)	(356.8)	(313.3)	(271.4)	(228.6)
After-tax interest expense	617.6	572.3	502.6	435.4	366.7
NOPAT	3,654.6	3,863.4	4,084.7	4,319.2	4,567.7
Depreciation	3,194.7	3,406.7	3,631.4	3,869.7	4,122.2
Amortization	39.3	38.3	37.4	36.4	35.5
Deferred taxes	1,537.2	1,029.0	702.2	492.9	359.4
Minority interest	0.0	0.0	0.0	0.0	0.0
Income from affiliates	0.0	0.0	0.0	0.0	0.0
Other noncash items	0.0	0.0	0.0	0.0	0.0
Changes in net working capital	2,676.0	(182.3)	(193.2)	(204.8)	(217.1)
Cash flow from operations	11,101.8	8,155.1	8,262.5	8,513.4	8,867.8
Capital expenditures	(4,000.3)	(4,240.3)	(4,494.7)	(4,764.4)	(5,050.3)
Other	0.0	0.0	0.0	0.0	0.0
Free cash flow	7,101.6	3,914.8	3,767.8	3,749.0	3,817.5
Terminal value (perpetuity)	0.0	0.0	0.0	0.0	59,696.5
Total free cash flows to capital providers	7,101.6	3,914.8	3,767.8	3,749.0	63,514.0
Valuation					
Firm value	56,227.4	54,297.2	55,178.6	56,432.3	57,957.7
Plus: Excess cash	2,848.0	3,318.9	3,818.0	4,347.1	4,907.9
Less: Debt outstanding	15,485.0	15,107.1	13,270.6	11,561.5	9,856.3
Less: Minority interest	0.0	0.0	0.0	0.0	0.0
Less: Preferred stock	0.0	0.0	0.0	0.0	0.0
Equity value	43,590.4	42,508.9	45,726.0	49,217.9	53,009.4
Value per share	**$64.53**	**$70.28**	**$75.60**	**$81.37**	**$87.64**
WACC Calculation					
Debt/Market equity	35.5%	35.5%	29.0%	23.5%	18.6%
Relevered beta	0.91	0.91	0.88	0.86	0.84
K_e	11.1%	11.1%	10.9%	10.8%	10.6%
WACC	9.2%	9.2%	9.3%	9.5%	9.6%

EXHIBIT 5
Daimler-Benz A.G. Income Statement (in DM millions)

| | 1995 | 1996 | 1997 | 1998 | 1999 | Projected | | |
						2000	2001	2002
Revenues	102,985.0	106,339.0	124,050.0	133,974.0	144,691.9	156,267.3	168,768.7	182,270.1
COGS (excluding depreciation)	75,581.0	77,816.0	91,422.0	98,735.8	106,634.6	115,165.4	124,378.6	134,328.9
Selling, general, & administrative	26,203.0	21,534.0	23,096.0	24,943.7	26,939.2	29,094.3	31,421.9	33,935.6
EBITDA	1,201.0	6,989.0	9,532.0	10,294.6	11,118.1	12,007.6	12,968.2	14,005.6
Depreciation	8,661.0	4,908.0	5,198.0	3,826.8	4,241.6	4,689.6	5,173.4	5,696.0
Amortization of equip on operating leases	2,444.0	2,018.0	2,323.0	2,807.7	2,339.7	1,949.8	1,624.8	1,354.0
Other expense (income)	(1,742.0)	(1,402.0)	(1,620.0)	(2,679.5)	(2,893.8)	(3,125.3)	(3,375.4)	(3,645.4)
EBIT	(8,162.0)	1,465.0	3,631.0	6,339.6	7,430.7	8,493.6	9,545.3	10,601.1
Interest (income)	(2,113.0)	(1,368.0)	(1,589.0)	(1,830.2)	(2,175.0)	(2,469.1)	(2,737.7)	(2,997.2)
Interest expense—straight debt	1,184.0	865.0	933.0	2,215.2	2,207.4	2,207.4	2,207.4	2,207.4
Interest expense—convertible debt	0.0	0.0	0.0	0.0	0.0	0.0	0.0	0.0
Interest expense—revolver	0.0	0.0	0.0	0.0	0.0	0.0	0.0	0.0
Pretax income	(7,233.0)	1,968.0	4,287.0	5,954.6	7,398.2	8,755.3	10,075.6	11,390.8
Income taxes	(1,620.0)	(712.0)	(1,074.0)	2,381.8	2,959.3	3,502.1	4,030.2	4,556.3
Minority interest	116.0	(89.0)	189.0	0.0	0.0	0.0	0.0	0.0
Extraordinary item (income)	0.0	0.0	(2,908.0)	0.0	0.0	0.0	0.0	0.0
Net income	(5,729.0)	2,769.0	8,080.0	3,572.8	4,438.9	5,253.2	6,045.4	6,834.5
Straight preferred dividends	0.0	0.0	0.0	0.0	0.0	0.0	0.0	0.0
Convertible preferred dividends	0.0	7.0	38.0	0.0	0.0	0.0	0.0	0.0
Net income to common	(5,729.0)	2,762.0	8,042.0	3,572.8	4,438.9	5,253.2	6,045.4	6,834.5
Earnings per share:								
Basic	NM	5.37 DM	15.59 DM	6.91 DM	8.59 DM	10.17 DM	11.70 DM	13.23 DM
Fully diluted	NM	5.35 DM	15.30 DM	6.80 DM	8.45 DM	10.00 DM	11.51 DM	13.01 DM

EXHIBIT 6
Daimler-Benz A.G. Balance Sheets (in DM millions)

	1995	1996	1997	1998	Projected			
					1999	2000	2001	2002
Cash and equivalents	12,176.0	14,340.0	20,520.0	25,235.1	29,139.4	32,588.8	35,853.3	39,075.8
Accounts receivable	10,581.0	10,864.0	12,006.0	12,966.5	14,003.8	15,124.1	16,334.0	17,640.8
Inventory	14,329.0	13,602.0	14,390.0	15,541.2	16,784.5	18,127.3	19,577.4	21,143.6
Other current assets	14,188.0	15,009.0	20,838.0	22,505.0	24,305.4	26,249.9	28,349.9	30,617.9
Total current assets	51,274.0	53,815.0	67,754.0	76,247.8	84,233.1	92,090.0	100,114.6	108,478.0
Property, plant, & equipment	63,983.0	65,231.0	69,376.0	77,057.7	85,354.0	94,314.0	103,990.8	114,441.7
Accumulated depreciation	47,407.0	47,006.0	48,720.0	52,546.8	56,788.3	61,477.9	66,651.3	72,347.2
Net property, plant, & equipment	16,576.0	18,225.0	20,656.0	24,511.0	28,565.7	32,836.1	37,339.5	42,094.5
Goodwill & other intangibles	10,330.0	13,892.0	16,846.0	14,038.3	11,698.6	9,748.8	8,124.0	6,770.0
Equity in income of affiliates	4,813.0	3,536.0	3,453.0	3,453.0	3,453.0	3,453.0	3,453.0	3,453.0
Deferred taxes and other	19,105.0	22,993.0	28,390.0	28,390.0	28,390.0	28,390.0	28,390.0	28,390.0
Total assets	102,098.0	112,461.0	137,099.0	146,640.1	156,340.4	166,518.0	177,421.1	189,185.5
Accounts payable	7,378.0	9,027.0	11,079.0	11,965.3	12,922.5	13,956.3	15,072.9	16,278.7
Other current liabilities (excl. S/T debt)	16,703.0	17,160.0	20,230.0	21,848.4	23,596.3	25,484.0	27,522.7	29,724.5
Total current liabilities	24,081.0	26,187.0	31,309.0	33,813.7	36,518.8	39,440.3	42,595.5	46,003.2
Straight debt	22,285.0	28,850.0	39,302.0	39,302.0	39,302.0	39,302.0	39,302.0	39,302.0
Convertible debt	0.0	0.0	0.0	0.0	0.0	0.0	0.0	0.0
Revolver	0.0	0.0	0.0	0.0	0.0	0.0	0.0	0.0
Total debt	22,285.0	28,850.0	39,302.0	39,302.0	39,302.0	39,302.0	39,302.0	39,302.0
Deferred taxes	3,460.0	2,253.0	2,003.0	6,293.4	9,841.9	12,936.1	15,762.8	18,442.9
Minority interest	1,324.0	936.0	1,170.0	1,170.0	1,170.0	1,170.0	1,170.0	1,170.0
Other long-term liabilities	28,088.0	27,842.0	28,230.0	28,230.0	28,230.0	28,230.0	28,230.0	28,230.0
Total liabilities	79,238.0	86,068.0	102,014.0	108,809.2	115,062.7	121,078.5	127,060.3	133,148.1
Straight preferred stock	0.0	0.0	0.0	0.0	0.0	0.0	0.0	0.0
Convertible preferred stock	0.0	0.0	0.0	0.0	0.0	0.0	0.0	0.0
Common stock (Par + APIC)	6,589.0	7,360.0	8,577.0	8,577.0	8,577.0	8,577.0	8,577.0	8,577.0
Retained earnings	16,271.0	19,033.0	26,508.0	29,254.0	32,700.7	36,862.5	41,783.8	47,460.4
Total liabilities & stockholders' equity	102,098.0	112,461.0	137,099.0	146,640.1	156,340.4	166,518.0	177,421.1	189,185.5

EXHIBIT 7
Daimler-Benz A.G. Discounted Cash Flow Valuation (values in $millions)

	Projected				
Discounted Cash Flow Analysis: WACC Method	**1998**	**1999**	**2000**	**2001**	**2002**
Net income	2,030.0	2,565.9	3,090.1	3,598.4	4,117.2
Interest expense	1,258.6	1,276.0	1,298.5	1,313.9	1,329.8
Tax effect of interest expense	(503.5)	(510.4)	(519.4)	(525.6)	(531.9)
After tax interest expense	755.2	765.6	779.1	788.4	797.9
NOPAT	2,785.2	3,331.4	3,869.2	4,386.8	4,915.0
Depreciation	2,174.3	2,451.8	2,758.6	3,079.4	3,431.3
Amortization	1,595.3	1,352.4	1,146.9	967.1	815.7
Deferred taxes	2,437.8	2,051.1	1,820.1	1,682.5	1,614.5
Minority interest	0.0	0.0	0.0	0.0	0.0
Income from affiliates	0.0	0.0	0.0	0.0	0.0
Other noncash items	0.0	0.0	0.0	0.0	0.0
Changes in net working capital	(723.9)	(795.3)	(874.1)	(955.3)	(1,044.1)
Cash flow from operations	8,268.6	8,391.4	8,720.7	9,160.6	9,732.4
Capital expenditures	(4,364.6)	(4,795.5)	(5,270.6)	(5,760.0)	(6,295.7)
Other	0.0	0.0	0.0	0.0	0.0
Unlevered free cash flow	3,904.0	3,595.9	3,450.1	3,400.6	3,436.7
Terminal value (EBITDA Multiple)	0.0	0.0	0.0	0.0	54,841.3
Cash flows to capital providers	3,904.0	3,595.9	3,450.1	3,400.6	58,278.0
Valuation					
Firm value	50,083.3	50,460.4	51,235.2	52,267.4	53,492.3
Plus: Excess cash	8,818.2	11,696.6	14,199.6	16,421.9	18,586.3
Less: Debt outstanding	22,330.7	22,717.9	23,118.8	23,394.0	23,675.9
Less: Minority interest	664.8	676.3	688.2	696.4	704.8
Less: Preferred stock	0.0	0.0	0.0	0.0	0.0
Equity value	35,906.0	38,762.8	41,627.8	44,598.9	47,697.9
Price per share	**$69.48**	**$75.01**	**$80.56**	**$86.31**	**$92.30**
Price per share	**DM 122.29**	**DM 129.77**	**DM 136.95**	**DM 145.00**	**DM 153.22**
WACC Calculation					
Debt/Market equity	62.2%	58.6%	55.5%	52.5%	49.6%
Relevered beta	1.06	1.04	1.03	1.01	1.00
K_e	11.9%	11.8%	11.7%	11.6%	11.6%
WACC	8.7%	8.8%	8.8%	8.9%	8.9%

EXHIBIT 8
Daimler-Benz A.G. Income Statements (values in US$ millions)

	1995	1996	1997	1998	1999	2000	2001	2002
						Projected		
Revenues	$71,517	$68,606	$69,302	$76,122	$83,637	$91,922	$100,458	$109,801
COGS (excluding depreciation)	52,487	50,204	51,074	56,100	61,639	67,744	74,035	80,921
Selling, general, & administrative	18,197	13,893	12,903	14,173	15,572	17,114	18,703	20,443
EBITDA	834	4,509	5,325	5,849	6,427	7,063	7,719	8,437
Depreciation	6,015	3,166	2,904	2,174	2,452	2,759	3,079	3,431
Amortization of equip on op leases	1,697	1,302	1,298	1,595	1,352	1,147	967	816
Other expense (income)	(1,210)	(905)	(905)	(1,522)	(1,673)	(1,838)	(2,009)	(2,196)
EBIT	(5,668)	945	2,028	3,602	4,295	4,996	5,682	6,386
Interest (income)	(1,467)	(883)	(888)	(1,040)	(1,257)	(1,452)	(1,630)	(1,806)
Interest expense	822	558	521	1,259	1,276	1,298	1,314	1,330
Pretax income	(5,023)	1,270	2,395	3,383	4,276	5,150	5,997	6,862
Income taxes	(1,125)	(459)	(600)	1,353	1,711	2,060	2,399	2,745
Minority interest	81	(57)	106	0	0	0	0	0
Extraordinary item (income)	0	0	(1,625)	0	0	0	0	0
Net income	(3,978)	1,786	4,514	2,030	2,566	3,090	3,598	4,117
Preferred dividends	0	5	21	0	0	0	0	0
Net income to common	($3,978)	$1,782	$4,493	$2,030	$2,566	$3,090	$3,598	$4,117
Shares outstanding (avg - basic)	513,000	513,900	515,700	516,748	516,748	516,748	516,748	516,748
Earnings per share (basic)	NM	$3.47	$8.71	$3.93	$4.97	$5.98	$6.96	$7.97

574

EXHIBIT 9
Daimler-Benz A.G. Balance Sheets (value in US$ millions)

	1995	1996	1997	1998	1999	Projected 2000	2001	2002
Cash and equivalents	$ 8,456	$ 9,252	$11,464	$14,338	$16,844	$19,170	$21,341	$23,540
Accounts receivable	7,348	7,009	6,707	7,367	8,095	8,897	9,723	10,627
Inventory	9,951	8,775	8,039	8,830	9,702	10,663	11,653	12,737
Other current assets	9,853	9,683	11,641	12,787	14,049	15,441	16,875	18,444
Total current assets	35,607	34,719	37,851	43,323	48,690	54,171	59,592	65,348
Property, plant, & equipment	44,433	42,085	38,758	43,783	49,338	55,479	61,899	68,941
Accumulated depreciation	32,922	30,326	27,218	29,856	32,826	36,163	39,673	43,583
Net property, plant, & equipment	11,511	11,758	11,540	13,927	16,512	19,315	22,226	25,358
Goodwill & other intangibles	7,174	8,963	9,411	7,976	6,762	5,735	4,836	4,078
Equity in income of affiliates	3,342	2,281	1,929	1,962	1,996	2,031	2,055	2,080
Deferred taxes and other	13,267	14,834	15,860	16,131	16,410	16,700	16,899	17,102
Total assets	70,901	72,555	76,592	83,318	90,370	97,952	105,608	113,967
Accounts payable	5,124	5,824	6,189	6,798	7,470	8,210	8,972	9,806
Other current liabilities (excl. S/T debt)	11,599	11,071	11,302	12,414	13,639	14,991	16,383	17,906
Total current liabilities	16,723	16,895	17,491	19,212	21,109	23,200	25,354	27,713
Straight debt	15,476	18,613	21,956	22,331	22,718	23,119	23,394	23,676
Total debt	15,476	18,613	21,956	22,331	22,718	23,119	23,394	23,676
Deferred taxes	2,403	1,454	1,119	3,576	5,689	7,609	9,383	11,110
Minority interest	919	604	654	665	676	688	696	705
Other long-term liabilities	19,506	17,963	15,771	16,040	16,318	16,606	16,804	17,006
Total liabilities	55,026	55,528	56,991	61,823	66,510	71,223	75,631	80,210
Common stock (Par + APIC)	4,576	4,748	4,792	4,873	4,958	5,045	5,105	5,167
Retained earnings	11,299	12,279	14,809	16,622	18,902	21,684	24,871	28,591
Total liabilities & stockholders' equity	70,901	72,555	76,592	83,318	90,370	97,952	105,608	113,967

EXHIBIT 10
EPS and Dilution Analysis, Pooling-of-Interests Transaction

Merger Scenario—Pooling of Interests (100% Stock)

Transaction Assumptions

Target Name	Chrysler Corp
Acquiror Name	Daimler-Benz
Transaction Type (1 = pooling; 2 = purchase)	1
% Cash (input % for all transaction types)	0.0%
Refinance target debt (1 = yes; 2 = no)	2
Refinancing rate:	
YTM on 10-Year Treasuries	5.4%
Spread	0.7%
Refinancing rate:	6.1%
Current weighted average cost of debt (Interest expense/Debt balance)	6.5%
Effective tax rate	38.4%
Base year for combination	1997

Note: Combination model excludes effect of transaction expenses (i.e., legal, banking, accounting fees)

Transaction Adjustments

Pro Forma Net Income (diluted)	1997	1998E	1999E
Daimler-Benz's net income	4,492.7	2,030.0	2,565.9
Chrysler Corp's net income	2,804.0	3,037.0	3,291.1
Unadjusted combined	7,296.7	5,066.9	5,856.9
Adjustments to Net Income: Expenses (−) or Credits (+)			
Goodwill amortization	0.0	0.0	0.0
New interest income (expense)	748.3	748.3	748.3
Refinancing adjustments	0.0	0.0	0.0
Assumed combination synergies	0.0	0.0	1,400.0
Pretax adjustments	748.3	748.3	2,148.3
Income taxes on adjustments	(287.7)	(287.7)	(825.9)
After-tax adjustments	460.6	460.6	1,322.4
Adjusted net income	7,757.3	5,527.5	7,179.3
Pro forma EPS	$6.48	$4.62	$6.00

Current Valuation	Chrysler Corp	Daimler-Benz
Price per share	$40.75	$99.63
Merger price	$99.63	
Implied premium	144.5%	
Exchange ratio	1.0000	
Shares outstanding (in millions)	648.4	516.7
Options/SARs/Converts	31.7	7.51
Total post-deal shares	680.1	524.3

Earnings per Share (basic)	1997	1998E	1999E
Chrysler Corp	$4.15	$5.02	$5.44
Daimler-Benz	$8.71	$3.93	$4.97
Source of Projections	Model		

1997 Financial Data (in $MM)	Chrysler Corp	Daimler-Benz
Revenues	61,147.0	69,301.7
EBITDA	8,259.0	5,325.1
EBIT	5,563.0	2,028.5
Net income to common	2,804.0	4,492.7
Existing goodwill amortization	0.0	1,297.8
Total cash & equivalents	7,848.0	11,463.7
Excess cash	2,848.0	8,670.4
Goodwill	1,573.0	9,411.2
Total assets	60,418.0	76,591.6
Total debt	15,485.0	21,956.4
Preferred equity	0.0	0.0
Common equity	11,362.0	19,600.6

Goodwill Created	
Cost of equity acquired	NA
Plus: Liabilities assumed	NA
Less: Excess cash	NA
Total consideration	NA
Less: Adjusted value of assets	NA
Goodwill created in transaction	NA
Goodwill amortization period	NA

Adjusted Asset Value	
Total assets	NA
Less: Goodwill	NA
Less: Excess cash	NA
Plus: Assumed asset write up	NA
Adjusted value of assets	NA

Summary Outputs — Pooling of Interests (100% Stock)						
Pro Forma Earnings Impact	1997	1998E	1999E	*1997 Contribution Analysis*	Chrysler Corp	Daimler-Benz
Daimler-Benz's stand-alone EPS	$8.71	$3.93	$4.97	Revenues	46.9%	53.1%
Newco's combined EPS	$6.48	$4.62	$6.00	EBITDA	60.8%	39.2%
Accretion/(Dilution)	−25.6%	17.6%	20.8%	Newco shares	680.1	516.7
				% Ownership	56.8%	43.2%
Additional pretax synergies required for no dilution	4,336.9	0.0	0.0			

576

EXHIBIT 11
Value Line **Report on Chrysler Corporation**

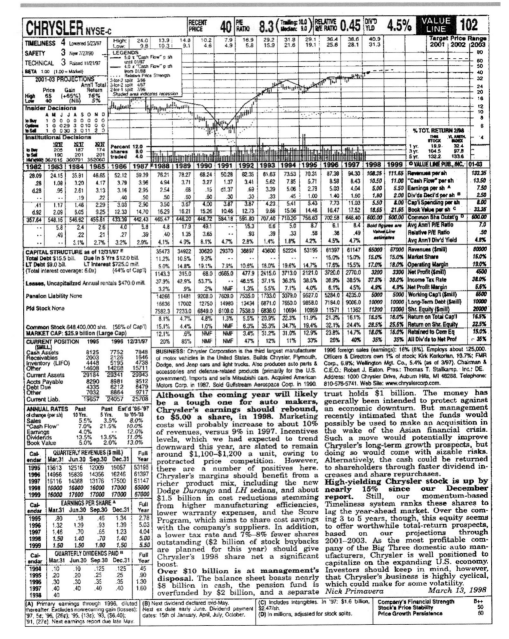

EXHIBIT 12
Value Line Report on Daimler-Benz A.G.

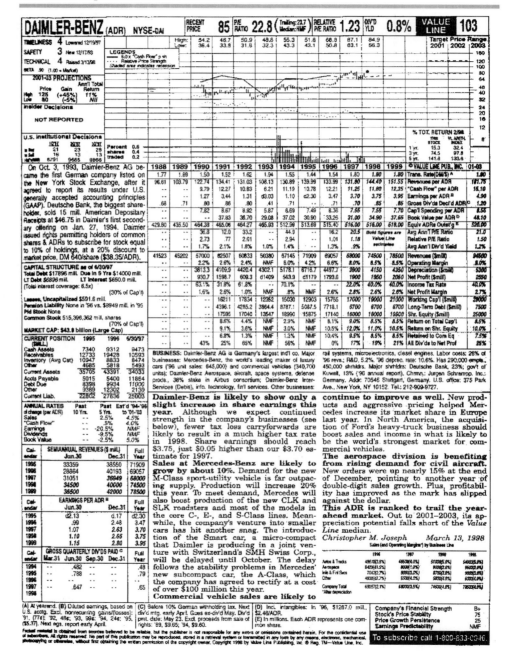

EXHIBIT 13
Comparable Automobile Manufacturers (in US$ millions, except where otherwise noted)

	Price Feb-98	1997 Revenues	1997 Profits	1997 EPS	1998E EPS*	1997 CF/Shr	Trailing P/E	Forward P/E	Price/ CF	Shares Out	L-T Debt	Debt/ Total Cap	Mkt/Bk Value	Beta**
U.S.														
Ford Motor	$37 9/16	$ 153,627	$ 6,920	$ 5.75	$ 5.38	$ 11.97	6.5	7.0	3.1	1,194	$ 80,245	64%	1.51	0.86
General Motors	68 15/16	166,445	6,276	8.70	7.97	22.82	7.9	8.6	3.0	721	41,972	46%	2.67	0.96
Chrysler	40 3/4	61,147	2,804	4.15	5.01	8.43	9.8	8.1	4.8	648	9,006	25%	2.33	0.85
Navistar	30 3/8	6,321	150	1.65	2.60	3.33	18.4	11.7	9.1	72	1,316	37%	2.83	1.03
Average, U.S.						*11.64*	*10.67*	*8.86*	*5.03*			*43%*	*2.33*	*0.93*
Japan														
Honda Motor	70 3/8	45,111	1,960	4.02	4.40	6.39	17.5	16.0	11.0	487	5,096	13%	4.55	0.80
Nissan Motor	8 7/8	49,358	382	0.30	0.55	3.34	29.6	16.1	2.7	1,257	12,554	53%	0.92	0.66
Toyota Motor	54 7/8	87,807	3,416	1.79	2.35	3.81	30.7	23.4	14.4	1,902	16,006	13%	2.70	0.63
Average, Japan						*4.51*	*25.92*	*18.49*	*9.36*			*26%*	*2.72*	*0.70*
Europe														
Daimler–Benz	99 5/8	68,951	1,764	3.38	3.75	11.50	29.5	26.6	8.7	517	9,564	16%	2.69	0.86
Volvo	27 1/8	23,118	400	0.88	2.20	2.99	30.8	12.3	9.1	442	2,913	20%	1.59	0.71
BMW (DM)	1,475	60,137	1,246	50.63	59.50	412.99	29.1	24.8	3.6	25	10,516	22%	3.59	0.88
Peugeot→+ (FFr)	867	186,785	(2,768)	(55.24)	48.20	336.97	NM	18.0	2.6	50	17,004	28%	0.82	0.88
Fiat (Lira)	6,292	89,658	2,417	459.90	379.60	2,141.76	13.7	16.6	2.9	5	10,938	25%	1.35	0.73
Audi (DM)	1,450	22,410	367	85.35	125.00	536.28	17.0	11.6	2.7	4	—	0%	2.93	0.68
Renault (FFr)	212	207,912	5,427	22.79	16.00	48.88	9.3	13.3	4.3	238	30,760	38%	1.16	0.78
Average, Europe						*NMF*	*21.57*	*17.59*	*4.84*			*21%*	*2.02*	*0.79*
Average, All Firms							*19.22*	*15.29*	*5.86*			*29%*	*2.26*	*0.81*

Note: Data is taken from *ValueLine Investment Survey* and Bloomberg, and may not match exactly with other data given in the case;
*Domestic EPS estimates are taken from Nelson's, International EPS Estimates are taken from *Value Line* and IBES.
**Beta is calculated against the S&P in all cases and is based on weekly observations between Mar-96 and Feb-98.

EXHIBIT 14
Recent Stock Price Information for Chrysler Corporation and Daimler-Benz A.G.

Chrysler Corporation		Daimler-Benz (ADR in US$)		Ratio of Chrysler
Month	Stock Price	Month	Stock Price	to Daimler
May-96	$ 33.31	May-96	$ 53.50	0.6227
Jun-96	31.25	Jun-96	53.00	0.5896
Jul-96	28.38	Jul-96	53.13	0.5341
Aug-96	29.25	Aug-96	54.25	0.5392
Sep-96	28.63	Sep-96	58.25	0.4914
Oct-96	33.63	Oct-96	64.50	0.5213
Nov-96	35.50	Nov-96	67.31	0.5274
Dec-96	33.00	Dec-96	71.00	0.4648
Jan-97	34.88	Jan-97	71.13	0.4903
Feb-97	34.00	Feb-97	76.00	0.4474
Mar-97	30.00	Mar-97	73.13	0.4103
Apr-97	30.00	Apr-97	78.00	0.3846
May-97	31.88	May-97	80.13	0.3978
Jun-97	32.88	Jun-97	82.13	0.4003
Jul-97	37.19	Jul-97	73.50	0.5060
Aug-97	35.13	Aug-97	80.75	0.4350
Sep-97	36.81	Sep-97	67.31	0.5469
Oct-97	35.25	Oct-97	69.44	0.5077
Nov-97	34.31	Nov-97	71.00	0.4833
Dec-97	35.19	Dec-97	68.75	0.5118
Jan-98	34.81	Jan-98	79.75	0.4365
Feb-98	38.75	Feb-98	99.63	0.3890
	High $ 38.75		High $ 99.63	0.6227
	Low 28.38		Low 53.00	0.3846
	Avg.: 33.36		Avg.: 70.25	0.4835
Adjusted Beta:[*] 0.85		Adjusted Beta:[*] 0.97		
Volatility:[**] 25.83%		Volatility:[**] 29.39%		

[*]Beta was calculated with respect to the S&P 500 Index from weekly data over the period 5/03/96 to 3/01/98 and adjusted for beta's tendency to converge to 1 according to the formula: Adj Beta = (.67)[*] Raw Beta + (.33)[*] 1.00.
[**]Volatility was calculated from daily data for the 260 most recent trading days.

Source: Bloomberg Financial Service.

EXHIBIT 15
Long-Term Debt Structure as of December 31, 1997 (in US$ millions)

Chrysler Corporation				
	1997	**1996**	**LTD Repayment Schedule (in millions)**	
Chrysler Corp. Debentures due 2027–2097	$ 1,588.0	$ 265.0	1998	$ 2,638.0
Chrysler Corp. Notes due 1999–2020	689.0	1,467.0	1999	3,423.0
Chrysler Finance Corp. Senior Notes due 1999–2018	9,335.0	8,437.0	2000	2,363.0
Chrysler Finance Corp. Mortgage Notes and Capital Leases	32.0	13.0	2001	431.0
			2002	470.0
Total	$11,644.0	10,182.0	Thereafter	2,319.0
Less current portion	2,638.0	2,998.0		$11,644.0
Total long-term debt	$ 9,006.0	$ 7,184.0		

Daimler-Benz (in US$)				
	1997	**1996**	**LTD Repayment Schedule (in millions)**	
Bonds and notes due 1999–2007	$ 5,619.0	$ 4,720.0	1998	$ 669.8
Long-term bank loans due 1999–2019	3,769.3	3,261.3	1999	1,315.1
Liabilities to affiliated companies due 1999–2004	309.5	245.2	2000	1,750.8
Capital leases and residual value guarantees	589.9	370.3	2001	1,553.6
Total	$10,287.7	$ 8,596.8	2002	1,426.3
Less current portion	669.8	313.5	Thereafter	3,572.1
Total long-term debt	$ 9,617.9	$ 8,283.2		$10,287.7

Source: Chrysler and Daimler-Benz 1997 annual reports.

EXHIBIT 16
Recent Acquisition Activity in the United States (values in US$ billions, except where noted)

	2nd Quarter 1997		3rd Quarter 1997		4th Quarter 1997		1st Quarter 1998	
	# Deals	Value	# Deals	Value	# Deals	Value	# Deals	Value
All Activity:								
U.S. acquisitions	1,365	$ 167.60	1,581	$ 178.10	1,719	$ 172.60	1,420	$ 162.70
Non-U.S. acquisitions	141	19.10	174	18.00	205	25.10	138	18.50
U.S. acquisition, non-U.S.	287	22.10	279	17.80	256	23.40	256	25.10
Total	1,793	208.80	2,034	213.90	2,180	221.10	1,814	206.30
# reporting price	739		877		1,051		809	
Divestitures only[*]	613	51.90	666	43.00	686	72.40	505	76.30
# reporting price	271		336		402		286	
LBOs only[*]	23	2.10	25	0.60	22	1.80	16	0.50
# reporting price	9		10		9		8	

Note: [*]*Included in all activity.*

Twelve-Month Moving Average Stock Premiums

1 Month before Announcement		1 Week before Announcement	
2Q97	35.31%	2Q97	29.53%
3Q97	47.97%	3Q97	39.61%
4Q97	36.51%	4Q97	28.34%
1Q98	37.11%	1Q98	31.61%

Mode of Payment

	Combined	Cash	Stock
2Q97	18%	54%	29%
3Q97	17%	57%	26%
4Q97	15%	59%	26%
1Q98	17%	58%	24%

Note: "Combined" includes mixture of cash
and stock.
Source: Mergers & Acquisitions, July/August 1998.

Revenue Volumes of Target
Companies 4/1/97–3/31/98

Sales	# Firms
$1–$5MM	154
$5.1–$10	144
$10.1–$15	103
$15.1–$25	184
$25.1–$35	103
$35.1–$50	107
$50.1–$75	104
$75.1–$100	65
$100.1–$500	301
$500.1+	179

Note: Sales are in millions.

EXHIBIT 17
Recent Jumbo M&A Activity (Greater than US$ 10 Billion) (In millions, except where otherwise noted)

Non-Financial Companies

Acquiror	Target	Date	Value	P/E	Premium to Stock Price One Week Prior	Outcome
Tracinda Corp.	Chrysler	Apr-95	$21,618	5.40	37.50%	Withdrawn
Walt Disney	Capital Cities/ABC	Jul-95	18,837	25.40	25.20	Completed
SBC Communications	Pacific-Telesis	Apr-96	16,490	15.50	36.20	Completed
WorldCom	MFS Communications	Jan-97	13,596	NM	60.00	Completed
CSX Corp.	Conrail	Jun-97	10,436	58.40	60.30	Withdrawn
Bell Atlantic	NYNEX Corp.	Aug-97	21,346	19.50	−0.40	Completed
Boeing Corp.	McDonnell Douglas	Aug-97	13,359	NM	22.70	Completed
CUC International	HFS Incorporated	Dec-97	11,343	40.30	3.00	Completed
Lockheed Martin	Northrup Grumman	Feb-98	11,831	28.00	41.20	Withdrawn
Starwood Lodging	ITT Corp.	Feb-98	13,748	24.70	98.30	Completed

Financial Companies

Acquiror	Target	Date	Value	P/E	Premium to Stock Price One Week Prior	Outcome
Chemical Banking Corp.	Chase Manhattan Corp	Mar-96	10,446	10.70	7.50%	Completed
Wells Fargo	First Interstate Corp.	Apr-96	10,930	13.10	36.30%	Completed
Dean Witter Discover	Morgan Stanley	Feb-97	10,573	10.70	12.80%	Completed
Nationsbank	Barnett	Jan-98	14,822	25.00	43.90%	Completed

Sources: Securities Data Company, Bloomberg.

EXHIBIT 18
Recent Economic Data: Germany and United States

	Unemployment			Inflation (CPI)			Annual GDP Growth			Industrial Production		
	U.S.	GR—Total	GR—West	U.S.	GR—Total	GR—West	U.S.	GR—Total	GR—West	U.S.	GR—Total	GR—West
1991	7.30%		5.70%	3.10%		4.20%	0.39%		3.30%	0.30%	−0.10%	
1992	7.40		6.50	2.90	3.30%	3.40	3.70	0.90%	0.30	4.40	−5.00	−5.50%
1993	6.50	9.60%	8.10	2.70	4.20	3.30	2.40	−0.20	−0.90	3.80	−1.50	−2.60
1994	5.40	9.30	8.20	2.70	2.50	2.50	3.30	3.40	2.70	6.80	6.80	5.90
1995	5.60	9.90	8.60	2.50	1.80	1.50	2.10	0.00	−0.20	2.30	−4.90	−5.10
1996	5.30	10.80	9.50	3.30	1.40	1.40	3.90	2.10	1.90	4.70	3.10	2.50
1997	4.70	11.80	9.90	1.70	1.80	1.70	3.80	2.30	2.50	5.70	3.20	3.70
1998	4.50	11.00	9.30	1.70	1.20	1.10	3.60	2.50	2.60	3.20	1.60	1.70

Source: Bloomberg Financial Service.

EXHIBIT 19
Current Capital Market Conditions

Prime Rates on Senior Bank Loans			Recent Money Rates (February 27, 1998)				Stock Market Indexes		
	Germany	U.S.		Germany	U.S.			Germany	U.S.
1988		10.50%						(DAX)	(S&P 500)
1989		10.50	Libor	3.76%	5.78%		1988	1,328	278
1990		10.00	3-mo. T-bill	3.43	5.30		1989	1,790	353
1991		7.50	6-mo. T-bill	3.48	5.31		1990	1,398	330
1992		6.00	1-yr. T-bill	3.66	5.39		1991	1,578	417
1993		6.00	3-yr. T-note	4.15	5.53		1992	1,545	436
1994		8.50	5-yr. T-note	4.49	5.57		1993	2,267	467
1995		8.75	10-yr. T-bond	4.93	5.61		1994	2,107	459
1996		8.25	30-yr. T-bond	5.49	5.91		1995	2,254	616
1997	6.75%	8.50					1996	2,889	741
Jan-98	6.62	8.50					1997	4,250	970
Feb-98	6.55	8.50					Jan-98	4,440	980
							Feb-98	4,710	1,049

U.S. Corporate Bond Ratings & Yields (1)

	AAA	A	BBB	BB
Dec-97	6.17%	6.44%	6.62%	7.85%
Jan-98	5.90	6.21	6.49	7.64
Feb-98	6.06	6.37	6.58	7.76

(1) Based on 10-year yields from the Bloomberg Index for selected Industrials.
Sources: Bloomberg, Federal Reserve Bulletin.

S&P Bond Ratings

Chrysler Corp.	A2/A
Daimler-Benz	A1/A+

Yield to Maturities of Selected Issues as of 2/27/98

Chrysler		Daimler-Benz	
7.95%/00	6.12%	10%/99	6.02%
6.95%/02	6.19	6.625%/00	6.00
7.45%/27	6.84	6%/02	6.10
7.45%/97	7.02	7.375%/06	6.36

Source: Bloomberg.

Palamon Capital Partners/TeamSystem S.P.A.

We want to make money by investing in change.

—*Louis Elson, Managing Partner, Palamon*

In February 2000, Louis Elson looked over the London skyline and reflected on the international private equity industry and the investment processes that would be necessary for success in this increasingly competitive field. Elson, a Managing Partner of the U.K.-based private equity firm Palamon Capital Partners, was specifically considering an investment in TeamSystem, S.p.A., an Italian software company. Palamon was interested in TeamSystem for the growth opportunity that it represented in a fast-changing market. Palamon had an opportunity to purchase a 51 percent stake in TeamSystem for €25.9 million. In preparing a recommendation to his colleagues at Palamon, Elson planned to assess TeamSystem's strategy, value the firm, identify important risks, evaluate proposed terms of the investment, and consider alternative exit strategies.

INTERNATIONAL PRIVATE EQUITY INDUSTRY

The international private equity industry was segmented into three sectors. Venture capital funds made high-risk, early stage investments in start-up companies. Generalist private eq-

This case was prepared by Chad Rynbrandt from interviews, under the direction of Professor Robert F. Bruner. Some details have been simplified for expositional clarity. The cooperation of Palamon Capital Partners is gratefully acknowledged, as is the financial support of the Batten Institute.

uity funds provided expansionary funding or transitional funding that allowed small companies to grow and eventually go public. And, leveraged buyout funds financed the acquisitions (often by management) of preexisting companies that had the capacity to take on debt and make radical improvements in operations.

Private equity funds raised capital primarily from individual investors, pension funds, and endowments that were interested in more attractive risk/return investment propositions than the public capital markets offered. Funds existed all over the world, but, not surprisingly, North America had the largest number of funds and largest dollar value of capital invested as of 1999. Europe and Asia had the next largest private equity industries. **Exhibit 1** presents the number and dollar value of private equity funds by global geographic region.

Most private equity markets saw rapid growth in the 1990s. In Europe, the amount of new capital raised grew from €4.4 billion in 1994 to €25.4 billion in 1999. Correspondingly, the amount of capital invested by the funds more than quadrupled from €5.5 billion to €25.1 billion over the same period. **Exhibit 2** summarizes the amount of new capital raised and the amount invested through the 1990s. Some key players in the mid-market sector in Europe included Duke Street Capital (€650 million fund based in U.K.), Mercapital (€600 million fund based in Spain), and Nordic Capital ([€760 million fund based in Sweden). Large investment banks like Dresdner, Deutsche Bank, and Banca de Roma also had notable private equity presences.

LOUIS ELSON AND PALAMON CAPITAL PARTNERS

Louis Elson began working in private equity in 1990, when he joined E.M. Warburg, Pincus & Co. Soon after joining the firm, he began focusing on European transactions and, in 1992, decided to relocate permanently to Europe. Elson became a partner of Warburg, Pincus in 1995 and was an integral part of a team which built a $1.3 billion portfolio of equity investments for the firm. The portfolio contained over 40 investments in seven different European countries. In late 1998, Elson and another of his partners, Michael Hoffman, saw a unique window of opportunity in the European private equity industry. They believed that the European economic landscape was changing in a way that benefited smaller, middle-market companies. Therefore, Elson and Hoffman recruited two additional partners and began laying the foundation for what would eventually become Palamon Capital Partners.

By August 1999, Elson and Hoffman had raised a fund of €440 million. They accomplished this despite macroeconomic obstacles like the Russian debt default, by marketing their unique pan-European private equity experience. With the fund closed, Elson and Hoffman grew the Palamon team to nine professionals. They hired people with experience in private equity, investment banking, corporate finance, and management consulting. Consistent with Elson and Hoffman's original vision, the Palamon team used their breadth of experience to build a portfolio of investments that would provide investors with a unique risk profile and substantial long-term returns. Essentially, Palamon was a generalist private equity fund that served the segment of investors interested in less risk than venture capital, but more risk than the leveraged buyout funds. Accordingly, Palamon targeted a 35 percent return on a single portfolio investment, and 20–25 percent blended net return on a portfolio, with an investment horizon of approximately six years. Louis Elson said,

> Our investors include large American public sector pension funds, corporate pension funds, major financial institutions, and large endowment funds. They look for us to beat the return on the S&P Index by 500 basis points per year on average. We have the best chance of getting funded again if we can beat this target, adjusting of course for risk. We look to pick up good businesses at attractive prices, and then add value through active involvement with them.

Like other generalist funds, Palamon's investment strategy was to make "bridge" investments in companies that wanted to move from small, private ownership to the public capital markets. Unlike many private equity funds, however, Palamon did not restrict itself to one specific European country, nor did it limit its scope to one industry. Instead, Palamon focused more broadly on small to midsized European companies in which it could acquire a controlling stake for between €10 and €50 million.

For companies that fit Palamon's profile, the transition from private to public ownership required both funding and management ability. Palamon, therefore, complemented its financial investments with advisory services to increase the probability that the portfolio companies would successfully make it to the public markets. Elson was optimistic about Palamon's investment strategy. As Elson sat in his office, Palamon was finalizing its first investment, a Spanish Internet content company, Lanetro, S.A., and had three other investments (including TeamSystem) in the pipeline.

INVESTMENT PROCESS

Palamon's investment process began with the development of an investment thesis that would typically involve a market undergoing significant change, that might be driven by deregulation, trade liberalization, new technology, demographic shifts, and so forth. Within the chosen market, Palamon looked for attractive investment opportunities, using investment banks, industry resources, and personal contacts. The search process was time-consuming with only 1 percent of the opportunities making it through to the next phase, due diligence. Due diligence involved thorough research into the history, performance, and competitive advantages of the investment candidate. Typically, only one company made it through this final screen to provide Palamon with a viable investment alternative.

Palamon brought its deal-making experience to bear in shaping the specific terms of investment. Carefully tailored agreements could increase the likelihood of a successful outcome, both by creating the right incentives for operating managers to achieve targets, and by timing the delivery of cash returns to investors in ways consistent with the operating strategy of the target. Deal negotiations covered many issues including price, executive leadership, and board composition. Once a deal had been completed, Palamon then offered value-added support to management.

To close the process, Palamon searched for the best exit alternative, one that would help them fully realize a return on the fund's investment. Classic exit alternatives included sale of the firm through an initial public offering in a stock market, and sale of the firm to a strategic buyer. **Exhibit 3** provides more detail about Palamon's process and the firm's investment screening criteria.

TEAMSYSTEM, S.P.A.

Palamon's theme-based search generated the opportunity to invest in TeamSystem, S.p.A. In early 1999, even before Palamon's fund had been closed, Elson had concluded that the payroll servicing industry in Italy could provide a good investment opportunity because of the industry's extreme fragmentation and constantly changing regulations. History had shown that governments in Italy adjusted their policies as often as four times a year. For Palamon, the space represented a ripe opportunity to invest in a company that would capitalize on the need of small companies to respond to this legislative volatility. With the help of a boutique investment bank and industry contacts, Palamon approached two leading players in the market. Neither company was suitable to Palamon, but both identified their most respected competitor as TeamSystem. Palamon approached TeamSystem directly and found a good fit. Due diligence was done and, by the end of the year, a specific investment proposal had taken shape. It was the one Elson now considered.

TeamSystem was founded in 1979 in Pesaro, Italy. Since its founding the company had grown to become one of Italy's leading providers of accounting, tax, and payroll management software for small-to-medium-sized enterprises (SMEs). Led by CEO and cofounder Giovanni Ranocchi, TeamSystem had built up a customer base of 28,000 firms, representing a 14 percent share of the Italian market.

TeamSystem offered its customers a compelling value proposition. The company's software integrated the financial information of business and automated tedious and complex administrative functions. The software also enabled SMEs and their financial advisors to stay on top of the frequently changing regulatory environment. To that end, TeamSystem continually invested in development to keep its software current. Customers were given access to these product upgrades in exchange for a yearly maintenance fee that the company collected (in addition to the initial purchase price of the software). TeamSystem had excelled in this customer service and developed loyal customers. Nearly 95 percent of its customers renewed their maintenance contracts every year.

In 1999, TeamSystem generated sales of lire 60.5 billion (€31.3 million) and EBIT (earnings before interest and taxes) of lire 18.5 billion (€9.5 million). These results continued a strong pattern of growth for TeamSystem. Since 1996, sales had grown at an annualized rate of 15 percent and operating margins improved. As a result, EBIT had grown at an annualized rate of 31.6 percent over the same period. **Exhibit 4** provides additional detail on TeamSystem's historical sales and profitability from 1996 through 1999. **Exhibit 5** contains balance sheet information for the same period.

As Elson looked through the numbers, he noted the current lack of debt on TeamSystem's balance sheet. In his opinion, this represented an opportunity to bring TeamSystem to a more effective capital structure that might lower the company's cost of capital. Elson also noted the "pro-forma" label on both financial statements. TeamSystem, given its private ownership and multicompany structure, did not have audited consolidated financial information for the past five years.

INDUSTRY PROFILE

The Italian accounting, tax, and payroll management software industry in which TeamSystem operated was highly fragmented. Over 30 software providers vied for the business of 200,000 SMEs with the largest having a 15 percent share of the market (TeamSystem ranked number two with its 14 percent share.) All of the significant players in the industry were family-owned companies that did not have access to international capital markets. **Exhibit 6** shows 1998 revenues for the nine largest players.

Analysts predicted that two things would characterize the future of the industry—consolidation and growth. Consolidation would occur because few of the smaller companies would be able to keep up with the research and development demands of a changing industry. Analysts pointed to three acquisitions in 1998–99 as the start of this trend. As for growth, experts predicted 9 percent annual growth over the period 1999–2002. This growth would come primarily from increased PC penetration among SMEs, greater end-user sophistication, and continued computerization of administrative functions.

THE TRANSACTION

After reviewing TeamSystem's past performance and the state of the industry, Elson returned his attention to the specifics of the TeamSystem investment. The most recent proposal had offered €25.9 million for 51 percent of the common (or ordinary) shares in a multipart structure that also included a recapitalization to put debt on the balance sheet:

- Palamon would invest lire 50.235 billion (€25.9 million) in the ordinary shares (i.e., common equity) of TeamSystem S.p.A. These shares would be purchased from existing shareholders of TeamSystem. Giovanni Rannochi would maintain a 20 percent shareholding while noncore employees would be diluted from holdings ranging from 3 to 8 percent to 1 percent each after completion.
- Over half of TeamSystem's lire 28.5 billion of cash was to be distributed to existing shareholders via two dividend payments: a lire 8.5 billion dividend to existing TeamSystem shareholders in April 2000, and a 6.5 billion dividend to be paid at time of closing. A cash balance of lire 13.5 billion would remain.
- With Palamon's assistance, TeamSystem would borrow lire 46 billion from Deutsche Bank, in a seven-year loan, offering a three-year principal repayment holiday and an initial cost of 1.0 percent over base rates (Italian government bonds). Shareholders would receive the proceeds of the debt at time of closing in another special dividend.
- Excess real estate would be sold by TeamSystem, thus removing the distraction of unrelated property investments. A group of existing shareholders had made an offer to purchase lire 2.1 billion of real estate at book value if the transaction closed.

The sources and uses of funds in this transaction are summarized in **Exhibit 7**. An income statement and balance sheet for TeamSystem, pro forma the transaction, are given in

Exhibits 8 and **9**. Palamon, as a majority shareholder, would have full effective control of TeamSystem, although the existing shareholders would have a number of minority protection rights. For example, Palamon would be unable to dismiss Ranocchi for a two-year period. But Palamon would have the ability to deliver 100 percent of the shares of the company to a trade buyer should this be the appropriate exit. Furthermore, more than 40 percent of the cash to be paid to the departing shareholders would be held in escrow for a period of at least two years, under the control of Palamon.

VALUATION

To properly evaluate the deal, Elson had to develop a view about the value of TeamSystem. He faced some challenges in that task, however. First, TeamSystem had no strategic plan or future forecast of profitability. Elson only had four years of historical information. If Elson were to do a proper valuation, he would need to estimate the future cash flows that TeamSystem would generate given market trends and the value that Palamon could add. His best guess was that TeamSystem could grow revenues at 15 percent per year for the next few years, a pace above the expected market growth rate of 9 percent, followed by a 6 percent growth rate in perpetuity.[1] He also thought that Palamon's professionals could help Ranocchi improve operating margins slightly. Lastly, Elson believed that a 14 percent discount rate would appropriately capture the risk of the cash flows. This reflected three software companies trading on the Milan stock exchange, whose betas average 1.44 and unlevered betas averaged 1.00.

The second challenge Elson faced was the lack of comparable valuations in the Italian market. Because most competitors were family owned, there was very little market transparency. The nearest matches he could find were other European and U.S. enterprise resource planning (ERP)[2] and accounting software companies. The financial profiles of these comparable firms are contained in **Exhibits 10** and **11**. See also exchange rates and capital market conditions in **Exhibits 12** and **13**. Looking through the data, Elson noticed the high growth expectations (greater than 20 percent) for these software firms and correspondingly high valuation multiples.

RISKS

Elson was concerned about more than just the valuation, however. He wanted to carefully evaluate the risks associated with the deal, specifically:

- *TeamSystem's management team might not be able to make the change to a more professionally run company.* The investment in TeamSystem was a bet on a small, private company

---

[1] This was roughly the sum of an expected long-term inflation rate in the euro of 3 percent, and long-term real economic growth in Europe of 3 percent.

[2] Enterprise Resource Planning (ERP) systems are commercial software packages that promise the seamless integration of all the information flowing through a company: financial, accounting, supply chain, customer, and human resources information.

that he hoped would become a dominating, larger player. The CEO, Ranocchi, had successfully navigated the last five years of growth, but had, by his own admission, created a management group that relied on him for almost every decision. From conversations and interviews, Elson concluded that Ranocchi could take the company forward, but he had concerns about the ability of the supporting cast to deliver in a period of continued growth.

- *TeamSystem was facing an inspection by the Italian tax authorities.* The inspection posed a financial risk, and therefore could serve as a significant distraction for management. Also, because it was "open-ended," the inspection might delay the company's ability to go public. However, Elson had quantified the risk through sensitivity and scenario analysis, and believed that the expected monetary impact of the inspection was low.

- *The company may not be able to keep up with technological change.* While the company had begun to adapt to technological changes like new programming languages, it still had some products on older platforms that would require significant reprogramming. In addition, the Internet posed an immediate threat if TeamSystem's competitors adapted to it more quickly than TeamSystem did.

Finally, Elson wanted to make sure that he could capture the value that TeamSystem might be able to create in the next few years. Exit options were, therefore, an important consideration for him.

CONCLUSION

Elson looked at all of the information that covered his desk and pondered the recommendation he should make to his partners. How much was a 51 percent stake really worth? What might explain the valuation results? What nonprice considerations should he make part of the deal? How might Palamon feasibly capture the value from the investment? Were the risks serious enough to compromise the value of the investment?

EXHIBIT 1
Size of Regional Private Equity Markets, 1999

Region	Number of Funds	Total Dollar Value of Funds (millions)
North America	8,376	$892,598
Europe	2,556	160,749
Asia	1,360	60,582
Middle East	130	6,469
Australia/Oceania	155	5,741
Central/South America	42	5,044
Africa	13	1,711

Source: Thomson Securities Data/Venture Xpert.

EXHIBIT 2
Historical Data on European Private Equity Market

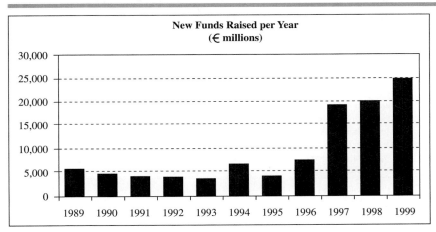

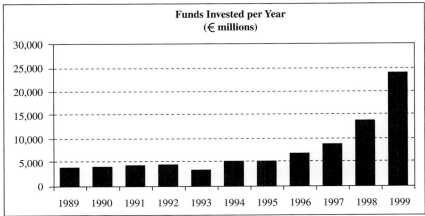

Source: European Private Equity & Venture Capital Association.

EXHIBIT 3
Screening Criteria and Investment Process

Investment Process

Palamon utilizes an investment process which has been proven over the past decade through economic cycles and across geographic regions. This process is underpinned by a core set of investment principles, which can be summarized by stage of the investment process.

- Determination of Investment Focus—Identify sectors undergoing significant changes, develop industry knowledge and take a contrarian stance when appropriate
- Pro-Active Deal Sourcing—Pro-actively pursue investment opportunities within identified sectors
- Rigorous Due Diligence—Execute comprehensive yet focused company due diligence; concentrate on "deal breakers" early on
- Sophisticated Deal Structuring—Base structuring on a sound knowledge of local practices without relying necessarily on ineffective customs; align objectives with the entrepreneur; avoid excess leverage.
- Value-Added Support—Provide strategic direction to portfolio companies; make international network of advisors and expertise available to management teams; commit to longer time horizons sufficient to ensure scope for company growth
- Proven Realization Strategies — Prepare for liquidity events; utilize in-house expertise to access public market capital or organize trade sales, creating exit options for all shareholders.

Investment Screening Criteria

The partners of Palamon are especially rigorous in their investment selection criteria, identifying those characteristics that will foster high growth combined with manageable risk. The following key elements are sought in each investment made:

- Superior management with unique capabilities and experience
- Leadership in core markets which are either expanding robustly or are experiencing dislocation due to technological, regulatory, or competitive changes
- High potential for operating leverage
- Opportunity to access alternative markets
- Access to undervalued assets

Source: Palamon Web site.

EXHIBIT 4
TeamSystem, S.p.A. Historical Pro-Forma Income Statement (values in millions of lire)

	1996	1997	1998	1999
Total Sales	39,665	42,922	50,694	60,499
Cost of materials	(9,979)	(11,430)	(12,258)	(15,179)
Cost of service	(9,380)	(8,692)	(10,889)	(12,389)
Rents and leasing	(328)	(394)	(1,493)	(1,553)
Total Operating Cost	(19,687)	(20,516)	(24,640)	(29,121)
Salaries	(4,875)	(5,382)	(6,282)	(7,151)
Social contributions	(1,855)	(2,047)	(1,917)	(2,011)
Other personnel costs	(456)	(481)	(572)	(753)
Total Personnel Costs	(7,186)	(7,910)	(8,771)	(9,915)
Other Operating Costs	(2,793)	(3,052)	(3,133)	(1,339)
EBITDA	9,999	11,444	14,150	20,124
Depreciation & amortization	(1,052)	(1,427)	(1,355)	(1,636)
EBIT	8,947	10,017	12,795	18,488
Interest expense	(185)	(144)	(154)	(210)
Non-op income	1,800	1,305	1,132	1,283
Pretax profit	10,563	11,178	13,773	19,562
Taxes	(5,870)	(6,699)	(6,437)	(9,525)
Earnings before minorities	4,693	4,479	7,336	10,036
Elimination of intercompany invest	(30)	(13)	(139)	(287)
Net Income	4,663	4,466	7,197	9,749

Source: Palamon memorandum.

EXHIBIT 5

TeamSystem, S.p.A. Historical Pro-Forma Balance Sheet (values in millions of lire)

	1996	1997	1998	1999
ASSETS				
Cash	13,092	19,134	21,144	28,513
Marketable securities				
Receivables	13,257	14,957	16,328	19,443
Inventory	1,333	1,087	1,195	1,235
Total Current Assets	27,682	35,178	38,667	49,191
Intangible assets	14	22	18	21
Land, PP&E	4,962	2,080	2,489	3,681
Other tangible assets	729	668	1,140	2,055
Deferred costs	327	1,947	1,738	1,865
Securities and other	1,434	1,173	1,229	1,226
Total Assets	35,148	41,068	45,281	58,039
LIABILITIES				
Accounts payable	7,661	8,932	8,969	9,669
Tax and other payables	6,796	9,827	8,660	9,956
Deferred income and accruals	1,200	1,127	1,257	4,156
Long term liabilities	2,688	2,094	2,235	3,055
Total Liabilities	18,345	21,980	21,121	26,836
Shareholders' Equity and Minority Interest				
Capital	4,580	4,580	4,580	4,580
Reserves	6,636	9,442	11,662	15,884
Net Income from operations	4,584	4,405	7,132	9,660
(Less special dividend)				
Total Shareholders' Equity	15,800	18,427	23,374	30,124
Minority interest	1,003	661	786	1,079
Total Shareholders' Equity and Minority Interest	16,803	19,088	24,160	31,203
Total Shareholders' Equity and Liabilities	35,148	41,068	45,281	58,039

Source: Palamon memorandum.

EXHIBIT 6
Revenues for Top Companies in Italian
Payroll Software Industry, 1998

Company	Revenues (Lire Billions)
TeamSystem	50.7
Inaz Paghe	47.0
Osra	38.0
Sistemi	37.0
Zuchetti	36.0
Esa Software	35.0
Omega Data	34.4
Axioma	26.0
Dylog Italia	25.0

Source: Palamon memorandum.

EXHIBIT 7
Sources/Uses of Cash
in Proposed Transaction

Sources:	
Debt	46,000
Excess Cash	15,000
	61,000
Uses:	
Special Dividend—April 2000	8,500
Special Dividend—Closing	52,500
	61,000

Note: This table refers strictly to the leveraged recapitalization of TeamSystem. Ignored in this table are (1) the lire 50.235 billion purchase of shares by Palamon from investors in TeamSystem and (2) a purchase of TeamSystem real estate for lire 2.1 billion by investors.

EXHIBIT 8

TeamSystem, S.p.A. Pro-Forma Income Statement (values in millions of lire)

	2000	2001	2002	2003	2004	2005	2006	2007	Assumptions
Sales Growth Rate	15%	15%	15%	6%	6%	6%	6%	6%	growth
Total Sales	69,573	80,009	92,011	97,532	103,383	109,586	116,162	123,131	
Cost of materials									
Cost of service									
Rents and leasing									
Total Operating Cost	(31,308)	(36,004)	(41,405)	(43,889)	(46,523)	(49,314)	(52,273)	(55,409)	45.0%
Salaries									
Social contributions									
Other personnel costs									
Total Personnel Costs	(10,784)	(12,401)	(14,262)	(15,117)	(16,024)	(16,986)	(18,005)	(19,085)	15.5%
Other operating costs	(2,783)	(3,200)	(3,680)	(3,901)	(4,135)	(4,383)	(4,646)	(4,925)	4.0%
EBITDA	24,699	28,403	32,664	34,624	36,701	38,903	41,237	43,712	
Depreciation & amortization	(835)	(900)	(975)	(1,010)	(1,046)	(1,085)	(1,126)	(1,170)	25.0%
EBIT	23,863	27,503	31,689	33,614	35,655	37,818	40,111	42,542	
Interest expense	(3,160)	(3,160)	(3,160)	(2,765)	(1,975)	(1,185)	(395)	—	6.9%
Non-op income	561	1,157	1,855	2,091	2,408	2,813	3,310	4,507	5.0%
Pretax profit	21,265	25,500	30,383	32,939	36,088	39,446	43,026	47,049	
Taxes	(10,207)	(12,240)	(14,584)	(15,811)	(17,322)	(18,934)	(20,652)	(22,584)	48.0%
Earnings before minorities									
Elimination of intercompany invest									
Net Income	11,058	13,260	15,799	17,129	18,766	20,512	22,373	24,465	

Source: Casewriter analysis.

EXHIBIT 9

TeamSystem, S.p.A. Pro-Forma Balance Sheet (values in millions of lire)

	2000	2001	2002	2003	2004	2005	2006	2007	
ASSETS									
Cash	13,500	15,202	17,482	18,531	19,643	20,821	22,071	23,395	19.0% of sales
Marketable securities	11,224	23,143	37,096	41,816	48,165	56,253	66,196	90,144	PLUG
Receivables	20,872	24,003	27,603	29,259	31,015	32,876	34,848	36,939	30.0% of sales
Inventory	1,391	1,600	1,840	1,951	2,068	2,192	2,323	2,463	2.0% of sales
Total Current Assets	46,988	63,948	84,021	91,557	100,891	112,142	125,438	152,941	
Intangible assets	20	20	20	20	20	20	20	20	
Land, PP&E	1,581	1,581	1,581	1,581	1,581	1,581	1,581	1,581	
Other tangible assets	1,739	2,000	2,300	2,438	2,585	2,740	2,904	3,078	2.5% of sales
Deferred costs	2,087	2,400	2,760	2,926	3,102	3,288	3,485	3,694	3.0% of sales
Securities and other	1,391	1,600	1,840	1,951	2,068	2,192	2,323	2,463	2.0% of sales
Total Assets	53,807	71,549	92,523	100,473	110,245	121,962	135,751	163,776	
LIABILITIES									
Accounts payable	11,132	12,802	14,722	15,605	16,541	17,534	18,586	19,701	16.0% of sales
Tax and other payables	11,132	12,802	14,722	15,605	16,541	17,534	18,586	19,701	16.0% of sales
Deferred income and accruals	3,479	4,000	4,601	4,877	5,169	5,479	5,806	6,157	5.0% of sales
Long term liabilities	46,000	46,000	46,000	34,500	23,000	11,500	—	—	
Total Liabilities	71,742	75,604	80,044	70,587	61,252	52,047	42,980	45,559	
SHAREHOLDERS' EQUITY AND MINORITY INTEREST									
Capital	4,580	4,580	4,580	4,580	4,580	4,580	4,580	4,580	
Reserves	25,544	(24,398)	(11,138)	4,661	21,789	40,555	61,067	83,440	
Net Income from operations	11,058	13,260	15,799	17,129	18,766	20,512	22,373	24,465	
(Less special dividend)	(61,000)								
Total Shareholders' Equity	(19,818)	(6,558)	9,241	26,369	45,135	65,647	88,020	112,486	
Minority interest	1,883	2,504	3,238	3,517	3,859	4,269	4,751	5,732	3.5% of equity
Total Shareholders' Equity and Minority Interest	(17,935)	(4,054)	12,479	29,886	48,994	69,915	92,771	118,218	
Total Shareholders' Equity and Liabilities	53,807	71,549	92,523	100,473	110,245	121,962	135,751	163,776	
Debt Repayment									
Starting balance	46,000								
	0%	0%	0%	25%	25%	25%	25%		
Principal due	—	—	—	(11,500)	(11,500)	(11,500)	(11,500)		

Source: Casewriter analysis.

EXHIBIT 10
Valuation Measures for Publicly Traded Enterprise Resource Planning (ERP) Software Companies

	Adjusted Mkt Value (a) as a Multiple of:			Equity Market Value as a Multiple of:			Long-Term Projected EPS Growth(b)	CY 1999 P/E to LTGR	Growth Rates 1 Year		LTM Margins	
	LTM Revenues	LTM Op. Inc.	LTM EPS	Cal. 1999 EPS Est. (b)	Cal. 2000 EPS Est. (b)	Cal. 2001 EPS Est. (b)			Rev.	EBIT	EBIT	Net
Tier 1—Large ERP Player												
Baan	4.0 ×	NM	NM	NM	NM	NM	26%	NM	8.2%	NM	−38.0%	−40.2%
JD Edwards	1.6 ×	26.2 ×	37.9 ×	NM ×	95.0 ×	74.9 ×	27	NM	44.2	77.0%	6.2	5.0%
Oracle	6.8 ×	32.0 ×	47.8 ×	42.1 ×	34.4 ×	27.8 ×	24	143%	23.6	32.7	21.2	14.6%
Peoplesoft	2.3 ×	23.6 ×	NM	NM	54.8 ×	44.3 ×	24	231	61.1	41.7	9.9	2.1%
SAP	8.3 ×	42.1 ×	75.2 ×	61.9 ×	45.8 ×	36.6 ×	25	182	41.9	17.4	19.7	11.1%
Low	1.6 ×	23.6 ×	37.9 ×	42.1 ×	34.4 ×	27.8 ×	24	143	8.2	17.4	−38.0	−40.2%
Mean	4.6 ×	31.0 ×	53.6 ×	52.0 ×	57.5 ×	45.9 ×	25	185	35.8	42.2	3.8	1.5%
High	8.3 ×	42.1 ×	75.2 ×	61.9 ×	95.0 ×	74.9 ×	27	231	61.1	77.0	21.2	14.6%
Tier 2—Middle Market Accounting Software Companies												
Great Plains Software	4.8 ×	8.1 ×	56.1 ×	48.2 ×	37.8 ×	28.0 ×	35%	108%	57.5%	590.5%	58.9%	9.5%
Intuit Inc.	5.8 ×	42.8 ×	43.6 ×	62.4 ×	52.4 ×	43.2 ×	21	247%	12.8%	40.1	13.6	16.3%
Epicor Software	1.5 ×	NM	NA	54.2 ×	18.1 ×	14.2 ×	28	66%	NA	NA	−10.0	−10.2%
Sage Group	16.0 ×	58.5 ×	84.3 ×	71.1 ×	58.2 ×	43.0 ×	35	165%	25.9%	26.6%	27.4	17.7%
Symix	0.7 ×	8.2 ×	12.6 ×	13.5 ×	12.1 ×	9.4 ×	28	43%	48.4%	68.0	8.4	5.1%
Low	0.7 ×	8.1	12.6 ×	13.5 ×	12.1 ×	9.4 ×	21	43%	12.8%	26.6	−10.0	−10.2%
Mean	5.8 ×	29.4	49.2 ×	49.9 ×	35.7 ×	27.6 ×	29	126%	36.2%	181.3	19.7	7.7%
High	16.0 ×	58.5	84.3 ×	71.1 ×	58.2 ×	43.2 ×	35	247%	57.5%	590.5	58.9	17.7%
Tier 3—Others												
Agresso	0.8 ×	40.2 ×	42.0 ×	15.6 ×	7.7 ×	3.5 ×	121%	6%	266.4%	3209.1%	2.1%	1.8%
Intentia	1.6 ×	−69.2 ×	NM	62.1 ×	29.5 ×	NA	NA	NA	51.7	115.6	−2.4	−5.5%
Navision	17.6 ×	79.6 ×	126.9 ×	41.6 ×	32.0 ×	NA	NA	NA	91.5	137.9	22.1	14.0%
Brain International	3.1 ×	NM	NM	72.7 ×	31.8 ×	NA	NA	NA	23.1	−66.0	−0.2	1.1%
Low	0.8 ×	−69.2 ×	42.0 ×	15.6 ×	7.7 ×	3.5 ×	121	6%	23.1	−66.0	−2.4	−5.5%
Mean	5.8 ×	16.9 ×	84.5 ×	48.0 ×	25.3 ×	3.5 ×	121	6%	108.2	849.2	5.4	2.9%
High	17.6 ×	79.6 ×	126.9 ×	72.7 ×	32.0 ×	3.5 ×	121	6%	266.4	3209.1	22.1	14.0%

LTM calculations are based on financial results reported in the most recent 10-K and 10-Q fillings and on quarterly earnings reported over the Dow Jones newswire. All revenues, operating expenses and EP have been restated to exclude ordinary credits/charges and discontinued operations. Revenues and operating expenses have been restated to exclude the effects of interest.

(a) Based on Adjusted Market Cap., which is defined as Equity market value + Long-term debt − Cash & equivalents
(b) Based on I/B/E/S estimates

Source: Datastream.

600

EXHIBIT 11
Financial Data for Selected Enterprise Resource Planning (ERP) Software Companies (dollars in thousands, except per-share data)

	Ticker	Share Price 9/3/99	Equity Market Value	Long-Term Debt	Cash & Equiv.	Adjusted Market Value (a)	LTM Revenues	LTM Op. Inc.	LTM EPS	Cal. 1999 EPS Est. (b)	Cal. 2000 EPS Est. (b)	Book Value
Tier 1—Large ERP Players												
Baan	BAANF	$ 12.81	2,637,618	200,546	121,697	2,716,467	674,664	(256,446)	$ (1.35)	$ (0.15)	$ 0.08	112,821
JD Edwards	JDEC	16.88	1,829,385	—	211,782	1,617,603	1,001,263	61,842	0.45	(0.08)	0.18	583,996
Oracle	ORCL	41.50	62,282,746	301,140	2,562,764	60,021,122	8,827,252	1,872,881	0.87	0.99	1.21	3,695,267
Peoplesoft	PSFT	14.25	3,611,452	—	498,155	3,113,297	1,333,095	131,978	0.05	0.09	0.26	664,292
SAP	SAP GR	400.78	41,907,460	718,858	693,411	41,932,907	5,052,321	995,535	5.33	6.48	8.76	2,096,138
Tier 2—Middle Market Accounting Software Companies												
Great Plains Software	GPSI	$ 48.19	767,893	—	123,683	644,210	134,907	79,489	$ 0.86	$ 1.00	$ 1.28	133,193
Intuit Inc.	INTU	93.81	6,476,010	36,043	1,761,200	4,750,853	814,889	111,009	2.15	1.50	1.79	1,673,405
Epicor Software	EPIC	3.80	154,977	—	47,304	107,673	73,688	(7,333)	NA	0.07	0.21	122,196
Sage Group	SGE LN	48.58	5,997,648	136,046	78,171	6,055,523	377,477	103,595	0.58	0.68	0.83	11,187
Symix	SYMX	11.50	84,421	4,109	3,261	85,269	123,010	10,374	0.91	0.85	0.95	36,749
Tier 3—Others												
Agresso	AGR NO	$ 1.85	88,554	1,398	18,680	71,272	85,973	1,771	$ 0.04	$ 0.12	$ 0.24	40,804
Intentia	INTB SS	21.95	557,217	36,833	12,655	581,395	352,988	(8,400)	(0.72)	0.35	0.74	104,085
Navision	NAVI DC	25.51	655,707	—	6,285	649,422	36,875	8,155	0.20	0.61	0.80	9,540
Brain International	BNI GR	40.08	256,499	19,991	39,283	237,207	76,686	(164)	0.13	0.55	1.26	65,365

LTM calculations are based on financial results reported in the most recent 10-K and 10-Q filings and on quarterly earnings reported over the Dow Jones newswire. All revenues and operating expenses have been restated to exclude ordinary credits/charges and discontinued operations. Revenues and operating expenses have been restated to exclude the effects of interest.

(a) Based on Adjusted Market Cap., which is defined as Equity market value + Long-term debt − Cash & equivalents
(b) Based on I/B/E/S estimates
Exchange rate of 1.84 DEM/$
Exchange rate of 7.02 DKK/$
Exchange rate of 0.94 Euro/$
Exchange rate of 7.84 NOK/$
Exchange rate of 8.20 SEK/$
Exchange rate of 0.62 GBP/$

EXHIBIT 12
Recent Lira/Euro Exchange Rates

At January 1, 1999, the European Community fixed the lira/euro conversion rate at LIT 1,936.27. The exchange rates that follow were estimated through euro vs. the dollar exchange rates,[1] and are proxies for open market rates of exchange.

Date	Lire/€
September 1999	1696.3
October 1999	1740.1
November 1999	1901.8
December 1999	1912.6
January 2000	2055.0

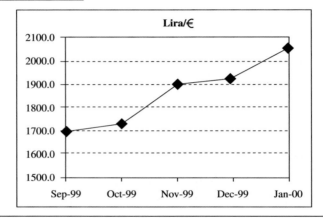

Source of data: Bloomberg Financial Services.

[1]For instance, in September 1999, the EUR/USD exchange rate was 1.0684 and the lira/USD exchange rate was 1812.32. Dividing the lira/USD rate by the EUR/USD rate yields an implied lira/EUR rate of 1696.3.

EXHIBIT 13
Capital Market Conditions (February 2000)

Instrument	Yield
EURIBOR[1]	
90-day	3.41%
6-month	3.78%
1-year	4.11%
Government Bonds (euro-denominated)	
Italy, April 2004	6.00%
Italy, July 2007	5.87
Italy, March 2011	9.25
Euro Area, 5 years[2]	5.16
Euro Area, 7 years	5.45
Euro Area, 10 years	5.61

Equity Market Index	Price/Earnings Multiple
Milan MIB30 Index	37.87
FTSE 100 Index (London)	28.75
DAX Index (Frankfurt)	57.47

Sources: ECB Monthly Bulletin, European Central Bank (March 2000); Bloomberg Financial Services.

[1]EURIBOR stands for euro interbank offered rates.
[2]Euro Area bond yields are harmonized national government bond yields weighted by the nominal outstanding amounts of government bonds in each maturity band.

General Mills' Acquisition of Pillsbury from Diageo PLC

On December 8, 2000, management of General Mills, Inc., recommended that its shareholders authorize the creation of more shares of common stock and approve a proposal for the company to acquire the worldwide businesses of Pillsbury from Diageo PLC. This transaction called for an exchange of shares of General Mills for the Pillsbury subsidiary that would leave Diageo as the largest shareholder in General Mills. Furthermore, it was agreed that just before the transaction, Pillsbury would borrow about $5 billion, and pay a special dividend to Diageo. Finally, General Mills would obtain a contingent commitment from Diageo that would pay General Mills up to $642 million on the first anniversary of the transaction, depending on General Mills' stock price. The proxy statement carried the opinions of General Mills' financial advisers that the transaction was fairly priced. Yet shareholders and securities analysts were puzzled by the contingent payment. What was it? Why was it warranted in this transaction? Would this deal create value for General Mills' shareholders? In light of answers to these questions, should General Mills' shareholders approve this transaction?

GENERAL MILLS, INC.

General Mills was a major manufacturer and marketer of consumer foods with revenues of about $7.5 billion in fiscal year 2000. The firm's market capitalization was about $11 billion. It was the largest producer of yogurt and the second-largest producer of ready-to-eat

This case was prepared by Professor Robert F. Bruner from public information with research assistance by Dennis Hall. It was written as a basis for class discussion rather than to illustrate effective or ineffective handling of an administrative situation. Copyright © 2001 by the University of Virginia Darden School Foundation, Charlottesville, VA. All rights reserved. *To order copies, send an e-mail to* dardencases@virginia.edu. *No part of this publication may be reproduced, stored in a retrieval system, used in a spreadsheet, or transmitted in any form or by any means—electronic, mechanical, photocopying, recording, or otherwise—without the permission of the Darden School Foundation.* Rev. 12/01. Version 2.6.

breakfast cereals in the United States. Headquartered in Minneapolis, Minnesota, the firm's segments included "Big G" cereals, "Betty Crocker" brand desserts, baking and dinner mix products, snack products, and yogurt marketed under the "Yoplait" and "Colombo" brands. Each of these businesses in the United States was mature, and offered relatively low organic growth. The firm pursued expansion opportunities overseas, through company-owned businesses, and through a cereal joint venture with Nestlé, and a snacks joint venture with PepsiCo. Through a program of aggressive share repurchases in the 1990s, the firm had increased its book value debt-to-equity ratio dramatically compared to its peers.

DIAGEO PLC

Diageo, headquartered in the United Kingdom, had been formed in 1997 through the merger of GrandMet and Guinness, making it one of the world's leading consumer goods companies. Its product portfolio consisted of prominent alcoholic drink brands such as Smirnoff, Johnnie Walker, Guinness, J&B, Gordon's, Tanqueray, as well as the Burger King fast food chain and Pillsbury. Pillsbury had been acquired by GrandMet, acting as a "white knight" acquirer to save Pillsbury from acquisition by Sir James Goldsmith, a well-known raider.

THE PILLSBURY COMPANY

Pillsbury produced and marketed refrigerated dough and baked goods under the familiar "Dough Boy" character, canned and frozen vegetables under the familiar "Green Giant" brand, "Old El Paso" Mexican foods, "Progresso" soups, "Totino's" frozen pizzas, and other food products. Pillsbury had been headquartered in Minneapolis, Minnesota, as an independent company, and still had significant administrative operations there. Revenues for the company in fiscal year 2000 were about $6.1 billion.

ORIGIN OF THE TRANSACTION

Seeking to build growth momentum, General Mills studied areas of potential growth and value creation in the spring of 1998. This had generated some smaller acquisitions, and a general receptivity to acquisition proposals by the firm. In early 2000, the firm's financial advisers suggested that Diageo might be interested in selling Pillsbury, in an effort to focus Diageo on its drinks business, and that Pillsbury would complement General Mills' existing businesses. In March 2000, Diageo's chief operating officer contacted General Mills' chairman and CEO to explore a possible sale of Pillsbury. General Mills submitted its proposed deal terms to Diageo in June 2000—the total proposed payment was $10.0 billion. Diageo submitted an asking price of $10.5 billion. The two sides would budge no further, and it looked as if the negotiations would founder. General Mills did not want to issue more than one-third of its post-transaction shares to Diageo, and believed that its shares were undervalued in the stock market. Diageo believed it was necessary to value General Mills' shares at the current trading prices. In an effort to bridge the difference in positions, the two firms agreed upon including in the terms of the deal a contingent payment on the first anniversary of the transaction that would depend on General Mills' share price. James Lawrence, chief financial officer of General Mills, said, "We genuinely believe this is a way in which they could have their cake and we could eat it too. There's no question in my mind that absent this instrument we wouldn't have been able to reach this deal." David Van Benschoten, General Mills' treasurer, added that the contingent payment was another example of the "development of the use of [options] in the past 20 years as finance has come to first understand, and work with, the constructs of optionality."[1]

On July 16, 2000, the boards of General Mills and Diageo approved the final terms. On July 17, the two firms issued press releases announcing the deal. In the week following the announcement, the shares of General Mills lost 8 percent of their value, net-of-market. But in late August, investors began to bid upward the General Mills share price, perhaps in response to the publication of the merger proxy statement and prospectus, and on news that the operating losses at Pillsbury had narrowed further than analysts had expected in fiscal year 2000. That fall, General Mills was the subject of several "buy" recommendations. **Exhibit 1** gives the recent trading history of shares in General Mills.

MOTIVES FOR THE TRANSACTION

General Mills declared in its proxy statement that acquiring Pillsbury would create value for shareholders by providing opportunities for accelerated sales and earnings growth. These opportunities would be exploited through product innovation, channel expansion, international expansion, and productivity gains. The resulting product portfolio would be more balanced. The combined firm would rank fifth in size among competitors, based on global food sales.

In addition to growth, the deal would create opportunities to save costs. Management expected pretax savings of $25 million in fiscal 2001, $220 million in 2002, and $400 million by 2003. Supply chain improvements (i.e., consolidation of activities and application of best practices in purchasing and logistics), efficiencies in selling, merchandising, and marketing, and finally, the streamlining of administrative activities would generate these savings.

---

[1]Quoted from Steven Lipin, "First Roll Out a Tool to Save Doughboy Deal," *The Wall Street Journal,* July 21, 2000, pp. C1 and C2.

TERMS OF THE TRANSACTION

The transaction proposed that an acquisition subsidiary of General Mills would merge with The Pillsbury Company, with Pillsbury surviving as a wholly owned subsidiary of General Mills. The agreement outlined several features:

- **Payment of shares.** General Mills would issue 141 million shares of its common stock to Diageo shareholders. After the transaction, Diageo would own about 33 percent of General Mills' outstanding shares. When the board of directors approved the merger in July, the company's shares traded at around $34.00–$37.00. In the first week of December, the company's shares traded at around $40.00–$42.00.
- **Assumption of Pillsbury debt.** General Mills agreed to assume the liabilities of Pillsbury at the closing, an amount expected to be $5.142 billion of debt. The Pillsbury debt would consist of about $142 million of existing debt, and $5.0 billion in new borrowings, which Pillsbury would distribute to Diageo before closing. Terms of the new debt were conditional upon the consent of General Mills, for whom a primary concern was that it should not lose its investment grade bond rating.
- **Contingent payment by Diageo to General Mills.** At the closing, Diageo would establish an escrow fund of $642 million. Upon the first anniversary of the closing, Diageo was required to pay from this fund an amount to General Mills depending on General Mills' share price:
  - **$642 million,** if the average daily share price for 20 days was $42.55 or more.
  - **$0.45 million,** if the average daily share price were $38.00 or less. This price reflected the price at which General Mills was trading at the time the deal was negotiated.
  - **Variable amount,** if the average daily share price were between $38.00 and $42.55. Diageo would retain the amount by which $42.55 would exceed the average daily share price for 20 days, times the number of General Mills shares held by Diageo.

Some financial professionals called this a "claw-back" provision, since it would reclaim some value for General Mills if its share price rose. Still other professionals referred to this as a "contingent value right" or CVR, a kind of collar that lived beyond the closing of the deal. CVRs were unusual corporate finance devices used to give the seller confidence in the value of the buyer's shares.

Merrill Lynch estimated that the transaction costs for this deal would amount to $55 million.

CONCLUSION

In evaluating this proposal, analysts considered current capital market conditions (see **Exhibit 2**). **Exhibit 3** presents a calculation of the historical share price volatility of General Mills from the past year's weekly stock prices, ending December 8, 2000—this volatility was 0.248. Using the same method to estimate the *historical volatility* for the year ending July 17, 2000 (the date of announcement of the deal), yielded an estimate of 0.249. Analysts knew that it would be possible to estimate the *implied volatility* from traded options on General Mills' shares—prices on these options are given in **Exhibit 4**. **Exhibit 5** presents the volatilities and financial characteristics of General Mills' peer firms. Contingent payments of the sort used in this transaction were rare. **Exhibit 6** outlines some prominent transactions where they had been used previously, mainly in combinations of pharmaceutical firms.

Analysts wondered why the contingent payment was used in this deal, and why it would be attractive to either side. Most importantly, they puzzled over the implications of the contingent payment for the cost of the deal to General Mills' shareholders. Finally, they sought to determine whether the total deal was fairly priced from the standpoint of shareholders of General Mills. The financial advisors of General Mills presented valuation analyses of Pillsbury and General Mills as a foundation for an assessment of the deal terms (see **Exhibit 7** for a summary of the valuation analyses). Nevertheless, some securities analysts remained uncertain about the deal:

> The deal is dilutive . . . we are concerned with the company's expectations that the acquisition will be dilutive to earnings until fiscal 2004. GIS notes the deal will be accretive to EBITDA by fiscal 2002, suggesting the investment community focus on this metric. However, we prefer to monitor traditional earnings growth in order to track a company's progress.[2]
>
> The sizable jump in debt concerns us. After the merger is complete, GIS will have borrowings totaling more than $8.5 billion. To help manage the high leverage, the company will likely suspend any share repurchases, using the funds expected to be received [from asset sales] . . . to work down the large debt load.[3]

Ultimately, these analysts sought to make a recommendation about how General Mills shareholders should vote on the proposed merger: for or against?

---

[2]*Value Line Investment Survey* (August 11, 2000): 1477.
[3]*Value Line Investment Survey* (November 10, 2000): 1476.

EXHIBIT 1
Weekly Stock Price of General Mills (GIS) Compared to S&P 500 Index
(prices indexed to 1.00 at January 13, 2000)

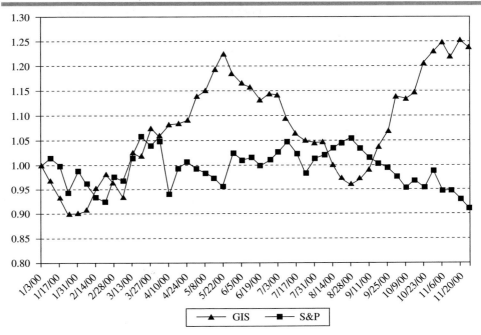

Source of price data: Bloomberg Financial Services.

EXHIBIT 2
Current Capital Market Conditions at December 8, 2000

Equity Market Indexes	
Dow Jones Industrial Average	10,373
S&P 500 Index	1315
NASDAQ OTC Composite Index	2645
Change in Equity Market Indexes over Last 12 Months	
Dow Jones Industrial Average	−5.6%
S&P 500 Index	−5.8%
NASDAQ OTC Composite Index	−21.1%
U.S. Treasury Yields	
Bills (90 days)	6.09%
Bonds	
1 year	5.22%
2 years	5.43%
5 years	5.32%
10 years	5.43%
20 years	5.74%
30 years	5.64%
Corporate Benchmark Rates	
Prime rate of lending	9.50%
LIBOR	6.45%

Sources of data: The Wall Street Journal (December 8, 2000); *Value Line Investment Survey.*

EXHIBIT 3
Estimation of General Mills Stock Price Volatility across 53 Weeks, November 29, 1999, to November 27, 2000

Date	Weekly Closing Prices	Price Relative	Log of Price Relative	Squared Error of Price Relative
29-Nov-99	$36.56			
6-Dec-99	33.55	0.918	−0.086	0.007731
13-Dec-99	32.47	0.968	−0.033	0.001212
20-Dec-99	32.65	1.006	0.006	0.000013
27-Dec-99	34.45	1.055	0.054	0.002695
3-Jan-00	32.67	0.948	−0.053	0.003028
10-Jan-00	31.76	0.972	−0.028	0.000914
17-Jan-00	30.61	0.964	−0.037	0.001518
24-Jan-00	29.39	0.960	−0.040	0.001802
31-Jan-00	29.51	1.004	0.004	0.000005
7-Feb-00	29.58	1.002	0.002	0.000000
14-Feb-00	31.15	1.053	0.052	0.002505
21-Feb-00	32.07	1.029	0.029	0.000721
28-Feb-00	31.46	0.981	−0.019	0.000444
6-Mar-00	30.49	0.969	−0.031	0.001111
13-Mar-00	33.52	1.100	0.095	0.008646
20-Mar-00	33.28	0.993	−0.007	0.000085
27-Mar-00	35.16	1.057	0.055	0.002816
3-Apr-00	34.63	0.985	−0.015	0.000293
10-Apr-00	35.43	1.023	0.023	0.000430
17-Apr-00	35.43	1.000	0.000	0.000004
24-Apr-00	35.61	1.005	0.005	0.000010
1-May-00	37.27	1.046	0.045	0.001882
8-May-00	37.63	1.010	0.010	0.000062
15-May-00	38.98	1.036	0.035	0.001101
22-May-00	40.14	1.030	0.029	0.000752
29-May-00	38.73	0.965	−0.036	0.001418
5-Jun-00	38.12	0.984	−0.016	0.000320
12-Jun-00	37.88	0.994	−0.006	0.000071
19-Jun-00	37.08	0.979	−0.021	0.000538
26-Jun-00	37.45	1.010	0.010	0.000062
3-Jul-00	37.41	0.999	−0.001	0.000009
10-Jul-00	35.81	0.957	−0.044	0.002092
17-Jul-00	34.82	0.972	−0.028	0.000893
24-Jul-00	34.33	0.986	−0.014	0.000263
31-Jul-00	34.27	0.998	−0.002	0.000014
7-Aug-00	34.33	1.002	0.002	0.000000
14-Aug-00	32.73	0.953	−0.048	0.002477
21-Aug-00	31.86	0.974	−0.027	0.000823
28-Aug-00	31.43	0.986	−0.014	0.000243
4-Sep-00	31.74	1.010	0.010	0.000061
11-Sep-00	32.36	1.019	0.019	0.000298
18-Sep-00	33.96	1.050	0.048	0.002150
25-Sep-00	35.01	1.031	0.030	0.000808
2-Oct-00	37.20	1.063	0.061	0.003454
9-Oct-00	37.07	0.997	−0.003	0.000028
16-Oct-00	37.45	1.010	0.010	0.000065
23-Oct-00	39.37	1.051	0.050	0.002320
30-Oct-00	40.05	1.017	0.017	0.000232
6-Nov-00	40.74	1.017	0.017	0.000223
13-Nov-00	39.81	0.977	−0.023	0.000630
20-Nov-00	40.99	1.030	0.029	0.000742
27-Nov-00	40.49	0.988	−0.012	0.000200
Sum		52.132	0.102	0.060218
Average	35.0548	1.003	0.002	0.001158

Number of price relatives:	52
Number of stock prices:	53
Adjusted weekly variance:	0.001181
Annual variance:	0.061
Annual Standard Deviation or Sigma:	**0.248**

Comment: In this table, stock prices are converted into price relatives (which are simply the ratio of today's price to yesterday's price). Then the price relatives are transformed into logarithmic values (in order to normalize the distribution). In the right-hand column, the squared deviations of the logarithmic values are computed from their mean value (0.002). The weekly variance is computed by dividing the sum of the right-hand column (.060218) by the number of price relatives (52) and then multiplying by a correction factor (52/51) to adjust for sampling bias. The annual variance is obtained by multiplying the weekly variance by 52. The standard deviation is the square root of annual variance. For a more detailed discussion of this estimation procedure, see J. Cox and M. Rubinstein, *Options Markets* (Englewood Cliffs, N.J.: Prentice-Hall, 1985), pp. 255–58.

EXHIBIT 4
Prices of Call and Put Options on General Mills Shares

Option	Call	Put
July 19, 2000		
Stock price = $35.00		
Expires July 22, 2000, Strike = $35	$0.25	$0.375
Expires October 21, 2000, Strike = $40	$0.50	$5.375
December 14, 2000		
Stock price = $39.9375		
Expires January 20, 2001, Strike = $45	$0.50	None traded

Note: The 90-day T-bill yield at December 14 was 5.92 percent. In mid-July, the 90-day T-bill yield was 6.14 percent.

Source of data: The Wall Street Journal (July 20, 2000, and December 15, 2000).

EXHIBIT 5
Financial Data on Firms Comparable to General Mills

Company and Business	P/E	Previous Year's Food Sales ($bn) (1)	Previous Year's Sales ($bn) (1)	Beta	Exp. Sales Growth (2)	Exp. Earnings Growth (2)	Expected Dividend Yield (%) (2)	LT Debt to Equity Ratio	Total Debt to Equity Ratio	Sigma (3)
General Mills, Inc. Cereals, desserts, flour, baking mixes, dinner and side dishes, snacks, beverages, and yogurt products	19.8	10.9	16.7	0.65	8.5%	11.5%	1.10	6.719	12.048	0.248
ConAgra Foods, Inc. Packaged foods (shelf-stable foods, frozen foods); refrigerated foods; agricultural products	20.7	17.1	25.4	0.80	4.5%	12.5%	0.90	1.287	2.391	0.398
PepsiCo, Inc. Snack foods, beverages, and juice	30.6	7.9	20.4	0.85	5.5%	11.0%	0.56	0.383	0.399	0.287
Unilever Plc Foods, detergents, personal & home care products	N/A	7.2	43.6	0.75	1.5%	8.5%	0.76	0.160	0.326	0.425
Sara Lee Corporation Packaged meats, frozen-baked goods, coffee and tea, shoe care, body care, insecticides, air fresheners, intimates	11.2	6.9	17.5	0.75	3.0%	8.5%	0.58	2.951	5.266	0.388
H. J. Heinz Company Ketchup, condiments and sauces, frozen food, soups, beans and pasta meals, tuna and seafood products, infant food	22.9	5.1	9.4	0.70	4.5%	9.0%	1.57	2.163	2.365	0.311
Campbell Soup Company Soup and sauces, biscuits and confectionery, and food service	19.7	4.8	6.3	0.80	3.0%	1.0%	0.90	9.050	23.850	0.375
Kellogg Company Cereals, cereal bars, toaster pastries, frozen waffles, bagels, and other products	18.8	4.4	7.0	0.70	5.5%	7.0%	1.10	0.699	2.164	0.365
Hershey Foods Corporation Chocolate and non-chocolate confectionery, pasta and grocery items	25.2	4.0	4.0	0.65	6.0%	9.0%	1.12	0.600	0.790	0.361
Quaker Oats Company Hot and cold cereals, pancake mixes and syrups, grain-based snacks, cornmeal, hominy grits, rice products, and pasta	37.0	2.4	4.7	0.65	5.0%	11.5%	1.14	1.539	1.730	0.337

1. Sales for fiscal year ending before July 17, 2000. PepsiCo's next earliest fiscal year ended in December 1999.
2. Expected sales, earnings, and dividend yield for the five years from 2000 to 2005.
3. Sigma (volatility) was estimated for the 54 weeks before and including July 17, 2000.

Source of data: Value Line Investors Services and casewriter analysis.

EXHIBIT 6
Terms of Other Contingent Payment Schemes in M&A

Deal	Eli Lilly and Company Buys 100% of Equity in Hybritech, Inc.	Rhône-Poulenc Acquires 68% of Equity in Rorer Group, Inc.	Dow Chemical Acquires 67% of Equity in Marion Laboratories	Roche Holding Ltd. Acquires 60% of Equity in Genentech
Closing date	February 1986	July 1990	July 1989	February 1990
Total est. payment (US$)	$412.8 million	$1,600 million	$5,700 million	$1,295 million
General structure	One-stage exchange per each Hybritech share: (1) $22.00 cash or par value of 10-yr. conv. notes paying 6.75%. Conversion price $66.31 per share. (2) 1.4 warrants to buy Lilly common stock at $75.98 per share. (3) One contingent-payment unit (CPU) paying up to $22.00 in dividends over 10 years.	Three-stage transaction: (1) Cash tender offer for 50.1% of stock in Rorer. At $36.50 for 43.2 million shares, the initial cash outlay is $1,577 million. (2) RP transfers its worldwide HPB to Rorer. Rorer pays RP $20 million and assumes $265 million of RP debt. Rorer issues 48.4 million new common shares to RP. (3) RP issues 41.8 million CVRs .	Two-step transaction: (1) Dow acquires 38.9% of Marion through a cash tender offer at $38 per share. (2) Dow contributes its pharmaceutical subsidiary, Merrill-Dow, and 92 million CVRs in exchange for new Marion shares.	Two-step transaction: (1) Roche purchases a 20% interest in Genentech through the purchase of newly issued shares at $22 per share. (2) All non-Roche common shares are exchanged for $18 cash and ½ share of redeemable common stock. Following the transaction, public shareholders will own 40% of voting stock; Roche will own 60%.
Contingent terms	Annual dividend of CPU equal to: [6% of sales + 20% of gross profits − ($11 million * (1.35^t)] divided by number of Hybritech shares. t = years since 1986. Sales and gross profits are for Hybritech.	CVR entitles holders to receive from RP the amount by which $98.26 a share exceeds either a $52.00 floor price or the average market value of Rorer's share price 60 days before the rights' maturity date of July 31, 1993. Maximum payout $46.26 per share. RP has the right to extend maturity of CVRs for an additional year to July 31, 1994. In that event, the ceiling rises from $98.26 to $106.12. Maximum payout increased to $54.12.	Similar to RP CVR: a "put" spread guarantees shareholder returns within a predetermined range of stock prices through 1992.	Redeemable common stock entitles Roche to redeem the shares at pre-determined prices until June 1995. Thereafter, these shares will automatically convert into an equal number of regular common shares. Redemption price starts at $38.00 at closing and rises $1.25 per quarter to the maximum of $60 per share in April–June 1995.

EXHIBIT 7
Valuation Estimates by General Mills' Financial Advisers

	Valuation Based on Comparable Firms	Valuation Based on Comparable Transactions	Valuation Based on Discounted Cash Flow Analysis
		Analysis of Pillsbury	
Analysis by Evercore Partners	LTM EBITDA: $8.6–$12.11 billion LTM EBIT: $8.97–$12.87 billion	LTM EBITDA: $10.59 billion LTM EBIT: $13.21 billion	Without synergies: $8.4–$10.5 billion With synergies: $11.3–14.2 billion
Analysis by Merrill Lynch	$8.598–$10.78 billion, based on LTM EBITDA and LTM EBIT	$9.553–$12.44 billion based on LTM EBITDA and LTM EBIT	Without synergies: $9.184–$11.204 billion With synergies: $11.836–$13.489 billion
		Analysis of General Mills	
Stock price at July 14, 2000: $36.31/share			
Analysis by Evercore Partners	LTM EBITDA: $34.60/share LTM EBIT: $37.17/share LTM Price/Earnings: $41.17/share	Comparable transactions are not an applicable basis for valuation of General Mills, because the firm is not a target in this transaction.	$34.69–$42.15/share
Analysis by Merrill Lynch	$31.75–$42.25/share		$38.50–$46.75/share

Note: Evercore's analyses were expressed in terms of valuation multiples rather than dollar figures. To permit easier comparison with the Merrill Lynch figures and to simplify student analysis, the Evercore multiples were converted by the casewriter into dollar figures using several simplifying assumptions.

Source of information: General Mills Definitive Merger Proxy Statement and Prospectus, filed with the U.S. Securities and Exchange Commission (August 22, 2000).

Printicomm's Proposed Acquisition of Digitech: Negotiating Price and Form of Payment

In December 1998, Jay Risher sat in his office at Printicomm seeking to structure the price and form of payment for the acquisition of Digitech. Risher was the vice president and controller of Printicomm, a communications company that offered "end-to-end" printing service by combining production capabilities with the ability to create finished copy and distribute the printed materials. He had identified Digitech as an attractive acquisition candidate and negotiated a letter of intent granting Printicomm the exclusive right to negotiate the purchase of Digitech. That exclusivity period would expire in two weeks. Due-diligence research revealed that the value of Digitech depended crucially on the managerial know-how of the two leaders of the firm. Risher had gained the agreement of these two individuals to remain with Printicomm for five years to manage the Digitech operations. With the benefit of their leadership, Risher concluded that the value of Digitech would be no greater than $30 million. These individuals believed, however that Digitech was worth $40 million. Since the closing of the transaction was approaching, Risher needed to decide on the appropriate deal structure to use given the existing disparity in the valuation of Digitech and the importance of retaining key Digitech employees after the acquisition.

Risher was impressed with the recent growth of Digitech and the likely prospects for growth in the future. Digitech's revenues had grown from $7 million in 1995 to $24 million in 1998 (see **Exhibit 1** for historical income statements). This rapid growth was attributable to the addition of several key large corporate accounts, which represented almost 40 percent of total revenue in 1997. Printicomm's acquisition of Digitech made strategic sense

This case was prepared from field research by Scott Stiegler under the supervision of Professor Robert F. Bruner. All names and financial data have been disguised. The case was written as a basis for class discussion rather than to illustrate effective or ineffective handling of an administrative situation. Copyright © 1999 by the University of Virginia Darden School Foundation, Charlottesville, VA. All rights reserved. *To order copies, send an e-mail to* dardencases@virginia.edu. *No part of this publication may be reproduced, stored in a retrieval system, used in a spreadsheet, or transmitted in any form or by any means—electronic, mechanical, photocopying, recording, or otherwise—without the permission of the Darden School Foundation.* Rev. 12/01. Version 1.6.

because of the complementarity of the company's products and markets and offered the prospect of significant growth potential. In addition, Risher thought that significant cost and revenue synergies might be realized after the acquisition.

Frank Greene, the founder and owner of Digitech, was 60 years old and wanted to sell the firm to achieve some investment liquidity before retirement. He was quite proud of the fact that the success of Digitech was totally a function of the hard work, knowledge, and expertise displayed by himself and his chief operating officer, Jepson ("Jep") Bucking-ham. Greene wanted to retire within the next few years to spend more time with his grand-children. But walking away from Digitech would be difficult for Greene because he had a rather strong emotional bond with his enterprise and the welfare of its loyal employees. He had chosen to sell the business at this time because he had felt that the current market-place was offering attractive valuations for companies like Digitech. Greene mentioned to Risher that he had recently seen several other firms like his sell for 10 to 12 times EBITDA. Although Greene was ready to recognize a return on his investment in Digitech by selling, he told Risher that he was willing to continue to run the day-to-day operations of Digitech until he retired.

Negotiations for this acquisition began in August of 1998 when Printicomm made a tentative offer of $11 million for Digitech.[1] Since Digitech's value was so strongly a func-tion of the owner's continued involvement, Risher did not initially feel comfortable em-ploying a financial forecast in excess of five years. Given Greene and Buckingham's continued involvement for a period of five years and effective conveyance of their know-how to Printicomm, Risher was prepared to pay a maximum going concern enterprise value of approximately $30 million. This valuation was based on both a discounted-cash-flow analysis (see Exhibit 1) and a review of comparable public companies (see **Exhibit 2**) pre-pared by Risher in his valuation analysis (see also **Exhibit 3** for yields on U.S. Treasury se-curities). Greene was firmly convinced that his business was worth at least 10 times EBITDA for an enterprise value of $40 million. Digitech financed itself with no debt.

The last negotiation between the two parties ended with Printicomm bidding $28 mil-lion and Digitech holding firmly at a price of $40 million. Given the strategic importance of this acquisition, Risher did not want the deal to fall apart over valuation, yet he was not willing to bid in excess of his estimate of $30 million as the maximum estimate of the en-terprise value of Digitech. Risher also knew that other competitors would move quickly to acquire Digitech if Printicomm failed in its attempt. Printicomm's exclusive right to nego-tiate the acquisition of Digitech ended in two weeks. Greene appeared unwilling to budge from his latest asking price.

In an effort to continue negotiating, Risher considered the possibility of proposing an earnout for the transaction. For simplicity, Risher had decided to propose two different earnout structures to Greene at the next meeting. The first earnout structure would extend

---

[1]This value is based on the present value of cash flows over the next five years excluding a terminal value. Printi-comm typically opens with a bid based on this type of valuation for companies such as Digitech that have a ma-jor component of value that is intellectual property.

payments to Greene and Buckingham over the next five years based on Digitech achieving certain operating income targets. Since this five-year plan left Printicomm exposed for a long time, Risher planned to incorporate high earnout targets into this structure. The second earnout structure would only provide for contingent payments over the following three years. Risher felt that the earnout targets should be lower for this structure, since there was less uncertainty about the future in the shorter time frame. The key would be setting the earnout targets in each structure such that Risher and Greene could each arrive at an acceptable enterprise valuation based on their views of the future.

PRINTICOMM

Printicomm was headquartered in Palo Alto, California, with key production facilities in Georgia, Massachusetts, North Carolina, Colorado, Maryland, New York, and Texas. The company was capable of handling electronic submissions of print copy throughout the United States and from 70 major cities abroad. Printicomm provided customers with integrated, "end-to-end" information and communication solutions. These involved a full range of creative, production, and distribution services.

The company was organized around two business units: Professional Communications, serving customers who published information, and Marketing Communications, serving customers who created and conveyed marketing messages. To these two markets, Printicomm offered services ranging across message creation, production, distribution, and fulfillment for well-defined market niches. Printicomm's services included: corporate identity marketing, advertising, custom publishing, direct marketing, financial communication, interactive media, point-of-purchase marketing, promotional marketing, specialty packaging, software duplication, catalog production, magazine and journal production, and general commercial printing.

PROFESSIONAL COMMUNICATIONS

Printicomm Journal Services

PrinticommJS was one of the world's largest producers of scientific, technical, and medical journals. This business unit provided traditional composition, printing, and distribution services, as well as a full complement of digital services, reprint, archiving, and content management for commercial and not-for-profit associations and special interest publishers. PrinticommJS offered a full range of solutions for publishers of journals, magazines, and other time-sensitive information. In order for PrinticommJS to remain an industry leader in journal services, it was going to be critical to stay focused on the rapid technological advances within the industry. The vision for PrinticommJS was to create a "Total Digital Pathway" that would enable complete digital workflows and the creation of a flexible digital content database.

MARKETING COMMUNICATIONS

PrinticommCom

PrinticommCom was a major integrated marketing firm that, in addition to its creative capabilities, offered in-house printing, production, and distribution. PrinticommCom's tactical capabilities included print and broadcast advertising, direct marketing, catalog and collateral design, publication development, and new media. The integrative approach of Printicomm-Com had proven to be attractive to customers who were interested in dealing with a one-stop shop that could be held accountable for all aspects of a communications program.

Printicomm Financial Communications

Among the top five financial printers in the nation, PrinticommFC specialized in the creation, production, and distribution of documents (electronic and traditional) to regulatory agencies and the investing community in over 70 cities worldwide. In addition to the private and public business sectors, PrinticommFC's primary markets included commercial and investment banking institutions, mutual fund companies, legal firms, and insurance companies.

Printicomm Graphic Solutions

PrinticommGS was in the business of integrating printing solutions with a wide variety of high-quality graphic communications services and consultation. Through its Corporate Partnership initiative, PrinticommGS offered analysis that reduced overhead, streamlined procurement systems, and provided innovative solutions to graphic communications challenges. It provided state-of-the-art commercial pre-press and printing, data archiving and management for repurposing content for electronic applications, finishing and binding, and a full array of mailing services. PrinticommGS also was the home of Printicomm Catalog Services, which specialized in providing end-to-end solutions in the catalog industry.

Printicomm Point of Purchase

PrinticommPOP focused on merchandising strategies and creative development, primarily for the quick-service-restaurant, beverage, retail, motor-sports, hospitality, and travel industries. PrinticommPOP handled in-house design, print production and assembly, on-demand production services, kit packing, fulfillment, and database management.

Printicomm Specialty Packaging & Promotional Printing

Printicomm Specialty Packaging and Promotional Printing produced CDs and floppy disks that served as distinguishable advertising vehicles as well as collateral materials that communicated marketing messages. Its services included structural design, production and distribution of high-quality, full-color external and internal packaging, dimensional mailers, corporate identity materials, product literature, computer documentation, and catalogs.

Printicomm Technology Solutions

A turnkey operation for software solutions, PrinticommTS handled CD and floppy-disk duplication, label printing, fulfillment and distribution, inventory and logistics management. PrinticommTS paired its comprehensive in-house services with strategic outsourcing relationships for auxiliary services needed by clients in the high-tech industry and those who wanted to incorporate technology into their customer offerings.

Over the past five years, Printicomm had completed 22 acquisitions in an effort to expand and enhance its capabilities. These acquisitions primarily involved premier marketing communications and publication services companies to complement Printicomm's strong core printing competence. Three of these acquisitions involved various earnout structures, most of which were economically successful. Because of the strong element of "intellectual capital" that typified the acquired companies in these transactions, reinvestment needs and asset values were not typically material elements of valuation. Printicomm found earnout structures to be a useful vehicle to substitute the risk of future cash flows from buyer to seller rather than seeking to mitigate risk by increasing its hurdle rate for the transaction.

DIGITECH

Greene started Digitech 10 years ago after he became frustrated working as a senior software engineer for a large technology firm. Soon after starting his firm, Greene recruited a former colleague, Buckingham, from their previous employer. Buckingham displayed a brilliance for creative programming and energized the development of important new products. One year after start-up Digitech had a market hit with Print-now software. Sales of this product spurred revenues to over $15 million by 1992. However, because of marketing-channel constraints and the fact that a large well-financed competitor quickly entered this market niche, this product's life cycle was short-lived.

Digitech's sales sputtered until the development of its Marketelegence software in 1995, which was the trademarked name for solutions for advertisers and publishers. Marketelegence used interactive technology to manage marketing messages from creation to ultimate placement to consumers. All photography and graphics were digitized and stored while the message and data repository was linked to a page layout program. Sales of this software skyrocketed with the addition of several major new large corporate customers in 1997. These customers represented over 40 percent of 1999's expected sales. Digitech had a great product but was severely constrained by its lack of marketing channel development and understanding. In Risher's view, management was focused on the development of new products, but lacked the managerial depth to manage a rapidly growing firm the size of Digitech.

INDUSTRY HIGHLIGHTS

Commercial printing was one of the nation's oldest and largest manufacturing activities. The industry was highly fragmented with approximately 52,000 printing establishments and one million employees that were dispersed geographically throughout the United States. The top 500 printers represented less than 1 percent of the total population of printers, while their revenues accounted for 34 percent of the total $73 billion of sales in 1998. Most printers competed on the regional, state, and local market level rather than a national level.

Most products of the U.S. commercial printing industry targeted the diverse needs of domestic consumers and businesses. The industry's economic fortunes tracked fluctuations in the nation's GDP and were closely tied to the level of U.S. advertising expenditures. Changes in U.S. demographics typically had a swift impact on the markets for printed products. Expansion of the school-age population generated more comics, textbooks, juvenile books, and youth-oriented periodicals. Growth in household formation promoted the interests of direct mail, newspaper insert, and catalog producers. New-business formation created markets for trade advertising, forms, directories, and financial and legal printing. An increase in the number of senior citizens increased the demand for newspapers and books.

Commercial printing was a mature industry that was undergoing a significant transition. Forces affecting U.S. commercial printing included changes in technology, shifts in the industry's structural dynamics, changes in the demand for print advertising, and imposition of new electronic media on traditional print markets.

Traditional printing operations were long centered on analog technology, a process dependent on photographic film, light-sensitive printing plates, solvent-based inks, and an array of chemicals and developers. This traditional technology was rapidly being replaced by digital technology. As a result, thousands of typesetting firms had been rendered obsolete by digital type produced on desktop computers. Also gone were the many platemaking and color-separation shops whose film-based skills had become worthless as digital processors produced color-corrected films or the digital text and images were applied directly to printing plates. Digital technology was also being applied to printing presses themselves. This yielded cost-effective, full-color short production runs of text and image variable printed products that were previously cost-prohibitive before the advent of digital imaging.

The rapid technological changes in the industry led to increasing consolidation in the industry as players sought economies of scale while attempting to retain a marketing focus that was sensitive to local and regional printing opportunities. A wave of merger and acquisition activities supported by a growing U.S. economy and rising stock market was consolidating ownership among a few dominant players. The most successful consolidators in the industry displayed many of the same qualities. First, they were geographically dispersed and had a specific business strategy. Second, they defined themselves as either a high value-added printer providing extra service in a specialized market niche or a specialized low cost producer in a narrow market niche. The goal of these firms was to become a one-stop shop that administered all their clients' communications needs.

While commercial printing's value of shipments closely paralleled fluctuations in GDP, the industry was largely dependent on U.S. expenditures on print advertising. Since 1980, U.S. advertising through various print media had held steady at approximately 60 percent of total advertising expenditures. Although print advertising's trends in the 1990s showed overall growth in nominal dollars, gains in advertising expenditures among print media varied significantly. Marginal growth was expected in the advertising revenues of newspapers and periodicals, while higher advertising growth was expected in the direct mail, catalog, and insert segments. The increased use of digital printing equipment was expected to enable U.S. printers to respond more rapidly to any changes in print demand that might have arisen from advertising expenditure fluctuations.

Although total demand for U.S. printed products continued to expand, the electronic media provided strong competition. Examples include CD-ROMs, which reduced the need for technical manuals, encyclopedias, and directories; web sites on the Internet, which provided electronic access to digital catalogs, annual reports, and other company information; and e-mail, including electronic commerce, which lessened the demand for newsletters and printed business information and forms. The Internet was used on a regular basis at work or at home by over 29 million U.S. residents age 18 or over. This sector represented 15 percent of the U.S. adult population. A doubling of this Internet-accessed sector over the next decade was virtually assured, guaranteeing further inroads in demand for selected U.S. printed products.

A series of favorable factors were expected to support the growth of U.S. printed product output over the next five years. The U.S. population was projected to reach 280.4 million by 2003, an increase of 8.1 million people. Higher levels of educational attainment and increasing personal income were expected to accompany this population growth. A rising U.S. economy, coupled with growth in aggregate demand for print advertising, were expected to support an inflation-adjusted annual growth rate of 2 percent over the next five years in the value of industry shipments. Competition from the electronic media was expected to reduce U.S. markets for some printed products, but commercial printing's aggregate demand was projected to stay relatively aligned with growth in the nation's economy. The costs of the printing industry's principal material input, paper, were expected to increase over the next five years, adversely affecting printers' profit margins.

SUPPORT FOR THE ACQUISITION OF DIGITECH

Printicomm was at a unique historical inflection point where the skills and competencies upon which its companies originally achieved success were less able to sustain profit growth and margins necessary for quality investment. This slow erosion of print margins and increase in the difficulty of maintaining or growing revenues had severely strained future internal growth. Continuing innovation in graphic reproduction threatened to obsolete current equipment and further increase industry overcapacity, forcing the demise or further consolidation of remaining companies.

Printicomm's strategy in this rapidly changing industry was to grow its business through strategic acquisitions that would provide the company with additional competitive advantages in its selected niches of the commercial printing industry. Risher believed that the acquisition of Digitech would have a significant positive impact on the performance of both the Printicomm Journal Services and Printicomm Point of Purchase divisions. Digitech's Marketelegence software would enhance the capabilities of these divisions by providing customers with the latest electronic marketing solutions.

ALTERNATIVES

Given the difficulty of the negotiations to date, Risher reflected upon some strategic alternatives before him.

Internally Develop Capability

One alternative for Printicomm was to pursue developing Digitech's technology in-house at Printicomm. The time and expense of creating a viable software program with the capabilities of Marketelegence were likely to be high, but a failure to reach a reasonable purchase price for Digitech may have made this a good option. According to some rough calculations performed by Risher, it would have cost Printicomm $50 million to develop the technology. Additionally, it would take approximately two years until Printicomm would have a working prototype that could compete in the marketplace.

Find Another Company to Purchase

Risher knew that it was not too late to pursue an alternative company to acquire. There were a number of other small software companies that had developed their own forms of digital technology for the commercial printing industry, but Risher felt that the Digitech technology was superior to the current competition and was worth a premium price if necessary. Risher also knew that Greene possessed strong managerial skills and that his level of qualifications would be difficult to find in another target company. In addition, it would be frustrating to have to start negotiations with a new company given the time and energy already spent on the Digitech transaction.

Fixed-Price Deal

Negotiations up to this point had focused on determining a fixed sales price for the acquisition of Digitech. A fixed-price deal would certainly be the easiest to consummate, requiring only a standard purchase and sale agreement that highlighted the total consideration in amount and form. Unfortunately, the two parties remained relatively far apart on their respective notions of a fair valuation for Digitech's business. Risher was also concerned that if Printicomm paid a premium price for Digitech, Digitech management would have little incentive to stay on at Digitech and continue to grow the business. Risher thought that the retention of Greene and Buckingham was critical to integrating the companies and transferring business knowledge between the two companies.

Earnout

Given his concerns about valuation and management retention, Risher had begun to consider the idea of using an earnout to move this potential transaction forward. Risher recalled that an "earnout" was an acquisition payment mechanism where some portion of the purchase price of the acquired company (Digitech) would only be paid by the acquiring company (Printicomm) if Digitech attained certain agreed-upon performance goals after the closing. Risher knew that there were three key elements in creating a successful earnout. First, the earnout should be based on achievable performance goals that increase the value of Digitech in the hands of Printicomm after the closing. Second, Digitech's management should receive adequate compensation for creating that value. Third, the earnout should provide Digitech's management with the resources and operating freedom necessary to achieve its performance goals.

Risher knew that an earnout made a lot of sense from an economic perspective, and if designed appropriately, could be viewed as a win-win situation for both parties. He also knew that the two key drivers that could be negotiated in designing an earnout were the time period and the earnout targets. As a result, Risher decided to develop two different earnout structures to present to Greene at their next meeting. The two proposals would offer alternatives that were on either side of the spectrum with regard to time period and earnout targets.

The first earnout structure would extend payments to Greene and Buckingham over the next five years based on Digitech achieving certain operating income targets. Since this five-year plan left Printicomm exposed for a long time, Risher wanted to incorporate high earnout targets into this structure. Risher decided to set the targets as follows: 1999—$2.5 million; 2000—$3.0 million; 2001—$3.0 million; 2002—$3.5 million; 2003—$3.5 million. These targets were purposely set close to Printicomm's projected operating income numbers for Digitech so that Printicomm would only pay additional monies for performance above the expected level. Risher also believed that the dollars paid out at closing could be set at a relatively low value of $20 million because of the potential future value offered to Digitech with a five-year earnout period.

The second earnout structure would only provide for contingent payments over the following three years. Risher felt that the earnout targets should be lower for this structure since there was less uncertainty about the future in this shorter time frame. Risher decided to set the targets as follows: 1999—$2.0 million; 2000—$2.5 million; 2001—$2.5 million. These relatively low targets provided Digitech with a good opportunity to earn additional monies in the earnout, but were still not expected to cost Printicomm much over the shorter time horizon. Since the shortened earnout provided Digitech with less time to capture value from the earnout, Risher believed that the dollars at closing would need to approximate the $28 million fixed-price offer that was already on the table.

The tax treatment of the earnout payments was under consideration by Printicomm's counsel. If Printicomm could deduct the payments as expenses, the cost of an earnout would be materially lower. But it was possible that the earnout payments might be viewed as a dividend, i.e., paid from after-tax earnings. As a starting point, Risher decided to make the more conservative assumption, that the earnout payments were not a deductible expense.

Each earnout would be valued differently by Printicomm and Digitech based on their respective views of the future. Risher decided that he would use a simulation-based valuation model that would use expected distributions for key value drivers. Risher believed that the key drivers of future value for Digitech were sales growth and profit margin. As a result, he set out to determine the appropriate distributions for these variables from the perspective of Printicomm. He projected that sales would grow by at least 5 percent a year, with a maximum growth rate of 15 percent. He further estimated that the most likely growth rate for sales in the future was 10 percent. Risher also decided that the same distribution of expected values could be used for expected future profit margins.

In order to anticipate how Digitech might view an earnout proposal, Risher decided to repeat the analysis, using the distributions that Digitech would likely use for the key drivers in their analysis. Risher reviewed the projections prepared by Digitech and concluded that Digitech's minimum expected future sales growth was 10 percent. He also determined that Digitech's maximum expected sales growth would be 30 percent, with the most likely growth rate equaling 20 percent. Risher expected the distribution for expected profit margins to be slightly tighter with a range from 15 percent to 25 percent, with 20 percent being the most likely.

After designing the two earnout options and determining the distributions for the key value drivers from the perspective of both parties, Risher thought it was time to simulate the values of the earnout proposals to determine the attractiveness of each earnout. Based on this analysis of the two proposed earnouts, he wondered which structure he would propose to Greene and why.

EXHIBIT 1
Historical and Project Income Statements and Cash Flows

Years Ended	Actuals Reported by Digitech							Projection by Printicomm			
	1992	1993	1994	1995	1996	1997	1998	Est 1999	Est 2000	Est 2001	Est 2002
Sales	$15,350	$10,633	$11,313	$6,747	$7,400	$18,651	$23,450	$28,140	$32,361	$36,244	$39,506
Nominal sales growth		−31%	6%	−40%	10%	152%	26%	20%	15%	12%	9%
Cost of goods sold	9,655	8,700	8,890	5,096	3,850	14,800	16,850	21,867	24,868	27,539	30,018
S, G & A	2,500	1,900	1,950	2,200	2,400	2,600	2,600	3,374	3,837	4,249	4,632
Depreciation and amortization	55	55	55	55	65	65	65	84	96	106	116
Total expenses	12,210	10,655	10,895	7,351	6,315	17,465	19,515	25,326	28,801	31,895	34,766
Operating income	$3,140	$(22)	$418	$(604)	$1,085	$1,186	$3,935	$2,814	$3,560	$4,349	$4,741
Operating ratio	80%	100%	96%	109%	85%	94%	83%	90%	89%	88%	88%
Operating income after taxes								$1,688	$2,136	$2,610	$2,844
Plus depreciation and amortization								$84	$96	$106	$116
Less capital expenditures 1% This year's sales.								$(281)	$(324)	$(362)	$(395)
Less additions to wkg. cap. 2% This year's sales.								$(563)	$(647)	$(725)	$(790)
								$929	$1,261	$1,628	$1,775

DCF Valuation: Printicomm's View
Discount rate	10%
Terminal growth rate	5%
PV of total free cash flows	$30,267

	Projection by Digitech			
	Est 1999	Est 2000	Est 2001	Est 2002
Sales	$28,609	$34,331	$40,167	$45,389
Nominal sales growth	22%	20%	17%	13%
Cost of goods sold	21,985	25,789	30,173	34,096
S, G & A	3,392	3,979	4,656	5,261
Depreciation	85	99	116	132
Total expenses	25,462	29,868	34,945	39,488
Operating income	$3,147	$4,463	$5,222	$5,901
Operating ratio	89%	87%	87%	87%
Operating income after taxes	$1,888	$2,678	$3,133	$3,540
Plus depreciation and amortization	$85	$99	$116	$132
Less capital expenditures 1% This year's sales.	$(286)	$(343)	$(402)	$(454)
Less additions to wkg. cap. 2% This year's sales.	$(572)	$(687)	$(803)	$(908)
	$1,115	$1,747	$2,044	$2,310

DCF Valuation: Digitech's View
Discount rate	10%
Terminal growth rate	5%
PV of total free cash flows	$40,285

EXHIBIT 2
Selected Industry Comparables (dollars in millions, except for share data)

Company	Sh O/s (mill)	Sh. price 31 Dec, 96 ($)	Beta (Lev.)	Beta (Unlev.)	Mkt.Val. Equity ($ mill)	Net Debt ($ mill)	Firm Value ($ mill)	Book Value ($ mill)	Revenues ($ mill)	EBIT ($ mill)	Net Income ($ mill)	1999(E) EPS	EBITDA
Champion Industries	9.714	10.25	0.54	0.49	100	17.86	117	90.62	123.06	7.87	4.15	1.14	11.49
Cunningham Graphics Intl	5.305	15.25	N/A	N/A	81	2.4	83	6.3	53.15	3.51	4.01	1.05	4.20
Baldwin Technology A	14.920	5.625	0.53	0.43	84	33.11	117	126.91	231.41	14.39	9.02	0.57	18.37
Polyvision Corp	14.093	2.0625	0.25	0.23	29	3.36	32	N/A	34.17	1	1	0.09	2
PrimeSource Corp	6.529	6.625	0.62	0.42	43	34.15	77	105.1	453.05	9	4	0.89	12
Tufco Technologies	4.426	5.00	0.10	0.07	22	17.7	40	65	76.97	2	0	0.13	5
IPI Inc	4.734	3.4375	N/A	N/A	16	0.05	16	32.48	8.53	1.95	2.03	0.43	2.37

	Enterprise Value as a Multiple of				Equity Value as a Multiple of	
	Revs.	EBIT	Net Income	EBITDA	1999(E) EPS	Book Value
Champion Industries	1.0	14.9	28.3	10.2	9.0	1.1
Cunningham Graphics Intl	1.6	23.7	20.8	19.8	14.5	12.8
Baldwin Technology A	0.5	8.1	13.0	6.4	9.8	0.7
Polyvision Corp	0.9	23.3	32.1	18.3	22.9	N/A
PrimeSource Corp	0.2	8.3	18.9	6.6	7.4	0.4
Tufco Technologies	0.5	17.8	120.7	8.2	38.5	0.3
IPI Inc	1.9	8.4	8.0	6.9	8.0	0.5
Low	0.2	8.1	8.0	6.4	7.4	0.3
High	1.9	23.7	120.7	19.8	38.5	12.8
Median	**0.9**	**14.9**	**20.8**	**8.2**	**9.8**	**0.6**

Sources: Bloomberg Financial Services and casewriter analysis.

EXHIBIT 3
Yields on U. S. Treasury Securities

Maturity	Current	1 Year Ago
1 year	4.69%	5.55%
2 year	5.00	5.69
3 year	5.04	5.70
4 year	5.08	5.73
5 year	5.11	5.75
10 year	5.22	5.74
30 year	5.57	5.90

Source: The Wall Street Journal.

Structuring Repsol's Acquisition of YPF S.A. (A)

Repsol will seek to negotiate with YPF to achieve a successful integration of the two companies.

—Repsol S.A.[1]

It was a shock to Alfonso Cortina, Repsol's chief executive, when he was cold-shouldered at his first YPF board meeting. . . . The Argentine company, under the leadership of Roberto Monti, appeared determined to resist Mr. Cortina's efforts to start integrating the companies' activities.[2]

In early April 1999, Alfonso Cortina reflected on the resistance of YPF to his firm's overtures. Repsol was the dominant oil company in Spain, and the 13th largest in the world in reserves. Seeking oil reserves and the advantages of larger scale, Cortina had embarked on a strategy of acquiring oil assets throughout Latin America. He began to acquire Yacimientos, Petroliferos Fiscales S.A. (YPF) when the Argentine government announced that it

---

[1]"Presentation to Security Analysts on 22 January 1999," Repsol's web site, www.repsol.com, accessed January 27, 2000.

[2]"Repsol: The Winner Must Oil the Wheels," *Financial Times,* accessed at ft.com-Mergers and Acquisitions/Case studies, 27 January 2000.

This case was prepared from public information by Fernanda Pasquarelli and Pablo I. Ciano under the supervision of Professor Robert F. Bruner. The financial support of the Batten Institute is gratefully acknowledged. Copyright © 2000 by the University of Virginia Darden School Foundation, Charlottesville, VA. All rights reserved. *To order copies, send an e-mail to* dardencases@virginia.edu. *No part of this publication may be reproduced, stored in a retrieval system, used in a spreadsheet, or transmitted in any form or by any means—electronic, mechanical, photocopying, recording, or otherwise—without the permission of the Darden School Foundation.* Rev. 12/01. Version 2.5.

would sell its block of shares in the firm. YPF was the largest oil company in Argentina, and the 12th largest in reserves. Management of YPF had resisted negotiating a friendly acquisition. To complete a takeover of the firm, Cortina would need to appeal directly to the shareholders in the form of a tender offer to purchase their shares. Unsolicited tender offers were extremely rare events in cross-border M&A and especially between developed and developing economies. It was very important to Repsol's management that an offer be structured that would receive the support of YPF's shareholders and repel potential competitors. A tender offer of this magnitude would be the biggest ever by a Spanish company, and the biggest ever in the energy sector.

The first step in planning the tender offer was to settle on the amount of consideration Repsol would pay for the 85 percent of YPF it did not already own. Cortina had decided to offer $44.78[3] per YPF share. The next step would be to determine the form of payment and financing for the offer. Repsol could offer cash, shares of Repsol stock, or conceivably a mix of the two. Any cash offer would need to be financed by an issue of debt or equity securities, since the cash reserves of the firm would not meet the total payment of $13.438 billion. Mr. Cortina contemplated the three possible financing alternatives. He wondered what were the comparative advantages and disadvantages of the alternatives, and how they should be analyzed.

HISTORY OF THE TRANSACTION

In January 1998, the Argentine government announced its intention to sell its 20.56 percent holding in YPF that remained after the firm's privatization several years earlier. But unexpected volatility in the equity markets caused the auction to be delayed. In September, the government invited 16 companies to bid for a block of 14.99 percent, with a minimum price of $38 per share. Of the 16 invitees, only six signed the confidentiality agreement to gain access to private information about YPF and to gain the right to bid in an auction for the block of YPF shares. These included Repsol, ENI SpA of Italy, Consolidated Natural Gas of Pittsburgh, Argentina's Perez Companc SA, and Britain's BP Amoco PLC.

On January 20, 1999, Repsol won the bidding at the minimum price of $38 per share, reflecting the absence of any other bidders. This bid was at a 30 percent premium to the market price of a few days earlier, $29.25. One analyst remarked, "It's a steal,"[4] noting that Repsol would be acquiring YPF's energy reserves at a comparatively cheap price of $3.65 per barrel. Another analyst team[5] opined that the bid was in line with the prevailing EBITDA multiples.

---

[3]Figures in this case are quoted in U.S. dollars, consistent with general practice in international oil transactions, and cross-border M&A. Also, the Argentine peso was convertible into the dollar at parity (i.e., one-for-one).

[4]Quotation of Vinod Sehgal in "Repsol Wins Stake in YPF with $2 Billion Bid," *The Wall Street Journal*, 21 January 1999.

[5]Irene Himona, Rachel Beaver, and Andrew Whittock, "Repsol-YPF: A Quantum Leap," *ABN-AMRO*, 6 September 1999.

A news report noted:

> Repsol is now likely to start a long and arduous courtship with YPF's loyal shareholders in an attempt to convince them that further integration with Repsol, and its Argentine oil and gas subsidiary Astra . . . makes sense. . . . YPF's bylaws say that any buyer who pays a premium for 15 percent of the company's shares or more must pay all other shareholders the similar premium in cash. That rule makes an all-cash tender offer for YPF difficult. . . . Repsol is likely to solicit a vote for an extraordinary shareholders meeting and then ask for a change in bylaws allowing for a tender offer via a stock swap. That move is bound to meet with some opposition, if only because there is a wise perception that Repsol has badly managed Astra, which it purchased a few years ago. "It has not struck my attention that Repsol is noted for its ability to cut costs and merge companies," said [one money manager].[6]

The Argentine government would maintain a "golden share."[7] The government would support a Repsol tender offer for the balance of YPF for a period of three years, including supporting changes to YPF's bylaws to facilitate an acquisition. Any third party interested in launching a tender offer for 100 percent of YPF would have to pay a premium of 25 percent over the price paid by Repsol for its block of YPF.

The securities markets expected Repsol's management to announce plans to increase control in YPF. Therefore Alfonso Cortina wanted to make a public announcement before the end of April. It was time to choose a form of payment (stock for stock or all cash) and financing (debt, equity, or a combination) for the transaction. Mr. Cortina understood that to meet investors' expectations and to minimize the cost of the acquisition he needed to assess conditions in the current debt and equity global capital markets, especially the increasing risk in emerging economies and volatile oil prices.

INDUSTRY OUTLOOK

After a long period of weak oil prices, 1999 was likely to be a year of recovery. Prices had been depressed in 1998 due to the Asian crisis, the expansion of Iraqi oil exports, and warm winters in Europe and North America. But oil prices had increased unexpectedly in recent months, increasing the attractiveness of firms with proven reserves. Inventories of oil in the United States and Asia were contracting as a consequence of strong demand. This, combined with OPEC's compliance with a landmark agreement reached in March to boost sagging oil prices by slashing daily output by 7 percent, was driving prices up. The rebound began in late March and industry analysts predicted that it would likely continue in the future, taking crude prices towards $18 to $20 per barrel. **Exhibit 1** shows oil price fluctuations during the last nine years.

---

[6]Ibid.

[7]Golden shares were a common feature of most privatizations of state-owned enterprises. They were first introduced by the British government in its privatization program that began in the 1980s under the leadership of Prime Minister Margaret Thatcher. In YPF's case, the golden share would permit the government to exercise veto power in (1) a merger of YPF with any other company, (2) acquisition by any other company of more than 50 percent of the capital, (3) sales of significant assets involved in exploration and production activities, and (4) dissolution of the company. Unclear was the possible influence of this golden share on the management of YPF.

Spot oil prices were trading at around $25 per barrel for January 2000 deliveries. Traders seemed anxious about what would happen in March 2000, when the actual OPEC agreement would expire. At a recent meeting, the oil cartel representatives expressed their interest in stable prices. With strong demand, observers speculated that they might increase production. Industry players still remembered OPEC's inaction for production restraint during 1998 that drove prices to a 30-year low, below $10 per barrel, seriously damaging the sector's profitability.

The natural gas sector also looked promising, especially in Latin America, which was enjoying strong demand coupled with the final stages of industry deregulation. The construction of various cross-border pipelines would reduce supply/demand imbalances and would make the product available to countries with perennial need for gas. Experts forecasted expected growth rates of natural gas volumes at 25 percent for Brazil, 12 percent for Chile, and 5 percent for Argentina.

A recent wave of very large mergers had suddenly changed the paradigm of competition in the oil industry. **Exhibit 2** compares recently announced "jumbo" deals to Repsol's contemplated takeover of YPF. Second-tier firms in America and Europe realized that they were too small to compete with the giants for the biggest of the multibillion-dollar projects in risky but important places such as China and Africa. Yet they were not sufficiently focused to compete effectively against niche firms with geographic or technical specialties.

An industry analyst likened the current merger madness to "the rush to find a partner, any partner, at a school dance after the big boys have picked the best ones." He suggested that remaining firms could try to succeed alone; but to do so they would have to rethink their strategies.

REPSOL S.A.

Repsol was an international integrated oil and gas company. In 1998, it was the largest industrial company in Spain in terms of revenue. Compared to other large competitors, it was the "oil company without any oil,"[8] with 1.1 billion barrels in proven reserves, ranking it 13th after YPF, which had 3.1 billion barrels.

Repsol was founded in 1987 when the Spanish government consolidated various state-owned oil and gas assets. Spain sold 24 percent of the firm to public investors in 1987, another 66 percent in 1996, and the remaining holdings in April 1997. Its shares were quoted on the Madrid Stock Exchange and in the form of ADRs[9] on the New York Stock Exchange.

Repsol had operations in 26 countries. Since 1996, the firm had been pursuing a strategy to create a new geographical dimension to its operations in markets with high growth potential. Latin America was the center of Repsol's strategy and accounted for $3 billion invested in the region since 1995. In Latin America, Repsol saw excellent opportunities to

---

[8]Quotation from an unnamed analyst in *The Wall Street Journal,* 21 January 1999.

[9]ADRs (American Depositary Receipts) are receipts issued by U.S. banks to American buyers as a convenient substitute for direct ownership of stock in foreign companies. ADRs are traded on stock exchanges and in the over-the-counter market. Foreign companies issue ADRs as a way of reaching the American stock market.

reinforce important pillars of its corporate strategy, in particular the desire to strengthen its upstream business and to strengthen its gas business, exploiting the links to electricity generation. Prior to the YPF bid, Repsol had acquired refining assets in Peru, and 67 percent of Astra, the fifth-largest energy company in Argentina. Astra derived the bulk of its earnings from exploration and production, and became a platform for the acquisition of other oil assets in Argentina. Cortina intended to merge YPF with Astra,[10] which, if it pushed through, would require Repsol to dispose of assets in order to satisfy Argentine antitrust authorities.

Exhibit 3 gives Repsol's recent financial statements. Repsol's share price had risen 27 percent to $16.74 at the end of March 1999 from $13.62 at the end of September 1998, reflecting the rise in oil prices in early 1999 and the market's reaction to the YPF deal. Historically, Repsol's P/E ratio had been similar to its European rivals but below major U.S. competitors. With a market capitalization of $15 billion, Repsol was perceived as a neutral or "hold" stock by securities analysts. Analysts agreed that if Repsol succeeded in a full acquisition of YPF, then the increase in size of the company, its more balanced revenue mix, and its geographical diversity would help the shares trade at higher earnings and cash flow multiples than in the past.

YPF S.A.

YPF was Argentina's largest company with a market capitalization of $15 billion. It was engaged in the exploration, development, and production of oil and natural gas, in electricity generation activities, and in the refining, marketing, transportation, and distribution of oil and a wide range of petroleum products, petroleum derivatives, petrochemicals, and liquid petroleum gas. **Exhibit 4** gives YPF's recent financial statements.

YPF played a key role in the energy industry in Argentina, accounting for 51 percent of the total estimated crude oil production, 58 percent of the total domestic and export sales of Argentine natural gas, 51 percent of the total refining capacity, and 37 percent of all service stations. The company had been pursuing an aggressive expansion strategy, mainly through joint ventures in areas in which it held concessions.

As part of the government privatization program, YPF completed an initial public offering in 1993. As a result, the Argentine government's ownership of YPF's equity was reduced from 100 percent to approximately 20 percent. **Exhibit 5** contains the current YPF structure of equity ownership. In addition, YPF restructured its internal organization and significantly reduced the number of its employees, from over 51,000 at December 1990 to 7,500 at December 1993. At December 1998, YPF had approximately 9,500 employees. Thanks to this restructuring, the firm outperformed its peer group of Latin American oil companies, and generally was regarded as an efficiently run firm.

Despite its low cost structure, strong management, commanding position in Argentina's downstream industries, and the strong export potential of natural gas to Brazil,

---

[10]"CMS Keeps Eye on YPF-Repsol Merger," *Alexander's Gas & Oil Connections, Company News, Latin America,* 11 June 1999, www.gasandoil.com, accessed 27 January 2000.

YPF's future performance could be affected by certain risk factors, such as economic and political risks in Argentina and other countries where YPF had operations, and volatility in oil prices. Argentina's economy experienced periods of slow or negative growth, high inflation, currency devaluation, and the imposition of exchange rate control measures. The currency board system[11] adopted by Argentina in 1991 brought more uncertainty about the peso, in that it differed from an orthodox currency board system. "An orthodox currency board system had no central bank and no room for discretionary monetary policy. Argentina's monetary system, in contrast, had a central bank with room for discretionary monetary policy."[12] Moreover, YPF's revenues in dollars and costs in pesos increased the risks of any change in the exchange rate policy in Argentina.

The tight link between Argentina and other emerging countries amplified uncertainty about the timing of this transaction. Emerging economies seemed to be recovering from the financial collapse that began with the Russian debt moratorium in August 1998 and was followed by the Brazilian currency devaluation on January 13, 1999 (five days before the Argentine auction of YPF shares). Investors remained reluctant to invest in emerging economies.

Foreign petroleum exploration, development, and production activities were subject to a variety of regulatory and political risks, including foreign exchange controls from other countries, expropriation of property, and risks of loss in countries due to civil strife and guerilla activities. These risks might interrupt YPF's operations. **Exhibit 6** presents the actual sovereign ratings for all the countries where YPF currently had operations, as well as capital market conditions.

Fluctuations in oil prices would affect the timing and reduce the amount of projected capital expenditures related to explorations and development activities, which in turn, could have a negative effect on YPF's ability to replace reserves. The ability to replace reserves was a crucial factor for companies in the commodity sector, because it suggested the company's ability to continue in the business. Credit ratings and cost of financing depended not only on the level of reserves but also on their estimated average life. For this reason, YPF's exposure to oil prices could ultimately increase investors' concerns about the future outlook for YPF.

M&A ENVIRONMENT[13]

M&A activity worldwide exploded from 1994 to 1998: the value of announced European transactions had grown at a compound average rate of 42 percent. In the first quar-

---

[11]Under Argentina's currency board system, the peso trades at a fixed rate one-to-one with the dollar and is convertible on demand. See Steve H. Hanke and Kurt Schuler, "A Dollarization Blueprint for Argentina," *Foreign Policy Briefing,* Cato Institute, 11 March 1999, 1.

[12]Ibid., 8.

[13]This section draws certain facts from presentations at the Mergers and Acquisitions Conference, Crédit Suisse First Boston, 14 May 1999.

ter of 1999, announced deals in Europe amounted to $449 billion, compared with $128 billion a year earlier. This reflected increases in both the number of deals and in the average transaction size. European M&A activity was driven by both global influences (such as deregulation, globalization, buoyant equity markets, etc.), and European-specific influences (such as the creation of the European Monetary Union, pressure by governments to create "national champions," and consolidation of previously fragmented markets).

In Latin America, many of the same forces exerted influence on M&A activity, though with an emerging-markets twist. Generally, the liberalization of markets through trade, deregulation, and privatization pushed firms to use their resources more efficiently. The rise of regional trading blocs (such as Mercosur) and globalization made it attractive for foreign buyers to establish "regional platforms" for business activities and further acquisitions in key markets. As business and capital markets matured, equity market volatility in those markets gradually declined. Strengthening business fundamentals and relatively low valuations meant that business assets might be acquired at reasonable prices. These factors combined created a compelling argument for foreign and domestic firms to seek to acquire in emerging markets.

M&A activity in Latin America had increased at a compound rate of 58 percent from 1995 to 1998. Latin American deal volumes in 1997 and 1998 were greater than the previous 10 years combined. European-based acquirers had increased their activity by four times between 1996 and 1998. Acquisition activity was not slowed by the Brazilian crisis in early 1999. Seventy-five percent of recent transactions were in Brazil, Argentina, and Mexico. Seventy-three percent of M&A volume occurred in capital-intensive industries.

MOTIVES FOR THE ACQUISITION

Repsol management noted several advantages from this transaction:

- **Geographic diversification.** YPF would deepen Repsol's business base in Argentina, and give it a material presence in other Latin American countries.
- **Business diversification.** Repsol's activities were concentrated in the "downstream" segment of the oil industry: refining and marketing. YPF had a substantial presence in exploration and production. Also, YPF would add a significant activity in natural gas.
- **Acquisition of reserves.** The transaction would convey YPF's substantial reserves at relatively low average price.
- **Competitive preemption.** Acquiring this dominant competitor in Latin America would deny other oil companies access to this market. YPF had a strong brand in Latin America.
- **Critical mass.** The transaction would elevate Repsol in the league tables of integrated oil companies. This would permit the exploitation of some economies of scale. More importantly, it would create the financial strength to permit exploration for new reserves and more aggressive marketing.

The precipitous decline in oil prices during 1998 (West Texas Intermediate grade was down by 34 percent over that year) had encouraged several high-profile consolidations in the oil and gas sector. Cost savings, economies of scale, concentration, and consolidation of capital spending motivated these. However, Repsol's full takeover of YPF was driven by a strategic step to take advantage of a unique opportunity.

For Repsol, the acquisition of YPF represented an opportunity to meet a number of its ambitions quickly. It would create an entity with a much better balance in a business sense, given that YPF's upstream business counterbalanced Repsol's orientation to the downstream. **Exhibit 7** shows the impact of the acquisition on Repsol's revenue sources. For both companies, the combined entity represented a geographical diversification from focused country-based current operations.

The acquisition reflected Repsol's four strategic objectives:[14]

Rank of Repsol-YPF among European and American Integrated Oil Companies:	
Total assets	8th
Operating revenues	9th
Operating income	7th
Net income	6th
Oil & gas production	9th
Oil & gas reserves	7th
Service stations	8th

1. Grow Upstream: YPF would strengthen Repsol's upstream business; oil and gas reserves would grow by over four times; oil and gas production would rise by 4.3 times.
2. International expansion: YPF would triple Repsol's presence in Latin America with 50 percent of the new group's total assets.
3. Diversify into gas/power generation: YPF would raise gas production eightfold.
4. Retain domestic market share: YPF's acquisition would complement Repsol's dominance in the Spanish market.

SYNERGIES

Repsol's operating management believed that a combination of Repsol and YPF would yield synergies in three areas:

- Cost savings after tax of $80 million in 1999, rising to $300–350 million by the end of 2000 achieved primarily through merging YPF and Astra. This savings amounted to 1.6 percent of the combined cost base of the two firms in 1998, and compared with 7.1 percent savings in the BP-Amoco deal. Some analysts believed that this estimate was too conservative and that the cost savings might amount to $500 million by 2002.
- More focused capital expenditure. By combining the two entities, the sum of the two companies' capital expenditure in the period 1999–2002 could be reduced from $15.6 billion to $13.6 billion, which would conserve cash as well as reduce net interest expense.

---

[14]Himona, Beaver, and Whittock, "Repsol-YPF: A Quantum Leap," *ABN-AMRO,* 6 September 1999.

- Better balance between upstream and downstream operations would generate increases in revenue from the enhanced integration and capital efficiency of the new group. These pretax synergies would start at $50 in 1999–2000 and were expected to reach $200 in 2003.

Repsol's managers also expected to divest noncore assets by 2002, yielding $2.5 billion after taxes.

FINANCIAL EFFECTS OF THE COMBINATION

Analysts believed that the new company, compared to the old Repsol, would have lower earnings volatility due to its more balanced source of profits (upstream versus downstream). At the same time it would have increased sensitivity to oil prices as a consequence of higher exposure to exploration and production activities. In sum, Repsol-YPF would enjoy lower earnings volatility at the expense of higher oil price sensitivity.

The acquisition of YPF by Repsol might increase Repsol's financial risk. The cost of capital might increase due to the political and economic risks that operations in an emerging region would bring. If the cost of capital were higher in developing countries than in developed countries, then it would seem that YPF's cost of capital would be higher than Repsol's. Combining the two firms could therefore result in a higher WACC after acquisition than for Repsol on a stand-alone basis, since 40 percent of the assets were going to be located in Argentina.

Repsol's capital structure and cost of capital would both be affected by the transaction. First, the diversification of business activities would affect the perceived *operating risk* of the new firm. Second, any choice of form of payment and transaction financing would affect the perceived *financial risk* of the firm. The cost of capital would be affected by leverage choices and investors' beliefs about default risk. **Exhibit 8** describes the calculation of the WACC for YPF (12.55 percent), Repsol (8.14 percent), and the new firm, Repsol-YPF (10.6 percent, if the all-debt financing alternative were chosen, or 11.07 with all-equity financing).

FORM OF PAYMENT

Repsol's management intended to make a tender offer to buy the 85.01 percent of YPF's shares that it did not own, at a price of $44.78 a share. A tender offer was simply a bid to acquire shares of another firm, made directly to the shareholders of the target. Mr. Cortina needed to make a final recommendation on the form of payment, i.e. cash, Repsol shares or a combination.

A reporter noted,

> Repsol had always planned to mount a stock rather than a cash offer to secure control of its prey. But with the YPF board opposed, a messy struggle to change YPF's statutes . . . appeared inevitable.[15]

---

[15]"Repsol: The Winner Must Oil the Wheels," *Financial Times,* accessed at ft.com-Mergers and Acquisitions/Case studies, 27 January 2000.

Endesa, a Spanish electric power company, had acquired the Chilean power company Enersis, and had attempted to assume control through a change in the bylaws of Enersis, but encountered resistance from Enersis. The cash deal seemed to be the easiest option to implement, because the acquisition could have been made based on the current YPF bylaws. The difficulty experienced by Endesa in Chile was not a promising precedent.

In a cash transaction, YPF's shareholders would receive a fixed price and would not participate in any additional gains or losses after the acquisition. Depending upon their expectations and uncertainties in the market, this option could be very attractive. This alternative would also signal the serious intention of Repsol's management to achieve the strategic synergies and to implement the growth strategy in Latin America.

However, in view of YPF's and Repsol's similar size, some analysts believed that a cash offer would be outside Repsol's financing capabilities. In addition, the short-term balance sheet risk that would be created by the abrupt increase in debt concerned Mr. Cortina. Financing would need to be arranged almost simultaneously with the cash offer in order to minimize the balance sheet risk and persuade YPF shareholders that Repsol could consummate the transaction.

On the other hand, a stock-for-stock deal offered important advantages. It would not be immediately taxable to YPF shareholders. Depending on the final price and capital gains obtained, YPF's shareholders might prefer a stock deal over cash in order to defer taxes. But a stock-for-stock deal might not be the best alternative given that Repsol's shares had recently underperformed the European market index by 19 percent.

FINANCING A POSSIBLE CASH BID

In order to support a cash bid, Repsol would have to put together a financing consortium to provide $13.4 billion of cash. However, Alfonso Cortina needed to decide on the most effective way to finance this cash outlay in the long run. The financial staff had analyzed three alternatives for financing a cash bid based on certain assumptions.

Alternative 1: Financing with Debt

Mr. Cortina explored financing a $13.4 billion cash offer by issuing a global bond. The possible terms of such an offer were not completely certain. Cortina asked his finance staff to recommend the possible structure of a globally issued bond including currency, maturity structure, coupon rate, fixed/floating rate, required yield, covenants, placement, and so forth. There were many variables to be defined in a short period of time.

The success of the bond issue would depend on the current situation in the debt capital markets. Two important crises affected the debt market recently. The first, triggered by the Russian debt moratorium in August 1998, caused a huge outflow of foreign investment from emerging economies, mainly in Asia and Latin America. The second crisis occurred in early January 1999, when Brazil sustained one of the most dramatic currency devaluations in its history. Once more, investors moved their portfolios to less risky instruments, such as U.S. treasury bonds.

Even though there were many uncertainties in the debt capital markets, Repsol's management was aware that debt financing tended to be cheaper than equity. If Repsol were successful in issuing the global bond, its net debt could move up sharply. Repsol's board was eager to capture the value represented by the tax benefits originating from tax shields. Moreover, the decrease in the combined enterprise's cost of capital was a factor that would create value for shareholders, especially in a scenario with future acquisitions and capital expenditures already being projected by YPF.

Possibly enhancing the chance of debt financing was the fact that Repsol had already proved that it could do a global bond offering. In early February 1999, Repsol issued a global bond for 1.1 billion euros at an interest rate of 3.81 percent, or only 45 basis points above the benchmark German government five-year bond rate. This was the largest fixed-income offer carried out by a Spanish company in international financial markets, and the second-largest ever denominated in euros. The purpose of the issue was to refinance the payment by Repsol for the Argentine government's shares in YPF.

Still, Cortina was reluctant to accept the debt offering as the best way to finance the tender offer for YPF's shares. A sudden increase in Repsol's leverage would almost certainly trigger a downgrade in Repsol's debt ratings and an increase in the cost of debt. **Exhibit 9** gives the S&P rating categories associated with different financial ratios. Cortina was determined to maintain a solid investment-grade rating—in fact, he aimed for a rating of no less than a single-A during 2000. In addition to the predictable effect on debt rating, increased leverage would undermine Repsol's ability to meet unforeseen financing requirements as they arose. **Exhibit 10** presents an assessment of the probability of default for Repsol under the three financing alternatives.

YPF's strength in "upstream" activities meant that the oil price level and trend would be crucial in determining the profitability of the new company. The all-debt option was highly sensitive to price changes since the company's repayment capacity was strongly linked to the macro conditions in the sector.

Among the many other concerns he had, Alfonso Cortina was not sure about investors' reaction to this huge debt issuance. There was also uncertainty about the final price or yield of the bond given the recent global financial crises in Russia and Brazil. Was the market ready for financing new investments in emerging markets? Was there liquidity for a $13.4 billion bond offer? How would the market react to the offer? What would a bond issue signal to the investor community?

According to the industry practice and to Repsol practice, long-term bonds were the most typical source of debt finance. In the 1990s, investment-grade corporations issued bonds with maturities ranging from 8 to 17 years and coupon rates from 6 to 8 percent. However, Mr. Cortina was aware that market conditions might have changed.

In order to keep the investment grade rating, the maturity would have to be shorter, around five years. And the coupon rate would have to include a spread of 300 basis points over U.S. treasury yields, reflecting the uncertainties relating to the size of the deal and the timing of the debt issuance in the capital markets.

Alternative 2: Financing a Cash Transaction with an Issue of Common Equity

The second option consisted of a bridge loan followed by a global stock issuance[16] after the acquisition had been consummated. Although the Latin American debt capital market was showing some signs of recovery after the Brazilian devaluation with bond yields falling at a fast pace, and the equity capital market was rebounding to record highs, analysts were not convinced that the financial crisis was completely under control.

Even though the outlook for the equity capital markets was cloudy, Mr. Cortina wanted to examine the implications of an equity transaction as an alternative to financing the $13.4 billion cash payment.

An issue of common equity offered some significant advantages. With an all-equity financing, the combined enterprise would maintain or expand its unused debt capacity, and as a consequence, be prepared to take advantage of sudden acquisition opportunities, especially considering YPF's strategy of aggressive growth in Latin America. Under this option, Repsol could maintain its coverage ratios and its credit ratings.

On the other hand, Repsol's board was concerned about the impact of an all-equity transaction on the cost of capital of the enterprise. How would the benefit of less gearing impact the cost of capital? Would the less-leveraged firm bring more focus on business risk?

Repsol's shareholders were also concerned not only about the impact on earnings due to dilution but also about the stock price reaction after the announcement of the financing. Demand for Repsol and YPF shares could be seriously affected by investors' perceptions about the future value of the enterprise. An all-equity transaction would be highly dependent on Repsol's share price. Was Repsol's stock being traded at a fair value? Overvaluation or undervaluation of the stock could bring key information about investors' perception regarding the value of the new enterprise. **Exhibit 11** shows YPF's and Repsol's historic stock prices.

Another issue that concerned management about the all-equity option was which type of investor would be the target clientele for Repsol's new shares. At the time of deciding between an all-cash or all-stock offer, it was clear that exchanging the YPF shares for paper in Repsol—a Spanish-based company—would have led to a large proportion of those holders selling their Repsol shares after the deal since most of YPF shares were held in emerging-markets funds where the shares in new Repsol-YPF would not fit the pure emerging-markets profile. It was not clear how the market would view the combined company with 50 percent of its assets in developing countries. Assessing this was important to determine the potential demand for and success of the new shares offering.

Alternative 3: Financing a Cash Offer with a Mix of Debt and Equity

A possible third option consisted of a mix of equity, equity-linked instruments, and debt. The finance staff modeled the following structure:

---

[16]A global offering would include listings on the following stock exchanges: Madrid, New York, London, Frankfurt, and Buenos Aires.

1. A global syndicated bank loan would finance the cash offer. This loan would be repaid by a series of issuances of long-term securities.
2. Issuance of $7.5 billion of common equity within six months of the transaction.
3. Refinance the remainder of the debt with $6 billion of long-term public debt issues. This would occur in a 12–18 month time frame. This debt would carry a 9 percent coupon rate at an A-rating, assuming Repsol could meet the requirements for that rating.

This alternative was by far the more complex, and would need to be completed in more than one phase. Less reliance on equity financing would reduce the dilution in earnings per share for the current Repsol shareholder. But it would also result in higher leverage.

This alternative, while bringing the advantages and disadvantages of the two pure ones, also added a timing concern. Given the complexity of the transaction, it required a medium term schedule of debt and equity issuances that would keep management busy in order to correctly launch each transaction. This fact could bring anxiety to the market that would prefer management to focus more on the implementation of the merger and less on the financial side of the deal.

Exhibit 12 provides a valuation analysis for the combined enterprise. **Exhibit 13** presents the balance sheet for Repsol-YPF under the three financing alternatives. **Exhibit 14** presents an analysis of potential EPS dilution under the all-debt alternative. **Exhibit 15** gives comparative financial information on peer firms in the oil sector.

CONCLUSION

Alfonso Cortina reviewed the analysis and assembled data. It remained for him to examine the trade-offs among the alternatives and make a recommendation. He would want to give special attention to how he should frame his recommendation to Repsol's board of directors. Strategic goals would be a significant influence on their willingness to endorse a recommendation. All of this would need to occur quickly to preempt any actions by competitors and any turbulence in capital markets and oil markets.

EXHIBIT 1
Oil Prices, 1991–1999
Oil Price, U.S. Dollars per Barrel, Brent Crude

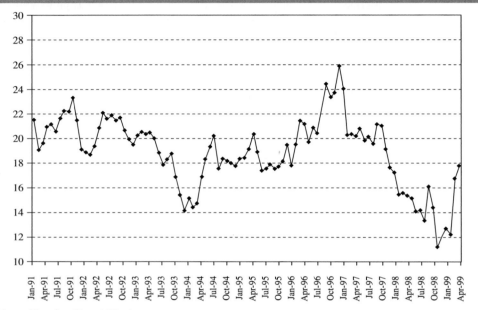

Source: Bloomberg Financial Services.

EXHIBIT 2
Information on Selected Recent Jumbo M&A Transactions

	Exxon	British Petroleum	BP Amoco	Repsol
Buyer	Exxon	British Petroleum	BP Amoco	Repsol
Target	Mobil	Amoco	Atlantic Richfield	YPF
Announcement date	1-Dec-98	11-Nov-98	1-Apr-99	TBA
Value of equity bid only ($ bn)	$78,945	$48,174	$27,233	$13,438
Value of equity bid and debt assumed ($ bn)	$86,399	$55,040	$33,702	$17,437
Form of payment	Stock	Stock	Stock	TBA
Accounting	Pooling	Pooling	Purchase	TBA
Lockup option	Exxon received right to acquire 14.9% of Mobil at 3.1% discount from offer price.	Amoco granted BP an option to acquire up to 19.9% of shares at a 72% discount from offer price.	None	14.99% preexisting stake from Argentine government auction
Attitude	Friendly	Friendly	Friendly	Unsolicited
Valuation multiples for target				
Price/Book	4.19	3.07	3.53	2.19
Price/Earnings	27.89	23.18	nmf	27.31
Ent. val./Sales	1.37	1.60	3.12	3.65
Ent. val./EBITDA	na	9.33	133.20	9.41
Ent. val./Opng. income	5.28	16.66	na	na
Premium of bid over stock price 4 weeks prior	32%	22%	54%	42%

Source: Securities Data Company, Merger and Acquisitions Transactions Database.

Note: "TBA" means "to be announced."

643

EXHIBIT 3
Repsol Financial Statements

Balance Sheet	1997	1998
Cash	$ 1,088	$ 1,144
Accounts receivable	2,907	3,185
Inventory	1,365	1,142
Total current assets	5,360	5,472
Total noncurrent assets	12,884	13,033
Total Assets	18,244	18,505
Accounts payable	3,520	3,674
Short-term debt	1,716	2,574
Total current liabilities	5,236	6,248
Total noncurrent liabilities	4,382	3,617
Total Liabilities	9,617	9,866
Minority interest	1,873	1,629
Shareholders' equity	6,754	7,010
Total Liabilities & Shareholders' Equity	18,244	18,505

Income Statement	1996	1997	1998
Net Sales	$ 21,891	$ 21,920	$ 22,227
Cost of sales	(20,325)	(20,324)	(20,285)
Operating income	1,566	1,596	1,942
Amortization of goodwill	(7)	(26)	(28)
Other income (expenses), net	(11)	39	(62)
Net financial items	(64)	(171)	(200)
Net income before tax	1,484	1,438	1,652
Income tax	(436)	(416)	(465)
Minority interest	(109)	(161)	(162)
Net income before preferred stock dividends	939	861	1,025
Net Income	939	861	1,025
Shares outstanding	900	900	900
Earnings per share	$ 1.04	$ 0.96	$ 1.14

N.B.: Shares outstanding and earnings per share are restated to reflect a stock split and recapitalization of Repsol that occurred in April 1999.

EXHIBIT 4
YPF Financial Statements

Balance Sheet	1996	1997	1998	1999E	2000E	2001E
Cash	$ 90	$ 142	$ 70	$ 88	$ 279	$ 409
Accounts receivable	1193	1132	1177	1070	1193	1316
Inventory	282	324	308	329	362	400
Total current assets	1,565	1,598	1,555	1,487	1,834	2,125
Total noncurrent assets	10,519	11,163	11,591	11,926	12,369	12,824
Total Assets	**12,084**	**12,761**	**13,146**	**13,413**	**14,203**	**14,949**
Accounts payable	886	882	788	839	935	1031
Debt	1,485	2,088	1,634	1,652	1,668	1,684
Total current liabilities	2,371	2,970	2,422	2,491	2,603	2,715
Total noncurrent liabilities	3,189	2,698	3,364	3,230	3,425	3,419
Total Liabilities	**5,560**	**5,668**	**5,786**	**5,721**	**6,028**	**6,134**
Minority interest	150	153	151	160	171	185
Shareholders' equity	6,374	6,940	7,209	7,532	8,004	8,630
Total Liabilities & Shareholders' Equity	**12,084**	**12,761**	**13,146**	**13,413**	**14,203**	**14,949**

Income Statement	1996	1997	1998	1999E	2000E	2001E
Net Sales	$ 5,937	$ 6,144	$ 5,500	$ 5,649	$ 5,846	$ 6,128
Cost of sales	(3,616)	(3,730)	(3,594)	(3,594)	(3,594)	(3,594)
Gross profit	2,321	2,414	1,906	2,055	2,252	2,534
SG&A	(782)	(782)	(760)	(760)	(760)	(760)
Operating income (EBIT)	1,539	1,632	1,146	1,295	1,492	1,774
Income on long-term investments	25	37	26	25	45	50
Other income (expenses), net	(93)	(50)	(44)	(15)	(18)	(35)
Net financial items	(246)	(239)	(264)	(316)	(280)	(285)
Net income before tax	1,225	1,380	864	989	1,239	1,504
Income tax	(369)	(479)	(264)	(306)	(382)	(466)
Minority interest	(12)	(15)	(11)	(10)	(12)	(13)
Net income before preferred stock dividends	844	886	589	673	845	1,025
Dividend on pref. stock of controlled companies	(27)	(9)	(9)	(2)	0	0
Net Income	**817**	**877**	**580**	**671**	**845**	**1,025**
Shares Outstanding	353	353	353	353	353	353
Earnings per share	2.31	2.48	1.64	1.90	2.39	2.90

Cash Flow	1996	1997	1998	1999E	2000E	2001E
Cash Flow from Operating Activities						
Net income	$ 817	$ 877	$ 580	$ 671	$ 846	$ 1,025
Adjustments						
Depreciation and amortization	1,065	1,093	1,061	1,131	1,230	1,323
Change in assets and liabilities	810	75	(1)	247	67	76
Net cash flow from operating activities	2,692	2,045	1,640	2,049	2,143	2,424
Cash flow from investing activities						
Acquisition of fixed assets	(1,817)	(1,593)	(1,351)	(1,400)	(1,600)	(1,700)
Acquisitions of long-term investments and intangible assets	(76)	(151)	(122)	(129)	(137)	(145)
Net proceeds on sale of investments	43	50	(67)	(71)	(75)	(80)
Other	*28*	39	31	33	34	36
Net Cash Flow from Investing Activities	(1,822)	(1,655)	(1,509)	(1,567)	(1,778)	(1,889)
Cash Flow from Financing Activities						
Proceeds from loans	1,964	52	115	0	0	0
Preferred shares redemption	(281)	(63)	0	0	0	0
Payments of loans	(2,261)	0	0	(100)	200	0
Dividends paid	(293)	(319)	(326)	(349)	(373)	(399)
Net Cash Flow from Financing Activities	(871)	(330)	(211)	(449)	(173)	(399)

EXHIBIT 5
YPF Shareholding Structure Before and After Argentine Government Sale

Shareholding Structure as of December 1998

YPF shares outstanding included 353,000,000 shares of common stock, with a par value of Argentine 10 pesos and one vote per share, which were fully subscribed, paid-in, and authorized for stock exchange listing. There had been no change in the number of shares since YPF's privatization in 1993. At the end of December 1998, YPF's shares were divided into four classes, as detailed below:

Owner	Number of Shares	Type of Share	Percent of Capital Stock
Government (1)	72,602,289	Class A	20.56%
Provinces	16,552,797	Class B	4.68
Employees	1,505,475	Class C	4.26
Public (2)	263,339,439	Class D	70.5

(1) The Argentine Government owned one "golden share" and could retain it indefinitely.
(2) 50 percent of the public shares were held by U.S. investors, mainly emerging market mutual funds.

YPF Shareholding Structure as of February 1, 1999

In January 1999, the Argentine Government sold to Repsol 52,914,700 Class A shares in block (14.99% of YPF's shares) at $38 per share, which were converted to Class D shares.

Owner	Number of Shares	Type of Share	Percent of Capital Stock
Government (1)	19,687,589	Class A	5.57%
Provinces	16,552,797	Class B	4.68
Repsol	52,914,700	Class D	14.99
Employees	1,505,475	Class C	4.26
Public	263,339,439	Class D	70.50

(1) The Argentine government kept the "golden share."

EXHIBIT 6
Capital Market Conditions, April 5, 1999

Treasury Obligations	U.S. Yields	Spanish Yields
90-day bills	4.38%	2.77%
1-year notes	4.66	2.84
5-year notes	5.05	3.47
10-year bonds	5.18	4.24
30-year bonds	5.62	5.14

Other Instruments	Yield
FED discount rate	4.75%
Commercial paper	
60 days	5.03
90 days	5.04
Certificates of deposit	
CD 3 months	4.87
CD 1 year	5.05
LIBOR	
Libor 3 months	5
Libor 6 months	5.05
Libor 12 months	5.24
Bank prime rates	
Argentina	8.73
United States	7.75

Source: Bloomberg Financial Services.

Sovereign	Date	Long-Term Rating
Argentina	Apr-97	BB
Brazil	Jan-99	B+
Chile	Jul-95	A−
Colombia	May-98	BBB−
Costa Rica	Jul-97	BB
El Salvador	Apr-99	BB+
Indonesia	Mar-99	CCC+
Mexico	Oct-98	BB
Peru	Dec-97	BB
Russia	Jan-99	Default
South Africa	Mar-98	BB+
Spain	Mar-99	AA+
United States	Jun-89	AAA
Venezuela	Aug-98	B+

Source: Standard & Poor's *Sovereign Ratings History,* April 1999.

EXHIBIT 7
Distribution of Repsol Revenues before and after the Transaction

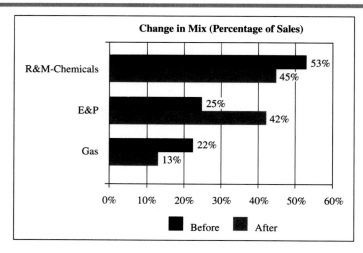

Note:
"E&P" stands for Exploration and Production segment of activities.
"R&M-Chemicals" stands for the Refining, Marketing, and Chemicals segment.

Source: "Quantum Leap," ABN-Amro Bank, 1 September 1999.

EXHIBIT 8
Estimation of WACC for Repsol Acquisition of YPF
(Suitable for Valuing U.S. Dollar Cash Flows)

	Repsol in Spain (stand-alone)	YPF in Argentina (stand-alone)	Combined Repsol-YPF Debt Financing	Combined Repsol-YPF Mixed Financing	Combined Repsol-YPF Equity Financing
Pretax cost of debt %	3.9%	6.0%	9.0%	8.2%	7.0%
Tax rate %	34%	34%	34%	34%	34%
Post-tax cost of debt %	**2.6%**	**4.0%**	**5.9%**	**5.4%**	**4.6%**
Asset beta	0.57	0.56	0.56	0.56	0.56
Beta in local market/relevered beta	0.8	0.75	0.96	0.78	0.68
Risk free rate % for U.S. $ investment	5.0%	5.0%	5.0%	5.0%	5.0%
Country beta versus U.S. market	1.15	2.00	1.59	1.59	1.59
Adjustment to U.S. risk-free rate for country risk	1.0%	3.0%	2.0%	2.0%	2.0%
Global equity market risk premium	6.0%	6.0%	6.0%	6.0%	6.0%
Cost of equity without country risk premium	**9.80%**	**9.50%**	**10.77%**	**9.70%**	**9.08%**
Cost of equity with country risk premium	**11.52%**	**17.00%**	**16.18%**	**14.47%**	**13.50%**
BV debt/(BV debt + MV equity)	38%	34%	51.6%	36.9%	23.7%
MV equity/(BV debt + MV equity)	62%	66%	48.4%	63.1%	76.3%
WACC with country risk premium	**8.14%**	**12.55%**	**10.90%**	**11.13%**	**11.40%**
WACC without country risk premium	**7.07%**	**7.61%**	**8.28%**	**8.12%**	**8.03%**
Market value of equity	15.066	15.807			
Weight Repsol and YPF market values	49%	51%			

Repsol's recently issued 5-year euro-denominated bonds yielded 3.81 percent.[1] The outlook was that Repsol bonds would be priced to yield 3.9 percent for 1999–2003 if Repsol remained on a stand-alone basis. Spanish government bonds were returning 5.2 percent; Repsol's beta was 0.8, and the Spanish market risk premium over the U.S. was 1 percent.

WACC Calculation Methodology
The financial forecasts are given in U.S. dollars. Therefore, the appropriate WACC is a dollar-based estimate, but reflecting the risks associated with doing business in Spain and Argentina. Estimating a WACC across borders must account for differences in political risk (through the political risk premium [pi] added to the U.S. risk-free rate), and equity market risk (through the use of a country beta that is multiplied by the beta in the local market). Accordingly, the general cross-border cost of equity model is an expanded version of the CAPM:

$$K_e = Rf_{US} + \pi + [\beta_{Country} \times \beta_{Firm} \times (\textit{Equity market risk premium})]$$

Source: Analysis by casewriters.

[1] At the time, yields on U.S. dollar- and euro-denominated instruments were similar.

EXHIBIT 9
Median Financial Ratios Associated with Long-Term-Debt Rating Categories,
(estimated for 1996–98)

	AAA	AA	A	BBB	BB	B
EBIT interest coverage (×)	12.9	9.2	7.2	4.1	2.5	1.2
EBITDA interest coverage (×)	18.7	14.0	10.0	6.3	3.9	2.3
Funds flow/total debt (%)	89.7	67.0	49.5	32.2	20.1	10.5
Free operating cash flow/total debt (%)	40.5	21.6	17.4	6.3	1.0	−4.0
Return on capital (%)	30.6	25.1	19.6	15.4	12.6	9.2
Operating income/sales (%)	30.9	25.2	17.9	15.8	14.4	11.2
Long-term debt/capital (%)	21.4	29.3	33.3	40.8	55.3	68.6
Total debt/capital (inc. STD) (%)	31.8	37.0	39.2	46.4	58.5	71.4

Source: Corporate Ratings Criteria, Standard & Poor's Corporation, 1999, 112.

EXHIBIT 10
Analysis of Default Risk for the Year 2000 Associated with the Three Financing Alternatives[1]

To: Alfonso Cortina, Chief Executive Officer
From: Carmelo Lopez, Chief Financial Officer

In an effort to estimate the default risk of Repsol-YPF under the three financing alternatives, the finance staff has prepared an estimate of the probability of not being able to meet interest payments. Specifically, default was defined as EBIT falling below interest expense. The probability was estimated across the three financing alternatives, and a range of possible cost saving synergies. We know that there are other benefits from the merger and restructuring, but decided to ignore them for the sake of conservatism. The assessed probabilities of default are given in the following table:

		Sensitivity Analysis for Synergies						
		Interest Coverage				**Probability of Interest Coverage < 1**		
	Debt	**Mix**	**Equity**			**Debt**	**Mix**	**Equity**
Cost Savings in Millions								
$ 50	1.2608	1.6656	2.9564	$ 50		24.05%	8.68%	1.21%
$150	1.2968	1.7131	3.0409	$150		21.13%	7.24%	0.94%
$250	1.3328	1.7607	3.1253	$250		18.43%	5.99%	0.72%
$350	**1.3688**	**1.8083**	**3.2098**	**$350**		**15.95%**	**4.92%**	**0.55%**	Base Case
$450	1.4048	1.8559	3.2943	$450		13.70%	4.01%	0.41%
$550	1.4409	1.9035	3.3787	$550		11.68%	3.23%	0.31%

Methodology

The simulations essentially run a sensitivity analysis of the EBIT coverage ratios under different oil price assumptions. We began by defining which business activities are exposed to oil price volatility. Two main sources appear: upstream and downstream operating income. For both, we considered a triangle distribution of oil prices based on market expectations and historical experience:

• Upstream operating income: This segment was calculated by taking the company's output prediction in barrels of oil, and subtracting the direct costs of this operation.

• Downstream operating income: This segment has different subproducts that are exposed to changes in oil prices in different ways. For the sake of simplicity, we took Repsol's stand-alone sensitivity to oil prices (since its income was mainly from downstream activities) and applied the same figure to the combined enterprise downstream business.

• Sensitivity summary: We added or subtracted all non-oil-price-sensitive charges to the operating income, and arrived at a Group EBIT.

[1] Analysis by the casewriters.

EXHIBIT 10
Analysis of Default Risk for the Year 2000—*Continued*

Analysis of Default Risk under Three Financing Alternatives
Detailed Results for "Base Case" of Cost Saving Synergies of $350 Million
Running the simulation through 1,000 trials on a base case scenario of $350 million in cost saving synergies yields the graphs below, and these results for the coverage ratio:

	All Debt	Mix of Debt and Equity	All Equity
Minimum	0.550	0.727	1.291
Mean	1.368	1.808	3.210
Maximum	2.307	3.049	5.412
Probability of Default	15.95%	4.92%	0.55%

Graphs of "Base Case" Probability Distributions of Coverage Ratio

Probability distribution of Repsol's EBIT coverage ratio if bid for YPF is financed by a blend of debt and equity.

Probability distribution of Repsol's EBIT coverage ratio if bid for YPF is financed entirely by an issue of debt.

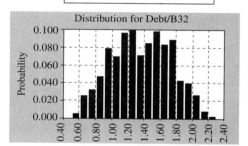

Probability distribution of Repsol's EBIT coverage ratio if an issue of equity finances bid for YPF.

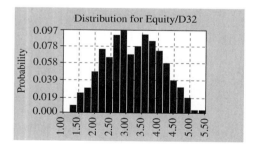

EXHIBIT 11
Recent Stock Prices of Repsol and YPF (values in U.S. dollars)

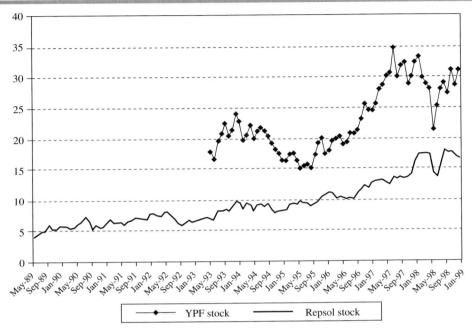

Source: Bloomberg Financial Services.

EXHIBIT 12

Forecast of Free Cash Flows for Repsol, YPF, and the Combined Firm, Repsol-YPF (values are in millions of U.S. Dollars)

Assumptions	YPF	Repsol	Combined		
Terminal value growth rate	4.0%	2.0%	3.0%		
WACC	12.5	8.1	10.6%		
Tax rate	34.0	34.0	34.0%		
Goodwill			6.229		
Return on assets			8%		
YPF Free Cash Flow	**1999E**	**2000E**	**2001E**	**2002E**	**2003E**
EBIT	1,295	1,492	1,774	2,046	2,291
Taxes	440	507	603	696	779
Earnings after tax	855	985	1,171	1,350	1,512
+ Depreciation	1,160	1,185	1,230	1,250	1,310
− CAPEX	(1,460)	(1,680)	(1,810)	(1,940)	(1,960)
− increase in WC	(65)	(75)	(89)	(102)	(115)
Free Cash Flow	490	415	502	558	748
Terminal value					9,093
Total free cash flow	490	415	502	558	9,840
Repsol Free Cash Flow	**1999E**	**2000E**	**2001E**	**2002E**	**2003E**
EBIT	1,948	2,285	2,554	2,754	2,889
Taxes	662	777	868	936	982
Earnings after tax	1,286	1,508	1,686	1,818	1,907
+ Depreciation	1,121	1,205	1,269	1,310	1,337
− CAPEX	(2,140)	(2,098)	(1,653)	(1,417)	(1,539)
− increase in WC	(97)	(114)	(128)	(138)	(144)
Free Cash Flow	169	501	1,174	1,573	1,560
Terminal Value					25,917
Total Free Cash Flow	169	501	1,174	1,573	27,478
Repsol-YPF Synergy Cash Flow Effects	**1999E**	**2000E**	**2001E**	**2002E**	**2003E**
Sales of assets	—	1,000	1,000	500	—
Adjustment to EBIT after sale of assets	—	(53)	(106)	(132)	(132)
Cost savings after tax	80	250	350	400	450
Revenue enhancement after costs and taxes	7	14	14	21	28
Reductions in capex less lost depreciation tax shields	393	386	380	373	366
Goodwill tax shield	106	106	106	106	106

Source: Casewriters' analysis.

EXHIBIT 13
Balance Sheet of the Combined Firm, Pro Forma the Acquisition under the Three Financing Alternatives
(assuming purchase accounting; values in millions of U.S. dollars except per-share amounts)

Amount to be Financed		$13,438
Financing Alternatives		**Percentage**
Debt	$6,000	45%
Equity	$7,438	55%
Assumed Price per Share	$20.41	
Option chosen	Mixed financing	

Gearings (Book values)	Pro-Forma 100% Debt	Pro-Forma 100% Equity	Pro-Forma Mixed Financing
Total debt	22,838	9,400	15,400
Total equity	7,073	20,511	14,511
Total capital	29,911	29,911	29,911
D/E	323%	46%	106%
D/C	76.4%	31.4%	51.5%
E/C	23.6%	68.6%	48.5%

Balance Sheet Repsol-YPF	Repsol	YPF	Adjustments	Pro-Forma 100% Debt	Pro-Forma 100% Equity	Pro-Forma Mixed Financing
Assets						
Cash	148	70		218	218	218
Accounts receivable	3,462	1,177		4,639	4,639	4,639
Inventory	2,337	308		2,645	2,645	2,645
Total current assets	5,947	1,555		7,502	7,502	7,502
Goodwill / asset revaluation			6,229	6,229	6,229	6,229
Total noncurrent assets	14,940	11,591		26,531	26,531	26,531
Total Assets	**20,887**	**13,146**		**40,262**	**40,262**	**40,262**
Liabilities						
Accounts payable	1,146	788		1,934	1,934	1,934
Loans	2,798	1,252		4,050	4,050	4,050
Other	1,046	241		1,287	1,287	1,287
Taxes payable	1,801	141		1,942	1,942	1,942
Total current liabilities	**6,791**	**2,422**		**9,213**	**9,213**	**9,213**
Long-term notes and accounts payable	56	53		109	109	109
Loans	2,663	2,578		5,241	5,241	5,241
Other	2,533	733		3,266	3,266	3,266
New Debt from acquisition			6,000	13,438	—	6,000
Total noncurrent liabilities	5,252	3,364		22,054	8,616	14,616
Total Liabilities	**12,043**	**5,786**		**31,267**	**17,829**	**23,829**
Minority interest	996	151		1,147	1,147	1,147
Preferred shares	775			775	775	775
New shares issued			364			364
New shares premium account			7,074		13,438	7,074
Shareholders' equity	7,073	7,209		7,073	20,511	14,511
Total Liabilities & Shareholders' equity	**20,887**	**13,146**		**40,262**	**40,262**	**40,262**

Source: Casewriters' analysis.

EXHIBIT 14
Analysis of Earnings per Share Dilution/Accretion

Pro-Forma Earnings Repsol-YPF		1999E	2000E	2001E	2002E	2003E
Repsol operating income (EBIT)		1,948	2,285	2,554	2,754	2,989
YPF operating income (EBIT)		1,295	1,492	1,774	2,046	2,391
Op. income before goodwill and amortization		3,243	3,777	4,328	4,800	5,380
Existing goodwill amortization		(40)	(40)	(40)	(40)	(40)
New depreciation of assets written up		(69)	(69)	(69)	(69)	(69)
New goodwill amortization over 20 years		(311)	(311)	(311)	(311)	(311)
Existing net financial expense		(684)	(713)	(652)	(623)	(590)
New financial expense	9.00%	(257)	(385)	(228)	(81)	56
Total interest expense		(941)	(1,098)	(880)	(704)	(534)
Other expense (income)		(15)	(18)	(35)	(40)	(50)
Associates income		25	45	50	55	60
Pretax income		1,892	2,286	3,043	3,691	4,435
Taxes	34%	(643)	(777)	(1,034)	(1,255)	(1,508)
Minorities		(178)	(193)	(212)	(233)	(256)
Reported net income		**1,071**	**1,315**	**1,796**	**2,203**	**2,671**
Cost savings after tax		80	250	350	400	450
Revenue enhancement		50	100	100	150	200
Reported net income with synergies		**1,201**	**1,565**	**2,146**	**2,603**	**3,121**
Number of shares original		900	900	900	900	900
New shares		364	364	364	364	364
Total shares		1,264	1,264	1,264	1,264	1,264
Repsol original EPS		1.23	1.45	1.71	1.88	2.1
New Repsol-YPF EPS excluding synergies		0.85	1.04	1.42	1.74	2.11
New Repsol-YPF EPS including synergies		0.95	1.24	1.70	2.06	2.47
Dilution (including synergies)		**−29.5%**	**−17.1%**	**−0.8%**	**8.7%**	**14.9%**
Debt Repayment						
Net income with synergies		1,201	1,565	2,146	2,603	3,121
Depreciation		2,371	2,525	2,684	2,843	2,979
Goodwill amortization		351	351	351	351	351
Equity income		(25)	(45)	(50)	(55)	(60)
Minorities		178	193	212	233	256
Operating cash flow		**4,076**	**4,590**	**5,344**	**5,975**	**6,648**
Dividends	45%	(540)	(704)	(966)	(1,171)	(1,405)
Preferred dividends	7.5%	(90)	(117)	(161)	(195)	(234)
Capex		(3,549)	(3,743)	(3,872)	(3,872)	(3,892)
Capex savings		400	400	400	400	400
Capex after savings		(3,149)	(3,343)	(3,472)	(3,472)	(3,492)
Cash from disposals		—	1,000	1,000	500	—
Financing cash flows		(3,779)	(3,165)	(3,599)	(4,339)	(5,131)
Cash Available for Debt Repayment		**297**	**1,425**	**1,745**	**1,637**	**1,517**
Debt outstanding		6,000	5,703	4,278	2,533	897
Debt repayment		297	1,425	1,745	1,637	1,517
Balance	6,000	5,703	4,278	2,533	897	(621)

Source: Casewriters' analysis.

EXHIBIT 15
Financial Comparison of Repsol (Stand-Alone) with Other Major Integrated Oil Companies

	Sector Average	Total	Shell	Chevron	ENI S.p.A.	Texaco	BP Amoco	Exxon Mobil	ELF	Repsol
Valuation Ratios										
Beta	0.8	0.85	0.81	0.57	0.94	0.32	NA	NA	0.84	1.00
Price to book	3.65	3.34	3.52	3.32	2.61	2.61	4.78	4.59	3.51	1.95
Price to cash flow	29.9	14.3	19.16	15.72	6.75	13.38	23.17	18.9	9.13	6.1
Price to earnings 1999	NA	21.8	26.2	31.3	15.2	30.6	30.9	27.9	24.0	18.6
Market capitalization (billion)	NA	30.48	67.09	62.44	48.98	29.52	166.3	270.1	34.96	16.27
Growth rates %										
Sales—5 Yr. Growth	8.49%	3.33%	−0.3%	−3.8%	0.8%	−1.4%	NM	NM	0.2%	na
EPS—5 Yr. Growth	10%	9.13%	−40.0%	1.0%	42.9%	−14.2%	NM	NM	37.0%	na
CAPEX—5 Yr. Growth	20.68%	10.19%	9.0%	3.2%	0.3%	5.9%	NM	NM	−5.7%	na
Financial Strength										
Current ratio	1.11	1.37	0.88	0.75	1.02	1.15	0.95	0.77	1.11	0.87
Total debt to equity	0.59	0.44	0.29	0.48	0.59	0.61	0.33	0.29	0.53	0.61
Interest coverage	10.05	NM	4.6	4.63	NM	2.98	6.92	17.39	4.32	na
Profitability Ratios (%)										
EBITD margin	15.6%	11.1%	14.6%	16.3%	27.9%	9.3%	18.4%	11.0%	16.1%	7.4%
Operating margin	4.3%	6.1%	6.0%	8.5%	13.1%	3.0%	10.7%	5.7%	4.5%	8.7%
Net Profit margin	2.9%	3.8%	2.5%	3.2%	8.5%	2.0%	4.9%	4.1%	1.9%	4.6%
Management Effectiveness										
RONA—5 Yr. Average	4.8	4.03	5.4	5.62	5.74	5.18	NA	NA	1.85	5.15
ROE—5 Yr. Average	10.49	7.95	10.29	12.62	20.49	13.57	NA	NA	4.11	14.50

Source: Market Guide, BT Alex Brown forecasts, May 1999.

Hostile Takeovers: A Primer for the Decision Maker

The game of professional investment is intolerably boring and overexacting to anyone who is entirely exempt from the gambling instinct; whilst he who has it must pay to this propensity the appropriate toll.

—*John Maynard Keynes*[1]

1. INTRODUCTION: TAKEOVERS ARE GAMES.

A hostile tender offer ("takeover") begins with an unsolicited offer by a bidder to purchase a majority or all of the target firm's shares. The bidder will set the offer for a particular period of time, at a price, and a form of payment, and may attach conditions to the offer. The target will ordinarily undertake evasive maneuvers. Research shows that the hostile bidder consummates a deal in about 20 percent of the cases. In roughly 30 percent of the cases, the target is acquired by another, usually "friendly," firm. And in the remainder of the cases, the target remains independent. The complexity, uncertainty, and drama of these events seem to defy an easy grasp.

Keynes' famous words afford a basis for understanding, analyzing, and designing or repelling hostile tender offers: takeovers are *games*. In the arena of M&A, the professional investor that Keynes cites is the arbitrageur. One can understand these events and the arbitrageur better by studying them the way one studies a game:

---

[1] Quoted from Keynes's *General Theory* on page 16, Smith (1969).

- Gain the perspective of the various players in the takeover scenario, their motives and be-
  haviors.
- Master important rules and defenses that constrain the players.
- Anticipate the paths that outcomes may take.

The analytics of hostile tender offers significantly entail the assessment of probabilities. Takeover attempts are bets on uncertain outcomes. The players' strategies are aimed at
tilting the odds in one's favor. The homework necessary to assess these odds and play them
well surely constitutes Keynes' "appropriate toll." Of course, understanding the game is no
assurance of likely success—it also takes skill. As John McDonald said about poker,

> *A knowledge of mathematical probabilities will not make a good poker player, but
> a total disregard for them will make a bad one.[2]*

2. BE AWARE OF THE PLAYERS, BOTH ON THE FIELD AND OFF.

One begins an introduction to a game by surveying the people gathered around the table.

Attacker (or in street parlance, a **bidder**). The popular press and halls of government view
bidders rather harshly, for it is the bidders who propose to wrest control, close plants,
lay off workers, and take other actions to enrich themselves. A more benign view is that
bidders are *entrepreneurs* who through research and initiative discover profitable opportunities. The hostile tender offer is the action taken to begin to harvest the profit.

Defender or **target** *is* the profitable opportunity. Usually, targets have underperformed
against one or more benchmarks, about which the target managers are doing little,
or floundering in attempts to improve performance. The bidder may see hidden or
underutilized assets that could be sold, or businesses that are draining cash and could
be restructured or closed.

It is naive to see the hostile tender offer as a contest simply between bidder and target.
The field is considerably more complicated. Viewed through a lens of economics, the contest embraces the following kinds of players:

Free riders versus the bidder. Free riders are shareholders who may not be well informed but who suspect that the bidder knows something they don't, and who are
tempted to participate in some of the profits flowing to the bidder. These shareholders seek to ride free in harvesting the profitable opportunity. The bidder would like
to quell the free riders, because they reduce the bidder's profit.

Groups within the target. One of the worst mistakes is to view the target as a solid
bloc of decision makers. In reality, the target harbors important divisions which the
bidder can exploit:

- **Managers versus directors.** Usually senior target company managers lose their
  jobs following a successful hostile takeover. Even if they do not lose them,

---

[2]John McDonald, *Strategy in Poker, Business & War* (New York: W.W. Norton, 1989), p. 22.

salaries and perquisites tend to be distributed less freely. In short, target managers have a strong incentive to oppose a hostile bid. A firm's directors, however, are bound by legal doctrines of the duties of care and loyalty to maximize the welfare of shareholders. Failing to do so exposes directors to micromanagement by courts of law, and possible personal liability for past errors. Obviously, the interests of managers and directors can diverge. The **Target's board of directors** is at the fulcrum of pressure and can reverse management's strategy in the game through such means as rescinding the firm's antitakeover defenses, and declaring an auction for the firm.

- **Insiders versus outside directors.** The board itself may consist of subgroups that harbor divergent interests. Inside directors are usually also managers. Other directors who side with the manager-directors may have links by marriage or work experience that tie them by loyalty more closely to managers than to shareholders.
- **Large shareholders versus small shareholders.** Not all target shareholders are equal; their relative voting power can have an influence on the board of directors.

Other potential buyers, who would have an interest in acquiring the target, but have yet to enter a bid. These might include friendly buyers (also called, "white knights"), and friendly investors in special controlling securities (also called, "white squires"[3]).

Arbitrageurs who make a living betting on price movements in takeovers. Once a takeover is announced, the "arbs" (as they are more popularly known) practically absorb all loose shares sloshing around in the stock market, and almost certainly become the crucial deciders of any contest—for this reason, they deserve careful examination.

3. THE ARB IS THE CONSUMMATE ECONOMIC ACTOR.

The arbs' outlook is rationalistic, impatient, and always oriented toward value maximization. Appeals to loyalty, tradition, or some vague plan will have little influence over them. They like immediate cash profits. Arbitrageurs are short-term investors driven only by economic motives. They invest funds in takeover situations and recapitalizations and try to limit the exposure to the likelihood of a deal not being consummated. They often provide liquidity to investors who do not wish to wait out a battle for corporate control.

Consider the example[4] of a target company, which receives an offer of $60 per share for all the shares of the company. If the shares are trading at $40 per share when the offer is announced, one could make a profit of $20 by buying instantaneously, and holding

---

[3] Warren Buffett has played the "white squire" to several firms, most notably Gillette. He has purchased convertible preferred stock, which if converted would represent a material minority of shares outstanding. The shares represented in these white squire positions require added investment on the part of a hostile bidder and thus have a deterrent effect.

[4] This example was drawn from "Takeover 1997 (A)," a Darden case study, UVA-F-1170, coauthored by Robert Bruner, John P. McNicholas, and Edward Rimland.

until the transaction is completed. Unfortunately, the Stock Exchange would probably suspend trading in the stock as investors flood the market with orders to buy or sell. When order has been regained, the stock will resume trading at a point where there are both buyers and sellers at the same price. At that point, the shares may be trading at $57 or $58 a share. Institutions and private investors would be able to sell shares immediately to the arbs at $57, reaping a $17 gain. The $3 difference or spread can be viewed as compensation to investors for any remaining uncertainty about whether the transactions will be consummated, and for the time remaining to closing of the deal. The bidder's share price declines $3 upon the announcement to close at $50, and remains there until the end of the arb's holding period.

The task for the arbs is to evaluate the likelihood of the deal being consummated and structure an investment position based on that view. The arb will seek to create a hedged position, whose risk is determined by the deal, rather than by general market conditions. A typical arbitrage position following a hostile takeover announcement would be to take a "long" position in the shares of the target company, and a "short" position in the shares of the bidder—this reflects the typical movement of share prices at the announcement of hostile bids, but the structure also cushions the arb against general movements in the stock market.

3.a. Return to the Arbitrageur

The following example calculates the return to the arb in the transaction described above:

(1) Position Taken: 100 Target Company shares bought at $57. 100 Bidder Company shares sold short at $50.
(2) Date Position Taken: June 1, 1996
(3) Date Shares Tendered: June 28, 1996
(4) Date Proceeds Received: July 10, 1996
(5) Total Time Involvement: 40 days
(6) Capital Employed:

Assets		
Long 100 shares of Target × $57/share =		$5,700
Liabilities and Capital		
Short 100 shares of Bidder × $50/share =	$5,000	
Borrowed 100 shares of Bidder =		$(5,000)
Bank Borrowings (70% of Assets) =	$3,990	
Capital (30% of Assets) =	1,710	
Total	$5,700	

(7) Net Spread Calculation:

$300 Gross Spread (Target: [$60 − $57] × 100 shares) plus (Buyer [$50 − 50] × 100 shares)
　(43) Interest Cost (10% for 40 days on credit of $3,990)
　(20) Short Dividends Forgone
　 30 Long Dividends Received
$267 Net Spread or Return on Investment

(8) Annualized Return on Capital

$$\text{Average Capital Employed} = \frac{40 \text{ days}}{365 \text{ days}} \times \$1,710 = \$187$$

$$\text{Annualized Return on Capital Employed} = \frac{\$267}{\$187} = 142\%$$

While this is a high apparent return on capital, the arb could sustain a sizable loss if the hostile bid does not succeed. Note also, that this ROI is very sensitive to small variations in waiting period, and dollar return.

3.b. The Arb's Choice between Tendering into a Hostile Bid and Waiting for the Target's Recapitalization

In deciding where to tender their shares in a contest for corporate control, the arbs will determine which offer gives them the highest annualized return on their invested capital. To continue our example, an arb would prefer $60 on July 10 as opposed to payment of $61 received in September. With capital costs of 30–40 percent per year, the timing of cash flows received is crucial to their decision. Lastly, the decision of arbs to tender their shares to a raider will, in almost all cases, mean that a company will not have ample time to complete its own recapitalization if it is calculated to have a lower blended value.

Assume the Target Company decides to mount its own recapitalization plan by buying back 35 percent of its shares at $85 per share. Furthermore, assume that the stub share (i.e., a share of the common stock remaining after the recapitalization) will be estimated to trade at approximately $55 per share afterward.

$$\text{Blended value} = (35\% * \$85) + (65\% * \$55) = \$65.50$$

Note that an arb would prefer a blended value of $65.50 if that value could be delivered on a timely basis.

More usually, risk arbitrageurs will play both sides of a hostile tender offer, taking a long position in the shares of the target, and a short position in the shares of the bidder. One of the leading arbs, Guy Wyser-Pratte, has written,

> An arbitrageur is not an investor in the formal sense of the word: i.e., he is not normally buying or selling securities because of their investment value. He is, however, committing capital to the "deal"—the merger, tender offer, recapitalization, etc.—rather than to the particular security. He must thus take a position in the deal in such a way that he is at the risk of the deal, and not at the risk of the market.[5]

As Wyser-Pratte suggests, the arb will be extremely sensitive to the values underlying the deal, and to its outcome. To illustrate why, consider **Table 1,** which expands the results of the example given above, and gives the annualized rates of return associated with different holding periods and payoffs.

---

[5]Quoted from Guy P. Wyser-Pratte, *Risk Arbitrage II* (New York: New York University, Salomon Brothers Center for the Study of Financial Institutions), Monograph 1982-3-4, p. 7.

TABLE 1
Sensitivity Analysis of Annualized Rate of Return to Variations in Length
of Holding Period and Expected Payoff from Investment

							Expected Value Per Share			
		$55	**$57**	**$59**	**$60**	**$61**	**$63**	**$65**	**$67**	**$69**
	20	−226%	−13%	201%	308%	414%	628%	841%	1055%	1268%
	25	−186%	−15%	156%	241%	327%	497%	668%	839%	1010%
	30	−159%	−16%	126%	197%	268%	411%	553%	695%	838%
	35	−139%	−17%	105%	166%	227%	349%	471%	593%	715%
Days in	40	−125%	−18%	89%	142%	195%	302%	409%	516%	622%
Holding	45	−113%	−19%	76%	124%	171%	266%	361%	456%	551%
Period	50	−104%	−19%	66%	109%	152%	237%	322%	408%	493%
	55	−97%	−19%	58%	97%	136%	213%	291%	369%	446%
	60	−91%	−20%	51%	87%	123%	194%	265%	336%	407%
	65	−86%	−20%	46%	78%	111%	177%	243%	308%	374%
	70	−81%	−20%	41%	71%	102%	163%	224%	285%	346%
	75	−77%	−20%	36%	65%	93%	150%	207%	264%	321%
	80	−74%	−21%	33%	59%	86%	139%	193%	246%	300%

Note: Shaded cell indicates example case in text.

The table reveals that apparently small variations (e.g. $2.00) in expected payoffs produce sizable swings in returns—returns vary directly with payoffs. The table also shows that returns vary inversely with holding period—the longer the period, the smaller the returns.[6] Plainly, a takeover consummated in 20 days results in dramatically higher returns than those taking 40 and 80 days.

The implication of Table 1 is that the arb will be extremely sensitive to variations in time and payoff. This sensitivity means that bidders and targets that seek the support of arbs must tailor their tactics to exploit this sensitivity.

4. THE ARB ASSESSES A RECAPITALIZATION PROPOSAL IN TERMS OF BLENDED VALUE.

One common response by takeover targets is to initiate a leveraged recapitalization of the firm. This entails borrowing substantially and paying a large one-time dividend to all shareholders and/or a large one-time share repurchase. Asset sales or other restructuring tactics may be involved also. The result is a highly levered acquisition target that is probably less

---

[6]The inverse relationship between holding period and return is true for all but the left-most column, in which the return is less negative, the longer the period. This is because at short holding periods, the annualization multiple (365 divided by days in holding period) has a huge effect in amplifying a negative return to be even more negative. For longer periods, the annualization impact is less pronounced.

attractive to a hostile bidder. The arb assesses the share-repurchase recapitalization as a blend of values.

Assume the target company decides to mount its own recapitalization plan by buying back 35 percent of its shares at $85 per share pro rata among all shares. Furthermore, assume that the stub share[7] will be estimated to trade at approximately $55 per share after the recapitalization is completed. The share value to the arb of this recapitalization is a blend of the two:

$$\text{Blended Value} = (35\% * \$85) + (65\% * \$55) = \$65.50$$

Note that in this example, an arb would prefer a blended value of $65.50 realized from the recapitalization (as opposed to the raider's $60 offer) if that value could be delivered on a timely basis. To continue the previous example, if the arb realizes a value of $65.50 per share, the return on investment for 40 days will be 48 percent,[8] and the annualized return will be 436 percent. As this second example illustrates, the high leverage of the arb's position causes the returns to swing dramatically with small changes in the gross spread per share.

In deciding where to tender their shares in a contest for corporate control, the arbs will determine which offer (i.e., the hostile bid, or the recapitalization) gives them the highest annualized return on their invested capital. To continue our example, an arb would probably prefer $60 cash on July 10 as opposed to cash and securities of $65.50 received on October 10.[9] With capital costs of 30–40 percent per year, the timing of cash flows received is crucial to the arbs' decision. Lastly, the decision of arbs to tender their shares to a raider will, in almost all cases, mean that a company will not have ample time to complete its own recapitalization if it is calculated to have a lower blended value.

5. TAKEOVER DEFENSES ALTER THE PROBABILITIES OF OUTCOMES.

Target management can undertake a series of maneuvers to delay or completely stop the consummation of a hostile acquisition. These are commonly known as "antitakeover defenses." Courts have shown strong reluctance to invalidate these defenses without some proof of conflict of interest, negligence, or fraud on the part of target management.

Classified boards dictate the election of a fraction of the total directors each year, thus delaying the attainment of control by the bidder through domination of the board.

The **supermajority amendment to the bylaws** specifies that a large percentage of the currently outstanding common shares must approve a merger between the company and an

---

[7]"Stub shares" are the shares of a company that remain after a major recapitalization. For instance, if a Parent Company decided, in the face of a hostile tender offer, to sell off two of its major business lines and borrow a significant amount of money to buy back two-thirds of its shares, the shares left over would be called stub shares.

[8]The gross spread is $65.50 − $57 × 100 shares, or $850 on the position in the Target, and $50 − $50 × 100 shares or zero on the position in the buyer. Deducting interest of $43.73 and dividends forgone from the short sale of $20, and adding dividends received of $30 gives a net spread of $816.27. Dividing the net spread by capital committed of $1710 gives a return on capital of 48 percent, which is annualized to 436 percent.

[9]Assuming a 40 percent annual discount rate, the present value of $65.50 received in four months is $58.55.

acquirer. Generally, acquirers would be hesitant to make an offer for a company if they believed they would not be able to complete the merger.

The **fair price amendment to the bylaws** requires that all selling shareholders receive the same price from a buyer. This prevents the implementation of a two-tier or "freeze-out" tender offer in which a controlling block of shares is purchased at a premium, and the remaining minority is purchased at a discount.

Golden parachutes grant target management generous severance payments if they are fired following an acquisition. This has the effect of raising the cost of acquisition to a bidder.

A **leveraged recapitalization** by the target entails borrowing heavily, and paying a large one-time dividend to target shareholders. Thus, a hostile acquirer will need to assume a large debt burden from the target. Moreover, many debt provisions in highly leveraged recapitalizations include **poison puts** that make the debt immediately payable upon a change of control of the target firm. Thus, the bidder must be prepared to refinance the target's debt upon acquisition.

The **shareholder right** (or "poison pill" as it is commonly called) is a nondetachable right to obtain common shares at nominal cost. All shareholders participate in the right except for an "interested person" who acquires more shares than allowed under the rights plan. Thus, the plan discriminates against an unwanted acquirer in favor of all other shareholders, making the acquisition more expensive (e.g. 25 to 50 percent more) than otherwise. Typically the right is effective for 10 years unless extended by the board of directors. Nondetachable rights are distributed pro rata to all common stockholders as a stock dividend. The rights are automatically transferred with the shares of common stock to which they relate but do not become exercisable (and indeed are not even represented by separate instruments) until the occurrence of a "Triggering Event." At that point, separate instruments representing the rights are distributed to shareholders. The rights detach from the common shares and become separately tradable.

- *Triggering event, "Interested Person":* The triggering event is defined as the acquisition by any person (or group of persons acting in concert) of a certain percentage (today, typically 10 percent) of outstanding common stock without the prior consent of the firm's board of directors. Such an acquirer is known as an "Interested Person." An "Interested Person" may not exercise the rights.
- *"Flip in" and "Flip Over" Provisions:* The rights plan may contain either or both "Flip In" and "Flip Over" provisions. The latter apply only when the Interested Person, having acquired voting control of the firm, attempts to merge the firm into itself. At that point, holders of the rights become entitled to purchase common shares of the surviving firm at nominal value. "Flip In" provisions entitle the holders to purchase common shares of the target firm at nominal value. Both the "Flip In" and "Flip Over" provisions impose significant economic dilution on the interested person.
- *Redemption:* The board of directors may redeem the rights at any time prior to the Triggering event and for 10 days thereafter at the redemption price of $0.01 per right. The rights become irredeemable after a 10 day "window."
- *Qualified Offer, "Dead Hand" Provision:* The board may also choose to exempt a qualified offer from the operations of the rights plan. A "Qualified Offer" is defined as an all-cash, any-and-all-shares tender offer, or merger proposal that has been approved by the board. After a "Change of Control," defined as the replacement of 50 percent of the board

in a proxy contest, the rights may be redeemed only by a majority of, but at least two, "Continuing Directors." A "Continuing Director" is defined as a person who was a member of the target board at the time the rights plan was adopted or was nominated by a majority of the directors then in office or their nominees

Poison pills are by far the most effective defense in the corporate arsenal. Pills have never been deliberately triggered, and, unless rescinded by target directors, are virtually guaranteed to halt a hostile takeover. But the poison pill defense is not without weaknesses. On occasion, courts have required boards to rescind poison pills. Some targets have appealed to directors and shareholders successfully to rescind pills (usually this is accompanied with a large acquisition premium).

6. COURT DECISIONS, LAWS, AND REGULATIONS AFFECT THE GAME CONSIDERABLY.

Government intervention in hostile takeovers influences the takeover process considerably. At the federal government level in the United States, securities law has been oriented toward creating a "level playing field" in the spirit of enhancing competition among bidders. Antitrust law has been oriented toward protecting consumers and generally enhancing competition in product markets. At the state government level, antitakeover laws have been oriented toward simply preventing unwanted takeovers. These and other laws and regulations constrain the behavior of bidders and targets and affect the odds of successful acquisition. The following government-imposed requirements give a sense of the constraints on bidder and target managements.

A. The acquisition of shareholdings in excess of 5 percent of a target's shares must be disclosed within 10 days to the Securities and Exchange Commission (Rule 13-D). Arbitrageurs, major trading houses, and financial institutions employ runners to transmit copies of these 13-D filings with the SEC immediately to their employers. Disclosures of major changes in shareholding become rapidly impounded in share prices. The effect of this requirement is to telegraph the intentions of a bidder to the target and the rest of the market, well in advance of acquiring control through open market purchases.

B. A tender offer must remain open 20 business days (Rule 14e-1(a)). Before the Williams Act, raiders could set a relatively short time to expiration of the offer, compelling hasty decision making on the part of the target shareholders and preventing action by target management. The effect of this rule is to give the target a window in which to organize a defense or a counterproposal to the arbs.

C. The bidder must honor all shares tendered into the offering pro rata, rather than on a first-come, first-served basis (Rule 14d-8). This relieves some of the target shareholders' compulsion to decide quickly in order to get in line early—offers for a controlling interest (e.g. 51 percent) rather than 100 percent of shares might be intended to induce a shareholder stampede. Similarly, this rule defuses somewhat the impact of the two-tier tender offer.

D. Target shareholders may withdraw their tenders for any reason in the first 15 days of a tender offer (Rule 14d-7(a)(1)). This permits shareholders greater flexibility in responding to competing offers, should they appear.

E. Tender offer time periods are extended by 10 days if a competing offer appears. (Rule 14d-7(a)(1)).

F. Directors must exercise duties of care and loyalty to the shareholders (case law). This extremely important doctrine prevents directors from giving much weight to the considerations of other stakeholders in the firm. Directors must do what is best for the shareholders first, and must do so in an informed and diligent manner.

G. Directors and managers must disclose *material* information about the company to the public (case law). For instance, receipt of a bona fide certain offer to buy a company that is communicated to management under some circumstances must be communicated to shareholders. However, what is "material" is a key matter of judgment. If management receives an offer then they must determine, with or without the assistance of an investment banker, if the offer is bona fide. For instance, an offer made by someone without financial support may not be deemed to be bonafide. If the offer is deemed to be bona fide, then at the very least the board of directors should be notified. At that point, legal counsel should be sought to make a determination of the disclosibility of the offer. The company should never lie to the press because to do so would make them liable to charges of fraud. They may elect, as a matter of corporate policy, not to comment on market rumors.

H. If it is determined that the company is to be sold, the directors must sell it to the highest bidder. (Case law, the "Revlon Decision.")

I. The courts are disinclined to intervene in, or second-guess, management decision making unless gross negligence or fraud can be proved. This is the "Business Judgment Rule" doctrine in U.S. federal courts. This puts the burden of proof on the bidder if the bidder seeks to have a court invalidate a target's antitakeover defenses.

J. In the event that a management group conducts an auction for the company, managers must be careful to maintain a level playing field during the auction process. They can give no bidder a preferred advantage in the bidding process.

7. SELLING SHAREHOLDERS FACE A PRISONER'S DILEMMA

The decision of whether or not to sell into a tender offer creates an unusual conflict of interests for the selling shareholders of target companies. On one hand, by waiting and not tendering, there may be a higher offer down the road—or management might reveal some hidden value justifying a higher share price and bid offer. On the other hand, selling now locks in a certain value. The only way to find out whether there is more value in the target firm is for target shareholders to band together, delay in tendering into the bidder's offer, and to wait to see if a higher value (or bid) emerges. The problem is that unified action among a highly atomistic shareholder group is difficult, if not impossible, to engineer.

This is the classic problem of the "prisoner's dilemma."[10] In this hypothetical case, two robbers are arrested by the police in the belief that they acted together in committing a

---

[10]The prisoner's dilemma was first discussed in Anatol Rapoport and A.M. Chammah, *Prisoner's Dilemma,* Ann Arbor: University of Michigan Press, 1965.

TABLE 2

		Prisoner B	
		Doesn't Confess	Confesses
Prisoner A	Doesn't Confess	I. A gets 5 years B gets 5 years	II. A gets 8 years B gets 3 years
	Confesses	III. A gets 3 years B gets 8 years	IV. A, B get 10 years each

crime. The prisoners are separated in different cells and interrogated independently. The prosecutor encourages each to confess, and implicate the colleague. If neither prisoner confesses, the prosecutor believes the court can be convinced to send the suspects to jail for five years. If both prisoners confess *and* implicate each other, the court will send the suspects to jail for 10 years. If one prisoner confesses and implicates the other, and the other neither confesses nor implicates, the one who confesses will get three years (time off for assisting the prosecution), and the other will get eight years. The "prisoner's dilemma" is whether to confess or not, and offers four possible outcomes, represented in **Table 2.**

Plainly, Quadrants II and III are the best outcomes for the two prisoners individually, since these result in lower jail terms for each. But if *both* prisoners take the incentive offered, they will wind up with the longest sentences, 10 years each. The safest course of action is for neither to confess, since it results in a jail term materially shorter than 8 or 10 years, and not much longer than 3 years. Unfortunately, with the prisoners separated and unable to communicate, the collaboration and mutual assurances necessary to achieve Quadrant I are unlikely.

The "prisoner's dilemma" illustrates how opportunism and the absence of joint action result in least-desirable outcomes. The model has been used to explain a wide range of phenomena in business and finance. The key here is in anticipating the probabilities and actions of other players in the game.

The decision facing target shareholders (especially arbs) is similar. **Table 3** recasts the prisoner's dilemma into a takeover setting. Here, two shareholders contemplate a two-tier tender offer of $80 cash paid per share for the first 51 percent of shares, and $60 in securities for the rest. Target shareholders face the payoffs shown in the cells of Table 2, associated with either tendering immediately, or waiting. With an immediate tender, the investor accepts the raider's offer. If both wait, the offer is defeated and the raider must raise its offer. If only one waits, the waiting shareholder becomes a minority investor in the firm, and eventually sells to the raider at a much-reduced price.

If the target shareholders act in concert and wait, they may obtain better information and a better price for their firm (Quadrant I). If some sell into the tender offer while others wait, those who sell may obtain a better deal than those who wait and wind up being minority shareholders in a firm that is dominated by the bidder. Absent joint action and communication, if all shareholders sell into the tender offer, the bidder takes the firm at the price he offered (Quadrant IV).

TABLE 3

		Investor B	
		Wait	Sell into Offer
Investor A	Wait	I. A gets $100/share. B gets $100/share.	II. A gets $60/share B gets $80/share
	Sell into Offer	III. A gets $80/share B gets $60	IV. A, B get $70 each[*]

[*]The $70 payoff in Quadrant IV assumes proration of the front-end and back-end payments, 50% times $80 plus 50% time $60.

To the extent that takeovers conform to this model, the "prisoner's dilemma" has important implications for bidders and target shareholders:

- Bidders benefit, and target shareholders lose by the asymmetric structure of payoffs and the difficulty of taking joint action among target shareholders.
- To heighten the bidder's benefit (and achieve Quadrant IV), the bidder should structure the asymmetry of incentives to the target shareholders to motivate all to "defect" to accept the bid. This might be achieved by offering one high and relatively certain price to those who tender early, and another, lower and less certain payment to those who tender late. Also, the bidder might send signals consistent with a likely future "minority shareholder freeze-out." The classic achievement here is the "two-tier" tender offer: cash is offered to shareholders who participate in the bidder's offer for 51 percent of the firm, to be followed by shares or high-yield bonds for the shareholders who delay and tender late, participating in the last 49 percent of the purchase. A minority that holds out entirely might see the assets of the firm stripped and sold piecemeal to the bidder, in essence liquidating the target. In 1997 Hilton Hotels Corporation bid $55 per share for ITT Corporation: for the first 50.1 percent of shares, Hilton would pay cash; for the rest of the shares outstanding, Hilton would pay $55 in shares of stock. The consideration was structured to be equivalent in value, though the cash payment appealed much more to arbitrageurs.
- A key problem for arbs and other target firms' shareholders is to assess the probability of other shareholders' actions. Nowhere does the gamelike nature appear in takeovers than in this fact: like the card-player who must assess the hands and probabilities of other players, the arb in this situation must assess the likely actions of other investors.
- Collaboration among selling shareholders may pay. This perhaps explains the appearance of ad hoc committees of target shareholder groups, and the appeals to take action together.
- Securities regulation regimes that favor equitable treatment of all shareholders and "level playing field" conditions will discourage asymmetric incentives that lead to Quadrant IV outcomes.
- Time is very valuable to the target shareholders, and is the enemy of the bidder. Searching for a white knight buyer, developing a recapitalization plan, or mounting defenses takes time. To the extent that the bidder can hasten the target shareholders' decision process, the less effective is bound to be the target management's evasive action.

8. TO SET A BID PRICE, THINK LIKE AN INVESTOR.

Given the panoply of laws and takeover defenses, the bidder faces the reality that the main instrument of success is *deal design*. The task of a bidder in a hostile takeover is to fashion terms such that the acquisition succeeds while preserving as much value as possible for the bidder. In the discussion that follows, the focus will be on price, although in reality, form of payment and the other dimensions will be very important considerations as well.

Given that arbitrageurs are the significant decision makers in a hostile tender offer, it is reasonable to assume that the highest price offered takes the company. The bidder presumably will offer to purchase shares at a premium to the preexisting share price. The key issue is how large the premium should be. The range of choice for the bid premium will be bounded on the high side by the bidder's most optimistic estimate of the target's intrinsic value (using DCF, multiples, and other valuation approaches to achieve this "high" value). At first glance, it would seem that the low end of the premium range would be determined by the preexisting share price. But the bidder needs to assume the possibility that the target might undertake a self-initiated restructuring that would release value to its shareholders in excess of the current share price—a leveraged restructuring would be an example of such an action. Since it is reasonable to assume that target management want to keep their jobs and that restructuring is the only alternative available if a white knight cannot be induced to enter the bidding, then in effect, this restructuring value becomes the other bound in the range of bid premia. Exactly where, within this range, the bidder will choose to make its offer is a matter of how likely the bidder believes a competing bidder will enter the action.

The advice to a bidder in a situation like this is to *think like the target shareholder.* The shareholder's choice is simple, accept the tender offer if:

$$\text{Value of tendering} \geq \text{Expected value of not tendering}$$

Since the value of the bidder's offer can be reasonably estimated, the core of the analysis lies in estimating the value of not tendering (EVNT). EVNT is a simple average of share prices under two uncertain outcomes: (a) no shares are tendered to the raider, the takeover fails, and share prices subside to the ex ante price;[11] and (b) no shares are tendered to the raider, but they are tendered to a higher competing bidder who buys the firm. These prices are multiplied times their probability of occurrence, and summed:

$$\text{EVNT} = (\text{Share Price}_{\text{No Competing Bid}} * \text{Probability}_{\text{No Competing Bid}}) + (\text{Share Price}_{\text{Competing Bid}} * \text{Probability}_{\text{Competing Bid}})$$

Thus, to succeed in the bidding, the raider must set the bid price somewhat higher than EVNT. Of course, this requires estimates of probabilities and the dollar offer of a competing bidder. If a decision maker is uncomfortable with this judgment, the EVNT formula

---

[11] When a hostile tender offer is successfully deflected, we observe that the target share price tends to subside back toward the level prevailing ex ante. Whether it returns to the ex ante price exactly, will depend on expectations of further takeover bids or possible changes in management policies.

TABLE 4
EVNT If the "Default Value" Is the Target's Ex Ante Share Price (Possibility A)

						Value of Competing Bid					
		$45.00	$50.00	$55.00	$60.00	$65.00	$70.00	$75.00	$80.00	$85.00	$90.00
Probability	10%	$45.00	$45.50	$46.00	$46.50	$47.00	$47.50	$48.00	$48.50	$49.00	$49.50
of a	25%	$45.00	$46.25	$47.50	$48.75	$50.00	$51.25	$52.50	$53.75	$55.00	$56.25
Competing	50%	$45.00	$47.50	$50.00	$52.50	$55.00	$57.50	$60.00	$62.50	$66.00	$67.50
Bid	75%	$45.00	$48.75	$52.50	$56.25	$60.00	$63.75	$67.50	$71.25	$75.00	$78.75
	90%	$45.00	$49.50	$54.00	$58.50	$63.00	$67.50	$72.00	$76.50	$81.00	$85.50

could be solved in reverse for those probabilities and competing bid prices that yield outcomes just better or worse than the bidder's possible offers. Then, the bidder can make some judgment about the reasonableness of the range of competing offers and probabilities as a final step to preparing a bid price.

To illustrate how the EVNT equation can be used to help frame a bidder's analysis, consider the following example. A hostile bidder wants to prepare an initial bid for ABC Corp. ABC's current share price is $45. Under an aggressive restructuring plan (calling for asset sales and a leveraged recapitalization), ABC would be worth $65 per share. The hostile bidder envisions some synergies with ABC, which, if applied entirely to the value of ABC, would justify a maximum bid of $77 per share. Plainly, the hostile bidder would like to appropriate as much of the middle range for itself as possible. At what price should the bidder commence the hostile offer?

As discussed earlier, the Raider's strategy will be heavily influenced by the Target's ability to counter with a value-creating restructuring plan. Thus, the Raider could consider two scenarios:

- **Possibility A: Target does not restructure.** In this instance, if the Raider's bid fails to attract the requisite number of shares, the Target's share price could be presumed to fall back to the ex ante level, $45.
- **Possibility B: Target announces a restructuring.** Here the shareholders would be unlikely to part with their shares for less than $65, if they were highly confident of the Target's ability to deliver this value. For simplicity, let's assume that the restructuring value is highly likely.

Table 4 gives EVNT for various combinations of competing bid prices and probabilities in the first scenario. The shaded region indicates the breakeven values for each probability and bid that the Raider must top in order to motivate the arbs to favor the Raider's bid. For instance, a competing bid of $70 and a 50 percent probability suggests that the Raider must bid *more* than $57.50 to motivate the arbs to tender their shares to the bidder. The task of the bidder must be to assess whether any other firm could possibly afford $70 per share, which is the same as asking whether the probability of a bid at $70 is really 50 percent.

Table 5 summarizes the results for the second scenario. Comparing the shaded areas of both tables shows that the Target's restructuring considerably reduces the buyer's room to maneuver.

TABLE 5
EVNT If the "Default Value" Is Driven by Target's Restructuring (Possibility B)

		Value of Competing Bid								
		$45.00	$50.00	$55.00	$60.00	$65.00	$70.00	$75.00	$80.00	$85.00	$90.00
Probability	10%	$63.00	$63.50	$64.00	$64.50	$65.00	$65.50	$66.00	$66.50	$67.00	$67.50
of a	25%	$60.00	$61.25	$62.50	$63.75	$65.00	$66.25	$67.50	$68.75	$70.00	$71.25
Competing	50%	$55.00	$57.50	$60.00	$62.50	$65.00	$67.50	$70.00	$72.50	$75.00	$77.50
Bid	75%	$50.00	$53.75	$57.50	$61.25	$65.00	$68.75	$72.50	$76.25	$80.00	$83.75
	90%	$47.00	$51.50	$56.00	$60.50	$65.00	$69.50	$74.00	$78.50	$83.00	$87.50

This analysis shows the enormous advantage that accrues to the first mover in hostile tender offers. Arbs must weigh the concrete offer by the first bidder against uncertain offers by potential competing bidders. Uncertainty discounts the value of these potential competitors such that it requires a relatively high probability of a high bid to dissuade arbs from tendering into a certain offer.

The practitioner (bidder or target) can use this analysis as follows:

1. Bound the bidding range on the low side by either the ex ante share price, or the value per share produced by any restructuring plan.
2. Set an upper limit on the bidding range, determined by the value of the target firm reflecting all synergies, and optimistic assumptions about operations and the ability to use financial leverage aggressively.
3. Estimate the EVNTs for various combinations of competing bids and probabilities—this is equivalent to the shaded areas in Tables 4 and 5.
4. After reflecting on competing bidders, their bid prices, and the likelihood of their entry into the contest, set an offering price that slightly exceeds the EVNT for that cell in your table.

Finally, EVNT offers general insights on two classic competing strategies: (a) start with a high bid; and (b) start with a low bid. Each has advantages and disadvantages:

- **Bid high.** A high initial bid is known in M&A parlance as a "bear hug"—presumably referring to the apparent expression of affection that kills all resistance. This strategy deters competitors and pressures the target's directors to accept the offer. Knowing this, and seeing the high offer, arbs will tend to support the bid. Accordingly, the high bid strategy probably wins the contest. The chief disadvantage of this strategy is that it gives value to target shareholders that might have been retained by the bidder with a lower-priced opening bid. Generally, this strategy is appropriate where the bidder fears other competitors, or is impatient.
- **Bid low.** This has the advantage of saving the gains from takeover for the bidder. But it may attract competing bidders, and almost certainly invites the target to announce an internal restructuring. This approach probably leads to a longer contest. The risk to the bidder is higher. Generally, this strategy is appropriate where the bidder is patient and/or confident of there being no or few other competing bidders.

9. CONCLUSION: THE GAME HAS IMPLICATIONS FOR DESIGN AND DEFENSE OF TAKEOVERS

The discussion in this chapter suggests that practitioners need to assess and exploit uncertainty in the design and execution of hostile offers. Specific implications include these:

- Clarity about the value of the target is an absolutely essential foundation for takeover attack and defense. Value should be estimated from a variety of perspectives: current stand-alone status, status if restructured or recapitalized, value to the primary hostile bidder with synergies, and value to potential competing bidders with their synergies. At the very least, this valuation effort anticipates the likely analysis of arbitrageurs who will figure importantly in deciding the contest.
- The hostile bidder should take actions that shorten the time to outcome, that forestall collaboration among target shareholders, that preempt potential competitors, that reduce investor uncertainty about the value of the bid, and that generally pressures the target board to cooperate. The target firm should do the opposite: delay, explore restructuring and white knight bidders, cast uncertainty on the hostile bidder and its bid, and generally pressure the target board not to cooperate.
- The focus of both attacker and defender should be the investor, particularly the arbitrageur. The arb is unimpressed with appeals to loyalty, tradition, or vague strategies. Cash value delivered in timely fashion will be decisive. Winning the game, then, is largely a matter of maximizing value.
- Government influence in the takeover game is immense. Courts and government agencies can intervene in the game often in unpredictable ways. An important second "front" for both attacker and defender to manage is the observance and exploitation of case law.

FOR FURTHER READING

Auerbach, Alan J., *Mergers and Acquisitions,* Chicago: University of Chicago Press, 1988.

Brams, Steven J. *Rational Politics, Decisions, Games, and Strategy,* Boston: Academic Press, 1985.

Fleisher, Arthur, Jr., and Alexander R. Sussman, *Takeover Defense,* 5th ed., (2 vols.) Aspen Law & Business, New York: Aspen Publishers, Inc., 1997.

Gilson, Ronald J., and Bernard S. Black, *The Law and Finance of Corporate Acquisitions,* 2nd ed. Westbury, The Foundation Press, Inc., 1995.

McDonald, John, *Strategy in Poker, Business & War,* New York: W.W. Norton, 1989.

Rapoport, Anatol, and A.M. Chammah, *Prisoner's Dilemma,* Ann Arbor: University of Michigan Press, 1965.

Smith, Adam, *The Money Game,* New York, Dell, 1969.

Thaler, Richard H., *The Winner's Curse: Paradoxes and Anomalies of Economic Life,* Princeton: Princeton University Press, 1992.

Wyser-Pratte, Guy P., *Risk Arbitrage II,* New York: Salomon Brothers Center for the Study of Financial Institutions, Graduate School of Business Administration, New York University, Monograph 1982-3-4.

The Hilton–ITT Wars

Professor William Z. Ripley of Harvard, the leading authority on corporations in the 1920s, warned President Calvin Coolidge that "prestidigitation, double-shuffling, honey-fugling, hornswoggling, and skulduggery" were threatening the entire economic system. Plus ça change, plus c'est la même chose.[1]

—Rand V. Araskog, CEO of ITT

Surprised by the announcement of ITT Corporation's (ITT) restructuring proposal, on July 17, 1997, Matthew J. Hart, the chief financial officer of Hilton Hotels Corporation (Hilton), reviewed the valuation analysis of ITT (see **Appendix**) and pondered the next step in his firm's hostile tender-offer contest for ITT. Hilton had commenced the tender offer on January 27, 1997. The financial community had responded favorably, but ITT's management had resisted firmly, selling assets and even refusing to call an annual meeting. Because ITT had a strong "poison-pill" antitakeover defense in place, it would be necessary to replace ITT's board and for that board to rescind the poison-pill defense before Hilton could consummate its purchase of ITT. But ITT had delayed calling an annual meeting at which a new board could be elected. In the six months since the initial Hilton offer, ITT had developed its "trivestiture" proposal, which it hoped would successfully fend off Hilton.

---

[1]Rand V. Araskog, *The ITT Wars* (New York: Henry Holt and Company, 1989), 228.

ITT Corporation's tax-free "trivestiture" proposal would split the company into three independent companies:

1. ITT Destinations, Inc., which would consist of the gaming and lodging businesses and own the Caesars and Sheraton brands;
2. ITT Information Services, Inc., which would publish international telephone directories;
3. ITT Educational Services, Inc., which would own and operate a chain of technical schools.

Under the proposal, ITT shareholders would get a share each of ITT Destinations and ITT Information Services and 0.25 shares of ITT Educational Services. ITT also announced a self-tender offer for 30 million shares (25 percent of the outstanding shares) at $70 a share and a tender for $2 billion of outstanding public debt. This proposal was to be put to a vote at the upcoming annual meeting of ITT shareholders.[2] Any attempt to acquire ITT Destinations after the restructuring would endanger the tax-free status of the trivestiture and the acquirer would be saddled with a $1.4 billion tax liability. Also, ITT Destinations had only one-third of its directors up for retirement every year, slowing the pace of any possible takeover of that business unit. The trivestiture appeared to be an attempt to lift ITT's share price by creating highly focused companies in three distinct industries through a tax-efficient separation and then delivering cash to shareholders through the self-tender.[3]

HILTON HOTEL CORPORATION

Hilton Hotel Corporation was the seventh-largest hotel company, with 1996 sales of approximately $3.9 billion and assets of approximately $7.6 billion. The company developed, owned, managed, and franchised hotel-casinos, resorts, hotel properties, and vacation-ownership resorts. The firm operated 241 Hilton hotels, casino-resorts, and riverboat casinos in 40 states and 11 Conrad International hotel-casinos in 10 countries around the world.[4]

ITT CORPORATION

ITT was formerly a wholly owned subsidiary of a Delaware corporation known as ITT Corporation (Old ITT). On December 19, 1995, Old ITT (renamed ITT Industries) distributed to its shareholders all the outstanding shares of common stock of ITT and ITT Hartford Group, Inc. In 1998, ITT Corporation was no longer affiliated with ITT Industries or ITT Hartford Group, Inc.

In 1996, ITT Corporation was one of the world's largest hotel and gaming companies. It had sales of approximately $6.6 billion and assets of approximately $9.3 billion. Its core

---

[2]Tom Lowry, "ITT Splits Three Ways to Fend Off Hilton," *USA Today,* 17 July 1997, B3.
[3]ITT Corporation Investor Presentation, 16 July 1997.
[4]Hilton Hotel Corporation Annual Report and 10-K Statement, 1996.

assets included ITT Sheraton, one of the world's largest hotel companies, with approximately 410 hotels and resorts in 60 countries, and Caesars World, the leading brand name in the gaming industry, with major casinos in Atlantic City, Las Vegas, and Lake Tahoe. Other assets included ITT Educational Services, ITT World Directories, and ownership interest in Madison Square Garden (in partnership with Cablevision) and in New York television station WBIS+ (in partnership with Dow Jones).[5]

HILTON'S HOSTILE OFFER AND ITT'S INITIAL RESPONSES

On January 27, 1997, Hilton offered to pay $55 a share in cash for 50.1 percent of ITT shares and $55 a share in stock for the rest. The acquisition would be accounted for as a purchase transaction. (See **Exhibit 1** for a complete summary of the offer.) If successful, this transaction would be the biggest takeover ever in the lodging and gaming industry. Many analysts believed that the ITT acquisition would make Hilton the world's biggest hotel and casino company. With ITT Sheraton's larger international presence, Hilton would be in a much stronger position to compete in the worldwide hotel industry. Moreover, ITT's "Caesars" brand name would solidify Hilton's presence in Atlantic City and Las Vegas. W. Bruce Turner, gaming and lodging analyst at Salomon Brothers, said, "The combination of Hilton and ITT represents a once-in-a-lifetime opportunity to create an unduplicatable global franchise twice as large as any hotel rival and four times as large as any gaming company."[6]

Wall Street was very excited about this tender offer; Hilton's shares increased 10 percent following the announcement, an unusual move for the stock of an acquiring company (**Exhibit 2** gives the share price of both firms during the period of the tender offer). Turner observed, "It's an indication of the market's enthusiasm for the proposal and the value Hilton could bring."[7]

Both ITT Corporation and Hilton Corporation were in a race to dominate the lodging and gaming industry. They competed for the same customers, more or less, in their main business segments, lodging and gaming. Both were acquiring hotel properties in the luxury and midscale markets. In the 1990s, it was cheaper to acquire than build. In the gaming business, ITT acquired Caesars World, Inc., in 1995; Hilton outbid ITT to acquire Bally Entertainment Corporation in 1996. This was not the only time that ITT and Hilton had crossed paths directly. ITT had approached Hilton to acquire its hotel business in 1960 and its hotel and gaming business in 1994. On both occasions, ITT's offer was rebuffed.

The hostile tender offer was no surprise because ITT management had declined to negotiate a friendly acquisition by Hilton. Even after the tender offer, ITT management refused to meet with Hilton management. While there was no negotiation, there was verbal jousting. Rand Araskog, ITT's chairman, said,

> We've never bothered to talk with Hilton, and our board has turned down their bid because we are a much better company with a brighter future, given the superior quality and location of our

---

[5]ITT Corporation Annual Report and 10-K Statement, 1996.
[6]Jonathan Laing, "Nasty Bout," *Barron's* (29 September 1997): 34.
[7]Ibid.

hotels and gaming facilities. Our Sheraton brand name is in the Four Seasons class, and no gaming operation has quite the same image that our Caesars operation has.[8]

Stephen Bollenbach, CEO of Hilton, said,

What Araskog has shown ever since we made our first offer in late January is that he will do anything just to try to fend us off and preserve his own job. That includes dumping so-called core assets, sacrificing 65 percent of his headquarters staff, riding roughshod over the interest of shareholders, and turning his company into a junk credit. He has spent his entire career acting like a beneficiary rather than as a steward of ITT assets, living like a sultan of Brunei in the process. And even more pathetic, he has been acting like a superweenie, hiding behind his board and advisers and refusing to talk with us.[9]

The Hilton offer of $55 a share amounted to a 29 percent premium over ITT's share price of $43, and was timed to exploit the imminent ITT general meeting at which all of ITT's directors would be up for reelection. At the annual meeting, Bollenbach planned to ask ITT shareholders to elect up to 25 Hilton nominees to the ITT board. These nominees were expected to facilitate the proposed merger. Hilton also planned to ask the ITT shareholders to repeal any bylaw amendments that ITT might adopt before the annual meeting that could interfere with the offer, the merger, or the election of Hilton's nominees—the chief among these would be to waive the activation of ITT's poison-pill antitakeover defense.

On February 12, 1997, ITT management rejected Hilton's offer, arguing, "The interests of ITT shareholders as well as ITT employees, suppliers, creditors, and customers would be best served by ITT's continued independence." They cited the following reasons to support their decision.[10]

1. The Hilton offer did not reflect the inherent value of ITT. ITT's response stated, "In the opinion of our financial advisers, Goldman Sachs and Lazard Frères, the Hilton proposal is inadequate."
2. The merger would lead to cannibalization and conflicts among properties managed by Sheraton and Hilton.
3. Hilton's proposal to license the Sheraton and Four Points names for franchising could lead to termination of numerous contracts.
4. The offer raised several potential antitrust and gaming-law issues.

In an effort to defend itself, ITT management deferred the general meeting by six months and initiated litigation to claim relief from the misappropriation and misuse of confidential ITT information acquired by Hilton after its recent acquisition of Bally Entertainment.

Hilton reacted immediately to ITT's rejection. It filed an injunction to force ITT to hold its annual meeting in May. It also communicated the following to the capital market:

- A potential annual synergy cash flow of more than $100 million in this transaction, pointing to Bollenbach's ability to squeeze out a $60 million annual synergy cash flow from the Bally acquisition as an illustration of its ability to realize the stated synergies.
- A strategy to create value for ITT's shareholders by monetizing and selling noncore assets of ITT.

---

[8]Ibid., 33.
[9]Ibid.
[10]ITT Corporation press release, 17 July 1997.

- A history of poor shareholder-value creation by current ITT managers, who were more interested in cashing in than performance.[11]

Following the unsolicited $6.5-billion hostile-takeover bid by Hilton, ITT started an aggressive effort to sell assets—the objective was to raise its stock price and keep Hilton from winning the takeover battle. In effect, ITT management sought to take the kinds of actions that Hilton management had proposed to do after the merger.

- February: Reduction in headquarters staff from 200 to 75
- February–March: Sale of investments in Alcatel Alsthom for $830 million
- April: Sale of interest in Madison Square Garden for $650 million
- May: Sale of interest in WBIS+ for $128.75 million
                                  Sale of five Sheraton hotels for $200 million

These actions by ITT resulted in an increase in share price to $63.50. Also, management refused to hold an annual meeting at which Hilton's proposal might be heard and voted upon. On April 4, 1997, the U.S. District Court for the District of Nevada denied Hilton's motion for a preliminary injunction requiring ITT to hold its annual meeting in May.

COUNTERING THE TRIVESTITURE

Now, on July 17, 1997, Matthew Hart knew that Hilton would have to fight this battle on two fronts: in the courtrooms and in the capital markets. Analysts' and arbitrageurs' expectations, as well as fear of a white knight and the repurchase of shares by ITT at $70 a share, convinced Hart that Hilton would have to raise its bid for ITT. He was unsure, however, what the next bid should be, what legal action he should initiate, and what message he should send to investors and the financial community.

As a foundation for considering the next steps, it would be necessary to take the view of investors and arbitrageurs who held ITT's shares. First, one needed to evaluate the bidding for a target's shares in light of the target's estimated intrinsic value. (The Appendix presents an estimate of value consistent with analysts' expectations before the bidding began.) Hart would want to update this analysis to reflect recent events and ITT's press releases. Second, it would be necessary to model the investor's decision and work backward from that to the bid by Hilton that reflected Hart's assessment of an even higher bid by ITT or a third party—this was the analysis based on the Expected Value of Not Tendering (EVNT). In short, intrinsic value and EVNT would provide benchmarks against which Hart could evaluate Hilton's past bidding for ITT and the range of possible future bids. Hart wanted to make sure that his next bid would compel the ITT board of directors to accept the Hilton offer.

---

[11]Over the 16 years of Araskog's chairmanship, ITT was able to deliver an average annual gain of only around 10 percent. The S&P over the same period gained nearly 16 percent per annum. Despite ITT's lackluster performance, Araskog earned a compensation of $11.4 million in 1990, a period when ITT's return to shareholders was in the bottom 30 percent of America's 406 largest corporations. In 1995, he negotiated a $13.5 million compensation package for himself.

EXHIBIT 1
Comparison of the Terms of the Actual Tender Offer and Proposed Tender Offer

	Actual Tender Offer as on January 28, 1997	Suggested Terms of Tender Offer Originally Proposed in Appendix
Offer	$55 a share cash and stock bid	$65–70 a share cash and stock bid
Terms	$55 a share in cash for 50.1 percent of outstanding ITT shares and Hilton shares worth $55 in exchange for the balance 49.9 percent of ITT shares	$65–70 a share in cash for 50.1 percent of outstanding ITT shares and Hilton shares worth $65–70 in exchange for the balance 49.9 percent of ITT shares
Assumed Debt	$4 billion	$4 billion
Total Value	$10.5 billion	$11.7 to 12.3 billion
Offer Expiry Date	February 28, 1997	One month from date of offer
Approvals	Hilton and ITT Shareholders	Hilton and ITT Shareholders
	Gaming Regulators	Gaming Regulators
	Anti-Trust Regulators	Anti-Trust Regulators
	National Basketball Association	National Basketball Association
	National Hockey League	National Hockey League
	Federal Communications Commission	Federal Communications Commission
Collar	Unspecified	Specified, based on Hilton's expected share price immediately after announcement of offer

Source: Casewriter's analysis.

EXHIBIT 2
Share Prices versus S&P 500 January 1, 1996, to July 17, 1997

ITT Corporation

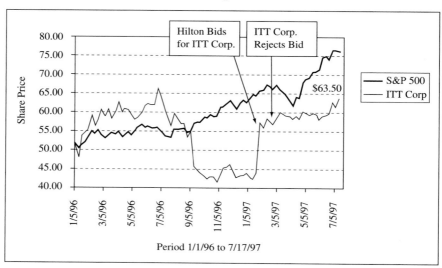

Period 1/1/96 to 7/17/97

Hilton Hotel Corporation

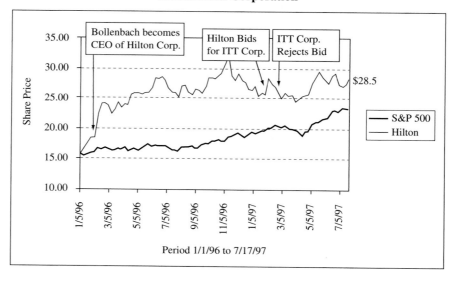

Period 1/1/96 to 7/17/97

APPENDIX

To: Matthew J. Hart,
Chief Financial Officer
Hilton Hotels Corporation

From: Jane Smith, Director
Corporate Planning

Subject: Tender Offer for ITT Corporation

Date: December 31, 1996

This memo summarizes our valuation of ITT and the proposed strategy for acquiring the firm. Sections and Exhibits are as follows.

1. Strategic Motives for the Transaction
2. The Tender Offer
3. Pricing and Timing of the Tender Offer
4. Suggested Terms of Proposed Tender Offer
5. Implementation of the Tender Strategy
6. Comparison of ITT Corporation and Hilton Hotel Corporation
7. Industry and Competitive Outlook
8. Valuation of Proposed Acquisition of ITT Corporation

Valuation Methodology

Exhibit A1 - Valuation of ITT Corporation
Exhibit A2 - Valuation of ITT's Lodging Business
Exhibit A3 - Valuation of ITT's Gaming Business
Exhibit A4 - Valuation of ITT's Education Business
Exhibit A5 - Valuation of ITT's Directories Business
Exhibit A6 - Valuation of ITT's Entertainment Business
Exhibit A7 - Valuation of ITT's Investments
Exhibit A8 - Valuation of Corporate-Level Expenses
Exhibit A9 - Valuation of Synergies from this Acquisition

Additional Financial Data

Exhibit A10 - Comparable Transactions
Exhibit A11 - Comparable Companies

Source: This appendix is a fictitious memorandum prepared from public information. The views and analysis herein are consistent with observations of knowledgeable observers outside of ITT and Hilton. This is intended to represent the range of concerns attendant to making a hostile tender offer and to stimulate student analysis rather than to illustrate effective or ineffective managerial decision making.

1. STRATEGIC MOTIVES FOR THE TRANSACTION

This acquisition is consistent with Hilton's corporate strategy of global expansion of its lodging business and market leadership of its gaming business. With the acquisition of the Sheraton Hotels, The Luxury Collection, Ciga and Four Point Hotels, Hilton will bolster its international presence in the lodging industry. The increase in capacity to 230,973 rooms will make Hilton the sixth largest lodging corporation in the world. Also, the proposed franchising arrangement with HFS will ensure the domestic and international expansion of the Sheraton and Hilton brands. The acquisition of the Caesars gaming business will add considerable muscle to Hilton's existing gaming operations. The critical size achieved will enable Hilton to emerge as a giant of the gaming industry with brands such as Caesars, Bally, Sheraton and Hilton Casinos in its portfolio of gaming assets. Additionally, the critical size and international presence achieved by this merger will enable the realization of synergies in the following areas.

1. International expansion through Sheraton's global presence will bring benefits of global diversification.
2. The consolidation of reservation services, catering, marketing and bakeries will result in pretax annual cost savings of more than $100–115 million. Also, the company will have increased bargaining power in negotiation with food and beverage suppliers, insurance brokers, telephone and telecommunication companies and computer hardware and software vendors.
3. Reduced capital expenditure will result in increased cash flow. This will enable Hilton to pay larger dividends to shareholders.

2. THE TENDER OFFER

It is proposed that Hilton Hotel Corporation make an unsolicited tender offer for any and all common shares of ITT Corporation. As you know, we have approached ITT Management and attempted to negotiate a friendly merger. Despite the unwillingness of ITT management to negotiate, we continue to believe that this combination offers substantial economic benefits that could enhance the wealth of both Hilton and ITT shareholders. Thus, we propose proceeding with a hostile tender offer and recommend the strategy set forth below:

- Integration of ITT hotels and casinos into the Hilton system.
- Eliminate duplicative selling, general and administrative expense, to be derived in part from the disposal of ITT senior management.
- Franchising of the Sheraton name to HFS Inc.
- Sale and/or monetization (through spin-offs or carve-outs) of noncore assets.

To be successful, this tender must be made at an opportune time and at a significant premium to the market price of ITT shares. It will also be necessary to comply with SEC disclosures, Section 13 and Section 14 of the Williams Act of 1968, Insider Trading sanctions, Racketeer Influenced and Corrupt Organizations Act of 1970, Nevada State

Business Laws, Securities & Exchange Act of 1934, ITT's internal bylaws, and antitrust regulations.

3. PRICING AND TIMING OF THE TENDER OFFER

In light of the current gaming and lodging industry dynamics, we believe there is a low probability of a competitive bidder with the financial resources and management capacity to run ITT. However, based on comparable transactions we believe that a premium of about 50 percent over the current $43–46.50 share price range would be appropriate, implying a bid price range of $65–70 per share. A tender offer in this range is higher than ITT's breakup value and will appeal to ITT's shareholders and will discourage other acquirers from entering into a bidding war. Moreover, with a high price, the probability of a successful tender offer is higher. The high probability will attract the support of risk arbitrageurs ("arbs") who, shortly after the tender offer, will likely become the critical swing "voters" in the control contest. If we can gain the support of the arbs, it is likely that our offer will succeed.

Late January is an ideal time to make this tender offer to ITT shareholders because:

1. ITT shares are expected to remain undervalued.
2. ITT's entire board of directors is up for reelection. This is a golden opportunity to oust all of the ITT directors at the next annual meeting.
3. A merger between ITT and Hilton may result in the cancellation of ITT's Tampa Hotel Project. The ambiguity around the merger will have a negative impact on ITT's projected earnings and ITT's share price.

4. SUGGESTED TERMS OF THE PROPOSED TENDER OFFER

Offer	$65–70 a share Cash and Stock bid.
Terms	$65–70 a share in cash for 50.1% of outstanding ITT shares and Hilton shares worth $65–70 in exchange for the balance 49.9% of ITT shares.
Assumed Debt	$4 billion
Total Value	$11.7 to $12.3 billion
Nature	Hostile tender offer
Offer Expiry Date	One month from offer date and prior to June 1997
Consummation Subject to These Approvals	Hilton and ITT Shareholders Gaming regulators Antitrust regulators National Basketball Association National Hockey League Federal Communications Commission
Collar	Specified, based on Hilton's expected share price immediately after announcement of offer.

5. IMPLEMENTATION OF THE TENDER OFFER STRATEGY

a.   **Purchase 4.9 percent of ITT's shares before the announcement.** At 5 percent, Hilton must file a Form 13-D with the Securities and Exchange Commission, thus announcing to the public its interest in Hilton. By purchasing just less than 5 percent, Hilton acquires a "toe-hold" number of votes, and a bloc of shares on which to profit if Hilton's bid is topped by another firm.

b.   **Commence the tender offer with a public announcement of the tender price, and with direct solicitation of major institutional stockholders in ITT.** The key points of persuasion are the attractive offer (at $65–70 per share) and the abysmal record of current ITT management. The offer must be outstanding for 20 business days before Hilton can purchase shares.

c.   **Restructure the ITT board of directors, and rescind the poison pill anti-takeover defense:** At the shareholder meeting Hilton management must ask ITT shareholders:

   • To elect up to 25 Hilton nominees to the ITT Board. These nominees will help facilitate the proposed merger.
   • To sanction this merger and repeal any bylaw amendments that ITT management might adopt before the annual meeting that could interfere with the offer, the merger or the election of Hilton's nominees.

It is essential that ITT's poison pill be rescinded—without this, the acquisition of ITT will become prohibitively expensive. ITT's bylaws give ITT's board the right to rescind the poison pill. Hence, restructuring ITT's board is essential.

The restructured board should give attention to other considerations as well:
1. Possibly limiting "golden parachute" payments, compensation to ITT management because of change in ownership.
2. Possibly limiting stock option exercise because of change in ITT ownership and management.
3. Managing the redemption of debt securities as a result of change in ITT ownership and management.
4. Limiting the negotiation of contracts that are not in the interest of the merged company.
5. Terminating defensive litigation.

d.   **Licensing the Sheraton name to HFS Inc.** After the ITT acquisition, Hilton should consider licensing the Sheraton Brand to Hospitality Franchising Services Inc. (HFS), which franchises Ramada, Days Inn, and Howard Johnson hotels. HFS would license Sheraton's franchise and management systems. The agreement with HFS should ensure that HFS pays a fee for the Sheraton trademark and shares earnings with Hilton from the franchise and management fees. This arrangement will give Hilton a secure cash flow stream from HFS and promote healthy competition between the Hilton and Sheraton brands.

e.   **Sale or Monetization of Noncore Assets** ITT Corporation consists of four distinct businesses: gaming, lodging, entertainment (Madison Square Gardens) and information systems (ITT Education and ITT Directories). They also have a 5 percent stake in Alcatel Alsthom, a French chemical company. As Hilton is interested in the gaming and lodging assets of ITT, it will be financially prudent to monetize the information system assets and sell off noncore assets, the entertainment business, and Alcatel Alsthom investments. The monies realized from the sale and monetization of noncore assets should be used to pay down the debt incurred during the acquisition.

f.   Financing the Acquisition The acquisition should be financed from a combination of internal and external sources. We recommend that Hilton use available cash, working capital, and existing borrowing facilities and also issue public debt. It should be possible to finance the acquisition in this manner, and maintain Hilton Hotel Corporation debt rating at "Baal."

6. COMPARISON OF ITT CORPORATION AND HILTON HOTEL CORPORATION

a. Corporate Strategy[12]

ITT Corporation	Hilton Hotel Corporation
To deliver near term value to shareholders while maintaining and building a platform for superior long-term growth and profitability	1. Access favorable capital markets and utilize strong balance sheet. 2. Take advantage of current economic conditions to acquire full-service hotels. 3. Be a winner in the consolidation of the gaming industry. 4. Invest in our brand through domestic franchising and expanding our international presence.

b. Investor Base[13]

Equity Ownership	ITT Corporation	Hilton Hotel Corporation
Management	4%	27%
Banks	12%	11%
Insurance Co.	13%	3%
Asset Managers	40%	30%
Mutual Funds	22%	23%
Others	9%	6%

[12]Hilton Hotel Corporation and ITT Corporation Annual Reports and 10-K Statements, 1996.
[13]O'Neil Database, December 1996.

c. Properties by Ownership Type[14]

	ITT Corporation		Hilton Hotel Corporation	
	Properties	**Rooms**	**Properties**	**Rooms**
Owned or partially owned hotels	68	22,856	31	23,092
Managed hotels	135	50,415	28	16,776
Franchised hotels	208	51,691	177	45,050
Owned or partially owned or				
Managed or franchised casinos	11	3,179	13	17,914
Riverboat casinos	1	0	5	0
TOTAL	**423**	**128,141**	**254**	**102,832**

d. Financial Performance[15]

	ITT Corporation		Hilton Hotel Corporation	
	1996	**1995**	**1996**	**1995**
Revenues	$ 6,597	$ 6,252	$ 3,940	$ 3,555
Operating income	$ 728	$ 568	$ 329	$ 355
Net income	$ 249	$ 147	$ 82*	$ 173
Total assets	$ 9,275	$ 8,692	$ 7,577	$ 3,443
Long-term debt	$ 3,894	$ 3,575	$ 2,606	$ 1,070
Shareholders equity	$ 3,074	$ 2,936	$ 3,211	$ 1,254
Shares outstanding	117	117	194	194
EPS	$ 2.11	$ 1.26	$ 0.42	$ 0.89

Note: All financials, other than per-share data, are in millions. ITT's financials adjusted for 1995 reorganization.
*Includes extraordinary loss of $74 million.

e. Recent Corporate Events[16]

ITT Corporation	Hilton Hotel Corporation

ITT Corporation

In January 1995, ITT completed a cash tender offer for the outstanding shares of Caesars World Inc., a gaming corporation, for approximately $1.76 billion.

In March 1995, MSG, a partnership between subsidiaries of ITT and Cablevision Systems Corporation acquired the business of Madison Square Gardens Corporation for approximately $1 billion.

In July 1996, ITT in partnership with Dow Jones and Co. purchased a television WNYC-TV (now renamed as WBIS+) station from The City of New York for $207 million.

Hilton Hotel Corporation

In February 1996, Steven F. Bollenbach was named president and chief executive officer of Hilton Hotels Corporation.

In June 1996, Hilton acquired Bally Entertainment Corporation and became the world's largest casino gaming company.

In August 1996, Hilton formed a strategic alliance with Ladbrook Group PLC (current owners of the Hilton name outside the United States) to reunite the Hilton brand on a worldwide basis.

---

[14]ITT Corporation and Hilton Hotel Corporation Annual Reports and 10-K Statements, 1996.
[15]Ibid.
[16]Ibid.

f. Share Price Analysis:

ITT Corporation	Hilton Hotel Corporation
Based on Figure A1 we conclude that in 1996, ITT shares underperformed the S&P Index by 32 percent. Total return to shareholders during this period was −16 percent. This poor performance is mainly due to shareholder expectations of poor returns from the gaming business segment.	Based on Figure A1 we conclude that in 1996 Hilton's share price outperformed the S&P Index by 50 percent. Total return to shareholders during this period was 68 percent. This has been mainly due to its aggressive growth strategy and market expectation of continued economic prosperity for this industry as a whole.

FIGURE A1:

Hilton Hotel Corporation, ITT Corporation, and S&P 500 Index Performance from January 1, 1996, to December 31, 1996

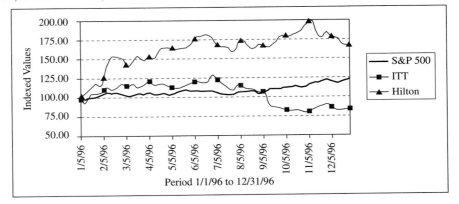

7. INDUSTRY AND COMPETITIVE OUTLOOK

a.   Lodging Operations[17]

We expect Average Daily Rates (ADR) to increase at rates higher than the overall inflation rate of the U.S. economy. Demand for hotel rooms will be fueled by moderate economic growth; however, there are indications that the robust growth experienced by the industry during 1995 and 1996 will soon ease. U.S. unemployment at 5.5 percent will lead to a hike in federal minimum wage and this will affect labor costs and margins adversely. Also, the $5.2 billion investment in hotel construction in 1996 is expected to create increased capacity and competition, which will reduce the growth rate of ADR.

Internationally, the emerging economies of Latin America, Eastern Europe, Southeast Asia, and China will fuel international growth of this industry. As foreign direct investment to various regions increases, there will be a demand for luxury, midscale, and budget hotels. New construction, strategic joint ventures or cross-border acquisition, and expansion of local hotel chains will fulfill this demand.

Many analysts believe that due to the absence of capacity in full service hotels in the luxury and midscale segments, it is more attractive (less costly) for companies to acquire

---

[17]S&P 500 Industry Report, October 1996.

existing properties. This market opportunity has resulted in a spate of equity issuance and mergers and acquisitions activity. Recently, Double Tree Corporation bought Red Lion Hotels for $1.2 billion and Marriott International bought Renaissance Hotel Group for $1 billion. For now, hotel companies and REITs are focused on acquisitions in their peer groups. Down the road, they are going to look further afield towards acquisition of other real estate related businesses including ski resorts and casino operations.

b.   Gaming Operations[18]

Revenues continue to rise in the gaming industry, but the conditions for long-term sustainable double-digit growth in the United States have weakened. No new states have approved non–Native American casinos since mid-1993. Although the development of glamorous and distinctive new facilities in Las Vegas and Atlantic City should boost the number of gambling visitors, for many Americans, a visit to a casino still requires a long-distance trip by plane, car, or bus. River boat gambling has mushroomed in popularity in the past decade as additional states—Illinois, Indiana, Iowa, Louisiana, Mississippi and Missouri—have approved the practice. This is an area of differentiation and one that will be very profitable in the long run.

Though geographic expansion prospects for the gaming industry look weak and analysts believe that the industry is plagued with overcapacity, gaming companies have taken a long-term perspective and have started attracting family customers by establishing themselves as destination resorts. Food prices, room rates, and entertainment income have skyrocketed and serious revenue streams have begun to flow as gaming companies have reinvented themselves to be in the "business of selling excitement." So if casino operations do not make money, the gaming businesses are insulated with higher room rates, lower food costs, and revenues from nongaming entertainment.

c.   Assessment of ITT World Directories[19]

One of the most important factors currently affecting the business of ITT World Directories is the changing competitive environment in the member states of the European Union in which it publishes telephone directories. Historically, the national telephone service provider in countries in the European Union awarded an exclusive contract for the provision of directories. ITT World Directories lost its exclusive contract with the national provider of telecommunications services in Belgium (Belgacom) and the Netherlands (PTT Telekom) in 1994 and 1993, respectively. In Belgium, ITT World Directories now actively competes with BDS, a joint venture between the local telecommunications provider, Belgacom, and a subsidiary of GTE Corporation. In the Netherlands, ITT World Directories now actively competes with directories published by a joint venture between the local telecommunications provider, PTT Telekom, and Telemedia Group. Although currently there is no meaningful competition for directory services in the other principal countries in which ITT World Directories' operates, there can be no assurance that such conditions will continue.

d.   Assessment of ITT Educational[20]

The postsecondary education market in the United States is highly fragmented and competitive, with no private or public institution enjoying a significant market share. ITT

---

[18]Ibid.
[19]ITT Corporation 10-K Statement, 1996.
[20]Ibid.

Technical Institutes compete for students with four-year and two-year degree-granting institutions, which include not-for-profit public and private colleges and proprietary institutions, as well as with alternatives to higher education, such as military service or immediate employment.

Competition among educational institutes is believed to be based on the quality of the educational program, perceived reputation of the institution, cost of the program, and employability of graduates. Certain public and private colleges may offer programs similar to those of ITT Technical Institutes at a lower tuition cost due in part to government subsidies, foundation grants, tax-deductible contributions, or other financial resources not available to proprietary institutions. Other proprietary institutions offer programs that compete with those of the ITT Technical Institutes. Certain of ITT Educational's competitors in both the public and private sectors have greater financial and other resources than ITT Educational.

8. VALUATION OF PROPOSED ACQUISITION OF ITT CORPORATION

As ITT consists of four strategic business units (SBUs), break-up valuation methodology has been used to value the corporation. We derived the estimate of each SBU by triangulating[21] from the results of several valuation techniques:

1. Comparable Companies
2. Comparable Transactions
3. Discounted Cash Flow

The comparable companies and comparable transaction valuations involved the use of enterprise value multiples (Revenue, EBIT, EBITDA, Adj. EBITDA and Net Income), and equity value multiples (PE's and Book to Market). To ensure the accuracy of the valuation these multiples were derived from financials of pure plays from each business segment.

The discounted cash flow valuation makes use of the capital asset pricing model to determine the discount rate. All discount rates were calculated based on pure play betas and target capital structures. For the purpose of valuation, terminal values were based on constant growth model. As a sanity check, other methods to calculate terminal values were also used.

---

[21]*Triangulate* is a term used by valuation practitioners to suggest the process of finding the likely intrinsic value of an asset from several estimates of value. This process entails judgment about the efficacy of the different value estimates (e.g. DCF, multiples, etc.) as well as valuation practice within the industry.

EXHIBIT A1
Valuation of ITT Corporation (in millions of dollars)

Business Units	Valuation		
	Pessimistic	Best Guess	Optimistic
1. Lodging	$ 4,200	$ 6,000	$ 7,000
2. Gaming	2,300	2,800	3,300
3. Information Services			
Education	330	425	498
Directories	880	1,050	1,280
4. Entertainment			
MSG	500	500	500
WBIS	104	104	104
5. Investments	877	877	877
6. Corporate-level expenses	(999)	(999)	(999)
Value of enterprise	**$ 8,193**	**$10,757**	**$12,559**
Less value of debt	(4,000)	(4,000)	(4,000)
Value of equity without synergy	**$ 4,193**	**$ 6,757**	**$ 8,559**
Shares outstanding	116.37	116.37	116.37
Per share value of equity without synergy	**$36.04**	**$58.07**	**$ 73.55**
Value of synergy	900	1,149	1,300
Value of equity with synergy	**$ 5,093**	**$ 7,906**	**$ 9,859**
Shares outstanding	116.37	116.37	116.37
Per share value of equity with synergy	**$ 43.77**	**$ 67.94**	**$ 84.73**

EXHIBIT A2
Valuation of ITT's Lodging Business (in millions of dollars)

	1997	1998	1999	2000	2001
EBIT	$ 465	$ 577	$ 645	$ 707	$ 763
(Less) Taxes	(186)	(231)	(258)	(283)	(305)
(Add) Depreciation	173	189	209	229	249
Subtotal	452	535	595	653	707
Change in noncurrent assets and liabilities	(21)	7	12	11	10
Change in working capital	390	16	30	28	26
Net capital investment	(465)	(431)	(534)	(532)	(530)
Free cash flow	$ 355	$ 127	$ 102	$ 159	$ 213
Terminal value					$ 5,882

DCF of ITT Lodging $4,009

WACC	10.90%	**PV of Terminal Value** (Constant Growth Model)		$ 3,507
W_e	84.46%	$(CF_n (1 + g) / (K - g)) / (1 + K)^5$		
W_d	15.54%			
K_e	12.07%	Growth rate		7.01%
K_d	7.55%	Inflation		2.70%
R_f	6.44%	Real		4.20%
R_p	5.40%			
Beta	1.04	**Other Terminal Value Estimates**		
		NOPAT/K		$ 3,853
		NOPAT $(1 - i)/(K - g)$		$10,815

Valuation Summary—Lodging	Multiples		Value	
	Low	**High**	**Low**	**High**
FCF valuation			$ 3,100	$ 4,500
Enterprise value as a multiple of 1996				
1 Revenue	1.03	12.45	4,566	55,191
2 EBIT	16.71	31.49	6,199	11,683
3 Net income	34.35	58.87	6,321	10,833
4 EBITDA	13.39	25.71	6,641	12,752
5 Adj EBITDA	23.14	30.80	3,271	4,354
6 Net assets	2.19	3.67	—	—
Equity value as a multiple of				
1 1996 EPS (A)	29.24	32.00	5,380	5,888
2 1997 EPS (E)	21.43	27.21	5,161	6,553
3 1998 EPS (E)	16.57	22.35	5,102	6,882
Triangulated enterprise value			$ 4,200	$ 7,000

Source: Casewriter analysis.

EXHIBIT A3
Valuation of ITT's Gaming Business (in millions of dollars)

	1997	1998	1999	2000	2001
EBIT	$ 233	$ 254	$ 271	$ 306	$ 327
(Less) Taxes	(93)	(101)	(108)	(122)	(131)
(Add) Depreciation & amortizations	120	131	135	139	143
Subtotal	260	283	298	323	339
Change in noncurrent assets and liabilities	26	5	7	5	8
Change in working capital	31	(4)	(3)	(6)	(3)
Net capital investment	(914)	(297)	(108)	(108)	(109)
Free cash flow	$ (598)	$ (11)	$ 195	$ 213	$ 235
Terminal value					$ 3,929

DCF of ITT Gaming	**$ 2,361**

WACC	9.11%	**PV of Terminal Value** (Constant Growth Model)	$ 2,540
W_e	77.54%	$(CF_n (1 + g) / (K - g)) / (1 + K)^5$	
W_d	22.46%		
K_e	10.44%	Growth rate	2.96%
K_d	7.55%	Inflation	2.70%
R_f	6.44%	Real	0.25%
R_p	5.40%		
Beta	0.74	**Other Terminal Value Estimates**	
		NOPAT / K	$ 1,286
		NOPAT $(1 - i)/(K - g)$	$ 1,904

Valuation Summary—Gaming	**Multiples**		**Value**	
	Low	**High**	**Low**	**High**
FCF valuation			$ 2,300	$ 3,000
Enterprise value as a multiple of 1996				
1 Revenue	1.72	3.64	2,210	4,677
2 EBIT	8.97	16.30	1,893	3,439
3 Net income	21.73	35.21	797	1,292
4 EBITDA	6.72	12.47	1,902	3,529
5 Adj EBITDA	9.78	13.26	1,762	2,389
6 Net assets	1.34	2.40	—	—
Equity value as a multiple of				
1 1996 EPS (A)	16.51	23.58	606	865
2 1997 EPS (E)	13.31	22.73	365	624
3 1998 EPS (E)	11.60	19.23	852	1,413
Triangulated enterprise value			**$ 2,300**	**$ 3,300**

Source: Casewriter analysis.

EXHIBIT A4
Valuation of ITT's Education Business (in millions of dollars)

	1997	1998	1999	2000	2001
EBIT	$ 24	$27	$31	$35	$ 40
(Add) Depreciation	7	8	9	10	11
(Less) Taxes	(9)	(11)	(12)	(14)	(16)
Subtotal	21	24	27	30	34
Change in noncurrent assets and liabilities	0	0	0	0	0
Change in working capital	6	8	9	10	11
Net capital investment	(8)	(8)	(9)	(10)	(10)
Free cash flow	$ 19	$24	$27	$31	$ 35
Terminal value					**$637**

DCF of ITT Education	**$485**

WACC	**9.77%**	**PV of Terminal Value** (Constant Growth Model)	$ 400
W_e	100.00%	$(CF_n (1 + g) / (K - g)) / (1 + K)^5$	
W_d	0.00%		
K_e	9.77%	Growth rate	3.98%
K_d	0.00%	Inflation	2.70%
R_f	6.50%	Real	1.25%
R_p	5.40%		
Beta	0.61	**Other Terminal Value Estimates**	
		NOPAT/K	$ 244
		NOPAT $(1 - i)/(K - g)$	$ 412
		NOPAT $[1/K + i(R - K)/K(K - g)]$	$ 465

Valuation Summary—Education	**Multiples**	**Value**	
		Low	**High**
FCF valuation		$400	$550
Market capitalization as on 12/31/96			642
Enterprise value as a multiple of 1996			
1 Revenue	2.92		678
2 EBIT	25.08		441
3 Net income	38.47		456
4 EBITDA	20.25		468
5 Net assets	4.13		536
Equity value as a multiple of			
1 1996 EPS (A)	36.21		429
2 1997 EPS (E)	30.00		424
3 1998 EPS (E)	23.33		376
4 1996 Book Value	16.91		1,162
Triangulated enterprise value		**$400**	**$600**

Source: Casewriter analysis.

EXHIBIT A5
Valuation of ITT's Directories Business (in millions of dollars)

		1997	1998	1999	2000	2001
EBIT		$ 218	$ 215	$ 209	$ 203	$ 203
Net of Dep + Cap Inv		1	57	1	1	0
Taxes		(87)	(86)	(84)	(81)	(81)
Change in working capital		1	57	1	1	0
Free cash flow		$ 133	$ 243	$ 127	$ 124	$ 122
Terminal value						$1,268
DCF of ITT Directories		$1,378				

WACC	**9.76%**	**PV of Terminal Value** (Constant Growth Model)	$ 796
W_e	78.03%	$(CF_n\,(1 + g)\,/\,(K - g))\,/\,(1 + K)^5$	
W_d	21.97%		
K_e	11.03%	Growth rate	0.00%
K_d	8.69%	Inflation	0.00%
R_f	6.50%	Real	0.00%
R_p	5.40%		
Beta	0.84	**Other Terminal Value Estimates**	
		Book Value	$ 317
		NOPAT / K	$1,251

Valuation Summary—Directories	**Multiples**		**Value**	
	Low	**High**	**Low**	**High**
FCF Valuation			$1,000	$1,400
Enterprise value as a multiple of 1996				
1 Revenue	0.76	2.24	491	1,449
2 EBIT	11.73	16.29	2,503	3,477
3 Net income	13.92	21.68	1,755	2,733
5 Net assets	1.04	1.89	421	766
Equity value as a multiple of				
1 1996 EPS (A)	12.80	13.00	1,613	1,639
2 1997 EPS (E)	11.82	12.66	1,544	1,653
3 1998 EPS (E)	10.82	10.33	1,399	1,336
Triangulated enterprise value			**$1,100**	**$1,600**

Source: Casewriter analysis.

EXHIBIT A6
Valuation of ITT's Entertainment Business (in millions of dollars)

MSG Sport Properties
Book Value $500.00

WBIS+ TV Station
Book Value $103.50

As both acquisitions were made in 1995–96, their book values are assumed to provide a reasonable estimate of their fair market values.

Sources: Financial statements and 10-K statement.

EXHIBIT A7
Valuation of ITT's Investments (in millions of dollars)

Fair market value of 7.5 million shares of Alcatel Alsthom	$599
Equity in 20%–50% owned companies	$261
Other investments	$ 17
Value of total investments	**$877**

Sources: Financial statements and 10-K Report.

EXHIBIT A8
Valuation of Corporate-Level Expenses (in millions of dollars)

	1997	1998	1999	2000	2001
Pretax impact of corporate-level expenses	$100	$104	$108	$112	$ 117
After-tax impact of corporate-level expenses	$ 60	$ 62	$ 65	$ 67	$ 70
Terminal value of corporate-level expenses					$1,216
PV of corporate-level expenses	**$999**				

Assumptions	
WACC	10.00%
Growth Rate	4.00%
Tax Rate	40%

Source: Casewriter analysis.

EXHIBIT A9
Valuation of Synergies from This Acquisition (in millions of dollars)

	1997	1998	1999	2000	2001
Pretax impact of synergies	$ 115	$120	$124	$129	$ 135
After-tax impact of synergies	$ 69	$ 72	$ 75	$ 78	$ 81
Terminal value of synergies					$1,398
PV of synergies	**$1,149**				

	Low	High
Value range of synergies	**$900**	**$1,300**

Assumptions	
WACC	10.00%
Growth Rate	4.00%
Tax Rate	40%

Source: Casewriter analysis.

EXHIBIT A10
Comparable Transactions

Selected Gaming and Lodging M&A Transactions ($ in millions, except for per share data)

Date Announced	Acquiror & Target	Implied Equity Purchase Price/Share	Implied Aggregate Equity Purchase Price	Total Announced Transaction Value	Enterprise Value as a Multiple of			
					LTM EBITDA	CFY EBITDA	CFY + 1 EBITDA	LTM Net Income
Lodging Comparables								
Jan-97	Extended Stay America/ Studio Plus Hotel	$22.86	$ 287.00	$ 253.60	26.4	22.6	11.1	55.2
Dec-96	Marriot International/ Renaissance Hotel Group	$32.70	$1,000.00	$1,061.90	16.4	16.5	13.9	30.0
Aug-96	Double Tree Corporation/ Red Lion Hotels	$30.49	$ 977.60	$1,154.40	15.8	10.0	9.3	30.3
				Low	15.8	10.0	9.3	30.0
				High	26.4	22.6	13.9	55.2
				Mean	19.5	16.4	11.4	38.5
Gaming Comparables								
Aug-96	Sun International Hotels/ Griffin Gaming & Entertainment	$22.00	$ 198.10	$ 271.80	5.6	6.5	6.5	20
May-96	Hilton Hotels/ Bally Entertainment	$26.59	$2,050.30	$3,097.00	11.1	10	9.1	58.8
Apr-96	Boyd Gaming Corporation/ Par A Dice Gaming Corp	$18.25	$ 174.60	$ 186.00	5.3	N/A	N/A	N/A
Mar-96	Hollywood Park/ Boomtown	$ 6.33	$ 56.80	$ 147.80	6.3	N/A	N/A	N/A
Mar-95	Circus Circus/ Gold Strike Resorts	N/A	$ 443.50	$ 590.40	8.3	N/A	N/A	N/A
Dec-94	ITT Corporation/ Caesars World	$67.50	$1,754.00	$1,824.50	9.6	7.7	7	23.8
				Low	5.3	6.5	6.5	20.0
				High	11.1	10.0	9.1	58.8
				Mean	7.7	8.1	7.5	34.2

EXHIBIT A11
Comparable Companies

Selected Gaming, Lodging, Education, and Publishing Comparables ($ in millions, except for per share data)

	Enterprise Value as Multiple of						Market Value of Equity as a Multiple of			
	Revenues	EBIT	Net Income	EBITDA	Adj. EBITDA	Net Assets	1996 (A) EPS	1997(E) EPS	1998(E) EPS	Book Value
Lodging:										
Marriot International 1996 a	0.91	14.64	30.09	11.73	24.35	1.92	24.67	22.10	18.73	5.58
HFS Inc 1996 a	13.00	32.87	61.46	26.84	32.15	2.45	46.32	22.46	17.37	3.83
Promus Hotel Corp 1996 a	7.49	18.94	27.34	14.94	17.77	2.82	23.70	20.15	16.55	6.15
Double Tree Hotels 1996 a	7.73	60.82	90.17	46.34	79.82	1.37	44.55	28.48	22.17	2.23
Gaming										
Circus Circus 1996 a	3.50	17.24	46.27	12.46	17.42	1.76	34.72	20.22	17.63	3.30
Mirage Resorts 1996 a	3.19	14.31	21.04	10.95	15.08	2.10	20.40	19.66	16.63	3.00
MGM Grand 1996 a	3.09	13.31	22.35	10.00	13.49	2.03	17.10	15.85	14.53	2.08
Harrah Entertainment 1996 a	1.82	9.53	29.26	7.14	10.39	1.56	20.92	17.28	13.25	2.73
Publishing										
McGraw-Hill 1996 a	1.67	12.16	10.39	9.65	NA	1.41	9.30	8.54	7.82	3.35
Donnelley 1996 a	1.03	15.99	29.55	17.47	NA	1.41	21.03	20.48	16.71	2.91
Dun & Bradstreet 1996 a	2.39	14.40	38.60	10.02	NA	2.39	30.45	13.57	12.50	−9.39
Education										
National Education Corp 1996 a	2.21	18.99	29.13	15.33	NA	3.13	26.29	21.79	16.94	12.28
Entertainment										
Florida Panthers 1995–96 a	19.75	NA	NA	NA	NA	14.20	NA	NA	NA	1.61
Boston Celtics 1995–96 a	2.62	10.67	10.74	10.47	NA	1.22	8.64	372.92	NA	7.25
Media—TV Stations										
King World Productions 1995–96 a	2.05	7.08	9.05	7.05	NA	2.66	9.27	9.65	9.83	1.84
Paxon Communications Corporation 1995–96 a	4.32	NA	NA	22.84	NA	1.29	NA	NA	NA	0.53

Source: Bloomberg, *Value Line,* and casewriter analysis.